Two Lucky People

Milton & Rose D. Friedman

TWO LUCKY PEOPLE

M E M O I R S

**Iona College
Libraries**

THE UNIVERSITY OF CHICAGO PRESS

CHICAGO & LONDON

The University of Chicago Press, Chicago 60637
The University of Chicago Press, Ltd., London
© 1998 by The University of Chicago
All rights reserved. Published 1998
Printed in the United States of America
07 06 05 04 03 02 01 00 99 98   1 2 3 4 5
ISBN: 0-226-26414-9 (cloth)

Library of Congress Cataloging-in-Publication Data

Friedman, Milton, 1912–
    Two lucky people : memoirs / Milton and Rose D. Friedman.
        p.   cm.
    Includes bibliographical references and index.
    ISBN 0-226-26414-9 (cloth : alk. paper)
    1. Friedman, Milton, 1912–   . 2. Friedman, Rose D.
    3. Economists—United States—Biography. I. Friedman, Rose D.
    II. Title.
    HB119.A3F75   1998
    330′.092′273—dc21   97-48951
    [B]   CIP

This book is printed on acid-free paper.

To Aaron Director
brother and mentor

Contents

Contents

✧ *Preface* ✧

{ *Rose and Milton* } In 1976, the *Oriental Economist,* an economic journal published in Japan, asked Rose to write a series of articles about her life with Milton Friedman. She wrote twelve articles, which covered our life through the Nobel award in 1976 and were published in issues dated from May 1976 to August 1977. The *Oriental Economist* subsequently asked Rose for permission to bring the articles together as a book to be published in Japanese and English. She agreed to their publication in Japanese but refused to let them be published in English because we already had in mind a more complete version that would be written by the two of us. This memoir is that more complete version.

Despite the urging of friends, we kept postponing writing our memoirs. Other activities seemed more urgent.

After we became octogenarians, we finally settled down to complete the work that Rose had started, only to have medical problems force an interruption of nearly two years. All in all, it has taken us far longer to complete these memoirs than we ever contemplated.

An element of conceit inevitably enters into the decision to write one's memoirs. We can plead only that we have experienced and participated in many of the major events and developments that have shaped our country's and the world's history for more than half a century—from the Great Depression to the fall of the Berlin wall.

We have tried to avoid writing an academic survey of history or, alternatively, an exposition of the results of our scientific research, or a presentation of our philosophical views. We have done that in other books and many articles. We have aimed rather to present a personal record of our lives and experiences.

Children of immigrants, and in Rose's case an immigrant herself, we are rather typical of our contemporaries, though less so of our successors, as the melting pot has increasingly been replaced by multiculturalism, and rugged individualism by a welfare state.

Both of us graduated from college and went on to graduate school, which is where we met, coming from opposite ends of the continent. We were married six years later, after starting on separate professional careers, both as economists. We have been blessed with a long and happy married life, fifty-nine years and still counting; have had two wonderful children and four grandchildren, and an active professional life, much of it as collaborators.

We are two lucky people. It was pure luck that Rose's mother brought her to the United States three months before the outbreak of World War I—a delay of three months and she might never have made it. It was pure luck that her brother Aaron went to the University of Chicago and brought her there. It was pure luck that Homer Jones was Milton's teacher at Rutgers and made it possible for him to go to Chicago. In all it was pure luck that brought us together and enabled us to have an extraordinarily rich and varied life together.

Though both of us were trained as economists, we have never been competitors. When Rose has been asked, as she has been time and again, the "secret" of our long and happy marriage, she has replied, "While our interests are common, our personalities and tastes are different, and we have each tried to accommodate to the other. Tolerance is the secret of a successful family life, as it is of a successful society."

An example has arisen in writing this book. We first tried to write it entirely in the "we" voice. We found that approach drained it of personality, and so, where appropriate, we have resorted to the "I" voice.

{ *Rose* } My greatest indebtedness is to my brother Aaron who in a very basic sense is responsible for all my good fortune. If he had not made it possible for me to go to the University of Chicago the story that follows would never have unfolded. Throughout my life he has been there when I needed help. And for this memoir he has provided missing bits concerning my early life that I was too young to remember.

My parents provided the love and caring in my formative years that unfortunately is missing in so many homes today. Material resources were limited, but they unstintingly denied themselves to help their children. Though they had little formal schooling, they were far from uneducated and strove to inspire a love of learning in their children.

My sister Becky, six years older than I, never had the opportunities that Aaron provided for me and never had as fulfilled a life (she died in 1985). Yet she never showed any resentment. On the contrary, she seemed to enjoy my fortune and share my troubles as though they were her own.

Dorothy Brady was one of my dearest friends who was always there in times of need. Her death left a void that has never been filled.

Arther Burns became my friend the first time we met and never failed me when I needed him.

{ *Milton* } My greatest indebtedness, aside from my parents, was unquestionably to Arthur Burns, who was my teacher at Rutgers, and thereafter my mentor, guide, and surrogate father (my natural father died when I was fifteen) for much of my adult life. Like Rose, I was indebted to him for his concern and kindness, but even more for his intellectual influence, which played a major role in shaping my scholarly activity.

Homer Jones, another of my teachers at Rutgers, was responsible for introducing me to the Chicago school and made it possible for me to go to Chicago for graduate work.

My first year at Chicago was unquestionably the most intellectually stimulating time of my life, not least because of my fellow students.

{ *Rose and Milton* } So many people have been important in our life, as teachers, personal friends, fellow students, academic colleagues, associates in public policy ventures, and in many other ways, that we hesitate to name any for fear of leaving all too many out. Many names will come up in the course of the tale that follows.

We must however mention the persons who have helped us directly in writing this book. Bill Jovanovich and Bill Peterson repeatedly urged us to write the book. Bill Jovanovich read some of the early chapters and so did Marianna Lee of Harcourt Brace Jovanovich, who suggested the use of the "I" voice. Gordon St. Angelo, at the time with the Lilly Foundation, arranged a modest grant for us so that we could get help to organize a lifetime accumulation of files. Lenore McCracken accomplished this task in exemplary fashion. Milton's longtime secretary Gloria Valentine not only typed more versions than we care to think of, in the process making many suggestions that improved the text, but equally important, did much research in the library and the archives, providing us with a steady stream of answers to detailed questions. Our son David also read the entire manuscript and was generous with constructive criticism. Bob Chitester, Michael Latham, and Eben Wilson, our colleagues in *Free to Choose,* read the relevant chapters and provided us with much original material from their files. Gale Johnson and Bruce Caldwell read a late draft of the manuscript and made helpful suggestions. We appreciate the help we have received from the University of Chicago Press, some anonymously, some from Penelope Kaiserlian, Julee Tanner, Sara Leopold, Perry Cartwright, and especially from Bruce Young, retired managing editor of the Press, who edited the final manuscript.

{ *Milton* } My vocation has been professional economics. Except for one book (*The Theory of the Consumption Function*), Rose played a secondary role in that part of my work, reading and critiquing everything that I wrote but not being a major participant.

My avocation has been public policy, and in that area Rose has been an equal partner, even with those publications, such as my *Newsweek* columns, that have been published under my name.

Milton Friedman
Rose D. Friedman
July 1, 1997

Chapter One

HOW WE MET

Monday, October 3, 1932, Professor Jacob Viner was presiding over the first session of his famous economic theory course, Economics 301, in room 107 of the Social Science Building at the University of Chicago.

To help him identify his students, Professor Viner arranged them alphabetically. This seated Rose Director, a recent graduate of the University of Chicago who had transferred there after two years at Reed College in Portland, Oregon, next to Milton Friedman, a recent graduate of Rutgers University who came from Rahway, New Jersey. Rose had never been east of Chicago; Milton had never before been west of the Delaware River.

Initial contact of two naive youths blossomed into friendship, then romance, followed by marriage six years later on June 25, 1938.

Why did it take so long? Primarily because of our economic insecurity. Times were tough and jobs in our chosen profession of college teaching were scarce—especially for Jews. We had only ourselves to depend on. Our parents could not help us with expenses at school let alone subsidize us after marriage. In addition, we regarded marriage as "till death us do part." As a result we did not want to take that step until we had a reasonable prospect of being able to support ourselves and a family.

This book is the story of our lives. It is now (1997), as we finish telling the story, sixty-five years since we met and fifty-nine years since we were married. We have had our ups and downs—the downs early, the ups later, but our love and confidence in each other was strengthened and deepened by the downs as well as by the ups. Our life has surpassed our wildest expectations: two wonderful children, four grandchildren, rewarding professional careers, and a loving partnership. Who could ask for more?

Chapter Two

EARLY YEARS—ROSE

I was born in Charterisk,* a small village in a part of Eastern Europe that was Russia before World War I, Poland between the two wars, the Soviet Union after World War II, and part of Ukraine since the collapse of the Soviet Union. I was two years old when I left Charterisk with my mother and siblings to join my father in Portland, Oregon. What little I know about life in Charterisk comes entirely from the reminiscences of my mother and older siblings. I did not get interested in family history until it was too late to ask questions.

Both Jews and Christians, whom the Jews always referred to as "Russians," lived in Charterisk, but there seems to have been no social contact between the two groups. Interaction was limited strictly to commercial transactions. Farmers in surrounding areas came to local markets to buy provisions and sell their wares. My aunt had a bar where the Russians congregated after the markets closed. My father worked in his father's mill, to which Russians brought wheat and other grains to be ground. I don't recall hearing any stories about pogroms such as are reported for other communities. Nevertheless, my parents and siblings made it clear that the Jews lived in fear of their Russian neighbors.

My mother was two years old when her mother died in childbirth. The baby, my mother's only brother, survived. Left with an infant and three young daughters, my grandfather lost no time in finding another wife—who came with two young daughters. My mother's stories about growing up were far from the conventional ones involving a cruel stepmother. On the contrary,

---

* My spelling of the name is based on its pronunciation by my parents. Maps we have consulted have a variety of spellings.

they frequently concerned cruelties that one of my mother's sisters, resenting a new mother, heaped either on the stepmother or on the stepsisters. After we left Charterisk, my mother kept in contact with her stepmother and sent her small sums of money whenever she could—evidence of the good relationship between the two parts of the family. And when the infant son grew up, he married one of his stepsisters. They had a large and apparently thriving family—affluent enough to send one daughter to France to study, as I learned when we visited Israel and for the first time met Malke, who had studied in France and was teaching chemistry at Haifa University. We also met her two daughters and her two sisters and their families. To the best of my knowledge, they and an aunt and her family who emigrated to the United States before we did are the only maternal relatives who survived. The others all died in the Holocaust. We have never learned where or how.

Before she married my father, my mother lived not in Charterisk but in a neighboring village. However, an older sister lived in Charterisk and must have known my father's family. I assume that was how the marriage was arranged. As an only son, my father was exempt from being drafted into the Russian army, a real advantage for a potential husband. I do not know when his mother died, only that she had died before he married my mother.

Life in Charterisk

My parents never had a home of their own until they came to the United States. They moved into my grandfather's home when they were married and lived there with their children until we left Charterisk. My father's two unmarried sisters also lived with my grandfather, whether as part of one household or a separate household in the same house, I am not sure. I conjecture that there were two households with some overlapping quarters. It is clear that my mother's life was not an easy one. One unmarried sister-in-law caused problems for my mother because she thought that my grandfather was partial to my mother. One tale concerned bread baking. Apparently both households used the same hearth. It took several hours to heat the oven before it was hot enough to bake bread. The jealous sister-in-law would get up very early in the morning to bake her bread so the oven would be cold before my mother was ready to do her baking. Such interpersonal problems simply added to the hardships associated with living in a small village in Eastern Europe in the late nineteenth and early twentieth centuries. Running water, electricity, indoor plumbing, washing machines, and the myriad kitchen conveniences that we take for granted were totally absent. When Milton and I took a bus trip from

Warsaw to Moscow (see chap. 20), I was reminded of my mother's stories about her early life. In the villages we passed, women were still doing their laundry at the village pump, and at night all was dark except for a single light in the village Communist party headquarters—the only thing that had been added.

Medical practice was primitive and superstition rife. For example, my mother had a long and very difficult labor with her first child. One remedy recommended to ease childbirth was to stretch a string from her bed to the synagogue, presumably to enlist the aid of the Deity. Another was to cut off the hair of all unmarried females in the household. I have never understood how this was supposed to help. Another story concerned my sister when she had what I assume was diphtheria at the age of two or three. My mother and sister were moved to the edge of a cemetery, which served as a place of quarantine, until the crisis was over. There were of course no antibiotics. But there were leeches. The doctor, after applying the leeches, said that if they fell off after a certain number of hours, my sister would live. If they did not, she would die. She lived, but I have no recollection of hearing whether or not the leeches fell off. (As an aside, there were still no antibiotics when I had pneumonia in the United States some fifteen years later, but medical practice had at least moved beyond leeches.) I bear a more lasting memento of medical inadequacy—a short index finger. Not long before we left Charterisk for good, my mother was standing on a stool hanging clothes to dry and I was crawling underfoot. As she got down she stepped on my finger. I have never learned whether a doctor was consulted. I only know that my finger was still bandaged when we left Charterisk and started our voyage to America.

I was born, according to family tradition and my own deduction, during the last week of December 1911, the youngest of a family of five. A sixth child had died as an infant long before I was born. Of my four siblings, two were boys and two girls. Lewis was closest to me in age and Aaron, next to the oldest. My sister Anne was the oldest and Becky came between Aaron and Lewis. The interval between siblings was roughly three years. Since there was never any discussion of sex in our family, I never learned how this more or less regular pattern of childbearing was maintained. There were, of course, none of the modern birth control devices.

Jewish children in Charterisk did not go to the same schools as Russian children, and only boys went to school at all. I know nothing about the schools the Russian children attended. My brother Aaron was the only one in our family who went to school. He attended classes with a few other youngsters in the home of the local learned man. I believe my parents paid the teacher in kind for the classes. All that the boys studied was the Talmud and commentaries on it.

Coming to the United States

My father made two trips to the United States, the first before I was born. I know little about why my father decided to go to "America," as his contemporaries would have referred to this country. His two sisters and their families had already made their way to the United States—one to Portland, Oregon, the other to Detroit, Michigan. Many of my father's cousins had also settled in Portland. In addition, my mother's sister, after first emigrating to London, had moved to Portland. I have often wondered why these relatives went to Portland rather than staying in New York as so many others did. I recently heard one possible explanation. An American manufacturer of furniture came to Poland looking for cabinetmakers whom he could bring to the West Coast to work in his furniture factory. Someone took up his offer, and relatives—not themselves cabinetmakers—followed in due course. The hypothesis sounds plausible, but there is no way to prove it now, since none of the original immigrants is still alive.

I am sure that my father heard from his relatives as well as from other emigrants about the wonderful country across the ocean. He was always very venturesome, so it is not hard for me to imagine him itching for new adventure. I can well imagine that my mother, for whom it meant being left behind with four young children and an elderly father-in-law, may not have been as enthusiastic. That would not have deterred my father. He would probably have tried to persuade her with glowing stories, but failing, he would stubbornly have done what he wanted to do. This was more or less the pattern I remember throughout my childhood.

I don't know how long my father stayed in the United States before returning to Charterisk, nor do I know anything about his life in the new country during this period. I know only that he returned at my grandfather's insistence. Neither do I know how long my father stayed in Charterisk before returning to the United States. I know only that he did not leave until after his father died and that he left rather precipitously and sooner than he intended. I suspect that he was going to stay until I was born but left prematurely as a result of a terrible accident in the mill that he had inherited from his father. It was my father, I believe, who improved the mill by converting it to steam. A young Russian who had brought his grain to be milled got his coat caught in the machinery and was dragged into the wheels of the mill and killed. My father feared for his life because of the anger in the Russian community. After hiding out for a few days, he departed a second time for the United States. I have never heard more than this about the episode. In particular, I have never heard anything about the reaction of the Russian community to the family that was left behind.

Fortunately, my father earned enough money to send for us shortly before the start of World War I. Had we not been able to leave then, we would probably never have been able to come or, at best, not until many years later. I realized what we were spared when a cousin who was not so fortunate told about her experiences during and after the war. Her husband made his first trip to the U.S. with us but left his wife and two children behind, one of whom died during the war. My cousin's stories were confirmed by a book on Poland written in 1938. It vividly describes what occurred in the "eastern provinces of Poland" where Charterisk was located:

> In order to delay the pursuit of the retreating Russian armies by the Germans in 1915, the Cossacks destroyed everything: railway stations, churches, houses, bridges; . . . they burned all crops and removed three million of the local population together with their livestock and implements to the interior of Russia. . . . [Further] misfortune afflicted these districts in 1921, when the three million Poles, White Ruthenians and Jews, driven six years earlier by the Cossacks from their homes, returned to their native land, fleeing from the hunger and famine that was raging in the interior of Russia. Those refugees found at home only abandoned trenches, a sea of barbed wire, remnants of conflagration, skeletons of buildings, empty shells and barren land covered with weeds. The only nourishment these people could find was that which they could dig out from the soil, uncultivated for the last seven years: mushrooms, roots, bark. Their only shelter was in abandoned dugouts. An epidemic of typhoid fever set in and raged throughout the whole winter.[1]

Voyage to America

My mother's only brother lived in Kovel, a short distance from Charterisk. When the time came for our departure, he came with his horse and buggy to take us to the train station and bid us farewell—as it turned out, never to see us again. We then went by train to the port of Libau or Libava, about five hundred miles from Charterisk, where we embarked for London. How long we stayed in port before embarking I do not know. My mother's story was that we were delayed because my injured index finger was still bandaged. Tales were rife at the time about the difficulties encountered by the flood of immigrants entering at Ellis Island, so I assume that the officers at the port of embarkation tried to keep people from starting if there was likely to be a problem. But that's only a guess.

Our voyage to the U.S. was in two parts, from Libau to London and then from London to Portland, Maine. I have always wondered why we entered the country at Portland, Maine, rather than Ellis Island, which seemed to be the most popular port of entry. My brother Aaron's hunch is that the reason was my damaged finger, plus the tales about the difficulties at Ellis Island.

My mother's story of the voyage was one of great discomfort: everyone seasick and the ship smelling of vomit for the whole voyage. She had so many questions and no one to answer them. The other passengers knew no more than she did, and those who could have given her answers, that is, the crew, did not speak Yiddish.

My brother Aaron's version, which he related to me only recently, was altogether different. Unlike my mother, who was responsible for a brood of five children of whom the oldest was sixteen, Aaron was young and carefree, twelve years old, eager to learn the new language and excited about the whole adventure. Even after these many years his recollection of the voyage from Libau to London and on to Portland, Maine, is very clear. The voyage from Libau to London was not long—perhaps one or two days and nights. There were no berths. Everyone huddled in one large room. Passengers brought their own food on board. Aaron spent most of his time on deck among the sailors listening to their conversation, eager to pick up a few words of English. He had no recollection of being miserable or seasick. For him, it was an exciting adventure.

We had relatives in London, so that made a convenient resting place between the two parts of the voyage.

An incident on our trip from Portland, Maine, to Portland, Oregon, as told by my mother, indicates the insularity of the early immigrants. A black man who was on the train with us was apparently very attentive to me, a two year-old, and my mother was petrified. She had never seen a black person but she did know about gypsies. Stories about their kidnapping young children were legion. I have no idea whether my mother actually knew of any children being kidnapped. Nevertheless, she was sure that the strange man would kidnap me. The trials of the trip were increased.

When I recall my mother's stories about her life in Charterisk and especially the break with that life that was involved in coming to a strange land, I am full of admiration for the immigrants of those days. The voyage itself was difficult enough, and when they arrived at their destination, they were on their own. Some had relatives in the new land, but these had come only recently and had little to share with the newer arrivals. Some private charities did exist in larger cities like New York. However, I do not recall my mother ever speaking of help for arriving immigrants in Portland, Oregon. They were accustomed to depending on their own efforts and not on government or private charity. Of the many immigrants of that era whom I met in later years, I never heard one complain about the lack of help or express regrets about coming. They never expected help and did not get any. Yet, to the best of my knowledge, few fell by the wayside.

My father presumably had arranged housing for us, but men in those days knew little about housekeeping and cared less. I shudder at the thought of what advance arrangements my father would have made. As an aside, my father never got so much as a cup of tea for himself, much less removed the cup when he had finished. That was the pattern, at least in our family, and I expect in most families at that time.

Life in Portland

Life in Portland was certainly a big step up from Charterisk. We had running water, even hot water, which I believe was heated by a wood stove in the kitchen. We lived successively in three houses—each a step up the ladder— all in the same neighborhood. I have no recollection of the first house. The third house was the first one we owned. It was the home from which I left Portland and which my parents occupied for the rest of their lives. We had no electricity but we did have gas lighting. Central heat did not come until my father found a secondhand furnace that he installed himself and was always fixing. My father was a wonderful fixer, whether it was a furnace or a washing machine or some other piece of equipment. I do not remember ever seeing a repairman of any kind around our house when I was growing up. My father always did whatever repairs needed doing. With the proper education, he would have made an excellent engineer. Until my father installed central heat, the only heat was from a kitchen stove and a potbellied stove in the dining room. We never thought that getting dressed in the morning around the kitchen stove was a hardship. We had no telephone until my sister Becky, who went to a commercial high school so she could go to work, finally had one put in so her boyfriends could call her.

I grew up in a strictly Orthodox Jewish home. My father went to the synagogue on Saturdays whenever he was at home. My mother ran a 100 percent kosher kitchen. Dinnerware and tablecloths for meat meals and dairy meals were kept separate and never did the two foods mix. My father was more fanatic about religion than my mother. I always had the impression that habit rather than conviction ruled my mother and that when she broke the rules it was without any sense of guilt. For example, when I was anemic as a child, my mother did not hesitate to fix my meat without the soaking demanded by kosher rules. She felt, I believe correctly, that soaking took all the food value out of the meat. She kept separate cooking utensils and dishes for me, however, so as not to contaminate the rest of the kitchen. Many years later, when I visited my parents with my children, my mother never hesitated to serve the children milk with their meat. By that time, she had become sufficiently emancipated as not even to use special dishes for them.

Superstitions did not disappear when we moved to the New World. I remember one in particular related to Yom Kippur, the Jewish Day of Atonement. As a child, I always dreaded that holiday. It was a day of fasting. My parents spent the day in the synagogue praying for forgiveness for any sins committed in the year past and for health and good fortune in the year ahead. There was much crying during the prayers. My mother always came home at sundown with a dreadful headache and went to bed as soon as she fed us. But the worst aspect of the holiday was associated with the custom of burning candles on Yom Kippur from sundown to sundown. The superstition was that if any candle went out during those twenty-four hours someone in the family would die during the year. I still recall the anxiety that followed a candle's blowing out one year. Even though no one died during that year, the superstition nonetheless persisted.

My Schooling

When I was about five I went to kindergarten, not in the public school but in what was known as the neighborhood house. I believe that it was not a government-funded institution but rather one financed and run privately. Miss Lowenberg, a descendant of earlier German immigrants, ran the institution. Her sister was the librarian in the local library. The neighborhood house was a place where people in the neighborhood, primarily immigrants, met for all kinds of activities. There were probably English classes in the evening for adults. I remember going to kindergarten there as well as to dancing classes and other activities. Long before I started grammar school, I spoke English like a native though I have always remained fluent in Yiddish as well.

Like my siblings, I attended Failing School, a public school that was a short walk from our home. As I remember it, the children all went home for lunch since they lived in the neighborhood. Although Jews were the dominant group in the neighborhood, there were other nationalities, and unlike Charterisk there was no social separation. We were all immigrants in a new land. One neighbor across the street was Italian and our two families became good friends.

School was very congenial. The teachers were always helpful and the atmosphere was friendly. I remember especially the year (I believe I was in the fourth grade) that I had pneumonia and was out of school for much of the term. This did not keep me from passing, however, probably because the teacher helped me make up the work. That winter is very vivid in my memory. I am not sure whether it was because of the stories I heard after I recovered about my behavior when I was delirious, or because that was the winter of a big snow storm, which was very unusual for Portland. Whatever the explanation, I can still see myself sitting at the dining room window watching the other children sledding down the hill.

I don't remember anything special about any of the teachers except the principal and her sister, who taught the eighth grade. Those two one could never forget. In my memory, they seem to be the tallest women I have ever seen. They always stood perfectly straight and had a stately appearance. Neither smiled much and yet I remember them as friendly. Classes were relatively small. As far as I remember, my mother never attended a parent-teachers meeting but she always took a keen interest in our progress at school. The periodic report cards told her how we were doing.

I attended Hebrew school for a year or so. The other pupils were all boys and I have never understood why I was sent. Hebrew was only just emerging in Palestine as a living language. The Hebrew school that I went to taught us only the Hebrew alphabet and how to pronounce words written in Hebrew. The aim was to enable us to "read," i.e., pronounce, the prayers in the Hebrew prayer books. That part of my education lasted a short time. However, I did go to Sunday school until I was thirteen. I still have the Bible I was given when I graduated. I have a vague memory of getting a medal; I'm not sure whether it was for good attendance or achievement.

My closest girl friend as a child was a black girl who lived either next door or a few houses away from the second house we lived in. I mention this only because to the best of my recollection there was no problem of race relations at that time in Portland. I have no recollection of feeling that somehow she was different from my Jewish girl friends. I recalled this early un-awareness of race many years later when I was married and living in Chicago. My five year-old daughter was entertaining a black classmate while the girl's mother was visiting with me. The two children were playing upstairs and after a while appeared in the living room, having exchanged clothes. They announced in unison that they had exchanged everything except their skin, and they couldn't do that. They were quite indifferent to the color of each other's skin. Their attitude was in sharp contrast to that of a black maid whom I left on one occasion with my three-year-old son. David asked questions about anything and everything, and the maid was indignant when I got home. She told me that he had asked her why her skin was black and his was white. She felt that the question was insulting and that I was at fault for not instructing him about the difference between white people and black people—and presumably telling him never to mention the difference!

After graduating from Failing School, I went on to Lincoln High School, which was also within walking distance but not close enough to come home for lunch, so we carried bag lunches in plain paper sacks, not the fancy containers that youngsters carry today. Nor, to the best of my recollection, was there a cafeteria.

I studied the usual subjects: Latin, math, civics, history, and English. I did no dating except for a graduation party. I can, I believe, vouch for the total absence of any pregnant girls. Though I was immature, and some girls were more advanced socially, I think I would have known if any girl had dropped out because she was pregnant. The classes were not large and I knew most of the students. I remember no problem of stealing, much less other crime. We walked around the neighborhood at any time of day without fear.

I took piano lessons from a very early age. I occasionally even dreamed of life as a concert pianist. My greatest disappointment in high school had nothing to do with report cards, because I was always a good student: it was not getting the lead for the class play. In the competition I lasted up to the final round and then lost out. It was a terrible blow.

My brother Lewis, who was about six when we came to Portland, also went to Failing School and had much the same primary school experience that I had. Since he was not scholastically inclined, he went on to a technical high school.

Schooling for Immigrant Children

My three older siblings, however, had a very different school experience. With only a poor command of English, they started their primary education in what was called an ungraded class. Each youngster progressed at his or her own speed and their progress determined how long it would take them to graduate. That has always seemed to me an effective arrangement for older youngsters. My oldest sister Anne, who was sixteen when we arrived, stayed in school only long enough to learn to speak and write some English and then went to work. My brother Aaron, who was twelve when we arrived, finished his primary education by the time he was fifteen and went on to Lincoln High School, a four-year high school from which he graduated in three years. My sister Becky, who was about nine when we arrived, started in the ungraded class but moved to the regular class when she learned English and reached the required level. When she graduated, she went on to a commercial high because she was eager to go to work.

After graduating from high school at age eighteen, Aaron went to Yale University. How could a youngster from an immigrant family get to a university at the opposite end of the country? What did he know about Yale or any other university? The answer is very little. He was lucky. As it happened, the principal of Lincoln High School was a Yale alumnus. Recognizing a bright youngster whose parents could certainly not afford to send him to college, he advised Aaron to apply to Yale and recommended him for a tuition scholarship. Until the G.I. bill came in after World War II, there was very little financial help other than tuition—and even tuition scholarships were few and far between. Two other immigrant youngsters who were friends attending Lincoln High also received tuition scholarships and the three went off to Yale University. The tuition scholarships were the only financial help that they received from the university. I do not know about the other two boys but Aaron was entirely on his own aside from an occasional five- or ten-dollar bill that my mother scraped up to send him by taking in boarders. He earned his living expenses at a variety of jobs. He spoke very little about the jobs he had but I know one was teaching in a Hebrew Sunday school on weekends. He graduated from Yale in three years.

My father, always very ambitious and hard-working, had moved up the economic ladder from peddling to owning a small general store in Portland. After a few years, when he saw other small-business entrepreneurs opening stores in rural areas and doing well, he decided that he too could move up the economic ladder if he sold his store in the city and opened one in the country. He chose to open a store in Wilsonville, a small town some miles from Portland. I don't believe there was another Jewish family in the town. My father wanted to have the family move to Wilsonville but he could not persuade my mother to do so. The idea of living in a totally gentile environment did not appeal to her. More important, she was sure that the schools in Wilsonville would be inferior to the schools in Portland. Though she had no formal education herself, she was determined that her children should have as good an education as possible. When I hear people today, discussing educational vouchers, argue that uneducated parents would not be interested or capable of choosing the right schools for their children if they had free choice of schooling, I recall my mother. Though totally unschooled, she certainly was interested in seeing her children get the best education possible.

My father, determined to have a store in the country whether the family moved with him or not, decided to live there by himself behind the store and come home whenever he could. I remember that my brother Aaron helped, but his help must have been very limited since he was going to high school at the time. I don't know how long my father had the store but I remember there were problems. As the only Jew, and an immigrant as well, my father encountered a fair measure of anti-Semitism, unlike our experience in Portland. About the time that Aaron graduated from high school and was making plans to leave for Yale, the store burned down in very suspicious circumstances. My father was asleep in the back of the store and was fortunate to get out with his life.

My father felt that this was not the time for Aaron to go off to college. His help was needed to put together the information about the fire for insurance and to make other arrangements to recover from the fire. My father argued that Aaron could postpone his departure and enter college the following year. My mother feared, probably correctly, that things would drag on and that Aaron would miss his opportunity to get a good education. She was determined that he leave, whatever the circumstances.

The only money resource that my mother had was a life insurance policy that she had taken out on Aaron. I have always been amused about the insurance policy story. It seems that Metropolitan Insurance Company sold the immigrants one-hundred-dollar life insurance policies for their young children for something like twenty-five cents a month. Why any of these parents would be interested in life insurance policies on their children, I have never understood. Either they did not understand what a life policy meant or it was sold to them as a savings plan because the children could cash them at a later date. This was what Aaron did and used the proceeds to get to New Haven. I too had such a policy that I cashed some years later when I realized how foolish a thing it was. I believe I used the cash to buy a dress—far less significant use of it than Aaron's.

Of the two boys who went to Yale with Aaron, one, Marcus Rothkowitz, became a well-known artist, changing his name to Mark Rothko. The other became a physician.

Aaron spent the year after he graduated from Yale hitchhiking, first around this country and then Europe. Except for a few incidents, he never spoke much about his experiences. He was interested in the labor movement, and I know he spent some time working in coal mines. At that period of his life, he was a socialist—an example of the old adage, "If one is not a socialist before age thirty, one has no heart; if one remains a socialist after thirty, one has no head." In Europe, he met his history teacher from Lincoln High, Mr. Schwartztrauber, who told him that the Labor Temple in Portland was looking for a director and suggested that Aaron might be interested in the job. Aaron returned to Portland and became director of the Labor Temple.

There was always a special relationship between Aaron and me. He was semi-sibling and semi-parent. As a twelve-year-old he carried me to the boat when we left Russia. He took me to school when I started at Failing Grammar School. When I graduated from grammar school, though he needed the little money he had, he gave me a beautifully bound copy of Edgar Allen Poe's poems with the inscription "Congratulations: May this be the first of many graduations." And he made it possible for me to have many graduations. In another way, he was my mentor. I earned a little money as a teenager by playing the piano for gym classes at the neighborhood house. After a couple of years of enjoying the munificent income of, I believe, five dollars a month, a new gym teacher arrived with her own pianist and I was out of a job. I was heartbroken. In addition to losing the income, in the current vernacular, my self-image was devastated. Aaron, who was working at the Labor Temple, came up with an interesting proposal. He would pay me the same sum I had been getting if I would spend a certain number of hours each week in his office teaching myself to type. This not only restored my self-image and my income but also resulted in my learning to type, which stood me in good stead all through college. It was also a learning experience of a different kind that I do not pretend to have appreciated at the time. He did not simply give me the money because I lost my job. I had to do something in return, even if it was something for my own good.

By the end of my third year of high school I needed only two more courses to graduate. Aaron was planning to leave his job at the Labor Temple that fall to enter the University of Chicago for graduate study. He had a teaching fellowship as well. He proposed that I take the two courses I needed to graduate during the summer and go to Chicago with him and enter the University of Chicago. I do not know how he thought we would live on his fellowship income, which was $2,000 or less, but he seemed to think that somehow we would manage. However, my mother vetoed that proposal. I was the youngest child and whether for that reason or because I had little in common with either of my sisters, I was very close to my mother when growing up.

Above all, my mother felt that sixteen was much too young for her baby to go two thousand miles to some place that she knew nothing about. Aaron had no arguments that could convince her. So I did not go to summer school and Aaron left for Chicago without me. Instead, I graduated from Lincoln High at midyear, January 1928, and so had nine months to spend before I could enter college. This gave me nine months in which to work and earn a little money. I was lucky because a new store—a Kresge five-and-ten—had just opened and was hiring staff. I worked at the toy counter, which suited me just fine—I enjoyed demonstrating the toys at least as much as my little customers enjoyed playing with them. I remember particularly my pleasure in demonstrating the little tin horn into which one hummed and made music. Except for working a few Saturdays at a department store while going to high school, this was my first real job and I was very proud of being able to earn thirteen dollars a week. As I remember, after a very short period, I was promoted to manager of the toy department, which consisted of two counters. I believe I then got a raise in pay of seventy-five cents a week.

That fall I entered Reed College and remained for two years. Reed was a small private school (about five-hundred students) with an excellent faculty, which maintained a close relationship with students. Many faculty members had an open house or tea for students regularly. The atmosphere was very academic. The school was run on the honor principle. Exams were not monitored and grades were not given to students, though they were kept in the office for students to use in applying to other schools for transfer or graduate study. There were some dormitories but, like most students, I lived at home and commuted to school, and hence took advantage of few extracurricular activities other than occasional faculty teas. The courses were more advanced and exciting than my high school classes and I met students from more varied backgrounds. Other than that, life did not differ much from my high school years.

In addition to economics, I took courses in history, literature, contemporary society, mathematics, and biology. A course in ancient history led to heated arguments with my father about the Old Testament. My father was sure that the Old Testament was literal truth. He also believed similar stories that he read in other Hebrew books. I, of course, insisted that they were all fables. My father had not met such insubordination up to this time.

The biology course convinced me, if I ever thought otherwise, that medicine was not my dish. It involved a considerable amount of lab work, primarily dissection. We started, as I remember, with a frog and ended with a cat. While

I was not at all squeamish about dissecting the frog, cutting up a cat and having to look at those lifeless eyes was almost more than I could bear. I am sure that if I hadn't felt that it was a sign of failure, I would have dropped the course. In any case I dissected the cat with a little help and skipped lunch many a day.

The summer between my freshman and sophomore years at Reed, I had strange physical symptoms that resulted in a week's stay in the hospital for observation and then an exploratory operation. Only a very inflamed appendix was found and it was removed. To the best of my memory, no one then had health insurance. We did not have routine medical checkups, but there was also never a question of not seeing a doctor because we were too poor. Doctors had a sliding scale for charges. I remember very well that my mother paid doctor bills in installments—sometimes over months. I don't remember her getting monthly bills. I believe she was told how much the charge was, either before or after the visit. If she felt the charge was more than she could afford she met with the doctor, not with a bookkeeper, and the charge was generally adjusted and the timing of the payments discussed. There was a very personal relationship between doctor and patient as well as patient's family.

It is hard to exaggerate the change in medical practice over the past sixty years. Of course, there has been a tremendous advance in the science. There were no MRIs, no antibiotics, and much, much more. But at the same time, medical practice has become less personal. The primary interest on a first visit to a doctor or upon entering the hospital seems to be what kind of insurance one has, not what ails one.

After my sophomore year at Reed, I transferred to the University of Chicago. In a sense, I was on my own for the first time in my life. In another sense, I was still protected and still taken care of. If I had a problem, Aaron was always there. Although he had a very modest salary, he always insisted it was enough for both of us and never encouraged me to work apart from a few modest research jobs that I did for Professor Paul Douglas, with whom Aaron was writing a book at this time. I also did some work for Professor Palyi. None of these jobs contributed much toward my living expenses. Tuition was three hundred dollars a year, but we paid only half because Aaron was on the faculty. I lived in a small dormitory that was across the Midway from the university and took my meals there. I did much of my studying in the library or in Aaron's office. If I stayed until dusk, he always insisted on walking me across the Midway. His excuse was always that there were many stories about girls being raped while crossing the Midway. He was skeptical about the stories but nevertheless always insisted on accompanying me. That gave me a chance to have many interesting conversations with him. As I remember, these were mainly not about economics but about much more general, philosophical questions. Was happiness the primary goal of life and what produced happiness? What was important in life? Aaron, like me, is a very private person, so we didn't discuss any personal problems. I never told him how very homesick I often was. Every now and then he asked me whether I needed any money. My recollection is I asked for very little. I had a pretty good idea of his income and, since my room and board and tuition were paid in advance, I needed little more.

My wardrobe, such as it was, was purchased either by my mother in Portland during the summer or by my sister Becky, who was married and living in San Francisco. She had worked at Montgomery Ward in Portland from the time she left school at about the age of seventeen. She started in a minor position but did such a good job that she was given more and more responsibility. When she married and moved to San Francisco she had no difficulty getting a comparable position with Ward's in Oakland. Differing six years in age and with different interests, Becky and I had little in common until we were adults. As a teenager she had no interest in a higher education but was eager to go to work so that she could have nice clothes. I was in many respects the opposite. Clothes were never very important. My interests lay much more in books and in school. Becky had a great interest in boyfriends—perhaps because she wanted to get married and leave home. I had very little interest in boys. When she grew up, Becky regretted her choice, became a voracious reader, and did a wonderful job of educating herself. As adults we became close friends. She and I spent many hours together when we were both on visits to Portland during the summer and when I visited her in San Francisco on my way to or from Chicago. She shared my interests and my problems and became my closest friend and confidante. There was never any resentment on her part because I had had greater advantages. On the contrary, with her own love of nice clothes, she enjoyed getting clothes for me whenever she had the opportunity.

As at Reed, I did not have an active social life during my two years as an undergraduate at Chicago. I had a few very close girl friends and only casual men friends. I have no recollection that this troubled me. I never thought much about finding a husband: I suppose I assumed that in good time he would come along—as he did. I was going to college to get an education, to make life more interesting, but even more to prepare me to earn my living.

Strange the things that one remembers or forgets. I have no recollection of the graduation ceremony in June 1932. I do remember very clearly that Aaron took me to lunch at the faculty club and how impressed I was that a number of faculty men came over to congratulate me. Then I left for the summer at home, knowing that I would return in the fall to start graduate work in economics.

People today often express surprise that in the early thirties a young woman went to college, majored in economics, and even did graduate study. Women's lib as it exists today, of course, was not in the picture in the thirties. However, I do not believe that young women were discriminated against in seeking admission to college. On the other hand, I do believe there was discrimination when it came to getting financial help. Marrying and having a family was the ultimate goal for most women, including those who went to college. Accordingly, it was deemed proper to favor men in granting financial help, since they were to be the primary support for a family. Getting started in a career was also more difficult for women for the same reason.

Change was needed and change has occurred. But the changes have also created many problems. I believe that absentee mothers and latchkey children are the cause of many of today's ills. The big problem is that women have different roles to play at different periods in life. One is raising a family and that is best pursued as a full-time career for a number of years. However, it is no longer a career for a lifetime. Properly performed, it may bear fruits that last a lifetime, but the activity does not. A second career should start when the first comes to an end, and that is not easy to achieve. Perhaps the technological changes that are rapidly transforming the workplace will enable women to perform both roles at the same time. If not, then sooner or later, the market will make the needed adjustments so that women may enter and leave the marketplace at different periods in their lives.

⤳ *Chapter Three* ⤶

EARLY YEARS—MILTON

My father, Jeno Saul Friedman, and my mother, Sarah Ethel Landau, were born in a small mostly Jewish town, Beregszasz, in Carpatho-Ruthenia—my father in 1878, my mother in 1881. Carpatho-Ruthenia was then in the Hungarian part of Austro-Hungary. After World War I, it became part of Czechoslovakia; after World War II, part of the Soviet Union; and after the collapse of the Soviet Union, part of Ukraine. The town is now named Berehovo.

Yiddish was doubtless the primary language in the home, but both my parents spoke Hungarian well and my father had some fluency in German.

At an early age my father went to live with a much older half-brother in Budapest. They had the same mother but different fathers. His half-brother's name was Friedman, and since my father was always referred to as "Friedman's brother," he took Friedman as his name, though it was not his biological father's. At one time, I knew his original name, but I'm too uncertain now to record my present impression. That sequence of events explains why, so far as I know, I have no blood relatives by the name of Friedman and have been able to send confident negative replies to people named Friedman in Russia, Australia, and elsewhere, who have written wondering whether we are related.

At the age of sixteen (1894), my father emigrated to the United States and settled in Brooklyn. I know literally nothing about the details of his emigration. My mother emigrated to the United States when she was fourteen (1895). Three older sisters had emigrated earlier and settled in Brooklyn. They encouraged her to emigrate, I assume both with persuasive arguments and with financial help and eased her early days in the new country.

I know even less about my parents' activities between their arrival and their marriage. I had the usual youthful egoistic lack of interest in origins when I could have learned about them. I do know, however, that very shortly after my mother's arrival, she started earning her own living by working as a seamstress in a "sweatshop." In view of the bad reputation of sweatshops, it is interesting that I never heard my mother make a negative remark about her experience. On the contrary, she regarded it as enabling her to earn a living while she learned English and became adjusted to the new country.

It served that function for many immigrants then, and to a lesser extent it still does. In those distant pre-welfare state days, immigrants were strictly on their own except for the assistance they could get from relatives and private charitable agencies.

I know even less about my father's source of income. I am under the impression that not long after his arrival he went into business on his own as a petty trader of some kind and remained self-employed for the rest of his life.

I do not know how my parents learned to speak, read, and write English, but I assume that it was by attending the night schools for immigrants that were common at that time.

My mother must have been very young when my father left his native town for the great entrepot of Budapest, and may never have met him in Beregszasz. However, their marriage doubtless sprang from their common roots. That is how networks develop and marriages are arranged in an immigrant culture.

Once my parents married, they wasted little time before having a family: first, three girls, Tillie, Helen, and Ruth; then I completed the family as the only male. I am the only one still living. I was born on July 31, 1912, at 502 Barbey Street in Brooklyn, New York, my parents' address, according to my birth certificate. My parents had the good sense to move out of Brooklyn to Rahway, a small town in New Jersey, when I was thirteen months old, so I have no early memories of Brooklyn.

Rahway

Rahway was a town of about fifteen thousand. It is twenty miles from New York on the main line of the Pennsylvania Railroad between New York and Philadelphia. It had some industry—most notably then and now, Merck, Wheatena, and Regina—but mostly it was a bedroom city for commuters to Newark and New York.

My parents bought a building on a corner of Main Street alongside the overhead tracks of the Penn and used it as both home and a small clothing factory, no doubt one that would be termed a sweatshop today. That venture was not very successful and they closed it after a few years, sold the house, and bought one across the street at 104 Main Street, where they opened a small drygoods store. I have only the vaguest recollection of the first house, except from seeing it when we were no longer living there, so the store must have been started when I was very young. For most of my youth, my mother ran the store while my father commuted to New York where he operated as what he termed a jobber. I do not know what that meant. The one thing I do know is that he never made much money.

The store apparently generated enough income to support our modest living standard. Like many immigrants, we lived above the store—the same phenomenon that we observe today in the San Francisco Chinatown near our current residence. Among my most vivid memories are heated discussions between my parents at night about where the money was to come from to pay incoming bills. Postponement was frequently the name of the game, often in two or more stages: first, by paying the bill with postdated checks; then, when the due date arrived, by frenzied scrambling to get a friend or friendly merchant to cash or endorse a still later postdated check. Years later, in the course of studying monetary arrangements in a number of countries, I discovered that my harassed parents were by no means unique in relying on post-dated checks. In many underdeveloped countries, such as Taiwan in 1962, where I first came across the phenomenon, postdated checks are a major and extremely convenient and flexible form of credit instrument.

We had few luxuries, but somehow our parents scraped together enough money to pay for music lessons for my sisters and me—violin lessons for me that were a complete waste of time and money. I have remained a musical illiterate who, to my regret and Rose's frustration, gets no pleasure from music, whether classical or popular. Music lessons, however were one expression of the high value that my parents, like the Jewish community in general, placed on education.

The common language within the household was English. My parents spoke Hungarian only when they wanted to keep something from the children or (as happened only rarely) when they had occasion to speak to Hungarian customers or friends. Most of their social contacts were within the small Jewish community of about a hundred families in Rahway. In those contacts the common language of conversation was often, perhaps usually, Yiddish. Accordingly, we children never learned more than a few words of Hungarian but did pick up a smattering of Yiddish, enough to understand the conversation of adults, but not enough to speak it fluently.

The house that we lived in dated back to the early nineteenth century. I have a vivid memory of exploring as a child a dark and dingy attic, discovering words apparently written with smoke from a candle on the ceiling under the eaves, and coming to the conclusion that the house, prior to the Civil War, must have served as a way station on the underground railway for slaves.

When I was eleven or so, my parents reconstructed our building, making two stores instead of the one plus a space that had been used as a garage. After unsuccessful attempts to rent the other store, they decided to open it up themselves as an ice cream parlor. By that time, my sisters and I were old enough to serve as clerks, which we did with great pleasure because of the availability of ice cream—though I may say we soon became satiated and stopped eating up the meager profits. The store, as I recall it, was never a financial success, but it continued in operation for some years. I no longer recall what replaced it. Perhaps its most important product was a husband for my oldest sister. Fred Porter delivered carbonated beverages to the store, met Tillie there, and a courtship ensued.

I recall several incidents connected with my father's Model T Ford. One relates to a 1918 explosion in a munitions factory in a neighboring community. My father's story was that when the explosion occurred, his Model T jumped several feet straight up, then landed back on the road and continued on. Another incident relates to my falling out of the passenger side of the same Model T, giving my father a great scare, though I suffered only a skinned knee. Some years later, when my father was driving the car into the garage, he hit a rock in the driveway and I went forward through the windshield. (That was, of course, long before either shatterproof glass or seat belts.) I suffered a deep cut on my lip that bled profusely and was incompetently sewed up, so that to this day I bear a slightly disfiguring scar on my upper lip.

My elementary school was Washington Public School, a relatively short walk from home. I have few clear memories of my early school years. Somehow, when I was in the sixth grade, a teacher decided that I should be advanced, and arranged a transfer in the middle of the year to the seventh grade at another school, Columbus School, a little farther away but still within easy walking distance. As a result, I completed the two years in one. The only clear recollection that I have of my new school was a nickname that I acquired. I tended to talk very loud, indeed shout, so that, when the proverb "Still water runs deep" came up in class one day, my fellow students dubbed me "Shallow."

One other recollection that has stayed with me relates to the preparations for graduation ceremonies from elementary school. In order to assign students their parts in the song that the class was supposed to sing, the music teacher asked each student to sing a few notes. When my turn came and I sang a few notes, the teacher's response was, "It doesn't matter." When I have told that story in later years, it almost always evokes expressions of indignation at the thoughtless cruelty of the teacher. That never was and is not now my reaction. It was a simple statement of fact and helped to instill in me a respect for facts. However, Rose has always felt that it worked to discourage any musical interest I might have developed.

Until I was bar-mitzvahed at the age of thirteen, I attended Hebrew school at the local synagogue. Hebrew school met in the afternoon after public school. Though we were taught some biblical history, the main purpose was described as teaching us to read Hebrew. In that context, reading did not mean understanding but simply pronouncing—learning the Hebrew alphabet, the punctuation symbols, and the pronunciation of Hebrew words, so that we could recite the prayers in the prayer book correctly. In addition, we memorized the responses that would be required from us at the bar mitzvah ceremony. My sisters did not have that experience. The idea of bas mitzvah for girls had not yet surfaced in Rahway.

Until not long before my bar mitzvah, I was fanatically religious, seeking to conform in every detail to the complex dietary and other requirements of Orthodox Judaism. I recall an incident from a Scout—presumably a Cub Scout—picnic that I attended when I was ten or eleven years old. It was held in a local park by a troop of boys from various religious backgrounds. There was to be a frankfurter roast. In order to avoid either eating nonkosher (traife) meat or making a public display, I sneaked away and ran home. Perhaps as a result of that incident, some other boys and I prevailed upon our Jewish local dentist, Sam Katzman, himself childless, to organize a Jewish Boy Scout troop with himself as scoutmaster. Thus began many happy years of scouting.

By the age of twelve or so, I decided that there was no valid basis for my religious beliefs or for the rigid customs that I had followed, and I shifted to complete agnosticism. I went through the bar mitzvah ceremony for the sake of my parents—who, I may say, were never as rigid as I was and displayed considerable tolerance for both my early rigidity and my later reversal. Rose has often remarked that I became fanatically antireligious, citing the difficulty she had in persuading me to accept a religious marriage ceremony for the sake of our parents.

My father suffered from angina for years. I vividly recall his popping nitroglycerin pills to surmount frequent attacks. He died at the age of forty-nine when I was fifteen years old and getting ready to enter senior year in high school. Jewish tradition, and my mother's desire, required that a son say kaddish—a prayer for the dead—every day for a year after his father's death. Despite my by then firm agnosticism, I conformed. The Jewish community in Rahway was so small that it could rally a minyan (ten Jewish male adults) only on Saturday, so for the next year I took a bus every day other than Saturday to the neighboring community of Roselle, which had a much larger Jewish population, to attend services at which I could say kaddish. I must say I was glad to see the year's end.

More than forty years later, I developed angina myself, and found myself being prescribed the well-remembered nitroglycerin pills. I was, however, spared my father's fate by the fortuitous perfection of by-pass surgery.

From 1924 to 1928, I went to Rahway High School. Like the elementary schools that I attended, it was within easy walking distance from home. One teacher who had a lasting influence on me was Mr. Cohan, who taught political science, or "civics" as it was then called. He also taught Euclidean geometry simply because he loved the subject. And he succeeded in passing that love on to at least some of his students, including me. Nearly seventy years later, I still recall his putting the classic proof of the Pythagorean theorem (the square of the hypotenuse of a right triangle equals the sum of the squares of the other two sides) on the blackboard, and stressing what a beautiful proof it was by quoting from Keats's "Ode on a Grecian Urn": "'Beauty is truth, truth beauty'—that is all ye know on earth, and all ye need to know"—thereby instilling a love simultaneously for mathematics and poetry.

My four high school years were pleasant and rewarding but mostly uneventful. I participated some in extracurricular activities, such as playing on the chess team and being an assistant manager or some other minor official for our baseball team. That was the closest I came then or in college to participating in a team athletic activity. I graduated in 1928 with what in retrospect I judge to have been a good grounding in language (two years of Latin), mathematics, and history.

One other activity that I engaged in in high school accidentally came to the surface when Rose discovered among some memorabilia a bronze medal, with my name engraved on the back, that was awarded in connection with a National Oratorical Contest on the Constitution sponsored by the *New York Times*. Apparently anyone who got beyond the first level to represent his or her school got a medal. That seems to have been as far as I got, according to the *New York Times* articles unearthed by my secretary, Gloria Valentine. However, it was doubtless the first time that my name appeared in a major newspaper.

The local public library played as important a role in my education as the schools that I attended. Thanks to it, I became a voracious reader, almost exhausting the contents of the small library.

Rutgers, 1928–32

Two of my high school teachers were recent graduates of Rutgers University and no doubt influenced my decision to attend Rutgers. A more decisive consideration was that the state of New Jersey had recently established competitive tuition scholarships to Rutgers for students who could demonstrate financial need. This was the first step in converting Rutgers from a small private university in New Brunswick to the public megauniversity with numerous campuses that it is today.[1] I took the exam for those scholarships, and also, as I recall it, applied to the University of Pennsylvania—about the only other college I had heard much about—for a scholarship. The Rutgers scholarship came through, the University of Pennsylvania scholarship did not.

Rahway is only twelve miles or so from New Brunswick, and both are on the main line of the Pennsylvania Railroad, so that there were frequent trains. As a result, many residents of Rahway who attended Rutgers lived at home and commuted. I was determined not to do so because I did not want my college experience to be simply a continuation of high school. I wanted to benefit from the extracurricular as well as the curricular experience of college. The many novels of college life that I had read left me with a romanticized picture of what college life was like. I roomed in one of the dormitories, Winants Hall, which, by a curious coincidence, has now become the home of the Rutgers Economics Department.

When I entered Rutgers in 1928, the economy was still booming, so I had little difficulty finding employment to pay my expenses other than tuition. I found a job as a part-time clerk in the men's department of a local department store, Roselle's, which paid me four dollars for a twelve-hour day on Saturday, and two dollars for an occasional afternoon. I was fortunate to retain that pay for the next four years, thanks to experience, while the occasional new hires were receiving half that amount by 1932. I also found a job waiting on tables at a restaurant across the street from my dormitory. Its main business was lunch, which was when I worked. My pay was a free meal, so I made sure that lunch was my main meal for the day. Generally, I could not eat until close to one o'clock. Since I frequently had classes that started at 1:30 some distance away, I had to eat fast, a bad habit that has lasted all my life.

The lunch job cost me the only C on my college record. I took an excellent course in European history that met at 1:30 in the most distant building on campus. As a result, I was frequently late. The instructor downgraded me to a C on that account, and when I protested, replied, quite correctly, that I was in college not to wait on tables but to learn. (Again, Rose disagrees with my reaction. Instead she believes that the instructor demonstrated a lack of under-standing or sympathy for a youngster who was determined to get an education whatever the difficulties.)

The lunch job also gave me firsthand exposure to the importance of entre-preneurship. When I first started working there, the restaurant was doing a flourishing business. A year or so later, the owner, whose name I no longer remember, sold it. After a few months under the new owner, the restaurant was in the doldrums, doing hardly enough business even to keep me on at the cost of a meal. The new owner then sold it back to the original owner for decidedly less than he had paid for it, and within a few months, business was booming again. That cycle was repeated at least once more during my tenure: under the control of the right person, a booming business; under some-one else, a dismal flop.

I supplemented my earnings from the two jobs by several entrepreneurial ventures during the school year and by earnings during the summer. The entrepreneurial ventures were in cooperation with Harold Harris, my closest friend from Rahway, who entered Rutgers the year after I did. Rutgers freshmen were required by long tradition to wear white socks and green ties, either for the whole of the first year or for much of it—I forget which. Hal's father had a department store in Rahway, and could get us the socks and ties at wholesale. So we conceived the idea of peddling socks and ties in the dormi-tories during Freshman Week. In order to do so, we needed permission from the dean of students, who obliged by giving us a letter of authorization. The socks-and-tie venture went very well and gave us a more ambitious idea.

In my junior year, we arranged with Barnes and Noble, then as now a major dealer in secondhand books of all kinds, including textbooks, to come to Rutgers toward the end of the school year and set up shop for a day in the restaurant where I worked, for the purpose of buying secondhand books. We advertised the sale and made all the logistic arrangements. In return, if memory serves, we received a commission of 5 percent of the amount Barnes and Noble spent on books, and the right to buy back any books we wanted at 45 percent of list price. We then interviewed each of the teachers of the large freshman courses to determine which texts would be reused, borrowed a few hundred dollars from our families (mostly from Hal's), and bought back all the copies of such texts that Barnes and Noble had purchased, with the idea of selling them to freshmen, along with green ties and white socks.

The bookstore got wind of our plans and protested to the dean that we were poaching on their territory. Fortunately for us, the dean's authorization of our peddling activities had not been limited to socks and ties, but was phrased so loosely that it covered almost anything we might decide to sell, and so we were able to proceed. If we had not been able to do so, the venture would have been a financial disaster. As it was, it was very profitable and, as I recall, we were left with only a handful of unsold books. Buying and selling was clearly in the genes of two Jewish boys.

My summer activities were of two very different kinds. In that benighted era, there were few if any restrictions on the sale of fireworks. Preceding the Fourth of July, dealers set up stands on the highway offering a great variety of fireworks. Beginning with my first or second year in high school, I had worked at and then run such a stand for a dealer whom I had somehow come into contact with, perhaps because he was a wholesaler who sold goods to my mother for her store. The job lasted only a couple of weeks, but the hours were long, the activity at times hectic, and the opportunity to cheat the often absent owner of the stand considerable, so the owner was willing to pay well for a person he was confident he could trust. I continued that activity throughout my college years.

My second summer activity was very different—tutoring high school students who had failed courses. I was on good terms with the principal of my high school (Mr. Smithers), who was concerned that the school was getting overcrowded and was anxious to enable students to make up failed courses. There was no public summer school. Instead, he at first recommended individual students to me to tutor. They could then take make-up exams, administered by teachers at the school. After I did this for two summers, I made an even better arrangement with him. I set up a summer school in the high school building, and taught classes in a number of different subjects for students who had failed them and were willing to pay, if my memory serves me right, 50 cents an hour. He, in turn, agreed to accept my certification of the students in lieu of a special make-up exam.

The summer school was extremely profitable. The classes lasted five weeks, and I cleared something like $450 a summer in 1930 and 1931. At the time, the average salary of full-time instructional staff in elementary and secondary schools was about $1,400, so in five weeks I earned the equivalent of four months' average earnings of a full-time teacher—not bad for a seventeen- or eighteen-year-old at a time of wide unemployment. Indeed, it was so profitable a venture that, when Mr. Smithers resigned or retired as principal after the 1930–31 school year, the assistant principal seized the opportunity to take over my summer school and run it himself as a sideline.

The summer school was not only profitable, it was also excellent experience. I taught everything from English and geometry to Latin—in which I had had two years of high school courses five or six years earlier—to the bottom tier of students. I truly learned something about pedagogy. My most lasting memory is of a class in Latin in which we were discussing English cognates of the Latin word "sanguinis," meaning bloody. One student spoke up and asked: "Mr. Friedman, is the English word sanguich derived from that?"

The result of the assistant principal's takeover of the summer school was that my leanest summer was 1932, after I graduated from college. I did make my usual sum selling fireworks, but I was unable to get any other job worth anything. As I recall, I tried door-to-door selling, of encyclopedias, I believe, but I made so little that I soon gave up and spent the summer doing some studying, I don't remember what.

Nonetheless, I had no reason to complain. I ended my college career with a nest egg of a couple of hundred dollars when I went off to the University of Chicago for graduate work. Moreover, my family, like me, escaped the worst ravages of the depression. One sister, Helen, had a job as a Western Union telegraph operator and did not lose her job. My other two sisters had occasional spells of unemployment but were able to find clerical jobs most of the time. My mother had hard times in the store but was able to tide over with some help from my sisters.

To return to my undergraduate years, Rutgers, one of the oldest universities in the country, founded in 1766 by the Dutch Reformed Church, was an excellent small undergraduate college, though it was clearly not "Ivy League." It had two campuses—the main campus "on the banks of the old Raritan," as the college song had it, housing Rutgers College for men, which I attended, and a campus several miles away on the other side of New Brunswick, housing Douglas College for women and an agricultural experiment station.

Rutgers College was sufficiently small, with a student body numbering under two thousand, that a youngster raised in a small town, who had graduated from high school in a class numbering about eighty, could feel at home. Yet Rutgers was sufficiently large that it offered a wide variety of courses and had a varied faculty, many of whom were excellent and dedicated teachers. Also, the campus was extensive and extremely pleasant, with many attractive college buildings and the usual fraternity row, which, given my limited resources, I saw only from the outside. I have nothing but good feelings about my undergraduate years, in terms of my personal life, the friends I made, and the education that I received.

My major extracurricular activity in college (other than earning money) was on the *Targum,* the student newspaper, where I finally ended up as copy editor, in charge of proofreading the text and writing headlines. A Reverend Mr. Sockman gave one of the regular Sunday talks in the Rutgers Chapel.

My headline for the story was: "SOCKMAN SPEAKS OF/SIN IN CHAPEL." That blooper was widely reprinted, and for all I know may still circulate as a cautionary tale for aspiring journalists; fortunately, headlines are anonymous.

The most memorable episode of my journalistic activity was accompanying William Freedman, then a journalism major and a *Targum* reporter, later a reporter for the *New York Times,* to Princeton to visit the parents of a Rutgers undergraduate who had committed suicide. The visit was macabre. We were welcomed into a living room with a coffin on trestles, candles burning—the family was from South America and piously Catholic—and talked to two heartbroken parents trying hard to maintain their dignity. Bill, dedicated to a journalistic career, regarded it as a great experience; by contrast, it banished from my mind any remote idea of making my career as a journalist.

At the time, two years of ROTC was compulsory for Rutgers undergraduates. I attained the rank of corporal by the end of the second year, but that was about all I got out of marching, learning to present arms and to disassemble and reassemble antique World War I rifles, and reading a textbook, of which the only thing I can remember is that we had one. Those students who stayed on for two more years to become reserve officers may have benefited both themselves and the country; I regarded ROTC as a burden to be borne with no significant benefits for me or for the country.

I originally intended to major in mathematics. The only paying occupation I had heard about that used mathematics was actuarial work, so I had informed myself about that and planned to become an actuary. An academic career never entered my mind. I stuck to my original intention for some years, going so far as to take some of the actuarial examinations required to become a fellow—by far the most difficult exams I have ever taken. I passed several and failed others before I abandoned the attempt. After a year or two, however, I changed my major from mathematics to economics.

Whatever the reason for that decision, it changed my life primarily because of my exposure to two remarkable men: Arthur F. Burns, who was teaching at Rutgers while completing his doctoral dissertation at Columbia, and Homer Jones, who was teaching between spells of graduate work at the University of Chicago. Both had a major impact on my life and both became lifelong counselors and friends.

As I wrote in a memorial tribute to Arthur after his death in 1987,

Save for my parents and my wife, no one has influenced my life more than Arthur—as my teacher, mentor, colleague, and friend. . . .

I first met Arthur fifty-six years ago, when I was a naive undergraduate at Rutgers. To my nineteen-year-old eyes, Arthur at twenty-seven was a sophisticated man of the world—mature, almost elderly. In fact, he was a callow young assistant professor in his first teaching job while simultaneously completing his dissertation. . . . The young Arthur was very different from the mature public figure that is freshest in our memory. Yet he was already addicted to a pipe, already had acquired an amazingly wide fund of learning and a deep intellectual and moral commitment. Already, also, he displayed the force of character, the maturity of judgment, that years later, on the occasion of his appointment as chairman of the Board of Governors of the Federal Reserve System, led John Davenport to title a note in *Fortune,* "Where Arthur Sits," and to end it by saying, "It has been said that no matter what job Burns holds, 'where Arthur sits, there is the head of the table.'"

Arthur's initial impact on me was in a seminar that ended up with two students—Lawrence Vass and myself—spending full time going over word for word, sentence by sentence, a draft of Arthur's doctoral dissertation, *Production Trends in the United States.* That seminar imparted standards of scholarship—attention to detail, concern with scrupulous accuracy, checking of sources, and above all, openness to criticism—that have affected the whole of my subsequent scientific work.

Another impact—and I do not recall how it came about—was to introduce me to the great nineteenth-century economist, Alfred Marshall. Arthur was a great admirer and thorough student of Marshall's *Principles of Economics,* and we spent many a pleasant hour then and in later years discussing the precise interpretation to be placed on passages from that magnificent book.

In concluding my memorial tribute, I wrote,

> as one looks over Arthur's life, one cannot but marvel at the human potential that a free society can release. A boy of ten arrived in America speaking not a word of English, the son of parents in poor economic circumstances who settled in Bayonne, New Jersey. Eleven years later, he was graduated from Columbia University as a Phi Beta Kappa and the same year earned a master's degree. His parents were able to provide little or no financial assistance. He earned his keep by a wide variety of jobs. In addition, he received some scholarship help for tuition.
>
> After two years of graduate work at Columbia, he became an instructor at Rutgers University, where I met him four years later. This young immigrant boy, without a word of English at the age of

ten, became a fluent speaker of English and a writer of rare distinction, precision, and style. He went on to become a world-famous scholar, a professor at a leading university, the director of research of a prestigious economic research institute, president of the American Economic Association, and subsequently a major public figure—all this entirely on the basis of personal qualities, not as a result of influence of any kind. . . . What a testament to the benefits that a policy of free immigration has conferred on the United States.[2]

While seemingly a digression, these final comments are highly relevant to the world that both Rose and I grew up in. My parents, Rose herself, and her entire family were immigrants. The statements about Arthur apply almost word for word to her brother, Aaron. All of us were products and beneficiaries of the transplanting of a Jewish emphasis on learning and scholarship, largely limited in Europe to Talmudic interpretation in yeshivas, to a country in which there was tolerance of national and religious differences. There was prejudice and discrimination, yes; but they were handicaps that could be overcome, not impenetrable fortress walls.

Homer Jones, the other teacher at Rutgers who had a major influence on me, came from a very different background. He had grown up on an Iowa farm. His parents presumably were Protestant, though I never recall discussing his background with him. He had graduated from the University of Iowa, where he had come under the influence of Frank H. Knight, and followed Knight to the University of Chicago for graduate work. Homer came to Rutgers as an instructor when I was a junior. Like Arthur, he appeared to my eyes to be a mature man of the world, though he was only twenty-four, in his second year of teaching. As low man on the academic totem pole, Homer was stuck with teaching, among other courses, insurance and statistics—two subjects that I doubt he had ever before been exposed to. Since I was still planning to become an actuary, I naturally took both subjects. Only later did I realize how fortunate I was. Insurance would hardly seem a subject of far-ranging significance, yet Homer made it one. His quizzical mind, his theoretical bent, yet withal his Iowa-farmer interest in down-to-earth practical matters, combined to lead us far beyond the dry matter-of-fact textbook into the more fundamental issues of *Risk, Uncertainty, and Profit,* as Frank Knight titled his magnum opus.

In statistics, Homer was clearly learning along with us, and that experience has always persuaded me that the blind can in fact lead the blind—or is the right aphorism that in the country of the blind, the one-eyed man is king? Because he was just learning, Homer could recognize the points of difficulty.

Because he was so mature despite his chronological youth, he had neither false pride nor false modesty. He did not try to hide his limited knowledge of mathematics and statistics, but neither was there any question, on his part or ours, that he was the teacher and we the students.

Homer first introduced me to what even then was known as the Chicago view. Like his mentor, Frank Knight, a product of the rural Midwest, he put major stress on individual freedom, was cynical and skeptical about attempts to interfere with the exercise of individual freedom in the name of social planning or collective values, yet he was by no means a nihilist. It has always seemed to me a paradox in Frank Knight, to a lesser extent in Homer—and I believe that others say the same about me—that they could be at once so cynical, realistic, and negative about the effects of reform measures and yet at the same time be such ardent proponents of the "right" reform measures.[3]

FROM MEETING TO MARRIAGE, 1932–38

Together at Chicago, 1932–33

{ *Milton* } It was in 1932, at the depths of the depression, that I graduated from Rutgers. By that time, thanks to Arthur Burns and Homer Jones, I was no longer set on an actuarial career. My horizons had widened. I applied for scholarships to a number of universities and was fortunate to receive two offers of tuition scholarships: one, from Brown, in applied mathematics; the other, from the Chicago Economics Department. Awards that paid more than tuition, fellowships, as they were called to distinguish them from tuition scholarships, were few and far between and hardly ever available for first-year graduate students. By this time, I had definitely transferred my primary allegiance to economics, so the choice was easy. Yet my having a choice is also a striking example of the importance of purely random events. Had Homer not chosen to spend a couple of years teaching at Rutgers, I would almost certainly not have gone to Chicago, but would have taken the Brown offer, and had a wholly different life and career.

In writing about the choice subsequently,[1] I referred to some famous lines of Robert Frost: "Two roads diverged in a yellow wood,/ And sorry I could not travel both/ . . . I took the one less traveled by,/ And that has made all the difference."

As I wrote then,

I cannot say I took the less traveled one, but the one I took determined the whole course of my life.

The reason I chose as I did was not only, perhaps not even primarily, the intellectual appeal of economics. Neither was it simply the influence of Homer and Arthur, though that was important. It was

33

at least as much the times. . . . The United States was at the bottom of the deepest depression in its history before or since. The dominant problem of the times was economics. How to get out of the depression? How to reduce unemployment? What explained the paradox of great need on the one hand and unused resources on the other? Under the circumstances, becoming an economist seemed more relevant to the burning issues of the day than becoming an applied mathematician or an actuary.[2]

I drove west to Chicago in the fall of 1932 with a couple of college friends, one of whom, Eugene Weiss, had a car and was headed for medical school at Northwestern.[3] It was an eye-opening experience. I had just turned twenty, and had never before been west of the Delaware River. The farther west we went, the friendlier and more hospitable the people. That trend, as I discovered when I traveled to Rose's home in Portland for the first time eight years later, continued beyond Chicago all the way to the West Coast.

My first year in Chicago, 1932–33, was my most difficult year financially. I did find a job as a lunchtime waiter at a restaurant on Ellis Avenue that was run by an elderly widow. It was across the street from the public entrance to Stagg Field, the university's football stadium, named for Amos Alonzo Stagg, the famous football coach. The spot is now marked by a sculpture by Henry Moore commemorating the first self-sustaining nuclear reaction, which was achieved in a squash racquets court under the stadium. As it happens, I played squash racquets in that court as a student and remember it well. The atomic experiments weakened the stadium structure so much that it had to be torn down. The building that housed the restaurant was also torn down many years ago in the course of building the Research Institutes.

The restaurant was crowded only on days when there was a football game in the stadium. For the rest of the time, it barely made expenses. My pay was one meal a day and a small room above the restaurant. I did manage also to be taken on as a salesman on commission on Saturdays at an O'Connor and Goldberg shoe store. However, as the most recent hire, I was allowed to serve a customer only when all the other clerks were busy. When my commission totaled seventy five cents after a twelve-hour day, I quit. All other attempts to find a paying job were unsuccessful. That was the first year that I did not meet my expenses from my own resources. I had to rely on a loan from my family of three hundred dollars, if my memory serves me right, supplied mostly by Helen, my telegraph-operator sister. I paid her back the next year out of the fellowship I received from Columbia.

In 1932, as now, the Economics Department had the deserved reputation of being one of the best in the country. The two stars on the faculty, Jacob Viner and Frank Knight, were joined by other eminent economists—Henry Schultz, Paul Douglas, Henry Simons, Lloyd Mints, Harry A. Millis, John Nef. Each had his special strength and left a unique imprint on the students. Controversies among faculty members, mostly on an intellectual basis, helped to make the department an exciting place to study, preserved an atmosphere of a search for the truth, and developed the tradition that what mattered in intellectual discourse was only the cogency of an argument, not the diplomacy with which it was stated, or the seniority or professional standing of the person who stated it. Equally important, a brilliant group of graduate students from all over the world exposed me to a cosmopolitan and vibrant intellectual atmosphere of a kind that I had never dreamed existed.

{ *Rose* } I had already experienced the intellectual atmosphere of the University of Chicago for two years as an undergraduate, more through contact with Aaron's friends on and off the campus than with fellow students. So, as a graduate student, the big change for me was increased contact with my fellow students.

Jacob Viner and Frank Knight were brilliant men who could hardly have differed more from one another. They alternated in teaching the first-year course in economic theory. Viner had an incisive and organized mind, was rigorous and not given to suffering fools gladly. Knight was far less organized, given more to philosophical and even sophistical reasoning. The same course was very different when taught by Knight than when taught by Viner. Many students, I among them, took the course from both men and learned from each.

The course in which Milton and I met (Economics 301, Price and Distribution Theory) was taught that quarter by Jacob Viner. It was the basic price-theory course at Chicago, taken by nearly every graduate student. Viner was an extreme disciplinarian in the classroom. Some students found the course forbidding and lived in fear of the man and of his subject. I found the course stimulating but the man forbidding, in part because of the tales I had heard as an undergraduate about how tough he was. The gossip was that he failed at least a third of the class every year. And because Aaron was on the faculty, I was nervous about embarrassing him by not making the grade. Viner opened a new world for both Milton and me. He presented economic theory with verve and color, making it an exciting subject. In Viner's hands, economic theory was a coherent set of tools, to be used with care and the utmost attention to logical rigor, but to be judged primarily by its usefulness in understanding and interpreting important economic events. He presented economics as, in Alfred Marshall's words, "an engine of analysis."

Though Viner had few peers for quickness of mind and tongue or ability to grasp new ideas or to spot and expose fallacies, he was less open to admitting error himself. There was a famous episode in which he instructed a draftsman (Y. K. Wong, who later became an eminent mathematician) to draw a graph for an article on "Cost Curves and Supply Curves" in a way that incorporated a mathematically impossible relation between two curves. Viner comments in a footnote that his stubborn draftsman "saw some objection to this procedure which I could not succeed in understanding. I could not persuade him to disregard his scruples as a craftsman and to follow my instructions, absurd though they might be."[4] That footnote made Mr. Wong's reputation among economists because his economics, and not only his mathematics, was correct.

As a brash student in Viner's class, Milton had a somewhat similar experience. In illustrating some economic proposition on the blackboard with a special example, Viner differentiated a function incorrectly. It was a clear mistake, yet for the rest of the class period he maintained that his mathematics was correct, while Milton as stubbornly asserted that it was not. After the class was over, and the rest of the students had left, Viner quickly admitted his error. That taught Milton a lesson—though one that he has often disregarded. In later years, we translated the lesson into a maxim for our children: if you make a mistake and refuse to admit it, you hurt yourself twice, once when you make the mistake and again when you refuse to admit it.

Frank H. Knight taught the History of Economic Thought our first year. He can best be described by quoting from a talk by George Stigler, a fellow student of ours, at the memorial service for him on May 24, 1972:

> He was a lovable, indomitable, improbable man, but his powerful influence did not derive from his eccentricities or his charm.
>
> One great source of his influence was the purity of his devotion to the pursuit of knowledge. Frank Knight transmitted, to a degree I have never seen equaled, a sense of unreserved commitment to the truth.
>
> He had an unfailing suspicion of authority, which, if anything, he may have overtaught some of us. Yet somehow his unwillingness to bow to any authority except reason did not lead him to arrogance but rather to a special sort of humility; in particular, there was not the slightest element of condescension in his relations with us students. He listened at least as hopefully to a suggestion from one of us as to one from a famous scholar and in fact it was sometimes

downright embarrassing to be accorded the respect with which he awaited our inadequate views.

I can attest personally to this respect, as I had the good fortune to serve as Frank Knight's research assistant from 1934 to 1936. Knight also instilled in his students a sense of skepticism which became part of their thinking and work—and, unhappily, in so doing discouraged some of them from making the contribution that they might otherwise have made.

Frank Knight was intensely intellectual, holding particular views with great conviction, but this did not prevent his abandoning them with equally great conviction. I recall his starting class one day with a diatribe about how absurd a particular interpretation of some author was, expressing amazement that any intelligent person could ever have held it, only to add, "of course, that was my view until" a short time ago. His copy of David Ricardo's *Principles* was literally unreadable because of the detailed handwritten notes on nearly every page, testifying to repeated rereadings.

Stories about Knight abound. He reacted to his early background in a fundamentalist religious family by becoming religiously antireligious in later years. His younger brother Bruce, who taught at Dartmouth College at a time when we had a second home not far away, once told us the following story. At a Baptist revival meeting, his father required Frank, then twelve or thirteen, and his three younger brothers to sign written pledges to Jesus. After the meeting, Frank collected his brothers, made a fire behind the barn, and induced them to join him in consigning the pledges to the flames, saying, according to Bruce decades later, "Pledges and promises made under duress are not binding." That was the Frank Knight we knew so well.

A Catholic priest doing graduate work in economics registered for Knight's course one quarter. His presence in clerical garb was doubtless an irritation to Knight. After two weeks or so in the course, the priest politely complained to the chairman of the department, "I registered for a course in the History of Economic Thought, not one in the misdeeds of the Catholic Church," and asked for, and received, a refund of the fee he had paid for the course.

During our first few months at Chicago in the fall of 1932, Knight gave one or more tongue-in-cheek lectures on "The Case for Communism," subtitled "Why I Am a Communist, by an Ex-Liberal." As we were walking out of the lecture room, we heard one (real) communist student say to another, "Knight means well, but I am afraid we will have to shoot him along with the rest." When asked some years later for permission to publish the lectures, Knight is said to have responded, "I wish I could unpublish them."[5]

We have often remarked that two-thirds of his students never got anything from him, and the rest never got anything out of two-thirds of his remarks, but that the remaining one-third of one-third was well worth the price of admission. To this day we find ourselves often prefacing a comment, "as Frank Knight would say."

Lloyd Mints, though less brilliant and exciting than Viner, served the same function for us in monetary theory that Viner did in price theory. His Economics 330 and 331 introduced us to the organic core of monetary theory. Like Viner, Mints concentrated on the fundamentals, not on institutional arrangements. He was thorough and meticulous in his presentations and, again like Viner, assigned us readings ranging over a wide variety of views. Neither used a textbook, but insisted that we read the original sources. In Mints's case that included Keynes's 1923 book *Monetary Reform* and his two-volume *Treatise on Money*. *The General Theory* was still in the future.

I had a very warm feeling toward Mints. He and Aaron were close friends and had adjoining offices. Since I spent a fair amount of time studying in Aaron's office while an undergraduate, I knew Mints as a friend as well as a teacher. In addition, I was grateful to Mints for what I considered a great kindness to me. My final exam in Mints's class immediately followed Viner's exam. I was so nervous at the end of Viner's exam that I could not read the questions in Mints's exam. When Mints saw me sitting there, he came over and asked what was wrong. I explained my problem. In a very fatherly way, he said, "Just relax for a few minutes and you will be fine." But that didn't happen. When Mints came around a second time and I was in no better mental condition, his answer was, "You can write a paper on Keynes's *Treatise on Money* instead, but you're making a mistake because you can easily answer the questions on the exam." Needless to say, I wrote the paper.

{ *Milton* } In that first year, Rose and I took one other course together: Henry Schultz's course in correlation and curve fitting. Schultz was a highly pedantic teacher and scholar, not original or profound, who had qualities of tenacity, patience, and industry that Rose and I did not value highly at the time. We have come to value them far more highly in retrospect. Schultz specialized in a narrow field: statistical demand curves. However, he dug that field very deeply, devoting many years to his magnum opus, *The Theory and Measurement of Demand* (Chicago: University of Chicago Press, 1938). I was later his assistant, working on that book.

The most important benefit that I received from the course was not what Schultz taught in class, though his systematic presentation of basic statistical techniques was valuable, but rather his urging me to study with Harold Hotelling at Columbia and his recommending me to Hotelling for a fellowship, which Hotelling secured. That also meant that Rose and I were separated for our second year of graduate work.

Rose and I worked together in the statistics laboratory at the time-consuming calculations Schultz assigned in the course—sometimes into the early morning. We spent more time together in connection with this course than with any other. As a result, we got to know each other better. We were often joined by a fellow student from Sweden, Sune Carlson, who became one of our closest friends during the years he was in the United States, but from whom we drifted apart after he returned to Sweden, where he had a distinguished academic career. By a curious turn of fate, he was a member of the Nobel committee that awarded me the Nobel Prize in 1976. We saw him there during the Nobel ceremonies, and again in 1991, when we returned to Stockholm for a Nobel jubilee, celebrating the ninetieth anniversary of the establishment of the prize.

Sune was somewhat older than we and much more sophisticated. The statistics lab was on the fourth floor of the Social Science building, and on many occasions, after we had finished our work for the day, the three of us would wait for the elevator together. When it came, Sune would push Rose and me into the elevator and run down the stairs himself. He thought he was encouraging a romance, but we were too immature to take advantage of his good intentions.

{ *Rose* }   Milton did not have any contact with H. A. Millis, who was chairman of the Economics Department for many years. His interest was labor and he was then writing a tome that would be published a decade later.[6] His courses, which I was foolish enough to take, consisted of reading word for word from his manuscript. Since his class met at 8:00 A.M., my recollection is that I missed more classes than I attended. That was no problem, because I had the manuscript and could read the part I had missed hearing. Millis was a fine fatherly man but not the most exciting of teachers.

{ *Milton* }   I was wiser in my choice of additional courses. They were primarily in the Department of Mathematics, where I took courses enough to have the equivalent of a master's degree in mathematics—which stood me in very good stead in my later career.

The graduate student body, while few in number, were of extraordinarily high quality. Two of our fellow students, Albert G. Hart and Kenneth Boulding, were somewhat senior to us as graduate students. Both went on to have distinguished careers, Al as a longtime professor of economics at Columbia University; Ken, first as the author of a widely used price-theory textbook, and then in the wider field of conflict resolution as Distinguished Professor of Economics at the University of Colorado, Boulder. Our most vivid memory is their vigorous manner of engaging each other in discussion. Both believed it was wasteful for only one person to talk at a time. So Al would proceed with his remarks at a machine-gun pace while Ken responded simultaneously in an inimitable stutter. Observing them at it hammer and tongs—an apt image, if ever there was one—was a favorite diversion of their fellow students.

Numerous visitors from overseas passed through Chicago for longer or shorter intervals, either as graduate students or as part of a traveling fellowship. For innocents like us, it was eye-opening to meet scholars from Britain, France, Germany and elsewhere, most often senior to us but of the same academic generation.

During our first year at Chicago, the deepest depression in U.S. history reached its nadir and the monetary system collapsed. As one of his first acts after taking office as President, Franklin Delano Roosevelt declared a national bank holiday. The Federal Reserve System itself, set up to avoid precisely such an event, closed its doors. The New Deal began. These events did not pass unnoticed in the Economics Department.

Some forty years later, when I was charged with engaging in "scholarly chicanery" for linking my restatement of the quantity theory of money to a "University of Chicago oral tradition," I wrote:

> I was myself first strongly impressed with the importance of the Chicago tradition during a debate on Keynes between Abba P. Lerner and myself before a student-faculty seminar at the University of Chicago sometime in the late 1940s (or perhaps early 1950s). Lerner and I were graduate students during the early 1930s, pre-Keynes's *General Theory*; we have a somewhat similar Talmudic cast of mind and a similar willingness to follow our analysis to its logical conclusion. Those have led us to agree on a large number of issues—from flexible exchange rates to the volunteer army. Yet we were affected very differently by the Keynesian revolution—Lerner becoming an enthusiastic convert and one of the most effective expositors and interpreters of Keynes, I remaining largely unaffected and if anything somewhat hostile.
>
> During the course of the debate, the explanation became crystal clear. Lerner was trained at the London School of Economics, where

the dominant view was that the depression was an inevitable result of the prior boom, that it was deepened by the attempts to prevent prices and wages from falling and firms from going bankrupt, that the monetary authorities had brought on the depression by inflationary policies before the crash and had prolonged it by "easy money" policies thereafter; that the only sound policy was to let the depression run its course, bring down money costs, and eliminate weak and unsound firms.

By contrast with this dismal picture, the news seeping out of Cambridge (England) about Keynes's interpretation of the depression and of the right policy to cure it must have come like a flash of light on a dark night. . . . It is easy to see how a young, vigorous, and generous mind would have been attracted to it. . . .

The intellectual climate at Chicago had been wholly different. My teachers regarded the depression as largely the product of misguided policy—or at least as greatly intensified by such policies. They blamed the monetary and fiscal authorities for permitting banks to fail and the quantity of deposits to decline. Far from preaching the need to let deflation and bankruptcy run their course, they issued repeated pronunciamentos calling for governmental action to stem the deflation—as J. Rennie Davis put it, "Frank H. Knight, Henry Simons, Jacob Viner, and their Chicago colleagues argued throughout the early 1930's for the use of large and continuous deficit budgets to combat the mass unemployment and deflation of the times."

There was nothing in these views to repel a student; or to make Keynes attractive. On the contrary, so far as policy was concerned, Keynes had nothing to offer those of us who had sat at the feet of Simons, Mints, Knight, and Viner.[7]

At the time that was written (1972), the Keynesian revolution was still dominant in the economics profession, as it had been from shortly after the appearance of the *General Theory* in 1936, though support was beginning to falter. During that period, the small minority of economists who did not succumb to the Keynesian revolution consisted disproportionately of Chicago-trained economists.

{ *Rose* } We had our first date only after our first year together as graduate students, and that was with Sune Carlson as our companion (or chaperon?). Chicago was the locus of a world fair—the Century of Progress, as it was labeled—and we decided to celebrate by going to the fair. That was the first of many world fairs that we saw together but undoubtedly the one we enjoyed the most. However, neither of us has any very clear or detailed recollection of the fair itself. One memory, however, lingers at least in my mind. When we returned to the campus, Sune left us. We sat on a bench for a while talking about what was ahead. Milton and Sune were going to New York the following year to attend Columbia University. I was going to return to the university after spending the summer in Portland. Then Milton attempted a goodnight kiss and, hard as it is to believe in today's culture, I refused to cooperate (I did not, however, regard it as sexual harassment).

Rose in Chicago, 1933–34

I spent the summer of 1933 in Portland, as I had earlier summers since going to Chicago, visiting old friends, reading for recreation, and studying for courses that I planned to take in the fall. I returned to Chicago by way of San Francisco and across the southern part of the country. The route from San Francisco to Chicago was extremely interesting for me since I had never seen the Southwest.

Coming back to the university for the second year of graduate study I had mixed emotions. I wanted to continue my education but I also was eager to be independent. Aaron in no way made me feel I was a burden. On the contrary, I believe that he got a good deal of satisfaction out of helping me and did not realize how I felt about being dependent on him—and foolishly I did not tell him. When I learned that he had told Professor Millis that I didn't need the fellowship that the department was prepared to offer me, I felt even stronger about making a change. However, I continued with the courses I had planned to take plus auditing Frank Knight's course in price theory. Many students followed this practice of taking the course from either Viner or Knight and auditing the other's course. I also took language examinations to satisfy the requirement for the Ph.D. However, I did not give up the idea of dropping out of the university and going to work.

The question was where to find a job. It was 1934 and few jobs were available. But it was also the beginning of the Roosevelt New Deal programs. These included make-work projects of all kinds from art to building to statistical studies. Though designed for the relief of the unemployed, these projects were planned and administered mostly by graduate students or faculty on leave. I learned that Philip Hauser, a professor in the Sociology Department at the university, was in charge of such a project, A Study of Closed and Open Unemployment Cases. I had met Hauser at the university but knew him only slightly. However, I decided to see him and try my luck. He offered me a job on the project. My recollection is that he did not stay with the project beyond its early days. The rest of the supervisory staff were all men I had never met before and have never seen since.

My title was editing supervisor and my job consisted of answering the questions of the people who were editing the schedules that came in from the field, and checking samples of the schedules for consistency. The employees were primarily men who had held responsible jobs before the depression. I recall no nonwhite men, though there may have been one or two. I do remember very clearly a nonwhite girl, who could easily have passed for white. I remember her because she complained bitterly to me that she had a particularly difficult time because black employers told her she could pass for a white and white employers were not eager to employ a black. I also remember the visit of a black supervisor from Washington. At that time few restaurants or hotels in Chicago or anywhere else welcomed blacks. Someone found a restaurant that would seat us for lunch or dinner and my guess is that he stayed with friends. The job was not very stimulating but I recall no unpleasantness. I stayed with the project until the end of the summer.

Sometime before the end of the spring quarter Professor Knight had arranged for the Social Science Research Committee to offer me an assistantship for the following academic year to work with him. That solved my personal problem. It meant that I could be financially independent and at the same time continue graduate work.

Aaron left the university sometime during the summer to accept a position at the Treasury Department in Washington. He had not received tenure at the university, thanks to his having transferred his allegiance from Paul Douglas to Frank Knight. That aggravated an ongoing feud between Douglas and Knight (well and amusingly portrayed in George Stigler's *Memoirs,* chap. 12).

With the beginning of the fall quarter, I left the project and returned to the university to work with Professor Knight and start what I thought would be my dissertation.

Milton at Columbia, 1933–34

{ *Milton* } At Columbia, where I spent my second year of graduate study— as I have written elsewhere—"Harold Hotelling gave me the same kind of feeling for mathematical statistics that Viner had for economic theory. In addition, Wesley C. Mitchell introduced me to both the institutional approach to economic theory and the various attempts to explain the business cycle, and John Maurice Clark, to his own inimitable combination of pure theory and institutional detail."[8]

Harold Hotelling, who undoubtedly influenced me most during that year, was a fascinating human being. Rotund at the time I first met him, he exuded pompousness, yet basically he was anything but. In class, he was concise, rigorous, and lucid. Basically a mathematician, his thinking, talking, and writing was always at a very high level of abstraction. Yet he also had an extraordinary instinct for picking problems and making contributions of the greatest practical importance. In economics, the "Hotelling (1931) rule" is referred to in a 1992 article in the *Economic Journal* as "the fundamental theorem of economics of exhaustible resources."[9]

Hotelling was extremely accessible to his students. His first wife had died some years earlier, and he maintained a bachelor apartment on Riverside Drive and also a country home somewhere in New Jersey. I attended many informal seminars at both places during my year at Columbia.[10]

Wesley Mitchell was the most distinguished of Columbia's then excellent faculty in economics. He was widely regarded as the world's leading expert on business cycles, thanks to his 1913 and 1927 books on business cycles and to the major ongoing research at the National Bureau of Economic Research, of which he had been one of the founders in 1920 and Director of Research from 1920 to 1945. A few years later (1937), I joined the NBER as an assistant to Simon Kuznets, and, still later, participated in its business-cycle research program, so I had extensive personal contact with Mitchell.

As a graduate student, however, my only contact with him was in attending two of his courses: one on the history of economic thought; the other on business cycles. In the first, he lectured largely from written notes (the texts of his lectures were available for many years in mimeographed form, and were subsequently published).[11] Mitchell was a fine stylist, in both written and oral exposition. I was particularly impressed that his extemporaneous answers to questions could hardly be distinguished from his carefully written manuscript: he answered in rounded, grammatically perfect, elegant sentences. A rare gift. As to content, I found the course on economic thought dull. Mitchell was clearly not a theorist of the caliber of Viner or Knight. To him the history of thought was much more a history of social and economic development. In sharp contrast to the history of thought as developed many years later by George Stigler, theories had no life of their own, were not regarded as developing out of the internal logic of the subject, but rather in response to external events. Moreover, it was clear that Mitchell was repeating ideas formed long ago and was not currently deeply interested in what he was teaching. The contrast between Chicago and Columbia was sharp.

His course on business cycles was a different matter. Though technical, and highly empirical, the subject matter was his life's work and presented current research. He displayed enthusiasm and engagement—and hence had a real impact on students—not seen at all in the course on economic thought. There was no overlap here with Chicago, but a different subject pursued in depth.

Next to Mitchell, John Maurice Clark was the best-known economist on the faculty. Unlike Mitchell, Clark had a real bent for economic theory which he applied to empirical problems. His *Studies in the Economics of Overhead Costs,* written in the early 1920s while he was teaching at Chicago, has become a classic. He was the son in one of the three famous father-son pairs in economics: James Mill and John Stuart Mill, John Bates Clark and John Maurice Clark, John Neville Keynes and John Maynard Keynes—all with first names starting with "J," and five out of six, John. John Bates Clark too had been a professor at Columbia for many years, and "from the middle nineties of the last century to his retirement in the nineteen-twenties, . . . held the unchallenged premiership in American economic theory."[12]

J. M. Clark was painfully shy in personal contacts. Eli Ginzberg, a fellow student of mine who became a close personal friend, was a disciple of Clark's (he and Moses Abramovitz, another fellow student, edited a collection of Clark's essays, *Preface to Social Economics: Essays on Economic Theory and Social Problems,* published in 1936). Eli told of a foreign student, a Swede I believe, who had come to Columbia specifically to work with Clark on overhead costs. He went to Clark's office to confer with him, asked a question and received no reply for so long a time that he asked a second, with the same result. He left indignantly, believing that Clark was trying to brush him off. When he complained, Eli advised him to go to Yale or some other university and mail his questions to Clark. He did so and received detailed, specific, and very helpful written answers. He ended by writing his thesis under Clark in absentia.

Another anecdote from my own experience. One day Clark came into class, pronounced confidently "It is obvious that . . ." such and such, which he wrote on the blackboard, "is true," stopped and stared at what he had written for what seemed a long time, walked out of the room, and returned some minutes later to stride confidently to the board and say "It is true that . . ."

In later years, in private contacts, we found him a delightful conversationalist. I recall particularly two conversations: one took place when he and Rose and I happened to be in the same car of a train on our way to an American Economic Association meeting. He went at great length into the story of the somewhat stormy early history of the association, a story he knew from his father. A second conversation took place at a small discussion meeting, when, to illustrate what had been happening to the distribution of income, he noted that his father had received a salary that was a multiple of a skilled carpenter's wage, while his own salary in the same position was roughly equal to that of a skilled carpenter.

Despite his hesitant lecturing style, which many students found disturbing, I regarded his course as second only to Hotelling's as the most rewarding of those I took at Columbia. It was theory with a different approach and in a different context from what I had been exposed to at Chicago, yet no less rigorous or relevant.

Of the other classes that I attended, James Angell's course in international economics was probably the most valuable, Vladimir Simkhovitch's on economic history, the most amusing. Simkhovitch had one fixed idea: the decline of the Roman, and every other, civilization was to be explained by the exhaustion of the soil. He had written some excellent articles—perhaps a book—on the subject and they were apparently his only claim to fame. He had a strong Russian accent and was an excellent and amusing lecturer, however limited his perspective. Ralph Souter, another of my professors, was a New Zealand economist. He had written a book titled *A Prolegomena to Relativity Economics,* which professed to be an original approach to economic theory but was almost unreadable, entirely abstract, and filled with jargon.

At Columbia, as at Chicago, the graduate students were a remarkably able group, some of whom have remained lifelong friends. I probably learned as much from interaction with them as from most of the courses I attended.

One friendship developed in an amusing way. At the time, Columbia, like most schools granting Ph.D.'s, required a minimal reading knowledge of two foreign languages. I chose French, in which I was reasonably fluent, and German, of which I had only a passing knowledge. One day, when I was in the library trying to study for the German exam by reading a difficult article in a German economic journal, a young man approached and said in a friendly way: "Pardon me, but can I be of any help? I am from Austria and I note that you have been on the same page of that German article for a very long time." That was the beginning of a lifelong friendship with Fritz (Friedrich) Machlup, who was in the United States at the time on one of the fellowships that the Rockefeller Foundation, with rare wisdom and foresight, was offering to scholars in Germany and Austria threatened by the rise of Nazism. Fritz later emigrated to the United States with his lovely wife Mitzi, and had a distinguished academic career, ending with a long stay at Princeton. He was one of that remarkable group of Austrian economists who have done so much to enrich economics as a discipline and, equally important, promote a better understanding of the role of the state: Gottfried Haberler and Joseph Schumpeter, both of whom received appointments at Harvard in the late 1930s; Ludwig von Mises; Friedrich Hayek and Friedrich Machlup, both participants in Mises' famous *Privatseminar*;[13] and a number of others.

Another graduate student, greatly affected by the rise of Nazism, who became a close friend was Wilhelm Kromphardt. He was a privatdozent (i.e., a beginning instructor on the first step of the professional ladder) at a German university, who had left a wife and at least one child in Germany while spending a period of time on a fellowship at Columbia. Needless to say, with his family in Germany and Hitler in power, he was in a delicate position. As a result, he was extremely circumspect in open discussions about developments in Germany. However, I became sufficiently intimate with him that he spoke frankly to me about his opposition to Hitler and Nazism. Indeed, I recall arguing about developments in Germany with a fellow student who made the most persuasive case I had encountered for Hitler. I later discovered that both his case for Hitler and mine against him derived from Kromphardt! An extremely able economist, Kromphardt told me that he planned to restrict his teaching to rigorous mathematical economics when he returned to Germany as the only way to avoid getting involved in political issues. For obvious reasons, I was unable to keep in touch with him after he went back, though I did receive one letter from him shortly after his return. I heard indirectly that he had survived the Nazi regime.

One amusing incident involved Sune Carlson, who was spending part of the academic year 1933–34 at Columbia. As a proud Swede, Sune thought I should be introduced to aquavit, so, shortly after Prohibition had been repealed, we went for dinner at a Swedish restaurant where Sune had in the past been able to get aquavit despite Prohibition. When Sune ordered aquavit, the reply was, "Sorry, we can't serve it to you because we haven't received our license yet!" After much palaver in Swedish with the proprietor, Sune persuaded him to take us out to the kitchen where we were served glasses of aquavit.

Another incident involved an evening when four of us ended up somewhat inebriated at the top of the Empire State Building late at night—Sune, Moe Abramovitz (still a close friend and a professor emeritus of economics at Stanford University), a fellow student whose name I don't recall, and I. We found a real novelty there, a machine for making a voice recording, and we jointly recorded a takeoff on Milton's "On His Blindness," produced on the spot, if my memory is correct, by Sune and Moe. I have no idea what happened to the record but for some curious reason the poem itself still comes to mind:

"When I consider how my life is spent/Studying profits, interest, and rent/ Smith, McCulloch, J. S. Mill, Ricardo Davy/Better drink aquavit, and join the navy." Not exactly a classic, but some indication of how immersed we all were in economics.

We also took advantage of the opportunities that New York offered at the bottom of the depression. My fellowship stipend was $1,500. Of that sum, $300 went for tuition (the total tuition for a full-time program for an academic year of two semesters at Columbia or three quarters at Chicago). The $1,200 that remained was enough to help me to pay back the debt I had accumulated the preceding year, pay for my dormitory room and meals, enable me to see more Broadway plays than I have ever since been able to see in a year, and leave enough to finance a summer spent with Moe Abramovitz at an isolated cabin in Canada—of which more later. The theaters were seldom sold out in 1933–34, so, when the urge struck us, we would take the subway (for a nickel fare) from Columbia (116th Street station) to Times Square, where Gray's Drugstore had a basement room devoted to cut-price tickets for that evening's performances. For fifty cents we could usually get a ticket in the first balcony for any one of a considerable number of plays, including even those regarded as hits.

New York at that time was very different from New York today. No doubt crimes, muggings, and theft occurred, but they were not the omnipresent reality that they have become. Harlem was predominantly black but had nothing like the population that it reached as a result of World War II in-migration. For us, it was simply another place for recreation. We did not hesitate to go to the famous dance hall, the Savoy Ballroom I believe the name was, with no fear of being mugged or accosted. Blacks and whites mingled freely, though there were few mixed couples. Indeed that was true ten years later, during the war, when I was again at Columbia with the Statistical Research Group. Similarly, the subways were not places of danger.

Doubtless this account owes something to nostalgia for youth, but at most it is an exaggeration, not a distortion. The depression brought distress and misery to many—as evidenced in the "ten cents a dance" halls that were fixtures in the Times Square region—but it did not destroy the social fabric as more recent developments are doing.

To return to the academic scene, I concluded from my own experience that the ideal combination for a budding economist was a year of study at Chicago, which emphasized theory, followed by a year of study at Columbia, which emphasized institutional influences and empirical work—but only in that order, not the reverse. Allen Wallis, who later followed the same route, confirmed that judgement.

My experience at both institutions persuaded me that fellow students are the most important contributors to the education of a scholar. As George Stigler wrote in his delightful and insightful intellectual autobiography, "I am convinced that at least half of what one learns at a college or university is learned from fellow students. They live together and they argue among themselves with a vigor and candor that are inappropriate in discussions with faculty members, even tolerant ones. If one could attract good students without a good faculty, one could run a fine university very economically."[14]

The role of professors, I decided after I had myself become a professor, is twofold: to attract good students and to provide them with topics for bull sessions. In addition, a good professor not only provides good topics, but also enough initial content to fuel intensive discussion. We teach ourselves; there is no Socratic dialogue that can match the bull sessions among young students seriously committed to their subject. That was certainly my experience at both Chicago and Columbia.

As I mentioned earlier, between my year at Columbia and my return to Chicago as a research assistant for Henry Schultz, Moe Abramovitz and I spent the summer in Canada. A fellow graduate student from Canada, Bill Conklin, had access to a cabin on the French River, which connects Georgian Bay and Lake Nipissing, about 150 miles north of Toronto. The plan was for the three of us to spend the summer there. At the last minute, however, a family matter came up that prevented Bill from doing so, but he arranged for Moe and me to use the cabin. Moe had a Model A Ford in which we drove from New York north to Canada, and then west to North Bay. We parked the car there for the (I think) six weeks that we were in the cabin, because the only access to it was by water. It was on the shore of the French River some six or seven miles from the nearest place for shopping. We had only one reasonably close neighbor, an Indian fishing guide, who berated us one day for scandalizing his wife and infant children by swimming in the nude. As our own experience with a canoe developed, we came to admire greatly his skill in canoe-handling. We became fairly good at it ourselves, but never approached his mastery.

One episode revealed our culinary incompetence. We decided to vary our monotonous diet and bought some rice. We had no cookbook and had no idea how to cook it. The clerk who sold us the rice told us to cook it in a double boiler, so we proceeded to put the rice in the top of a makeshift double boiler and water in the bottom. The water boiled and boiled and the rice got a little warm. Finally, it got through our thick skulls that we should put some water in the top of the double boiler. When we did so the rice started to expand exponentially, and before we were done, every container we had was filled with boiled rice.

We spent most of our time working on a manuscript about business cycles to which for some strange reason we initially gave a German title, something like: "Wie ist das cumulation möglich." We ended up with an extremely lengthy manuscript entitled "Hoarding." We never completed it, though I still have a copy and extensive subsequent correspondence with Moe on revisions. However, it undoubtedly shaped both Moe's and my future approach to the theory of business cycles. In my case, I believe it was the beginning of my skepticism about whether there is indeed an economic phenomenon justifying the designation "cycle," or whether the economic fluctuations glorified by that title are not merely reactions to a series of random shocks, along the lines of a famous 1927 article by Eugen Slutsky.[15] In any event, both intellectually and personally, it was a wonderful summer, to which I look back with much nostalgia.

Together in Chicago, 1934–35

{ *Rose* } In the fall of 1935, Milton and I both returned to Chicago, he to work as an assistant to Professor Henry Schultz, I as an assistant to Frank Knight.

I was assigned an office next to Knight's, which made frequent communication convenient. Though my relationship with Knight was friendly—during my undergraduate as well as graduate days at the university I had had many pleasant Christmas and Thanksgiving dinners with the Knights—I never called him Frank, contrary to the more recent custom, and it was only after a considerable time that he would address me as Miss Rose. I have no recollection of his ever reproaching me or telling me he was busy and could not see me. He discussed his thoughts about whatever he was working on (mostly Ricardo at the time) and took my comments as seriously as he would those of any advanced scholar. I will add that I was more hesitant to offer comments than he was to receive them.

It was a great privilege to work closely with Frank Knight. Some of my friends thought it would be a strain to work with so brilliant a man, but he was so modest about his own ability and, equally important, so very human that I never felt the slightest strain. To illustrate, I remember coming in one Monday morning feeling more than a little guilty because I had spent the weekend making myself a dressing gown instead of working on capital theory—which my conscience told me I should have been doing. When Professor Knight asked me how I had spent the weekend, I answered truthfully, but I am sure apologetically, that I made a dressing gown for myself. Instead of frowning, he smiled and said that was wonderful; I had something tangible to show for my weekend of work and that was more than I would have had if I had spent the weekend on capital theory. Was he sending me a message? I don't think so. I believe he thought well of me. As evidence I can only say that after the first year of my assistantship, he asked the Social Science Committee to continue it for another year.

After considerable discussion with Professor Knight, I decided that I would concentrate on a history of capital theory as a Ph.D. thesis topic. It would fit into my assisting him with his research, and was a kind of research that I found interesting. Knight approved, adding, "I have been working on that for twenty years without success but perhaps you will succeed." I never did. During Milton's and my honeymoon, I completed drafts of the contributions to capital theory by Longfield and Senior. However, when we started life in New York, I went to work for the National Bureau on a bond study postponing, I thought temporarily, my dissertation. I never have finished it.[16]

My work for Professor Knight consisted of reading and discussing his interpretation of Ricardo with him, checking on any questions he might have and going over the final manuscript. He always took my suggestions seriously and acknowledged my help in a footnote to his article on Ricardo.[17]

{ *Milton* } Back in Chicago, I was on easy street, being paid $1,600 a year to serve as a research assistant to Henry Schultz, with no tuition to pay. I was able to sit in on courses and did so, and also to take the preliminary exams for the Ph.D. degree, so that I ended up satisfying the requirements for a Ph.D. other than the dissertation at both Chicago (where I had received a master's degree in 1933) and Columbia. (I eventually took the degree at Columbia for purely practical reasons.)

Professor Schultz had completed a draft of his book on statistical demand curves. My assignment was to go over the manuscript, suggest changes and draft revisions or additions, with special emphasis on the purely mathematical and theoretical analysis.

Professor Schultz was a pleasure to work for—as I have realized more in retrospect than I did at the time. Diplomacy was not my long suit. When I found what I regarded as errors or omissions in his manuscript I pointed them out to him bluntly. I did not realize how rare it is for a senior and established academic to accept readily and with a thoroughly open mind such unvarnished criticism from a youngster—though Rose found much to her pleasure that Frank Knight was the same. In later years, I discovered that openness to criticism, if not unique to Chicago, is much rarer elsewhere. It was and remains one of the chief characteristics that has made the University of Chicago such a powerful center of scientific innovation.

Professor Schultz treated me as an equal and was concerned only with getting it right, not with who erred. At the time, I regarded the number of errors I found, and on occasion the difficulty he had in understanding the argument, as evidence of limited intellectual capacity—and indeed, sheer analytical ability was not his forte. Only later did I come to appreciate that his disinterested pursuit of truth and his persistence in digging deep in a narrow field enabled him to contribute far more to economic understanding than many an abler but less disciplined and less tolerant scholar.

Professor Schultz died at the age of forty-five on November 26, 1938, only a few months after his magnum opus, *The Theory and Measurement of Demand,* had been published. He had just learned to drive and had acquired his first car in order to take his family (wife and two daughters) on a vacation in California. Driving on the coastal road (U.S. Route 1), the car left the road and plunged down a steep cliff. The whole family was killed. A great tragedy and a loss to economic research.

I learned much about research from my year with Schultz, and even more about the pure theory of demand and supply, and the statistical analysis of time series. Schultz demonstrated his personal character in the generosity of his acknowledgments to me in the book.[18]

In the course of revising one section of Schultz's manuscript, I took the liberty of including a reference to an unpublished paper of mine, and Schultz retained the reference in the final version. Some fifty years later, a Japanese reader of Schultz's book (Professor Kotaro Tsujimura) came across the reference, found it relevant to his work, and wrote to me asking for access to a copy. As it happened, I did have the original article and was able to send him a copy. He later sent me a reprint of a paper of his that used some of the concepts in my paper, and asked for my permission to publish a Japanese translation of my paper along with his paper. In granting permission, I added, "I write mainly to express the great satisfaction at something which I did fifty years ago turning out to be practically useful today" (letter of May 29, 1984).[19]

My first published paper was a by-product of my work with Schultz. It was a criticism of "Professor Pigou's Method for Measuring Elasticities of Demand from Budgetary Data," as the article was titled. Since Pigou was then the professor at Cambridge University, I submitted it, at Henry Schultz's suggestion, to the *Economic Journal,* of which the longtime editor was John Maynard Keynes, and simultaneously sent a copy to Pigou. Keynes replied, "I cannot accept it." He went on to say, "I have discussed it with Professor

Pigou," and summarized the reasons that Pigou thought my criticism invalid. That was one of only two letters I ever received from Keynes, the other also a rejection!

I resubmitted the article to the Harvard *Quarterly Journal of Economics*, of which the longtime editor was Professor F. W. Taussig. He accepted it on the recommendation of Professor Joseph Schumpeter and it was published in November 1935. Pigou objected vigorously to Taussig, saying that he had pointed out to me the error of my ways. Fortunately, when I first submitted the article to Taussig, I told him that it had been submitted to and rejected by Keynes, and listed and answered Pigou's criticisms. The end result was a reply by Pigou to my article and a rejoinder by me, both published in the May 1936 issue of the *Quarterly Journal of Economics.*

My next contact with Pigou was nearly thirty years later (1953–54), when I spent a year as a Fulbright scholar at Cambridge. He was then retired but living at King's College, of which he had been a Fellow for the whole of his career. I wrote to him saying something like, "You may recall that you and I had an interchange in the *QJE* many years ago. I hope you will forgive my youthful indiscretion and grant me the great privilege of a visit with you." Pigou replied in a handwritten note, which unfortunately we did not save, something like,"I am 196 years old and allergic to economic conversation. Nonetheless, if you insist on coming and can get some one like Kaldor to hold my hand during the operation, you are welcome to visit me." I was annoyed but prepared to visit Pigou anyway. Rose was indignant and persuaded me instead to send a note saying that, under the circumstances, I would not disturb him. I have always regretted that I took Rose's advice. However idiosyncratic (Pigou was well known as an eccentric, a mountain climber, a member of the famous Apostles, and, like many of them, a homosexual, and was later accused of having served as a link in the Cambridge group that spied for the Soviet Union), Pigou was a great economist, a successor to Alfred Marshall, and a pioneer in welfare economics.

{ *Rose* }   The delight of having Milton back in Chicago added to the satisfaction of being back at the university and working for Knight. The old adage about absence making the heart grow fonder seemed to apply to us. Though we pretty much took up where we had left off, we seemed to be closer than we had been our first year. We were of course no longer sitting in classes together or working in any statistical lab, but we were still two students who found each other's company very pleasant. We were joined by two students, W. Allen Wallis and George J. Stigler, who were not at Chicago our first year, but whom I had already met: Allen was a graduate of the University of Minnesota, where his father, a distinguished anthropologist, was on the faculty. George came to Chicago after a year of graduate work at Northwestern University. Like us, their future spouses were also at the university: Allen's, Anne Armstrong, was majoring in art history; George's, Margaret Mack, always known as Chick, was majoring in social work. We soon formed a sextet whose lives were intertwined from then on. Anne and Chick, I fear, often tired of the rest of us talking almost nothing but economics, economics, economics.

In addition to the time with our friends, Milton and I also spent a good deal of time alone. When Milton's assistantship with Schultz came to an end and mine with Knight was to continue the following year, there was a second parting. At least for me, this parting was sadder than the first.

{ *Milton* } Outside of economics, the most lasting of Rose's and my friendships was undoubtedly with Leo Rosten, at the time a graduate student in political science, who went on to become a world-famous writer and true polymath—humorist, novelist, author of screen plays, as well as of scholarly books. When I first met him, he was finishing his course work in political science. He was interested in writing a dissertation on the role of the media in politics, and for that purpose applied for and received a Social Science fellowship to finance a year of study and writing in Washington, so he and I went to Washington at about the same time. He has always taken credit for persuading me to pop the question to Rose. He maintains he did so in the course of a long talk about my personal problems, while we were floating down the Potomac in a rented canoe. You will not be surprised that Rose and I have been unwilling to give him as much credit as he claims—though he clearly deserves some.

I have emphasized the role of chance in determining my own career. Leo's case is equally striking. His wife, Pam (Priscilla Mead), whom he had married while still a graduate student, fell sick while they were in Washington and had to quit working, putting great pressure on the family finances. To meet the financial need, Leo started writing "The Education of H*Y*M*A*N K*A*P*L*A*N," a series of humorous articles that he submitted to, and were accepted by, *The New Yorker*. Fearing that writing popular fiction would disqualify him for an academic career, Leo signed the articles with a pseudonym, Leonard Q. Ross. They were published under his own name only later, as his Hyman Kaplan stories became immensely popular and developed into a true classic of American literature. The stories were based on Leo's own experience teaching English to immigrants in night classes while he was attending the University of Chicago.

Though Leo always kept one toe in the academy, earning his Ph.D. with his book *The Washington Correspondents*, writing a long scholarly book on Hollywood, and doing occasional stints as visiting professor, the success of the *New Yorker* articles undoubtedly led to his pursuing a literary rather than an academic career.

Our long friendship with Leo, now deceased, was one of the great joys of our life. He was a wonderfully entertaining, yet also wise, friend, with incredibly wide interests and knowledge.

A steady stream of foreign visitors came through Chicago. One visitor was Oskar Lange, a Polish economic theorist, who later became a member of the Chicago Economics Department, leaving at the end of the war to become Poland's representative to the United Nations, and then returning to Poland to become a cabinet minister in the communist government of Poland.

He left Chicago in 1945, a year before I arrived to join the faculty, so I never got to know him better, though I later reviewed a book of his.[20] His lasting fame in economics is mainly for devising, along with Abba Lerner, a market-oriented model of socialism. He maintained that a socialist system could combine efficiency and freedom by playing at capitalism. The technical economic analysis is excellent—Lerner was a first-rate theorist and Lange the rare socialist who had truly mastered economic theory—but the analysis is essentially static and does not acknowledge the system's inability to simulate the incentives provided by rights to personal property.[21] Lange himself did not escape the corruption of power after he returned to Poland. By all reports, he ended up a tragic figure, a willing puppet of the communist regime, never able to achieve in practice what he had preached in theory. His personal life, also, was devastated. He abandoned his wife, who returned to the U.S., a sad and lonely figure. When he traveled abroad, it was with another woman, widely suspected of playing a dual role as companion and communist watchdog.

The year 1934–35 was extremely productive for me in many ways. At the end of it, however, I needed a job. No offer of an academic job was in sight. However, the New Deal was in full flood, providing an expanding market for economists and statisticians. Allen had gone to Washington a few months earlier and had landed a job with the National Resources Committee. He persuaded his boss, Hildegarde Kneeland, to offer me a job—which I gladly accepted. So off I went to Washington, leaving the sheltered academic cloister at Chicago and the warmth of my close relationship with Rose.

1935 to Marriage in 1938

{ *Rose* } Milton left Chicago on August 19, 1935. I went in the opposite direction four days later. Professor Knight was going to be out of residence for about six months—the fall and winter quarters of 1935–36—so I was free either to stay in Chicago and work on my thesis or get a temporary job and extend my assistantship at Chicago. Knight was amenable to either arrangement but staying in Chicago had no great attraction for me at this time. So I decided to go home to Portland for a visit and then get a job somewhere for those six months.

I had hoped to get a job in Washington, where so many of my former classmates (including one special one) had gone. Clark Tibbets, whom I knew from my work on the employment project, was planning a census survey that he hoped to get approved, and he thought that there might be a job on that project for me in Washington. But he also mentioned the possibility of other projects of the kind I had worked on in Chicago that were being planned for the West Coast.

The first stop on my journey to Portland was therefore San Francisco, where I pursued the leads I had about jobs in San Francisco and Oakland. I received encouragement but no job offers because the projects were still in the planning stage. So, after a brief visit with my sister Becky and her husband, Milton, in San Francisco, I went on to Portland for what I hoped would be a brief visit. My sights were still set on Washington.

Unfortunately, the census survey I was counting on did not get approval. Along with this disappointing news from Clark Tibbets came the suggestion that perhaps my best chances were on a project back in Chicago. I had hardly digested this unpleasant information when another note from Mr. Tibbets informed me that a Mr. Kenneth McGill would interview me "this week if possible." I had no notion who Mr. McGill was or what he would interview me about, whether this meant I would be going back to Oakland or, as I hoped, to Washington. But I did not have to wait long to find that the interview involved neither Oakland nor Washington. The project Mr. McGill was interviewing for was on health under the auspices of the Public Health Service and would be located in Portland. He offered me the position of editing supervisor—the same position that I had held in the Chicago project—at $130 a month, which was about what I had been getting as an assistant to Professor Knight essentially working on my dissertation.

With nothing else on the horizon and my mother's delight at having me home for a longer period, I again became a government employee. This job was not very different from the one I had in Chicago. However, because this was a smaller office with a much smaller supervisory staff, I had more responsibility. Portland was to be the chief training center for the whole Pacific Coast, so once we were in operation, we also had the job of training people for the other offices in the western region. I was not a very patient teacher and the students were not the brightest.

Initially, the job involved long hours training our own enumerators and editors and enumerators for other offices in Oregon and the state of Washington. In addition, changes were constantly coming in from the head office in Washington, D.C. We would just be getting things running smoothly when some new change would come, which meant more reorganization and more retraining. We also had frequent visits from Washington bureaucrats. I remember them in the main as older men, but perhaps that was just because anyone over thirty seemed old to me. My recollection some sixty years later is that their visits were pleasant socially but not very productive for the project.

As I remember, the supervisory staff consisted of five people. A young student who was my assistant and I were the only females. Mr. McGill, who was in charge of the whole area, was a gentle, fatherly man and did not spend much time in our office once the planning was over. The director of our office was not a local man, and I didn't like him much because he was very bureaucratic and took himself too seriously. The young man in charge of the fieldwork was the one I liked the best and worked with the most. He had dropped out of medical school because of the depression and the health problems of his wife. He was somewhat older than I but we were close enough in age to have similar interests and concerns. Neither his job nor mine was very arduous after the first few weeks and we both felt more comfortable with each other than we did with the men from Washington or the project director. As a result, we spent a good deal of time talking when we were both in the office. He told me about his problems and I talked about mine. He had many more problems than I had. While I could do nothing to help him solve them, I probably helped by serving as a sounding board. As for me, I missed my life and friends in Chicago and so found it comforting to talk to someone about life there. In addition, absence, plus seeing some of my earlier boyfriends, made me realize how much I missed Milton, and therefore it was pleasant to have someone listen sympathetically when I went on about his virtues.

After the first flurry of work—planning, organizing, and teaching—the job became dull and monotonous. I tried to keep myself from getting too bored by spending time in the library at Reed College reading current economic articles in the journals, reviewing general material in preparation for the prelims which I hoped to take when I returned to Chicago, and in general thinking about my dissertation. Some of this I did in the evenings, but much was done on government time when I had nothing else to keep me busy. I can't say that I made much progress on my thesis. Boredom about life in general is not a good prescription for doing original work.

Although my thoughts and hopes were all about how and when I could get to Washington, I turned down a feeler from Day Monroe, head of the Bureau of Home Economics, about my interest in a job on the Study of Consumer Purchases—a cooperative project conducted by the National Resources Committee, where Milton was working, the Bureau of Labor Statistics and the Bureau of Home Economics. Much as I was tempted by the possibility of getting to Washington, I felt that I was morally committed to stay with the Health Survey until I returned to Chicago, and I had only three months left. I am sure that this feeler from Day Monroe was a result of the efforts of Milton and other friends in Washington.

I have no idea what the many studies conducted during the depression years contributed to the store of human knowledge. I had given little thought to that question until I started looking back over my life in the course of writing this book. Some, I am sure, added to our knowledge about the economy; others just added to the collections in the archives. Their greatest contribution was to provide employment for many people who needed support. As I look back, I keep comparing the condition of the unemployed people who were working on the project with today's unemployed. There were no unemployment insurance programs and no extensive welfare programs. Workers then seemed to appreciate the help they were receiving rather than feeling it was society's fault that they were unemployed and therefore up to the government to provide for them. Ironically, it was the government, i.e., the Federal Reserve Board, that was primarily responsible for the depth of the depression but neither the unemployed nor others were aware of this.

{ *Milton* } By 1935, the New Deal was in its second year and still gaining steam. In later years, Rose and I came to be among the best-known critics of the growth in centralized government that the New Deal initiated. Yet, ironically, the New Deal was a lifesaver for us personally. The new government programs created a boom market for economists, especially in Washington. Absent the New Deal, it is far from clear that we could have gotten jobs as economists. Academic posts were few. Anti-Semitism was widespread in the academy. Although George Stigler got a teaching post at Iowa State College in 1936, and Allen Wallis at Yale in 1937, to the best of my recollection I was not offered any academic post until I went to Wisconsin for a year as a visiting professor in 1940—and anti-Semitism helped make that only a one-year appointment (see chap. 6).

Of course, none of that entered our minds at the time. The depression had been an unprecedented disaster for the country. Rose and I had been exceedingly fortunate personally to be able to complete our graduate work. However, we were very much aware of what the nation had been through—after all, we witnessed at close range the collapse of bank after bank in Chicago during our first graduate year there. Like our teachers and fellow students at Chicago, and indeed most of the nation, we regarded many early New Deal measures as appropriate responses to the critical situation—in our case not, I hasten to add, the price- and wage-fixing measures of the National Recovery Administration and the Agricultural Adjustment Administration, but certainly the job-creating Works Progress Administration, Public Works Administration, and Civilian Conservation Corps.

In any event, Rose and I were much more concerned with our personal affairs than with these cosmic issues. We were on the verge of beginning our careers, and though young and naturally optimistic, our outlook and habits throughout our lives were greatly affected by the depression.

The National Resources Committee

Allen Wallis was the first of our group to go to Washington. In the spring of 1935 he took a job for the summer at the National Resources Committee. He was with a group, headed by Hildegarde Kneeland, that was planning a nationwide study of consumer purchases, as a WPA project. At Allen Wallis's recommendation, Miss Kneeland offered me a job, which I accepted. My salary with Schultz in Chicago had been $1,600, and that had been adequate to enable me to improve my standard of life and accumulate some savings. My salary at the NRC was munificent by comparison: $2,600 a year.

To digress in order to make these numbers meaningful in current terms, according to the data collected by the Study of Consumer Purchases, only 10 percent of all consumption units (families and single individuals) in the United States and only 5 percent of single individuals had an income that exceeded $2,600. My federal income tax in 1936, the first full year that I was in Washington, was $45.53, or less than 2 percent of my income; prices, as measured by the consumer price index, were more than eleven times as high in 1996 as in 1935; and tax rates have risen sharply. In 1996, it would have taken a salary of more than $36,150, paying a tax of roughly $7,000, or 19.3 percent of income, to yield an after-tax income with the same purchasing power as what I received in 1935.

And even that comparison greatly understates the relative munificence of my salary. Real incomes, and not only dollar incomes, have risen over the past half century. In 1935, my salary yielded more than 2.2 times the after-tax average annual earnings of a full-time employee in all industries. In 1994 (the latest year for which I have readily available figures on average annual earnings), it would have taken a salary of around $71,000 to yield 2.2 times the after-tax earnings of a full-time employee—not a bad salary for a twenty-three-year-old just leaving graduate school. The tendency for Washington to take care of its own is hardly a recent development.

When I arrived, Allen and our mutual friend Russell Nichols were rooming with a young Washington couple, Lois and Ellsworth Clark, who had rented an apartment that was larger than they required for their family (the two of them and one infant), and were renting out rooms to supplement Ellsworth's income as a government-employed junior attorney. When Allen left a couple of months later to go to Columbia University for graduate study, I took his place at the Clarks'. That led to a lifelong friendship. At one time or another, Rose and, years later, our son David stayed with them. By then, it was Clark hospitality, not financial need, that accounted for David's staying with them during part of a summer he spent in Washington as a congressional intern. Indeed, David has commented that his main problem was to keep Lois from giving him money for bus fare when he left in the morning to go to work.

Lois came from South Berwick, Maine; Ellsworth, from nearby Portsmouth, New Hampshire. They were distantly related, and Lois, who was a few years older than Ellsworth, loved to boast about how she had pushed Ellsworth in his baby carriage. They were wonderful people, now deceased, whose hospitality and friendship knew no bounds. During later summers, when we had a second home in New Hampshire and they occupied Lois's natal home, we exchanged many a visit, in the process being introduced to lobster, which was cheap and plentiful on the Maine coast. We still eat many of our meals on an ancient yellow pine table that we salvaged from Lois's grandfather's attic and refinished.

New Deal Washington

New Deal Washington was a wonderful place for a young economist—and young lawyers, political scientists, journalists, and no doubt others—and not only because it offered well-paying jobs. The explosion of government, combined with the paucity of academic and business jobs, attracted the best and brightest to Washington, and enabled them to achieve positions of far greater responsibility than was possible under more static conditions. There was a sense of excitement and achievement in the air. We had the feeling—or illusion—that we were in at the birth of a new order that would lead to major changes in society. The many young people created an active social life, enabling people from different backgrounds, fields of expertise, and universities to get to know one another. All of this was especially true in the early years of the New Deal. Things settled down by the end of the thirties.

The Study of Consumer Purchases

The study was designed to collect detailed information from a large sample of families on their incomes and outlays. Though it owed its ambitious size to the job-creating objective of the WPA, the study was of a kind that had been conducted on a smaller scale repeatedly, not only in the United States but in many countries, primarily to accumulate information necessary for calculating an index of the cost of living. In computing such an index, it is necessary to assign different weights to the prices of different commodities, depending on their importance in consumers' budgets.

The Study of Consumer Purchases raised many new problems of sampling and organization. Our group at the NRC was assigned the task of planning the project as a whole: designing the schedule (the detailed questionnaire that was to be filled in for each family), the sample, and the sampling procedure; developing plans for tabulation and analysis, and preparing a final report on the results, which was published in two volumes in 1938 and 1939.[22] The Bureau of Labor Statistics of the Department of Labor and the Bureau of Home Economics of the Department of Agriculture collected the data. They had traditionally collected such information for urban and rural communities respectively.

Hildegarde Kneeland, who headed our group at the NRC, was a remarkable woman, one of the first to receive a Ph.D. in economics—from the Brookings Institution in Washington, which for a brief interval in the twenties was a degree-granting institution. She had risen to a responsible position at the Department of Agriculture when she was asked to take charge of the planning of the Study of Consumer Purchases. A demanding boss, she worked long hours herself and expected others to do the same. She was highly intelligent, extremely knowledgeable in the field of consumption, very open-minded, and personally likable and warm. Both Allen and I, and later Rose, who joined our group for a few months in late 1936, became close to her and saw her subsequently for many years. Rose and I have a picture of Hildegarde, as we came to call her instead of Miss Kneeland, admiring our baby daughter in Central Park nearly ten years later.

Allen's, Rose's, and my academic training in statistical techniques and theory, though highly relevant to designing the study, had hardly fully equipped us to deal with bureaucratic Washington. However, Hildegarde Kneeland, Faith Williams at the Bureau of Labor Statistics, Day Monroe, and Hazel Stiebling at the Bureau of Home Economics were longtime civil servants who had been involved in earlier budget studies and, at least as important, knew the bureaucratic ropes.

I became completely immersed in the project. It was challenging, different from anything I had ever done, and greatly widened my perspective, both substantively and personally.

Initially, I found it incredible that people interviewed in their homes would be willing to spend several hours answering highly personal and extremely detailed questions, let alone have the ability to answer them, though I was assured by the veterans that they would. My skepticism disappeared when I went into the field with a crew that was testing a preliminary schedule. I discovered that many of the people interviewed—mostly wives who were at home while their husbands were at work—were bored stiff and delighted to spend several hours with someone who was interested in their personal affairs. They had no hesitancy in telling a stranger what their income was and how much they had spent in the past week or month or year on toothpaste or toilet paper or various items of clothing, and so on in incredible detail. Today's counterpart is the tolerance so many people display toward the phone calls they receive polling them on an apparently endless number of issues, or selling products or asking for donations, calls that in our experience seem invariably to come just as we are having dinner.

As a remark in a letter of August 8, 1936, to Rose indicates, the experience was broadening for me in more ways than one: "It's been fun to see the different offices in operation. I went out near Mansfield, Ohio, with an agent while he took a schedule from a farm family and found out what a farm looks like."

The preparation of the schedule raised all sorts of interesting questions of how to classify items of expenditure. One case I remember very well was whether to classify wine as "food" or in some category such as "recreation." Hazel Stiebling, a dietary expert, was initially strongly opposed to classifying wine as food. She changed her mind after analyzing some reported French diets for nutritive adequacy and discovering that they would qualify as adequate if and only if wine was included.

Perhaps the most difficult statistical problem was how to design the sample. Some aspects of the theory of sampling were well developed, but not with respect to the design of stratified samples for field studies. The theory of designing such samples has developed greatly since then and I have no idea how the sample we devised would be judged by today's standards.

{ *Rose* } I was delighted to return to Chicago on April 12, 1936, to continue my work with Knight. However, the place seemed different. As I wrote in a letter to Milton, "I was rather lonely when I got back to Chicago just a week ago yesterday. The places were the same but most of the faces strange. . . . I have seen most of the people I know—even most of them seemed quite different after seven months absence—or perhaps it's I that am different." Although my appointment with Knight would not terminate until September, my thoughts were already focused on what would come after that. I continued my research but my heart was clearly not in it. And what by now seems obvious, it was more than just having a job that was involved. I wanted a job in Washington. I started making inquiries about possible openings both through people I knew in Washington and through Professor Millis, the chairman of the Economics Department at the university. He was very nice and fatherly, and suggested that he would be in touch with friends in Washington but didn't really see the necessity of doing anything since I would not be ready to go for six months.

It is interesting, looking back, that he was the only faculty member who I thought could help me find work in Washington, and his help was only due to some of his cronies there. In contrast with the situation today, senior academics were not very influential then in Washington, though economists at our level flooded the place.

At Knight's suggestion, I went to see Viner about my thesis. As I wrote in a letter to Milton, "I did feel more inclined to work when I left his office than I have been for some time. Though we'd all agree that all in all, F. H. is the greater man, I'm quite sure Viner is really much more helpful as an adviser. I'm really sorry I didn't consult him sooner but I didn't think it was the tactful thing to do last year." With this boost, I got back to work, finishing an article on Longfield and one on fixed capital in Ricardo's economics. Professor Knight was very pleased with them and thought the one on Ricardo might be an article for the *Journal of Political Economy* with a little more work. Apparently the work was not completed, since it was never published. I was trying at this point to finish up whatever I was working on since I planned to leave Chicago by September.

In the course of a field trip, Milton was able to visit Chicago and we had a very pleasant weekend, with much talk about my getting to Washington. One of the complications we discovered at this point was that I was not a U.S. citizen. For some reason, which I have never understood, my father never bothered to become an American citizen. My sisters got their citizenship by marrying husbands who were citizens. Aaron and Lewis were naturalized. I had taken out my first papers as soon as I could but had not as yet received my second. The citizenship question did come up in connection with jobs in Chicago and Portland, but having my first papers was considered sufficient evidence of good intentions. The problem of citizenship became crucial only when employment in Washington, the mecca of government, was involved.

The first letter from Milton after he returned to Washington informed me that Hildegarde Kneeland had inquired about the possibility of my getting employment without citizenship and was told that (even though it was a matter of a very brief period before I would have my second papers) it was out of the question. However, Miss Kneeland, I suspect as a result of urging from Milton and Allen Wallis, went to a great deal of trouble to find a way that I might be hired. It turned out that previous government employment provided a loophole.

Sometimes things happen rapidly in Washington. The next letter from Milton informed me that I would be getting an application blank from the National Resources Committee "with a covering letter whose ambiguity will be exceeded only by its indefiniteness." Along with very specific suggestions about how to fill out the application blank came the advice not to expect anything to come of this.* (Milton had by this time become a knowledgeable government bureaucrat.)

Two weeks later I got the good news that my appointment had been approved and a letter from Milton telling me how surprised they all were at the rapidity with which the appointment had gone through: "We can make no guess as to the magic behind the move. It looks like merely an attempt once again to prove the utter unpredictability of administrative action. Whatever the explanation, I was delighted." Learning in later years how important whom you know in Washington is in getting anything done, I suspect that either Miss Kneeland, or one of the several people I had been corresponding with about a job, had something to do with the application getting the attention it did.

The appointment was for three months and was not extended. After a very brief period of unemployment, I got a job at the Bureau of Home Economics, working on drawing wiring diagrams to be used in tabulating the results of the Study of Consumer Purchases—an extremely dull and repetitive job that

---

* Milton's letter informing me that a request was being made by Miss Kneeland for my employment had a postscript by Allen Wallis saying, "While M. Ickes occasionally passes up something absurd, refusing your appointment would be so extremely absurd that I am afraid the chances of his overlooking the opportunity are not great. But I am generally too pessimistic (I have to show some signs of intelligence), so don't give up hope. Milton and I won't be the only ones here who will be plenty disappointed if this does fall through, either; HK will also join the weeping."

I was delighted to leave to accept an offer of a position at the Division of Research and Statistics of the Federal Deposit Insurance Corporation. The corporation was established after the disastrous collapse of the banking system in early 1933 to insure bank deposits against loss in the event of a bank failure.

My appointment initially was for six months as an assistant to Homer Jones—the same Homer Jones who was instrumental in Milton's going to the University of Chicago to study economics, an episode without which this story would never have come into being.

My job involved work that is fairly typical in a research division in government: preparing material and writing rough drafts of testimony for the chairman to present on the Hill, working on the annual report, answering letters forwarded by congressmen from their constituents. In addition, because Homer was a scholar at heart not a government bureaucrat, we engaged in general research in the field of banking. There was then, as there still is, much interest in branch banking and group banking as ways to improve the banking system. I spent a good deal of my time exploring banking arrangements in other countries and writing reports on them.

Homer was a delight to work with. He would come in every morning with some remark about something he saw in the morning paper and we would talk about it for a while before getting down to work. But it was not idle talk. It always had some relevance to our work. He was a perennial student. Our interests were very similar. Like me, he was much more interested in exploring new answers to old questions than in the typical Washington practice of defending existing arrangements, sometimes even when one didn't agree with them. Homer and I shared an office and for the most part I worked directly with him and he in turn with Donald S. Thompson, Chief of the Division of Research and Statistics.

I had already told Homer that I would leave in June the following year because I was getting married and we would be living in New York (which, as a good friend of both Milton and me, he already knew). Since he was my friend as well as my boss, however, after some cracks about not letting me leave, he said he did not intend to pass the information on. Sometime later, he confessed to me that he had inadvertently told Thompson of my plans. Nevertheless, that did not prevent Thompson's converting my six-month appointment into a permanent position.

On occasions when Homer was out of town, I worked directly with Mr. Thompson. I remember one such occasion because we talked about personal things as well as the testimony we were preparing for Chairman Leo T. Crowley to give on the Hill. We discussed the problem of my getting a job in New York. After suggesting that perhaps I could persuade my family (i.e., Milton) to move back to Washington, he was encouraging about my getting a position in New York on a study of the securities markets that the National Bureau of Economic Research was planning in cooperation with Moody's and possibly the FDIC. He proposed writing to a Dr. Blattner who was running a larger project for the bureau and Winfield Riefler who was an advisor. I am sure that helped pave the way for me.

Life in Washington at this time was exceedingly satisfying. I enjoyed my work and associates at the FDIC. I had many friends, some from student days in Chicago, others whom these friends introduced me to. There was always much activity, social and intellectual. In addition to all of this, there was always Milton and we spent a great deal of time together; some serious, some just fun. But all too soon, that part of life in Washington came to an end when Milton left on September 20, 1937 for New York to work at the National Bureau.

{ *Milton* } By the end of my two years full-time at the NRC, I had become an expert on consumption studies, and had acquired experience with practical statistics that supplemented my knowledge of mathematical statistics, something that stood me in good stead throughout my scientific career. I had also acquired the interest and knowledge that some fifteen years later enabled me to write what I consider my scientifically best piece of work.[23] Similarly, Rose's work on the Consumer Purchases Study contributed to later articles on consumption that she wrote jointly with Dorothy Brady, a lifelong friend we made as a result of our working on the study.

One incident of a purely personal character that I vividly recall had a permanent effect on me. A difference of opinion about some feature of the study—just what I no longer recall—led me into a bitter controversy with Faith Williams of the Bureau of Labor Statistics. In the course of a meeting about the issue, I lost my temper and accused her, a much older woman and a senior official, of underhand tactics—in the modern jargon, of dirty tricks. I later discovered that I had been wrong and she had been right. It taught me a real lesson in humility and I believe that I never again lost my temper under similar circumstances, though Rose may consider that a slight overstatement.

A Digression on Bermuda

In February 1937, by which time the NRC's part in planning the Study of Consumer Purchases was largely completed, and the task of analyzing the final returns had not yet begun, I took a long vacation in Bermuda, my first, I believe, since I had joined the NRC staff nearly two years earlier. In a letter to Rose, I described the "manifold charms and virtues—as well as the opposite—of Bermuda":

Bermuda is . . . a study in pastels. Everything is in light shades. There are pink houses and pink beaches, yellow houses and yellow and red flowers, all surrounded by a deep, deep blue sea. And everything else is likewise in pastels. Life is easy and leisurely—no automobiles to rush you—only innumerable bicycles and carriages and a Toonerville Trolley train that makes the 24 miles from one end of the island to the other in two hours.

Even the economic situation of the populace is easy and pastel-like. Wealthy people there are to profusion—but they are for the most part Americans, Canadians, or English who have homes here. Among the 33,000 or so real Bermudans—2/3 of whom are negro—there seem few enormously wealthy families. And, at the other extreme, poverty while by no means absent is certainly inconspicuous. Thanks to the enormous growth of the tourist trade, work is easy to find. Wages are not high but the needs are simple.

Don't take me, however, to be picturing an island paradise. There is the seamy side as well. The dominant white group uses every means to suppress the negroes. Only men owning £60 ($300) worth of land can vote. As a result only 2,500 people have the right of suffrage and only six of the thirty-six members of the legislative body are negro. Incidentally, to be a legislator it is necessary to own £240 worth of land.

Income taxes, inheritance taxes and real estate taxes are nonexistent; this in order to attract wealthy foreigners. Government revenue is thus largely derived from heavy import and excise taxes on the necessities. The educational system is none too good and is not entirely free. A small charge is imposed for each pupil. About three or four times as much money is spent annually on the Trade development board as on education.

Simon Kuznets and the Income Conference

In early 1937, I attended the first meeting of the Conference on Research in National Income and Wealth, a group which had been organized the prior year at the initiative of Simon Kuznets of the National Bureau of Economic Research.

The NBER, which was to play an important part in my professional life for decades thereafter, was "organized in 1920," primarily at the initiative of Wesley C. Mitchell, "in response to a growing demand for scientific determination and impartial interpretation of facts bearing upon economic, social, and industrial problems."[24]

During its early decades, the NBER concentrated on two principal areas: measurement of national income, a subject on which one of its founders, Willford I. King, had done pioneer work; and the analysis of business cycles, a subject on which Mitchell had become a recognized authority thanks to his monumental book, *Business Cycles,* published in 1913. The Bureau had remained the leader in national income measurements, and accordingly, when the Department of Commerce undertook to prepare official estimates, it asked the Bureau to cooperate with it. Simon Kuznets was assigned to the Department of Commerce, where he headed a group that produced the first official estimates of national income, published in 1934 as a Senate document under the title *National Income, 1929–32.*[25] In 1936, Simon Kuznets organized the income conference to bring together the large number of people in universities and government agencies who by that time were actively working on various aspects of national income and its distribution. The Kneeland group at the NRC was invited to participate because one of its tasks was to use the income data from the Study of Consumer Purchases to construct a distribution of family incomes by their size. I was given the opportunity to be one of the representatives of the NRC at the conference.

I may have met Simon Kuznets earlier because of my closeness to Arthur Burns, who was Kuznets's colleague on the research staff of the NBER. However, the conference was certainly my first occasion for close contact with him—another of those fortuitous events that do so much to shape a career and a life. As a result of that contact, and no doubt also of Arthur's recommendation, Kuznets later in the year offered me a job as his assistant at the National Bureau.

The Analysis of Ranks

One important by-product of my work at the NRC after I returned from Bermuda was the development of a new method of analyzing cross-classified data of the kind being collected by the Study of Consumer Purchases: for example, amount of savings cross-classified by the incomes of consumer units. Modern computers were still far in the future and our calculations had to be done on desk calculators (Marchants, Monroes, and Fridens were the major varieties). The best of them were slower and more limited than the ubiquitous modern hand-held electronic calculator. As a result computation was slow, tedious, and expensive, and the cost of computation was a major consideration in designing any research strategy. This was a major impetus for my developing "the analysis of ranks," as I called my new method by analogy to "the analysis of variance," then and now a standard technique for analyzing cross-classified data. Computational simplicity was a major advantage of my new method but not the only one—as is evidenced by my discovery a few years ago, much to my delight, that "Friedman's test" was included as one item in statistical software packages for personal computers. Apparently, the method is still used enough to justify inclusion in a computer package more than half a century after it was developed

I terminated my full-time employment at the NRC in mid-1937. I spent the rest of that summer, before going to New York, working full time revising my memorandum and making supplementary calculations. The resulting article was published in the *Journal of the American Statistical Association* in December 1937.[26] In retrospect I marvel at the brevity of the interval between my submission of the article and its publication. The academic and other changes of the past half century seem to have made such brevity an endangered species. Apparently, nostalgia is not the only basis for my belief that not all change in the academy has been progress.

I remember with great pleasure the work schedule I adopted during that summer: working until 4:00 a.m., and then sleeping until noon. The early morning hours were by far the most productive: quiet, no chance of disturbing phone calls or other personal interruptions. After marriage, we maintained that schedule whenever we could until the arrival of our first child rendered it impossible. One long-standing remnant was my insistence whenever possible on scheduling classes in the afternoon.

The National Bureau of Economic Research

In September 1937, I moved to New York to assume my new job with Simon Kuznets. He had in mind two major tasks for me, one general, one highly specific. The general task was to contribute in various ways to filling in what he and other income experts regarded as a major lacuna in data on income and wealth, namely, distribution of income and wealth by size. The specific task was a by-product of his work at the U.S. Bureau of the Census in producing the initial official estimates of the national income accounts. Simon had found a serious lack of data on the incomes of independent professional practitioners. To fill this gap, he distributed questionnaires to samples of physicians, dentists, lawyers, accountants, and consulting engineers. Initially he used the data solely to estimate their average incomes. On returning to the bureau, he brought the questionnaires with him for more detailed study, and wrote a preliminary manuscript analyzing them. However, he was diverted to other tasks and the professional-income manuscript languished. He expected me to assist him in analyzing those data.

The bureau opened a new world for me, one that was to play a large role in shaping the rest of my academic life. As I wrote to Rose a few days after I started to work (on September 25, 1937):

> I know I shall enjoy it. . . .
>
> For the moment I'm working on getting the income book [the conference volume] ready for the press. Then I most likely shall turn to exploratory studies in the field of the distribution of income by size. There's none of the Washington hustle and bustle around here; more of the academic quiet and ease.
>
> Nobody cares when you come in or leave or what you do in the meantime.
>
> Most pleasing, however, is the attitude towards research. If in Washington they set somebody to work on the distribution of income by size, they'd expect a completed distribution in three months. Here, Kuznets says, we know you can't possibly make a decent estimate as things are now. The thing to do, says he, is to spend two or three years on exploratory studies designed to lay the basis for decent estimates. That is the way to do research!

One of my first tasks after I went to the National Bureau in the fall was to edit the proceedings of the conference that I had attended in the spring. Subsequently, I served as the secretary of the conference for its first few years and in that capacity edited the second and third of the proceedings volumes.[27] The meetings, the planning of the programs, and the editing of the three volumes made me an expert on national income accounting, and more important, put me in contact with some of the most fertile and active workers on a wide range of statistical and economic issues. Simon Kuznets continued to be active in the conference until his death in 1985. I remained active until 1943, when I temporarily left economics for work as a mathematical statistician on war research, and did not participate actively thereafter. The conference recently celebrated its fiftieth anniversary, and is still going strong.[28]

As part of my work on the distribution of income, I advised on two studies, one in Delaware, one in Wisconsin, that were being undertaken at the suggestion of the income conference. Delaware had a unique body of data on the distribution of income because it was the only state that required every resident, whether subject to tax or not, to file a return. This was at the initiative of Pierre S. Dupont who, as tax commissioner, contributed substantial private funds to improve tax collection, and who believed that only universal filing would minimize tax evasion. He was pleased to find that in the process he had produced data of interest to scholars and not only agreed to their tabulation but also, I believe, underwrote much of the cost.[29] From my personal point of view, the study provided valuable professional experience in organizing and analyzing the unique body of data, and, incidentally, led to occasional visits to Wilmington which enabled me to bring back to Rose early samples of nylon stockings then being developed by Dupont and available nowhere else.

The Wisconsin data were significant for a different reason. Wisconsin was and for all I know may still be the only state in which the income tax returns were available to the public, without any guarantee of confidentiality. It had been one of the early states to introduce a personal income tax, had a good record in administering the tax, and had a far more varied population and industry than Delaware. Moreover, a number of people at the University of Wisconsin, Professor Harold Groves in particular, were interested in analyzing the data. The Wisconsin study was partly responsible for my spending a year at the University of Wisconsin in 1940–41 (see chap. 6). I wrote a foreword to the book produced by the study.[30]

Professional Incomes

My major assignment at the National Bureau was to revise and complete the preliminary manuscript that Simon Kuznets had written on the incomes of independent professional practitioners. His first draft was incomplete and needed much further work. Once I took over, both the statistical analysis and the preparation of the manuscript were in my charge. The result was a completely rewritten manuscript.

The final product was a book, *Incomes from Independent Professional Practice,* that was essentially complete by 1941, but was not published until 1945.[31] The delay was caused partly by the diversion of all of our activities by World War II, but mostly by a controversy about one part of the manuscript.

The book dealt with two major topics: first, an explanation of the differences in average income among the five professions we studied—one of the earliest empirical studies in what has become an important area of research, generally dubbed "human capital"; second, the distribution of incomes among individuals and its dynamic development over time.

Human Capital

Controversy arose about one part of our study of human capital: our attempt to explain the roughly one-third by which the average income of physicians exceeded that of dentists. We concluded that "factors associated with the free working of supply and demand," such as differences in length and cost of training, could at most account for only half of the observed excess average income of physicians. The rest, we concluded, was explained by the difference in ease of entry, produced at least in part by the success of the American Medical Association in limiting entry into medicine. At that time, there was no effective control of entry into dentistry.

I hasten to add that the AMA has lost power over time as its monopoly has been increasingly replaced by a government monopoly. Unlike economic power, political power is close to a zero sum game; as Washington has come to play an increasing role in medicine, the power of the AMA has declined. I did not anticipate that outcome when I was working on the book in the late 1930s.*

Dynamics of Income

A second major set of problems that we explored was the distribution of incomes among individuals and its dynamic development over time. It had long been realized that the distribution of income for any single year—data showing the fraction of a particular group that had income less than, say, $5,000, between $5,000 and $10,000, $10,000 and $20,000, etc.—could be a misleading indicator of the inequality of income because incomes changed over time. What really mattered was inequality over a longer time period. The professional income data had the rare quality that they gave the incomes of

---

* Incidentally, this study led me to form the opinion, later expressed in our book *Capitalism and Freedom,* and in other writings, that licensure of occupations does more harm than good. The experience of one member of the medical faculty of the University of Chicago who strongly agreed with my position on licensure provides an interesting commentary on the situation during the thirties. He had practiced in Austria and had achieved some eminence in his profession before Hitler took over. Being Jewish, he fled to the United States. In order to get a license to practice in the United States, he had to retake two years at a medical school, so he could be a graduate of an "approved school," and then intern for one year in an "approved hospital." Despite this waste of three years, by the time I knew him he had again become eminent in his specialty. The effectiveness of the AMA's control of entry into medicine is demonstrated by the fact that the number of foreign-trained physicians admitted to practice in each of the five years after Hitler came to power was less than three hundred or 5 percent of the total number licensed, and showed no tendency to rise, despite the flight of so many professional persons from Germany and Austria. For a full discussion, see *Incomes from Independent Professional Practice,* pp. 8–21.

the same individuals for a period of years—a brief period in the context of a lifetime, but a major improvement over data for just a single year.

Accordingly, we studied the correlation of incomes of the same individuals in successive years and compared the professions in respect of stability of relative position in the income scale over time. As part of that analysis, I developed a theoretical approach that decomposed the actual income received by an individual in a given year into components that I termed permanent, quasi-permanent, and transitory. This decomposition provided a means of estimating the long-run distribution of income from data on incomes of the same individual for a few years. This model of income composition, in a somewhat simplified form, constitutes a major element of the permanent-income theory presented in my book on the consumption function (see chap. 16). By now the terms "permanent" and "transitory," referring to components of any time series, whether of income or output or other magnitudes, have become common coin in the profession.

I believe that this part of the analysis of our book has had considerable influence on future research in the profession, though it is not of much direct interest to the public at large.

As an aside, my analysis of the dynamics of income change was in considerable measure inspired by a 1933 review by my teacher, Harold Hotelling, of a book in which the author presented evidence purporting to show that business enterprises were converging in size. Hotelling pointed out that "the seeming convergence is a statistical fallacy, resulting from the method of grouping." The author had grouped the enterprises by their size in the initial year of a period, and then traced the average size of these groups in succeeding years. Those averages converged. Hotelling pointed out that grouping the enterprises by their size in the final year would produce seeming divergence.

Since our data consisted of observations for the same individuals in successive years, we were in danger of falling prey to the regression fallacy if we simply grouped the income data by the size of income in the initial year. Instead, I developed the more sophisticated analysis mentioned above.

More than a half a century later, I published a brief note under the title "Do Old Fallacies Ever Die?" in the *Journal of Economic Literature* (December 1992), pointing out that exactly the same fallacy had recurred in a review in that journal of a 1989 book on productivity and in the book itself. As an example of how widely prevalent the fallacy is, I wrote: "For example, 'everyone knows' that job creation comes mainly from small firms. That proposition may be true but the evidence for it that I have seen classifies firms by size in an initial year and traces subsequent levels of employment—precisely what Secrist [the author of the book reviewed by Hotelling] did. I have yet to see what the data show if firms are classified by their terminal size, or by their average size over a period."

A few weeks after this note appeared, I received from an economist a copy of an article in which he and a colleague had examined this question for manufacturing and had classified the enterprises by average size during the period. What his results indicated was that, as so often is the case, what "everyone knows" is not so. New firms start small and are responsible for initially creating a disproportionate number of jobs. But new firms are also very likely to fail, in the course of which they destroy a disproportionate number of jobs. As a result, firms that are on the average small during a period do create many new jobs, but also destroy many jobs, so that their net job creation or destruction is not the major factor in the change in the aggregate number of persons employed.[32]

I cite this example to illustrate the devious, and often random, process by which science develops. Hotelling's review came to my attention mostly because I was his student when it appeared. It had a considerable effect on my analysis of professional incomes, which in turn played a crucial role in my permanent-income theory of consumption. Yet Hotelling's insight is forgotten and needs to be recalled to the attention of today's economists—and this cycle will undoubtedly recur in the future.

The Controversy

I was young and innocent at the time, and did not realize that a storm of protest would develop from accusing the American Medical Association of monopolistic practices that raised the cost and reduced the supply of medical care. I soon learned better. Under the rules of the bureau, adopted to ensure that its publications presented "to the public important economic facts and their interpretation in a scientific and impartial manner . . . a copy of any manuscript proposed for publication shall . . . be submitted to each member of the Board." The resolution from which these words are quoted, and which was part of the front matter of every book published by the bureau, went on to specify the procedures to be followed before approval of a book for publication. Those procedures included a "special reading" committee of directors appointed to evaluate the manuscript and recommend to the board of directors whether it should be published. As it happened, one of the members of the board who was named to the "special reading" committee was C. Reinhold Noyes, who was in the pharmaceutical business. He protested our finding in no uncertain terms. In a memorandum dated October 27, 1941, he recommended strongly against publication on the grounds that in the part of the book "about which economic theory has speculated," i.e., the part dealing with reasons for differences of income in different occupations, "the authors have allowed that theory to blind them." In particular, he wrote, "I suggest that the subject of freedom of entry is a hot poker and be dropped."

Three years of back and forth discussion followed, with Wesley Mitchell, the Director of Research at the bureau, trying to mediate, while consistently supporting the scientific freedom of bureau authors. By this time, I was working full- and overtime at the Treasury. Nonetheless, over the next two years, Simon and I prepared four separate memos, totaling eighty pages, replying to successive blasts from Noyes, and made numerous revisions in the organization and content of the manuscript, partly to include qualifications such as, to cite two examples, "For our purposes it is sufficient to describe this role [of the AMA] in terms of its overt expression and its effect on the supply of physicians. . . . The social desirability or undesirability of the changes here described has been much debated, but that large issue lies outside the scope of this investigation" (pp. 20–21), and "We are led to the highly tentative conclusion, based on many questionable figures and uncertain assumptions that . . ." (p. 133).

In later years I came to appreciate how rare is the combination of toughness and diplomacy that Mitchell demonstrated in defense of our scientific freedom.

I am indebted to Wesley Mitchell not only for defending our scientific freedom but also for teaching me a lesson about writing that has stood me in good stead. After reading my draft of a proposed bulletin on our early results, Mitchell came into my office and gave me a dressing down about the quality of the exposition. As I recall more than half a century later—itself testimony to the deep impression it made on me—he said, "There is some excuse for Simon if he doesn't write clearly. After all, English was not his native language and he did not learn it until his late teens. But there is none for you. English is your native tongue. People often excuse bad writing by saying that they know what they mean, and simply have difficulty expressing it. That is nonsense. If you cannot state a proposition clearly and unambiguously, you do not understand it." I took that lesson to heart. I learned that trying to write something clearly and unambiguously was the best way to find errors and omissions in my reasoning and to clarify my own thought. I was greatly assisted by Arthur Burns, himself a student, disciple, and successor to Mitchell who was generous in his textual criticism of much that I wrote.

Many of my future students, especially those who wrote their dissertations under my supervision, heard the same stern lecture. One example recently came to my attention in going over early correspondence in preparation for writing these memoirs. It was in a letter to Gary Becker in May 1954, when I was in Britain, referring to a draft of his thesis that he had sent to me: "Nine times out of ten," I wrote after criticizing his exposition, "sloppy writing reflects (and advertises) sloppy thinking." I am sure that Gary, who received the Nobel Prize for economics in 1992, appreciates my lecture as much as I appreciate Mitchell's.

Personal Life

Thanks to Eli Ginzberg, a close friend from my year of graduate study at Columbia who was teaching at the Columbia School of Business, I was offered and accepted the opportunity to teach a course in elementary economics at Columbia Extension. It was my first experience of formal teaching since the summer school for failing high school students that I had conducted half a dozen years earlier.

In addition, I also retained a consulting capacity with the NRC, which enabled me to make occasional weekend trips to Washington, expenses paid. That was a great pleasure to both Rose and me at a time when there were no inexpensive ninety-minute flights between the two cities, but only trains that took some six or more hours. Government transportation vouchers financed Pullman travel, enabling me to leave New York after my Friday evening class at Columbia and arrive rested in Washington early Saturday morning. The rest of Saturday was generally spent at work, but Saturday evening and Sunday were free for other purposes, and the ever hospitable Clarks provided shelter and elaborate Sunday morning breakfasts.

Aside from these weekend trips, letters flew furiously back and forth between New York and Washington: no fewer than 138 in the nearly ten months that elapsed between my departure for New York and our marriage, or about two each way each week! Such a pace was possible only because the postal service had a dependability that we can only envy today: with few exceptions letters bearing a three-cent stamp, posted in the evening in New York, were delivered the next morning in Washington (there were several deliveries a day in that unenlightened period). And when Rose visited her family in Portland for a month before our marriage, a letter bearing a six-cent stamp posted in the evening in Portland reached me in New York in the morning mail two days later, thanks to the recently established air mail service. As a result of our regular correspondence, we can document our activities during this period in far greater detail than for any other comparable period in our life, since neither Rose nor I has ever kept a diary.

In one of the letters from me to Rose in late 1937, I remarked with feigned surprise, "I just received a letter from 'your obedient Servant,' J. M. Keynes, Secretary, the Royal Economic Society, informing me that the Council will at their next meeting take up my application for life membership. . . . They certainly must be interested in having me as a member if they are willing to contribute $50 for me. Little did I realize my reputation had spread that far or was that great. . . . It's a swell idea anyway, for I certainly could think of few nicer things than receiving the *Economic Journal* for the rest of my life without having to give the matter any thought." Rose had given me a life membership as a gift, surely one of the most financially rewarding investments she, or we, ever made. A life subscription to what was then the premier economic journal in the world cost a little over fifty U.S. dollars, when the annual subscription was a little over ten dollars. I continue to receive the journal currently when the annual subscription is $65, and have now done so for sixty years.

Needless to say, the developments leading up to World War II did not pass unnoticed. As I wrote in a letter to Rose of March 17, 1938,

> I must say this damn European situation certainly is lousy. Here the world is going to pieces over our heads and we sit worrying about means and standard deviations and professional incomes. But what the hell else can we do?
>
> One thing the U.S. could certainly do would be to provide asylum for political refugees and I wish there were some way pressure could be brought to bear to do that. But such proposals would immediately bring a yowl about the need of taking care of our own unemployed, etc.
>
> Well, I suppose we can't do much but go our own individual futile ways and try patiently to await the obvious end.

And two days later: "Hell seriously seems to have started abroad. God only knows where the taking of Austria by Germany will lead; probably nowhere but to increased German arrogance and insolence."

The turmoil in Europe led to a flow of foreign economists to the U.S. Most visited the bureau or talked at a seminar that I attended at Columbia. Among them was Gunnar Myrdal, who was engaged in his famous Carnegie Corporation–financed study of the negro in the United States, published in 1944 as *An American Dilemma: The Negro Problem and Modern Democracy*. One of his assistants, Richard Sterner, became a good friend whom we saw frequently for several years.

During this period a group of present and recent Columbia economics students organized weekends in Connecticut, at one of which Myrdal was present. In a letter to Rose commenting on the weekend (with special reference to my humiliation at losing a cigarette case she had given me for Christmas), I commented that Myrdal was "an awfully charming and intelligent fellow. He started out as a technical economic theorist, as you doubtless know, and has since gone into politics. He is now a member of the Swedish parliament. He is a fascinating speaker and of course there is much of interest to economists in the Swedish situation."

My recollection is that this was not the only contact I had with Myrdal. At the time, Myrdal was a relatively mild reformer, a New Deal type, not the more extreme proponent of an extensive socialist welfare state that he later became. He proved to be one of the most important intellectual advocates of the "middle way," as Swedish policy came inaccurately to be designated thanks to an influential book by Marquis Childs with that title.

Myrdal received the Nobel Prize in 1974 jointly with Friedrich Hayek, the most famous opponent of socialism in all its forms. When the Nobel Memorial Prize in Economics was established in 1969 by the Bank of Sweden, it was specified that the prize was not to be awarded to a Swede for at least five years. In 1974, the sixth year of the prize's existence, and here I resort to conjecture, the Swedish committee in charge of awarding the prize wanted to honor Myrdal but feared criticism because of his notoriety as an extreme leftist. Hence they decided to link him with an equally notorious rightist. Some time later, Myrdal publicly stated that he had made a mistake in accepting the award under those conditions. Whatever may have been true of Myrdal, the award was a lifesaver for Hayek. In his middle seventies, he had become extremely depressed, withdrawn, and unproductive. The award gave him a shot in the arm and unleashed an incredibly productive fifteen or so additional years. The world owes much to the Nobel committee's sensitivity to criticism, if my conjecture is correct.

{ *Rose* } I lived in a rooming house a short distance from the Clarks' apartment. I was always welcome and we spent many pleasant evenings together plus many meals. I remember and so does Milton many Sunday brunches. Lois provided some wonderful steaks smothered in onions and I became an expert at making potato pancakes. They never tasted quite as good to me as my mother's, but the others, especially Milton, thought they were wonderful. I have often said he married me for my potato pancakes. Unfortunately, thanks to the advances in dietetics, recognition of the ill effects of fat and cholesterol, to say nothing of old age, we rarely have potato pancakes today.

When Milton left Washington on September 30, 1937, I moved to the

Clarks and lived with them until we were married. Their home remained a second home for both Milton and me for many years.

After Milton left for New York, daily visits with each other were succeeded by almost daily letters. At first most of the correspondence dealt with stock transactions, which were very complicated in spite of their minuscule size— complicated because they all concerned partnership arrangements with Russell Nichols, a friend who along with Milton lived with the Clarks, and Ellsworth, our friend and landlord. No one of the three had enough money to deal in the stock market on his own. There was much uncertainty about just where the market was heading and there was the problem of dividing the invested capital when Milton left Washington. I functioned principally as an inter-mediary except for one small investment of my own, when I decided to buy a few shares and Russell decreed that I should buy them from him (and so relieve him of his debt while saving broker's fees). Once the financial ar-rangements were settled, the letters continued, with contents of a different sort.

The primary theme was when and how we could get together. For a while it looked as though I might get a trip to New York on FDIC business, in connection with a project by the Reserve Bankers on Consumer Credit and Installment Selling. When that fell through because a more senior staff mem-ber wanted the trip, and when it appeared that Milton had no plans to come to Washington to confer on the consumer project, I decided to make the trip at my own expense. The result of the weekend was the decision that separation with intermittent weekends together was most unsatisfactory—so we decided to get married. I felt that I should stay at the FDIC for a total of one year, which meant we would not marry until June of 1938. I have never understood how two people who love each other and want to spend their lives together can be satisfied with careers that involve living separately during the week and getting together for weekends.

On an early visit to New York, Helen Burns invited Milton and me for Sunday lunch. That was the first time that I met Arthur and Helen, of whom I had heard so much from Milton. Arthur was going to Washington that afternoon on the same train that I was taking. However, he had a reservation in the club car, I in coach. Arthur endeared himself to me when he changed his reservation so that he could ride with me. When we arrived in Washington, he became my friend for life by taking me home and spending about three hours discussing the history of capital theory, my proposed doctoral thesis. I had many later occasions to be indebted to him for his kindness and concern.

In addition to my work at the FDIC and trying to get together some of the things I thought we would need for our future household (reports of this provided much of the contents of letters after the stock market arrangements had been settled), I was also reviewing for the finance exam required for the Ph.D. degree which I still planned to get. I passed that exam and had left only the one in theory to satisfy that part of the requirements.

An interesting tidbit: We planned to combine one visit together with attending the American Statistical Association annual meetings in Atlantic City at the end of December 1937. Milton took on the task of making reservations for both of us. In his letter to me on December 1, he wrote:

> When I got to the office Monday morning I found a program from the American Statistical Association indicating that the meetings were going to be at the Chalfonte-Haddon Hall. I immediately wrote for reservations at $3 and today received an answer saying that they were all out of $3 rooms but were reserving two rooms for us at $4.
>
> Consequently, I'm writing to another hotel which is just a block away asking them to reserve two rooms for us at $3. If they can, I'll cancel the reservations at the Chalfonte-Haddon. If not, I guess we'll have to pay $4—that's a hell of a price, however.

It would have been cheaper if we had stayed in one room but that never occurred to us!

{ *Milton* } Reading Rose's story of this incident reminds me of another. About a week before the convention, I went somewhere on a Fifth Avenue bus carrying in an envelope the original and all the carbons of the finished paper that I was scheduled to deliver in Atlantic City. After I got off the bus, I discovered to my horror that I had left the envelope on the bus! Desperate, I crossed the street and boarded every returning bus to ask whether someone had turned the envelope in to the driver. Sure enough, after about an hour, a driver handed me the undisturbed envelope! Miracles on Fifth Avenue did occur in those long bygone days.

{ *Rose* } Our next activity was finding a place to spend our honeymoon. Since most of the people at the bureau left for the summer and continued their work wherever they spent the summer, we could spend the whole summer on our honeymoon. Of course, as if I didn't know it already, Milton informed me that he at least would have to work as well as play. I intended to do the same, so we wanted a place that would be suitable for working, especially late into the night, since it seemed that both of us were night people. After much effort on Milton's part, input from Lois Clark, and much writing back and forth concerning pros and cons, we settled on a house on Lake Kezar, North Lovell, Maine, where our friends the Abramovitzes had spent the previous summer on their honeymoon.

Since my family was on the West Coast and Milton's on the East Coast, and we planned to live in New York City, we decided to get married in New York. That meant that none of my family would be present at the wedding. People in my parents' economic class did not travel, especially across the continent, in those days as they do today. My brother Aaron, who would have represented the family, was in Europe for the year. His letter to me, when told of our plans, indicated his approval.*

In lieu of my parents' attending the wedding, I went home to see them, as well as friends and other relatives before the big event. My friends in Washington gave me a wonderful send-off. That plus a telegram from Milton with a new kind of calendar (DN—days before Nirvana) sent me off in a high mood.

My visit was full of the usual celebrations for an upcoming bride. Our relatives, of whom there were many, plus friends, were invited to celebrate the coming event. Since my parents had given my two sisters large weddings, I suppose they felt they should do something special for me. Except for the pleasure of being with my mother and sister Becky, who came to visit when I did, I would have preferred to stay in New York but I did my duty and, in the process, collected some nice wedding presents from my relatives!

This time I returned directly to New York, arriving only three days before the wedding. Milton had real reservations about a religious wedding ceremony. However, he bowed to my wishes, or rather arguments, and made the arrangements. I should say here that I was no more religious than he, but I knew very well that both my parents and his mother would be very unhappy if we were not married by a rabbi. Unlike him, I had no scruples about going through the religious act, whereas he felt it was hypocritical to do so.

---

* "I am never particularly good at composing the right sentiments on important occasions. Nor is Birchin Lane, off Lombard Street, very conducive to such composition. This you must know. I would have welcomed any person you chose. In this case I have real pleasure in so doing. Milton is a fine person, whom I always liked. There is universal agreement on his very superior ability. What more can one ask?

"I do not urge the founding of an economic dynasty, but common interests lend attraction. (Tell him I shall not hold his very strong New Deal leanings—authoritarian to use an abusive term—against him.)" Aaron Director to Rose Director.

{ *Milton* } Our marriage ceremony on June 25, 1938, was held at the Jewish Seminary, thanks to Rose's persuasive powers in overcoming my objections to taking part in a religious ceremony. As so often proved to be true in the years that followed, she was entirely correct. Both Rose's parents and my mother would have been greatly upset at our being married solely in a civil ceremony. As I gradually came to realize over the years, this gesture to please them involved no fundamental sacrifice of principle on my part. It was a matter of pure form, not substance.

We had a very small wedding. My mother, sisters, and brother-in-law were present. Lois and Ellsworth Clark came up from Washington, and Doris and Arnold Beichman, who had become my friends in New York (Arnold had married Doris Modry, who had been a friend of mine when she was an undergraduate at Chicago), made up the rest of the company. The ceremony was a traditional Orthodox Jewish ceremony, with a chupa (a canopy held up by four males who had to be Jews, so Ellsworth was disqualified, and my brother-in-law Fred and Arnold had to be supplemented by two of the officiating rabbis), and the crushing of a wine glass underfoot after Rose and I had drunk from it.

The next morning we left by car, a Ford that I had acquired about a year earlier, bearing the total of our worldly possessions, to begin married life in North Lovell, Maine.

Chapter Five

BEGINNING MARRIED LIFE

{ *Rose* }   Our first view of the cottage that was to be our home for the next three months was a delight. It was a stone cottage in the woods, with a view of Lake Kezar and a path that led to a private landing on the lake. Our cottage was the guest house of Mrs. Paisley, a novelist, who had a larger house on the lake. As I remember, she was not there during our stay and we had the private use of her landing plus a canoe. The cottage was wired for electricity but current had not yet reached the area. However, the house was equipped with wonderful Aladdin kerosene lamps that provided us with good light for working far into the night. I cooked on a wood-burning stove—with which I was very familiar. My mother always did her cooking and baking on such a stove even after we had persuaded my father to get her a combination wood and gas stove. She could bake better cakes in her wood stove without even using the thermometer on the oven door than most modern cooks can produce with present-day fancy equipment. I should say, however, that I had never done more than boil water on my mother's stove, since she did not believe in children doing their own cooking or any other housework for that matter. But somehow, whether because of my mother's genes or my good luck, I managed to provide us with adequate if not elaborate meals.

{ *Milton* }   Like her mother, Rose has always been a marvelous cook, and I can offer the evidence of nearly sixty years of enjoying her food. If indeed her mother did not teach her, her culinary ability is strong testimony to the importance of genes!

{ *Rose* }   With or without modern conveniences, our days were idyllic. Thanks to our wonderful lamps, we could work late into the night on our dissertations: Milton on professional incomes and I on capital theory. There was never any question about how we would share the work that had to be done. We shared typing each other's manuscripts, as well as household chores. I was better at some chores, like cooking. He was better at others, like chopping wood. It was never a question of woman's work or man's work. It was only a question of who had the comparative advantage, including the time for the job at hand.

Most afternoons were spent swimming or canoeing on the lake. I had never learned to swim, and Milton insisted on teaching me before he would let me go out in the canoe. I never became a really good swimmer, but competent enough to satisfy him. Other afternoons we went for walks in the surrounding countryside or for drives in the area.

On one trip, we visited our friends the Clarks at the home of Lois's grandparents in South Berwick, Maine. Lois's parents had both been killed in an accident when she was very young so she and her two brothers had been brought up by their grandparents. Lois felt great responsibility and love for them, in particular for her grandfather, who was one of the most delightful gentlemen I have ever met. No one could help loving him. Our visit to South Berwick was the first of many visits, continued in later years after we began to spend our summers in New England. To the best of my recollection, however, we never saw the grandparents again.

The details of our first three months together have faded. What remains is the memory of a delightful summer. Of course, adjustments had to be made since we had both led independent lives for some years. We hit on a very useful way to make some adjustments easier as well as save time, namely, using numbers to substitute for certain frequent expressions. Our recollection is that we got to 10 but only one has remained to this day. It is "number 2," which stands for "I was wrong and you were right." That one has stuck because it is so much easier to say "number 2" than to admit to being wrong.

At the end of the summer, we decided to visit Quebec before going to New York, which would be home for the next two years. So we packed our few belongings in the car and started north through sparsely settled and heavily wooded areas. I remember the trip very well. The rain was pelting down, the wind was howling, trees had been uprooted. As we drove along, we noticed as it got dark that there were no electric lights in the houses and motels we passed. Occasionally we spotted a candle in a window. This seemed strange, but we still did not connect the absence of lights with the storm we had been driving through. When we finally spied a motel and decided to stop for the night, we were informed by the person at the desk that we had driven through a major hurricane. We learned later on that 1938 had become "the year of the hurricane" for New Englanders.

Car radios were not as common then as they have become and we had none in our car. Even if we had had a radio, the details of weather would have been nothing like so complete as they are today. However hard it is to believe, we were totally oblivious of any disaster in progress. Were we stupid or so absorbed with each other that the outside world did not really matter?

By the time we got to Quebec, the hurricane had blown over and the sun was shining. We had an enjoyable visit in Old Quebec and then turned around and drove to New York.

We had not rented an apartment before we left for the summer so we went to a hotel and started our hunt the next day. I do not recall looking at many apartments before we settled on what was really a luxury apartment in a recently built building at the corner of 104th Street and Central Park West. The location was ideal for Milton since the NBER was located at Columbus Circle (Broadway and 59th Street) and so was just a few subway stops away on the Eighth Avenue subway, which was a pleasure to ride in those days long gone. I hoped it would be convenient for me too when I went to work. The neighborhood, which I gather is questionably safe now, was clearly an upper-class location then. Arthur and Helen Burns had an apartment just a few blocks away, at 97th and Central Park West. That was doubtless one reason we looked for an apartment in the area.

We furnished the apartment slowly. As has been true during our entire lifetime, both of us believed that purchases should be made for cash, with the single exception of a house. Also, since this was to be our dream home, we wanted it to be perfect. When we finished furnishing it, including some beautiful bookcases that Milton made, it was the most elegant home either of us had ever had, and we luxuriated in it. (I don't remember where he did the carpentry but assume in an empty living room. Actually, he had done no carpentry since "manual training" in high school, but carpentry remained one of his main hobbies.)

We had many friends in New York and led an active social life. Except for the Burnses, our friends were all, like us, in the early years of marriage and had not started their families. Most, though not all, were classmates of Milton's from his year at Columbia. Again, most of them have remained friends throughout our life even though we have lived in other parts of the country much of that time. Since we traveled frequently, we have renewed our friendships whenever possible.

Of the five couples who were guests at a dinner party pictured in a home movie we came across recently—Helen and Arthur Burns, Moe and Carrie Abramovitz, Lowell and Agnes Harriss, Allen and Anne Wallis, Rollin and Jane Bennett, we lost touch with only one couple, the Bennetts. Perhaps this was because Rollin left academia, where all the others' careers were centered. And even that loss has been repaired. We recently visited them in their California retirement home.

The men in our group were all economists and some of the wives were as well, so parties were an opportunity to discuss the economic problems that were very much in everyone's minds at the time. In addition, the deteriorating world situation troubled all of us. The war that broke out in Europe in September 1939, almost a year before we left New York, was a major subject for noneconomic discussions.

Milton's friendship with Arthur Burns started earlier than any of the others and lasted until Arthur's death in 1987.

Whether it is a reflection of the mores of the time, or of our special group or our special circumstances, or a combination, our friends all remained married to their first spouses. Only death separated them and the survivor did not remarry. Agnes Harriss died a few years ago. Anne Wallis developed Alzheimer's disease in her seventies and died after a long illness.

Leo Rosten was living in Hollywood but visited New York occasionally. Leo, who died in February 1997, was always a wonderful storyteller. Loquacious and egocentric, Leo took over the stage at any gathering at which he was present. Eli Ginzberg, who was also both loquacious and egocentric, also liked to hold center stage at any party. On one of Leo's visits, we decided it would be great fun to invite both Leo and Eli and two or three other friends for dinner and see who would win center stage. The competition was intense but long before the evening was over Leo was, as we had anticipated, the champion.

One other incident at this dinner always sticks in my mind. Because Milton and I were both working, we indulged ourselves by employing a part-time maid. I have never forgotten Fanny. She came in the early afternoon and stayed through dinner. I believe she worked five days a week. We paid her $7 a week, which was the going rate in New York at this time. She was very happy with her job and we were delighted with her. She was not humble and we were not condescending. The dinner at which we entertained Leo illustrates her attitude best. This was the period when Father Divine was famous as a Harlem evangelist. At some point during dinner, Eli started talking about Father Divine in his usual healthy voice then guiltily lowered his voice, realizing that Fanny was close by. The kitchen was not completely separated from the dinette where we were seated. Fanny called out, "You don't have to whisper. I'm not one of Father Divine's angels!"

Not long after we settled in New York, I went to work, as I had hoped, as assistant director of a bond survey that was a cooperative project of the

National Bureau, the Federal Deposit Insurance Corporation, and the Federal Reserve Bankers Association. This was the project that I had discussed with Mr. Thompson in Washington as a possible position for me after I moved to New York. I did not stay to see the project to its conclusion because we left New York in June 1940, when Milton was offered an appointment as a visiting professor in the economics department of the University of Wisconsin (see chap. 6). Leaving a job before its completion has in a way been the pattern of my working career, by choice.

Although we both started our life together as economists, there was a difference. From the beginning, I never questioned whose career came first. I left my job at the Federal Deposit Insurance Corporation because I have never wanted a part-time marriage and Milton was not interested in a Washington career. When we left New York for Wisconsin, I gave up my job. In part this attitude on my part was probably a reflection of the times. Women's lib was not yet on the horizon. Few married women with families had full-time careers that involved being away from their families most of the day. Those few of our friends who did had a widowed mother or mother-in-law who lived with them and took the place of the mother. Both Milton and I felt strongly that when we had a family, which we were anticipating, my primary career would be as a mother; the economist would come second.

In addition, in all of life's activities, the personal element is crucial. From the beginning, I have never had the desire to compete with Milton professionally (perhaps because I was smart enough to recognize that I couldn't). On the other hand, he has always made me feel that his achievement is my achievement. In an interview for the San Francisco Sunday *Examiner* on March 18, 1984, I was asked, as I often am, how I deal with the fact that we do not share equally in the popular limelight. My answer: "Fortunately, I was not born with a strong competitive gene, so his fame is our fame. I will never be a Nobel laureate, but I am very proud to be the wife of one. In addition, he is more gregarious and outgoing and less self-conscious than I, so he is better suited for the limelight."

Milton had never been farther west than Chicago. In addition, he had met only two members of my family: my mother, who visited us in New York after we were married, and my brother Aaron. We decided to spend the summer before moving to Madison, Wisconsin, driving west to Portland for a visit with my family and friends.

{ *Milton* } Sometime during the preceding two years we had gotten rid of the Ford that I had bought not long before leaving Washington. For our trip west, we bought a slightly used Mercury convertible for $795. It gave us great service for the next six years until we sold it in Portland, Oregon, for $1,350 after our second trip there in 1946. Our paper profit was a result of wartime inflation, higher car prices in the West, and a shortage of cars, thanks to the suspension of production of civilian passenger vehicles during the war and to the price controls that were still in effect. We did not buy another car for a year or so, and when we did, we had to settle for a Kaiser (which was not subject to price control because it had not existed before the war—and which did not last very long after the war).

{ *Rose* } We left New York in July 1940 and spent the summer on a grand tour of the United States by car. Perhaps it is only nostalgia, but we look back on this trip as one of our most enjoyable. Though an extensive itinerary was planned in advance, our schedule was deliberately flexible. If we liked a place, we stayed longer. If we found it dull and uninteresting, we moved on. We traveled very simply, stopping in motels and not hotels, picnicking beside a brook or on a mountain peak if we were lucky or just in an open field if nothing better was available. In the national parks, we stayed in campground cabins.

The campgrounds did not have many of the conveniences they now have but also they were not as crowded as they are today. As nearly as I can recall, we did not make a single reservation ahead for a place in which to spend the night on that whole trip.

Neither of us had done much traveling up to this point and there were many places we wanted to visit. A look at our itinerary gives evidence that we left very few out. We covered the United States from north to south and east to west and made excursions into Canada and Mexico.

Our first excursion into Canada came early in the trip when we visited Montreal. An incident there highlighted a difference between Milton and me in patterns of expenditure that has been consistent throughout our life together. The question was how to go to the top of Mount Royal, a standard tourist attraction. Milton wanted to take a horse-drawn carriage. I thought we should walk up and save the money. However, I did not hesitate to buy a set of bone china, whereas Milton thought dime-store china was fine. We "compromised." I bought the china *and* we walked up the mountain. The Study of Consumer Purchases had just issued tables on expenditure, by family size and income, for various budgets. The agreement was that I was to save enough money during the next year on our food budget by comparison with the average for our size of family and income level to pay for the china. I also had a glass container full of pennies that I had saved the previous year. That was my first installment. I must admit I cheated a bit. Meals eaten out were not included in *my* food expenditure. I have long forgotten how this all ended but I still have the china.

On our way west, we stopped in Madison to choose a house for the following year. I say choose because our good friend Helen Groves, whose husband Harold Groves was responsible for the Wisconsin offer, had already canvassed the market and selected a number of houses for us to look at. We rented one that was in a development called Frost Woods. It had been built by a student of Frank Lloyd Wright and suited our needs perfectly. With that chore completed, we continued on our way west.

One long stop was an unplanned but not unpleasant sojourn in Banff, Canada, because of an accident we had. While I was driving from Jasper to Banff, we hit a wet spot as we came round a curve, and the car skidded and turned over. This was one of the many events that demonstrates to us that we were born under a lucky star. Our car was a convertible and seat belts had not yet been introduced. Fortunately, we had put the top up because of a rainstorm we had just driven through—which was why the road was slippery—but a convertible top is not much protection. Nevertheless, we both crawled out without a scratch though the car was badly damaged. I didn't hear then, nor in the many years since did I ever hear, a single word of criticism from Milton. He has always said it was not my fault, it was the wet road.

As always happens with any disaster on the road, people stopped, some to see if they could help, others out of curiosity. One comment we have never forgotten: viewer after viewer remarked, "Look, the car is badly smashed, yet the eggs didn't break!" As it happened, we had some hard-boiled eggs in our picnic basket and when the trunk of the car popped open on impact, they had rolled out. Indeed, they were not broken, only cracked!

While our car was being repaired in Calgary, we spent a pleasant week in Banff in a tourist home run by a delightful Scotswoman who made us scones each afternoon for our tea (something Milton has never forgotten), and we saw all the local sights. Our car repaired, except for a badly smashed trunk lid, we went on to Portland.

Thanks to the delay we had to eliminate some of our planned itinerary in order to get to Portland on the promised date. We arrived in the middle of the night because I had forgotten what the road was like between the Dalles and Portland. What I remembered as a two-hour trip down the Multnomah Highway turned into something like six hours. The two-lane road snaked along the Columbia River with sharp curves one after another. Although I made my way quietly into the house through a well-remembered bathroom window, the family was on the alert for our arrival and heard us. Everyone woke up.

For the next week, we spent nearly full time visiting relatives. My sister Becky had come home from Reno with her ten-year-old son, Barry. The two of them joined us when we left Portland, and Milton became Becky's hero from the first. In addition to his friendliness with my family and his tolerance for all the social activities with people whom he didn't know and was really not interested in, she was particularly taken by his patience with her young son. Barry wanted to stop at every attraction along the way to San Francisco and Milton accommodated almost every request.

We had already visited two world fairs, our first in Chicago in 1933 and the second in New York in 1939. But we couldn't pass up the Golden Gate International Exposition on San Francisco's Treasure Island, celebrating the new Golden Gate Bridge and the San Francisco/Oakland Bay Bridge. I believe it was on our way east that we went to the Grand Canyon. Though I'm not sure just when it was, I have a very vivid memory of a few events during that visit, in particular our trip into the canyon on burros. I have no difficulty seeing the two of us standing up to eat our dinner that night and can almost bring back the pain.

Although I had made the trip from Chicago to Portland many times when I was a student at the University of Chicago, I had never made the trip by car—and that is the only way really to see the country. We were both impressed by the great variety of people we met along the way. We had never before been so aware of the diversity, not only of nature but also of people in our country. After twelve weeks and thirteen thousand miles, our trip came to an end in Madison, Wisconsin, our new home.

⤳ *Chapter Six* ⤳

VICTIM OF CAMPUS POLITICS

{ *Rose* } Harold Groves, who was responsible for Milton's being offered a visiting professorship at the University of Wisconsin for the year 1940–41, was a professor of public finance at the University of Wisconsin, where he was supervising a study of Wisconsin incomes. As a result he was an active participant in the Income Conference, of which Milton was the initial secretary. That was how they met.

Harold Groves was a man of great personal force and the very highest character. He and George Sellery, dean of the College of Letters and Science, felt that the Economics Department at Wisconsin had deteriorated and needed new blood. Impressed with Milton's work at the NBER, Groves thought that bringing him to Wisconsin would strengthen teaching in statistics and also in economic theory, where the department had always been weak.

He first wrote to Milton in February 1940 to inquire whether he would be interested in an appointment with the rank of associate professor at a salary of about $4,000. Groves was aware that he might have difficulty in persuading his colleagues to approve such an appointment. He disagreed with his colleagues about the future of the department and several feuds were raging. Sides were being chosen and feelings hurt—a not-unusual situation in campus politics.

Professor Groves was an optimist and I think considered himself a better politician than he was. After Milton indicated that he was interested in at least thinking about the prospect, Groves wrote, "I should say that the prospect itself is quite uncertain. But we have a considerable staff working on our project [the income study] and all of us could organize a very considerable conspiracy on your behalf. . . . at least it would be worth trying."

In further correspondence, after Professor Groves had indicated that the situation in the Economics Department was not conducive to an easy approval of a permanent appointment, Milton suggested that, given his own doubts about a permanent post at Wisconsin, the preferable arrangement might be a one-year appointment instead of a permanent one. In response, Groves proposed that the position be divided between teaching in the department and assisting on the income project. In retrospect, after going over many documents dealing with events of that year, I am inclined to believe that Groves was using the income study as a Trojan horse to bring Milton to the Department of Economics.

The department finally recommended an appointment as a visiting professor for 1940–41 to advise on the Wisconsin income project and to give two courses each semester (it was specified that the two courses were not to include two named statistics courses in order to reassure the persons then giving those courses that they were not being replaced). The note from the secretary of the Board of Regents offering Milton the appointment described it as lecturer in statistics, with rank of professor, for the academic year 1940–41, at a salary of $4,000 for the period. It did not mention the income project.

Obviously the standard academic load was very different in those days than it is now. Two courses each semester would now be regarded as a normal, or even a heavy load, at a research university. Then, it was considered a half-time load, the other half being reserved for the income study.

We were young and naive about campus politics and, like Groves, Milton has always been an optimist. In addition, we were unencumbered by either children or worldly goods, and so found new experiences challenging. Finally, Milton was eager to get started in academia, where he hoped to make his life career. So we were game to take the chance and accepted the challenge.

The house in Frost Woods that we had rented on our way west three months earlier proved to be very comfortable and livable. The neighborhood was more rural than suburban, with a lake nearby. All in all, that aspect of our year in Madison was very pleasant.

Our first few weeks confirmed the picture that Harold Groves had painted for us. There were indeed two camps. As protégés of Groves, we had already been placed in one of them. The other faction in the department welcomed us in muted fashion though without open hostility or improper behavior. But to the best of my recollection, only two couples in the department ever entertained us. One was the Groveses, who tried very hard to bring us in contact with the other side, feeling that if they knew us they would like us. It didn't work. The other couple was Selig Perlman, the only Jew on the tenured faculty of the Department of Economics, and his wife Fanny. We were also welcomed by some members of the Law School—in particular Willard Hurst and Charles Bunn, who, when Milton withdrew his name from consideration for an appointment at the end of the year, expressed the hope that "Sometime, when all this has blown over, we hope you will return."

I don't remember that we were particularly disturbed by the indifference of the other side. The Groveses and the Perlmans were lovable people and more than made up for the ones we didn't get to know. More important, we felt closer to the graduate students and junior research assistants or instructors than to the senior faculty. We were of their generation, younger than some and slightly older than others. Like them, we still had the enthusiasm and curiosity of the young, which many senior faculty members had lost if they ever had it. Our home was always open to students, and the more mature among them took advantage of the opportunity. The favorite entertainment was conversation. Among this group were Walter Heller, later chairman of the Council of Economic Advisers under Presidents Kennedy and Johnson; Joseph Pechman, for many years a tax specialist at the Brookings Institution, the home away from home for Democrats out of office; Herb Klarman, later a distinguished scholar in the field of health economics; Henry Buechel, for many years a professor of economics at the University of Washington; and Ben Stephansky, who had a varied and distinguished career, including service as U.S. Ambassador to Bolivia and the Organization of American States, and as director of the Institute for Employment Research. All remained friends even though we were frequently in different political camps.

At Thanksgiving, we invited some of the students and junior faculty for dinner. That proved a truly new experience for me. I had ordered a turkey from a local farmer. He delivered it on time but, to my dismay, though dead, it was fully clothed. I had never dressed and cleaned a bird and did not know where to begin, although I had watched my mother do so. Our trusty Boston Cooking School Cookbook, which Lois Clark had given me and which I still have, came to our aid. Milton read the instructions from page 330 line by line and I followed orders. After much travail, a fully dressed, cleaned and stuffed turkey made its way to the oven, in time for a good dinner.

{ *Milton* } The contrast between the eagerness and ability of the young graduate students and assistants, and the dullness and lack of scholarly interests of many, though not all, of the senior faculty made a deep impression on me. In subsequent years, I observed what happened to my own graduate students and have been dismayed at the same contrast between what so many display as students and then later as tenured faculty. I have often wondered what we do to them as students, or what academic life does to them in later years, that converts so many promising intellectuals into second-rate, pedantic, unenterprising faculty.

{ *Rose* } The early influence of John R. Commons (1862–1945) predisposed the Wisconsin faculty and students to political activism, modern liberalism and Keynesian economic policies. Commons was the dominant figure in the Wisconsin Economics Department from the time he joined the faculty in 1904. According to one authority, he "drafted much of the reform legislation that made Wisconsin the laboratory for other states and the federal government, notably legislation on civil service, public utilities, workman's compensation, and unemployment insurance. He was also active in monetary policy."[1]

These topics furnished grist for many a bull session. Strong disagreement never led to ill feeling. As Leonard Silk put it thirty-five years later, after discussing the still strong influence of Commons at the University of Wisconsin in 1940, "The image which Friedman's arrival at Wisconsin suggests is that of a libertarian Daniel walking into the institutionalist lion's den—a historic confrontation between the 'Chicago' and 'Madison' doctrines." He adds, "In fact there was no such confrontation. Although Friedman's ideological sympathies lay with the free market, he had not yet actively taken up the cudgels in its behalf. His asssociation with Wesley Mitchell—the student and admirer of Thorstein Veblen, and himself the most 'scientific' of American institutionalists—gave Friedman impeccable credentials."[2] The confrontation may not have been historic, but the difference between the views that Milton and I had absorbed at Chicago and those that were conventional at Wisconsin certainly was striking.

The war in Europe was the other major topic for bull sessions. At the time the United States was neutral, though sentiment throughout the country was favorable to Britain and her allies. Wisconsin was something of an exception. Populated largely by immigrants from Germany, there was strong pro-German feeling reinforced by a general sentiment for neutrality that characterized most liberal intellectuals during the 1920s and 1930s. Milton and I were strongly anti-Nazi and pro-British, very much in favor of U.S. assistance to the Allies and even of the U.S. entering the war as an active combatant. Though never discussed openly among the faculty, this issue was one of many that colored the atmosphere during the year.

The graduate students and assistants were very much aware of the deficiencies in the Wisconsin economics program and were eager to have Milton appointed to a permanent post. The University of Wisconsin was, and probably still is, as vulnerable to leaks as Washington. When the graduate students learned that the faculty had failed to approve an offer to Milton after Dean Sellery had suggested that they offer him an associate professorship for three years without tenure, seventeen members of the junior teaching and research staff signed a written request to the faculty of the Economics Department recommending an expansion in the number and variety of courses in theory and statistics and expressing the hope that Milton would stay at Wisconsin. Before the whole affair was over, many of this group led a protest in his favor. The faculty did not appreciate what they considered unwarranted intrusion into their bailiwick by the students.

{ *Milton* } In later years, Walter Heller and I were often on opposite sides of public policy issues, on one occasion engaging in a well-publicized debate on monetary versus fiscal policy.[3] Similarly, Joe Pechman and I remained good friends though often disagreeing. As late as 1988, in a letter to the organizers of the fiftieth-anniversary celebration of the founding of the Income Conference, Joe noted that "at the end of the [academic] year [1941] the graduate students—led by Walter Heller—petitioned the Department of Economics to add him as a member of its faculty. The department rejected our petition and the University of Wisconsin lost the opportunity to persuade Milton to remain in Madison." Walter and Joe, both of whom are now deceased, long took pleasure in informing newsmen who assumed that political difference necessarily implied personal hostility that they had carried picket signs on my behalf at Wisconsin. We remained lifelong friends.

{ *Rose* } Unlike some of the faculty, the students did not feel that Milton threatened them in any way. They based their wish to have him stay on his merits; not on whether he threatened their position or was being offered a salary that was higher than anyone at a comparable level was getting, or on whether Professor Groves hadn't been fully open in his efforts to bring Milton to the department. Many considerations that were key ingredients in the faculty's deliberations were totally irrelevant to whether he would be a good or bad addition to the faculty—which, generalized, explains why so many university and college departments end up with mediocre faculties.

Milton spent much time planning and organizing his lectures. The rest of his working hours were spent either in consultation on the income project or working on the manuscript of his *Income from Independent Professional Practice*.

This was my first year without a full-time job since student days. I took advantage of my leisure to take some "hobby courses"—one in pottery and another in hooked rugs. I enjoyed these very much for about three months, when I began a difficult pregnancy that was not conducive to much activity.

That year's annual meeting of the American Economic Association was held in New Orleans and we decided to drive there. After the meeting, we drove to Biloxi with our friends the Machlups who were also attending the meetings. It was a pleasant vacation except for my nausea in the morning, and general feeling of malaise. I was not sorry to start the trip home. But what a return. We arrived in Frost Woods on New Year's Eve to discover that the house was cold, the water in the toilets starting to freeze, thanks to an empty oil tank. The standing order to keep the tank full had been overlooked.

The first thing that Milton did was to build a fire in the fireplace and put me down in front of it. Then he went into action. He found the emergency number for the oil company and probably gave vent to his anger freely, no doubt explaining, as he always does in such situations, that he knew the person answering the telephone was probably not responsible for the negligence. He must have made the situation clear, however, because before long the owner of the company arrived in a full dress suit to fill our tank. He had been at a New Year's Eve party when he got the message and lost no time in coming. Though the era of liability suits had not yet arrived, he knew what the freezing temperatures of a Wisconsin winter could do.

Except for on-and-off bouts of illness connected with a pregnancy that seemed ill-destined from the beginning, the winter quarter passed without incident. In contrast to the coldness of many of the faculty, I was touched by the thoughtfulness and friendliness of a neighbor. Whenever I returned from brief stays in the hospital she would leave baskets full of her cooking or baking on our front porch. She was also a good friend in other ways during that winter. I was saddened to hear later on that her husband had divorced her and left her with three children to bring up.

One pleasant memory from that year in Wisconsin was Christmas with our friends the Groveses, who were Quakers. As the years have passed since that Christmas and values and customs have changed so drastically, I frequently look back and compare today's Christmas celebrations—especially the emphasis on presents, the more expensive the better—with the presents of the Groves family. I don't remember all of them but I do remember some. One child brought a little bundle of kindling wood that he had split, tied with a pretty ribbon. Another brought some dishcloths that she had hemmed. And so on. The parents' presents to the children were all things that the children apparently had asked for or needed—tennis shoes for one, snowshoes for another. Similarly, the presents to and from other relatives were all useful rather than showy. And most important, everyone was pleased with what he or she received.

So far as we knew at the time, nothing overt happened concerning our future at the university until April. We heard rumors that the dean had proposed and the president had approved a tenured appointment, and I guess we were aware that there were difficulties in getting the department to approve. However, it was only in 1990 that we learned the full details, when, in the course of preparing a history of the department, Professor Robert Lampman of the Wisconsin Department of Economics sent Milton an early version of his section on "The Milton Friedman Affair, 1940–41." His draft contained much that we had known nothing about and was accompanied by copies of many documents that we had never seen.[4]

The next thing we were told was that to facilitate approval the dean had changed the proposed appointment of a tenured position to a three-year appointment as associate professor without tenure. Milton has always been opposed to tenure in academia, but, because of the opposition of the Economics Department to an appointment for him, with or without tenure, he was apprehensive about accepting a three-year appointment. He expressed his apprehension to the dean in a letter dated April 11, 1941, asking for help in judging what the outcome of a three-year appointment might be, given the possibility that the faculty would repeat their present action. Milton went on, "if I thought the renewal of the appointment depended solely on my performance and competence, I should have no hesitancy in accepting it [the three-year appointment] and would have no basis for objecting to its termination at the end of three years. I am not averse to taking risks. . . . I recognize, of course, that competence and performance are the grounds on which you and the president will judge the issue; but I fear that these may not be the grounds on which the department will." He went on in the letter to give his analysis not only of what the ultimate outcome might be but also what the three years' experience might be like. (I have not come across any reply from Sellery to this letter, but subsequent memos make it clear that Milton did accept. The dean wrote in a note to the president, handwritten on a copy of a letter to Professor Edwin Witte, chairman of the department, "I have already told Friedman the job was his and he has accepted—none too gladly. To let him out I will not agree to.") Determined to push ahead with what he considered the good of the department and the university and with the approval of the president, the dean decided to go ahead without the approval of the department.

At this point, some member or members of the faculty called in the media, not an unusual practice at this or other universities. On May 14, 1941, the *Capital Times* (which had welcomed us to Wisconsin the prior year) headlined a story on the front page, "Fireworks in U.W. Econ Department as Instructor May Get $3,500 Prof's Job." The article starts with a brief statement of events, beginning with the first meeting of the department budget committee in

March when the appointment was first considered and withdrawn when it became apparent that objections would be raised not only to an appointment as associate professor with tenure but even to an assistant professorship without tenure. The article then goes on to suggest that the appointment will be recommended to the regents at their next meeting in spite of the department's objections. It then quotes essentially in its entirety, though without attribution other than to "one prominent member of the department," a letter written by the chairman (Professor Witte) to the dean and the president, explaining why the appointment should not go forward. The reasons given are that "while a promising young man, [the former Columbia instructor] is not so pronouncedly superior that he merits a rank and salary above that of others of like training and experience. He is still in his middle twenties. . . . In his advanced courses at Wisconsin, he has proven himself a good teacher and he has had good experience as a statistician. . . . Generally he is a man of promise, but can hardly be said to have arrived as yet. Certain it is that he has no great reputation in the profession."*

The *Capital Times* story refers also to an unofficial "investigation" of the teaching of certain phases of economics made by Milton and the circulation of his report claiming inefficiency in teaching practices, and quotes the last two sentences of Milton's report as though they were the gist of the report. (More on this "unofficial investigation" below.)

The last paragraph of Witte's letter quoted by the *Capital Times* is sort of a mea culpa: "Without criticizing any one, it is undeniable that many unfortunate incidents have occurred in connection with the promotion and consideration of Mr. Friedman for a position in our department, which have aroused bitterness, both within the department and in the associated department of agricultural economics and the school of commerce."

The *Capital Times* story was of course followed by others in the *Times* on the following days as well as in the *State Journal* and the campus paper. The only thing these follow-up stories added was that the regents did not consider the matter of the appointment in the May 26 meeting as the *Times*

---

* In 1951, Milton was awarded the John Bates Clark medal by the American Economic Association. This medal is awarded every other year to the "American economist under the age of forty who is adjudged to have made the most significant contribution to economic thought and knowledge." Edwin Witte was present on the occasion, and, with some apparent embarrassment, heartily congratulated Milton on a well-deserved award. At the time, Milton thought this was pure hypocrisy. But one of the items in Lampman's record suggests that we were too harsh on Witte. The item is a letter to James Earley, a member of the department on leave in Washington, in which Witte wrote, "He [Milton] was an innocent victim and throughout the whole time behaved like a gentleman. I certainly wish him well and think that he will not suffer by reason of his unfortunate experience."

had anticipated. Actually, to the best of our knowledge, though there were various statements about the regents' consideration of the appointment, no consideration took place because we had already decided that we did not want to become enmeshed in the many and complicated quarrels of the Economics Department, and had communicated this to those involved.

Accordingly, on June 2, 1941, Milton wrote formally to President Dykstra, "I should appreciate your withdrawing my name from consideration by the Board of Regents for appointment to an associate professorship in the Department of Economics." The ostensible reason he gave for withdrawing his name was "The emergency in which our country finds itself, the pressures on me to work on defense problems, and my own very strong conviction that only energetic prosecution of the defense effort and multiplied aid to Britain can preserve democracy and freedom." While an accurate statement of Milton's feelings about the war, this was not his reason for withdrawing his name from consideration. President Dykstra's reply is also interesting. After saying that he understood Milton's desire to do something about the national situation, he goes on, "As you leave us, after a year of successful work on the campus of the University of Wisconsin, I think you ought to know of the common agreement there seems to be about your capacity, your ability, and your success as a teacher. Everything I have heard on these subjects is most complimentary to you and therefore I want to congratulate you upon your year with us."

Everything President Dykstra said may have been true but, for all that, it was highly misleading. Dean Sellery's letter to Wesley Mitchell on June 28 gives a more accurate picture: "It is a matter of deep regret to me and to President Dykstra that our proposal to give Dr. Milton Friedman an associate professorship did not go through. Friedman's work and personality are very pleasing; he is a gentleman and a scholar. Unfortunately, he was caught in the crossfire between two factions in our department of economics. The best men, by and large, in the department wanted him. The opposition to him did some dirty publicity work and he decided to decline to stand for appointment."

The rest of the story comes from Professor Lampman's report referred to earlier. He sent Milton copies of many letters and memoranda with the hope that Milton might be able to fill in some details. From this material, we learned much about what went on behind the scenes during that year. As I read Lampman's coherent and well documented account, I was impressed anew by the many different strands, plus some bungling, that determined the ultimate outcome. Some members of the faculty feared that Milton's appointment would threaten their position and that of others who were teaching the courses he would teach. Others thought that his appointment would impede their efforts to establish a separate School of Commerce rather than one within the College of Letters and Science. Dean Sellery and President Dykstra felt very strongly that putting Economics in the School of Commerce would mean that Commerce would dominate Economics and, as Sellery wrote to the President in a note, "that would be dangerous." Personal rivalry for power played a part. And so did anti-Semitism on the part of at least two members of the Economics Department.

Another issue used by some members of the School of Commerce was a memo that Milton wrote at the request of Professor Groves. From the evidence, there is a real question whether any member of the department actually read the memo. The reaction to it was based on two things—the title and the last two sentences. The title unfortunately was "Proposed Program in Statistics at the University of Wisconsin with special reference to the Social Sciences." The last two sentences, which were repeated whenever the memo was mentioned either by the members of the department or the media, are "A student cannot secure training at the University of Wisconsin sufficient to qualify him to teach advanced statistics or to do independent work in the field of statistical methods. Even if he takes all the work offered he will be but indifferently qualified to do research involving the application of modern statistics."

The main body of the report was about the revolutionary changes that had taken place within the field of statistics, and how these changes affected the teaching of statistics overall. This aspect of the report was never mentioned. Milton and Allen Wallis were tentatively committed to writing a statistics text, and the memo circulated at Wisconsin was based on a draft of a proposed preface to the text. Of the ten or more pages of the report, the first seven contain only one passing reference to Wisconsin. The final three pages deal specifically with the Wisconsin situation and start with the disclaimer, "The following classification of the courses now being given in the social science department or the mathematics department is based exclusively on catalogue descriptions." No specific course or teacher is criticized. And then there are those last two sentences which were interpreted as cruel criticism of the teaching or of the teachers in the department.

Interestingly, the memo played a more constructive role later on. A little more than a year later (October 7, 1942), Allen Wallis wrote in a letter to Milton, "[Prof. Harold] Hotelling has expressed considerable interest in your manuscript on a proposed program in statistics. . . . He is on a committee of the Institute of Mathematical Statistics which is to report at Christmas on the general subject of the 'teaching of statistics,' which is the reason for his being especially interested in your document." The memo led to Milton's becoming a member of Hotelling's committee and the Wisconsin memo was in part incorporated in the committee's final report.[5] That report contributed to the subsequent establishment of separate statistics departments at a number of universities, including Wisconsin.

In addition to collecting contemporary memos and other material, Professor Lampman asked Walter Morton to write his recollections of the "Friedman affair," which he did on September 18, 1979. Morton, regarded as anti-Semitic and strongly pro-German at the time, had been a key player in the affair, consistently opposing Milton's appointment. His recollections (written thirty-nine years after the event, when he was eighty years old), contain some clear errors, such as that Milton was "then a student at Columbia" (Milton was a student at Columbia in 1933–34). More interesting, Morton's references to Milton contain not one negative comment about him—either his ability or his person. For example: "Milton Friedman made an excellent impression both on the faculty and the students. He was able, intelligent and very lively in the classroom and was favored by many of the graduate students for an appointment in the Department. Without doubt he was an excellent teacher and an able economist." Why then did he vote against the appointment? Morton recalls that after expressing a favorable opinion of Friedman in a conversation with Dean Sellery, the Dean "indicated to me that since I considered Friedman a very able young fellow with an excellent knowledge of economics, a lively instructor, popular with the students and a good teacher, he thought I ought to vote for the appointment and did not give much weight to my explanation that I did not think it was handled very well by Groves and that I was hesitant to [be] offensive without cause to Professors Fox, Gaumnitz and Earley with whom I would have to live day after day in the Department. Moreover, I did not believe that any professor should be tricked out of his job as apparently Fox and Gaumnitz believed Groves was trying to do. Dean Sellery then told me that he would appoint Friedman anyway, adding: 'This is not the Third Reich.'"

At least in his later years, Morton apparently felt guilty about the anti-Semitism that he undoubtedly displayed in the earlier period. In a letter in 1981 to Mark Perlman, the son of Selig Perlman, thanking him for sending a copy of an article dealing with anti-Semitism,[6] Morton wrote: "The whole matter boils down not to anti-Semitism but to stupid political maneuvering by Harold Groves." He repeats his conversation with the Dean praising Milton and then concludes, "I was therefore partly responsible for Sellery's action because I told the truth about Milton's capacity."

Throughout both Morton's 1979 memorandum to Lampman as well as his 1981 letter to Mark Perlman, all blame is put on Groves, all praise on Milton. Of course, by this time, Milton's promise was no longer in the future, his reputation was well established, and he had won the Nobel Prize!

Memorandum after memorandum included in the Lampman report points up problems in the Wisconsin affair that are endemic to faculty politics everywhere: basic dissension among members of the faculty plus the usual backbiting and smallness. One report on a meeting in the office of the dean on April 16, 1941, gives the flavor: "The Dean explained the purpose of the meeting. He said it was painful to him to call together grown-up men in order to discuss their conduct. He referred to the weakened morale of the department due to internal dissension and criticism of colleagues by one another." And then the rest of the meeting was spent essentially calling names and questioning the morals of various members. When the discussion began about the Friedman appointment, one member pointed out that this was beside the point since the meeting was held to discuss the problem of smearing among the faculty. The Dean agreed and all agreed that another meeting should be held.

Clearly, the bitterness and backbiting lasted long after we left. As late as 1979, in his memorandum to Professor Lampman, Walter Morton could not resist adding something about the effect of the Friedman affair on salary raises the following year: "Hence the Friedman affair was financially profitable to those favoring the appointment and very unprofitable to those opposing it."

James S. Earley was an assistant professor on leave during the year we were at the university. Though his name was mentioned occasionally as being threatened by Milton's joining the faculty, he himself played no part in the quarrel. Indeed, in a letter to Lampman in 1989, he wrote, "I did . . . agree fully with Groves and the graduate students that the Department needed radical 'restructuring.' Like the others, I recognized that U.W. economics had suffered grievous decline since its heyday, and I was in favor, then as later, of restructuring it. Theory and statistics were specially weak and important areas. Generally, I saw that the Department had suffered badly from inbreeding and the associated protégé system." Earley also wrote, "I tend to view the Friedman affair as part of the running battle, that became really acute after WWII, between Walter Morton and others over the control of the Department and its development. That war was not settled until Ed Young became Chairman."

{ *Milton* } The year we spent at Wisconsin was my introduction to full-time academic life—and to academic politics. I became a pawn in an internal departmental controversy and learned how small-minded and petty respected academic figures can be in such controversies. The more trivial the issues, the dirtier seem to be the politics. Fortunately for me, I learned this lesson early, and under circumstances that blunted any future impact on my career, for the wartime economy was destined to provide me, for at least the next few years, with an alternative to an academic career other than a return to the National Bureau. Under other circumstances, the Wisconsin Affair, as it became known, might have done far more harm to my academic prospects than it actually did—another example of how lucky I have been. As it was, it simply faded away, leaving only a bad taste in our mouths.

Though I have myself been extremely fortunate in my later academic career and, minor episodes aside, have escaped getting deeply involved in campus politics, the impressions that I formed at Wisconsin have been amply confirmed since. Let a member of an academic department win a prize of millions in a lottery, and his colleagues will clap him on the shoulder and tell him what a lucky fellow he is. Their undoubted envy will not be corrupted by malice. The reaction will be less generous if the new-found wealth comes from a best-selling text or other book, but it will not compare to the reaction to his getting a better raise (be it by no more than a hundred dollars) than they, or being assigned a better office. Envy is the least relevant motive; malice, the most. What matters is the invidious distinction that is perceived between him and them. They will feel demeaned.

I hasten to add that the same phenomenon occurs in the nonacademic world, though it may take different forms.

{ *Rose* } After the end of the school year and our decision not to stay at the University of Wisconsin, we headed east, Milton by car and I, following the advice of my doctor, by train. We met in New York, where I saw the obstetrician who was to take over. As it happened, he was a friend from our earlier stay in New York. He advised me on do's and don'ts, since I was still having problems and gaining far too much weight.

We then headed for Norwich, Vermont. Milton had earlier agreed to collaborate with Carl Shoup and Ruth Mack on a study of the use of taxes to prevent inflation, to be carried out in Norwich. The study was submitted to the Treasury Department in the fall of 1941 and was published in 1943 under the title *Taxing to Prevent Inflation.* Carl Shoup was a leading expert on public finance and a professor at Columbia University whom Milton had come to know primarily through the Income Conference.

Except for my physical discomfort, the summer was pleasant. We had many friends from the National Bureau and from Columbia as well as friends from the Dartmouth faculty. Arthur and Helen Burns spent their summers in Norwich and later had a house in Ely, Vermont, in the same part of New England where we spent our summers from 1948 on, and near where we built a house in 1968 in West Fairlee, Vermont. Ruth and Eddy Mack had a house in Thetford. An incident that summer which seems amusing now but wasn't then involved a dinner at the Macks. Their house was at the top of a very steep and rugged hill. We drove over from Norwich with the Burnses. When we reached the bottom of the hill, Arthur, who in those days and for many years after behaved in loco parentis to us, insisted that I get out and that Milton and I walk up the hill. In my condition the bouncing of the car could be dangerous for me!

We left Norwich sometime in July to be on the safe side for the expected arrival of our firstborn. But the baby was not as eager to enter this world as we were to have it and the wait seemed endless. In the end it was also futile. After an extremely difficult and prolonged labor, the infant was stillborn. As I look back, this blow was more devastating to us than our Wisconsin experience. However, sharing the pain of both of these experiences seemed to bring Milton and me even closer than we already were. In addition, we were no longer children; suddenly we had grown up.

{ *Milton* }   One outcome of the summer project was the offer of an attractive position with the Division of Tax Research of the Treasury Department. With war raging abroad, and the strong likelihood that the U.S. would get involved, working at the Treasury was more appealing than returning to the bureau. Accordingly, after a short convalescence for Rose, we left for Washington.

At the time, Aaron was living in Rockville, Maryland, where he had bought an old farmhouse that he planned to remodel himself and he suggested that we live with him. We had agreed to do so when we were all looking forward to a successful birth. Before going to Wisconsin, we had sublet our New York apartment furnished. On returning from the summer in Norwich we sent our furniture to Rockville in preparation for our move there after the baby arrived. Though we had no baby to join our little family, we still decided to stay with Aaron.

Chapter Seven

WASHINGTON, 1941–43

{ *Rose* } When we arrived in Washington, Lois Clark took me to Rockville to show me what was to be our new home. It was a gray rainy day and the farmhouse looked desolate. It only increased my feeling of emptiness and I broke down. I could not face spending long hours by myself in what seemed such a cold environment while Milton and Aaron were away in Washington. Lois immediately suggested that we live with them until we could find a place of our own in Washington. I knew that Aaron would be disappointed but also that he would understand—and he did.

Washington was expanding and it didn't take us long to find an apartment house under construction near Dupont Circle, with completion promised for about a month later. We signed up for an apartment, as did our friends Lowell and Agnes Harriss. Like Milton, Lowell, a student of Shoup's, had come to Washington to work at the Treasury Department. After we all moved in, Lowell and Milton frequently walked together the mile or so from Dupont Circle to the Treasury Building.*

{ *Milton* } The outbreak of war in Europe in 1939, and particularly U.S. active involvement in the war after Pearl Harbor on December 7, 1941, recreated the ferment that had characterized the earlier New Deal years. Washington again became a magnet, and again provided academics of my generation with the opportunity to participate in important events. I am impressed with the similarities of the two periods when I was in Washington: 1935–37 and 1941–43. Many people whom I had gotten to know during the first period

* Lowell and Milton have birthdays a day apart and Lowell has never missed sending a card to Milton on his birthday for the past fifty-odd years.

had either remained there or returned during the second period. The friendships formed during the first provided important links during the second.

One big difference between the two periods for me was professional. In the first, I was operating entirely as a technician in statistics and in economics, and had no contact with or responsibility for the formation of policy. In the second, I was at the Treasury in the Division of Tax Research and was involved in the formation and development of policy. But in both periods, I had greater responsibility than my age would ordinarily have entitled me to. In the first, I played a significant role in designing the largest and most comprehensive budget study that had ever been conducted, costing tens of millions of dollars. In the second, I was able to play a significant role in a major revision of the tax structure designed to contribute to the financing of the war. Those revisions shaped the subsequent peacetime structure for better or for worse, and were more radical than any that have occurred since. Both experiences added greatly to my understanding and shaped my future career.

During World War I, the number of federal government employees in Washington, D.C., had peaked at around 120,000, from which level it rapidly fell, once the war ended, to a low of 64,000, and then started gradually to rise. By 1933, when the New Deal got underway, it was 70,000. By 1940, it had roughly doubled, to 140,000. Under the impetus of the war, it doubled once again to 285,000 by 1943.

Washington was not then what it has since become. Its population was slightly larger, close to 700,000 compared to slightly over 600,000, and rapidly rising whereas now it is slowly falling. The surrounding bedroom communities, in Maryland and Virginia, which are now among the highest income areas in the nation and which, together with Washington, have a total population of about 4 million, were still largely rural and lightly populated.[1] For example, Rockville, where Aaron lived, was more country than city. Unlike Aaron, most government employees lived in the city, a large fraction, like Lowell and me, within walking distance of their places of work. Not yet had the later hordes of lobbyists descended in force to populate the surrounding communities. A subway had not yet been built, to fill the city in the morning and empty it at night.

More important, the racial composition was precisely the reverse of what it is now: 70 percent white, whereas it is now 70 percent black, though the Washington-Virginia-Maryland metropolitan area as a whole is about three-quarters white. Washington was a predominantly white middle-class city, not a predominantly black lower-class community with an enclave of high-income whites and blacks. Crime was not the problem it has become. It was, or at least seemed to be, safe to walk the streets at night anywhere in the city.

For middle-class professional persons like ourselves, it was the same attractive city that it had been when we had lived there a few years earlier. As earlier on, the "best and brightest," mostly young and full of energy, worked hard, with much overtime, and played hard. Despite long hours at the office, social activity flourished with much cross-agency business being done at parties, where bureaucratic and political gossip was the staple of conversation. As always, gossip centered on who was up and who was down. As in every governmental capital around the world, leaks and bureaucratic intrigue were a mainstay of the social scene. When we came to Washington, a few months before Pearl Harbor, orders from Britain and its allies, U.S. assistance to Britain, and the buildup of our own military forces had already converted the U.S. to a wartime economy. The early stage of a wartime boom was raising serious concerns about the danger of inflation. While consumer prices rose only 1 percent from 1939 to 1940, they rose a further 5 percent from 1940 to 1941.

Work at the Treasury

The Treasury was girding for war. Memories of World War I were still fresh. Tax revenues had financed less than one-third of total government spending during that war, borrowing, the rest. And much borrowing was a concealed form of printing money. Commercial banks that were members of the Federal Reserve System were encouraged to lend money to their customers to finance the purchase of government bonds. They obtained the reserves required to back the resultant increase in deposits by discounting the loans at the Federal Reserve—i.e., borrowing from the Federal Reserve on the security of loans for which government bonds served as the collateral. As a result, while high-powered money—currency and deposits at the Federal Reserve—increased by $2.5 billion (or 60 percent), only about a tenth of that represented direct purchase of government securities; the remainder consisted of credit extended to member banks.

The end result was an increase in the money supply of about 50 percent, which led to a more than doubling of the price level. That, in turn, was followed by a sharp postwar contraction from 1920 to 1921, during which prices fell sharply—wholesale prices by 44 percent. The powers that be at the Treasury Department were determined to do better this time.

Taxing to Prevent Inflation, the study that Carl Shoup had persuaded the Carnegie Foundation and the Institute of Public Administration to finance, was one result of this determination. A substantial expansion of the Division of Tax Research was another. On Carl Shoup's recommendation, Roy Blough, who was head of the Division of Tax Research and many years later a colleague of mine at the University of Chicago, added Lowell and me to the division.

When we joined it, the division had already embarked on preparing a major revision of the tax structure in all its parts: personal and corporate income taxes, excise taxes, estate and gift taxes (Lowell's special field of expertise). The next two years saw major revisions that still determine the key features, and many of the details, of the federal tax system. Though not always precisely what the division favored, the revisions were in the main its work.

{ *Rose* } I had not intended to go back to work when we planned our move to Washington since we thought taking care of our baby would be more than a full-time job for me. Without a baby, and another pregnancy postponed on the advice of my obstetrician, we had to rethink our plans. I spent the month we stayed with the Clarks recuperating psychologically and physically. I could not have asked for a better psychiatrist than Lois. As it happened, she too had lost an infant at birth recently and though she already had two children the sense of loss was there. She spent a great deal of time cheering me up and, by the end of the month I was ready to take on the chore of first moving and then getting settled in our new apartment. That took about another month.

Both Milton and I felt that children were an important part of a full and happy life. The fear of not being able to have any children haunted me. The first thing I did was to check with Lois's obstetrician, one of the most delightful doctors I have ever known. An older man, he was the head of Doctor's Hospital in Washington. He treated me as he would a child who had to be comforted, and he did his best to relieve me of my fears. When I asked for a promise that he would perform a Caesarian and not attempt a natural birth, he hesitated at first. But when I said I could not go through nine months with the fear of a repetition of my first experience, he gave me his promise that he would do as I asked. He kept his promise when the time came even though he said he was very embarrassed by having to confess to younger doctors that he had performed a Caesarian when the infant weighed only six pounds. However, that promise did more for my mental state than almost anything else.

I decided that the time of waiting before I could think of starting another pregnancy would pass more rapidly if I went to work for at least part of the period. Since this was definitely to be a temporary job I did not even consider going back to the Federal Deposit Insurance Corporation. Dorothy Brady, whom we first met when we were all working on different parts of the Consumption Study, was working at the Bureau of Home Economics. She was engaged in research on the relationship between savings and income.

As a human being, Dorothy came closer to perfection than anyone I have ever known. Perhaps because of her own experience, she always seemed to sense other people's emotional situation. She certainly always sensed mine, and came to my rescue more than once. No one was quicker to help when help was needed. Although her life was far from easy, Dorothy seldom complained. She had a Ph.D. in mathematics, rare for a female in those days, and had been married to Robert Brady, an economics professor at the University of California, Berkeley. They were divorced soon after their son Michael was born. From then to the time Michael was on his own, he was Dorothy's responsibility. Despite a full-time and highly productive professional career, she never shortchanged Michael. Her resources seemed limitless. She was interested in everything: mathematics, music, physics, gardening, and had a wealth of knowledge in almost every field. She could be as resourceful entertaining children of all ages as she was with adults. She became one of our closest friends as well as, later on, our children's friend—to whom she was always Dor-Dor.

In later days she would spend long visits with us at our summer home in New Hampshire when the children were young and later yet in Vermont after they were grown. She not only entertained us all but also solved problems in such a way that the solution became play. I will always remember one example. The summer was over and it was time to pack up for the journey to Chicago. In the garden there were still many lovely green tomatoes on the vines. And the children, then about five and seven, were very restless. Dorothy put those two situations together by offering to pay the children one penny for every tomato that they picked, wrapped in newspaper, and put in a box for transport to Chicago. This solved everything. The children were delighted; a penny was worth something in those days. The end result was that we took back to Chicago a good supply of green tomatoes that ripened in coming months.

As soon as Dorothy knew that I wanted to go to work, she got busy, and the first thing I knew I had a temporary job working with her on her research. I could not have found a better place to forget myself. How much I contributed to Dorothy's research I won't venture to say, but with her usual generosity Dorothy insisted that the article that resulted from our work be coauthored.[2]

New agencies connected with the war were being set up and old agencies were being expanded. I was enjoying my work with Dorothy when I got a call from the War Shipping Board inquiring about my availability for a temporary appointment there. Dorothy, of course, was agreeable to any arrangement I wanted to make, so we decided that I would take a leave from Home Economics and move to the Shipping Board.

As it turned out, this move was a fiasco. The day after I arrived, the man I was to work with went to the hospital for surgery. My desk was in a large office that I was to share with him. When he suddenly left and there was no word about when he would return, another newcomer to the Board, Dr. Tjalling Koopmans, moved into my office. It was only a matter of days before Dr. Koopmans decided that he should have the office to himself and peremptorily had me moved out. In today's terminology, that was clearly sex discrimination, but at the time I regarded it only as bad manners. It colored my opinion of Tjalling then and later when, for some years, he was a colleague of Milton's at the University of Chicago. With no word about when my absent boss would return and no one who seemed to know or have any interest in why I was hired, I was not at all unhappy to return to Home Economics and my friend Dorothy.

After about six months, my doctor decided that we could begin to think of another pregnancy. Because we were so anxious, of course, the miracle did not occur as promptly as we had hoped. We decided that quitting my job and resting more might help. That, plus encouragement of various sorts from my doctor, did the trick and we were on our way.

{ *Milton* } For me, the period that we spent in Washington was hectic, fascinating, and extremely instructive. It was my first involvement in the actual making of government policy, my first exposure to the problem of getting legislation enacted, of preparing testimony for Congress, of writing speeches for others to give, and of testifying before congressional committees. I came to understand firsthand the pull that Washington has for so many intellectuals, the sense of shaping the destiny of a nation, the excitement of the political process—and also experienced the manipulation, dishonesty, and self-seeking that are an intrinsic part of the process. The disinterested pursuer of the public interest and the interested promoter of self are not always easy to distinguish.

My experience in those years shaped the advice I regularly gave my graduate students in later years: by all means spend a few years in Washington—but only a few. If you stay more than two or three you will become addicted and will be unable effectively to return to a scholarly career.

One example will illustrate the interaction between bureacratic self-seeking and supposedly objective analysis. In the spring of 1941, the president by executive order created the OPA (Office of Price Administration) to prevent "price-spiraling, rising costs of living, profiteering, and inflation." He named as its head Leon Henderson, an economist who had been active in the New Deal and had gained a considerable measure of fame by correctly predicting that a recession was coming in 1937. (As I recall, it was his third straight yearly prediction of a recession, and the two prior predictions had been wrong.

However, since he had been in a minority all along, his incorrect predictions attracted no attention, while his correct prediction was widely heralded. I later used this example as the basis for a sure-fire way to establish a reputation as a forecaster.) John Kenneth Galbraith was assistant and then deputy administrator in charge of the Price Division during the period that I was at the Treasury. Its economic research section, of which Richard Gilbert was the major figure, at one time or another employed a considerable number of well-known economists, including George Stigler, Walter Salant, and Herbert Stein.

One of my first assignments at the Treasury, following on from the Shoup project, was to participate in constructing estimates of the amount of additional taxation that would be required to stem inflation. We discussed our results with the economic research group at the OPA, as well as with economists at the Federal Reserve and others throughout the government. Though we were supposedly using much the same (Keynesian) analysis, the OPA economists' estimates of the amount of taxes needed were at first very much lower than ours, and they fought stubbornly to defend their estimates. In the bureaucratic infighting they were successful in preventing our estimates from being accepted by the administration as the basis for a request to Congress for additional taxes.

Early in February 1942, the OPA economists suddenly appeared with revised estimates that were much higher than ours! In retrospect, the explanation was simple. In late January, Congress passed, and on January 30, 1942 the president signed, the Emergency Price Control Act, which gave the OPA the legal authority to fix prices and wages. In the process of lobbying Congress for that act, the OPA had argued that price and wage control, however unpopular, was the only way to stop inflation. They did not want the Treasury to muddy the waters by offering the alternative of higher taxes. Hence, their successful campaign to keep the Treasury from requesting Congress to enact higher taxes.

Once the OPA had the legal authority it had been desperately seeking, the interests of the OPA economists changed. They knew as well as we did that siphoning off income by taxes would reduce upward pressure on prices and wages. The Treasury now became an ally, not a competitor. Supposedly objective scientific estimates of taxes needed were revised sharply upward. The OPA now urged the Treasury to request even larger tax increases than we had estimated were needed. Crass promotion of their own power? Or necessary tactics to achieve what they firmly believed was a public good? Whatever the answer, the manipulation of the estimates seemed to me then, and still does, dishonesty pure and simple.

My own files contain few documents from the two years that I spent at the Treasury. No doubt, the numerous memoranda, reports, and letters that I wrote during those two years are buried somewhere in the files of the Treasury Department. However, I have made no attempt to get access to them. As a result, I warn the reader that the account that follows is based primarily on my necessarily imperfect recollections of those two hectic years more than half a century ago, plus examination of some published documents, which means that it will consist primarily of memorable episodes, rather than a coherent documented account of my participation in the process by which the tax system was revolutionized.

One document that has survived is a statement that I made before the House Ways and Means Committee on May 7, 1942—probably the first time that I ever testified before a congressional committee. (Before the end of my stay at the Treasury, I had become a veteran.) The statement is a highly academic presentation of the forces making for inflation, the role of taxes in offsetting those forces, why avoiding inflation would reduce "the real economic cost of the war to the American people," and why the income tax "is more effective in preventing an inflationary price rise and . . . leads to a better distribution of the cost of the war" than a sales tax. I summarized my statement by saying that "the inflationary pressure on prices is already large and is becoming larger month by month. . . . If inflation is to be prevented, this pressure must be neutralized by measures that restrict consumer spending. Taxation is the most important of those measures; unless it is used quickly and severely, the other measures alone will be unable to prevent inflation."

Why such academic testimony at this time? The only reference to proposed legislation is a single number: "The 8.7 billion of additional taxes recommended by the Treasury is the smallest amount that is at all consistent with successful prevention of inflation." The occasion for my so testifying was a dispute within the Treasury about some aspects of the tax proposal. The Treasury had been scheduled to testify on the details of the proposal but was not ready to do so, so I was sent up at the last minute as a stopgap to fulfill the Treasury's obligation. (Though the testimony was given on May 7, the typed copy of the statement is dated May 14, indicating that it was not prepared in advance as most statements were, but revised from a stenographic account.)

The most striking feature of this statement is how thoroughly Keynesian it is. I did not even mention "money" or "monetary policy"! The only "methods of avoiding inflation" I mentioned in addition to taxation were "price control and rationing, control of consumers' credit, reduction in governmental spending, and war bond campaigns." Equally Keynesian is a comment I wrote somewhat earlier on a paper titled "The Inflationary Gap," by Walter Salant, one of the authors of the OPA's estimates, in which he contrasted the OPA approach with the Shoup-Friedman-Mack approach.[3] When I reprinted my comment in 1953, I made "additions to correct a serious error of omission in the original version," noting that "the omission from that version of monetary effects . . . is not excused but may perhaps be explained by the prevailing Keynesian temper of the times."[4]

Until I reread my statement to Congress in preparing this account, I had completely forgotten how thoroughly Keynesian I then was. I was apparently cured, or some would say corrupted, shortly after the end of the war.

Aside from participating in general discussions of our tax policy and of the tactics to follow with Congress, my special assignments were personal income taxation and the taxation of insurance companies. The latter assignment proved extremely instructive in one respect that may interest the general reader. I dealt with two classes of insurance companies: (1) Large life insurance companies, like Metropolitan Life, Prudential Life, mostly mutual but with a few stock insurance companies—like Jefferson Standard, the CEO of which was a crusty Kentucky colonel, whose name I've forgotten. His company, though one of the smallest, paid, as I recall, about one-third of all the taxes paid by all life insurance companies, thanks to a defect in the law. This made the colonel an important participant in our deliberations. (2) Medium-sized casualty companies, mostly from the Midwest, dealing in the main with fire and accident insurance. The large companies were represented by salaried lawyers and actuaries; the medium-sized companies (including Jefferson Standard) by their CEOs, who typically also had a large equity stake in them.

The attitudes and responses of the two groups of representatives differed markedly. The CEOs were open to arguments in terms of the national interest, of the need for higher taxes to prosecute the war. We were able to engage in a reasonably objective discussion of the fairness and reasonableness of the changes we were proposing. They were spending their own money, regarded financing war expenditures as an important objective, and hence were willing to agree that certain changes in the law were justified even though the result would be higher taxes on themselves. The lawyers and actuaries from the large companies were a different matter. They were spending other people's money, and while, offhand, one might expect them to be indifferent to higher taxes, the reverse was the case. They were hired guns who had a single criterion by which they would be judged: their success in minimizing taxes on the companies they represented. Arguments from fairness and reasonableness made no impact on them. It was in their own, personal self-interest to be more single-mindedly self-interested on behalf of their employers—in that narrow sense of "self-interest" so often used to denigrate private enterprise—than the individuals who were spending their own money. Intransigent bureaucracy is not restricted to government.

I learned an important lesson from another isolated episode. I was testifying before the Senate Finance Committee. Senator Tom Connally of Texas—a colorful character whose trademark was a flowing black neckpiece in place of the usual four-in-hand or bow tie—asked why we had made one detailed change. I proceeded to answer in a thoroughly academic fashion, saying something like "there are three reasons, first . . . , second." Before I could continue, the senator stopped me and said, "Young man, one good reason is enough."

Still another lesson about human beings was implicit in the reaction of members of Congress to proposed changes in income-tax rate schedules. As I recall it, members of Congress were paid a salary of $15,000 at that time. Whenever we testified before a congressional committee on proposed changes, we could count on one of the first questions being: "Now, take a special case, for example, $15,000." That reaction explains why our proposed schedules were often very convoluted around the $15,000 level.

National income accounts were a fairly recent development, yet they came to play a large part in tax considerations. Senator Robert A. Taft of Ohio, a member of the Senate Finance Committee, wanted to become knowledgeable about the new sets of data and asked the Treasury to assign someone to inform him. By great good luck, I received the assignment, so I had the unique experience of tutoring a famous senator and four-time candidate for presidential nomination. He proved to be an apt student. I would rank him with Richard Nixon as one of the intellectually ablest political figures with whom I have had close contact. He would have been an outstanding member of any university faculty.

Another member of the Senate Finance Committee, Robert M. La Follette, Jr., offered a sharp contrast. A second-rate intellect, he had been elected first in 1925 to fill the unexpired term of his famous father, who had died a few months earlier. His reelection for three successive terms is strong evidence of the power of incumbency, and the appeal of a famous name. Having spent 1940–41 in Wisconsin, a state that had been dominated by the La Follettes, I was particularly interested in what "Young Bob," as he was known in Wisconsin, would be like, and much disappointed when I found out. I should note that I never had any run-ins, or indeed any unpleasant encounters, with him, so these comments are based solely on observing him in action during the many hours I spent at Senate Finance Committee meetings, occasionally as a witness, more frequently as a source person for the Secretary or other Treasury officials.

Another amusing tidbit is that Treasury offices dealing with high policy had three typewriters: a regular typewriter, one with especially large type, and one with very small type (that was before the invention of the IBM Selectric with its changeable type ball). Secretary Henry Morgenthau, Jr., was presbyopic, but also vain, and liked to be able to read memos without putting on glasses. He was tolerant of long memos so any destined for him were in large type, however long. On the other hand, FDR insisted on memos for him being on one page, but was not particular about size of type, so any memos for the president that would otherwise exceed one page were typed in small type and, if necessary, on legal-size paper. Many a document ended up being typed on all three typewriters.

Occasionally, I would be called on to draft speeches for the secretary or for Randolph Paul, general counsel of the Treasury and tax adviser to the secretary. That was my only experience with writing talks for others to give. I found it rather enjoyable. I could let myself go. Someone else was to speak the words, so I had no hesitancy in using clichés of a kind that were common in political speeches but that I could not have used myself in a public speech without smirking. The experience was instructive for a different reason: I was forced to express complex and technical material in terms that would be accessible to the proverbial "man in the street." Mitchell's lecture on writing stood me in good stead.

Thanks to my intimate involvement in what was a major concern of the Treasury, reforming the tax system to help finance the war, I had a great deal of contact with the secretary and, indeed, he came to rely on me to provide backup at congressional hearings, going so far as occasionally to call to make sure that I was going to be at a hearing at which he was to testify. The secretary was a person of high character, impeccable integrity, and unbounded loyalty to the president. A close friend of Roosevelt, Morgenthau had served in various minor capacities in the New York state government when Roosevelt was governor, and accompanied Roosevelt to Washington in 1933, where he served in various capacities until he was named secretary of the treasury in January 1934, a position that he held until July 1945, when he resigned shortly after Roosevelt's death—a longer tenure than any secretary of the treasury except Albert Gallatin (1801–13). To my surprise and disappointment, I found the secretary to be quite limited in his intellectual capacity. I repeatedly was amazed that anyone with such limitations could occupy so important a position. I have since learned better. Objective evidence of his meager intellectual capacity was readily available. One sign was his insistence on having backup support at all hearings. Another was how often, when asked a specific question at a hearing, he would refer it to a subordinate to answer. I recall, on at least one such occasion, a representative or senator saying: "Mr. Secretary, I want your opinion, not the opinion of your subordinate."

A more amusing example was his habit during our meetings with him of saying something like, "We're going to have to make that clear to the ordinary citizen. Take, for example, my daughter Joan, she's in high school. I want you to say that so Joan could understand it." At one such session, it must have been in the fall of 1942, he began to say something like that, and then stopped, saying: "I guess I can't use Joan as my example any more. She's in college now."

The Treasury and the Federal Reserve had a joint lunch on a regular schedule attended by Secretary Morgenthau, Marriner Eccles, chairman of the board of governors of the Federal Reserve System, and the professional persons at the two agencies. Like Morgenthau, Eccles was a close adviser of FDR. The contrast between Morgenthau and Eccles was striking. Morgenthau seldom spoke and then uttered mostly pleasantries or other innocuous comments. Eccles dominated the conversation, speaking lucidly and at length about a wide variety of topics, always knowledgeably and thoughtfully. He clearly had an independent mind, and had no hesitancy about expressing unorthodox opinions. I was fascinated by him and formed a high opinion of his intelligence, though I found his loquacity a bit off-putting. His opponents sometimes described him—unfairly—as having "a diarrhea of words and a constipation of ideas."

Eccles played an important role in the Federal Reserve from his appointment to head the board in November 1934 to his resignation from the board in July 1951. His independence led to a clash with Truman after Truman was elected president, and the president refused to reappoint him as chairman in April 1948.[5] Eccles stayed on the board despite his having to hand over the chairmanship—to the best of my knowledge, one of only two board chairmen ever to do that. In 1951 he became so disturbed at Truman's efforts to influence the supposedly independent Fed that he called a press conference for a Sunday, when all Federal Reserve and other government offices were closed, to make public the story of a recent White House meeting at which Truman had insisted, improperly in Eccles's view, that the Fed change its policy. Thereupon, Eccles resigned.

Morgenthau's limited intellectual capacity meant that he was inordinately dependent on consultants and subordinates. Many people are unwilling to have as subordinates persons who are abler than they or even their equal. It speaks well of Morgenthau that he was completely free of that character flaw. He surrounded himself with an extraordinarily able group of subordinates. From almost the beginning of his tenure as secretary, he relied heavily on our former teacher, Jacob Viner, as an outside adviser. Viner, in turn, was responsible for recommending able people for positions at the Treasury, some of whom, despite their ability, turned out to be highly controversial because of their left-wing sympathies.

Harry Dexter White

Morgenthau's most prominent internal adviser was Harry Dexter White, head of the Division of Monetary Research. White had been a professor of economics at Lawrence College in Wisconsin when he came to the Treasury. As head of the Division of Monetary Research he became a close adviser to the secretary and established an intimate relationship with him. I recall one meeting in the secretary's office, with perhaps a dozen or so persons present, at which there was a difference of opinion about something or other and the discussion became very heated, with White somehow differing with the secretary. Suddenly, White stood up, face livid, and said something like, "I'd better leave before I say something I shouldn't," and stomped out of the room. The atmosphere was like that of a schoolboy squabble.

Another incident that I vividly recall occurred in the fall of 1942. During the summer we had developed a proposal for a "spendings tax" as a supplement to the income tax and in lieu of higher tax rates.[6] In a pamphlet, *How to Pay for the War,* published in 1940,[7] Keynes had made a different radical proposal: compulsory saving, to be repaid after the war as a way simultaneously to reduce purchasing power during the war and to expand it after the war to offset the postwar depression that Keynes and his disciples feared. Harry White, and perhaps others at the Treasury, were very much taken with this idea and had been looking for an occasion to propose it. They came up with the idea of combining the two novel proposals: using spending rather than income as the basis for extracting funds from the public, and treating at least some of the funds raised as compulsory savings instead of taxes. Those of us in the Division of Tax Research who had developed the spendings tax were strongly opposed to combining the two novel ideas.

The day before we were to propose the spendings tax to the Senate Finance Committee (September 2, 1942), the dispute had not yet been resolved, so a special meeting was called in the secretary's office to settle the issue. As I recall, some seventeen of us were present. After much discussion, the secretary called for a vote. The result: 16 to 1: 16 in favor of proposing it as a tax; one, Harry White, as partly compulsory saving. The one proved an adequate majority for the secretary, who decided that we should propose it as partly compulsory savings. The end result was that the proposal got nowhere. It was in effect laughed out of court: to introduce such a novel device, and not even raise a penny in taxes! "What a silly idea" was the reaction of the Finance Committee members.

Harry White was widely regarded as responsible for what became known as the "Morgenthau plan," which proposed "converting Germany into a country primarily agricultural and pastoral in its character." It was tentatively adopted by the wartime allies in September 1944, but subsequently replaced by a more moderate program. Of more lasting influence was White's role in the Bretton Woods Conference held in July 1944, out of which came the International Monetary Fund and the International Bank for Reconstruction and Development (the World Bank). White and Keynes were the two leading figures at the conference, the "White" and "Keynes" plans the two leading alternatives considered, and a combination of them the basis for the institutions that emerged. By this time, I had left the Treasury and was working as a mathematical statistician on purely military problems (see chap. 8), so I had no direct knowledge of those activities.

White became a highly controversial figure after the war during the investigation of communist influence. A number of witnesses before the House Un-American Activities Committee mentioned White's name as a member or sympathizer. Whittaker Chambers in his book *Witness,* refers to his frequent meetings with White and his receiving information from him. Indeed, the following passage from *Witness* first persuaded me that Chambers's testimony was accurate:

> Harry Dexter White . . . was not a party member, but a fellow traveler. . . .
>
> He talked endlessly about the "Secretary" (Henry Morgenthau, Jr.) whose moods were a fair barometer of White's. If White's spirits were up, I knew that the Secretary was smiling. If he was depressed, I knew that the Secretary had had a bad day.[8]

That was precisely the White I knew, as my earlier comments on White's close relationship with the secretary indicate. From my observation, White was extremely able and quick intellectually, but not profound. After brief reflection on any issue, he would come up with a better analysis than most people qualified to evaluate the issue; but after three days, his analysis would remain the same, whereas some analysts would have dug far deeper. I was also persuaded that while he was not a communist, simply because he so obviously valued his independence, he would not hesitate to leak confidential material to the communists—with the best of motives. He had enormous confidence in his own judgment, and if he thought that it was in the interest of the United States for confidential information to be passed on to the Russians, he would not have been restrained from doing so by the fact that his superiors believed otherwise. On less important matters, whenever there was a leak to the press, it was the common view of us underlings at the Treasury that White was responsible.

White was called to testify before the House Committee on Un-American Activities on a number of occasions, on all of which he maintained his innocence. Three days after one such session in 1948, he had a fatal heart attack, which his family attributed to the stress produced by the long and tiring testimony.

Personal Income Tax: The Doubling-up Issue

The revision of the personal income tax involved many detailed issues: how to handle medical care, which involved determining a base amount (5 percent of income) such that only the excess of medical expenses over that base would be allowed as a deduction in computing taxable income; the exemptions and tax schedules for joint and separate returns; the treatment of capital gains; and so on in infinite detail. An overriding issue was the rate schedule to be recommended. All this involved preparing estimates of the effect on revenue of one or another change in the base, and of one or another rate schedule. In addition, all sorts of suggestions came our way, from members of Congress and others, that required analysis, sometime including estimates of effects on revenue.

I recall one particular suggestion of this kind, that a tax be imposed on increases in income from one year to the next. It was not an idea that we looked on favorably for rather obvious reasons, but it came from an influential source and had to be taken seriously. So I found myself spending one weekend trying to estimate the revenue that would be generated by such a tax. There was no reliable evidence on which an estimate could be based—and of course no computers to permit rapid and complex computations if there had been such evidence. I do not recall how I made the calculation but I do know that I came up with some kind of a number.*

Two major issues stand out from this welter of day-to-day concerns: first, the so-called forgiveness problem; second, withholding at source. Both derived from the same concern: to achieve current collection of taxes on income.

---

* As it happened, the work I had done on professional incomes and income distribution at the National Bureau proved to be highly relevant both to my estimate of the appropriate base amount for medical care and to estimating the yield from a tax on increases in income.

Prior to 1942, the tax on income received in one year was due and payable in quarterly installments the next year. There was no collection at source, and no advance payment of taxes. The taxpayer was left to his own devices to come up with the sum necessary to meet his tax liability. That raised few problems so long as the income tax was fairly low and only a small fraction of the population was subject to the tax. Even though the top tax rate had been raised from 24 percent in 1929 to 79 percent by 1939, the high rates applied only to extremely high incomes and affected relatively few people. As late as 1939, fewer than four million taxable returns in all were filed, and total taxes collected were less than $900 million, or 4 percent of net taxable income. As an upper middle-class family with two earners, we were one of those four million. However, our total tax on 1939 income was $119, or less than 2 percent of our taxable income. It was no great hardship to pay that in a single check on March 15, 1940. By 1943, only four years later, the top rate was 88 percent, the number of returns filed had multiplied ten-fold, and the total taxes collected, nearly fifteen-fold, amounting to 15 percent of net taxable income. In our own case, our income was only a little higher than in 1939, thanks to having only one earner, yet our tax was $1,704, or 23 percent of our taxable income. It would have required considerable advance planning to be prepared to pay that amount in four installments in 1944, let alone in one check.

It was clear to all of us at the Treasury, as we set out to multiply the amount of revenue to be collected from the personal income tax, that it would be impossible to do so unless we could develop a system to collect the taxes as the income was earned, not a year later.

One problem raised by shifting to current collection was how to handle the problem of two years' taxes coming due in one year. Under the former system, the tax for 1941 income was due and payable in 1942. But under a system of current collection, the tax for 1942 income would also be due and payable in 1942. Something had to be done to avoid that outcome. Many alternatives were suggested, both inside the Treasury and outside, almost all involving some degree of forgiveness of one of the two years' taxes or part of both. But which year, and how? The discussion of alternatives became very technical and heated, and is no longer of anything but antiquarian interest. What remains interesting to me was what the discussion taught me about the press.

We naturally had our own proposal at the Treasury. The chief outside proposal came from Beardsley Ruml, who at one point had been dean of the Social Sciences at the University of Chicago, but had left the academic world and at the time was treasurer of R. H. Macy & Co. (then located entirely in New York), and chairman of the board of directors of the Federal Reserve Bank of New York. His plan essentially called for simply forgiving the whole of the tax on 1941 income if current payment was introduced for 1942 income.[9] The *New York Times,* and most of the New York financial community, strongly favored the Ruml plan.

As one of the architects of the alternative Treasury proposal, which involved much less forgiveness of taxes, I naturally followed the news coverage closely. I was outraged at the biased coverage of the dispute by a number of major papers, especially the *New York Times.* When Ruml first testified before the Senate Finance Committee, his testimony was covered in a front-page story in the *Times* (July 28, 1942), followed by at least three editorials (August 14, 26, 29), and two signed opinion pieces, all in favor of the Ruml plan. One opinion piece was by Arthur Krock (August 28, 1942), perhaps the best known commentator on public affairs at the time; the other, by Godfrey N. Nelson, described as "an authority on taxation," which appeared on the front page of the Sunday financial and business section (August 23, 1942). When Randolph Paul, general counsel of the Treasury, attacked the Ruml plan in a radio address over a nationwide network, the story ran on page 22 (September 1, 1942), "among the garter ads," as the saying went. And the same treatment was repeatedly accorded testimony by the secretary or by Paul before congressional committees.

I could understand the *Times* taking an editorial position for Ruml and against the Treasury, but I did not expect the news columns to be so partisan. The one newspaper that clearly separated editorial opinion from news was the *Wall Street Journal.* Editorially it supported Ruml, though less fervently than the *Times,* but its news columns gave a fair coverage to both the principal proposals, correctly reporting shifts of sentiment within the Senate Finance Committee first in favor of and then against the Ruml plan. For example, the Paul radio address attacking the Ruml plan was given full coverage on page 3 of a sixteen-page issue, and was referred to on the first page. I have had no reason to alter that initial judgment about those two papers in the more than half century that has elapsed since then.

The final version, signed into law by President Roosevelt as the Current Tax Payment Act of 1943 on June 9, 1943, incorporated a modification of the Ruml plan. It canceled ("forgave" in the language of the opponents of the Ruml plan, or "abated" in the language of proponents) one year's tax obligations of $50 or less and 75 percent of the required tax on the lower of 1942 or 1943 income, requiring the remaining 25 percent to be paid in two equal annual installments. The compromise was reached after endless debate spanning well over a year. The *New York Times* labeled its editorial after the passage of the bill "The Tax Compromise" (June 3, 1943, p. 20); the *Wall Street Journal,* "A Gain for Sound Taxation" (June 3, 1943, p. 6).

Withholding at Source

Two devices were enacted at that time, and mostly still prevail, to collect taxes currently: for wages, collection at source from the employer at the time wages are paid; for other income, advance estimates by the recipient. (Withholding at source was initially proposed for and is currently used for some income other than wages, such as interest and dividends, but the enactment into legislation of such withholding was a later development.) If you were to ask a current official of the Internal Revenue Service whether it would be possible to collect the present level of income taxes without withholding of taxes on wages at source, he would tell you in no uncertain terms that it would be impossible. In 1942, the officials at the Internal Revenue Service were the chief opponents of collection at source. In August 1942, the *Wall Street Journal* reported on the "testimony given to the [Senate Finance] Committee . . . by Guy T. Helvering, Internal Revenue Commissioner," noting that "while the details of the commissioner's argument were not revealed, it was understood that he contended any withholding tax would place an almost insuperable burden on the collecting agency" (August 21, 1942, p. 2).

The first law of bureaucracy—that the only feasible way of doing anything is the way it is being done—was further impressed on me when we consulted experts on the British and German tax systems. Both countries were collecting taxes on wages at source, but in different ways. In both, the amount collected at source (in Germany, on current income; in Britain, on past income), was treated as final payment and there was no retrospective adjustment. We insisted on developing a system under which the amount collected at source would be a tentative advance payment on a total tax to be determined after the end of the year, with additional payments or refunds to adjust for any difference between the final tax assessed and the advance payments. Both the German expert, a refugee from Nazism, and the British expert assured us that they had considered such a possibility and had found it thoroughly impractical, that only final payment was possible.

In order to flesh out the details of our proposal, and also to foster the full cooperation of the Internal Revenue Service and persuade them of the feasibility of our proposal, we formed a number of joint teams of IRS officials and members of the Division of Tax Research to make trips into the field to study the payroll practices of a few enterprises, and confer with them about how to set up withholding in the most effective way. The group I joined visited Detroit, Toronto, New York, and Wilmington.

My most vivid recollection is the contrast between the payroll practices of Hudson Department Store and Ford Motor Company, both in Detroit.

Hudson had one of the most efficient and automated systems we came across, and we learned a great deal from studying it. Ford, by contrast, had about as inefficient a system as any that we observed. Essentially all enterprises at the time paid their employees by check; Ford almost alone paid in cash. The reason was simple. Ford, too, had paid its employees by check before 1931 or 1932. But during the financial disturbances of the Great Depression, when many banks failed and currency exchanges arose to perform some of their functions, the exchanges, and perhaps also some banks, charged a fee to cash checks. Henry Ford, Sr., still very much in charge, was outraged that his employees would have to pay to get their pay, and he decreed that all wages should henceforth be paid in cash! We found it ironic that a representative of such an ancient industry as retail trade should be so technologically advanced in its payroll practices, while a pioneer of modern mass production should be so backward.

In any event, we ended up with a system that was very different from either the German or British and that achieved all our own objectives. No doubt, had I been asked a few years later to advise some other country how to set up a system of collection at source, I would have told them that our way was the only way to do it!

Far more important, without a system of current collection, it would have been impossible to collect the amount of income taxes that we collected during the war. At the time, we concentrated single-mindedly on promoting the war effort. We gave next to no consideration to any longer-run consequences. It never occurred to me at the time that I was helping to develop machinery that would make possible a government that I would come to criticize severely as too large, too intrusive, too destructive of freedom. Yet, that was precisely what I was doing.

Rose has repeatedly chided me over the years about the role that I played in making possible the current overgrown government we both criticize so strongly. That is in jest, since withholding would have been introduced had I been involved or not. The most I accept blame for is helping to make it more efficient than it otherwise might have been. There is an important lesson here. It is far easier to introduce a government program than to get rid of it. There is almost always, as in this case, a good reason for introducing it, but the program will not go out of existence if the initial need for it passes. Truly, the road to Leviathan is paved with good intentions. It may be worth noting that this proposition is equally true for nonprofit organizations. The March of Dimes, organized to collect funds for the treatment and prevention of polio, did not close up shop once polio was largely eradicated by the development of an antipolio vaccine. It simply adopted a new cause.

{ *Rose* } Our stay in Washington after I stopped working was for me very pleasant and very relaxed. We had many old friends, and new ones came along. There were always visitors from the real world to entertain. Since I had no other commitments, I enjoyed the domestic experience. Milton kept me up to date on what was going on as he has for most of our life together. While from one point of view the time did not pass as fast as I would have liked, everything went so well that I did not mind. When the end of February rolled around, Dr. Lawson decided that the time had come to bring our daughter into the world. On the morning of February 26, I packed the few articles that I would need at the hospital and Milton and I took off. By noon we were the proud parents of a beautiful little girl whom we named Janet—the best-looking in the nursery, everyone agreed.

There had been no labor pains, no waiting for just the right moment to be moved to the delivery room, sometimes the use of instruments to help the baby out and sometimes, as in my first experience, no baby after all the agony. I have heard all the arguments on the subject of natural birth, but sometimes (I do not know how frequently) nature lets you down. Whether to have a Caesarian section is still best left to the parents and the physician. My only question is whether the information about the positives and negatives of the two methods is as unbiased as it should be. Caesarian sections are generally performed when difficulties have already arisen. Hence the mortality rate is of course higher. (I cannot say that I have studied the statistics. This is an uninformed opinion.)

{ *Milton* } Janet's birth was the happiest event of our second stay in Washington—and also marked its end. By this time, whatever contribution revising taxes could make to the war effort had been made.[10] Hence, I welcomed the suggestion that Allen Wallis had been making for some months that I join him in New York, where he was primarily responsible for organizing the Statistical Research Group at Columbia University to do war research. I spent the rest of the war years as a mathematical statistician rather than economist.

My only regret is that, had I remained at the Treasury, I might have participated in the postwar financial reconstruction that took place at Bretton Woods, which the Treasury did so much to shape.

Chapter Eight

WAR YEARS IN
NEW YORK, 1943–45

{ *Milton* } Allen Wallis, one of my closest friends, was the director of the Statistical Research Group at Columbia University, organized in 1942 as part of a program to mobilize scientists for war work.[1] He asked me to join the SRG as associate director. The work promised to contribute far more to the war effort than further refining the details of tax legislation. It involved direct contact with the military, working on problems that they considered important. It was an opportunity to apply my training in statistics to a class of problems wholly different from those that I would encounter in a standard career as an economist, and to collaborate with able scholars in disciplines other than my own—physical scientists, engineers, and mathematicians. As it turned out, my two and a half years at the Statistical Research Group were among the most varied, interesting, and indeed exciting, professional experiences I have ever had. The experience unquestionably had a major influence on my subsequent work, in many different ways, not least in some of the friendships formed.

The Statistical Research Group was housed in an apartment at 401 West 118th St., one block from Columbia University.[2] I joined the group on March 1, 1943, just three days after our daughter Janet was born. Rose was still in the hospital. We did not actually move to New York for another two months. In the interim, I commuted to New York for two or three days each week and worked in Washington the rest of the time. This arrangement was possible because the headquarters of the principal SRG clients—notably the Navy— were in or near Washington. On one of my trips to New York, I rented an apartment for the family at 467 Central Park West, three blocks north of where we had lived from 1938 to 1940.

The ease with which I was able to rent an apartment will come as a shock to anyone who has current experience with housing conditions in New York. I simply scanned the advertisements in the newspapers, selected a few that seemed promising, and chose one. We wanted to live within walking distance of the SRG and close to Central Park, and the apartment I selected met those requirements.

The housing market then was efficient. The classified ads listed numerous apartments for rent. I had only to choose. I know that sounds like a pipe dream today. The problem now is to *find* an apartment in New York for rent. That may involve such stratagems as watching the obituary column. The reason for the difference is clear. Price control, including rent control, was imposed in 1942 but had not made much of a dent by early 1943 when I rented our apartment. The legislation that abolished rent control nationwide in 1949 gave any state or city that wished to do so the option to retain rent controls. New York was the only city in the country that chose to do so at the time. Fifty years of rent controls have produced the present housing situation in New York City.

{ *Rose* } Returning to New York ushered in a completely new way of life for me. For Milton, it was a temporary change of career. For me, it was much more—a complete change, being a mother instead of an economist, and, for the duration of the war, living in a style unlike any that we enjoyed before or since. Our style of living had already changed somewhat when we moved to Washington. Milton no longer did much of his work at home as he had been accustomed to doing; it was all done at the Treasury office. Evenings we spent in more social activities.

The SRG meant a more significant change. Because his work was confidential or secret, and documents had to be locked up when he left the office, Milton was unable to do any work relating to his job at home. More important, we could not even discuss what he was doing except on the most general and superficial level. Our talk was about what was going on in the world, how I spent my day, and, most important, how our daughter spent her day. The statistical work that Milton did at home involved keeping detailed records and charts of her weight, how much formula she consumed during the day (an important item, since she was not a big eater), her physical and, as the months went on, her intellectual progress. We had records of her first word, when she first combined words, and so on. We compared her progress with the stages described in a popular baby book by Arnold L. Gesell. Of course she was always at the head of the class. She was an unusually "good" baby, so we always looked forward to her waking hours during those early months.

Even after all these years, I vividly remember Milton's trying to keep her awake for her 10 o'clock feeding by tickling her toes while I tried desperately to get her to nurse. Keeping her awake was probably more difficult than writing the reports that Milton later told me about. But both were accomplished, and her weight, recorded daily, did increase, though not very rapidly. Looking back, it is hard to believe that one infant kept me busy all day and her father occupied, in one way or another, every evening.

We must have had some social life but, try as I may, I can't remember having a babysitter until I hired a neighborhood teenager during her summer vacation. Her babysitting consisted primarily in taking Janet across the street to Central Park in her baby carriage and keeping her in the fresh air and sunshine all day! I came across with her bottle every four hours.

Two comments: first, at that time, sunshine was considered to be very healthy for infants and adults (my pediatrician was most enthusiastic about Janet's tanned body when he saw her in the fall); second, it's hard to believe today that there was ever a time when Central Park was considered to be a safe place for a teenage girl and an infant to spend the day. I cannot remember ever hearing any concern expressed about safety in the park then. There were always many older people who spent long hours in the park and they were interested in the beautiful baby who was always there.

I am sure our teenager also sat for us when we went out in the evening. Unlike the current practice of taking babies along to restaurants or to friends' homes in the evening, I don't remember taking either of our children to a restaurant until he or she was old enough to sit at the table as an adult, except when we were traveling and had no choice. Similarly, I always fed the children by themselves before we had dinner. Perhaps this was my way of having some time alone with Milton but I always felt it was also best for the children because they had our full attention.

I had what many young mothers today would consider other foolish ideas about bringing up babies. Milton's mother and sisters lived in Rahway, some twenty miles from Manhattan, but we did not take Janet to Rahway her first year because I was afraid that she would pick up some bug on the train. Although we had a car, I have no recollection of using it during that period, probably because of gas rationing. I always encouraged Milton's family to visit us instead. In addition to Janet's being so special for us because of the loss of our first child, I did have one excuse for behavior that may seem neurotic. When Janet was about six months old, she developed *celiac disease,* which the dictionary defines as a deficiency disease of young children caused by faulty absorption of food in the intestines, characterized by diarrhea and malnutrition.

Two things saved my sanity during the roughly eighteen months that the disease persisted: a wonderful pediatrician and a supply of bananas. Our pediatrician, Dr. Murray Bass, who had replaced Dr. Bela Schick (of the Schick test) at Mt. Sinai Hospital, diagnosed the disease almost immediately and explained to me that the disease had two characteristics: (1) there was no known cure and (2) it eventually disappeared as suddenly as it appeared. The important thing was to keep the child from becoming malnourished. That was where the bananas came in, because bananas were one of the few foods that a celiac patient could tolerate. Dried bananas did not appear in the market, or at least I had no knowledge of them, until late in the course of Janet's disease. Wartime price control made bananas difficult to get, but we managed while we were in Manhattan since by this time we were well known at the market. However, when I spent a month at Fire Island with Janet in the summer of 1944, bananas were not available at the island stores at any price.

Milton and I both remember vividly his arriving for weekends with a large suitcase filled not with clothes but with bananas that he had collected during the week—not always an easy task. I used them very carefully since they had to last until the new supply arrived the following Friday night. Three close friends, Anne Wallis, Jane Bennett, and I, and our children shared the house at Fire Island that summer. All three husbands were on the staff of the Statistical Research Group, and came to the island only on weekends. Since the house could accommodate only two families at a time, we decided that each of us would share the house with each of the other couples for two weeks. My hoarding of bananas until I was sure they would last the week was understood by my friends and, as far as I can remember, there was no problem even with the children. I was about two months pregnant with our second child at this time and my good friends were very helpful about that as well.

Perhaps because I was too busy taking care of Janet or because I was just getting accustomed to that state, I don't recall any difficulty with the third pregnancy. However, unlike some women who find pregnancy a delightful period, I was much relieved when our second child turned out to be a boy: because the child I lost was male, I somehow felt that that loss could only be completely filled by another male child. Or perhaps I just felt that one of each sex would be more interesting. In any event, my first question to Milton after the birth, even before I was entirely awake, was, "What is it?" His answer, "A boy." My reply, "Thank God, I don't have to go through this again," spoke volumes. I was very fortunate in the obstetrician who was recommended by Dr. Bass. When I suggested a second Caesarian, he not only agreed but announced that if he were a woman and pregnant, he would hike from New York to California, where Caesarians were more common, if necessary, to get a doctor who would perform the operation. This was so different from the standard attitude about Caesarian sections at that time (and still today) that I was much impressed by his freely expressed opinion.

Though eager to see her new granddaughter (at the time, she only had one other), my mother did not come from Portland to New York until Janet's second Christmas. I remember very clearly several things about this visit. Orthodox Jews, of course, do not celebrate Christmas. However, just as, when I was a child, my mother had permitted me to have a Christmas tree one year when my friend had one,* she not only tolerated our having a Christmas tree, she even strung popcorn to hang on it. Our Christmas tree as I remember was not much bigger than Janet and I still have a vivid picture of Janet carrying the tree around the house, to the delight of her parents and grandmother.

My other "mother story" is quite different. As it happened, Janet came down with a strep throat while my mother was visiting. Sulfa drugs were not yet in common use. Upon making his home visit (physicians still made house calls at that time), Dr. Bass warned us that one of us must be at Janet's bedside throughout the day and night because she could at any time begin to choke. While I don't recall just what we were supposed to do in that event, I do remember that Milton and I took turns sitting or lying beside her crib. The point of this story was my mother's reaction. She was certainly concerned about Janet, but she was even more concerned about me, protesting my either lying or sitting beside Janet a good part of the night in my condition (I was seven months pregnant). To her, I was still her baby and she had to protect me! For me, my own baby was all-important.

Janet was still sleeping in a crib when her sibling was due to arrive. We did not want to buy another crib, so we decided to move Janet into a twin bed. However, we were very much concerned that she might fall out of bed. How to prevent this? Milton has always been very good at what in our day were known as Rube Goldberg solutions. He decided that if he could build some kind of a canopy over the bed and I would crochet a loose curtain to hang from it, this would keep Janet from falling out. How long this activity took, I no longer remember, but I have no difficulty remembering the result. The first night we put Janet into her new bed we heard a bump in the night: Janet had gone right through the curtain and was on the floor, landing with no ill effects. So far as I can recall, she never fell out of the bed again once the curtain and canopy were removed.

---

* Though I have no very clear recollection of the restrictions surrounding my having a Christmas tree, I suspect that my father, who was not nearly as amenable as my mother to breaking the rules if it involved something the children wanted, was the one who decided that the tree had to be set up in the basement, not in the living room.

The next big event was David's birth. My sister Becky, whose only son, Barry, was old enough to be left at home in the care of his father, came to New York to take care of Janet while I was in the hospital. This was the first time she had seen Janet. Janet was a handful: as adventuresome a two-year-old as Becky had encountered. Janet had one characteristic almost from the day she was born: she was always attempting activities before she was really ready for them. She tried to walk before she was ten months old, and we have movies of these early attempts—two steps and then kerplunk. She never grew discouraged, however, and, little by little, there were more ups than downs. When she got her first tricycle there were many bruises, but Janet never became discouraged. No slide in the park was too much for her. Becky didn't trust her not to fall off and climbed the steps of the slide after Janet, and then ran around to catch her when she slid down.

{ *Milton* } Becky had never been east of Reno before she came to take care of Janet while Rose was in the hospital. To her, New York was a wholly new, very different, and not very attractive world. The most revealing incident occurred one evening when I got tickets to a Broadway play for Becky and me. Because of wartime rationing of gasoline, the rules against sharing taxicabs had been loosened for the duration. The cab that took us downtown had another couple in it. We rode to our separate destinations without any conversation between the two couples sharing the cab. When we left the cab, Becky burst out with: "How can people live that way? Riding all the way downtown and never saying a word to one another! That could never have happened in Reno." Another bit of evidence to support the generalization I had reached a decade earlier when I first traveled west of the Delaware River: the farther west, the friendlier the people.

I will add, however, that the taxicab experience is misleading. Beneath the convention of strictly minding one's own business, people are just as friendly in New York as elsewhere, but only within close circles, not with strangers.

{ *Rose* } Since Becky had to get back to her own family soon after I came home from the hospital, we had hired a nurse on the advice of a friend. Not long after we had gone to bed the first night, the three of us, Milton, Becky, and I, who were all sleeping in the living room, since we had given the nurse and David our bedroom, were awakened by the loud crying of our young son. As I remember, all three of us marched into the bedroom to find the nurse snoring away while our poor baby was yelling because he didn't like being wet and dirty. We refrained from sending her packing in the middle of the night, but when morning came we gave her her walking papers. Her idea and ours about taking care of a baby were very different. After a few days on our own, we lucked out. Another friend recommended an Austrian grandmother, who turned out to be a treasure. For six weeks, she took care of Janet, David, and me, plus preparing some wonderful food for us.

Becky formed a strong attachment to David from the moment she took him in her arms when I came home from the hospital—an attachment that lasted until her death in 1986. I have always wondered what there is about a week-old infant that can create such a bond between that infant and an adult. David in turn made the attachment mutual on his first extended exposure to Becky at age 2. David named his daughter, born in 1990, Rebecca in her memory.

When summer approached, our friends the Shoups, who planned to spend the summer at their second home in New Hampshire, suggested that we move to their home in Riverdale for the summer instead of staying in our apartment. We gladly accepted their offer and as a result spent a delightful summer with our two babies. Since gas rationing was still in effect, Milton took the train to Columbia. To the best of my recollection, I was so comfortable that I never left the house. But we did eat, so I must have gone out at least to do the marketing. However, that remains a total blank in my mind and Milton's. I do remember, however, that Janet's battle with celiac ended about the time that David was born.

At the end of the summer, the Shoups returned and we moved back to our apartment. I, in particular, regretted having to leave our temporary home. It was the first time that I had enjoyed the luxury of a washing machine and a dishwasher. I did have the use of a washing machine in the basement of our apartment house but there was no dishwasher in our kitchen. When I expressed my gratitude for such wonderful equipment to Ruth Shoup, she replied that there was only one postwar luxury she looked forward to and that was a full-time maid! I guess everything is relative.

{ *Milton* } The Statistical Research Group was the first demonstration on a substantial scale of Allen Wallis's extraordinary talent as an administrator. Seemingly effortlessly, Allen organized a group of eighteen principals, including some of the most eminent statisticians of the time, and others who attained that distinction in later years, as well as a large support staff, while at the same time making significant contributions to the group's substantive work. The group proved extremely useful to its military clients and, in the process, developed new statistical procedures that have become part of the discipline of statistics.*

In an article on the SRG that Allen published in 1980, thirty-five years after it had been disbanded, he wrote:

> SRG was composed of what surely must be the most extraordinary group of statisticians ever organized, taking into account both number and quality. . . . SRG was in many respects a model that has not been equaled of an effective statistical consulting group. . . .
>
> SRG's sole purpose was to serve the Army, Navy, Air Force, Marines, OSRD [Office of Scientific Research and Development], and a few suppliers to these. . . .
>
> We were under steady pressure to deliver—there was a war on, as the saying went. Our work, however excellent, was in effect not delivered if it had no influence; so we had to understand the client's viewpoint and needs and be persuasive and accommodating.
>
> Perhaps the strongest encouragement was the fact that when we made recommendations, frequently things happened. Fighter planes entered combat with their machine guns loaded according to Jack Wolfowitz's recommendations about mixing types of ammunition, and maybe the pilots came back or maybe they didn't. Navy planes launched rockets whose propellants had been accepted by Abe Girshick's sampling-inspection plans, and maybe the rockets exploded and destroyed our own planes and pilots or maybe they destroyed the target. During the Battle of the Bulge in December 1944, several high ranking Army officers flew to Washington from the battle, spent a day discussing the best settings on proximity fuzes for air bursts of

---

* Later on when Allen and I were both at Chicago, he did a similarly effective job in organizing an independent Department of Statistics, of which he served as chairman for nearly a decade. When, in 1956, he was asked to become dean of the Business School at the university, I tried to persuade him to turn it down, arguing that he could make a greater contribution as an original and innovative economist and statistician than he could as an academic administrator. I was clearly wrong. With his typical good judgment, he accepted the offer, did a brilliant job as dean of the School of Business, raising its standing to the very top rank of business schools in the country by broadening its scope and giving it a distinctive character. He recruited George P. Shultz to succeed him when he departed in 1962 to accept the presidency of the University of Rochester, and later the chancellorship. Thanks to his leadership, Rochester was one of the few major universities in the country to come through the period of student unrest in the 1960s without a serious crisis. When he retired in 1982, Rochester had gained greatly in national stature, distinction of its faculty, and financial resources. After retiring from Rochester, Allen served with distinction as George Shultz's undersecretary of state for economic affairs.

artillery shells against ground troops, and flew back to the battle to put into effect advice from, among others, Milton Friedman, whose earlier studies of the fuzes had given him extensive and accurate knowledge of the way the fuzes actually performed. We were never wholly responsible for what happened. In fact, we seldom knew whether we were slightly responsible or even knew exactly what happened and to whom. But this kind of responsibility, although rarely spoken of, was always in the atmosphere and exerted a powerful, pervasive, and unremitting pressure.[3]

An additional comment in Allen's article is worth quoting in the current atmosphere of "affirmative action." After discussing the staff of the SRG, he added, "Recruiting was by the old-boy network pure and unabashed: no advertising, no competitive examinations, and no attention to race, sex, age, physical handicaps, or apparent nationality or surname." In a footnote attached to this comment, he adds, "in spite of this 'negative action' recruiting, SRG included a high proportion of women, two blacks, and two persons with severe physical handicaps."

All in all, in its slightly more than three years of existence, the SRG produced 572 substantive reports, memoranda, and letters for its military clients, most of them classified confidential or secret at the time. As a by-product, after the war four books in statistics were published which contained spin-offs from SRG's wartime work. One, Abraham Wald's book *Sequential Analysis,* was truly pathbreaking; the others have all proved influential.[4]

On a light note, I confess to a bad habit of having an extremely messy desk. In a skit one year at the traditional annual party given by graduate students at Chicago to celebrate the end of the preliminary examinations for the doctorate, a student playing me was in a room behind a closed door. Another student knocks on the door. My double says "just a minute," picks up a cardboard carton filled with assorted papers, dumps them on the desk, stirs them up thoroughly, and says, "Come in."

The two and a half years I spent at SRG are the only period during my professional career that I have ended each day with a clean desk! All classified material had to be locked up when not under direct supervision. So at the end of the day, I swept everything on my desk into a large drawer that could be securely locked. Rose has always regretted that the clean desk proved a strictly temporary aberration.

The ninety-eight reports and memos that I wrote dealt with five major topics. The sections on these topics that follow are, to quote Allen Wallis, "reminiscence" rather than "history."[5]

Aircraft Vulnerability

One early assignment that I received was to evaluate a suggestion by a Navy officer about a possibly more effective antiaircraft shell. The standard shell was a high-explosive shell which, on explosion, shattered into a large number of fragments varying widely in size and shape. The suggestion was that it might be more effective to use a shrapnel shell (analogous to a shotgun shell), which, on explosion, would project forward a stream of spherical pellets. The supposed advantage would come from being able to control the size of the pellets, which could be uniform and of optimum size. The problem I was given was two-fold: determine the optimum size of the pellets; and compare the effectiveness of the resulting shell with the standard shell. (Not exactly what I had been doing at the Treasury.)

I did not of course start from scratch. Studies had been made of the effectiveness of a standard high-explosive shell; the distribution in space of the fragments into which the shell burst; their velocities; the vulnerability of the aircraft assumed to be the target, and so on. Some of the most useful of these came from Britain. In addition, I had computational, clerical, and research assistance. Nonetheless, the task of using this information for the particular purpose was far from trivial.

I mention the details of the problem because the results illustrate a proposition that has broad relevance. The basic problem in judging the optimum size of the pellets was the trade-off between size and number. Large pellets would do a great deal of damage if they hit, but a shell could contain only a few of them, which meant that there was little chance of hitting the target. At the other extreme, one of many tiny pellets would be more likely to hit, but would do little harm to the target. The officer making the initial request suggested that, as a starting point, "the shrapnel shell be assumed to contain spherical steel bullets, numbering perhaps 16 balls, each 1.75″ in diameter." Our conclusion was that the optimum shell would contain 307 spherical steel bullets 0.65″ in diameter or nineteen times as many balls.

That contrast is instructive. The advantage of size is generally far more apparent than the advantage of number. Ask people to name the most important industries in the United States and they are likely to name automobiles or steel—or more recently, computers. Hardly anyone will name printing and publishing, let alone the restaurant industry, yet the printing and publishing industry employs more people than automobiles, steel, and computers combined, and "eating and drinking places" employ more than three times as many as the printing and publishing industry. The reason is simple. GM, Ford, and Chrysler; US Steel (as it used to be) and Bethlehem; IBM, Microsoft, and Apple, these are the kinds of names that spring to mind in free association with "major industries." There are no similarly dominant enterprises in the printing and publishing industry or in the restaurant industry—not even McDonald's in the restaurant industry. These industries have a very large number of small firms that collectively more than make up for the absence of large, dominant firms.

The same bias helps to explain the appeal of centralized government versus dispersal of power among many small government units; of government planning versus competition; of large mega-universities versus small dispersed colleges. Some years ago the phrase "small is beautiful" spread as a result of a book trying to offset this bias—without much apparent success. In our military advisory work we came across the same bias again and again in areas in which we were not directly involved as well as those in which we were: large versus small aircraft carriers; battleships versus destroyers; and so on. In every case, size tended to be overvalued relative to number.

This assignment was one of a series of assignments involving aircraft vulnerability. I recall vividly one trip I made in that connection. It was to Eglin Field in Florida, where test firings were being conducted: a gun would be fired at a disabled aircraft on the ground in a way that simulated combat conditions; after each burst, experts would examine the hits on the plane and judge how much damage had been done. In the course of the visit I observed some of the firings from a bunker located behind the target plane. The sounds we heard were eerie. The first sound after a firing would be the projectile striking the target. Then, a few seconds later, we would hear the gun going off. The explanation: the bullets traveled faster than sound so they reached the target before the sound of the gun firing. I recall none of the results of the firings, only the eerie sound pattern.

I made one study in response to a request to evaluate the vulnerability of the B-29, a new and larger bomber intended to replace the B-17, known as the Flying Fortress. That study led to a trip in a relatively small military plane from Albuquerque to Alamogordo, New Mexico. Alamogordo was the base at which the plane was being developed. It was also the base for Los Alamos, where the Manhattan Project was being conducted, but we knew nothing about that at the time, given the extreme secrecy of the project.

I recall that trip because of two events that occurred during the brief flight from Albuquerque to Alamogordo. The pilot, a former American Airlines pilot, had also been trained as a fighter pilot and offered to demonstrate for us the kind of evasive action that a pilot would take in combat. The demonstration shook us up mightily, including my hitting my head sharply on the overhead of the cabin—I suppose we did not have seat belts. The other event was altogether different. Over mountains to the west of us, I saw a perfect 360-degree circular rainbow. It was magnificent and the sight has remained with me ever since. I have never seen another, although commercial pilots I have talked with do not regard the phenomenon as exceptional. It is only our limited horizon that cuts off the rainbows we see from the ground.

Proximity Fuse

The most extensive work I did involving aircraft vulnerability was in connection with the development of a new type of fuse for antiaircraft projectiles, a proximity fuse. The standard fuse used on high-explosive antiaircraft rockets was a time-delay fuse that could be set to explode after a specified period. Three numbers must be fed in to aim such a projectile: azimuth, elevation, and range. The so-called "director" controlling the gun converted range into time delay. As the name suggests, a "proximity fuse" was designed to explode the projectile when it was in the neighborhood of the target. Its great advantage was that only two numbers had to be fed in to aim it: azimuth and elevation. That advantage was particularly important for air-to-air combat and for defense against dive bomber attacks on ships because, in both cases, the range changes so rapidly in the course of the combat that accurate estimates are almost impossible.

We were asked to assist in the design and development of the fuse. As an initial step, we analyzed data from a large number of test firings of rockets containing the fuse against simulated targets in order to determine the distribution of the points of burst in relation to the target. That turned out to be a challenging statistical task. Standard statistical distributions, such as the normal curve, or even the sum of two normal curves, did not fit the data adequately. We were finally led to fit the data by the sum of two exponential, i.e., very sharply peaked, distributions.

I mention this technical detail because it is a marvelous example of how work in one field can carry over to what seems a wholly different field. As Allen Wallis reports, "Friedman's inspiration to fit the fuze data by joining a positive and a negative exponential distribution, thus generating a sharp-pointed mode, followed an evening of conversation about economics with Arthur F. Burns, who questioned the assumption, which is made a priori by economists, that no economic series or distribution ever has a discontinuity in the first derivative—or probably any other derivative either."[6]

To complete the story, I was impressed with how much the distributions of points of burst looked like the distributions of income by size that I had worked on at the National Bureau. Later on, that led me to wondering whether the same method could not be used to describe income distributions. As a result, the idea was incorporated in, and was part of the stimulus for, an article "Choice, Chance, and the Personal Distribution of Income" that I published in 1953.[7]

The work on the proximity fuse was not only intellectually challenging, but also very successful in achieving its objectives. We were able to suggest design changes that we estimated would double or triple its effectiveness, and were able to apply our analysis to a variety of projectiles and targets.

Because of its importance, strict secrecy was maintained on the proximity fuse. None were initially made available in the European theater because of fear that they would fall into the hands of the Nazis who could use them to blunt severely the heavy aerial bombardment they were being subjected to. The ban was lifted for the Battle of the Bulge, and as Allen indicated earlier, this necessitated hurry-up instruction in what the fuse was and how to use it. The fuse proved, if not crucial, extremely helpful in that battle. After the war, we learned that the worst fears of the guardians of the fuse had been realized: the Nazis had captured a box of proximity fuses; fortunately, they never realized what they were and never made use of them.

The fuses were extremely valuable for the Navy in the Pacific in defense against dive bombers and suicide bombers.

Sequential Analysis

By common consent, the major direct contribution of SRG to the postwar discipline of statistics was the invention of sequential analysis. The story of how it happened is of human as well as scientific interest.

In order to understand the story, it is necessary to have an idea of a simple statistical problem, and of the standard procedure for dealing with it. The actual problem out of which sequential analysis grew will serve. The Navy has two alternative designs (say A and B) for a projectile. It wants to determine which is superior. To do so it undertakes a series of paired firings. On each round it assigns the value 1 or 0 to A accordingly as its performance is superior or inferior to that of B and conversely 0 or 1 to B. The Navy asks the statistician how to conduct the test and how to analyze the results.

The standard statistical answer was to specify a number of firings (say 1,000) and a pair of percentages (e.g., 53% and 47%) and tell the client that if A receives a 1 in more than 53% of the firings, it can be regarded as superior; if it receives a 1 in fewer than 47%, B can be regarded as superior;

if the percentage is between 47% and 53% for both, neither can be so regarded.

When Allen Wallis was discussing such a problem with (Navy) Captain Garret L. Schyler, the captain objected that such a test, to quote from Allen's account,

> may prove wasteful. If a wise and seasoned ordnance officer like Schyler were on the premises, he would see after the first few thousand or even few hundred [rounds] that the experiment need not be completed, either because the new method is obviously inferior or because it is obviously superior beyond what was hoped for. . . .
>
> This was early in 1943, after Milton Friedman had joined SRG but before he had been able to move his family to New York. He was commuting from Washington to New York for two or three days each week. He and I regularly had lunch together, and came to realize that . . . it might pay to use a test which would not be as efficient as the classical tests if a sample of exactly N were to be taken, but which would more than offset this disadvantage by providing a good chance of terminating early when used sequentially. Milton explored this idea on the train back to Washington one day, and cooked up a rather pretty but simple example. . . .
>
> When Milton returned to New York we spent a great deal of time at lunches over this matter, and we began to get so interested that our conversations carried over into the office; and there began to be a noticeable interference with the work we were supposed to be turning out. We finally decided to bring in someone more expert in mathematical statistics than we.

In the next couple of days, we talked about our idea on several separate occasions with Jack Wolfowitz but were utterly unable to arouse his interest. As Allen wrote, "there seemed to be something distasteful about the idea of people so ignorant of mathematics as Milton and I venturing to meddle with such sacred ideas as those of most powerful statistics, etc. No doubt this antipathy was strengthened by our calling our new tests 'super colossal' on the grounds that they are more powerful than 'most powerful' tests." Wolfowitz insisted that it had been proved mathematically that the classical tests were the most powerful possible tests and hence we had to be wrong.

We finally gave up on Jack Wolfowitz and turned to Abraham Wald, a brilliant statistician, who made seminal contributions to statistics. Like so many who contributed to victory in World War II, Wald was a refugee from

Nazism. He was Jewish of Rumanian birth, and a resident of Austria at the time of the Anschluss, escaping to the United States in 1938. He had been teaching at Columbia when he joined SRG. He died at an early age along with his wife in a plane crash in India.

As Allen put it,

> We presented the problem to Wald in general terms for its basic theoretical interest, and as a practical example, cited the problem of comparing two fire control devices with a hit or miss classification of each round.
>
> At this first meeting Wald was not enthusiastic and was completely noncommittal. I am inclined to attribute this to the fact that Wolfowitz had spoken to him the preceding evening, after our appointment had been arranged.
>
> The next day Wald phoned that he had thought some about our idea and was prepared to admit that there was sense in it. . . . He added, however, that he thought nothing would come of it; his hunch was that tests of a sequential nature might exist but would be found less powerful than existing tests. On the second day, however, he phoned that he had found that such tests do exist and are more powerful, and furthermore he could tell us how to make them. He came over to the office and outlined his sequential probability ratio [test] to us. . . .
>
> It was quite a while before Wald worked out all of the theoretical justifications of his initial results. Actually it was a very short time in view of the amount of work he achieved.[8]

One could hardly ask for a better example of the intolerant reaction of specialists in a particular field to amateurs venturing to question accepted dogma. At the time, I had nothing but scorn for Wolfowitz's attitude, but over the many years since, I have become more sympathetic as I have received literally thousands of missives from amateur economists professing to point out basic fallacies or brilliant insights. The bulk are obvious fallacies, however confidently set forth. But every once in a great while, as in this case, there is an exception, and these compensate for the rest.

Three of the four postwar books that grew out of the work at SRG dealt in whole or in part with sequential analysis, one, authored by Wald, with the theory; the other two, with applications. Much further work has been done on sequential analysis since then. In his article on sequential analysis in *The New Palgrave,* James O. Berger lists three books by various authors on sequential analysis published since Wald's original book. As Allen wrote in 1980, "Sequential analysis even today, 37 years after its discovery [as I write, more than 50 years] continues to exert a strong influence on statistical research."[9]

Sampling Inspection

An important activity at SRG was consulting with the military on procedures for inspecting batches of material submitted by suppliers to determine whether they met specifications and should be accepted or rejected. Such acceptance inspection, and the closely related problem of inspecting samples of items coming off the production line to control quality, are of long standing, and standard procedures had been developed well before the war. The contributions of SRG were of two kinds. The first was simply to advise the military about relevant procedures and to assist in drafting manuals for various groups to use. The second was to improve the existing procedures. The development of sequential analysis and its application to specific problems was the main contribution of this kind. These activities led to a request that SRG prepare an inspection manual for the Navy.

Because of the obvious peacetime importance of sampling inspection, the work we had done during the war was published after the war in a volume entitled *Sampling Inspection: Principles, Procedures, and Tables for Single, Double, and Sequential Sampling in Acceptance Inspection and Quality Control Based on Percent Defective.*

Many people at SRG were involved in this activity, though I assumed major responsibility for preparing the inspection manual for the Navy, wrote a few reports on various topics, and was one of the editors of the book just referred to.

The Navy request that we prepare an inspection manual was made in March 1945. On June 4, 1945, a version of the manual was distributed. Such rapid progress was possible only because of the earlier work that we and others had done on the problem. We prepared and conducted a course for the sampling-inspection representatives based on the manual at Hershey, Pennsylvania, June 18–22, 1945, attended by forty-three Navy representatives from all over the country. I cite this succession of dates to illustrate the pace of work under wartime pressure.

My main recollection of that course has nothing to do with its content but rather with its location. It was held at Hershey, Pennsylvania. We stayed at the Hershey Hotel, on the corner of Cocoa Avenue and Chocolate Boulevard, across the street from the Hershey Junior College, where the actual instruction took place, a block or so from the Hershey Department Store. The town was extremely neat and pleasant; all the houses were, I believe, owned by the Hershey Company. Their occupants, Hershey employees in the main, were required to maintain them to meet Hershey standards. The stench—or perfume—of paternalism was heavy in the air: both its good points—order, decency, concern for employees—and its bad—enforced conformity, absence of color and diversity—were only too apparent.*

One request for assistance on a problem of sampling inspection was rather unusual. It had to do with an inexpensive item that was extremely important for an unspecified application. The item could only be tested by destructive testing. We were asked to design an acceptance testing procedure that would give a level of assurance approaching certainty that accepted items would work, even if that involved destroying a large fraction of the items purchased. There is no sampling procedure that can give that assurance. Suppose nine hundred items out of a lot of one thousand are tested and not a single one fails to work. Does that assure you that the remaining one hundred are all good? Obviously not. Perhaps only one in the thousand items is defective. If so, there would be one chance in ten of not including it in the sample of nine hundred tested.

Happily, there is a simple solution. If only one item must work, multiply the number of items used. If on the average 10 percent of items are defective, duplicating the number used means there is only one chance in a hundred that both will be defective; tripling the number used, only one chance in a thousand that all three will be, and so on.

---

* Nearly half a century later, I referred to this episode in an op-ed piece I wrote for the *Wall Street Journal*, "The Folly of Buying Health Care at the Company Store." That produced a letter from R. A. Zimmerman, Chief Executive Officer of Hershey Foods, bringing me up to date:

"I . . . found your comments about Hershey, Pennsylvania quite interesting. We certainly spent many years as the quintessential company town: conceived, built and to all intents run by our founder, Milton S. Hershey. As many of our older residents will affirm, it was paternalism heavily laden with concern both for residents' quality of life and for their ability to independently manage their own affairs. It was a fortunate mix as the community struggled with its own growing pains, two wars and the Great Depression.

"Certainly, it is a different community today. I regret to say that the Cocoa Inn (the one you remember as 'the Hershey Hotel') has been reduced to rubble—a victim of declining traffic to its center-city location. Hershey Junior College, which was privately financed and open to children of all employees and township residents, fell victim to high costs and the emergence of local community colleges; fortunately, it lives on as part of the Harrisburg Area Community College.

"The building which housed the Hershey Department Store still stands. While the store itself failed to survive the appearance of shopping centers, today a variety of local merchants lease the building's first floor and help maintain a retail presence downtown" (Letter of February 10, 1993).

We later discovered that the request had come from the Manhattan Project, that the item was an inexpensive detonator to be used to set off the atomic bomb, so that there was no objection to multiplying the number of detonators to give a very high probability that one would work.

High-Temperature Alloys

In the middle of 1944, I embarked on a new assignment that was to prove both challenging and instructive.

For some time, a large-scale research program had been underway to improve the performance of the alloys used for the blades of turbosuperchargers and gas turbines. The military was interested because the performance of aircraft depends critically on the efficiency of the turbosuperchargers which in turn rises rapidly with the temperature at which they can be operated. Hence the importance of alloys for turbine blades that can withstand high temperatures. (In later years, the same considerations were important for the alloys used to line jet engines.)

I recall the pride that one of the leaders of the research, Commander Bruce Old, showed in his handiwork when he told the story of a trip in a military plane across the Atlantic. Looking out the window, he saw red-hot turbosuperchargers working steadily without failing and helping the plane achieve high speeds. Only possible, he said, because of the improvements in the alloys used.

In the early period of the wartime research, progress was so rapid that refined statistical techniques were of no great importance. But then, improvement slowed and anomalies arose: alloy A would test better than B, B than C, and then C would test better than A. The result was a request that SRG help the research people design their experiments and analyze their research. The task was assigned to me, and constituted a major part of my activity until the end of the war.

As a result, I was thrust into learning something about metallurgy, a subject about which my ignorance was absolute. I found the subject, or as much as I could understand and absorb, fascinating.[10]

I served as something of a clearing agency for the results of the various experiments in progress, as an adviser on the statistical design of experiments, and as an analyst of the results. After a few months, I started issuing a monthly bulletin to the researchers in the field, in which I summarized both work that I had done and work that was underway at various research institutions, notably

MIT and Batelle Memorial Institute. "These bulletins," I wrote in the final report I submitted at the end of the project, "were intended to be as full as possible, including preliminary results; . . . they thus provide a fairly complete record of the work done on the study. The specific problems covered in the bulletins covered a wide range. Many of them consisted of detailed analyses of specific data in order to measure experimental error, or to determine the effect of such factors as testing laboratory, treatment given an alloy, chemical composition, and size of specimen on the properties of specific alloys."[11] All told, we issued and circulated eight substantive monthly bulletins in the course of the study.

The procedure in testing an experimental alloy was to hang a specified weight on a standard turbine blade made from the alloy, put it in a furnace capable of generating a very high temperature, and measure the time it took for the blade to break. At one point, I thought it might be possible to summarize the test data from all the separate experiments by calculating a single equation (a multiple regression) that would express time to fracture as a function of stress, temperature, and variables describing the composition of the alloy, and from which it would be possible to predict the strength of alloys as yet untested. I assured myself that the form of the equation I planned to estimate was consistent with metallurgical theory. The result of this ambitious experiment was to have a major effect on my approach to empirical work for the rest of my professional life.*

The major problem then, trivial now, was to compute the parameters of the equation and the associated test statistics. That was the age of the electric—not electronic—desk calculator and the Dolittle method of computing regressions. The labor involved in that method increases exponentially with the number of independent variables. For the number I wanted to use, we estimated that it would take three months for one of our highly skilled operators to calculate the equation. Fortunately, we discovered that there was one

---

* I had occasion to publish this story recently as an addendum to an article by Anna Schwartz and me responding to an attack by a couple of statisticians on one of our monetary books. They had attacked us for using insufficiently sophisticated econometric analysis in our analysis, in particular, for not using highly complex multiple regressions, along lines that David Hendry, one of the authors, had elaborated. I labeled the addendum "A Cautionary Tale." I have drawn on that account in this and the following paragraphs. See Milton Friedman and Anna J. Schwartz, "Alternative Approaches to Analyzing Economic Data," *American Economic Review* 81 (March 1991): 48–49. Our article was a reply to David F. Hendry and Neil R. Ericsson, "An Econometric Analysis of U.K. Money Demand in *Monetary Trends in the United States and the United Kingdom* by Milton Friedman and Anna J. Schwartz," *American Economic Review* 81 (March 1991): 8–38.

large-scale computer in the country that could perform our calculations—the experimental Mark I at Harvard, itself not electronic but built from a large number of IBM card-sorting machines housed in an enormous air-conditioned gymnasium. We were granted time on the machine to perform our calculations. Today's statisticians will be interested to know that, not counting data insertion, it took forty hours to calculate a regression that I can now calculate on my desktop computer in less than thirty seconds—my favorite story to illustrate what has happened to our computing power.

I was delighted with the calculated regression. It fit the data extremely well by every test that I knew of then, more than fifty years ago. I immediately set to work to create some new and better alloys. The technical details are irrelevant for the present purpose and I could no longer reproduce them in any event.

The bottom line is that I ended up formulating two new alloys (which with hope combined with caution I labeled F-1 and F-2). According to the calculated regression, each would take several hundred hours to rupture at the very high temperature I proposed to test them at, a sizable multiple of the best recorded time for any previous alloy. This was physics, not economics, so I did not have to wait years to see whether the predictions from my equation were correct. I phoned an MIT lab that was working on alloys of a similar type, and asked them to cook up and test my two alloys. I was sufficiently skeptical—or perhaps just cautious—as not to tell them what to expect. A few days later they phoned the results: my two alloys had ruptured in something like one to four hours, a much poorer outcome than for many prior alloys. F-1 and F-2 were never heard of again.

Ever since, I have been extremely skeptical of relying on projections from a multiple regression, however well it performs on the body of data from which it is derived; and the more complex the regression, the more skeptical I am. In the course of decades, that skepticism has been justified time and again.

One final point on the gas turbine. The scientists working in this area were unanimous that the gas turbine was the engine of the future. I recall being told that within five years after the end of the war the gasoline engine for cars would be obsolete. Cars would be powered by gas turbines the size of a shoe box. Unfortunately that dream has not been realized. Major auto companies have spent many millions, perhaps hundreds of millions of dollars, trying to develop a commercially feasible automobile powered by a gas turbine, but so far without success. I believe, though I am no expert, that the key problem is how to handle the high temperatures required for efficiency. The shoe box remains in our future.

VJ Day

When Japan surrendered on August 15, 1945, SRG's reason for existence came to an end, and my command of mathematical statistics reached its peak; it has been all downhill ever since. Loose ends had to be gathered up, and there was continued activity to publish the four books that were our contribution to the discipline of statistics. But demobilization, as throughout the war effort, was in order.

We were spared participation in combat and so did not suffer the hardships and dangers of the active combatants. And yet, I can understand Robert E. Lee's "It is well that war is so terrible, or we should grow too fond of it," and William James's plea for the "moral equivalent of war." The atmosphere in our group and in related groups was altogether different from any that I have experienced before or since. It was different from the atmosphere at the Treasury Department, even though there also, promoting the war effort was our major task. At the Treasury, we were too far from the actual battlefront, too much concerned with usual peacetime activities, to have a feeling of urgency, of direct connection with what was happening in combat. Politics, seeking personal advantage, the usual intermix of all sorts of human motives ruled the field. Moreover, most people involved in the process were simply performing their usual peacetime tasks and filling their regular career positions.

At SRG and related groups under the OSRD, the situation was very different. Essentially everyone involved was diverted to wartime work of a kind he or she would never have been doing in the ordinary course of a career. The rest of the world was in a sense cut off. Economists, physicists, chemists, statisticians, mathematicians, were all cooperating with one another under intense pressure with a single objective: contributing to the effectiveness of our fighting forces. I saw less internal bickering, less office politics, less self-interested manipulation, more concentrated hard work, during that period than I have in any comparable period before or since.

Surprisingly, social scientists turned out to be extremely useful in wartime operational research—indeed, typically more useful than natural scientists. The reason was simple. Social scientists were accustomed to working with lousy data, and wartime operational data certainly fitted that category. Natural scientists were accustomed to dealing with carefully controlled experimental data, and were often at a loss how to handle the kind of data turned out in wartime.

We have all read in history or fiction about the kind of fellowship that grows up on the front lines under common danger. Something of the same kind of feeling grew up in the SRG and related groups under the Office of

Scientific Research and Development. Few things bind people together so much as working cooperatively for a common, relatively short-term, achievable objective.

Of the various people who served at SRG, Harold Hotelling had been my teacher; Allen Wallis and George Stigler were fellow students at Chicago and among my closest friends; Rollin Bennett had been a fellow student at Columbia and a good friend. The rest were noneconomists, mostly statisticians and mathematicians, whom I came to know and respect in the course of our intensive collaboration.

One among them stood out especially and became one of my close collaborators: L. Jimmie Savage, one of the few people I have met whom I would unhesitatingly call a genius. Jimmie was severely handicapped. His eyesight was so poor that it met some legal definitions of blindness, yet Jimmie, as he was always called, was a voracious reader. When he graduated from high school, the school refused to recommend him for college. Only the persistence of his remarkable father enabled him to go to college. He went on to get a Ph.D. in an esoteric branch of mathematics and then, partly as a result of his experience at SRG, ended up as a mathematical statistician. After the war, he taught at the University of Chicago, where he and his wife became our close personal friends. Later he taught at Michigan, and finished his career at Yale, dying in 1971 at the age of fifty-three.

Jimmie had an extraordinarily wide-ranging curiosity and imagination—the world was his domain and he was determined to experience as much of it as possible. I recall one occasion when he collaborated with Arctic explorers and lived on nothing but pemmican for some six months or so in an experiment to test whether pemmican could provide a fully balanced diet. He did this in close collaboration with the physicians at Billings Hospital at the University of Chicago. I collaborated with him on a number of purely statistical papers published in the SRG volumes. He collaborated with me on a number of papers in economics that introduced what has come to be known as the Friedman-Savage utility function.

His fundamental contribution was a book titled *Foundations of Statistics* that is widely regarded as initiating something of a revolution in the field of mathematical statistics. It laid the groundwork for the subsequent explosion of so-called Bayesian statistics.

Though the SRG did not formally end until September 30, 1945, and Allen Wallis spent a few additional months dealing with final arrangements before returning to Stanford from which he was on leave, the rest of its principals started making plans for their life after the war.

{ *Rose* }　George Stigler had some months earlier returned to the University of Minnesota, from which he had been on leave. Milton had severed his connection with the Treasury, except as an occasional consultant, when he moved to the SRG. Presumably he could have gone back to the Treasury but that was the last thing he wanted to do. A government career was never Milton's choice. He could always return to the National Bureau, but I knew that that too was not Milton's preference. An academic career was what he wanted.

By early September, when we moved back to our apartment in Manhattan, Milton had received no offer for the fall. As an inveterate worrier always fearing the worst, I was not happy. I remember very well a visit from the Burnses and Arthur's attempt, while Milton was temporarily out of the room, to reassure me by telling me that Milton was very gifted and would make it to the top and that I had no reason to be concerned. I needed no reassurance about Milton's ability, but we now had two small children and it was time to put down roots.

Fortunately, I did not have to worry very long. Thanks to our friend George, the University of Minnesota offered Milton a one-year appointment and we were on our way. Since we did not plan to return to New York, and we had no assurance that we would be staying at Minnesota for more than a year, we decided to sell our furniture and rent a furnished house in Minnesota for the school year. Rent control in New York had already made possessing an apartment a great advantage, so we had no difficulty selling our furniture as a condition for transferring our lease on the rent-controlled apartment.

We decided to make the move to Minnesota separately, I with the children by train and Milton by car. In order to allow Milton enough time for the drive plus time to rent a furnished house, the children and I went first to Washington and spent some time with Aaron and his wife, Katherine. Milton drove first to Washington and after a few days, to Minnesota. After a couple of weeks with Aaron and Katherine, we continued our trip by train to Minnesota, where we were again reunited.

→ *Chapter Nine* ←

MINNESOTA

{ *Rose* } The friendly environment in Minnesota was very different from what we had experienced in Wisconsin. Our friends the Stiglers were there and we quickly got to know other members of the faculty, some our age and some older. Bruce Mudgett, a statistician, and his wife were lovely and friendly people. In later years they retired to Thetford, Vermont, not far from where we later had a second home and we saw them frequently and renewed our friendship. Bruce's great passion was woodworking. He was a master craftsman and produced beautiful pieces of furniture.

I saw much of Edith Marget and her young son, Jonathan. Edith was lonely since her husband, Arthur, was in Europe on military duty as Chief, Finance Division, U.S. Element Allied Command for Austria. I was home a great deal with my two children. Edith and I enjoyed each other's company and had many interests in common.

Our house was very much like the house I grew up in—an old house with few if any modern appliances. It was not at all like the two newly built apartments we occupied in Washington and New York. My taste has always been for modern houses and I certainly appreciate modern appliances. We did have an electric washing machine that I shall never forget. It had an old-style wringer—the roller type. Whether because I was in a hurry or just careless, I once caught my hand between the rollers. As I remember, I reversed the rollers and my hand rolled out but the damage had been done and the swelling was immediate. Fortunately, it was on a Sunday and Milton was at home. Unfortunately, I had my wedding band on and could not get it off because of the swelling. Milton used my manicure tools, a nail file and cuticle scissors, to cut the ring. We applied the usual home remedy for swelling— soaking in cold water—and on Monday an X-ray removed our fears about possible bone fractures but the pain and swelling lasted for some time, and the ring was never the same.

Our good friend Allen Wallis, who had grown up in Minneapolis, warned us about the severity of the winters. Facetiously, I am sure, he told us not to touch door knobs except when wearing gloves because the skin would stick to the knob. I never wore gloves and my hand never stuck to the knob. In fact, I did not find the cold weather unpleasant because it was a dry cold. I often ran across the street in the middle of winter coatless to check on my daughter who had a playmate there. However, I did find the long snowy winter depressing. I remember that the first heavy snow came the night before Thanksgiving. As it happened, we had been invited to have Thanksgiving dinner with Anne Wallis's parents. Milton got more than his quota of exercise clearing the long driveway before we could get out. My recollection is that I did not see the ground again before I left for Portland in the late spring to spend the summer with my family. Milton thinks I exaggerate the length of the winter.

Although Milton's appointment at Minnesota was initially for one year, both sides were satisfied, and long before the academic year was over, he was offered, and accepted, a tenured position with the rank of associate professor. We started to make plans for what we thought was to be our home for many years. Our first step was to look for a house. We found a very nice one that we bought for $10,000 and were looking forward eagerly to moving. As will unfold later, we actually stayed at Minnesota only a year and never occupied that house. We managed to sell it before we left, making a profit of $1,000 as I remember.

{ *Milton* } I taught two courses a semester: one on statistics, the other on economics. The students were primarily undergraduates, though Minnesota had then, and greatly expanded later, a sizable, highly ranked graduate program in economics. I already knew some of the economists at Minnesota, and quickly came to know the rest. The atmosphere of the department was in happy contrast to what we had experienced in Wisconsin. There were no factions, the members were all on good terms with one another, and we soon found ourselves accepted as equals.

What I remember best about the time I spent at the University of Minnesota is sharing an office with George Stigler. We had been close friends since our student days at Chicago, but sharing an office sealed an intimacy that was to last until George died in 1991. He was a delightful office companion, a stimulating conversationalist, a highly constructive critic, and, like myself, lived, breathed, and slept economics.

One day in the winter George came into the office nursing his elbow after slipping on the ice. I examined it and declared that it was nothing but a minor sprain. He subsequently had it X-rayed to find that he had fractured a bone. He never ceased ribbing me about the episode. Ever after, on any medical matter, I was *Dr.* Friedman.

We jointly authored a pamphlet during the year attacking rent controls. The catchy title, "Roofs or Ceilings," implying that there was a choice between roofs over our heads or ceilings over rents, was undoubtedly George's. World War II price controls, which had included controls on rents, had been imposed in 1943 and were still in effect when the pamphlet was published by the Foundation for Economic Education as volume 1, number 2, of "Popular Essays on Current Problems" in September 1946. As a result, the issue was both topical and controversial. A condensed version of the pamphlet was provided by the Foundation to the National Association of Real Estate Boards, which circulated some 500,000 copies as part of its campaign of opposition to rent controls.

It was my first taste of public controversy. An unfriendly reviewer in the *American Economic Review* (Robert Bangs) characterized "this well-written, closely reasoned, popular pamphlet" as "a political tract." The same reviewer ended a column in the popular press blasting the pamphlet by saying, "Economists who sign their names to drivel of this sort do no service to the profession they represent."* An unfriendly correspondent wrote, "If your students still have respect for your opinions after having read your pamphlet, I feel sorry for them—not you."

A very different controversy also arose over the pamphlet. The Foundation for Economic Education had recently been established by Leonard Read, a remarkable man with whom we had much contact over the years. However, this initial collaboration was stormy. Read and his associate, Orval Watts, objected strenuously to one paragraph and asked us to delete it, contending that it could be interpreted "as an endorsement by the Foundation of certain collectivist ideas which are repugnant to us." The objectionable paragraph reads as follows:

> The fact that, under free market conditions, better quarters go to those who have larger incomes or more wealth is, if anything, simply

* He must have had an uneasy conscience about his attack on the pamphlet because only six months after his review appeared, he wrote me a letter to compliment me on an article that I had published. He had only recently become employed in the Division of Tax Research of the Treasury, and he added, "in my present work . . . I have found a couple of your old memoranda dealing with capital gain and loss to be among the most helpful documents in the received doctrine of the Division" (letter of November 18, 1947).

a reason for taking long-term measures to reduce the inequality of income and wealth. For those, like us, who would like even more equality than there is at present, not alone for housing but for all products, it is surely better to attack directly existing inequalities in income and wealth at their source than to ration each of the hundreds of commodities and services that compose our standard of living. It is the height of folly to permit individuals to receive unequal money incomes and then to take elaborate and costly measures to prevent them from using their incomes.

We refused to delete it, stating that instead of doing so we would withdraw permission to publish it and forgo the modest fee the foundation had offered us. Whether that reflected our youth and idealism or was the proper response may be open to question, but we were certainly justified in being outraged by what happened subsequently. The paragraph was included in the published pamphlet but, without asking our permission, an anonymous "Editor's Note" (no editor was mentioned by name in the pamphlet) was appended to the paragraph:

The authors fail to state whether the "long-term measures" which they would adopt go beyond elimination of special privilege, such as monopoly now protected by government. In any case, however, the significance of their argument at this point deserves special notice. It means that, even from the standpoint of those who put equality above justice and liberty, rent controls are the height of folly.

We both regarded this note, which in effect accused us of putting equality above justice and liberty, as inexcusable, and for some years we refused to have anything to do with the foundation or with Leonard Read.[1]

I was finally reconciled with Leonard when we were both stranded in Paris's Orly Airport after a meeting of the Mont Pelerin Society, with hours to wait for our common connection. In the course of those hours we resolved our dispute and I discovered what a charming and principled person Leonard was, and from then on he was one of our fast friends.

Leonard had been chief executive of the Los Angeles Chamber of Commerce in the late 1930s, when he became persuaded that freedom was endangered by the increasing intervention of government into the economy sparked by FDR's New Deal. Toward the end of the war he managed to raise enough money to establish the Foundation for Economic Education in Irvington-on-Hudson, New York. Under his firm guidance, FEE became one of the few principled and effective defenders of a free society—economic, social, and

political freedom—at the time. He refused to compromise his principles—
our spat was evidence of that and so also was his not bowing to major contributors who objected to his firm defense of complete free trade. He was especially
effective in the seminars he organized for members of the business community.

FEE also provided an intellectual home for Ludwig von Mises, the noted
Austrian economist who was never offered a position at any major university
after he emigrated to the U.S., undoubtedly because of his intransigent defense
of free enterprise and free markets. He conducted a famous seminar at New
York University, but was able to do so only because it was subsidized by
private, nonuniversity financing.

In addition to Leonard's effectiveness in presenting the case for free markets, he was also a gourmet cook and, on several visits to Chicago, cooked
gourmet meals for us and a few favored friends.

{ *Rose* } I remember very well the first time that Leonard came to our house
to cook bouillabaisse for us and about ten guests. He sent Milton a letter
listing the ingredients required for the dish. They were extensive, including
a live lobster and various other shellfish. The last requirement was a "little
girl to fetch and carry." That item tickled Milton the most. He replied to
Leonard that there was only one little girl in our household who fetched and
carried and she would take care of getting the ingredients. Actually Leonard
required very little help either in preparing the meal or in taking photographs
of every ingredient as it appeared.

{ *Milton* } Wherever rent controls have been enforced in the U.S., Canada,
Britain, France, or elsewhere they have had the destructive effects that George
and I foresaw. As a result, our pamphlet has been reprinted repeatedly.

National rent controls in the U.S. were ended along with other price
controls in 1949, though localities were given the option to continue them,
and they were reinstated temporarily on August 15, 1971, as part of President
Nixon's imposition of price and wage controls. Earlier in 1971, I published
a *Newsweek* column with the same title as the pamphlet, noting, "New York
City—with that unerring instinct for self-destruction—is the only major city
still controlling rents." It still controls rents but it is no longer the only city
doing so. A number of other cities adopted controls during the inflation of
the 1970s.

In 1979, when San Francisco was contemplating introducing rent control,
I persuaded the *San Francisco Chronicle* to reprint my *Newsweek* column with
a head note commenting,

As a recent resident of San Francisco, I am dismayed that rent control seems about to be enacted. In light of the experience of other cities and countries and of the extensive literature documenting the harm that rent controls do, I find it hard to believe that anyone other than a knave or a fool could, after even cursory examination of that evidence, vote to impose rent control on San Francisco.

That will not only harm the city, it will hurt most the less fortunate and poorest residents of the city. To indicate my personal interest, I own a cooperative apartment. The shortage of housing that would be produced by rent control would undoubtedly drive up the price of cooperatives and condominiums. As a result, I, or my heirs, would reap a financial windfall from the enactment of rent control.

Though the members of the Board of Supervisors were neither knaves nor fools, that did not prevent them from enacting rent control for short-term political advantage. And the expected consequences did follow, including a sharp rise in the market value of our cooperative apartment.

{ *Rose* } Life in Minnesota proceeded at the usual pace of academic life until the spring. That story we will let George himself tell as recorded in his memoirs:

> In the spring of 1946 I received the offer of a professorship from the University of Chicago, and of course was delighted at the prospect. The offer was contingent upon approval by the central administration after a personal interview. I went to Chicago, met with the President, Ernest Colwell, because Chancellor Robert Hutchins was ill that day, and I was vetoed! I was too empirical, Colwell said, and no doubt that day I was. So the professorship was offered to Milton Friedman, and President Colwell and I had launched the new Chicago School. We both deserve credit for that appointment, although for a long time I was not inclined to share it with Colwell.

Milton thinks it reveals a great deal about George's generosity of spirit that Milton's benefiting at George's expense never had the slightest effect on the closeness of their friendship.

{ *Milton* } Instead of going to Chicago, George went to Brown for a year, and then to Columbia where he stayed for a decade, despite several attempts to lure him to Chicago. Finally, in 1958, Allen Wallis, then Dean of the

Business School, induced George to return to Chicago where he belonged. This whole episode and its effect on both our careers is another example of the extraordinary role that pure chance plays in most people's lives.

Rose and I were both delighted at the prospect of going back to Chicago, which had remained our intellectual home and where we had many friends on the faculty. We had been treated very well at Minnesota, the faculty had been extremely congenial, and we were not at all reluctant to remain there before the Chicago offer came along—though the prospect of George's leaving when Chicago first approached him reduced substantially the attractiveness of Minnesota. The only actual negative was never seeing the ground between Thanksgiving and Easter.

Once the Chicago appointment was final, I went to Chicago to find housing for our move in the fall. Rent control made it impossible to find a satisfactory house or apartment to rent, so we reluctantly decided to buy a house—though we would have preferred to rent first and take our time looking for a permanent home. But even buying a house was not easy. The pressure on the housing market created by rent control and inflation, plus the inertia in adjusting house prices to the market, meant that potential buyers outnumbered sellers. As it happened, one extremely conveniently located house at 5725 Kenwood Avenue was available for sale. It was owned by a woman who owned the house next door and who happened to be from Minnesota. That turned out to be the chance event that made us the successful bidder rather than another willing buyer! Hearing that I was teaching in Minnesota, she took me to be a "landsman," to use an expressive German-Jewish phrase, and gave me the edge.

The house was far from ideal for us. It was a big three-story house that had been occupied by a student cooperative and was in terrible shape. The price was $12,500, yet it was inferior in every respect to the house we had bought in Minneapolis for $10,000 and sold for about $11,000.

{ *Rose* } When Milton returned from Chicago after purchasing a house that he described as having only one redeeming feature—its location—it was his turn to stay in St. Paul with the children while I went to Chicago to see what could be done to make the house livable. The Knights had suggested to Milton that I stay with them on my visit. That was one aspect of the trip I looked forward to. When I arrived, Mrs. Knight offered to accompany me when I went to view the house. The outside of the house impressed me only as being monstrously large. Every house on the block with one exception looked the same. They had all been built about the time of the World's Columbian Exposition in 1893. Some had presumably been renovated on the inside and looked as though they had undergone some sprucing up on the outside. The house was empty, and I had the key. Mrs. Knight and I ventured in. We started on the first floor. The kitchen was bigger than any kitchen I had ever seen, but had no cabinets in it. It did have a large blackboard with instructions on it for previous tenants—the students who had occupied the house before we bought it. All the walls were grimy; the linoleum on the kitchen floor was cracked and broken. The floors in the living room and dining room were scuffed and worn. So up we went to the second floor, which consisted of four bedrooms and a bath. For some reason I've always been hypersensitive to cracks in plaster ceilings and walls, and the bedrooms had no shortage of these. The third floor held little interest for me, as I had no intention of using it. As I remember, neither of us had much to say as we went through this exercise. But as we went out the front door, Mrs. Knight said it all: "I'm so glad, Rose," she sighed, "that you're young!"

Before returning to St. Paul I must have made a list of the repairs and cleaning that I considered essential. Milton then returned to Chicago and made arrangements for these things to be done during the summer.

We spent that summer in Oregon, partly with my family in Portland, but mostly in a rented cabin at Cannon Beach, a lovely ocean spot some one hundred miles northwest of Portland. My sister Becky and her son Barry joined us for most of our stay, and we all had a fine vacation. The one event that marred our happiness that summer was the sad news that Henry Simons, Aaron's closest personal friend, whom we had known and liked from our student days and looked forward to joining in Chicago, had died, apparently a suicide, leaving behind his wife and very young daughter.

➤ *Chapter Ten* ❖

SETTLING IN AT CHICAGO

{ *Rose* } Coming back to Chicago in September 1946 was like coming home. The physical surroundings and many of the faces were familiar. As an added bonus, my brother Aaron came back from Washington the same year to join the Law School faculty as one of the first economists to occupy a full-time position on a law school faculty. One advantage, probably the only one, of having our big house was that Aaron and Katherine could live on the third floor while the house they had bought was being remodeled.

The physical surroundings at the university were unchanged, but we were not. We were no longer the young graduate students who had left Chicago more than a decade before. That decade had encompassed grindingly hard times for the country, followed by total war. Nonetheless, it had been a good decade for us personally: we had started life together; Milton had made a beginning on what was to become a great career; he had gained experience in academia as well as Washington, plus experience as a statistician during the war. And we were richer by two children. As I wrote in the short biography that appeared in the *Oriental Economist*:

> Looking back, it seems natural that my husband should have come to Chicago to replace Jacob Viner, who had just left to join the Princeton faculty. They were very similar physically. Both were short but broad-shouldered, and therefore not slight. If one saw them seated, one was always surprised to find how short they were when they stood up. Their minds were very similar—sharp, precise, logical and organized. But their personalities were very different. . . .
>
> When my husband first came to Chicago, I believe that he tried to emulate Viner's reputation for being a tough teacher and, in one sense, he succeeded. Many fell by the wayside in his classes as they

did in Viner's. But I doubt that any of his students, looking back at their experience in his classes, would describe him as cold and aloof. They would remember his warm smile, his friendliness, his interest in the whole student not just in his class work. As with his professional peers who criticize freely his writing or his policy positions, but always remain his friends, so his students have become his friends. Their children have heard him discussed with such warm feeling that they often think of him as a relative.[1]

Our first year was a busy one both for Milton and for me. Milton spent most of his time on the courses he was teaching for the first time, getting to know his colleagues, and, in general, adapting to the university. While I appreciated the necessity of his doing this, I also felt I needed more help from him with the job of making our house livable. In the end, deciding that we had spent too much on the house to make it a cheap place for us to live, yet too little to make it comfortable and attractive, we sold the house less than two years after moving in.

Although we could readily have sold the house without the help of a realtor, we let a local real estate company act as our broker in return for finding us a rental apartment. (Even so, we did make a profit of some $600.) The rent-controlled apartment they found for us was on the same block as our house (5701 Kenwood Avenue). That apartment was not one I would have chosen in a free market, but we did not own it and could move out whenever we found a better place—which we did in 1950. Again, it was on the same block (5731 Kenwood). In our opinion, this was the best house in the area. Like our first house, it had been built at the time of the 1893 World's Fair. But unlike our first house, it had been completely remodeled inside and out in the 1930s, when it was converted from a single three-story dwelling to a two-story dwelling plus two small apartments on the third floor with a separate outside entrance. The price of the house was more than we felt we could afford, $41,500. However, two things made the purchase feasible. The university was willing to provide a second mortgage at the same low interest rate (4.5 percent) as the first mortgage, and the two apartments, though under rent control, provided income to help meet the monthly payments. We lived happily in this house until 1962.

I started Janet in nursery school soon after we came to Chicago. David was still too young for that, so he stayed home with me—and was not very happy, because he missed his sister. That was remedied the following year when both were enrolled in the university nursery school. I still felt that David was too young, but he was unhappy without his sister and having them both at the nursery school for part of the day gave me a little extra time to do other things. And David enjoyed having his nap at school.

In April 1947, Milton made his first trip out of the United States to attend the founding meeting of the Mont Pelerin Society. I did not accompany him. Instead, I took the children to Reno to visit Becky and her Milton during the time that my Milton was in Europe. We must have stayed close to six weeks, because I remember joking about establishing residency in Nevada so that I could get an easy divorce if Milton didn't treat me well. It was a wonderful vacation for me. The children received an extra dose of love from my sister and her husband. In addition, Becky's friends took to the children and made them feel very much at home. So, all in all, I didn't mind not accompanying Milton to Europe.

{ *Milton* } The trip to Mont Pelerin and my later connections with the society have been important events in my life. Three of the original thirty-eight members were from the university (Frank Knight, Aaron, and myself) and two others joined the university faculty a few years later (Hayek and Stigler). The trip provided my first opportunity to go abroad, introduced me to distinguished scholars in economics, as well as other fields, some of whom became close friends, and it strengthened my incipient interest in political philosophy and public policy. Those effects matured over the years and are discussed at length in chapter 21. The cost was an extended separation between me and the rest of the family, by far the longest until then, and not to be repeated until I went to India in 1955 (chap. 18), a trip that ended less happily.

I no longer remember how I was able to arrange my academic schedule so as to be away for six weeks, but given Chicago's flexibility, and the willingness of department members to cooperate in shifting schedules, I don't think that was a serious problem.

I owe my invitation to the Mont Pelerin meeting to Aaron, who had met Hayek while spending a year at the London School of Economics. Aaron was instrumental in getting the University of Chicago Press to publish *The Road to Serfdom* and was one of the persons whom Hayek consulted in arranging the conference. As a result, George Stigler and I were among those invited to attend, expenses paid, a ten-day conference to be held at Mont Pelerin, Switzerland, from April 1 to 10, 1947.

The prior December, in a letter to me referring to correspondence with Hayek on the Giffen paradox, George had written, "a junket to Switzerland in April is contemplated to save liberalism. I assume you and Aaron will go. If this comes off, (1) train Aaron on bridge, and (2) let's find a fourth liberal;

and teach him." (We never did "train Aaron on bridge," though we did find a fourth liberal at Mont Pelerin, Trygve Hoff of Norway, with whom we had some memorable bridge games and who became a lifelong friend.)

The three of us went to Europe on Cunard's *Queen Elizabeth,* refitted from its wartime service. (That was long before transatlantic travel by air had become a commonplace, though George did return by plane.) It was George's and my first trip abroad.

We disembarked at Southampton and proceeded to London, where we stayed for several days at the plush Dorchester Hotel. (When Aaron and I returned to spend a few days in London after the meeting, at our own expense, we stayed at a cheaper hotel!) Britain was still in a sad way two years after the war. Food was rationed and poor. Price, wage, and exchange controls were extensive and rigid, and appeared to be widely accepted and respected. Black markets doubtless existed, but they were small and well hidden.

The situation was very different in Paris, our next stop. The food was better and there was a feeling of vigor and movement absent in Britain. George loved to tell the story, as he does in his memoirs, "of approaching the clerk at the Grand Hotel, where we were staying. 'Could you direct me to the closest outlet for the black market in currency?' I asked. 'Go no further, gentlemen,' was the response as he extracted a wallet from his jacket."

As we left Paris, George summarized his impressions: "I now know the difference between Britain, France, and the United States. The British obey all laws, the French obey no laws, the Americans obey only the good laws." That was his succinct summary of our having observed Britain being strangled by obedience to law (remember this was fifty years ago; the British have since learned better, or degenerated—take your choice), while France was being saved by the black market.

Interesting as was my first sight of Europe, the real payoff was Mont Pelerin—as I wrote to Rose, "the place is unbelievably wonderful." As to the conference, "we've been meeting three times a day—morning, afternoon, and night. . . . It's pretty wearing, but also very stimulating." Here I was, a young, naive provincial American, meeting people from all over the world, all dedicated to the same liberal principles as we were; all beleaguered in their own countries, yet among them scholars, some already internationally famous, others destined to be; making friendships which have enriched our lives, and participating in founding a society that has played a major role in preserving and strengthening liberal ideas.*

---

* This marked the beginning of my active involvement in the political process.

Years later, John A. Davenport, one of the participants in the first meeting, and a well-known journalist, recalled that first meeting:

> From the station platform at Vevey, Switzerland, a little funicular railway pointed up the mountain-side. As I swung aboard and as the cables tightened, I was vaguely conscious that something new and exciting lay at the top.
>
> It did, for the first meeting of what became known as the Mont Pelerin Society . . . was indeed a unique gathering and a turning point in the life of most participants.[2]

Our reaction to a T.

Davenport described some of the participants as follows:

> Hayek, then in his fifties and in those days much given to drawing on a briar pipe; Ludwig von Mises, the father figure of the Austrian School of economics and mentor of Hayek, Fritz Machlup, and Gottfried Haberler; the jovial and Jovian William Rappard, head of the École des Hautes Études in Geneva and chairman of many a stormy session (for while united in purpose Mont Pelerin was far from being a united group in what Plato dubbed "opinion"); Wilhelm Röpke, also of Geneva, who presently was to set in motion the great German currency reform of 1948 in alliance with Walter Eucken of Freiburg University; John Jewkes of Oxford, author of *Ordeal by Planning*, and Karl Popper, the diminutive philosopher and logician (a proposition is scientific if it can be refuted); Henry Hazlitt, indefatigable defender of enterprise even when associated with the New York Times; plus to be sure, a sprinkling of what became known as the Chicago School: Frank Knight, Aaron Director, and Milton Friedman, who then had some distance to travel on his road to *Free to Choose*.[3]

One participant who made an especially strong impression on me was Walter Eucken of Germany. I shall never forget his pleasure at eating the first orange he had seen in seven or eight years. More important, he made vivid what it was like to live in a totalitarian country, as well as in a country devastated by war and by the rigidities imposed by the occupying authorities. His courage in resisting the Nazis became legendary. He was a teacher of Ludwig Erhard, and helped inspire Erhard's currency reform in 1948, which initiated what came to be called the German economic miracle. More generally, his theory laid the groundwork for West Germany's "social market economy."

Although all of the participants shared the same basic values, they were by no means agreed on how to counter the attack on those values, or on the policies required to implement them. As a result, our sessions were marked by vigorous controversy over such issues as the role of religion and moral values in making possible and preserving a free society; the role of trade unions, and the appropriateness of government action to affect the distribution of income. I particularly recall a discussion of this issue, in the middle of which Ludwig von Mises stood up, announced to the assembly "You're all a bunch of socialists," and stomped out of the room, an assembly that contained not a single person who, by even the loosest standards, could be called a socialist.

Our differences extended to the name to be given to the proposed society. The name finally settled on, Mont Pelerin, after the place where the meeting was held, was not inappropriate since "pèlerin" means pilgrim, but it was selected only because it did not offend anyone, as every other proposed name had.

Similarly, it took the genius of Lionel Robbins to draft a "Statement of Aims" that was acceptable to all but one of the participants.[4]

The working sessions were suspended on Saturday and Sunday for an excursion to Schwyz and *Einsiedeln* by a private railroad car. The excursion, like the conference as a whole, exhibited Swiss efficiency at its best. The arrangements were all handled by a Swiss businessman, Dr. Albert Hunold. He had been responsible for raising the funds to finance the conference in Switzerland and served as the secretary of the society for many years. The traveling expenses of the Americans were financed by the Volker Fund of St. Louis.[5]

The excursion was not only most enjoyable; it provided an opportunity for the kind of informal interchanges that always play a key role in any conference. After the conference was over, Hunold produced a book of photographs, along with a few of the original documents. It is one of our most treasured mementos.

{ *Rose* } For nearly ten years after the initial meeting, neither Milton nor I attended any of the Mont Pelerin meetings. By 1957, however, the children were old enough so that I had no hesitancy in leaving them with my sister, and we both attended the Mont Pelerin meeting in St. Moritz that year. Thereafter, Milton attended almost all subsequent meetings, and I accompanied him on most (see chap. 21).

{ *Milton* } During the thirty years that I was on the faculty at Chicago, we lived a split life. My contract called for teaching three quarters each year; the fourth quarter was free, though it was understood that it would be devoted primarily to scholarly activities. After spending the summer of 1947 in Chicago, Rose and I decided that the city was no place to be in summer. From then on, we spent the summer quarter—and later on, two quarters—elsewhere, usually in New England. As it turned out, much if not most of my research and writing was done during those out-of-residence quarters. When I was in residence, teaching, faculty meetings, supervising students who were writing dissertations, attending seminars, occasionally lecturing off campus, and similar activities left too little time for research.

We always enjoyed both our time in residence and our time out of Chicago, finding that the two complemented each other. It was a happy combination that enabled us to enjoy the best of two worlds.

✦ *Chapter Eleven* ✦

OUR SUMMERS, 1948–80

{ *Rose* } Having decided not to spend our summers in Chicago, we had little doubt that New England was where we wanted to be. We had started our married life there in 1938 and had fond memories of the summer we spent there after the Wisconsin episode. Several friends from Columbia and the National Bureau spent their summers there and, finally, it was far enough away from Chicago that Milton would not be tempted to go back for some event or other during the summer. In all the summers that we spent in New England he never did go back to Chicago.

Leaving the children with our cousins the Mosleys, Milton and I made a brief trip to Vermont in the spring of 1948 and with the help of the Burnses, who were spending the spring vacation at their second home, we rented a house on the shore of Lake Fairlee for the coming summer. It was rather primitive. As I remember, we had running cold water but no hot water and, for our first summer, no modern refrigerator. When it became more and more difficult to have ice delivered, we arranged to share with our landlady the expense of buying a second-hand electric refrigerator our second summer.

The choice of this location in New England was not random. Lake Fairlee was about twenty-five miles north of Hanover, New Hampshire, the home of Dartmouth College. This made a good library available within a reasonable distance. Access to a library was a must for doing research until the technological explosion of recent years. That was why scholars from Columbia and the National Bureau had chosen that location.

The lack of conveniences in our rented cottage did not interfere with our enjoyment of those two summers. Being on the shore of Lake Fairlee was both pleasant and convenient. The children enjoyed playing on the dock while I could remain comfortably on the porch reading or doing some work and at the same time keeping an eye on what was happening at the dock. This prevented what could have been a catastrophe. Three-year-old David could not swim, but he loved to push his sister into the water. This was all right for a while, because she had taught herself to dog-paddle in the wading pool at nursery school. But Janet tired of the game before David did and, being unable to persuade him with words, pushed him off the dock into the water and then screamed "Mommy" as he went under. I got down to the dock before he went under a second time and all was well. He was unharmed and wiser for the experience. However, I believe the episode instilled a fear of the water that took him years to overcome.

Toward the end of our second summer, we decided to make New England our permanent summer location and began looking for a summer cottage that we could afford to buy. Before long, we found a delightful cottage that had been built by an artist, Mr. Maginnis. It was in the same general area but across the Connecticut River in Orford, New Hampshire. We called it "The Hideaway" because it was hidden from view by a thick grove of pine trees leading from a country road to a studio and then some three hundred feet further on to the house.

Mr. Maginnis had built the studio with a huge window on the north side, which gave him ideal light for painting. Most of Milton's research and writing was done in that studio. In addition to a small table that he used as a desk, it had a standard-size Ping-Pong table, the top of which always had to be cleared of Milton's papers before we could use it. But piling up the papers never kept us from playing Ping-Pong. An abandoned icehouse filled with sawdust was attached to the studio. In use, the ice had been cut in the winter from Upper Baker Pond, which was only about a quarter of a mile away. However, it had outlasted its usefulness since we had an electric refrigerator—an antique G. E. "Monitor Top." It was still in working order when we sold the house almost twenty years later.

{ *Milton* } It also was a nearly ideal place for me to work. The studio was far enough away from the house to insulate me from household noises and the light was perfect. We had no telephone until Janet was old enough to drive.

In those days, before Dartmouth had a summer school, it was nearly certain that any book the splendid Baker Library owned was available. The library was generous in granting use of its facilities to visiting scholars. Indeed, the visitors, rather than the Dartmouth faculty, were the most likely competitors for books.

My associates at the National Bureau—Arthur Burns, Solomon Fabricant, Geoffrey Moore—were all within easy reach for consultation. In addition, while working on *A Monetary History,* I benefited very much from discussions with Bray Hammond, who had written the classic history of pre–Civil War banking and had been the longtime secretary of the Federal Reserve Board before retiring to Thetford, Vermont. A former student of mine, Colin Campbell, was teaching at Dartmouth, and he and his wife, Rosemary, who jointly wrote one of the leading texts in money and banking, became intimate friends. Aside from social interaction and helpful discussions on areas of common interest, they were extremely helpful in facilitating my use of Dartmouth facilities.

In the early days, many, perhaps most, country roads were dirt roads, not hard-surfaced. For years, we made a game of trying to find a route from Orford to Hanover that was entirely on dirt roads. As the years passed, that became more and more difficult, though it did lead to interesting excursions on back roads and by roundabout routes. Eventually we had to surrender to the onward march of asphalt.

During our first few years at Orford, I was writing *A Theory of the Consumption Function,* a subject on which both Rose and two of our frequent guests, Dorothy Brady and Margaret Reid, had done and were doing much research. I can recall many a pleasant summer evening discussing consumption data and theory in front of a blazing fire in a fireplace constructed of massive local stones. David remembers "lying in the bed on the balcony falling asleep to adult voices down below and the firelight."

My major research at Orford was on the monetary study that I was doing jointly with Anna Schwartz. We discovered that collaborating at a distance, and without a telephone, had real advantages. It meant that everything had to be written down, avoiding the inevitable misunderstandings that arise from verbal communication. We found that practice so satisfactory that even when telephonic communication was available we seldom resorted to it. The only computing facility I had was an electric desk calculator, which I occasionally was able to inveigle Janet into operating for me. The IBM computing facilities were in New York at the National Bureau. As a result, Anna handled whatever computing was to be done—not so much for *A Monetary History* but a great deal for *Monetary Statistics* and *Monetary Trends.*

{ *Rose* } Janet and David had no friends of their age close by. Our friends' children who were their ages could be seen only when we went visiting. They had guests from Chicago occasionally but not as a regular thing. In the main, they just had each other. They shared many similar interests and got along very well. Both were avid readers, and liked walks in the surrounding woods.

There were many camps in the area—one within walking distance, Camp Mooselauke, where we arranged for Janet and David to go horseback riding. Another, Pemigewasset, was on the shore of Lower Baker Pond, where we went swimming almost every afternoon.

One year when Milton was going to be away for part of the summer, and two of David's best friends from Chicago were going to be at "Camp Pemi," I thought that David might enjoy a summer there so we decided to be extravagant and send him to Pemi with his friends even though our house was close by. It was a mistake. He enjoyed none of the usual camp activities and spent much of the summer collecting rocks and mounting and identifying them. Years later we came across a note that David had written at the end of that summer in which he said it was the worst summer of his life.

It was a good many years before David again went to camp. This time he went to a YMCA camp on Lake Fairlee (Camp Billings) and enjoyed it enough to be a junior counselor there for a summer or two. His next camp experience was very different. When he was in college, he spent one or two summers as a counselor at a camp for gifted children in New York. This was one of David's most interesting summer experiences. He was greatly impressed by the youngsters and became very close to some of them. In particular, I remember his reaction when one of the boys, who had leukemia, died soon after the end of the summer. David, fond of writing poems, was moved to write one about this youngster's death.

Janet too had the experience of going to camp for one or two summers. She went to a Campfire Girls camp in Berlin, New Hampshire, and enjoyed the experience. One of the most popular activities was swimming. Janet, unlike David, has from a very early age loved the water. The girls at her camp, which was in the northern part of the state, above the White Mountains, swam in a pool that was fed by glacially cold waters. It was far too cold for us when we visited, but not for Janet.

Janet, David, and I all engaged in horseback riding during our summers in New Hampshire. The riding master was a wonderful old man whose name was Schulenberg and whom we all called Schulie. The riding ring he used belonged to a family whose only daughter was an enthusiastic horseback rider. It was about ten miles from our place. Schulie was a stern master but an excellent teacher. He was too old and too fat to get on a horse himself when we met him. He would sit in a corner a good part of the time and call out his orders. From the beginning, Janet was the best and most enthusiastic rider of the family and has remained so to this day. She now rides her own horse, specializes in dressage, is raising a young filly, and is using her organizing ability to run horse shows. David has, I believe, not been on a horse since we left Orford. Neither have I.

{ *Milton* }   Another summer activity we all engaged in was mountain climbing. Richard Ware, Director of the Earhart Foundation, whom I had gotten to know through the Earhart fellowships that he had introduced, was a summer resident of New Hampshire and an enthusiastic climber. So also were Rosemary and Colin Campbell. The three of them all earned much prized membership in the Four Thousand Footer Club, which required climbing every one of the forty-six New Hampshire summits over four thousand feet in height.

With Dick, Colin, and Rosemary as the organizers, every summer saw a number of mountain-climbing expeditions participated in by a changing selection of summer visitors and their children. In a copy of the White Mountain Guide that Colin gave me, I find that in the course of these expeditions during the years from 1957 to 1972 we climbed fourteen of the selected group as well as a fair number of lesser peaks.

One expedition that stands out vividly was to Mount Washington, the highest peak in New England. Rose did not go on that trip but David and Janet did. When we finally got home after a series of adventures, I complained grumpily to Rose about what a spoiled daughter she had, citing the difficulty I had had getting her up and down the mountain—only for Rose to discover that Janet was running a high fever! As it happened, the problems with Janet were only the starter. After we got into our car and started home, our ancient Kaiser suddenly went off the road and into a ditch, thanks to a defective steering mechanism. We had to leave the car there, hitch a ride to the nearest rest place, where, fortunately, we had arranged to meet others of our group and so got a ride home.

{ *Rose* }   The mountain-climbing experience was really the second time that Milton misjudged Janet's behavior; the first occurred when Janet was a little over a year old. Janet and I spent a month in Connecticut with a friend who had a little girl somewhat older than Janet. Milton came up for weekends. The other little girl was accustomed to postponing bedtime by calling down for water and anything else she could think of. Her demands were always met. One evening during the weekend, Janet called down from her crib. I don't remember what she called down for; I only remember that her father insisted that we not go up to her because he was sure she was learning bad habits from the other little girl. I steeled myself for as long as I could but finally went up. When I got to her crib, I found that the poor child had vomited all over herself and was calling for help. I didn't let Milton forget that episode for some time.

{ *Milton* } Another climbing episode of a different kind concerned a neighbor of ours, subsequently governor of New Hampshire, Meldrim Thompson, who won election on the slogan "Ax the Tax," and did succeed in keeping New Hampshire free of both a general income and general sales tax. The closest mountain to our place was the relatively low Cube Mountain. One route to its top was, at least in part, on the Appalachian Trail, and ran through Thompson's "Mt. Cube Farm." One year Janet and a girlfriend who was visiting decided to climb Mt. Cube. An hour later, the two of them were back, Janet in tears. When they started up the trail, Mr. Thompson came barging out and berated them for trespassing on his land without his permission and forbade them to continue. I drove over with them and, explaining to Mr. Thompson that the Appalachian Trail was a public trail, induced him to relent and let the girls continue.

This was by no means an isolated episode. Indeed, there were so many complaints to the authorities in charge of the trail that it was rerouted to bypass Mt. Cube Farm.

{ *Rose* } Having been city dwellers until we went to New England for summers, we learned many things from our country experience—most added to our enjoyment, but a few, and they are the most memorable, did not. One of the latter concerned mice in the kitchen. One summer, when we plugged in our ancient toaster for our first breakfast at Orford, we were assailed by an unholy stench. Investigating, we discovered that a mouse had been using the toaster as a bed in our absence and was toasted to a crisp. A second experience with mice was even more unpleasant. One summer Aaron and Katherine were touring New England and met us en route as we were on our way to Orford for the summer. Shopping for food, I thought it would be fine to have a roast of beef for dinner. Nothing seemed to be amiss when I surveyed the kitchen on our return. (A neighbor, Donald Tatham, opened the house before we came and had it cleaned.) But not long after I turned on the electric stove to prepare the roast, a sickening smell permeated the kitchen. The smell clearly came from the oven, but what was the source? Careful examination and much consultation convinced Milton and Aaron that somehow the smell emanated from the insulation around the oven. So they started pulling out the insulation bit by bit. After our experience with the toaster, I had a vague feeling that somehow a mouse had again entered our life. And sure enough, before all the insulation was removed, the remains of a dead mouse emerged. I remember the incident well but I don't remember how the roast got cooked. Since the nearest hardware store where fresh insulation could be purchased was ten miles away, and was doubtless closed by the time the contretemps occurred, I'm sure we didn't have roast beef for dinner that night.

We learned about porcupines, too—from sounds not smells. Not long after settling into the house our first summer we heard a peculiar sound during the night, which Milton interpreted as electric sparking. We were puzzled and the next day we asked Donald Tatham about the sound. He laughed and said, "Oh, that must have been a porcupine; they like kitchen floors." Milton crawled under the kitchen and discovered that porcupines had eaten through the original kitchen floor before we bought Hideaway and were now busily working on a second layer that had been added later.

We learned a good deal about porcupines in ensuing years: first, that porcupines like salt, which is why they are attracted to kitchen floors; second, that they were plentiful. A neighbor informed us that in earlier years the state of Vermont paid a bounty for the nose of a porcupine and New Hampshire paid a bounty for the ear (or perhaps it was vice versa). He claimed to have paid his taxes for years by setting out a salt lick to attract the porcupines. When they came, he shot them and redeemed their noses in Vermont and their ears in New Hampshire. (I suspect that today there would be loud complaints by animal-protection people if the bounty was still in existence.)

Milton learned that his most effective weapon for killing porcupines was a baseball bat. The trick was to hit it on the nose, and though he didn't like to get that close, he learned the trick. Hitting it anywhere else as hard as he could, the bat would simply bounce off, yet the merest tap on the nose seemed to be fatal. Porcupines were also very unreasonable and came in the night, usually in the midst of that first deep sleep. So far as we were concerned, the ugly beasts had nothing to redeem them. We continued to have problems with them after we moved to our Vermont home, but that was better built, so they were not able to get under the main house, only under the porch.

Raccoons are something else. They are not interested in kitchen floors, only garbage cans and vegetable gardens, especially newly ripened sweet corn. And they are very clever. It is almost impossible to fix a garbage can so they can't open it. As for corn, they wait until it is perfectly ripe, and then manage to circumvent ordinary fences, electric fences, and traps to get more than their share of the corn. In addition to being clever, however, unlike porcupines, they are very cute. In California we still have problems with raccoons, but thankfully not with porcupines.

{ *Milton* } We also learned a great deal about water. When we first looked at the Orford house, we noticed that, in addition to the standard faucet in the kitchen sink, there was another faucet jutting out of the wall just above the floor. Mr. Maginnis told us that an excellent dug well provided water by gravity flow, but that toward the end of summer the water occasionally got too low to run from the sink faucet and they used the low faucet to get water from the well. He did have, he said, a supplementary source of water from a creek in the woods a few hundred yards from the house, which he had dammed and piped down to the house.

City dwellers accustomed to turning a tap and invariably getting water from it, we took it all at face value, much to our subsequent discomfiture. "Occasionally" had a way of becoming every summer. And "end of summer" had a way of being late July or early August. Our first reaction was for the kids and me to go in for dam-building and try to harness more effectively the miserable creek that was the alternative source of water. We replaced Mr. Maginnis's lead pipe with galvanized pipe, and some of the lead pipe ended up being melted and poured into molds by David and me to produce an army of lead soldiers. When that proved inadequate, we installed a pump on top of the well, but even that was sometimes not enough and we had to bring water in jugs.

Later owners, who winterized the house, finally did what we probably should have done and had a deep well dug.

{ *Rose* } Our summer cottage in Orford served us well as long as we spent only the summer months away from Chicago. When the children went off to college we decided it would be nice to spend more time in New England so Milton could devote more time to research and less to teaching. We first thought of winterizing Hideaway but soon gave that up because, while the place had much charm, it was not built to withstand New England winters. And we felt that making a substantial house out of it would destroy the charm. (And so it did, as we discovered many years later when we visited Hideaway after new owners had enlarged and winterized it.)

Besides, we really thought it would be exciting to plan our own house. We also felt that we might retire to New England and wanted a more substantial house if we did so. (We changed our minds about where to retire after two or three early winters in Vermont.)

Our first move was to look for land. We had a very clear idea about what we wanted. Milton had a fondness, that the children and I shared, for driving on back roads in out-of-the-way areas as a form of recreation—many was the time we had to build a road to get across a patch of mud. In the course of motoring around New England, we would always take special note of acreage for sale on a hilltop. That was what we wanted.

As economists, we should have looked for land in New Hampshire—since that was one of the few states that had no income or general sales tax. But that did not enter our minds.

Our friend Geoff Moore, who had a summer place in Vermont, told us about a farm on a hilltop that had about 120 acres mostly in timber (maple, birch, oak, and other hardwood), with an old house and barn that were falling apart. It was owned by the same farmer from whom Geoff had bought his land some years earlier. This sounded like just what we were looking for, so we lost little time before viewing it. We were delighted. It had a lovely view over the valley down to Lake Fairlee, and off to the mountains beyond. Acreage in New England at this time, though dearer than when we first came to Vermont, was still very cheap. After some bargaining, we paid $50 an acre for 120 acres.

Although we bought the land in 1965, we did not start to build for a year. In dreaming about plans for our future home, we remembered Milton's enthusiasm about the lodge at the Freedom School in Colorado Springs. In 1963, he had given a series of lectures at the school, which was a very unusual enterprise. It was run by Robert Lefevre, an extreme libertarian, and a group of like-minded disciples and associates. They had built their own buildings, all log cabins, using logs obtained from burnt-over areas and consequently thoroughly air-dried. They prided themselves on their independence from the government, and financed themselves by charging fees for short courses they held in the philosophy and practice of freedom.

Milton stayed at the main lodge, which not only served as the chief meeting place for large groups, but was also Lefevre's home. Milton was enchanted with it, and shared his enthusiasm with me when he returned. He tried to describe it verbally and on paper but without much success. We decided that I must see it. On a subsequent trip to the West Coast, we stopped off in Colorado Springs to visit the Freedom School. I was as enchanted with the lodge as he had been. Bob Lefevre was extremely helpful and more than willing to provide us with a set of building plans. In return, we made a modest contribution to the school.

This was not a conventional house. First of all it was a hexagon. Each side was twenty-two feet long and it had a cathedral ceiling that was supported by a hexagonal fireplace in the center. In building our own house we used redwood plywood rather than logs for the siding, and modified the plans by adding a summer wing. The hexagon was well insulated and electrically heated for year-round use. It contained a very large living room, a small bedroom, one and a half baths, and a kitchen, just enough for the two of us. Lefevre's fireplace was constructed of fieldstone, ours of cement blocks faced with Vermont tricolored slate. It was not only a joy to look at, but extremely efficient. The hexagon was heated with baseboard electric heating. It was an all-electric house because, at the time, the rate was lower the more electricity one used, very different from the situation later. On one occasion, when the power was off for nearly two full days, we were able to stay comfortable with the fireplace as our only source of heat because the house was so well insulated. The summer wing consisted of four bedrooms, each opening on a balcony with a magnificent view overlooking Lake Fairlee, two miles to the south. Milton used one as his study. The wing was not winterized; it was for summer use only.

It was not the kind of house that country builders were accustomed to constructing but we were dreamers and our dreams came true. We tried to get estimates from a couple of Hanover builders but were discouraged by the range of the estimates, so decided to take a chance with a local builder on a "cost-plus" basis. Building permits were not required for anything at this time in the New England countryside. We signed no contracts: everything was on trust, and we have never since had so satisfactory a result. I was fond of saying that the only papers we signed were a collection of little pieces that had my name at the bottom.

There was one other paper we had to sign, and that was to give the electric company permission to put poles on our land to bring us electricity. We tried to persuade them to put all the wires underground but they talked us out of that when they suggested that if something happened to the underground wire in the depth of winter, with the ground frozen and snow several feet deep, it would be very difficult to get the electric company to come to our aid promptly. We discovered later that there were many blackouts—generally because trees fell over wires. They did agree, however, to put the wires underground at the house level. We got used to the poles and they did not really interfere with our view.

We hired a neighbor to cut down some oaks, birches, maples, and butternut trees in our forest, and persuaded a local lumber company to mill them and have the planks kiln-dried. We then had the living room paneled in 3/4-inch white oak, the kitchen in butternut, and used the birch and maple to have much of our furniture—beds, dressers, and so on—built in. The final result fully matched our dreams.

As a result of our experience in Orford, I had two specific conditions. One, we would not start building until we were assured of enough water from a drilled well. Two, the house had to be mouseproof. The first condition was satisfied when, after watching nervously while the well drillers went down one hundred and then two hundred feet without getting a trickle, suddenly, on September 16, 1966, the drill hit an aquifer yielding more gallons of water a minute than we could ever need. Water rose in the well so that the pump was actually installed at the hundred-foot level. For the mouseproof proviso, I had only the contractor's assurance, but that was enough. We had a mouse in the house only once, when the house was broken into during our absence, and the door leading into the house from the basement was left wide open.

After our dream house was finished we thought it would be nice to have a pond on our property. This was not a problem since there was a marshy area with natural springs below the surface. So we had a four-acre pond dug that was fourteen feet deep in the center and was fed entirely by springs. We stocked it with trout fingerlings two summers in a row but never ate a fish. The neighbors were never sure whether an otter or a raccoon was the thief but we gave up after the second try. The man who put in our pond also raised mallards and he brought us four but they too did not survive. He clipped their wings so that they would not fly away while getting habituated to our pond, but unfortunately that meant that they also could not get away from predators who liked the taste of baby mallards. The pond was splendid for swimming and provided a home for our aluminum canoe.

We named our dream house "Capitaf," hoping that the royalties from our book *Capitalism and Freedom* would pay for it. And in the long run, we think they did. Our brief visit after it was completed in late 1967 was an experience that I have never forgotten. We decided to spend the Christmas holidays at Capitaf before going to Washington, D.C., for the American Economic Association meetings in December 1967. (We had brought a load of furniture up from Chicago that spring.) Before we went to Washington, the weather was fair and there was no snow. On our return after the meetings, we discovered at the Lebanon airport that a heavy snow had fallen in the interim. That didn't keep us from doing a big shopping so we would not have to shop for the rest of our stay. Since the roads from the airport to the foot of our property had been plowed, we had no problem until we came to our own driveway, which had not been plowed, and on which the car immediately got stuck. We had no choice but to take our bags of groceries and start hiking up the quarter-mile, steeply-sloped driveway in our city clothes— high heels for me, no boots for either of us. I made it but have never forgotten the struggle. To add insult to injury, after I got to the top of the hill without falling, I landed in the snow about twenty feet before reaching the house!

{ *Milton* } I arranged to have my salary adjusted so that I could teach only two quarters and spend the rest of the year on research. Accordingly, we planned to spend June to January at Capitaf and January to June in Chicago. After two years of very heavy snow, however, with my spending too many hours clearing the snow from the driveway with our four-wheel-drive Blazer and snow plow, we decided to accept reality and change our schedule. However, the spring had its own problem—the mud season. We conquered that by having the driveway black-topped. Now the snow problem was solved, but we wanted to see the fall colors, which were not at their peak until after classes started in the fall. So Rose stayed on through the middle of October and I flew back to Vermont for that heavenly weekend almost every year.

{ *Rose* } In addition to an education about the trials of country living, we also learned a good bit about New Englanders. Unlike the picture often painted of them, they are neither taciturn nor standoffish. Far from silent, they will talk your head off once you get them started. Like people everywhere, they come in different sorts. New England has both its ne'er-do-wells and its hard-workers.

Our neighbors at Capitaf provided examples of both. All were named Godfrey, but one Godfrey—William—claimed no relationship to the others. He was the most enterprising man I believe I have ever known. He was the local auctioneer and a very good one. He was the funeral director and had his own mortuary. He was an insurance agent. He collected sap from his maple trees, made excellent syrup by boiling it down, and marketed it. We were once at Capitaf during the maple-syruping time. Mr. Godfrey invited us to see his syruping operation. The syruping house was the steamingest, sweetest place I have ever been in. I believe that it was on this visit that Milton was inspired to tap a couple of our own sugar maples. My recollection of the experience is that the amount of sap we managed to collect always boiled away before it got to the syrup stage. This was not surprising when we learned that it took thirty to fifty gallons of sap to make one gallon of syrup.

Our nearest neighbors were Arthur Godfrey and his wife. They were poor but worked hard and as far as we knew never depended on handouts. They also sugared but in a much less mechanized manner than William Godfrey. It was Arthur Godfrey who cut the trees in our woods that went into the walls and furniture of our house. Toward the end of our stay at Capitaf, however, Mr. Godfrey got Alzheimer's disease and we would find him wandering around our grounds not knowing his way home. He died some years before we left and his wife sold the property to a Dartmouth astronomy professor, Forrest Boley, who not only did a considerable amount of renovation on the house but mechanized the syrup collection and boiling apparatus, and marketed the syrup. Forrest grew up on a farm and turned the Godfrey property into a more active farm. He had a few cattle, mostly for atmosphere I believe, and for his own and our consumption. He used to say that he did his best thinking when sitting on a tractor.

The Arthur Godfreys had two sons and two or three daughters. We never met the daughters, since they lived elsewhere. However, we did get to know the two sons, who lived on what was either their father's farm or small plots adjoining. The eldest son was a handsome-looking fellow who, we understood, suffered from many ailments and hence depended on handouts of one kind or another. When we first came to Capitaf, he and his wife were living in a deserted schoolhouse at the bottom of the lane. He spent several years building a house on his father's property soon after we came to Capitaf. My recollection is it was never really finished.

The second son we knew as "Peanut," though he was not particularly small. He was more enterprising than his older brother. Peanut had no special skills but did a variety of chores for us, like cutting wood for the fireplace from our forest, clearing the trees from our meadow, etc. He did similar chores for other summer people, I am sure. To the best of our knowledge he had no regular employment. I assume he also got some help from the government but we knew nothing about this. Peanut and his wife had three children.

After we moved to California in 1977, we tried for a while to keep Capitaf as our second home. We soon decided that it did not make much sense to maintain residences on the two coasts. Given California's equable climate, it made more sense to get a second home in California that we could use year-round (see chap. 31). Nineteen-eighty was the last summer that we spent at Capitaf.

The decision to dispose of our dream home was not easy, given how much of ourselves we had invested in its construction. We finally disposed of it by selling it at a bargain price to the University of Chicago. We were delighted when they in turn sold it to a colleague at the university's Business School, Bob Aliber, with whom we are in touch from time to time. He has become as attached to it as we were.

Chapter Twelve

AN AUTUMN IN PARIS, 1950

{ *Milton* } In the spring of 1950, former students who were working for the Marshall Plan agency in Paris asked if I would be interested in spending a few months in Paris as a consultant to their agency. When a formal invitation followed, I arranged with the university for leave in the fall quarter. As a result, we ended the first summer at our newly acquired Orford house by leaving for Paris rather than for Chicago.

{ *Rose* } We first drove to New York where we stored our car for the rest of the year and boarded the Holland American steamship. My only earlier Atlantic voyage was in the course of coming from Russia to the U.S. Though I have no recollection of that voyage, I am sure that this trip was a far pleasanter one. We traveled with our good friends the Burnses, who were going to London. They disembarked at Southampton while we went on to Cherbourg.

The U.S. had taken over the Hôtel Wagram on the rue de Rivoli as a temporary abode for Americans working in Paris on government business. We stayed there for about a month until we found other accommodations. Our first task was to choose a school for Janet and David, aged seven and five. We decided they would benefit from attending a French school, even for a brief period. After consulting French friends, we chose a small school on the Left Bank called l'École du Père Castor.

Our children knew no French and neither David's kindergarten teacher nor Janet's second-grade teacher nor any of the other pupils spoke English, but that did not prevent communication. Facial expressions, hand signals, and no doubt other expedients substituted for words until Janet and David had acquired some French, which they soon did. Indeed, we were astonished by how much French they managed to acquire in three months.

In addition to the difference in languages, they were exposed to a very different environment from what they had been accustomed to. The French children brought wine (mixed with water) in their lunch boxes; our children brought milk. The French children were much more disciplined than ours and had far better table manners.

Since l'École du Père Castor was on the Left Bank and the Hôtel Wagram on the Right Bank, and the traffic was frightening, I took the children to and from school by taxi. After depositing them at their school I wandered around Paris exploring different areas and practicing my French en route. I would then return at the appropriate time to bring the children home.

One incident that I have never forgotten occurred on one trip home from school. Upon arriving at the Hôtel Wagram, David got out of the cab before I did and started off for the hotel—unfortunately, in the wrong direction. As soon as he realized he was lost, he stopped a young lady beside him and in halting French tried to ask for directions to the Hôtel Wagram. David was taken aback when she gave him directions in English, since like him she was an American in Paris.

After a month at the Hôtel Wagram, we learned that one of the men at the American Embassy was going home on leave for two months and was interested in subletting his house located in the sixteenth arrondissement. That suited our needs perfectly since we were scheduled to stay in Paris for just two more months and did not enjoy living in a hotel, especially with small children. As part of the deal we also acquired a housekeeper and the use of a car.

The house was grander than anything we had occupied up to this time, and having a housekeeper made for a delightful two months. The only fly in the ointment was that the food was so rich that we all gained too many pounds and had to shed them on our return. Though a wonderful experience for a short time, I decided that this kind of living also had its shortcomings, perhaps because I was not accustomed to such luxury. Our housekeeper, a friendly Czech woman who garbled the French language, made me feel that I was a guest in my own house—incapable of getting even my modest breakfast of toast and coffee. She was upset if I did not sit down in the dining room and wait for her to bring me my breakfast. I always felt uncomfortable about it. On the other hand, it was very pleasant when we entertained our French or American friends at dinner to be treated as a guest in my own house. In addition, having a live-in babysitter made it easier for us to go out in the evenings to sample Paris's famed entertainments.

A favorite outing for the family was to the butte Montmartre, overlooking the city and teeming with artists and art studios and good restaurants. Seeing so many artists stimulated us to have portraits of our children painted as a souvenir of our stay in Paris. So every afternoon for a week, while the children sat for their portraits, I spent the time either watching the sitter or enjoying the view from the butte. I liked the scene so much that we bought a painting of it that we saw in the artist's studio. I don't believe that Monsieur Fremaux, our artist, ever became famous, but we still enjoy both his painting of Montmartre and the portraits of the children.

We made the obligatory visit to Notre Dame cathedral, including climbing the many flights of stairs to get a bird's-eye view of the famous gargoyles. Like the good first-time tourists that we were, we bought plaster reproductions of several of the more outrageous gargoyles, two of which still grace—if that is the word—the patio in our second home at Sea Ranch.

We accompanied our friends Maxwell Obst, a former student of Milton's working in Paris, and his wife to view the parade down the Champs-Élysées on Armistice Day. The crowd was tremendous and all went well as we waited patiently, in a hollow square with an open side toward the street, for the parade to arrive. But when it arrived, that unstable formation immediately collapsed as people rushed forward to see better. Our children disappeared in the melee. There were some nervous moments before we spotted them or they spotted us and we were reunited.

I remember also a trip to the Chartres cathedral, not only for the majestic beauty of the cathedral, but for my embarrassment when David suddenly decided to run around the cathedral while a service was in progress and I tried as inconspicuously as possible to catch him.

An unforgettable experience, of a very different kind, was lunch with Maurice Allais in his apartment. Allais was at the time a bachelor accustomed to what I will refer to as a French lunch. Neither Milton nor I had ever seen or consumed such a lunch, nor have we since. I don't recall exactly how many different wines were served but I do remember the result. My head was spinning by the end of the meal, when it was time to pick up the children at school. I don't know how I made my way to a taxi, got to the school, and picked up the children. But I do remember that I went to bed as soon as we arrived home and didn't wake up until the following morning. The best sleeping pill I have ever taken.

We also enjoyed our trips in the very early morning—the middle of the night to us—to Les Halles, the central wholesale market at the time in Paris for foods of all kinds, since dismantled and decentralized. The attraction was not primarily watching the stores of food for Paris being brought in and redistributed but the justly famed onion soup, the taste of which we nostalgically believe we have never been able to duplicate. We made several trips to the

French flea market and bought some wonderful copper pots—also a dueling pistol that is one of David's treasures. As we were traveling home by ship, baggage was not a problem, and since this was my first trip to Europe I wanted to buy everything. By the time we left Paris our trunk was overflowing. Much of the contents, like some wonderful Quimper dishes, were broken before we got them home.

{ *Milton* } This visit provided an occasion for renewing my friendship with both the French economists I had met at Mont Pelerin, Maurice Allais and Bertrand de Jouvenel. In addition we met other French economists; among them, Jean Fourastié, an economic historian of note, and Louis Rougier, an economic philosopher. We saw the Rougiers regularly on later visits to Paris.

{ *Rose* } In the course of his work, Milton found it necessary to go to Frankfurt, Germany, and we made this an occasion for the whole family. We drove from Paris to Frankfurt by car (a small Renault "Quatre Chevaux") and thus got an impression of the ravages of war in a way that no newspaper description or even television program could have given us. Driving through the German villages in the Ruhr valley, which still showed all the destruction from the Allied bombing, brought the war years back so vividly that we almost felt we were reliving those horrible years. None of the buildings showed any sign of repair.

We also learned something on this trip about ourselves—how deeply the war years had affected us. We thought that we were rational individuals who recognized that most Germans were no different from other people, that the majority had the same antipathy and revulsion to the atrocities of the Nazis that we had. But, when we saw German police directing traffic dressed in white tunics that reminded us of the Nazi Storm troops, the feeling of revulsion and fear was so great that we could not bring ourselves to stop for lunch until late in the afternoon when we reached an American military snack bar on the autobahn. (Parenthetically, when we crossed into East Berlin from West Berlin many years later, while the wall was still standing, that same feeling returned and we did not stay very long.)

We did, however, have to stop for gasoline, and this provided an interesting exercise in economics. During that period of Allied occupation, German tradesmen were not permitted to accept any foreign money. On the other hand, we had not bothered to get any German currency before leaving Paris because we were going to the American Mission in Frankfurt and would receive an allotment of Germany currency there to meet our expenses. How to pay for the gasoline? In Milton's poor German, he managed to convey our dilemma to the woman serving us, and she was very cooperative. She replied, "Haben sie keine wäre? Kaffee?" (Don't you have any goods? Coffee?) Milton replied that we had no coffee but that we did have a carton of cigarettes. The woman nodded her approval. She sold us the equivalent of four dollars' worth of gasoline. To her, a carton of cigarettes was worth four dollars. So we gave her our carton of cigarettes for the gas. We, on the other hand, had paid only one dollar for the cigarettes at the PX in Paris and would have paid one dollar for the gas if we had bought it at the PX in Frankfurt. In other words, she sold us four dollars' worth of gasoline for four dollars' worth of cigarettes, and we paid her one dollar in cigarettes for one dollar in gasoline. What happened to the other three dollars? This tale turned up as an exam question in later years.

My insecurity continued after we arrived at Bad Hamburg, where we stayed while Milton was consulting in Frankfurt. The hotel that had been taken over for U.S. personnel was in a lovely park, where I took the children for walks. It was very difficult for me to let them run freely as they were accustomed to do at home because always there was the nagging fear that they might suddenly disappear. Of course I knew that there were no Nazis in the park but somehow there was always in my subconsciousness those terrible stories about what happened to Jewish children during the Nazi era. That trip to Germany haunted me for many years.

{ *Milton* } The invitation to spend a quarter as a consultant in Paris came from the agency that had been set up in Paris to monitor Marshall Plan aid to Europe.[1]

The Schuman Plan

My principal assignment was to analyze the Schuman Plan—the proposal first made in May 1950 by the French foreign minister Robert Schuman to establish a common market in Europe for coal and steel. The outcome of that proposal was a treaty signed in April 1951 by six countries (France, West Germany, Italy, and the three Benelux countries) to set up the European Coal and Steel Community, the precursor of the European Common Market.

The United States became deeply involved in the discussions for obvious reasons: the proposal involved the use of Marshall Plan funds. It also had significant implications for international trade and finance—as the subsequent development of the Common Market was to demonstrate. It was viewed by both the French sponsors and the American policy makers as a step toward

"A United States of Europe" that could end once and for all the centuries-old rivalry between Germany and France that had been so conducive to war—an objective that still exists behind the proposed introduction of a common currency.

In a lengthy report dated October 25, 1950, I noted that "the Plan raises fundamental problems about the general kind of world trade that is desired. Is it desirable to proceed to the establishment of preferential trade areas largely insulated from one another but enjoying a great degree of freedom within their borders? Or is it preferable to have a more modest liberalization of trade on a broader basis?" That question is still very much with us, though, unfortunately, in my opinion, the example of the European Common Market has clearly been winning, as witnessed by the recent negotiation of the North American Free Trade Agreement.[2]

Re the plan itself, I argued that "the present draft of the Schuman Plan seems to me clearly unacceptable in light of United States policies. The admirable objective of creating a single competitive market has been used to cloak the granting of power to the High Authority and to regional groups whose aggregate effect is very likely to be the substitution of a single super-monopoly for the present collection of monopolies. . . . The provisions in the present draft designed to prevent this outcome are little more than glittering generalities that would offer no real barrier."

I went on to specify the modifications that I thought were required for the plan to be acceptable to the U.S. In a subsequent memo commenting on further developments (dated November 29, 1950), I stated that these developments "are exceedingly disturbing, to say the least. They confirm our worst fears that the fine words about 'competition' and 'single market' have been interpreted to mean centrally directed and controlled industries."

In a reply the next summer to a letter from a Belgian senator seeking my advice on whether to vote for or against the Schuman Plan in the Belgian parliament, I summarized my views thus: "In conclusion, then, if I had to vote for or against the Schuman Plan I would certainly vote against it if the final plan provides permanent exceptions to the single market. If it does not, I would be inclined hesitatingly and with considerable uncertainty to vote for it on the grounds that the gains from increased freedom more than balance the chance that the positive powers will be effectively and fairly continuously exercised."

In retrospect, my reservations about the Schuman Plan have proved amply justified. One of its main initial objectives was to eliminate excess capacity and establish a single competitive market in steel. The *Wall Street Journal* reported forty-three years later, in a story about the success of British Steel,

"Now the industry is in crisis again. . . . On the Continent, where state-owned steelmakers view the industry as a source of employment and national pride, most would rather subsidize than cut back. Defying European Community efforts to reform the industry they hobble from calamity to calamity" (December 29, 1993, p. A4).

Exchange Rates

The occasion for the trip to Frankfurt was another assignment that I received. Germany was having balance-of-payment problems and I was asked to analyze the problem and suggest how it could best be handled. In the memorandum I submitted, I analyzed the various alternative solutions and concluded that the best would be for Germany to float the exchange rate, i.e., allow it to be determined by private transactions in a free market. I went to Frankfurt before I completed my memo to discuss this issue, particularly the political feasibility of floating the mark, with the German authorities. The result was unambiguous: I could elicit no sympathy whatsoever for floating the mark.

Accordingly, I concluded in my memo, "Dramatic evidence of the superiority of a flexible exchange rate to other currently available devices for meeting the German exchange crisis is provided by the document submitted . . . by the German government outlining the measures it proposes involving numerous detailed interventions into particular aspects of economic activity. . . . All would be rendered utterly unnecessary if the simple step were taken of letting the exchange rate go free, and many if not most would then seem positively mischievous. . . . And to cap it all, there is no real confidence that these measures will solve the crisis."[3]

This was the origin of my later much-republished and cited paper on "The Case for Flexible Exchange Rates."[4]

We returned to the U.S. on the French liner *La Liberté*—one of the most delightful voyages we have ever made. It was over New Year's, which made it particularly festive. In addition, in the best French tradition, the children went to their own play area where they were supervised, entertained, and fed—a real treat for them and for their parents. After this wonderful holiday, we returned to Chicago ready to move into our new home on Kenwood Avenue where we lived for the next thirteen years.

→ *Chapter Thirteen* ←

THE UNIVERSITY OF CHICAGO

{ *Rose and Milton* } The University of Chicago is famous for its intense and stimulating intellectual atmosphere. Concentration on ideas; intellectual discourse among equals judged by scholarly ability, not status; tolerance for unconventional ideas; interaction among scholars in different fields—these are the hallmarks of what we continue to regard as *our* university. Potential students or faculty who are not interested in so intense an intellectual experience find Chicago unattractive.

Robert Maynard Hutchins was unquestionably the dominant figure both when we were students and when we returned in 1946. Named president of the university in 1929 at the age of thirty, after two years as dean of the Yale Law School, he was a remarkable and charismatic individual, full of good ideas and determined to bring them to fruition. It was impossible to be with him for more than a few minutes without feeling that you were in the presence of a truly great person.

Hutchins was extremely critical of American higher education. It was, he insisted, too specialized, concentrating on vocationalism at the expense of general education, and gave far too much importance to extracurricular activities, particularly athletics. Chicago had long been a member of the Big Ten, and a major football power in the 1920s. Yet, at Hutchins's insistence, it abandoned intercollegiate football in 1939.

"Hutchins," writes Edward Shils, "was one of the very few university presidents of his time—perhaps the only one—who believed in the value of intellectual life as an intrinsic good, who believed that intellectual achievement in teaching and research was the only worthwhile objective for a university to pursue. This gave the University of Chicago a distinctive tone. . . . He helped to keep the University alive as a university devoted to intellectual things and

183

not just as an institution to handle the administrative and financial burdens of self-enclosed departments and to enable strong-willed, gifted and mediocre individuals to get on with their specialized research and teaching. . . . In Robert Hutchins the University of Chicago had at its head a man of great moral qualities and of rarely equaled consecration to things of the mind."[1]

A story, perhaps apocryphal, about Hutchins and Abraham Flexner, author of the famous 1910 Flexner report on medical schools, illuminates one facet of Hutchins's character that many thought a defect—his impatience to get things done. As an official of a major foundation in the 1920s, Flexner sponsored a fellowship program directed to improving the quality of university administrators by financing a year abroad to study the administration of foreign universities. He offered Hutchins, then at Yale, such a fellowship and was turned down. At the inaugural festivities occasioned by Hutchins's installation as president at Chicago, the story goes, Hutchins said to Flexner as he went through the receiving line, "You see, if I had accepted your offer of a fellowship, I would not now be president of the University of Chicago." "No," Flexner is supposed to have replied, "You would not be, but you might be qualified to be."

President and then chancellor of the University of Chicago from 1929 to 1951, Hutchins was full of good ideas both for the university and the community. With the cooperation of Mortimer Adler, a philosopher whom Hutchins brought to the University of Chicago, he promoted study at the university and among the general public of the so-called Great Books, the list of which I believe they formulated. He and Adler for years jointly conducted a seminar on the Great Books. Saint Thomas Aquinas was Adler's favorite philosopher, and many of the Great Books were in the Catholic tradition. During the Hutchins-Adler era, a favorite wisecrack was that the University of Chicago was a Baptist institution to which the good Presbyterians sent their children to be converted to Catholicism by a Jew. It was said that Adler himself had never successfully converted to Catholicism because he could not demonstrate the requisite humility.

Two of Hutchins's most important projects were (1) the Chicago Plan for undergraduate education and (2) the 4E contract for faculty. He thought, correctly, that four years of high school was too long. So his plan had two parts. First, the college would admit students after their sophomore year in high school. And second, all requirements for a bachelor's degree could be met at any time by passing comprehensive exams in a range of subjects. Both ideas are excellent. There is much waste of time both in high school and college, and surely knowledge and not time served is the right basis for granting degrees. One of my brightest Ph.D.s took full advantage of this program, earning his bachelor's degree in less than two years, and his Ph.D. in another three.

Hutchins expected that many universities would accept the early degree as satisfying the requirement for admittance to graduate training and professional schools. Unfortunately, Chicago was about the only university to do so, and, over time, there was much reversion to standard practice, even at Chicago. (One change was a reduction by one year in the standard elementary and high school course at the University Laboratory School. Both our children graduated from the Lab School; Janet after eleven years, David after ten years.)

Hutchins was so impatient to get his way that he did not suffer gladly those who differed with him, and he was willing to use questionable tactics to override them.*

One striking example was Hutchins's desire to appoint Rexford Guy Tugwell to the faculty. He asked the Economics Department to recommend an appointment for him. After lengthy consideration, the department decided that Tugwell's quality as an economist did not justify an appointment and refused to recommend one. Undaunted, Hutchins established a new Institute of Planning in the Social Sciences Division in 1946, and appointed Tugwell as its first and only director. The institute lasted until Tugwell retired, when it was abolished, and its remaining members were transferred to other departments, mainly Political Science. One such member was Ed Banfield, who became a close friend and one of the leading political scientists in the country. He ended his career at Harvard.

Another Hutchins innovation that backfired was the introduction of the so-called 4E contract in 1944. It was patterned on a practice that then prevailed in the Medical School. It required new faculty, and sought to induce existing faculty, to give full time to the university and to turn over any outside earnings above a trivial amount to the university. It represented a major departure from prevailing practice. So far as we know, no other university in the country had a similar contract for all its faculty. Like so many of Hutchins's other ideas, it embodied an excellent principle, but was seriously flawed as a practical arrangement. Hutchins believed that an academic appointment should be a full-time activity, with outside activities engaged in only if they

---

* Professor Leonard White, who was head of the Political Science Department when Hutchins came to Chicago, told us this story. The night before the faculty meeting that was to vote on Hutchins's plan for admission of students to the university after two years of high school, he promoted to tenure a number of his followers in order to assure that a majority of the faculty would be on his side. At the meeting, Hutchins voted for the plan as a professor of philosophy. The result was a tie vote, so Hutchins then voted again, in his capacity as chairman, to break the tie. White and many of his colleagues were outraged.

contributed to academic performance. Yet it was something of a scandal then, and is even more of one today, that many college and university professors engage in extensive outside activities that have little or no relation to their academic duties. The 4E contract was designed to end this practice by leaving faculty free to undertake any outside activities they wished but requiring them to turn over any net earnings to the university. In compensation, faculty members who shifted to the 4E contract were given a raise, and newly recruited faculty members were paid more than the prevailing salary for the usual contract. For example, Milton's starting salary was $6,250 a year, compared with $3,500 at Minnesota.

It soon became apparent that the 4E contract was expensive to the university and unattractive to many faculty members. The estimate for one year was that $300,000 extra was paid to those on the 4E contract but that far less was turned over to the university ($15,000 in 1944–45, $35,000 in 1945–46, and approximately $90,000 in 1946–47).[2] Like all such bureaucratic measures, the 4E contract involved much paperwork, annoying to the faculty and costly to the administration. Faculty members felt that many outside activities that contributed to their professional development involved extra effort and inconvenience that justified and required additional compensation. Like all taxation, the effect was to alter the activities faculty members engaged in: painting their own house instead of earning the money to hire a professional painter (an actual case reported in the reaction against the 4E contract), and so on in infinite variety.

{ *Milton* } My own experience was typical. Initially, I expressed myself as "strongly in favor of the intent of the 4E contract."[3] As time went on, I became more and more dissatisfied with it. It was much too rigid and impersonal a system, and involved too much paperwork. Moreover, the main beneficiary of those activities that faculty members engaged in despite the lack of any financial incentive was not the university but the sponsors of the activities. They quickly learned about the 4E contract and accordingly offered only token payments.

In 1950, Phil Hauser, a professor of sociology, and I organized a petition drive among the faculty objecting to the 4E contract. The protest kept building, and a year or two later the 4E contract was made optional. The alternative involved a lower salary, and required the faculty member to get clearance for any outside activity that would absorb more than 10 percent of working time, but permitted the faculty member to keep any earnings. That proved a far better arrangement.

{ *Rose and Milton* } When Hutchins resigned as chancellor in 1951, he left the university in a financial bind. In pursuit of his favorite ideas, he had exploited every loophole available that enabled him to use endowment funds for current purposes. In the process, some such funds no longer conformed to the specifications under which they had been accepted, greatly reducing the willingness of large donors to the university to make restricted gifts. Lawrence A. Kimpton, who followed Hutchins as president, performed a great service to the university by careful and austere financial management that enabled him to restore deficient endowment funds and thereby regain the confidence of large donors.

As this final tale suggests, Hutchins was not an unmixed blessing for the university, but on the whole his contribution was highly positive. His spirit lingers on.

One notable episode during his tenure had a direct relation to George Stigler's joining the university a dozen years after President Colwell's initial rejection of his appointment. As George summarizes it in his *Memoir*, "Mr. [Charles R.] Walgreen, Senior, had withdrawn his niece from the University of Chicago in 1936, and accused the University of teaching such subversive doctrines as free love . . . and communism. The legislature of Illinois had created an investigating committee after the case was heated up by the *Chicago Tribune*. The University was exonerated. Mr. Walgreen was convinced of its innocence, and he gave $500,000 for [what ultimately became the Charles R. Walgreen Professorship] in American Institutions. I became the first holder of the chair some twenty years later" (p. 157). What George does not bring out was the key role that Hutchins played in the outcome. He refused to knuckle under to the public pressure and insisted on fighting for the academic freedom of his faculty. He testified extensively, eloquently, and persuasively before the legislative committee. Experience both then and since, particularly during the sixties, but also now during the "political correctness" craze, shows how rarely university administrators display such courage.

{ *Milton* } After leaving the university, Hutchins was appointed associate director of the Ford Foundation and in 1954 became president of the Fund for the Republic, the sole activity of which was to finance the Center for the Study of Democratic Institutions in Santa Barbara, California, of which Hutchins was the director and Tugwell a leading member. Years later, at the request of a financial supporter of the university and one of Hutchins's close friends, I spent a few days at the center to evaluate it. I was impressed as always by Hutchins's charisma and intelligence but depressed that his great talents had ended up presiding over what could only be described as an ongoing bull session for over-age adolescents.

One of the most attractive features of the university is the friendly relations between departments and the extensive interaction both within and between departments. For example, unlike the situation in many universities, where the business school and the economics department are intense rivals, at Chicago the relation between the two has always been cordial and cooperative. Students in the Economics Department take courses in the Business School and students in the Business School take courses and attend seminars in the Economics Department. Many of the best students in my classes were registered in the Business School.

Our personal relations were especially close with the Law School thanks to Aaron's membership on the Law School faculty. Aaron's close associates at the Law School—Ed Levi, Bernie Meltzer, Wally Blum, and their wives among others—all became personal friends with whom we interacted both socially and professionally.

Regular departmental seminars were supplemented by many interdepartmental seminars. One example was a seminar that Aaron conducted on law and economics that attracted participants from law, economics, business, and political science. After Aaron retired, it was continued as an "industrial relations workshop" by George Stigler.

Another example was a seminar that Friedrich Hayek started not long after he came to the Committee on Social Thought (1950). For several years, it dealt with problems of methodology.

One session in particular made a deep impression on me. The guest lecturer was Enrico Fermi, the famous physicist and prime mover in achieving the first nuclear reaction on the squash racquets court in the university stadium. He discussed the problem of measurement, which he defined as the making of distinctions. He insisted that distinguishing between a cat and a dog was a primitive form of measurement. The finer the distinction, the more precise the measurement. He gave many interesting examples of the problems of measurement, and how concepts were affected by the circumstances. One that I remember concerned what would happen to what we think of as a precise concept of length on the surface of the sun, where the temperatures are so high as to render all metals fluid or gaseous. Many sessions in Hayek's seminar were of great interest but none in my recollection approached Fermi's rare combination of subtlety of thought and simplicity of exposition. Hayek's seminars were attended by economists, sociologists, political scientists, philosophers, and no doubt others from time to time.

Fermi's comments were directly relevant to a quotation from the great physicist Lord Kelvin that is carved in stone over the entrance to the Social Science Research Building: "When you cannot measure, your knowledge is meager and unsatisfactory." The story goes that on contemplating it one day, Frank Knight was heard to mutter, "And if you can't measure it, measure it anyway." Fermi's seminar was the final clincher to my belief that Knight completely misunderstood Kelvin. Kelvin's point was not that measurement was a way to create science, but that, in Fermi's words, the ability to make "fine distinctions" was an end product of science and a test whether scientific knowledge had been attained.

Another university activity in which I participated was the University of Chicago Round Table, an NBC half-hour radio program broadcast on Sunday morning. For many years, until television achieved complete dominance, the Round Table was one of the most popular talk shows on the air. The program consisted of a conversation on a topical issue, generally among three persons with differing views, one of whom served as both moderator and participant. The participants were generally Chicago faculty members, though others were often included. The procedure was for the participants to meet Saturday night for dinner with the producer and discuss the issue at great length. The producer would then construct an outline of the issues. It would be available the next morning to guide the discussion. A transcript of each program was published as a pamphlet in a continuing series.[4]

The program that I recall most vividly was an unusual one. It was broadcast on April 18, 1948, from Toronto, Canada, rather than from the usual location, the radio studio at the top of Mitchell Tower at the university. The topic was "Canada and the Problems of World Trade," and it dealt with problems of trade between Canada and the United States. At the time, Canada was struggling with a trade deficit and having difficulty maintaining the fixed exchange rate to which it was committed under Bretton Woods. Donald Gordon, deputy governor of the Bank of Canada, was one participant. In the discussion Saturday evening as well as on the broadcast, my position was that the right policy was for Canada to float the dollar. Apparently, this was the first time that Donald Gordon, an extraordinarily able executive, had ever heard this solution put forth seriously and he and I had a vigorous argument about it. This discussion played a major role in the adoption of floating rates by Canada on September 30, 1950.

The Quadrangle Club, established as a private club to which all faculty are entitled to belong and to which some persons from the broader community who had close relations to the university could also belong, provided an excellent meeting place. Departmental lunches were held there. In addition, a number of large round tables were set aside, one for the social science faculty, one for the physical science faculty, etc. They provided an excellent mechanism for interdepartmental communication. They were so popular that it was often difficult to find a seat at them. The club was also convenient for meetings of members of the community with faculty members. In addition, many university social activities took place at the club.

All in all, it was our great good fortune to enjoy a more stimulating intellectual environment at Chicago than any we have ever encountered elsewhere.

→ Chapter Fourteen ←

THE DEPARTMENT
OF ECONOMICS

{ *Milton* }   The Chicago Department of Economics has been a leading center of graduate economics ever since the founding of the university in 1890.
James Laurence Laughlin, the first chairman of the department, who was recruited by President Harper from Cornell, set a pattern that has been maintained ever since. Himself a hard-money man of rigidly conservative views,
he demonstrated an extraordinary degree of tolerance in staffing and guiding
the department. He brought with him from Cornell Thorstein Veblen, a leading and highly controversial critic of classical economics, who remained in
the department for fourteen years, the longest period Veblen spent at any
single university during his stormy career. As one of his first acts at Chicago,
Laughlin founded the *Journal of Political Economy,* with himself as editor and
Veblen as managing editor. The journal quickly became, and has remained,
one of the leading professional journals in economics.

As John U. Nef (longtime professor of economic history at the University
of Chicago and one of Rose's and my teachers) wrote in his 1934 obituary
notice of Laughlin: "Laughlin frequently chose the best men when they were
of very different persuasions from his own. . . . And so it came about that
one of the most conservative heads of an economics department in the country
had politically the most liberal and economically the least orthodox department."[1]

Laughlin's emphasis on quality rather than ideology was combined with
an emphasis on research by his faculty, as well as by graduate students as part
of their training. A corollary was his belief in personal teaching as opposed
to formal lecturing. These have remained key characteristics of the Chicago
Department of Economics from that day to this.

In more recent years, as in Laughlin's day, the department has been widely regarded as a stronghold of proponents of a free-market economy. That reputation was justified in the sense that throughout the period the department had prominent members who held these views and presented them effectively. But they were always a minority. The department has been characterized by heterogeneity of policy views, not homogeneity. The economists at Chicago who held the generally fashionable views—who were "liberal" in the twentieth-century sense—could be matched at other institutions; the ones who were "liberal" in the nineteenth-century sense could not be.

George Stigler made this point well in 1964, during the Johnson-Goldwater campaign. "The Chicago department was," he said, "the only department in the country that could readily staff a Council of Economic Advisers for either Johnson or Goldwater. Many others could do so for Johnson; a handful could do so for Goldwater; but no other for both."

That diversity, plus emphasis on economics as a serious scientific subject, capable of being tested by empirical and historical evidence, and of being used to illuminate important practical issues of conduct and policy, made Chicago economics unique. These were Laughlin's bequest to the department he built.

Theodore W. Schultz had only recently become chairman of the department when I joined it in 1946. He continued as chairman for the next fifteen years. He was a splendid chairman, scrupulous in consulting members of the department on possible appointments and other departmental matters, patient in not moving until he had managed to build a strong consensus, consistent in judging potential recruits solely in terms of academic promise, not personality or ideology, and repeatedly demonstrating excellent judgment about the academic qualities of persons being considered for appointment. Under his chairmanship, the department ran smoothly, relations with the rest of the university were cooperative and cordial, and there were none of those bitter personal fights that we had experienced at Wisconsin and that are so common in academia. Personally, I am very much indebted to Ted Schultz for the role he played in making Chicago so favorable an environment for my own teaching and research.

Before coming to Chicago in 1943, Ted had been head of the Department of Economics and Sociology at Iowa State College for nearly a decade. There too he had demonstrated his unusual knack for recognizing ability by recruiting a collection of young scholars who had yet to earn a reputation but later became leaders in the profession. Many were from the University of Chicago—including George Stigler, Homer Jones, Albert Hart, and Kenneth Boulding. His own initial field was agricultural economics, and his department at Iowa State came to be recognized as outstanding in that field.

He demonstrated his commitment to principle when he left Iowa State partly because of a controversy that arose from a pamphlet by one of the younger members of his department, Oswald Brownlee. Schultz sharply and publicly castigated the administration of the college for failing to protect academic freedom.*

That is how it came to pass that the University of Chicago, a strictly urban university, became the preeminent center of teaching and research in agricultural economics.

Ted Schultz's interest in agriculture led to his studying agriculture in underdeveloped countries, which in turn led to pioneering work in economic development and in the systematic study of human capital. He was awarded the Nobel Prize in Economics in 1979.

Brownlee and another student of Ted's, D. Gale Johnson, came with him to Chicago. Brownlee subsequently moved to the University of Minnesota, where he had a distinguished career. Johnson stayed at Chicago and was a valued colleague throughout the thirty years that I taught there. He became dean of the Division of the Social Sciences, and still later, provost of the university, but never severed his membership in the department or stopped doing important and influential research.

Our revered teacher, Frank Knight, was an active member of the department when I arrived and remained so until he retired in 1955. Our relationship with him was particularly close, both before and after he retired, partly

---

* The pamphlet by Oswald Brownlee was one of a series of "Wartime Farm and Food Policy Pamphlets" prepared by the economics and sociology departments. Brownlee's "pamphlet, *Putting Dairying on a War Footing*, . . . argued for a dairy policy" that would lead to the decreased production of butter and the increased consumption of margarine, and "noted that the increase of margarine consumption was impeded by restrictive legislation, both federal and state. It commented that properly fortified margarine 'compared favorably' with butter in nutrition and palatability. The pamphlet was vigorously attacked by representatives of organized groups and the Iowa Farm Bureau."

The controversy raged for months, attracting national attention. The president of the college was more interested in appeasing the dairy interests than in defending academic freedom and retracted the pamphlet, announcing that a revision would be "undertaken cooperatively" with the dairy interests. Professor Schultz was outraged and wrote a long letter to the president criticizing this and other actions of the college and announcing his intention to resign. He also published an article in the *Des Moines Register* entitled "Iowa State College and Social Science Research," accusing the college of violating the fundamentals of academic freedom. Schultz's resignation was accompanied by "an exodus from Iowa State College which broke up one of the most active, productive, and influential social science groups in the country," according to the author of a detailed account of the episode. Some of the others who left accompanied Schultz to the University of Chicago. The quotations and the information on the margarine episode are from Charles M. Hardin, *Freedom in Agricultural Education* (Chicago: University of Chicago Press, 1955), chap. 10, pp. 119–25.

because of Rose's closeness to the Knights, partly because of Aaron's continuing intimacy with Knight.

Knight frequently, and especially when visitors were passing through, hosted bull sessions at his house on the other side of the Midway but within easy walking distance for those of us who lived in Hyde Park. The group varied a great deal in composition, but Aaron, Gregg Lewis, of whom more later, and Rose and I were regular participants. We recall particularly clearly two such sessions.

One involved a spirited discussion about floating versus fixed exchange rates. One participant was Melchior Palyi, a Hungarian who had gained a reputation as a student of banking during the late twenties and early thirties in Europe and then emigrated to the United States. He taught for a time at the University of Chicago before settling down as an official of a major downtown bank. Rose remembers him well, because she did some research work for him when she was an undergraduate. She first handed him a handwritten report, which he criticized sharply. When she then typed it up without changes and gave it to him, he thought it was a wonderful piece of work. He was also notable for his strong accent, so that his comments on the "development of banking" came out as "the devil upment of banking." At this particular session, as a "gold bug," he was outraged by my defense of floating exchange rates, and ended up calling me a communist for holding such views. A day or so later, he telephoned, or wrote, I don't remember which, to apologize.

We remember another session for a very different reason. Charles O. Hardy, an eminent economist who had taught at the Business School, but was then ensconced at the Brookings Institution in Washington, was the guest of honor. We discussed one possible government reform program after another. Hardy consistently objected to them, insisting that each would do more harm than good. Finally, with some exasperation, Frank said, "Tell me, Charles, is there anything wrong with the world?" Hardy's response was instantaneous and classical, "Yes, indeed, there are too damn many reformers."

Though Aaron was not a member of the Economics Department, he added greatly to the intellectual atmosphere. As we noted earlier, the University of Chicago Law School was one of the first law schools to have an economist on its staff. Henry Simons had been the first economist to hold that position, while remaining a member of the Economics Department. Aaron was the second, and was responsible for generating a great deal of interaction among members of the Law School faculty, the Economics Department, and the Business School. He also was a founder of the discipline of law and economics, both through his teaching and by starting the *Journal of Law and*

Economics, of which he served as editor for its first five years (1958–63). This field has exploded over the past few decades, and is the field in which David has specialized. Aaron, like Knight, lived in the neighborhood and was an occasional host for bull sessions—as indeed over the years were most members of the department.

John Nef and Chester Wright, economic historians whose lectures Rose and I attended as students, were still active in the department, though Wright was approaching retirement. He was an enthusiastic and regular tennis player—as in later years I became. In one doubles game at the Quadrangle Club in which Wright was a participant, the total age of the players was 280, though one was *only* in his fifties! The story was that every afternoon after tennis, bottles of gin and vermouth would emerge from Wright's locker and be converted into martinis for Chester and his group because Mrs. Wright was strait-laced and would not permit alcohol at home.

John Nef was independently wealthy and had broad interests in the humanities. He believed that it was desirable to have a group broader in scope than the individual departments. Accordingly, he founded, and helped to finance, the Committee on Social Thought that still flourishes at the university. Many of its members had interests that overlapped ours in the department, notably F. A. Hayek, who joined the committee in 1950.

Paul Douglas, another member of the department whom Rose and I knew from our student days, was a remarkable individual. Born in 1892, he had already acquired a reputation as an economist specializing in labor economics when he joined the Chicago faculty in 1920 as an assistant professor of industrial relations. He was extraordinarily prolific. Erica Schoenberg, who was his assistant when we were students, complained that he could write articles faster than she could read proof on them. He had widespread interests, was active in public affairs, serving as an alderman for the ward surrounding the University of Chicago from 1939 to 1942, and was a leading defender of greater government intervention in the economy. Aaron originally came to the University of Chicago in 1927 to work with Douglas, and coauthored a book with him.[2] They subsequently drifted apart after Aaron became greatly influenced by Knight.[3]

Douglas's most lasting contribution to economics was his work on production, which made the "Cobb-Douglas production function" almost a household word among economists.

Rose remembers Douglas as an extremely colorful teacher. In the Principles of Economics course she took with him her first year at the university, he arrived in class one day with a bag of oranges to demonstrate diminishing marginal utility. He proceeded to toss oranges to the students one by one until they yelled "no more." After this demonstration, how could anyone forget diminishing marginal utility?

She also remembers Douglas fondly because of his kindness to her when she did a bit of research for him during her first year at the university. While his manner was fatherly, it was not condescending and as a result good for her ego or, in today's verbiage, her "self-esteem."

Though a lifetime Quaker, Douglas was so deeply moved by the behavior of the Germans and Japanese culminating in World War II that he enlisted in the Marines as a private at the age of fifty. He rose to lieutenant colonel before he was discharged in 1946, a disabled arm bearing witness for the rest of his life to his participation in active combat. He then returned to the University of Chicago the same year we did. In 1947, he was president of the American Economic Association, devoting his presidential address to a highly statistical answer to "Are There Laws of Production?"[4] In 1948, he ran for and was elected to the U.S. Senate as a Democrat, and served for the next eighteen years in the Senate.

My relations with him during the two years we were on the faculty together were friendly but not particularly close. Later, when Douglas was chairman of the Congressional Joint Economic Committee, I testified several times before his committee. On any economic issue that did not have immediate political consequences for him, Douglas could be relied on to be on the right side. He was an excellent economist, and we frequently were allies on issues of monetary and fiscal policy, as will become clear in later chapters.

After Douglas was defeated for reelection in 1966 by Charles Percy, himself a graduate of the University of Chicago and a member of the university's Board of Trustees, George Stigler invited Douglas to give a Walgreen lecture at the university. When a number of us had lunch with him, I commented that he looked far more relaxed and in much better physical shape than he had while in office or during the campaign, and said, "So, Paul, maybe your defeat was a blessing in disguise." He reacted violently, saying, "Oh no! It's the worst thing that ever happened to me. There's no better job in the world than being a U.S. Senator."

H. Gregg Lewis, an assistant professor in the department in 1946, had been Douglas's research assistant some years earlier. He subsequently taught labor economics and earned a reputation as an outstanding scholar in that field. Though never chairman, he could be counted on to assume a good deal of administrative responsibility for varied tasks and to execute them efficiently and on time. At the same time, he compiled an enviable scholarly record and supervised many dissertations. In 1975, he accepted an offer at Duke University, where he spent the rest of his career.

Gregg and his wife Julia lived near us. He joined Aaron and me in joint carpentry projects in Aaron's basement, which contained an extremely well-equipped carpentry workshop. Gregg was a meticulous, painstaking craftsman in carpentry as in his academic work, but like me he recognized Aaron as the master craftsman. The joint project I remember best was building six sofas, two for each of us, of solid walnut—far less expensive then than it has since become. That project occupied many enjoyable evenings and weekends and produced what were truly works of art. Our two couches still adorn a room in our second home, and Aaron's in his home, no worse after more than three decades of constant use. I lost touch years ago with Gregg's couches.

An important group associated with the department when I joined it was the Cowles Commission for Research in Economics, which was founded in 1932 by Alfred Cowles "to advance the scientific study and development . . . of economic theory in its relation to mathematics and statistics." Originally located in Colorado, it relocated to the University of Chicago in 1939, where it remained until it moved to Yale University in 1955. The Cowles Commission played a major role in promoting the use of mathematics and statistics in economics. It was the pioneer in the United States in the construction of large-scale statistical models of the economy. Lawrence Klein, who received the Nobel Prize in Economics in 1980 for his contribution to the construction of such econometric models, did his early work at the Cowles Commission, and published the results as a Cowles Commission monograph.[5] Three other economists who were at the Cowles Commission in its Chicago days later received Nobel Prizes: Kenneth Arrow in 1972, Tjalling Koopmans in 1975, and Trygve Haavelmo in 1989.

Though the Cowles Commission was an independent research group with its own staff and budget, it was closely linked with the department through joint appointments of two of its leaders as professors in the department: Jacob Marschak, who was its director of research from 1943 to 1948, and Koopmans, who had been with the commission since 1944 and succeeded Marschak as director of research. The result was a great deal of interaction between Cowles and the department. Cowles had a stream of research associates who subsequently became leaders in mathematical economics and econometrics and who made the frequent Cowles seminars exciting events in which I and other members of our department participated regularly and actively. Indeed, I developed a reputation as something of a hair shirt since I was, and still am, a persistent critic of the approach to the analysis of economic data that became known as the Cowles approach. Similarly, Cowles staff participated in and contributed to departmental seminars. Cowles also enlivened the intellectual atmosphere by sponsoring lectures by visiting scholars.

In 1955, Cowles moved to Yale in spite of the effort made by the department and the university to persuade Alfred Cowles to keep the commission at Chicago. I believe that the reason we failed was a combination of Cowles's ties to Yale, of which he was a graduate, and financial incentives offered by Yale that Chicago was apparently not able to match. Whatever the reason, the move was a significant loss to Chicago.

Marschak and Koopmans both began their scholarly careers abroad. Marschak, born in Russia, had his first teaching post in Germany at the University of Heidelberg. When Hitler came to power, Marschak emigrated first to Britain, then to the United States, rapidly acquiring a reputation as an innovative and productive scholar. Koopmans was born in the Netherlands, where he worked with Jan Tinbergen, one of the joint recipients of the first Nobel Prize in Economics. Koopmans emigrated to the United States in 1940, where he worked for the War Shipping Board before he joined the Cowles Commission in 1944.

Marschak and Koopmans had very different personalities. Marschak was a warm, outgoing human being. Koopmans by contrast was rather cold and authoritarian. Marschak was a truly learned person who had wide interests and contributed to different areas of economics. He and I both taught courses in money in the department and as a result we frequently served together on departmental committees to draw up and grade the Ph.D. preliminary examination in the field of money, always amicably—though we often differed in our judgment of individuals.

Koopmans was highly disciplined and formal. He specialized very narrowly on theoretical issues, both economic and statistical, involved in modeling the economic system via a set of simultaneous equations. This is the work for which he later received the Nobel award. Unlike Marschak, he was much less cooperative in departmental matters. I recall one episode in particular that impressed me deeply. The department had decided to award an annual prize for the best article in the *Journal of Political Economy*. A small committee was appointed each year to make the final selection from articles nominated by members of the department, each of whom, as I recall, was asked to name three articles. One year, when I was chairman of the selection committee, I had received nominations from all members of the department other than Tjalling. I phoned him and asked for suggestions. He replied that he had voted against the awarding of a prize and as a result did not feel obliged to participate in the selection of the winner. That episode led me to think seriously about the fragility of any social organization based on majority rule.

The same year that I came to Chicago, Allen Wallis, who had returned to Stanford after the termination of the Statistical Research Group, was induced to accept an appointment in the School of Business, primarily to teach statistics. In doing so, Allen had to reconcile himself to not getting an earned Ph.D., although he had completed all the requirements at Chicago except for a dissertation. However, Chicago had a rule that it would not award earned degrees to tenured members of the faculty—an excellent rule to maintain standards. Having a Ph.D. was not as crucial a requirement for success then as it has since become. Judging from Allen's subsequent career, not getting an earned Ph.D. did not turn out to be a major sacrifice. He later received a number of honorary doctorates. His coming to Chicago was a great boon for us, both intellectually and socially, as well as to the university.

In that same year, Jimmie Savage came to the Institute of Radiobiology and Biophysics of the University of Chicago as a special Rockefeller Fellow to study applications of mathematics to biology. The next year he was appointed to teach statistics in the Mathematics Department, and subsequently, when a separate Department of Statistics was created at Chicago, he served for some years as its chairman. Jimmie—without question one of the most original and creative people I have ever met—and I had collaborated at the Statistical Research Group (as I recounted in chapter 8), and we jointly wrote two papers on choices under uncertainty after he had come to Chicago.[6] These papers have been and still are widely cited in the professional literature dealing with uncertainty. In addition, he greatly influenced my understanding of the foundations of statistics—particularly the interpretation of the concept of probability.

This survey of the persons in the department that I joined in 1946 is not complete—I have omitted a number of colleagues—but it does indicate how wide was the range and how high the quality of the group that I was privileged to join. Later additions to the faculty enriched it still further. Two of the most notable were Harry Johnson and Al Harberger.

{ *Rose* } We have very pleasant memories of our friends of the Chicago days. Some of the closest were from other departments: Ed and Laura Banfield from Political Science, who left Chicago before we did. Fortunately, they chose the same area in Vermont that we did for their summer residence so our friendship flourished. We spent wonderful summer days together either at their home or ours partaking of good food and good conversation. Alma and Donald Lach, from History, whose daughter Sandy and our Janet were classmates at the Laboratory School and good friends after school. As a renowned cook, Alma was not only the source of some excellent gourmet dinners but shared a few recipes with me. They still have their spot in my cookbook as "Alma's pie" or "Alma's edible peas." Dan and Ruth Boorstin, also from History, who almost persuaded us to move to the suburbs with them when safety became an issue in the neighborhood. We resisted. They left but returned after a short time and bought a house in Hyde Park. Dan went from the university to be director of the Smithsonian Institution and then Librarian of Congress. Wally and Natalie Blum, Bernie and Jean Meltzer, and Edward and Kate Levi from the Law School—Edward was dean of the Law School and then president of the university. There were others but these were the closest.

The friendly atmosphere within the Economics Department carried over to social relations. One of Chicago's great advantages was the fact that most of the faculty lived in Hyde Park or Kenwood, within walking distance of the campus. We never lived more than four blocks from campus. This made getting together easy and informal. Most of us were roughly the same age and had children of similar ages, many of whom went to the Laboratory School. Especially in the early years, dinner parties were very simple. Domestic help was scarce. We cooked and served our own dinners with help in cleaning up from other wives.* Women's lib had not yet made its appearance in any of its manifestations. Husbands did not share domestic activities. And it was only in later years, when we were somewhat more affluent, that we occasionally indulged ourselves in having dinners catered.

Conversation during and after dinner varied with the company. When it was a Law School party, for example, the conversation was social and general. At Economics Department parties, the conversation quickly moved to economics, something that had come up in class or appeared in the newspaper. After dinner, the company often separated into two groups, the wives in one and the husbands in the other. As an economist, I was generally more interested in the men's conversation but would join the women for part of the time.

Not surprisingly, our closest friends were the ones we knew from our student days—the Wallises and, when George joined the department, the Stiglers. Although George and Chick lived in the suburb of Flossmoor, that did not keep us from getting together frequently. George often stopped in for coffee on his way to or from the university. The Wallises, like us, lived in Hyde Park.

---

* Not long after we joined the university, we were invited to have dinner at the Nefs'. As mentioned earlier, the Nefs had independent means, and the dinner reflected this. It was served in the old tradition, with excellent wine and wonderful service, and after dinner the men retired to the library for brandy and cigars while the women went to repair their makeup and talk among themselves. I remember that dinner vividly because it was so different from all the others.

In addition, much social activity was connected with department activities. Whenever there was a seminar or a visiting speaker, for example, one of the faculty members would invite the group home for more discussion and light refreshments. At least once a quarter, we invited the members of Milton's workshop for refreshments and conversation. The conversation was always the more important part of the evening. Taken as a whole, the department was like a big family; we were closer to some but friendly with all. And that relationship still exists. We may not see one another for long periods, but when we do, the intervening years seem to fade away and we are again members of the family.

✦ Chapter Fifteen ✦

TEACHING

{ *Milton* }   During thirty years at Chicago, I taught mostly price theory (from 1948 to 1962, and again from 1971 to 1976) and monetary theory (an elementary course in the early years, the advanced course from 1963 to 1970). I also conducted seminars in assorted economic topics and in 1953, I established a Workshop in Money and Banking. My scientific writings covered a wide range, especially in the early years, but then concentrated more on monetary economics, where the workshop provided both stimulus and criticism for my own work, and an opportunity to supplement what I did with related work by students and colleagues. This combination gave birth to what came to be known as the Chicago School of Monetary Economics.

The Early Years and the G.I. Bill

The end of the war, reinforced by the G.I. Bill, produced a teaching environment that has been unique in my experience. Enrollment in institutions of higher education, which had fallen sharply during the war, more than doubled in the early postwar years. Our department had to accommodate a major influx of students. More important, the students were very different from the usual crop. They were more mature; many had been officers in the military and had exercised considerable responsibility; a large fraction were married; and essentially all were serious students, eager to complete their training and get started on their careers. They were unquestionably the ablest and most interesting students that it has been my privilege to teach.

The university had to make extraordinary efforts to accommodate the influx. I well recall the temporary housing on a previously vacant block on 58th Street that I passed each day on my way from home to office. Children, tricycles, bicycles, baby carriages—all the cheerful activity of a concentrated group of young families—sped me on my way.

The department too had to make adjustments. My major assignment was to teach the initial economic-theory course for graduate students—the course that Rose and I had taken from Jacob Viner fourteen years before. When we took it, the class numbered around thirty, and so it did also in later years. But when I recently went over some class lists dating from my early years at Chicago, I was reminded that some classes had as many as sixty students to accommodate the bulge. In addition, in several years I taught two separate sections in the same quarter. I recall that I initially thought that would be terribly boring. I was surprised to find that it was not, and that practice, if it did not make perfect, did improve the presentation, so that those in the second section benefited from what I had learned in the first.

I taught two sections for only a few years. For a longer period, I taught the two-quarter theory course twice a year, once in the fall and winter quarters, and a second time in the winter and spring quarters. In those early years, I also taught a one-quarter undergraduate course in money and banking. The courses typically met for fifty minutes three times a week. A normal full-time teaching load in our graduate department was two courses, or six teaching hours. To nonacademics that always sounds like a very light load. I am reminded of a story about a state legislature that was considering the appropriation for the state university. One legislator, a farmer, asked, "How many hours do they teach?" After being told "twelve," he remarked, "Not a bad day's work."

Of course, the actual time devoted to teaching is always some multiple of class hours because of the time spent in preparation of material, consultations with students, and grading of exams. In addition, our department prepared and administered what were called "preliminary examinations" that all students had to take to qualify for master's and doctor's degrees. Those examinations covered a subject-matter field, not the content of a specific course, and were prepared and graded by a committee of faculty members. Finally, supervising master's and doctor's theses is generally more time-consuming than classroom teaching—but also very rewarding, since it typically complements a scholar's own research.

When I retired from active teaching at the age of sixty-five, I said, half-seriously, that I was doing so because I had graded enough exam papers in my life. I have always enjoyed teaching and interaction with students. Grading exams, on the other hand, is something else. I have never been satisfied with multiple-choice questions that can be graded mechanically, feeling that any examination is a waste of time if its only function is to grade the student. An exam should contribute to the education of the student and serve as a stimulating experience. I always tried, therefore, to avoid questions that called for pure regurgitation of material from class discussions or assigned readings and to include questions that required the students to apply the principles they had been taught to a problem they had not encountered. Grading such questions is tedious work: reading perhaps thirty to sixty answers to the same question. More troubling, however, is the blow to one's self-confidence. Time and again you find that the students have not really understood what you thought you had made crystal-clear. They may be able to repeat it, but only a few can apply it in a new context. Your own failures as a teacher are what make grading papers not only a tedious but a depressing task.

Interestingly enough, many of those same students, when they took the preliminary examination in the same field a year or two later without having taken additional courses, demonstrated an understanding that they earlier lacked. As I first realized while a student myself, students learn more from one another and by themselves than from their professors.

Price Theory

Like Viner, I stressed original sources in my reading list, using the course as a way to introduce students to the great economists of the past as well as to more recent developments. Like him also, I taught economic theory as, in Alfred Marshall's words, an "engine for the discovery of concrete truth,"[1] not as a branch of mathematics. This was, and I believe remains, the distinctive feature of "Chicago economics," in sharp contrast to economic theory as taught at some other leading centers of graduate economics. As George put it in his memoirs, the "Chicago tradition . . . proceeded from the assumption that modern price theory is a powerful weapon in the understanding of economic behavior, not simply a set of elegant theoretical exercises suitable for instruction and the demonstration of one's mental agility."[2]

I based grades in the course not only on a written examination but also on take-home problems that I assigned. These generally dealt with puzzles in the application of economic theory to concrete issues, puzzles most of which had arisen in conversations with colleagues, especially George and Aaron, and to which no answer had yet appeared in the literature at the time I assigned

the problem. In the course of time, the problems generated a substantial literature by former students or colleagues.*

I was led to follow that practice by an experience during one of the first
years that I taught the course. I had assigned a problem in class to which the
most original and penetrating answer had been given by a Chinese student,
who at the end of the term did very poorly on the written exam. Although
he had mastered the theory and was highly original in applying it, he did not
have a quick mind and had difficulty in replying spontaneously to a series of
questions on a written exam. That episode persuaded me that written exams
alone were inadequate and that I should base my judgments of quality at least
as much on take-home problems as on the exam.[3]

A few years after I started teaching the course on price theory, two enterprising students (David I. Fand and Warren J. Gustus) collaborated in preparing summaries of my lectures in the course. After revision and additions by

---

* A sample problem:

Medical Care Financed by Taxation

Suppose a plan for medical insurance were adopted under which individuals paid for
medical care in the form of taxes levied on them in the same manner as other taxes. Assume
that no additional fee is charged, so that patients may call on physicians of their own choice
at any time without specific charge, and that no drastic changes were made in the organization
of medical practice. Assume also, for 1, 2, 3, and 4 below, that the number of physicians is
the same as before the system was adopted. As an economist,

1. What would you expect to be the reaction of patients? Explain in terms of demand
curves.

2. What would you expect to be the reaction of physicians if each physician were paid a
flat fee by the state for each patient-visit? Would the reaction be different if the physician were
paid an annual lump-sum salary? If so, how?

3. What variable might be expected to produce an equilibrium? How would it operate?

4. What conflict would arise between the reactions of patients and physicians? Would the
conflict be affected by the manner in which physicians were paid? Can you suggest any means
for resolving the conflict, subject to the limitation of a given number of physicians?

5. Suppose the conflict were resolved by an adjustment in the number of physicians, the
state paying whatever was required to get the necessary number and the entire cost being financed by taxes. What kind of adjustment would be required? *If* you accept individuals' judgments as final and as the sole consideration, and *if* you neglect entirely any effects on the
distribution of income, what, if anything, can you say about the effect of the change in the
manner of handling medical service on the efficiency of allocation of resources? State your
answer in terms of the relevant rates of substitution.

6. Why the two "if" clauses in 5?

Here are the titles of a few other problems: "Sears, Roebuck & Co., Allstate, and Diversifi-
cation," "The Economics of Tie-in Sales," "The Economics of Internal Pricing," and "The
Economics of Toll Roads."

Sample problem and titles from Milton Friedman, *Price Theory*, rev. and enlarged ed.
(Chicago: Aldine, 1976), pp. 330–34.

me, these summaries formed the basis for mimeographed versions that were used in my classes and also by other faculty members who taught the course. I wrote in the preface to *Price Theory: A Provisional Text* when it was published in 1962:

It is now more than a decade since the contents of this book were first mimeographed and used in classes in price theory at the University of Chicago. Throughout that period, I have been extremely reluctant to have these notes offered for general sale. The reluctance has derived from my dissatisfaction with their scrappy nature, from my intention to use them as a basis for a fuller and more satisfactory treatment of price theory, and from my optimistic belief that I would be able to turn to the preparation of the fuller treatment momentarily. As an empirical economist, however, I cannot neglect the evidence that has accumulated in that decade. Clearly, I must reject the hypothesis that a fuller treatment is imminent. Moreover, it has not been feasible to keep the mimeographed notes from getting fairly wide circulation. Hence, despite my continued dissatisfaction with them, it has seemed best to make them generally available.

In accordance with the term "provisional" in the title of the book, it was published in a rather flimsy large-size paperback version. Fourteen years later, in 1976, a revised and expanded edition was published, this time in hardback, and titled simply *Price Theory*. I wrote in the preface to that edition:

Shortly after the initial edition of this book was published, I shifted for nearly a decade from teaching price theory to teaching monetary theory. Three years ago, I resumed teaching price theory. Next year (the academic year 1975–76), I plan to teach it for the last time. Hence, if I were ever to revise substantially the provisional version that was published in 1962, now seemed the time to do it.

I cannot pretend that the present version is the finished treatise that I had in mind (or in youthful dreams) in the earlier years of teaching the course. But it is a much expanded and, I hope, improved version. . . .

I cannot end this preface without recording the great personal satisfaction that I have derived from teaching price theory to successive generations of able and enthusiastic graduate students. The formal structure of price theory has an aesthetic quality that has always reminded me of the famous last lines of Keats's "Ode on a Grecian

Urn": "'Beauty is truth, truth beauty'—that is all ye know on earth, and all ye need to know."[4]

(The reader may recall that these lines of Keats had been impressed on me by a high school teacher of plane geometry in a not unrelated context.)

Though never a bestseller, the book has had considerable use as a textbook and still continues to sell respectable numbers year after year. The earlier version was translated into Spanish, Portuguese, and Japanese; the later version into German and French. More important from my own personal point of view, the availability of the mimeographed notes and, later, the printed version enabled me to cut down on formal lecturing when giving the course—reserving that simply for the addition of new material—and to use class time for discussion with the students, which I believe they—and certainly I—found more rewarding than formal lectures.

I cannot resist boasting of one trick that I used to assure that students would get to class on time. At the second meeting of the class, one or more students would invariably come in late. When each did so, I would stop the person and say something like, "If you come in late, you impose costs on all other members of the class. If you simply stay away, you impose costs only on yourself. Hereafter, if you can't arrive on time, why don't you simply skip the class?" By that device, I assured prompt attendance and also implicitly taught a fundamental economic concept: external effects.

Monetary Theory

I shifted to teaching monetary theory partly because my research had come to be concentrated in that area but mainly because the department felt that the contents of the price theory course had largely stabilized, while the teaching of monetary theory had lost coherence after Lloyd Mints, under whom Rose and I had studied the subject, retired in 1953. In the following decade, the course was taught by several different members of the department and its content varied widely. Though my research had come to be specialized in monetary economics, I had not been teaching monetary theory. As a way of avoiding excessive specialization, I preferred to teach in a field other than the one in which I was doing research.

Initially, I intended to prepare a textbook in monetary theory on the basis of my lectures, and indeed taped the lectures and had a transcript of the tapes made for that purpose. However, the transcripts of the tapes were extremely poor. After Rose spent a great deal of time trying to put them in reasonable shape, we decided that the effort required was greater than we could justify.

The Workshop in Money and Banking

In 1953 I introduced a version of the natural-science laboratory, patterning it after some earlier experiments along the same lines at the University of Chicago, particularly by Ted Schultz. The Workshop in Money and Banking and similar workshops in other areas at Chicago proved so successful that they have been copied at many other universities.

The initial workshop was located in a basement room in the Social Science Building that I managed to get assigned to me and furnished with discarded tables and chairs. With funds from a grant by the Rockefeller Foundation, I provided financial assistance to a number of students, and bought three second-hand electric desk calculators. (As I recall, I paid $300 each, a sum that would be equivalent to about $1,800 in 1996 prices. It is a measure of the extraordinary progress in computing technology that electronic hand-held calculators now used as advertising giveaways, or costing at most $10, can do everything those bulky desk calculators could do, and much more.)

The workshop was made up of about ten or so graduate students doing research in the field of money. They met once a week to discuss their problems and, as their work progressed, to present their results to the group for criticism and suggestions. As time passed, other faculty members at Chicago, from the Economics Department and the Business School, joined as members. In addition, scholars at other institutions occasionally presented preliminary research findings.

Throughout the more than quarter-century that I conducted the workshop, it had two key operating rules: first, no representation without taxation—i.e., no one was admitted unless he or she was doing active research in the monetary field (broadly interpreted) and was willing to present one or more papers; second, all meetings were on the basis of written papers circulated in advance, and their authors were permitted only five minutes or so to correct any errors in the paper or make qualifying or additional remarks.

I am persuaded that these rules contributed greatly to the success of the workshop. They made it a group of active research workers who met to help and criticize one another and prevented its becoming just a series of informational lectures—a useful but very different function performed by many graduate seminars.

The workshop was successful in teaching students methods of research, in fostering the rapid completion of doctoral dissertations, and in deepening the quality of work done in the field of money, both at Chicago and elsewhere, because the workshop gradually became a kind of testing ground for monetary research wherever located. Most of the research stimulated by the workshop ended up not simply in doctoral dissertations buried deep in library stacks but also in journal articles and books. The workshop itself published four books whose contents consisted mainly of dissertations done in the workshop. Some of the articles in these books have become classics on the topics they covered.[5] The cumulative effect of the work of different people approaching related problems in different ways has done far more to deepen our understanding of monetary phenomena than the work of any single scholar could have done.

While on the faculty at Chicago, I spent a year at Cambridge University in Britain, where I experimented with the tutorial method of teaching. That episode is covered in chapter 17. In addition, I taught for one quarter each at the University of California at Los Angeles and at the University of Hawaii, and I occasionally did briefer stints of a day or a few days elsewhere.

UCLA

The winter quarter of 1967 (January–March) that I spent as a visiting professor at UCLA was a very pleasant interlude. We had many friends on the UCLA faculty. Indeed, the UCLA Economics Department and Business School was for a long time referred to as Chicago West, because it was one of the few university departments other than Chicago that had a strong representation of proponents of the free market: Armen Alchian, Bill Allen, Jack Hirshleifer, Neil Jacoby, Clay LaForce, for a time, James Buchanan, and a number of others. In addition, I met a number of people in the business community who were politically active—most important, Henry Salvatori, a close friend, supporter, and promoter of Ronald Reagan.[6] He introduced me to Reagan, with whom I had a long and thoroughly enjoyable visit. At the time, Reagan was governor of California and very much involved in educational issues, especially at the University of California but also at the elementary and secondary levels. I was delighted to find that he was not only a warm, attractive human being, but that his views on educational issues were very much in line with my own.

One of Governor Reagan's proposals was to raise substantially the tuition at state colleges and universities. That was of course highly unpopular with the students at those institutions and produced a wave of student protests and demonstrations. At UCLA, the Economics Department—or perhaps it was a student economics society—decided to stage a debate on the issue. Professor Michael Intriligator of the economics faculty was designated to argue against the proposed raise in tuition, and I agreed to defend it. Not surprisingly, I was greeted with subdued boos when I walked into the room, and my opponent with hearty cheers. However, he had a weak case, and I a strong one. I told the students that they were objects of charity, that there was no government program that so clearly transferred income from low- to high-income people as government subsidization of higher education: that, to put it dogmatically, the people in Watts were paying the college expenses of the people from Beverly Hills—an image particularly appropriate for a debate conducted in Los Angeles.

This debate made a deep impression on me, because of the reaction of the audience. As the debate proceeded, the atmosphere changed from hostility to support, and, at the end, the audience voted by a large majority in favor of the position I was defending. It was an ironic outcome. Economists generally rely on people to pursue their own self-interest, rather narrowly defined. Yet here I was, an economist, appealing to the students to rise above their own self-interest, and they did so, at least for the time being. All of us when young tend to be more idealistic than we are later, and much more readily rise above self-interest. However, the capacity to interpret self-interest broadly is present at all ages. Adam Smith's *Wealth of Nations* is balanced by his *Theory of Moral Sentiments*.

One side benefit from our quarter at UCLA was cementing a friendship with Troy Allen, a Los Angeles broker, who had telephoned me out of the blue several years earlier to inquire whether I would be willing to talk to him about financial matters from time to time. He said he would like to pay me a small fee every time he called. This appealed to me not because the fee was significant but because he was the first person ever to call for advice who did not want something for nothing. We first met him in person during that winter quarter. By this time, Troy was running a modest financial enterprise that made Small Business Administration–guaranteed loans to small businesses. Years later, when we went to Palm Springs for a stay while I recuperated from a by-pass operation, we found, courtesy of Troy, a rented car in the garage of the condominium that Armen Alchian had leased for us, an electric coffee pot, and some wonderful coffee in the kitchen. Our last visit with Troy was a very sad one. He was then dying of lung cancer, and we met him at the Fairmont Hotel in San Francisco for a last good-bye.

Hawaii

During the winter quarter of 1972 I was a visiting professor at the University of Hawaii. My duties included teaching an elementary course in economics to undergraduates, something that I had never done. I had been approached by a number of publishers to consider writing an elementary text, and in response I had speculated on a possible unorthodox approach to teaching principles of economics. Indeed, while we were in Hawaii, Thomas Horton, an agent for Prentice-Hall, presented me with a fat mock volume of a "principles-of-economics" text supposedly authored by me in an attempt to whet my appetite. The ruse did not succeed, as I had long believed that a good text could be written only by someone who had taught such a course a number of times. However, it did continue a friendship with Tom that has lasted to this day. He later started his own publishing company which, on a suggestion from me, he named Thomas Horton and Daughters, since he had only daughters and no sons. His company later published several editions of a collection of some of my *Newsweek* columns.

Instead of first discussing the abstract principles of supply and demand in a competitive private market, as most elementary textbooks do, and then turning to the complications introduced by monopoly and government, I reversed the order, organizing the course around government price controls. Specific price controls—such as floors on agricultural prices and ceilings on rents—led into the concepts of demand and supply in particular markets—relative price theory. General price controls—such as had been imposed by President Nixon the year before—led into the determination of the general price level and monetary theory. Government fixing of exchange rates—again a hot topic in 1972 after Nixon's closing of the gold window in 1971—led into the theory of international trade and finance. So far as we could tell, the course was very successful. Unfortunately, I never had the occasion to repeat and fine-tune the approach.

In addition to the undergraduate course, I also led a graduate seminar, and conferred with both faculty and graduate students on their research projects. The faculty was very congenial, included at least one former student and several longtime acquaintances, and led to a number of new friendships.

My duties at the university left ample time for us to enjoy the physical, climatic, and cultural attractions of Hawaii. We devoted many weekends to visiting the islands other than Oahu, none of which we had ever visited before. We swam and snorkeled in the warm ocean, visited active volcanoes, enjoyed the varied tourist attractions, and explored superficially some of the jungle areas. We also sampled many of the cultural attractions of Hawaii's harmonious and prosperous multiracial society. I gave a number of talks to business and other groups and we both enjoyed the extraordinary hospitality that seems natural to residents of Hawaii.

Conclusion

As I look back on my thirty years of teaching at the University of Chicago and elsewhere, I realize how lucky I was. Those were enjoyable as well as productive years. Teaching supplemented and complemented my research. Teaching a subject is far and away the best way to learn it—and to discover what you do not know about it. The student body at Chicago was of consistently high quality, and did not hesitate to make it clear if you failed to explain something to their satisfaction. I learned as much from them as they learned from me. The faculty at Chicago was also of high quality. In addition, thanks to the leadership of Ted Schultz and his successors as chairmen, we were almost entirely spared the kind of faculty politics that is so common at institutions of higher learning and that we had endured at Wisconsin. Most of the faculty lived in the Hyde Park area around the university, as we did, which encouraged social interaction among the faculty members and between the faculty and students, producing a highly collegial atmosphere.

Teaching is not confined to the classroom. The teaching experiences described in this chapter are simply the formal organized part of a lifetime of teaching and learning under many circumstances and in many places. For example, one of the doctoral dissertations that was published by the Workshop in Money and Banking was by Michael Keran, who never spent a day as a student at the University of Chicago, but whom I met during a visit to Japan. He is not the only person who never took a formal course from me whom I would instinctively call my student. And he and many others are also my teachers. Teaching is very much a two-way process.

→ *Chapter Sixteen* ←

SCHOLARLY WORK

{ *Milton* } The public at large knows me best for my involvement in public policy and for Rose's and my writings on public policy and political philosophy. However, these have been an avocation, not a vocation. The bulk of my publications are in technical economics and, to a lesser extent, statistics. Public policy has always been a part-time activity.

Technical economics and public policy are intimately connected. Every public-policy issue involves two steps: predicting the consequences of a suggested policy and evaluating those consequences as good or bad. The first step is the domain of science, the second, of values. The distinction is easy to state but it is far from easy to keep the one domain from intruding on the other. (This issue is discussed further below.)

During our first few years at Chicago, my scholarly publishing consisted of articles in professional journals. In 1953, at the suggestion of Alex Morin at the University of Chicago Press, I collected some of these articles, plus two new ones, in a book titled *Essays in Positive Economics*. The two new articles, "The Methodology of Positive Economics" and "The Case for Flexible Exchange Rates," became two of my most widely cited and influential articles. Roughly half of the book consists of papers on "Monetary Theory and Policy," a field in which I had already begun to concentrate my research, thanks to rejoining the National Bureau of Economic Research in 1950 to assume responsibility for their monetary study.

Studies in the Quantity Theory of Money, published in 1956, was a product of the Workshop in Money and Banking and consists of a long introductory chapter by me plus four chapters summarizing doctoral theses written by student members of the workshop. Several of those chapters have become classics,[1] and all the authors have since had productive scholarly careers.

213

A Theory of the Consumption Function, published in 1957, was a long-delayed by-product of my involvement two decades earlier in the Study of Consumer Purchases. Its permanent-income theory of consumption expenditures has since become part of standard economics.

My collaboration with Anna J. Schwartz on the National Bureau monetary study produced three major scientific publications: *Monetary History of the United States* (1963), *Monetary Statistics of the United States* (1970), and *Monetary Trends in the United States and the United Kingdom* (1982).[2] The *Journal of Monetary Economics* has documented the significance of the *Monetary History* by publishing three retrospective reviews of the book to commemorate its thirtieth birthday.[3] In addition, selected journal articles are reprinted in *The Optimum Quantity of Money and Other Essays* (1969). Finally, in 1992, *Money Mischief,* subtitled *Episodes in Monetary History,* included some chapters that had been published earlier in professional journals, in addition to new material. Unlike most of my other academic work, it is written to be of interest to the general public as well as the academic community.

"The Methodology of Positive Economics"

I doubt that anything I have written has been responsible for so large a volume of secondary literature as this introductory article in *Essays in Positive Economics.* The controversy it engendered shows few signs of dying out four decades after its appearance. As J. Daniel Hammond writes, "It is almost trite to point out that Milton Friedman's essay . . . is a classic . . . work. The essay has been many things to many people since it was published in 1953. . . . Generations of graduate students have learned a lesson (*the* lesson for most) in what it means for economics to be a science. Philosophers and methodologists have seen it as Friedman's introduction of this or that philosophy of science to economists, or have used it as a whipping boy to expose the philosophical naiveté of economists, or to frame the parameters of the 'Chicago School.' "[4]

One reason for the controversy is doubtless that, as Thomas Mayer wrote forty years after its initial publication, "Friedman's essay is broadly consistent with the methodology that most economists now affirm, at least in principle."[5] The major source of disagreement is my contention that a theory should be judged by the conformity of its implications with observation and not by the realism of what are called its assumptions. As Mayer says, "In the context of its time, it was a plea for a positivistic interplay of theory and observation. On such a reading Friedman's plea for unrealistic assumptions becomes much more defensible."[6]

I conjecture that another reason it has stimulated so much secondary literature is that, after publishing it, I decided that I would rather do economics than spend more time writing about how economics should be done. As a result, I decided that I would not respond to any criticisms of the article. That left an open field for others—particularly philosophers concerned with scientific methodology—to conjecture about what I "really" meant, whether I was an "instrumentalist" or a "conventionalist" or a "Popperian falsificationist" or a "realist." The most recent manifestations of the secondary literature generated by the article are a 1990 book by Abraham Hirsch and Neil de Marchi, *Milton Friedman: Economics in Theory and Practice,* and a 1996 book by J. Daniel Hammond, *Theory and Measurement: Causality Issues in Milton Friedman's Monetary Economics.*

The essay had a long gestation period. An early draft dates from 1947, six years before it was finally published, and I had already embodied its central thesis in a 1946 book review. I no longer remember what got me started on methodology. It may have been the discussion at the time about the recently formalized theories of imperfect competition, and even more directly the questioning of orthodox marginal analysis on the ground that interviews with or questionnaire studies of businessmen indicated that businessmen "do not in fact reach their decisions by consulting schedules, or curves, or multivariable functions showing marginal cost and marginal revenue."[7]

Shortly after I had completed a first draft, George Stigler and I had long discussions with Karl Popper in 1947 at the founding meeting of the Mont Pelerin Society. The part of those discussions that I remember best had to do with scientific methodology. Popper's book, *Logik der Forschung,* published in Vienna in 1934, had already become a classic analysis of the methodology of the physical sciences, but my German was too limited for me to have read it even though I may have known about its existence. It was not translated into English until 1959, when it was published as *The Logic of Scientific Discovery,* so these discussions at Mont Pelerin were my first exposure to his views. I found them highly compatible with the views that I had independently come to, though far more sophisticated and more fully developed. That conversation had a good deal of influence on the final version of the essay, as did comments by George, Arthur Burns, and Dorothy Brady on successive drafts.

A more important influence on the content of the article was my interest in statistics and my close friendship and collaboration with Jimmie Savage. At the time, he was in the process of writing *The Foundations of Statistics* (1954), a book that was destined to revolutionize the philosophical foundations of statistics. He regarded statistics as a method of reaching decisions, and replaced the concept of objective probability, which had been the key notion in the classical statistics that I had learned, with personal probability, which is the key notion in what has come to be known as "Bayesian" statistics. To oversimplify, Jimmie would say, "The role of statistics is not to discover truth. The role of statistics is to resolve disagreements among people. It's to bring people closer together."

Similarly, I argued in my essay that the role of positive economics was to contribute to resolving differences among economists. And the essay itself was devoted to discussing "how to decide whether a suggested hypothesis or theory should be tentatively accepted as part of the 'body of systematized knowledge concerning what is'."[8] To put my central thesis in a nutshell, it was that "the ultimate test of the validity of a theory is not conformity to the canons of formal logic but the ability to deduce facts that have not yet been observed, that are capable of being contradicted by observation, and that subsequent observation does not contradict."[9]

A Digression on Why Economists Differ

Economics is widely believed to be rife with differences of opinion among equally eminent and reputable economists. The extent of disagreement is grossly overstated. On many issues, economists are nearly unanimous. However, on some issues, disagreement has persisted despite numerous studies directed at resolving the disagreement. Rose and I have disagreed for decades on the reason why economists differ. She explored the difference in one of her articles in *The Oriental Economist,* writing:

> In his [1953] essay on methodology, my husband wrote: "Laymen and experts alike are inevitably tempted to shape positive conclusions to fit strongly held normative preconceptions and to reject positive conclusions if their normative implications are unpalatable." But he ventured the judgment that especially in the United States "differences about economic policy among disinterested citizens derive predominantly from different predictions about the economic consequences of taking action—differences that in principle can be eliminated by the progress of positive economics—rather than from fundamental differences in basic values, differences about which men can ultimately only fight." He goes on to cite as one obvious example, minimum wage legislation, where there is surely an underlying consensus on the objective of achieving a living wage for all. The difference is largely based on an implicit or explicit difference in predic-

tions about the efficacy of this particular means in furthering the agreed-on end. "Proponents believe (predict)," he says, "that legal minimum wages diminish poverty by raising the wages of those receiving less than the minimum wage as well as of some receiving more than the minimum wage without any counterbalancing increase in the number of people entirely unemployed. . . . Opponents believe (predict) that legal minimum wages increase poverty by increasing the number of people who are unemployed . . . and that this more than offsets any favorable effect on the wages of those who remain employed." Other examples he cites are the appropriate role and place of trade-unions and the desirability of direct price and wage controls and of tariffs.

It is not difficult to see why different laymen might have different predictions about the economic consequences of certain actions when the experts disagree. One does not expect the layman to have an independent judgment about the direct results to say nothing of the side effects of certain medical treatment. In medicine, the layman is content to take the expert's judgment, and, as a rule, *one* expert's judgment. Though the experts in medicine, I sometimes believe, disagree about their predictions as much as do the economists, they do not proclaim their differences as eagerly as do the economists. Moreover, it is generally believed that once the evidence on a particular medical treatment is gathered, the medical experts will, in the main, agree.

In 1953, my husband made the same judgment about differences among professional economists in their policy views that I have made about medical experts. It was on the hypothesis that this was a valid judgment that he concluded "that a consensus on 'correct' economic policy depends much less on the progress of normative economics proper than on the progress of a positive economics yielding conclusions that are, and deserve to be, widely accepted." Consistent with his views on methodology, however, he said, "Of course, my judgment that the major differences about economic policy . . . are of this kind is itself a 'positive' statement to be accepted or rejected on the basis of empirical evidence."

On this issue, my husband and I have always differed though I am inclined to believe that he is moving in my direction. I have always been impressed by the ability to predict an economist's positive views from my knowledge of his political orientation, and I have never been able to persuade myself that the political orientation was the consequence of the positive views. My husband continues to resist this conclusion, no doubt because of his unwillingness to believe that his own positive views can be so explained and his characteristic generosity in being unwilling to attribute different motives to others than to himself.

By 1968, in the introduction to another collection of essays dealing with inflation, monetary policy, and the balance of payments (*Dollars and Deficits*) my husband modified and expanded his earlier judgment about why economists disagree. Referring to the minimum wage rate again, he admits that "it would be hard to find a reputable economist—of whatever political persuasion—who does not agree that legal minimum wage rates increase unemployment among the unskilled. It would be almost as hard to find one who regards other consequences of legal minimum wage rates as sufficiently favorable to outweigh the adverse effects on employment." And he concludes that most economists remain silent on the issue because they do not want to be regarded as "reactionary" and "hard-hearted."*

He suggests as another explanation of the differences among economists their tendency to mix economic judgments with judgments about political feasibility. Differences about the price of gold and of the dollar is one example. Though most economists favored flexible exchange rates, there was a general belief that they were not feasible politically, so they did not advocate them. As history once again demonstrated, economists are poor judges of what is politically feasible.

A final explanation which he gives for the differences in policy choices among economists is their differences in time perspective. "Given the same scientific judgments, the choice among policies will often depend on the importance attached to the short-term vs. the long-term consequences of the policies."

"Interestingly," he goes on, "there tends to be a close connection between beliefs about the role of government and time perspective . . . the person who gives primacy to freedom and believes in limited government tends to take the long view, to put major emphasis on the ultimate and permanent consequences of policies rather than on the immediate and possible transitory consequences. The modern lib-

* Our friend, Leo Rosten, has since provided a dramatic example. At a session with economists at MIT, he asked about their opinion of minimum wages. He was surprised to find agreement that they were harmful. "How is it," he said, "that I don't read your saying that to newspaper reporters?" The reply: "We couldn't do that or people would think we were agreeing with Milton Friedman."

eral—the person who gives primacy to welfare and believes in greater governmental control—tends to take the short view, to put primary emphasis on the immediate effects of policy measures."

The final paragraph of the essay on "The Methodology of Positive Economics" reads: "Progress in positive economics will require not only the testing and elaboration of existing hypotheses but also the construction of new hypotheses. On this problem there is little to say on a formal level. The construction of hypotheses is a creative act of inspiration, intuition, invention; its essence is the vision of something new in familiar material. The process must be discussed in psychological, not logical, categories; studied in autobiographies and biographies, not treatises on scientific method; and promoted by maxim and example, not syllogism or theorem."

To me, this seems subconsciously autobiographical, for it describes so well the personality traits that account for my husband's seminal contribution to economics and for the influence he has had on his students.[10]

As Rose said, by 1976, when her remarks appeared in print, I was already moving in her direction. I must confess that I have continued to move in that direction and that I am much less confident now that I am right and she wrong than I was more than four decades ago when I wrote the methodology article from which she quoted. I have repeatedly experienced attacks on what I regarded as scientific findings by economists who seemed driven more by their values than their objective judgment. The attack on George Stigler's and my *Roofs or Ceilings* discussed in chapter 9 was an early and mild example. Many more were to come.

"The Case for Flexible Exchange Rates"

This article had its origin in a memorandum that I wrote in the fall of 1950 when I was serving as consultant to the U.S. agency administering the Marshall Plan (see chap. 12). At the time the article appeared, it ran counter to conventional wisdom, though a number of professional economists had taken the same position earlier, including Henry Simons and Lloyd Mints. Over time, it gained the support of perhaps the majority of monetary economists in the U.S. But in the early 1950s, Bretton Woods was still in its infancy. It was based on a system of fixed exchange rates subject to change from time to time, presided over by the International Monetary Fund. High hopes were held that it would combine stability and predictability with the capacity through cooperation among the major countries to make necessary adjustments from time to time.

As repeated balance-of-payments crises arose despite the best efforts of the IMF, I engaged in many discussions of the issue.[11] I recall two in particular that together were amusing. Both were at meetings of bankers from around the world, one in 1969 in Copenhagen, the other in 1972 in Montreal. Between the two meetings, the Bretton Woods system collapsed when, on August 15, 1971, President Nixon announced, as part of a major package of economic measures, that the U.S. would no longer live up to its obligation under Bretton Woods to sell gold to other central banks at $35 an ounce. At both meetings, I shared a platform with the secretary general of the IMF—a different one on each occasion. At the first meeting, the secretary general dismissed my proposal for floating exchange rates as utterly impractical, as visionary theorizing by an academic who did not understand the real world. At the second meeting, his successor described floating exchange rates as the only practicable system, and dismissed fixed exchange rates as having been completely discredited by recent experience.

Two points are suggested by this episode. The first is how economists like myself exercise influence. I have long believed that we do not influence the course of events by persuading people that we are right when we make what they regard as radical proposals. Rather, we exert influence by keeping options available when something has to be done at a time of crisis. Such a crisis arose in 1971. If the alternative of floating exchange rates had not been fully explored in the academic literature, by me and by such other prominent economists as James Tobin and Gottfried Haberler, to mention only two, it is not clear what solution would have been adopted. It might well have been even more extensive capital and exchange controls. As it was, flexible exchange rates provided a clear alternative to the existing system.

The second point has to do with the immortality of bureaucratic organizations. The IMF was established at Bretton Woods to oversee a system of fixed exchange rates; the World Bank, to provide funds for reconstruction and development to war-ravaged and underdeveloped countries. When the fixed-rate system collapsed, the IMF lost its function. It should have been abolished. Of course it was not. Instead it recreated itself as a junior world bank to provide loans and advice to countries having balance-of-payments or other problems. In my opinion, it has done much harm in pursuing such activities, but that has not prevented it from growing in size and gaining enhanced prestige.

Despite the collapse of Bretton Woods, fixed exchange rates have retained their appeal, though they have not gained viability. The European Economic Community has tried to maintain fixed exchange rates among themselves: first, the so-called snake, which lasted from 1972 to 1979, though not without exits from and entries into the system and many changes of exchange rates. The snake was followed by the European Monetary System, a more formal arrangement. It lasted until 1992, though again not without numerous changes in exchange rates. A small remnant remains.[12] The Community is now trying the more ambitious venture of establishing a single currency.

Discussion of this issue is confused by the failure to distinguish between "pegged" exchange rates and a "unified" currency. All the above systems involved commitments by countries to assure a fixed price for their currency in terms of other currencies by following appropriate monetary policies. In every case, each country retained a separate central bank. The commitments are price-fixing commitments, like commitments to "peg" the price of wheat. They almost invariably break down.

The relation between the Hong Kong dollar at present and the U.S. dollar is very different. The Hong Kong monetary authority simply promises to give 7.8 Hong Kong dollars for one U.S. dollar and conversely. It can always do the first since it can authorize the printing of any required number of Hong Kong dollars. It can always do the second because it holds a volume of U.S. dollar assets sufficient to redeem every dollar of Hong Kong currency in circulation. This system unifies the Hong Kong and U.S. dollars, in much the same way that a dollar in San Francisco is unified to a dollar in New York. Similarly, in the heyday of the gold standard, the various gold standard currencies were all unified. Pound, franc, mark, dollar, etc., were simply different names for specified amounts of gold.

Unified currencies often make sense, especially for small economies. A small economy like Hong Kong can benefit by unifying its currency with that of its major trading partner. In order to do so it must refrain from having a central bank, which few countries are willing to do. If countries are unwilling to give up their central banks, then the best system is one of freely floating exchange rates. Experience since I reached that conclusion in 1950 has only strengthened my confidence in its validity, while also, as I wrote a few years back, "making me far more skeptical that a system of freely floating exchange rates is politically feasible. Central banks will meddle—always, of course, with the best of intentions. Nevertheless, even dirty floating exchange rates seem to me preferable to pegged rates, though not necessarily to a unified currency."[13]

A Theory of the Consumption Function

A Theory of the Consumption Function, published in 1957, comes closer than anything else that I have written to adhering faithfully to the precepts of my essay on methodology. That is one, but by no means the only, reason why I have long regarded it as my best purely scientific contribution, though not the most influential. And I am not the only one of that opinion. In an article that he wrote about my work for *The New Palgrave,* Alan Walters commented, "as an accomplishment of the intellect, one suspects that most of Friedman's peers would still regard his work on the consumption function as the maximum maximorum of his contributions to economics. . . . One closed *A Theory of the Consumption Function,* not with the feeling that nothing more need be said, but that whatever was discovered in the future must fit neatly into this superb and satisfying framework. The architecture could accommodate, and indeed so far has shaped and absorbed all new contributions."[14]

As I wrote in the preface of the book,

> The theory of the consumption function proposed in this book evolved over a number of years. During most of this period, I was not engaged in empirical work on consumption. Indeed, prior to writing this book, I had done none since 1935–37, when I was connected with the planning of the Study of Consumer Purchases. I nonetheless kept in close touch with empirical research on consumption, thanks to the combined accident of my wife's occasional interest in the field and of our joint friendship with Dorothy Brady. Mrs. Brady's unrivaled knowledge of the empirical evidence from family budget data, penetrating insights into their explanation, and deep understanding of the scientific problems involved in their analysis occasioned a series of conversations on the interpretation of consumption data, in which discussions Margaret Reid subsequently joined. Miss Reid, with characteristic enthusiasm, persistence, and ingenuity proceeded to put to a critical test the hypothesis that had been evolving out of these conversations. . . . When it seemed to be passing the test with flying colors, she pressed me to write up the underlying theory so that she could refer to it in a paper presenting her conclusions. This book is the result, and though my hand held the pen, and though I am fully responsible for all its defects, it is in essential respects a joint product of the group, each member of which not only participated in its development but read and criticized the manuscript in its various stages (p. ix).

After it was published, the theory went through the usual process of new scientific hypotheses: criticism, misunderstanding, rejection, exploration of alternatives, and after a long interval, clarification, grudging acceptance, and finally incorporation as part of the conventional view.

The book was part of an outpouring of research on the consumption function that followed the publication of John Maynard Keynes's *General Theory,* which initiated the Keynesian revolution in economic thought. A centerpiece of Keynes's theory was the relation between expenditures on consumption and income, or, equivalently between savings and income, which he termed the consumption function. Center stage was occupied by "the marginal propensity to consume," the fraction of an additional dollar of income that would be spent on consumption rather than saved. It was, he wrote, "a fundamental psychological rule of any modern community" that this fraction was less than one. He also conjectured that "as a rule . . . a greater *proportion* of income [is] saved as real income increases," i.e., the average propensity to consume declines with income.[15]

The exact size of the marginal propensity to consume determines the "multiplier," another key concept in Keynes's theory. It professes to tell how many dollars will be added to total income by an extra dollar of investment or government deficit spending. The multiplier was happily welcomed by governments as a scientific justification for what they were eager to do anyway, namely spend more without raising taxes.

Keynes's conjecture that the marginal propensity to consume fell with the level of income was a major component of the "secular stagnation" thesis propounded by Professor Alvin Hansen of Harvard in the late thirties. Professor Hansen was a late but ardent convert to Keynesianism and became the major missionary of the Keynesian vision to the unconverted. He claimed that as the U.S. had become wealthier, the propensity to save had increased, while the opportunities for investment had become exhausted. As a result, the U.S. was condemned to stagnation unless the government came to the rescue by higher government spending financed by deficits.

Under these circumstances, it is easy to understand why the consumption function became an object of a great deal of empirical research. As I wrote in chapter I of the book:

Theoretical interest stimulated empirical work. Numerical consumption functions were estimated from two kinds of data: first, time series on consumption, savings, income, prices, and similar variables available mostly for the period after World War I; second, budget data on the consumption, savings, and income of individuals and families available from numerous sample surveys made during the past century and a half. Both sources of data seemed at first to confirm Keynes's hypothesis. Current consumption expenditure was highly correlated with income, the marginal propensity to consume was less than unity, and the marginal propensity was less than the average propensity to consume, so the percentage of income saved increased with income. But then a serious conflict of evidence arose. Estimates of savings in the United States made by Kuznets for the period since 1899 revealed no rise in the percentage of income saved during the past half-century despite a substantial rise in real income. According to his estimates, the percentage of income saved was much the same over the whole of the period. The corresponding ratio of consumption expenditure to income—the constancy of which means that it can be regarded as both the average and the marginal propensity to consume—is decidedly higher than the marginal propensities that had been computed from either time series or budget data. Examination of budget studies for earlier periods strengthens the appearance of conflict. The average propensity to consume is roughly the same for widely separated dates, despite substantial differences in average real income. Yet each set of budget studies separately yields a marginal propensity decidedly lower than the average propensity. Finally, the savings ratio in the period after World War II was sharply lower than the ratio that would have been consistent with findings on the relation between income and savings in the interwar period. This experience dramatically underlined the inadequacy of a consumption function relating consumption or savings solely to current income. (Pp. 3–4)

One appealing hypothesis to explain these anomalies was proposed by Rose and Dorothy Brady in a jointly authored article.[16] They suggested "that a consumer unit's consumption depends not on its absolute income but on its position in the distribution of income among consumer units in its community." Other scholars proposed a variety of alternative hypotheses at about the same time, some very similar to Rose and Dorothy's relative-income hypothesis.

It occurred to me that a way to interpret income data that I had developed in studying professional incomes might provide the basis for a more general hypothesis of which the relative-income hypothesis suggested by Dorothy and Rose would be a special case. This is a nice example of serendipity in scientific work. A mode of analysis developed to explain incomes of professional persons turned out to be highly fruitful for the very different purpose of explaining the relation between the income of people and how much they spend on consumption. Still later, the same idea turned out to be fruitful in understanding monetary phenomena.

The idea that I borrowed from the study of professional incomes was to interpret actual or measured income as the sum of a number of components. In the professional income context, I had used three components: permanent, quasitransitory, and transitory. For the consumption theory, I simplified the approach by considering only two components, permanent and transitory.

The central theme of the book is embarrassingly obvious. People do not decide how much to spend on consumption each day or week or year by how much they receive in income on that day or week or year but on some longer-term expectation of the amount that they will have available to spend. Similarly, the flow of consumption services that people enjoy during any day or week or year does not depend on how much they spend that day or week or year but on their accumulated stock of goods providing services (such as owned home, car, refrigerator, etc.).

Almost all budget studies presented data on average consumption spending during a period for consumer units grouped by their income receipts during the same period. Consider the consumer units in the lowest income group. If they do not, in some sense, belong in that group it will be because their incomes are abnormally low. But in that case, it is not surprising that the amount they spend on consumption in that year is related to what they perceive to be their "usual" or "normal" or, in my terminology, "permanent" income rather than their measured income, and may well exceed their measured income. Savings for the group will be abnormally small or even negative.

Similarly, units classified in the highest income group are far more likely to be there because their incomes are abnormally high than because they are abnormally low. As a result, their average consumption will tend to be relatively low compared to their average measured income. Their average savings will be abnormally high.

These considerations explain why the observed budget data, with units classified by income, invariably show consumption rising with income but less than in proportion, producing the appearance that Keynes's marginal propensity to consume is less than unity and less than the average propensity for the sample as a whole.

If units were classified by amount spent on consumption rather than income received, the same considerations would tend to make average income in the lowest consumption class high relative to consumption and conversely at the other end of the consumption scale. Accordingly, consumption would rise more rapidly than income, indicating a marginal propensity to consume greater than unity and greater than the average propensity (see also the discussion of regression fallacy in chapter 4).

These considerations can explain qualitatively the apparent conflict between the results for time series and budget data. National income and consumption average out the transitory elements special to individual consumer units, though leaving in any transitory influences on the community as a whole. However, these are likely to vary much less from year to year than among individual units in a single year. Hence, any bias resulting from transitory influences is likely to be smaller. It is still true that the two opposite ways of estimating the consumption function, plotting consumption against income or income against consumption, will give different results, but they will not differ much and there is no difficulty in accepting the observed evidence that national consumption equals roughly the same percentage of national income for a long period of years.

As noted, all this is embarrassingly obvious. The task is to translate this qualitative discussion into a specific model that can be used to interpret observed data, to extract from it implications sufficiently specific and well enough defined as to be subject to rejection when confronted with the relevant data, and to see whether the hypothesis is in fact rejected when it is so confronted.

The consumption book was devoted to that task. The final chapter, after stating the hypothesis formally and summarizing the evidence adduced in support of it, went on to list generalizations about consumer behavior derived from it, and outlined some of its implications for research, economic understanding, and economic policy. The chapter, as well as the book, concludes by saying, "An enumeration of the implications of acceptance of a new hypothesis can never hope to be exhaustive. Indeed, one of the main implications is that it will stimulate people to think in new directions and new ways that cannot possibly be specified in advance. Even though I have ventured in this section well beyond my empirical evidence and the areas of my own competence, I have no doubt omitted more of the ultimate implications of the permanent income hypothesis than I have included. This is at once the appeal and the justification of what we flatter ourselves by calling 'pure' research."

About the same time as the consumption book was published, two other scholars, Franco Modigliani and Richard Brumberg (who had been a student of mine a few years earlier), proposed and published a hypothesis inspired by the same general approach, the life-cycle theory of consumption, which viewed consumer behavior as directed at smoothing consumption over a life cycle.

Both hypotheses were initially sharply criticized. To give the flavor of the discussion that was generated, one early review of my book presented extensive statistical evidence that was said to contradict the permanent-income hypothesis, and yet to be a test that I myself had suggested. The review concluded that "the permanent income hypothesis may yet become a useful tool of economic analysis. As of now it must be regarded as a novel idea whose interest lies neither in its theoretical plausibility nor its empirical validity, in both of which respects it is unsatisfactory, but in the further research which it is likely to stimulate."[17] Six months later in the same journal came a reply, not by me but by another economist, pointing out that the first reviewer had misinterpreted the test that I had suggested and that when the test was performed correctly, it tended to confirm rather than contradict the hypothesis. The commentator went on to make what he regarded as an even more stringent test that proved consistent with the hypothesis. The initial reviewer conceded that the test he had made was inappropriate, but concluded, "the process of testing the hypothesis has only just begun," a proposition that was to be amply confirmed.[18]

With the passage of time, the permanent-income and life-cycle hypotheses have, in one version or another, become part of conventional wisdom. The large volume of further research generated by the hypotheses has not confirmed either specific hypothesis in every detail, and indeed has produced many examples of detailed behavior inconsistent with them. But it can surely be said that the further research has strongly supported the general approach and has demonstrated repeatedly its fruitfulness in generating testable implications.

Though the permanent-income hypothesis generated much controversy, it was of a wholly different kind from that generated by the study of professional incomes. The controversy was within the profession, not outside it, and concerned technical matters rather than prominent public institutions. It did have important implications for public policy but not of a kind that was the subject of popular dispute. As a result, the reviewing process at the National Bureau went smoothly and there was no significant delay in the publication of the book. The period between the gestation of the hypothesis and its publication was more than four years, but I was responsible for most of that by my attempt to make the evidence presented as extensive as I could.

Monetarism versus Keynesianism

In 1950, Arthur Burns, who had taken over from Mitchell as director of research, asked me whether I would take responsibility for the part of the study dealing with the role of money in business cycles. Both his invitation and my acceptance of it demonstrate the interest that I had already developed in the role of money, as manifested in the articles on the subject reprinted in my *Essays in Positive Economics.*

Accepting his invitation had a major effect on my scholarly activities for the next three decades. It was one of the chief reasons I established the Workshop in Money and Banking several years later. The combination of the university and the bureau proved to be extremely productive. It is not too much to say that for the next several decades they accounted for the bulk of significant scientific work in the English-speaking world on the role of money and monetary policy in the economy.

By 1950, the triumph of Keynesianism had relegated the classical quantity theory of money to the ash heap of discarded shibboleths.[19] The conventional view in the economics profession had come to be that "money does not matter," that what mattered was "autonomous" spending—primarily government spending plus private investment. Fiscal policy was crucial, monetary policy a minor adjunct.

The situation today is entirely different. The simple form of Keynesianism that ruled the roost in the 1950s is dead. The language remains, but the substance is gone. Almost all economists—whether they label themselves Keynesians, monetarists, rational expectationists, or believers in a real business cycle—recognize that money does matter, that what happens to the quantity of money has important effects on economic activity in the short run and on the price level in the long run.

The publication in 1956 of the workshop's *Studies in the Quantity Theory of Money* was the first major step in a counterrevolution in monetary theory that succeeded in restoring the classical quantity theory to academic respectability under the unlovely label of "monetarism." My introduction, "The Quantity Theory of Money—A Restatement," came to be regarded as defining a "modern quantity theory" which offered an alternative to Keynesianism, and other essays in the book as showing the fecundity of such an approach.

A Commission on Money and Credit organized by the Ford Foundation in 1958 to evaluate the financial structure and make recommendations for changes indirectly led to a second step. The members of the commission were prominent public figures, including commercial bankers and representatives of other financial institutions. It had a professional research staff and farmed out numerous projects to outside consultants. One member of the commission was Gaylord A. Freeman, Jr., at the time general vice-president of the First National Bank of Chicago. In a personal letter to me nearly twenty years later, he reported an episode that illustrates the general attitude at the time: "I am sure that I have told you that, during the Commission on Money and Credit

Rose's parents, Samuel and
Sarah Director, about 1930

Milton's parents, Sarah and Jeno Friedman with, *left to right*, Helen, Milton, Ruth, and
Tillie, 1917

Rose at age six, 1918

Milton at graduation from Rutgers University, 1932

Rose and Milton in Washington, D.C., during cherry blossom season, 1938

Milton, George Stigler, and Aaron Director at the founding meeting of the Mount Pelerin Society, 1947

Rose, Milton, David, and Janet, 1947

David and Janet with their paternal grandmother, Sarah Friedman, 1949

Friedman family on a ship to Europe with Arthur and Helen Burns, 1950

George Stigler, Milton, and W. Allen Wallis in the 1950s

Top, David at thirteen with his maternal grandfather, Sam Director, 1958

Bottom, Rose and Dorothy Brady at the Hideaway, 1966

Milton with President Nixon and Secretary of the Treasury Shultz in the Oval Office, 1971

Rose and Milton with Gatsha Buthelezi and Barbara Feldberg in South Africa, 1976

Milton at the Nobel ceremony, 1976

Rose and Milton at the Nobel Ball, 1976

Milton picking up the mail at Capitaf, about 1975

Rose receiving an honorary degree from Pepperdine University, 1986, with Richard and Jill Rosenberg, Jo An and Barry Gumbert, and Milton.

hearings, I repeatedly asked them to have you as a witness. The staff finally agreed to have you, but after dinner, as an entertainer, because they didn't feel they should take your economic theories seriously."[20]

I talked to them on March 11, 1960, and submitted a proposal for research for which they gave me a grant of $10,000, which came in very handy to help finance my workshop. The paper I submitted and which was published in one of the commission volumes was a joint paper with David Meiselman, "The Relative Stability of Monetary Velocity and the Investment Multiplier in the United States, 1897–1958."[21] The paper questioned the validity of one, if not the central, tenet of Keynesianism, the stability and importance of the "multiplier," and aroused a strong reaction from the Keynesians. The resulting controversy dominated an entire issue of the *American Economic Review,* what with two critiques, our reply, and rejoinders by the critics. The controversy came to be referred to as the battle of the radio stations, since our paper was referred to as FM, and the major critique as AM, for its joint authors, Albert Ando and Franco Modigliani.[22]

As we wrote in our reply to the *AER* papers, "Because [our article] questioned the new orthodoxy, we expected it to provoke controversy. That it has done so impresses us less than the large area of agreement between our critics and ourselves." Not surprisingly, the critics in their rejoinders denied any such agreement. The course of this controversy is one that I have experienced repeatedly. The initial reaction of defenders of an orthodox view is to reject out of hand any criticism of their central doctrines. Then if the criticism continues and even gains some support, they reluctantly concede that the criticism may have some validity, but, they add, the criticism is too extreme. In this case, their initial position was close to "money does not matter." They subsequently abandoned that position but accused me of claiming that "money is all that matters," whereas reasonable people like themselves recognize that money does matter but "autonomous" expenditures are even more important.

The commission issued its report in 1961, before it had received or published most of the research studies it had commissioned. One session of the 1961 meeting of the American Economic Association was devoted to a discussion of the report. My review of the report was highly critical, maintaining that it begged all the important issues.[23] The other four members of the AEA panel were for the most part much more favorable to the report than I, and several went out of their way to distinguish their reaction from mine, further evidence of the extent to which my views were regarded as idiosyncratic.

Anna Schwartz's and my *Monetary History* was published in the same year as the FM paper and it undoubtedly played a more important role in changing the tide of professional opinion by presenting extensive evidence from history on the consistent relation between monetary change and subsequent economic change.

For example, in a 1965 review article in the *AER*, James Tobin, a leading Keynesian and 1981 recipient of the Nobel Prize in Economics, while strongly critical of some of our conclusions, is on the whole very favorable, commenting,

> Many controversies on monetary theory and policy pit Friedman and his followers against the rest of the profession. But consensus among Friedman's opponents generally extends no further than the proposition that Friedman is wrong. In the course of their narrative, F&S frequently pause to point out error and to allege harm from Keynesian ways of thinking.
>
> But as F&S led me through major decisions of monetary politics and monetary policy of the past century, I did not find their Monday morning quarterbacking very controversial.

And he ends his twenty-one page review, "This is one of those rare books that leave their mark on all future research on the subject."[24]

My next important contribution to the ongoing controversy between Keynesianism and what had come to be dubbed "monetarism" was my presidential address to the American Economic Association in December 1967.[25] I there questioned the validity of the Phillips curve—the notion that there was a permanent trade-off between inflation and unemployment, so that policy makers could choose from a menu of alternative rates of inflation and unemployment; the higher the rate of inflation they were willing to tolerate, the lower the rate of unemployment they could achieve. I argued that any such trade-off was strictly temporary, and resulted solely from unanticipated changes in inflation. As employers and workers caught on to what was happening, any trade-off would disappear. I introduced the concept of a "natural rate of unemployment" to which the level of unemployment would tend whatever the rate of inflation, once economic agents came to expect that rate of inflation.[26] To keep unemployment below the natural level requires not simply inflation, but accelerating inflation.[27]

By now, the concept of a natural rate of unemployment and the temporary character of any Phillips trade-off are conventional wisdom—indeed a book has recently been published, edited by Rod Cross, entitled *The Natural Rate of Unemployment: Reflections on 25 Years of the Hypothesis*. At the time, however, as I noted in the paper, it went very much "against the grain of current thinking," and indeed still does for lay and journalistic opinion. The acceptance of the view that I expressed owed a great deal to the graphic demonstration in the 1970s that a policy of using monetary policy to reduce unemployment did indeed, as I had claimed, lead to accelerating inflation rather than to permanently lowering unemployment. The unlovely term "stagflation" was invented to describe a situation for which there was no place in the Keynesian lexicon. James Tobin, still an unreconstructed Keynesian, gave me a backhanded compliment when, in his contribution to the Cross volume, he referred to my presidential address as "very likely the most influential article ever published in an economics journal. Its influence reached way beyond the profession—for example, to European and Japanese governments and central banks and to *The Economist* and other opinion leaders. Europe has never really recovered from the recessions of 1974–75 and 1979–82, and now the entire democratic capitalist world is stagnating"[28]—all because of the dreadful influence of my article!

After the *Monetary History* was published, a number of reviewers "criticized the absence of an explicitly stated theory of the role of money in income determination capable of generating the propositions supported by the extensive empirical investigation." In response, I published two strictly theoretical articles in 1970 and 1971 in the *Journal of Political Economy*. Robert Gordon, coeditor of the *JPE* at the time, solicited "critical reviews from a number of noted monetary theorists." These were published in the *JPE* along with an extensive reply by me. Gordon then assembled them all and published them as a book, *Milton Friedman's Monetary Framework: A Debate with His Critics.*[29]

When this book was published, Keynesianism was still dominant in the profession, although its hold had been greatly weakened. President Nixon was quoted as saying that "Now I am a Keynesian in economics," and *Time* magazine (December 31, 1965) quoted me as saying "We are all Keynesians now." As I explained in a letter to *Time* (February 4, 1966), the quotation is correct but taken out of context. As best I can recall, the context was: "In one sense, we are all Keynesians now; in another, nobody is any longer a Keynesian." The second half is at least as important as the first—the first sense had to do with rhetoric, the second with substance.

The real body blow to Keynesianism was delivered by the experience of the 1970s. As Bob Lucas wrote in a review of a book by Tobin,

> Friedman and Phelps had no way of foreseeing the inflation of the 1970s, . . . but the central forecast to which their reasoning led was a conditional one, to the effect that a high-inflation decade should not have less unemployment on the average than a low-inflation de-

cade. We got the high-inflation decade, and with it as clear-cut an experimental discrimination as macroeconomics is ever likely to see, and Friedman and Phelps were right. It really is as simple as that. This view seems to me to remove most of the mystery as to the origins of recent challenges to Keynesian orthodoxy. They did not spring out of nowhere."[30]

I do not want to leave a misleading impression. Keynesianism is still far from dead, especially with respect to its influence on public policy. Moreover, approaches other than the monetarism and Keynesianism that I have been discussing have been and are being developed. Yet the state of opinion is very different from that of the early 1950s.

The Monetary Volumes

The National Bureau of Economic Research had long devoted much of its effort to research on business cycles—essentially an attempt to expand and improve Wesley Mitchell's classic 1913 volume *Business Cycles*. As director of research at the National Bureau, Mitchell himself published, as author or joint author, three volumes on business cycles, and sponsored the publication of others in the bureau's series, "Studies in Business Cycles."[31] In addition, he accumulated an extremely lengthy typewritten draft of what he planned to be a definitive work on business cycles. When he decided that he was not himself going to be able to complete his initial plan, he parceled out the separate chapters to different scholars who would each prepare a monograph on a specific topic.

Prior to my undertaking this task, the bureau had assembled much relevant data, analyzed according to standard NBER statistical techniques. More important, Anna Jacobsen Schwartz, a staff member in charge of the accumulation and analysis of monetary data, was assigned to work with me on the project. Her skills, which are extraordinary, happen to complement my own to a remarkable degree. Moreover, we got along extremely well personally. As I said at a conference honoring Anna for her many years of productive research, "We have collaborated with one another for over thirty years. . . . During those thirty years, I do not recall any kind of personal acrimony or altercation, even though we had many differences of opinion about individual items. . . . I always knew that everything she did was going to be done right. It was going to be precise, it was going to be accurate, it was going to be thoughtful. Moreover, both of us were prepared to change our views or to change what we had done or written if the other provided evidence that we were wrong or that there was a better way."[32]

Of the three major volumes we produced, the first, *Monetary History of the United States,* has unquestionably been the most influential. I have already referred to its effect on the Keynesian-monetarism controversy. In addition, the book's reinterpretation of the Great Depression had a significant influence on the broader issue of the appropriate role of the government in guiding the economy.

The depression led to a drastic change in public opinion about the role of government: to oversimplify, from the view that government was a necessary evil to the view that government was the solution to almost any social or economic problem. Conventional scholarly opinion reinforced the change in public opinion especially after the publication of Keynes's *General Theory.* The depression—so it was widely believed—occurred despite the best efforts of the Federal Reserve, and demonstrated the limits of monetary policy. In an image that became common, it was said that monetary policy was like a string: you could pull it (i.e., use it to restrain a boom) but you could not push on it (i.e., use it to offset a recession or depression).

We demonstrated that the actual situation was very different, that the Fed was largely responsible for converting what might have been a garden-variety recession, though perhaps a fairly severe one, into a major catastrophe. Instead of using its powers to offset the depression, it presided over a decline in the quantity of money by one-third from 1929 to 1933. If it had operated as its founders intended, it would have prevented that decline and, indeed, converted it into the rise that was called for to accommodate the normal growth in the economy. Far from the depression being a failure of the free-enterprise system, it was a tragic failure of government.

The chapter on the four years of the Great Contraction covers more than one hundred of the seven hundred pages devoted to the ninety-three years from 1867 to 1960, and has been reprinted as a separate book. There remain many differences of opinion about the precise explanation of the Great Depression, and much work has been done on that subject since our book appeared. However, almost every analysis currently regards the decline in the quantity of money as playing a major role. That view is now conventional whereas, before our book appeared, it was idiosyncratic.[33]

One amusing recent incident about the *Monetary History.* Anna Schwartz and I published an op-ed piece, "A Tale of Fed Transcripts," in the *Wall Street Journal* on December 20, 1993, dealing with recent congressional concern about the Fed's resistance to providing information about its meetings. We wrote:

This recent and continuing brouhaha recalls our own experience with the Fed when we were writing our "Monetary History" (published in 1963). At the time, the Fed made public only . . . summaries of the Board's or FOMC's policy decisions. . . .

After we had completed our semifinal manuscript we sent a copy on Jan. 5, 1962, to William McChesney Martin, chairman of the board at the time, asking for criticisms and, in particular, the correction of any factual errors we might have made because we lacked access to minutes of Fed meetings.

We received a courteous reply dated Jan. 15, acknowledging the receipt of the copy and saying, "We will do the best we can to let you have any comments or suggestions by Feb. 15, but as I am sure you realize we are under considerable pressure at that time of the year." We never heard another word—no criticisms, no corrections of errors, nothing. Despite the official silence, we learned through unofficial channels that a lengthy review of our manuscript had been prepared at the Fed for internal circulation, but we were unable to get a copy.

Now the amusing part. A few weeks after the op-ed piece appeared, I received a letter from David Townsend, a professor at Sam Houston State University, reading as follows: "I was fascinated by your recent contribution to the *Wall Street Journal*. . . . A copy of the Fed's in-house review of your 'Monetary History' is enclosed. I was not aware that my review was not sent to you and the National Bureau. If you read my comments written 32 years ago, perhaps you will understand why the Fed stonewalled."

Enclosed was a memo to the Board of Governors from Guy E. Noyes, then director of the Division of Research and Statistics, reading, "The attached review of Professor Friedman's forthcoming monumental work on money was prepared by Professor Townsend of the University of Texas, who is working here for a year on leave of absence. The style differs from that of the typical Federal Reserve staff memorandum, but I am circulating it without revision, with the thought that you may find the change refreshing."

The review (dated February 8, 1962) is on the whole extremely favorable and ends with the statement, "It is very difficult to do justice to this important work in a short review. Perhaps the principal task of a staff reviewer is to provide sufficient inducement for the Board and its staff to invest their time in reading the entire book."

The review does contain some criticisms and suggestions that would have been useful to us at the time. But, as Townsend predicted, reading his review enables us to "understand why the Fed stonewalled."

The American Economic Association

At the 1965 annual meeting of the American Economic Association, I was elected to serve as president-elect for 1966.[34] The president-elect is responsible for organizing the program for the next annual meeting, and then automatically becomes president for the following year, responsible for presiding over the affairs of the association and winding up his term by giving a presidential address at that year's annual meeting.

I regard shepherding through the conversion of the *Journal of Economic Abstracts* into the *Journal of Economic Literature* and the appointment of Mark Perlman as its first editor as my greatest contribution as president. Mark served with distinction in that position for fourteen years. By the end of his editorship, the *JEL* was established as the world's outstanding journal for reviews and summaries of the flood of economic literature. (As an aside, Mark is the son of Selig Perlman who played an important role in our Wisconsin episode many years earlier. See chapter 6.) After my term, the editorship of the *American Economic Review* also became vacant and I chaired the committee that named the new editor. We chose George Borts, a former student of mine, who served with distinction for eleven years.

I had two reasons for favoring the establishment of a new journal devoted exclusively to surveys of economic literature. The first, and by far the more important, was the belief that such a journal was badly needed. That belief grew out of discussions some quarter of a century earlier among George Stigler, Arthur Burns, and myself in which we expressed dismay about the quality of the reviews of economic books that appeared in the various professional economic journals. We felt that they were cursory, and tended to be unduly favorable because of the old-boy network combined with the signing of the reviews. More important, we felt that we needed critical and thorough surveys not merely of individual publications but of important areas of research. In our idealistic speculation, we conceived of a permanent staff of competent economists who would check the accuracy of the evidence presented— whether data or citations—evaluate the current state of understanding in a designated area, and publish their conclusions anonymously, so that there would be no barrier to utter frankness. The seed planted by these discussions flourished.

George wrote a number of articles on the accuracy of citations and quotations in published articles, finding that there were numerous errors. When I became president-elect of the AEA in 1966, I encouraged the appointment of a committee, which I chaired, on the two publications then issued by the association: the *American Economic Review* and the *Journal of Economic Abstracts*. During the next two years, we explored the possibilities and ended by recommending the replacement of the *Journal of Economic Abstracts* by a journal very like the one we had dreamed of decades earlier, except that it was never feasible to hire a permanent staff of reviewers or to enforce anonymity. In the years that followed, Mark Perlman did a splendid job arranging for extensive reviews of branches of literature, as well as lengthy reviews of important new books, while continuing briefer reviews of the many new books appearing each year, listing the contents of an increasingly wide assortment of economic journals, and abstracts of many of the articles in those journals.

My second reason for favoring a new, extensive, and expensive AEA journal was financial. Thanks to the careful husbanding of the association's resources and wise investment, its longtime secretary-treasurer, James Washington Bell, had managed to build up a substantial endowment for the association by the time he retired as secretary-treasurer in 1961 after twenty five years of service. When I became president in 1967, the endowment was roughly a half million dollars. It has long been my opinion that professional associations should avoid accumulating an endowment, that they should operate on dues and other current income. An endowment is a continuing temptation for the association to get involved in extraneous activities (such as promoting particular political views, or subsidizing individuals who are temporarily in positions of power). The new journal seemed to me an excellent way to use much of the endowment in a professionally productive way, and so it proved. It is not often that youthful dreams can be realized decades later!

An interesting episode during my tenure had to do with Greece. In April 1967, the military staged a coup and assumed power there, arresting a large number of prominent politicians whom they regarded as dissidents. Among those arrested, and later given a nine-year prison sentence, was Andreas Papandreou, which provided the link with the AEA. Papandreou was the son of Georgios Papandreou, who for many years was prime minister of Greece, and its major political figure. As a youth, Andreas had emigrated to the United States, where he was trained as an economist and entered on an academic career.

I first met Papandreou when he was teaching at Berkeley, where he became chairman of the Department of Economics. In the 1960s, he set up a "Center of Economic Research" in Athens, which was my base in January 1963 on a round-the-world trip. As late as December 1962, he gave a paper at the annual meeting of the AEA, listing himself as Department of Economics, Berkeley.[35] He undoubtedly was a member of the AEA at that time. I do not know whether he was still a member in 1967, by which time he had become one of the foremost and controversial political figures in Greece, and a leading proponent of a socialist economic policy.

His arrest and prison term elicited worldwide protest. As president of the AEA, I was pressured to support Papandreou's release in the name of his fellow economists. After some hesitation, I did so, sending a cable on behalf of the AEA to the "Colonels," as they were termed, who were running the country, urging his release. In response to the worldwide protest he and a number of other dissidents were released just before Christmas 1967.

He subsequently resumed his political career, became prime minister, and introduced highly socialistic and anti-American policies. George Stigler repeatedly teased me with being responsible for his rise to power! No more absurd than the responsibility seriously attributed to me for the Pinochet regime in Chile, of which more later (chap. 24).

→ *Chapter Seventeen* ←

OUR FIRST YEAR ABROAD

{ *Rose* } Feeling that we were settled, at least for the time being, and eager for new adventures, Milton applied for a Fulbright fellowship for the academic year 1953–54, supported by an invitation to serve as a visiting fellow at Gonville and Caius College of Cambridge University. The invitation had been arranged by Stanley Dennison, one of the participants at the first Mont Pelerin meeting. Stanley, a first-rate economist, was a Fellow and Senior Tutor at Caius, and had raised the possibility of Milton's visiting Caius when Milton saw him in 1952 during a visit to London to lecture at the London School of Economics.

The fellowship was granted. A request from the president of the American Economic Association to represent it as one of its delegates to a meeting of the International Economic Association, in Santa Margherita Ligure, Italy, in August 1953, gave us the opportunity to tour Italy before going to Cambridge.

The voyage to Italy on the *SS Constitution* by the long southern route took about ten days and was "wonderful, phenomenally smooth all the way over," as Milton wrote to Anna Schwartz, his most consistent correspondent because of the monetary study they were engaged in. We arrived at Genoa on August 29 and went directly to Santa Margherita.

The beach at Santa Margherita was a great disappointment. Remembering the happy times I had spent at the beaches in Oregon and Washington as a child, I thought a few days on the Italian Riviera would be a delightful way to start our holiday. Unfortunately, the Italian Riviera (like most of the French Riviera, as I was to discover) was nothing like my vision. No lovely white sand, just rocks, rocks, and rocks—none big enough to sit on, only big enough to stub one's toe on.

{ *Milton* } While Rose was being disappointed about the beaches and busy taking care of Janet and David, I was sitting in on interesting sessions on economics. I no longer remember the content of the sessions, but I remember one feature of them very well. Most participants could speak English and nearly all talks were delivered in English. The outstanding exception was the French. They gave their papers in French, even if they were fluent in English. One of their delegation, who had spent the war years in Washington, deigned to make his comments in English, to accommodate the English-speaking. As a result, he was ostracized by the other members of the French delegation. It was not my first experience of French chauvinism, but it was a particularly striking example.

Another American economist who was present at the meeting was Evsey Domar, who had spent the preceding year as a visiting Fulbright Scholar at Oxford. Through the academic grapevine somehow we had made a deal with Evsey to buy his secondhand Hillman Minx. In good academic fashion, at the end of our year in England, we sold it to another economist, Alexander Gerschenkron, who was going to spend the following year in Britain.

For some reason that is buried in history, the car was registered in France, so after the meetings we drove with Evsey to Nice to transfer ownership. Thinking this wouldn't take much time, I left Rose and the children on the rocky beach, while Evsey and I went on to encounter the French bureaucracy. Of course, the transfer took far more time than I had expected, leaving Rose stranded on the beach. It grew late, the beach emptied, the temperature dropped, and Rose became fearful that something had happened to us. She finally decided to take the children to our hotel, and once there, considered calling the police to report a missing husband. Before she actually did, however, I finally arrived, to find a most uncomfortable and frightened family.

{ *Rose* } The next day was much pleasanter. We spent it at Juan les Pins, an artificial beach formed by clean sand that had been trucked in. Then followed three weeks touring Italy. It was our first trip to Italy and we wanted to go to all the places of interest that we had heard or read about. Needless to say, that was impossible in three weeks but as typical tourists we tried our best. And despite having both children fall sick in Florence and missing the Blue Grotto at Capri because of high seas, we saw and did most of the standard tourist things.

Arriving in Cambridge, we found that although Stanley Dennison had selected a lovely house with a beautiful English garden for us (15 Latham Road), it would not be available for two or three weeks, so we settled in at the Garden House Hotel. This was our first taste of middle-class English food and it lived up (or down) to its reputation. What I remember best was the dessert trolley of tarts in all colors of the rainbow. All tasted the same. Our only excitement at the Garden House was when David, riding his new bicycle along the river Cam, toppled over and fell in.

Our rented house had three floors, of which we occupied the first two. A couple who worked for the owner lived on the top floor. We were told that the house had central heating but soon discovered that this meant something very different to the British than it meant to us. We had to close off the lovely big living room soon after we moved in because a wood-burning fireplace and the meager central heat was not enough for comfort. Instead, we made the dining room, which was smaller and had a gas fire, our main sitting and dining room. The bedrooms were icy most of the time but fortunately we had been advised to bring electric blankets and these made the beds comfortable. Getting out of bed was another matter.

One episode in Cambridge was a first for us. For some two weeks the temperature dropped below freezing. Going into the powder room in the entry hall, we were astonished to see an icicle hanging from the faucet. Outdoors, our neighbors were on the roof, pouring water down the outside pipes to keep them from freezing. We were told that the pipes were on the outside so that when they froze they wouldn't damage the interior walls. There may be similar arrangements in the U.S. but we had never encountered them.

On Stanley Dennison's advice, we enrolled David in the Perse School for Boys, founded in 1615 by Dr. Stephen Perse, a Fellow of Caius. The teachers at this time were all women. We discovered the first morning, however, that the little fellows all greeted their teachers with a cheery "Good morning, sir!" When we met the headmaster, one of our first questions was, "Why do the little boys greet their female teachers as 'sir'?" He answered that traditionally the teachers had been male, but wartime manpower pressure had enforced a shift to women. However, they still expected to revert to male teachers before long and did not want to confuse the little boys! The female teachers did not seem to object. I wonder whether the teachers are still women and whether they are still addressed as "sir."

As was the custom in Britain, at least in the "public" schools, the boys wore a uniform. At Perse, it was purple with black stripes from head to toe. David was pleased and I thought he looked very good, but Milton described the uniform in a letter as "repulsive." David certainly looked neater than he ever had before or has since.

Our impression of the school was mixed. There was more discipline and less spontaneity than we were accustomed to. We had no objection to the discipline but felt that the rigidity and routine frustrated the young imagination and stifled the innate curiosity of the brighter youngsters. Our young son had then and still has the same kind of curiosity and independence of mind as his father. He had never been willing to do things simply because he was told to do them. He always wanted a good reason for doing or not doing something. The Perse teachers were not used to this attitude and it must have been difficult for them and equally frustrating for him. However, like his father, he also has a most winning smile and generous disposition and these, combined with his being a foreigner, produced a good deal of tolerance. At least there were no complaints to the parents. We were delighted with the training that our children received in writing. A short essay was a daily requirement. The emphasis on literature, history, and geography was most welcome. On the other hand, the time that David had to spend every evening practicing penmanship seemed a waste of time and did not improve its appearance. The house had a good classical library and David, who invariably woke long before the rest of us, spent those hours systematically going through the library, supplementing what he was assigned at school. Among others, he became a devotee of Kipling, and ever after has been able to quote his verse at great length.

I had another reaction to discipline. We have always heard that English children are better behaved than American children. After watching a number of the little boys who came to the house to play, we concluded that they might be very proper when parents were around but on their own were just as unruly as our children. They never hesitated to run noisily up the stairs and slide down the banisters whenever they pleased. They seemed to know when to be proper and when they could let go.

We enrolled Janet in the Garden House School, which had originally been located in London but was moved to Cambridge during the war. Janet's experience was somewhat different from David's. Her school was more permissive or, as some would say, more progressive. On the other hand, she was just under the age of eleven, the most critical age for a British youngster, thanks to the 11+ examination at that time. The examination separated the youngsters who would go on to grammar school from those destined for technical school. Because performance in the 11+ examination was so important, Janet's classmates were pressured to devote all their spare time to school work. There was no after-school play. And the school work itself was directed—almost exclusively—to preparing the girls for the examination—and thus to raising their recorded IQ. For Janet, this was a game, since the results of the exam could not affect her future. She was disappointed that she was not permitted to take the exam. I don't think it has ever been established whether or not one's recorded IQ can be raised, but the training removed any tension on Janet's part about taking exams.

Janet's exposure to English history at this time had a lasting effect. For some time after our return, she continued to be interested in the British royal family and its history and collected pictures of the royal family. Her love of horses and riding also grew. She started jumping, too—something she loved, but which worried me. I was impressed with the Spartan spirit of the British as I observed the riding classes. On one occasion, a horse turned its head round and bit a youngster riding nearby. Janet was not the victim but I seemed to be more disturbed than the parent or the instructor, who both passed it off as a trifle. When Janet fell off her horse while learning to jump, I could hardly get to the spot soon enough, but the instructor seemed unconcerned. Again, we were impressed with this same insouciance when we saw firecrackers being thrown into a crowd on Guy Fawkes Day.

Milton and I were both fascinated and disturbed by one feature of our experience at Cambridge University. We were dismayed at the cleavage that different political and economic philosophies had created, especially among economists. The dominant group favored a centrally controlled and planned economy as the only way to solve economic and social problems. A smaller yet important group believed, as we did, that individual freedom is the prime objective of social arrangements and that planning by millions of individuals unfettered by government controls is the most efficient kind of economic system. Because we were foreign guests—and, Milton always adds, more extreme than either group—we were entertained by both groups. The other guests at a gathering were always from one group or the other, but never from both.

What disturbed us most was the bitterness and hostility that the two groups exhibited toward each other and the almost complete absence of any intellectual dialogue between them. We were accustomed to being in a minority with respect to our political and economic views on most campuses in the United States at this time. However, we have never been on a campus in the U.S. where the cleavage was as deep or as emotional as it was in Cambridge. After 1953, the balance at Cambridge shifted at least for a time even more toward believers in a highly centralized government. Unfortunately for Britain, some of these became advisers in the Labour government and were responsible for many of the measures that pushed England closer and closer to a totalitarian state until the ministry of Margaret Thatcher. Our friends, Stanley, Peter Bauer, and others, left Cambridge and went elsewhere.

{ *Milton* } As a Fulbright lecturer, I was not required to do any teaching. However, curious about how Cambridge students compared with ours and about the tutorial system of teaching, I asked Stanley Dennison, who was senior tutor at Caius, to select six students in economics for me to tutor: two of his worst, two of his average, and two of his brightest students.

As I wrote to Anna, as to innate IQ, the students "aren't much different [from ours], but they are much more literate, can write and speak much better than ours. They are less mature socially and personally, and take themselves much more seriously. They, or many of them, explicitly recognize that they are here to be trained as the future ruling class of Britain and act accordingly." I concluded that the big difference between Britain and the U.S. was in their secondary schools. In accordance with the general difference between class-structured Britain and democratic U.S., there is a far larger difference between their top secondary schools and the ones most youngsters go to than in the U.S., except for a very small number of elite private secondary schools in our country.

My experience with tutoring turned me into a strong admirer of the British system. The tutees, generally in groups of two, meet with the tutor for an hour a week, and he assigns readings and a topic on which they are to write a brief essay to be discussed the next week. The three pairs I was tutoring started out at the same level, but by the end of the year, they had reached very different levels of sophistication in economics. The brightest were at what we would regard as a graduate level, the least bright still in Economics 101. One from the brightest pair was Samuel Brittan, today a writer for the *Financial Times*. The other was Keith Marsden, who has had an outstanding career at the International Labor Organization in Geneva.

At first glance, individual tutoring seems far more expensive than our practice of teaching classes of twenty or thirty or occasionally more. But when I made a detailed calculation, allowing for the other respects in which the systems differ—such as shorter terms and lectures by selected members of the faculty to large audiences—I concluded that it was far from obvious which method was less expensive. A major offset is that lecture series are relatively brief, perhaps eight in what we would call a quarter, but each lecture is well-prepared and thorough. The lecturer may entertain a few questions at the end of the period, but there are no interruptions during the lecture. I recall the story of an English professor who was invited to serve as a visiting professor at an American university, and told that he would be expected to meet each of two classes three hours a week for eighteen weeks. He was appalled, wondering how he could stretch the content of an eight-hour series of lectures to fill fifty-four hours. He saw his deliverance in the first student hand that went up shortly after he started his first lecture.

All in all, I calculated that combining tutoring and lecturing, the Cambridge system made no greater demands on its faculty than ours, and provided the students with much more individualized instruction.

Aside from my tutees, the two people at Caius with whom I interacted most were Stanley Dennison and Peter Bauer—the economists at Gonville and Caius College at the time. Stanley, who had done important work during the war in the government, and was a highly respected scholar, left Caius some years later to become vice-chancellor (essentially the CEO) of Hull University, where he remained until he retired. Peter left Caius to become a professor of economics at the London School of Economics. Both at Caius and later he specialized in development economics and particularly the effects of foreign aid. He became the world's outstanding expert on these issues, as accumulating evidence discredited the earlier orthodoxy, which regarded development as a more or less automatic consequence of an increase in the ratio of capital to labor. In particular, Peter has argued for decades that foreign economic aid in general does more harm than good to the recipient countries—a view that I have long shared. For most of that period, his was a voice in the wilderness. At long last, it is increasingly recognized that he was right all along. Peter was named a life peer by Margaret Thatcher for his contributions to the theory of development, so he is now Lord Peter Bauer. Stanley died in 1993. Like us, Peter, is still active. Indeed, he had dinner with us in San Francisco the evening before I typed this sentence.

Two episodes involving Peter at Caius are of interest. One day, he related to me with indignation an experience with one of his tutees, with whom he had been discussing the theory of wages. In the course of the discussion, he pointed out that the theory implied that trade unions which succeeded in raising wages thereby reduced the number of people employed in that trade, creating unemployment or lower wages elsewhere for those who would otherwise have been employed. "But," he reported his tutee as saying, "surely, Mr. Dobb wouldn't agree with that." (Maurice Dobb was a famous Marxian economist at Trinity College.) "What kind of science is economics," Peter exploded, "if such differences can exist about a simple logical implication of agreed-on basic principles?" (Incidentally, one gold star for Rose's side of our longstanding difference about why economists disagree.) That evening, I happened to have dinner at the college, and to sit at high table next to R. A. Fisher, the great statistician and geneticist. I repeated the incident to him, as indicating the special problems of economics. He pooh-poohed that idea, saying that it was no different in his field. As soon as he knew a visitor's political views, he also could predict where he would stand on the nature-versus-nurture issue in genetics (Rose's position, of course).

The other incident is of a very different kind. One day when I was chatting with Peter in his rooms, he showed me a letter he had just received from Richard Kahn, who had developed the concept of a "multiplier" that played such a key role in Keynes's *General Theory* (and who succeeded him as bursar of King's College). For some reason that I no longer remember, Peter was outraged by the content of the letter. As soon as I saw it, I lost interest in the content because of the writer's distinctive handwriting, with the separate lines sloping very sharply downward. "Kahn," I said to Peter, "is certainly an extreme pessimist." (I had become persuaded that handwriting contains reliable information on character by Wilhelm Kromphardt when we were fellow students at Columbia, in 1933–34, and have been an amateur graphologist ever since.)

As it happened, I was scheduled to have lunch with Kahn the next day at the Cambridge Arts Theatre (one of Keynes's projects for Cambridge). We were discussing Keynes's and Kahn's policies as bursar. In the course of that discussion, Kahn remarked, "The big difference is that Keynes was an inveterate optimist and I am an inveterate pessimist." I again lost interest in the substance and said, "Does Keynes's handwriting behave like this [demonstrating sharply upward-sloping lines]?" Kahn replied that he didn't have the slightest idea, but added that he would show me some samples when we attended a sherry party at his rooms.

The sherry party was, like all such occasions, segregated, not by race but by ideology: left versus right. After a while, I reminded Kahn about handwriting, and he produced some specimens of Keynes's. Sure enough, the lines did slope sharply upward, as I had predicted that they would, the characteristic tipoff to optimism. Naturally that led to various people producing specimens and asking me to analyze them. By this time, I had had a good deal of sherry, so my imagination reigned freely. Finally, Joan Robinson, a leading Keynesian and radical, produced a specimen for me to analyze. I said something like, "This is obviously the writing of a foreigner, so it's difficult for me to analyze. But I would say it is written by someone who had considerable artistic but not much intellectual talent." It turned out to be the writing of Lydia Lopokova, the world-famous Russian ballerina whom Keynes had married. That was surely my greatest triumph of the year at Cambridge!

Joan Robinson was an extremely controversial, and remarkable, economist, with whom I got along well personally, though we were worlds apart in our views. She had married Austin Robinson, another economist, in 1926, and achieved professional recognition by a path-breaking book on imperfect competition that she published in the 1930s. She had gone on to teach at Cambridge and had become one of the leading members of the so-called Cambridge Circus, a group of young disciples of Keynes who had been closely involved in criticizing successive drafts of Keynes's *General Theory*. She had also become an extreme-left radical. To me she seemed schizophrenic. On the one hand, she was a first-rate technical economist, with whom one could have a rewarding discussion on technical economic issues. On the other hand, she was a committed ideologue who found it possible to rationalize and praise every feature of Russian and Chinese policy. She was an extreme example of a phenomenon that we have referred to repeatedly: the apparent ability of able economists to keep their scientific work from determining their policy views.

As an example of the first side of her character, a friend called me one day and reported that Joan planned to criticize my advocacy of flexible exchange rates in the next lecture in the series that she was giving. He suggested that I attend. Accordingly, I phoned Joan and asked if she would mind if I attended. She encouraged me to do so. At the lecture, she announced that I was in the audience, that she and I had different views about flexible exchange rates, and asked me if I would come to the podium and discuss with her the basis of our disagreement. She went on to say that both of us were competent technical economists, so our difference did not represent a mistake in logic or reasoning and hence must reflect differences in our factual assumptions or our values and that the students would find it instructive to have us explore those differences. An excellent discussion between us followed.

Several examples of the ideological side. In a lecture on her impressions after a visit to China, she found nothing wrong and everything remarkably good in China. She insisted that, thanks to good government policy, there was not a fly left in China, that the level of honesty was incredibly high. She told a story of a foreigner visiting China who accidentally opened his wallet while driving through a crowded area in an open car. His paper money flew all over the street. According to her story, the people on the street rushed to pick up the money and every single yuan was returned to the astounded foreigner. One such extreme story after another. She found absolutely nothing to criticize in the Mao regime.

Another example occurred some years later when she was in Chicago to give a lecture at the university under the auspices of our department. We had a dinner for her and some of our colleagues at our home. She arrived, wearing her trademark Indian sandals, and announced that she had just been in Cuba and that "what Americans cannot stand is the spectacle of an island ninety miles south of their shores in which there is no unemployment, no poverty, and no racial discrimination."

Richard Kahn, Joan Robinson, and Nicholas Kaldor were the leaders of the Keynesian faction at Cambridge. Kaldor was a Hungarian who had emigrated to Britain in the 1920s. He studied and then taught at the London School of Economics, and then became a Fellow of King's College and later a professor at Cambridge. He was a close adviser of the Labour Party and Labour government, and was made a life peer in 1974, some years after a peerage had been conferred on a fellow Hungarian economist, Thomas Balogh. Kaldor and Balogh were known as the "Budapest Lords," and the common saying was that it was easy to know which was Buddha and which Pest. Kaldor was large, somewhat obese, and very cheerful—clearly Buddha; Balogh was thin, austere, and dour, truly a pest. When I engaged in a television discussion (debate) with him some years later—in Chicago but for the BBC—I infuriated him almost to the point of speechlessness by insisting on calling him "Mr." rather than "Lord." He correctly interpreted it as a mark of my lack of respect for him.

I first met "Nicky" Kaldor in 1934–35, my second year at Chicago as a student, when he came through on a Rockefeller fellowship and stayed some weeks in Chicago. He was a first-rate technical economist, with whom I had many interesting discussions, particularly about capital theory, and the ideological differences that developed over the years never affected our personal relations, though we had no hesitancy in criticizing each other's views in print. He and his wife were helpful to us in Cambridge.

The intellectual leader of the smaller "conservative" or non-Keynesian faction was unquestionably Sir Dennis H. Robertson, although he had come to assume that position inadvertently. A shy, withdrawn, pure intellectual, he had specialized in monetary theory. He was a student of Keynes and then became his close personal friend from sometime before World War I to Keynes's death in 1946. To judge from the extensive correspondence reproduced in the complete works of Keynes, they regularly exchanged drafts of manuscripts with one another, and were brutally frank, yet always friendly, in criticizing them. Robertson went over repeated drafts of the *General Theory,* making detailed suggestions for change. Despite Keynes's extensive attempts to meet his criticisms, Robertson found himself unable to accept Keynes's new theory and never joined the Keynesian revolution. That strained their personal relation, yet Robertson differed far less from Keynes than he did from such radical disciples of Keynes's as Kahn, Kaldor, and especially, Joan Robinson.[1] Robertson was not only a brilliant economic theorist; he was also, like Keynes, a remarkable stylist. His little book entitled *Money,* first published in 1922, remains one of the most lucid and profound presentations of the central principles of monetary theory.

I was privileged to attend a weekly meeting of the Political Economy Club that Robertson hosted in his rooms at Trinity College. It attracted the ablest undergraduates interested in economics as well as many of the younger economists serving as fellows or lecturers and so was a very lively forum. Each week a paper on some economic topic, generally prepared by an undergraduate, was read and discussed. One Monday evening the paper was on British agricultural policy. In part, it dealt with the laws then in effect that provided for supervision by county agricultural committees over the use of agricultural land. The laws provided for sanctions to assure that the land was used "properly."

In the course of the discussion, I remarked that if land rents and other prices were competitively determined, I could see no justification for governmental control of the use made of the land. If the land was badly used, the operator of the land, whether tenant or owner, bore the full cost of the bad use. Sir Dennis lit into me vigorously, asserting that my argument simply demonstrated how far apart we were in our basic philosophical positions, and how hopeless further discussion was.

That ended the immediate exchange. However, I knew from past experience that Sir Dennis, like so many scholars trained in the Oxford-Cambridge tradition, was much more comfortable in written than in spoken discourse. Accordingly, a few days later, I continued the discussion in a letter. An amicable exchange followed, in which any difference between us was narrowed greatly. Nearly twenty years later, after Sir Dennis's death, I happened to run across the correspondence and showed it to Harry Johnson, who was then my colleague at Chicago and with George Stigler, coeditor of the *Journal of Political Economy.* I had first come to know him during our year at Cambridge when he was at King's College. Harry thought the correspondence had general interest, and with my permission and the permission of Robertson's niece, published it in the *JPE*.[2]

All in all, the three "terms" of eight weeks each that we spent at Cambridge that year were extremely stimulating and instructive, and led to my forming close professional friendships that paid dividends for decades.

{ *Rose* } In addition to the cleavage resulting from the intellectual and philosophical differences, I found the place of women in Cambridge as in all of Britain frustrating. For example, by contrast with the United States, when a foreign economist visited Cambridge, he was entertained by the men at the college. Wives rarely if ever had any contact with him. In addition, most Fellows at Cambridge regularly had their meals at the college rather than with their wives and children. I would have found this intolerable. Fortunately, Milton felt as I did and took his dinner at the college only on special occasions.

We broke with custom in other ways as well. We had many pleasant evenings at our home with Fellows from Caius, as well as with other new friends and visitors from abroad. One feature that we specially liked about the college system at Cambridge was the opportunity it gave us to meet non-economists as well as economists. We had the good fortune of getting to know Sir Ronald A. Fisher, a Fellow at Gonville and Caius. He was a brilliant scholar of many and varied talents. His interests ranged widely, from church history to astronomy, and he was thoroughly informed about every subject he was interested in.

We have often retold the story of Sir Ronald's visit to our home. When Milton went to Fisher's rooms to pick him up for dinner, he took David with him. Milton introduced Fisher to David as Sir Ronald, whereupon David asked, "What kind of a knight are you?" and received the reply, "I am a knight bachelor with five daughters and two sons." During the evening, David tried to impress Fisher with his knowledge. He began with dinosaurs, but discovered very soon that Fisher had forgotten more about dinosaurs than David ever knew. So David tried astronomy, with the same result. In desperation, David turned to comic books. Upon finding that Fisher was more knowledgeable about that as well, he gave up, with great respect for Sir Ronald.

At Caius, two copies of each day's London *Times* were ordered for the common room, solely for the famous *Times* crossword puzzle. Two groups formed to solve the day's puzzle, one working cooperatively, the other observing Fisher solving it on his own. The legend was that Fisher invariably won but that he sometimes peeked at the puzzle earlier. Incidentally, Milton tried taking up the puzzle, but even by the end of our year in Cambridge, he could count on getting at most one-third of the subtle clues.

We already had friends in London and Oxford whom we had met in the United States or whom Milton had met at the founding meeting of the Mont Pelerin Society. I had met Lionel Robbins, not yet a lord, many years earlier when he was visiting Aaron in Washington. Lionel and Iris visited us in Cambridge and we had many visits with them in London. Herbert and Lisl Frankel, originally from South Africa, then at Oxford, were our visitors in Cambridge and we spent a delightful weekend with them at Oxford. Our trips to London with the children, for sight-seeing, generally included visits with friends as well. We found the intellectual atmosphere at the London School of Economics much healthier and more congenial than that of Cambridge. Milton did not have tutorials every day, and so there were long weekends for our trips around England.

{ *Milton* } Several episodes brought home to us the contrast between the rigidity and class structure of Britain, and our far more fluid society at home. On one occasion, we had as guests Peter Bauer and a friend of his, George

Szasz. Both had been born in Hungary and had attended secondary school there. Both had emigrated, Peter to Britain, George to the United States, where he was employed as a physicist. We asked both of them the same question: "What are you?" Without hesitation, Peter replied, "A Hungarian"; George, "An American."

On another occasion we had as a visitor George Schwartz, a columnist for the *Sunday Times,* who had been trained as an economist at the London School and had taught there for a while. George was born in England, but because his father had emigrated to Britain from Germany, George had been barred from engaging in war work during World War II, along with other "enemy aliens," even though he had talents that would have been highly useful. I recall his standing in front of the fireplace and referring to "them," meaning the British. He still did not regard himself as one. Similarly, Friedrich Hayek, an Austrian who had emigrated to Britain in 1931 to accept the offer of a professorship at the London School, was excluded from war work even though he had become a citizen by 1938. That had the serendipitous consequence of giving Hayek the leisure to write his great classic *The Road to Serfdom* when the London School was moved to Cambridge to avoid the bombing of London.

The aristocratic character of England led to a greater inequality in almost everything than in more democratic U.S. The biggest cars were bigger; the smallest cars, smaller. The largest houses were bigger; the smallest houses, smaller; the truly wealthy appeared wealthier, as judged by the way they lived; the poor, poorer. Regional accents differ much more from place to place in small Britain than in large U.S. So too do accents and customs among the classes. We were amazed to have the plumber arrive in suit and tie, a sign of deference to upper-class values. And indeed, the relation between the upper classes and the "working class"—a category we may have but do not recognize—was one of automatic assumption of superiority and deference, not the easy assumption of familiarity that every taxicab driver in the U.S. displays toward his customers, regardless of their status.

Another indication. At Cambridge grants to students included an allowance not only for tuition and for ordinary living expenses but also for formal attire. Recipients were not expected to earn any part of their costs, but to live as "gentlemen." By contrast, in our experience at home, most undergraduate scholarships, and many graduate ones, covered only tuition and not living expenses; and a large fraction of students worked their way through school.

Though much has changed in Britain since we were there, I believe that the contrast with the U.S. is still large. The main change, I believe, is easier access to the upper class. However, there is still an upper class and a working class, and which a youngster will end up in is almost always decided by his teens. There is much less movement up and down thereafter. Several tutees I had at Caius came from working-class families and were much disturbed at the difficulty they had in communicating with their parents. They spoke in a Cambridge accent, no longer in their parents' idiom. Radio and television have done a great deal to alter that situation since.

{ *Rose* } One of our trips to London was especially memorable. We managed to get tickets to attend a session of the House of Commons. We were there for question time and, to our delight, Winston Churchill was present and answered some questions. We were struck with how old he looked. As Milton wrote in a letter to Anna Schwartz, "He looked every bit of his age, from his waddling entrance, the difficulty with which he got up after sitting down, his insertion of a hearing aid in his ear, and his worn and weary face. At the same time, he seemed to be intellectually all there. The initial questions are written and his initial replies he read from a script, but then there was some discussion afterward which he clearly followed and to which he gave appropriate and well-worded replies, with a great smile on his face." While we were delighted to have the opportunity of seeing Churchill, we were also very sad to see how old he looked.

Shopping in Cambridge was a real experience for me. I couldn't remember how many years it had been since staples like rice, sugar, flour etc., had been sold in bulk, as they were at the store in Cambridge where I shopped. The scene, with wooden barrels filled with a variety of flours, pasta, etc., reminded me of the Vermont Country Store. Frozen foods were very popular by this time in the U.S. but were very limited in Cambridge. There was more service, such as delivery of groceries to the door every day, than I was accustomed to, but little attention was given to the possibility of spoilage. For example, fish was wrapped in newspaper and left on a table in the back hall. There didn't seem to be a shortage of food at this time but it was inordinately dull, especially in restaurants. Lots of potatoes, brussels sprouts—the usual and often the only vegetable—and no salads. Meat had been removed from rationing but then was again rationed. We did not feel that we were short of meat, but the quality was poor. Waiting in a queue was a most frustrating experience when I did some shopping in London or waited in line for a bus, but the English housewives never seemed to get impatient. Visiting with neighbors in the line seemed to be their relaxation.

{ *Milton* } Experience with waiting in line for most everything led me to invent my one and only original riddle: Query: Every country has a national flag, a national motto, and other national symbols. But Britain is the only country that has a national letter. What is it? Answer: Q.

{ *Rose* } We appreciated especially the Cambridge schedule—eight weeks of term and four weeks of vacation. The long vacations enabled us to get acquainted with much of Europe. During the Christmas recess, Milton drove to Zurich to give some lectures, while the children and I stayed behind for a few days to finish their school term. We were supposed to follow him by air from London to Basle where Milton would meet us, and we would all go on to Arosa, Switzerland, for our first exposure to skiing. Getting to London was easy. Getting out of London was not. After sitting in the London terminal all day, with hourly announcements by British European Airways that the flight was delayed, we heard a final announcement simply saying, "The flight is canceled; if you will go to the ticket office, you can get your money back." Milton in the meantime was in contact with BEA in Zurich and was assured that we would be taken care of. Being taken care of apparently meant they would return our money, not that they would put us up or arrange for a flight the next day. I was so annoyed with BEA that I refused to fly with them for many years.

Getting from London to Basle turned out to be an interesting, if somewhat harrowing, experience. A young man from Switzerland, who knew his way around better than we did, and a woman with a little girl from Rio de Janeiro, who were also going to Basle and were as lost as we were, teamed up. We decided that the surest way to get to Basle was by train, so we proceeded to the railroad station. Informed that there were no more trains for Basle that day, we made arrangements for the the next day's trip and found a seedy hotel close to the station where we all spent the night.

In the morning we boarded the train and set off. One rewarding aspect of the trip for me was Janet and David's behavior. It was an overnight trip and we had to change trains in France. The only sleeping arrangements we could get were couchettes for—as I remember—six persons. The train was very crowded and the line to the dining car so packed that we couldn't make our way there. A young girl who occupied one berth provided the only food we had for dinner—a couple of chocolate bars—but I heard no complaints from the children. Instead, they consoled me. When we finally arrived at the station, Milton's beaming face when he saw his family was even more welcome than usual.

Arosa was a veritable fairyland. As Milton wrote in a letter to Anna Schwartz, "Everything a tourist could possibly want at prices reasonable by American standards (under $6 a day for each of us for food and board at a clean, warm, comfortable pension that served excellent food and plenty of it)."

Friedrich Lutz and his wife, Vera Smith, both excellent economists, joined us at Arosa for skiing. We also spent New Year's Eve with them before leaving Arosa. We were all enthusiastic about skiing and determined to continue when we returned to Chicago. For a brief time, we did so, but skiing there was nothing like Arosa and gradually, one by one, we dropped out except for Milton. I was the first to get discouraged. The children followed when they left home for college. Milton still skied until 1995, when physical problems forced him to quit.

After two weeks in ski heaven, we returned to Cambridge by car through Germany, Belgium, and Holland as we had planned. Germany, as on our earlier trip, aroused mixed feelings and in the main we were rather depressed by the absence of any real development of democratic ideas throughout Europe.

Our next trip was unexpected. Milton was invited to give two lectures in Madrid and he decided to accept. This trip we made without the children. It was, for me, the first time I had been away from them for more than a couple of days. Fortunately, a former student and his wife, Rondo and Claydeen Cameron, came to stay with Janet and David. The wife of the couple who lived on our third floor and did some housekeeping for me did the cooking and other chores. As nearly as we could tell when we returned, we were not missed and the Toledo sword and other things we brought back more than made up for the absence of parents.

Our Madrid visit was extraordinarily interesting. First of all, we had never experienced such hospitality or felt so much like visiting dignitaries. When we arrived at the airport, I saw a man at some distance carrying a bouquet of flowers. Jesting, I said to Milton, "I'll bet those are for me." Not jesting, he replied, "Who do you think you are, a Hollywood celebrity?" Imagine his and my surprise when the gentleman came straight to us and handed me the flowers. When I thanked him he replied, "We do this for all our foreign guests"—which I must say removed any illusions that I was special. He was from the Spanish Visitors' Bureau. On Easter Sunday, Easter lilies arrived at the hotel. The same kind of effusive welcome continued throughout our visit.

When we were taken on a visit to Toledo by some Spanish professors who were among our hosts, we wanted to buy some of the lovely examples of Toledo craftsmanship, but discovered quickly that as soon as we admired anything, our hosts immediately bought it for us. So we refrained from doing much admiring. Part of this was customary Spanish hospitality, but it must also have been a result of the isolation that Spain had endured for some time.

It was evident that the Spanish people felt closed in and were eager to make contact with the rest of the world.

The lecture was scheduled for something like 8 o'clock one evening. We were told that we would be picked up at our hotel before the scheduled lecture. We were, of course, ready and waiting about 7:30. Our welcoming delegation arrived in leisurely fashion closer to 9:00 p.m. than to 8:00. We then assumed that once we arrived at the university we would immediately proceed to the lecture hall, but instead we were told that the president of the university and a few other dignitaries were waiting to welcome us in the president's office. When we were finally escorted to the lecture hall at close to ten o'clock, we were aghast to find the hall outside the lecture room full of students, who I suppose had been there since eight, The lecture hall was empty. Spanish courtesy demanded that no student enter until the lecturer and his accompanying entourage had gone in.

In an entirely different way, reality in Spain was very different from our expectations. Spain was a fascist dictatorship, yet people spoke quite freely, criticizing Franco and the regime. There were no pictures of Franco except on the money. The university library contained a wide selection of magazines, including the left-wing *New Statesman and Nation.* When we visited El Escorial, we were amazed when our host at lunch began to criticize Franco—and not in a whisper. He was speaking in English of course but said that he was sure many of the waiters and others within hearing distance could understand English, but there was no problem. He did not hesitate, he explained, because it was quite safe so long as one did not criticize the church or the military and so long as one did not publish the criticism. There seemed to be much more freedom than we had expected. Milton was free to choose his own topic for the lecture and was not asked in advance what he was going to talk about.

On the economic side, we were surprised to find that Spain was in many ways a socialist state, much like England at that time: extensive social security, employers unable to dismiss workers, increasing nationalization of industry, government control of investment and of foreign exchange. Industry we were told was not a powerful force. The power was in the military, the church, and the Falange.

The great inequality between rich and poor and the extent of the poverty did not surprise us. We saw little of that in Madrid, a lovely city with the most exciting museum we had ever visited, the Prado. On our trip to Toledo, however, wherever our hosts stopped so we could admire the view, children and a few adults would gather to beg. Our hosts were embarrassed and tried to ignore them.

Our next vacation, in the spring, was spent in Holland, Denmark, and

Sweden. Our trips were all by car, in part because we have always felt that was the best way to see a country, and also because it was the cheapest way to travel. It was too early in the spring to include Norway so we had to forego that until many years later. We felt very comfortable in Sweden. It was amazingly like the U.S. When we first drove out into the countryside, David said, "This smells like New Hampshire," and it certainly did. It was the same kind of rolling country, with many rivers and lakes, the same kind of trees—spruces, pines, firs, birch, etc. Here, unlike most of the rest of Europe but much like the U.S., houses were built of wood and for the same reason. Again, like the U.S. but unlike most of Europe, we saw individual farms rather than strip farming.

Like so many of our trips, this one was a combination of work and vacation for Milton. We met many economists, whom we visited in their homes, and Milton was asked to lecture at several universities. In Sweden, he gave the lecture "Why the American Economy Is Depression Proof," later reprinted in *Dollars and Deficits,* a collection of some of his papers. By depression, he meant, of course, the devastating kind of contraction that the world experienced in the thirties, not the mild recessions that periodically punctuate an economy. The main factors he cited to justify his conclusion were the establishment of federal deposit insurance and the shift in the intellectual atmosphere from a fear of inflation to a fear of, and determination to avoid, true depression at any cost.

As we drove into Cambridge at the conclusion of our trip, the sun was shining brightly, the trees were blossoming, and almost in unison we all exclaimed, "Spring is here." But when our friend Stanley paid us a visit soon after our return and I told him I had packed away all our winter clothes, he said, with a smile, "I wouldn't be in a hurry." How right he was. It wasn't long before I unpacked.

Our final trip before leaving Britain took us first to the Lake District, then to Wales and Scotland. In spite of unpleasant weather, Milton and David climbed Ben Nevis so that they could forever boast that they had climbed the highest mountain in the British Isles. For both Milton and me, it was exciting to visit the place where Adam Smith grew up, and then his burial place. The burial plot, though larger than any other in the cemetery, was the most barren and neglected. Milton felt the neglect was more likely a result of bachelor Smith's having no descendants than the decline in the acceptance of his philosophy, as I did.

Our trip to Scotland over, we returned to Cambridge and packed for our departure. There was much luggage, including two bicycles that had been purchased in Cambridge for Janet and David to go to and from school and which of course they would not think of leaving behind. I do not remember much about our voyage home but I remember very well our arrival at the dock in New York. After depositing the children and me with all our belongings, Milton took off to get our car, which we had left with his sister in Rahway, never thinking of leaving me the keys so that I could open the bags for customs inspection. Again, my luck or innocent face paid off. The customs agent by forethought or accident chose to look at the one unlocked bag which contained our dirty clothes from the trip and he spent very little time looking at that. Even without any mishap, by the time we got through customs inspection, Milton had gone to Rahway and returned. We took off for Orford to spend the rest of the summer until school started in Chicago for Milton and the children.

→ *Chapter Eighteen* ←

ASSIGNMENT IN INDIA

{ *Milton* } In the summer of 1955, Arthur Burns, at the time chairman of President Eisenhower's Council of Economic Advisers, asked Neil Jacoby, a former member of the council and dean of the UCLA School of Business, and me to go to India under the auspices of the International Cooperation Administration (as the foreign aid agency was dubbed at the time) to advise the Indian government. Never having been to India, I welcomed the opportunity and arranged to take a leave of absence from the university for the fall quarter.

India was socialist in its orientation, its intellectual atmosphere having been shaped largely by Harold Laski of the London School of Economics, and his fellow Fabians. A series of left-wing advisers, including Oskar Lange and Michael Kalecki from Poland, and Nicholas Kaldor and John Strachey from Britain, had visited India since independence. American advisers financed by the Ford and Rockefeller foundations were for the most part highly sympathetic to the central planning propensities of the Indian authorities.

At the time, the Indian government was engaged in preparing its Second Five-Year Plan—a practice reflecting the strong influence of the Soviet experience. In that connection, the Indian government asked the Eisenhower administration for assistance. The administration recognized an opportunity to counter the influence of the left-wing advice by sending two strong proponents of free markets. Jacoby was assigned directly to the Planning Commission, and I to advise Mr. Deshmukh, the finance minister of India.

Whatever its value to India, the activity was personally most rewarding, though it was marred by an unfortunate incident in Chicago that led me to cut the trip short. I left from Los Angeles on Saturday, October 8.[1]

This was before the days of jet travel, so it was a long trip from Los Angeles to New Delhi, by way of Tokyo, Hong Kong, and Bangkok. I went to Tokyo on a Pan American Boeing Stratocruiser that had two levels, a passenger level above and a lounge below. The plane also had a limited number of very comfortable berths. The U.S. government had thoughtfully provided me with a berth, for which a fellow passenger who had not been able to get one offered me a hundred dollars (equivalent to nearly six hundred 1997 dollars)—or as I wrote back to Rose, "10¢ a minute of sleeping time." I resisted the temptation and slept soundly. En route to Tokyo, we stopped at Honolulu, then the next morning at Wake Island, where we stayed for an hour while we had breakfast, then on to Tokyo. All in all, while the trip took a lot longer than it would today, each hour was far pleasanter than an hour in today's mammoth crowded planes.

In Tokyo, where I arrived on Monday, thanks to losing a day on crossing the international date line, I stayed in the original Frank Lloyd Wright Imperial Hotel, famous for having been the only large building in Japan that survived the 1923 earthquake. As I wrote to Rose, "It is something of a disappointment. It looks a lot like an extended version of the Robie house on the corner of Woodlawn and 58th Street—same kind of brick and emphasis on horizontal lines. But nothing very exciting. Inside it is fine except it is almost impossible to find one's way around—you wander and wander." I spent much of the next day going to a Kabuki theater and wandering around Tokyo, shepherded by Professor Kitamuru, an economist with whom I had had some correspondence, and whom I had met the preceding evening at a dinner party in the home of Professor Shigeto Tsuru, a Harvard-trained economist, of whom we shall hear more in chapter 20.

I was greatly impressed by the cleanliness and beauty of the objects in the stores, the masses of people on the street; and the poverty. "The poverty was impressive and depressing. We really have no idea," I wrote, "how poor people can be and still live," a phenomenon that has impressed me again and again in the decades that have followed and has led me to assert that there is no level of income below which it is impossible for people to live.

By today's standards, even adjusting for the inflation that has occurred in the interim, prices were very cheap. But not by my standards then. As I wrote to Rose, "The hotel room is quite nice, with a private bath, but not particularly cheap. It will come to $8 or $9." I had lunch with Professor Kitamuru at a tempura restaurant for what was then as now a deluxe meal. "It all cost about $3 apiece—I paid of course for both and with true Japanese hospitality my Japanese friend made no protest, it probably would have been a week's salary, so I can't blame him." Relative to the cost of the hotel, the cost of the meal seems high. What struck me as I was rereading my letters to Rose was the extraordinary contrast between the image I then had of Japan as a poverty-stricken though advanced country and the image we have now. What a remarkable change in four decades!

I left that evening on an overnight flight for Hong Kong, where the government had reserved a room for me at the Peninsula Hotel, even then one of the great hotels of the world. I asked the clerk what the rate was for my room, and reacted in shock when he said $50. Observing my shock, he hastened to assure me that that was in Hong Kong dollars. At the time, it took six Hong Kong dollars to buy one U.S. dollar—so a single room at the elite Peninsula was about $9 American. Inflation alone cannot account for the difference between then and now. That difference is a tribute to the transformation of Hong Kong from a backward colonial outpost to one of the great cities of the world.

While I was registering at the desk, an attractive young Chinese female approached me, pleading poverty, and asking me to do her the great favor of letting her sleep in my room since she had no place to go. With some regret, I turned her down. As I wrote to Rose, "You begin here to see China's teeming millions."

I had just one day between planes in Hong Kong, and spent that sightseeing, in the morning in Kowloon, in the afternoon on the island. As I wrote to Rose, "Hong Kong before the war had about 800,000 people. Thanks to refugees from Red China it now has perhaps 2,500,000 or 3 million. We saw the quarters built by the municipality to house the worst-off of the refugees. Indescribable. A space perhaps 16 × 10 or so for a family of 5 or 6. Numbers galore." That problem has long since been resolved as Hong Kong prospered and Kowloon became filled with housing units for the continually growing and increasingly well-off population. However, a counterpart remains today as a result of the boat people from Vietnam, who in some ways pose a more intractable problem because the authorities do not wish to let them become permanent residents as they did the Chinese refugees.

The next morning (Thursday) I flew from Hong Kong to Bangkok. Though my travel arrangements did not call for stopping in Bangkok, it so happened that the BOAC plane to New Delhi on which I had reservations made a stop there, so I arranged to lay over and go to New Delhi on the same flight the next day. As it turned out, "on landing, I was told that the Friday flight was a day late and would not go out until Saturday, which pleased me even better—might just as well arrive Saturday night as Friday night."

Re Bangkok, I wrote to Rose,

This is a dirty, filthy, unattractive town, hardly relieved by the truly beautiful and in general well kept-up temples and government buildings that punctuate it. The overwhelming impression it leaves is filth and overcrowding. Masses of people wherever you turn. More shops and markets than you could dream of—I believe there must be more shopowners than customers. Every street and dirty little alley is lined with them. . . . Imagine Maxwell Street many times dirtier and more spread out and you have a vague idea.

The Thai people seem very pleasant and decent. They are cheerful and quiet. . . . The tour of the floating market was the most interesting part of the stay here. It consists mostly in riding around in a boat, first down the river, and then down some of the numerous canals that cover the city. The people, or very many of them, literally live and work on the river. The canals and water are everywhere and everywhere you observe people on it on small boats that they use, e.g., in picking the rice, somewhat larger boats that they may live on, or use for transporting goods, or use as floating stores or food-serving affairs. And the sides of the canals are lined with houses or shacks. As we went down the river, we observed numerous people taking their morning bath in the river or bathing their babies—there are babies and babies everywhere—or washing their dishes or their clothes or soaking cloth that they were dyeing, etc., etc. And this in a river that is bringing down 500 miles or more of refuse and debris from god knows where. The water is brown and muddy. . . . The morning tour also took us to one temple and to see the Royal barges. As always apparently in poor countries, the churches or their equivalent are magnificent.

I finally arrived in New Delhi Saturday evening, October 15, just one week after leaving Los Angeles—four days of actual traveling compared to perhaps fifteen hours on a direct flight today via Singapore.

I "was met at the airport by Mr. and Mrs. McClelland—he is a chap I saw in Washington this summer when he was there for a while on home leave [he was at the time Economic Advisor, Public Services Division, Technical Cooperation Mission to India]; she is a former student of mine, long ago at Columbia, when she was Anne Friedman, so I remembered her and her name well; also an Indian boy, Mohan Malhotra who had been a student at Chicago. . . . They immediately took me off to a cocktail party, supposedly in my honor."

To continue the saga of prices then and now, as I wrote Rose, "I am staying at the Hotel Ambassador just now at least temporarily—in a suite of a large living room, bedroom, and bath—all for $11 a day including meals.

I am going to try to get a cheaper room, which I understand I can get, but at the moment they tell me they don't have one." In a later letter I reported that Neil Jacoby and I had been able to arrange for a suite at "$6 a day apiece including food."

While Tokyo, Hong Kong, and Bangkok had introduced me to dire poverty, India was another step down, even in New Delhi, which, like most government capitals, was relatively prosperous. A better sample was provided in nearby Old Delhi, jammed with people, many living on the street, almost all dressed in what looked like rags, barbers plying their trade by the side of the road, oxcarts in the streets and roads, many unpaved dirt, and beggars everywhere. As I wrote to Rose, "one was struck by their generally ragged clothes but even more spindly legs." But I was not to see the pits to which poverty can descend until Rose and I spent a few days in Calcutta some seven years later. As a colleague in the New Delhi office of the U.S. Aid agency remarked, "You can stand a quarter square mile of slums, but when, as in Calcutta, they go on for square mile after square mile, it is nearly insupportable."

As in most poor countries, the contrast between the masses and the classes is extremely striking. In New Delhi, the latter consisted largely of members of the government, including the top civil servants, representatives of foreign governments and businesses, and a sprinkling of well-to-do businessmen, landowners, and the like. A first-time visitor is struck by what seems the hardhearted attitude of the upper classes to the poor, but it soon becomes clear that it would be impossible for affluent residents to survive unless they either developed such an attitude, or in effect joined the masses, like a Gandhi— of whom there are understandably few.

Several episodes impressed me with the cheapness and accompanying prodigal use of labor under such circumstances. One minor example was playing tennis (early in the morning to escape the heat) and having three boys running after balls for one doubles game, as well as "a so-called 'marker' who is a kind of professional tennis coach, who played with us. After we finished playing, I asked the friend who brought me whether we didn't have to tip. Oh no, he said, that was included in the $5 a month dues!" Or, again to Rose, "You would be convulsed at the sight of me walking into my Indian office here. First thing that happens is that my 'peon' runs down the hall to grab my bag and keep me from carrying it. . . . Then outside of each door are benches at which at least two 'peons' are sitting for its occupants. They all rise and salute as I walk past. It is really a sight that would be degrading if it weren't so funny. I think I told you I have a full-time peon outside my door to jump when I ring! What a waste of manpower when I'm only there a couple of hours a day."

The ICA staff and our then ambassador to India impressed me very favorably: "The staff are deeply involved in and concerned about the Indian problem; they are a dedicated group to whom their work really means a great deal." As to the ambassador, John Sherman Cooper, "I am delighted with him. He is an able, effective, and most attractive person. Our administration doesn't do so badly."

Similarly, I was more favorably impressed with the quality of the higher levels of the civil service in India than I had anticipated, even though I disagreed strongly with some of the policies they had adopted. Before independence, which India achieved in 1947, the British developed the Indian Civil Service, consisting of the ablest Indians they could attract, whom they sent to Britain to be trained. A highly elite group, almost all graduates of Oxford or Cambridge, they were few in number but were given great authority and independence. They ruled the vast and populous country. I have never met a more able or dedicated group of civil servants than the members of the ICS with whom I came in contact. Since independence, the Indians have established the Indian Administrative Service (IAS), a much larger, less select, and less well-trained group, that has by now completely replaced the ICS.

The minister of finance whom I was to advise, C. D. Deshmukh, was a fairly typical member of the ICS: "He is certainly a very intelligent and impressive person. He is quiet and an excellent listener, but with a keen mind and a not unsympathetic approach." The leading member of the Planning Commission (Nehru was the nominal chairman), to which Jacoby was assigned, was Professor P. C. Mahalanobis, a noted mathematician and head of the Indian Statistical Institute. He had been a classmate of Prime Minister Nehru at Cambridge, and was both a close friend of Nehru and one of his principal advisers.

I believe that mathematicians, whether pure mathematicians or economists or statisticians, tend to be favorable to central planning. Close contact with Mahalanobis during my stay in India reinforced my belief and led me to formulate an explanation. First, suggested solutions to mathematical problems are either clearly right or clearly wrong and "first-rate" mathematicians will agree which it is. Second, mathematical ability is frequently recognized at an early age. As a result, individuals who have exceptional mathematical ability get early deference, and develop great confidence in their ability to solve problems. When they enter a field like economics, they carry over the belief that all problems have clear-cut solutions and that they are competent to find them. As Adam Smith wrote in a famous passage, "The man of system . . . seems to imagine that he can arrange the different members of a great society with as much ease as the hand arranges the different pieces upon a chess-board; he does not consider that the pieces on the chess-board have no other principle of motion besides that which the hand impresses upon them; but that in the great chess-board of human society, every single piece has a principle of motion of its own, altogether different from that which the legislature might choose to impress upon it."[2] As a result, in economics there are frequently no clearly "right" or "wrong" answers that need only to be clearly formulated to be recognized by competent economists as the one or the other.

I do not want to misrepresent the situation. Mahalanobis was certainly open-minded in the sense of being willing to listen to different ideas, to discuss and consider them on their merits. For example, he was much taken, though not persuaded, by my suggestion that India should auction off whatever foreign exchange it proposed to make available for private use, rather than allocate it by rationing (though auctioning was clearly a second best from my point of view to the elimination of exchange controls and the floating of the rupee). But when it came time to fish or cut bait, he would come down in favor of the Planning Commission rather than the market. Deshmukh was much less opposed to the market, which is perhaps why he resigned as finance minister the next year to assume the unimportant position of chairman of the University Grants Committee.

Before I left the United States, I had boned up as much as I could on the situation in India, including comments of Indian economists on the proposed Second Five-Year Plan, of which more later, and had accumulated as much data as I could on economic magnitudes in India, so I did not arrive a complete innocent. I spent the next three weeks in extensive discussions with a wide range of Indian officials, persons at the U.S. Technical Cooperation Mission to India and the U.S. embassy, and representatives in New Delhi of the Ford and Rockefeller foundations; intensive study of data organized for me by the Finance Ministry and the Planning Commission; and a few visits to varied Indian private concerns—one of which, incidentally, took us to Agra, where we could combine it with viewing the Taj Mahal ("the most beautiful building I have ever seen"). That trip was to visit "the small scale shoe industry there— a retarded, backward segment that is being propped up by the government" and "a Community Development village, which was much more encouraging and hopeful."

At the end of the three weeks, I wrote an eleven-page memorandum, dated November 5, 1955, entitled "Some Initial Comments on Current Problems of Economic Development in India." A simple listing of the headings and subheadings will suggest the contents:

1. The goal
2. Investment policy
   a. Over-emphasis on capital-output ratio
   b. Emphasis in investment policy on the two extremes against the middle
   c. Attempt to do too much in the public sector
   d. Attempt to control private investment in too rigid and detailed a fashion
3. Policy toward the private sector
   a. Protection to inefficient methods of production
   b. Coddling of private industry in certain directions combined with severely restrictive controls in others
4. Monetary policy
   a. Erratic policy
   b. Deficit financing
5. Resources available to the public sector
6. The foreign-exchange problem
   a. The foreign-exchange gap
   b. Exchange controls
   c. Alternatives to exchange controls
7. Concluding note

I quote the concluding note in full:

> If these comments have concentrated largely on the financial machinery of economic organization, it is not because I consider it the only or even the most important problem facing India but rather because, on the one hand, it is more within my own special competence, and on the other, it seems to me the area in which current policy can be improved most.
>
> I am myself convinced that the fundamental problem for India is the improvement of the physical and technical quality of her people, the awakening of a sense of hope, the weakening of rigid social and economic arrangements, the introduction of flexibility of institutions and mobility of people, the opening up of the social and economic ladder to people of all kinds and classes. And what gives an outsider like myself a feeling of optimism and hope about the future of India, makes him feel that it is on the move and will continue to move, is that so much is being done and such a good beginning has been made

on this fundamental problem of creating the human and social basis for a dynamic and progressive economy.

As I write this more than forty years later, it is clear that my optimism, to say the least, was premature. However, in the past few years, in the atmosphere generated worldwide by the fall of the Berlin wall and the collapse of the Soviet Union, India has begun to move in the direction of giving a greater role to the market, of privatizing state enterprises, and of opening up foreign trade and investment. So the optimism may finally be justified. Let us hope so.

The only contemporary reaction to my memorandum that I know about was an article in *The Statesman,* a leading Indian newspaper, headed "Inflationary Effect Certain" and subtitled "U.S. Economist's View of India's Deficit Financing." The article was clearly based on a leaked copy of the memorandum and referred to my numerical estimates of the maximum deficit financing that would be consistent with avoiding inflation.

The government had appointed a committee of academic economists to advise on the proposed Second Five-Year Plan. I met some eight of the eighteen or nineteen members of the committee at a dinner given by J. J. Anjaria, the chief economic adviser to the Planning Commission and the finance minister, shortly after I arrived. Unfortunately, one member, whom I came to know well later, was not in that group: Professor B. R. Shenoy of the University of Ahmedabad, a remarkable and courageous man. When the committee finally turned in a report it contained a dissenting opinion, signed by Shenoy, and Shenoy alone. In my view, that dissenting opinion was head and shoulders above the rest of the report in competence and relevance. Though independently arrived at, its criticisms largely overlapped mine, but were even more unqualified. It is perhaps not easy for an American to realize how much courage it took in so conformist and rigid a society as India to dissent from the rest of the committee and to stand alone in defending reliance on the market and private enterprise rather than on government planning. Shenoy continued to demonstrate that courage. He was (he died in 1978) an absolutely first-rate economist who called the shots as he saw them. He became a member of the Mont Pelerin Society and we got to know him well. His wife is a published poet; a daughter, Sudha Shenoy, has followed in his footsteps both by becoming an economist and favoring free private enterprise. She has emigrated to Australia where she is Lecturer in Economics at the University of Newcastle in New South Wales.

Though I originally had planned to stay three months, I left almost immediately after I finished the memorandum, after a stay of about a month, because of the unfortunate incident at home that I adverted to earlier. Let Rose tell the story.

{ *Rose* } Milton was somewhat reluctant to go to India since that would be the first time he would be away from his family for so long a time. I was even more reluctant for the same reason but, in the end, we felt the experience would be instructive for him, and I had the children so I knew the time would be well taken care of. In addition, Milton and I had grand plans for me to come when his stint was over and we would have an exciting trip together.

Security in the university area had been declining slowly but we had not witnessed any real violence and I felt perfectly secure in our home, so we did not even think of having another adult come in to stay with us. But as well-laid plans often go astray, ours certainly did. Not long after Milton took off, I had the most traumatic experience of my life.

I went to a meeting at the Lab School one evening. When I came home the children were asleep upstairs. I did a little work that I hadn't completed before going off and went to bed. The next thing I was conscious of was my shoulder being shaken. The next events have always been like a dream since I was only half awake. I remember a gun, a masked face, and the words, "Where is your money?" I must have said "downstairs on the bureau," because that was where I kept my purse. But since he had already taken that, he wasn't really interested but said "get it for me." Again like an automaton I got out of bed and in my nightgown, in bare feet, with a gun pointed at me and a hand on my shoulder, I walked down the stairs. Upon reaching the bottom, I pointed to my purse and said, "There it is," but instead of taking it he made a suggestion that suddenly woke me up and I started shrieking "No." At this point he was the one who was startled. I had been so docile and accommodating up to then that my sudden reaction resulted in his flight through the open door in the kitchen. He had apparently planned an exit through this door but I'm sure he did not expect it to be such a sudden one. Though awakened as from a dream, I was not really rational. I rushed to the front window and started yelling for Milton and Aaron and other men including our neighbor, Dick Meyers. If I had been rational, I would have known that neither Milton in India nor Aaron two blocks away could possibly hear me, but Dick, who was still up, did and rushed out. Unknown to me, there was a sort of alert in the neighborhood because there had been a rash of such occurrences, all in homes where husbands were out of the country and wives were home alone. Several neighbors were soon on the street trying to track down the intruder but without success.

As for me, I was in a daze and not only for that night. Someone called Aaron, who came over immediately and stayed the night. Someone also called the police who arrived very promptly but had no suggestions for the future except getting a dog. Bars on the window through which the man had entered would not keep intruders out, they said. I could not remain in our house alone with the children at night. Plans had to be made but I was not capable of making them. Temporarily, my cousin Pauline Mosley, who lived a few blocks away, took the children the next night and I stayed at Aaron's. A police report over the radio informed the community and the news traveled quickly from Chicago to Washington. Margaret Reid, a close friend, was on her way to Washington where she was meeting with our friend Dorothy Brady who was working in Washington at that time. Being Dorothy, she did not wait to communicate with me but took the first flight to Chicago, and on the second day appeared at our house. Dorothy took over until my sister Becky arrived from Reno. In the meantime Arthur Burns, on learning the news, either called or wired Milton with the message to come home. There was much activity and Milton did cut short his visit but not immediately.

{ *Milton* } It was hard to get a clear picture of what had happened because of the difficulty of long-distance communication. I tried repeatedly to phone to Chicago, but without success. Cable, which we finally resorted to, was the only quick means of communication available. That explains why I did not cut my trip even shorter than I did. When I finally decided to do so, both the AID office and the Indian government people expressed sympathy and regret and suggested that we try to make arrangements for me to return the next spring. (That never did work out: Rose and I returned some seven years later but not in any official capacity.)

I have no record at all of how I came back from India, in contrast to the detailed record I have of going out. I only know that I did not return in the leisurely style in which I had gone out, but whether I went via the European route, or back across the Pacific, I have no recollection. Rose recalls that weather prevented the plane I was on from landing in Chicago, and forced it to land at an alternate airport, perhaps Detroit.

{ *Rose* } My sister stayed with me until Milton returned and, in addition, Earl Hamilton, who like so many was much disturbed by the incident, did not think we should be in the house without a man and arranged to have a student move into our spare room until Milton returned. We got along so well that the student (Bob Snyder) moved into one of the apartments on our third floor soon after Milton returned, and stayed there until he left the university. Needless to say, the plans for my trip to the Orient were forgotten since I was in no mood for any trip. All I really wanted was to get away from the house and from Chicago. Unfortunately, I couldn't do that until we went to Orford for the summer and then after another school year to California for the year. In the meantime I had to be satisfied with just having my husband home. There was never another extended separation!

The tremendous rise in violence in this country in the intervening years makes it hard to appreciate the deep emotional reaction to my experience by all of our friends. I was not hurt physically, only emotionally. But attempted forcible rape was a much rarer event in those days, and publicity about such events even rarer.[3] The individuals and families who experience the violence react in the same way but for many not themselves affected, the reaction, I fear, has changed. Though the feminist movement has made it easier to convict perpetrators of rape, the change in sexual morality has tended to devalue the crime.

{ *Milton* } The memorandum that I wrote in 1955 was not published at the time, though I expressed similar views in a note in January 1957 in *Encounter* magazine.[4] In 1989, the East-West Center of the University of Hawaii held a conference entitled The Modern Political Economy of India. One of the organizers of the conference, a young Indian by the name of Subroto Roy, who knew about the existence of my memorandum, invited me to attend and asked me to permit circulation of the piece. The proceedings of the conference were published in 1992, so my 1955 memo was finally published thirty-seven years after it was written! In commenting on it, the editors wrote,

> Of all the advice that the Government of India had elicited from numerous British and American economists in the 1950s and 1960s, Milton Friedman's memorandum of 1955 was unique in its content and also in the fact that it was wholly neglected and has never been published before, as far as is known by its author or by the editors. The aims of economic policy were to create conditions for rapid increase in levels of income and consumption for the mass of the people, and these aims were shared by everyone at the time from P. C. Mahalanobis to Milton Friedman. The means recommended were different. Mahalanobis advocated a leading role for the state and an emphasis on the growth of physical capital. Friedman advocated a necessary but clearly limited role for the state, and placed on the agenda large-scale investment in the stock of human capital, encouragement of

domestic competition, steady and predictable monetary growth, and a flexible exchange rate for the rupee as a convertible hard currency, which would have entailed also an open competitive position in the world economy. While it is impossible to tell what we would have been like today with an alternative history for forty years, it seems clear that if such an alternative had been more thoroughly discussed at the time, the optimal role of the state in India today, as well as the optimum complementarity between human capital and physical capital, may have been more easily determined.[5]

One final, rather amusing side effect of my visit has for long led me to take responsibility for John Kenneth Galbraith's becoming ambassador to India. Let Galbraith tell the story:

> We dined with Richard Kahn of King's College, Cambridge. . . . The other guest, a tall, slender, deeply featured and powerfully self-assured Indian, was Prasanta Chandra Mahalanobis. Mahalanobis, then sixty-two, had been a prize scholar in physics at Cambridge during the first World War. . . . He was now the head of the government supported but largely independent Indian Statistical Institute. . . . Mahalanobis was also a member of the Planning Commission of the Government of India of which Jawaharal Nehru, to whom Mahalanobis was adviser, friend and confidant, was chairman. . . .
>
> Mahalanobis spoke that evening in Geneva of India's Second . . . Five Year Plan. And more particularly he told of his generally successful efforts to bring scholars to his Institute from both the socialist countries and the West to counsel on the Plan and India's development in general. He had gone to the Eisenhower Administration for help, and it had offered him Milton Friedman then of the University of Chicago. I responded thoughtfully to the news, noting that to ask Friedman to advise on economic planning was like asking the Holy Father to counsel on the operations of a birth control clinic. Mahalanobis was pleased by my metaphor and proposed that I come to India instead. . . . We agreed to go early the following year.[6]

To the best of my knowledge, this was Galbraith's first exposure to India, the beginning of his long interest in the country.

→ *Chapter Nineteen* ←

CENTER FOR ADVANCED
STUDY, 1957–58

{ *Milton* } The Center for Advanced Study in the Behavioral Sciences was founded by the Ford Foundation to promote interaction among the different newly christened behavioral sciences—the social sciences plus other sciences such as biology and psychiatry dealing with individual behavior. As the center's current brochure says, "To reach this goal, outstanding or very promising scientists have been selected and placed in an attractive setting offering complete freedom from other obligations and distractions and all the necessary support to facilitate individual and collaborative scholarship." The center opened in September 1954 with Ralph Tyler, who had been dean of the Social Sciences at Chicago, as director. The setting was attractive: a splendid facility on the rolling Stanford hills, with separate cabins spread over the extensive grounds to serve as individual studies for the Fellows, fully equipped with desk, book shelves, etc., but without telephone, and with inviting clusters of benches outside encouraging leisurely interchange among Fellows.

I had a standing invitation from Tyler to come to the center. Ted Schultz and Allen Wallis had been Fellows during the academic year 1956–57. Both gave glowing reports of their experience. So I accepted Ralph Tyler's invitation for 1957–58.

{ *Rose* } I was delighted with the idea of spending the year in Palo Alto. It was a welcome change from winter in Chicago. In addition, I would be closer to Becky in Reno and my parents in Portland. I thought we could make frequent trips to San Francisco, which I had fallen in love with on my first visit twenty-seven years earlier. It has never lost its appeal for me. Not counting short visits, it took me twenty years to get back. (I must say, however, we did not make nearly as many trips to San Francisco from Palo Alto as I had anticipated.) Janet, though reluctant to go to California at first, had on her first visit the same reaction I had had. She vowed to come back and never leave. She did not wait as long as her mother to return. After two years at Bryn Mawr, she transferred to the University of California at Berkeley where she got her B.A. and went on to get her law degree at Boalt Hall. She has practiced law in California since then and has never left the state except for brief trips.

Unlike me, Janet and David did not look forward to another year away from their friends and their activities in Chicago. So we spent considerable time during our summer in Orford planning activities for the year to come. The promise of making the return trip to Chicago a camping adventure was a subtle bribe for David. The opportunity for regular horseback riding helped to persuade Janet. So also did the possibilities of skiing trips to Mount Hood when we visited my parents in Portland, plus interesting trips to places like Disneyland and Mexico.

The Mont Pelerin meeting was to be in Saint Moritz in 1957. Milton had not attended a meeting of the society since the founding one in 1947 and I had never attended one. We thought we would like to attend the meeting in Saint Moritz and go from there to Palo Alto. My sister Becky suggested that the children stay with her in Reno while we went to Saint Moritz.

So after a pleasant summer in Orford, we packed and went to the airport in Lebanon for the short trip to Boston where we parted, Janet and David to Reno and Milton and I to Saint Moritz. Though I remember little about the program of lectures and discussions at the sessions, I enjoyed meeting some of the people Milton had told me about who had been at the first meeting, as well as all the other interesting people who attended. In those days, the number attending was rather small, so we had the opportunity to get acquainted.

Somewhat before the end of the meeting, I left Saint Moritz in order to start Janet and David in their new schools. Traveling without Milton has never seemed to work out very well for me. (I sometimes wonder how I managed before he came along.) The trip from Saint Moritz was no exception. The train trip to London was pleasant. I had as a companion Anthony Fisher, who had started the Institute of Economic Affairs in London. However, when I arrived in London and went to the airport, I was told that I had no reservation for the trip from London to San Francisco because the person in Saint Moritz who was supposed to confirm the reservation had neglected to do so. I spent a good part of the night in the airport waiting for another flight. I finally got one and left.

Met by a friend, Mel Reder, at the airport, I eventually got to the house that the center had rented for us. The car that we had bought from Allen

271

Wallis when he left Palo Alto was in the garage, and so with a house and a car I was ready for Becky's arrival the next day with Janet and David. They had enjoyed their visit in Reno and were ready to start their new experience. Janet was beginning her first year in senior high, at Cubberley High School, which was just a block from our house. David started his last year in junior high, at Jordan Junior High School which also was within walking or biking distance. Both schools were considered good public schools.

While I don't remember much about Janet's class experience at Cubberley, I do remember that, going on fifteen, her interest in boys and dating blossomed, second only to her continuing interest in horses. School was old hat and there wasn't much to report, but dates were something new. I remember two of David's school experiences—both from his social science class. The first involved the Piltdown man. As David remembers the story, the teacher included Piltdown man in her list of ancient men. When David said that Piltdown man was a hoax, the teacher said he was wrong. He brought in his evidence the next day. The teacher never conceded her error in class, but when we met the teacher at a parents' meeting somewhat later, she made a point of saying that of course she knew about the hoax and just wanted David to bring in his evidence. The second incident involved a paper that the same teacher returned to him with a note that she hadn't read it because it was illegible. (All the practice in penmanship that David had in Cambridge did nothing to improve his atrocious writing. This was due to a gene he inherited from his father.) In any event, I typed the paper for David and he handed it back and got an A. Not long after that, David learned to type. Now, he uses the computer.

I too went to school but not to write my dissertation. I went back to something I started to do in Wisconsin and dropped abruptly when I got pregnant—a pottery class. I did somewhat better in Palo Alto and still have some of the things that didn't get broken in the years that followed.

In addition to the social activities at the center—picnics, square dancing, and many others, we enjoyed getting together with our friends Moe and Carrie Abramovitz as well as other friends who were not at the center. Most of all, I enjoyed the frequent visits from Becky and my mother, who was reluctant to travel to Chicago but was persuaded to visit us in Palo Alto. Also, we found it much easier to go to Portland by plane or car from Palo Alto than from Chicago. Since, wisely or not, we brought up our children in a secular home, they had never experienced the Jewish holidays, the happy ones and the sad, that we had known as children. Passover (Pesach) is one of the happy holidays so we went home to Portland for that. It had always been my favorite holiday and the ceremony on the first two nights benefits greatly from the presence of children. Our children enjoyed the festivity and my parents of course were overjoyed to have the children with them.

{ *Milton* } The roster of Fellows at the center that year was extraordinary in both the range of disciplines included and the distinction of the Fellows— a real tribute to the success of Ralph Tyler and his associates in selecting Fellows. The forty-seven Fellows were from five countries and thirteen disciplines. There were three other economists: Melvin Reder, then at Stanford, later at Chicago; Robert Solow, then as now at MIT; and George Stigler, then at Columbia, but scheduled to move to Chicago the next year. Three of the four economists subsequently received the Nobel Prize in Economics.

Five other Fellows were from Chicago in fields other than economics.[1] Louis Gottschalk, a historian whom I had known only casually in Chicago, organized a weekly poker game through which we got to know him and his lovely wife Frooma far better. As I recall, George Stigler and Sidney Siegel, an extraordinarily innovative and imaginative psychologist and inspired poker player (who died at an early age), were among the other Fellows who participated. The games continued irregularly and with changing participants for some years after we returned to Chicago.

Joseph Ben-David, a sociologist from Israel, was one of the foreign Fellows. He and his wife Miriam became close friends and we saw them in later years either when Jossi, as we called him, came to the University of Chicago Sociology Department on extended visits or when we visited Israel.

Another Fellow whom we got to know well on a social as well as professional level was Frank Newman, a law professor at Berkeley who later was a member of the California Supreme Court. His son, about the same age as Janet, started dating her, to the pleasure of both families.

One Fellow whom I knew from my wartime work at the Statistical Research Group was John Tukey, a brilliant mathematical statistician, one of the few people I have met in my life whom I would unhesitatingly label a genius.* He and I spent many hours exploring the relation between the world of economics and dynamic engineering structures, saying that we had to develop the analogies further, but never doing so. He did instill in me a serious

---

* I find it fascinating that of the people whom I have met whom I would label geniuses, so many are mathematical statisticians: R. A. Fisher, Jimmie Savage, Harold Hotelling, John Tukey.

A Tukey wartime episode that comes to mind is from a session at the Statistical Research Group (or perhaps its neighbor and associate, the Applied Mathematical Group) that was engaged in discussing a problem that had baffled some of their best mathematicians for days. Tukey, after hearing the problem for the first time, walked confidently to the blackboard and said, "The solution is . . ." And so it was.

interest in the possible use of spectral analysis for economic research. For several years thereafter, I spent much time on spectral analysis, experimenting extensively with its application in my own monetary research and stimulating a number of Ph.D. theses on the subject. I finally concluded that it was an unsuccessful experiment for me, though I continue to believe that the technique holds much promise for economics. Tukey also distinguished himself by his love of square dancing, which I believe he introduced at the center.

Another Fellow whom I knew from the Statistical Research Group was Ted Anderson, like Tukey a mathematical statistician. He and I collaborated on an article that tied up a loose end from the work done at the SRG more than a decade earlier.[2] It was one of the last papers I wrote in pure statistics.

For me, the center fully lived up to its promise. I was able to make rapid progress on the book that I was writing jointly with Anna J. Schwartz on monetary history. I wrote a number of journal articles, interacted with the scholars from other disciplines, and withal had ample leisure for family and social activities—as well as to play a lot of tennis, especially with George.

We did a fair amount of traveling within California to make good on our promises to the children, but I made only one trip by myself and that was to participate in a nationally televised program on CBS entitled "How Strong Is Our Economy?," the third in a much publicized series entitled "The Great Challenge," moderated by Howard K. Smith, a popular CBS Washington correspondent. This was my first experience with television, though I had had a fair amount of experience with radio thanks to the University of Chicago Round Table (see chap. 13).

The television program was doubtless more dramatic than the radio Round Table but to my mind less effective as a means of presenting content. As I wrote to the producer subsequently, "there were . . . too many people"— seven in addition to the moderator—"too many views and too free ranging and undisciplined a discussion."[3]

This experience was the first of many that impressed on me the different ways people react to TV and to radio. The mail response to a radio discussion tends to be much more negative and critical than to a TV discussion. The reason, I believe, is that the voice over the radio is disembodied; if the listener disagrees with the ideas presented he has no difficulty in demonizing the person who presented them; on the TV screen the ideas presented may be the same, but they are coming from a real human face. Ideas play a much larger role, irrelevant theatrical aspects a much smaller role, in radio than in television. Unfortunately, television is so powerful a medium that it has largely displaced radio for popular discussions, at least until the recent explosion of talk radio.

Of the several talks I gave while I was at the center, the most memorable was my participation in a debate organized by a local chapter of University of Chicago alumni on July 25, 1958. The subject was a new book by Mortimer Adler and Louis Kelso, which was receiving a good deal of publicity, entitled *The Capitalist Manifesto*. Adler and Kelso defended the book; I and Ithiel de Sola Pool, a political scientist from MIT and a Fellow at the Center, were on the other side; Clark Kerr, the chancellor of the University of California at Berkeley, was the moderator. The thesis of the book was that Marx had it backward, that it was capital, not workers, that was exploited. According to Marx, labor produces the whole of the product but only gets part. According to Adler and Kelso, capital produces 90 percent of the product but only gets 20 or 30 percent in return—as I put it at the debate, Marxism upside down with a 10 percent discount for cash.

The book's economics was bad, reflecting a complete lack of understanding of the forces accounting for returns to factors of production; the interpretation of history, ludicrous; and the policy recommended, dangerous. At a dinner prior to the debate attended by Adler but not Kelso, I asked Adler, whom I had known casually from his Chicago days (which ended in 1956), why he had lent his name to such economic nonsense. Adler replied that the economics was all Kelso's and he took no responsibility for it; he coauthored the book because he agreed with its intentions!

Kelso used the book to promote his solution for all the economic ills of the nation: ESOPs, employee stock ownership plans, which he claimed would convert workers into capitalists. He subsequently made a career of promoting and introducing such plans in many businesses. They were very popular because they constituted an ingenious tax evasion device for business.

One feature that made the debate memorable was not only the extremely large audience that it attracted, but even more that Clark Kerr, who arrived on crutches thanks to an accident, was so outraged by the Adler-Kelso line that he lost his cool as a moderator and attacked them vigorously.

On a very different topic, George Stigler's transfer from Columbia to Chicago was arranged during the year at the center. George had rejected several earlier attempts by Ted Schultz to attract him to Chicago. The successful offer was arranged by Allen Wallis, thanks to his pulling off the coup of getting control of the Walgreen Fund.[4]

That was very good news. It meant that for the first time since 1945 the three of us, Allen, George, and I, would be at the same institution. It did not, however, last for long. In 1962, Allen left to assume the presidency of the University of Rochester. Although we continued to keep in close touch with one another, never again were we all at the same institution.

{ *Rose* } When our year at the center came to an end, we set out to make good on our promise of a camping trip home. To my surprise, the camping trip, which I approached with some apprehension, turned out to be a delightful experience.

An exception was an early stop at Las Vegas. Our car was not air-conditioned, as few if any were at the time. As we got farther south, and entered the desert approaching Las Vegas, it became unbearably hot. We got relief at an air-conditioned motel. I recall that we purchased what was advertised as an air cooler for a car. I never did understand how it was supposed to work. It consisted of a cylinder that hung on a car window and was filled with water, the evaporation of which was supposed to cool the air. What I do recall is that every time I pulled a string that was supposed to improve the operation of the gadget, I got a shower of water.

From Las Vegas, we proceeded on a tour of national parks: first to Zion, with its extravagant colors; then to Bryce Canyon, with its extraordinary stone formations, the viewing of which on awakening in the morning, David today regards as "one of the most memorable moments in that trip"; to the Grand Canyon, the Petrified Forest National Park, Rocky Mountain National Park, and finally, Yellowstone. In each case we registered at the park campground when we arrived, Milton and David would unload the carrier on top of the car that held our camping gear and set up our tent, while Janet and I would make the necessary preparations for our evening meal. We would then stay a day or two before packing up and proceeding to our next stop. The parks then may have been less elaborate than now, but they were well maintained and far less crowded. As I recall, we made no advance reservations at any of the parks.

David and Milton planned to hike to the bottom of the Grand Canyon and up the other side—unquestionably the high spot of the trip for them. So we drove first to the north rim, where all of us went part way into the canyon on burros. Then Janet and I did our part by driving the car from the north rim of the canyon to the south rim and had the luxury of staying in a hotel for one night.

{ *Milton* } As David and I went down into the canyon on our hike, we moved from a temperate zone into an increasingly torrid zone—indeed one of the fantastic features of the trip down and up the canyon is the range of temperature zones and accompanying flora and fauna encountered on the way down and up. At the rim, we started in a temperate zone. At the bottom, we were in the tropics.

Around noontime, it was already getting very hot. We found a lovely little nook with a small waterfall keeping it relatively cool where we stopped for lunch. While having lunch, we heard noises that we did not recognize at the time, but learned a few days later, when we visited a rattlesnake farm, that they were rattlesnake rattles. After lunch, we discussed whether to rest for a few hours in the nook until the heat of the day had started to decline or continue on. We decided on the latter course for one reason only: the brochure for the Phantom Ranch at the bottom of the canyon, where we were to spend the night, showed tempting pictures of a swimming pool.

Accordingly, we continued on through increasingly intense heat. When we were shown to our cabin at the ranch, we asked the attendant where the swimming pool was. She pointed us in the right direction and went on her way. We put on our swimming trunks, which we had brought with us in anticipation of this moment, and proceeded to the pool, only to find when we got there that it had only mud in it, and was in the process of being cleaned out! Imagine the attendant not telling us that it was empty!

Nonetheless, David and I greatly enjoyed our walk up and down. The transition from one climate zone to another is accompanied by a corresponding change in vegetation and small animals. The trip down is more pleasurable, though of course less challenging, not only because it is down not up but also because it is a much milder slope that makes it possible to enjoy the scenery.

Rose and I had come down and up the southern side nearly two decades earlier, but that time on the backs of burros. This time, David and I climbed down and up on our own feet. Though more tiring, we did not experience the aftereffect of difficulty in sitting down for days, as Rose and I had earlier. We took it in leisurely fashion, and we were both in pretty good shape. I would not like to try it now! But David and I both relish having done it once.

At Yellowstone, on our final morning there, Rose was holding a piece of bread on a long fork over a fire to toast it when her back went out. She apparently dislocated a disk and could hardly move. We laid her down flat on the back seat of the car, packed as expeditiously as we could, and went on to the first decent motel we could find—I believe in Billings, Montana. We stayed there for nearly a week until Rose felt she could go on—an unexpected addition to our trip but not unpleasant for me and the kids as it was for Rose.

{ *Rose* } After we returned home, Janet went back to U High as a junior. It was time to start thinking about college. At the end of the school year, Milton took Janet on a tour of the schools she had selected as possibilities. She fell in love with the Bryn Mawr campus. In addition, thanks to the interest in British history that she developed during our year in Cambridge, she was attracted by the presence on the faculty of Caroline Robbins, a noted historian.

She was not interested in applying for admission to any other college but applied early at Bryn Mawr and was accepted.

On registering for courses when she matriculated in 1960, Janet discovered that Professor Robbins was on leave for the year, and another professor was taking her classes. Before the year was over, she was very unhappy about the substitute. Whether for that reason or some other, Janet came home in the spring and said she wanted to transfer to the University of California at Berkeley. We were not very happy about her changing schools and persuaded her to return for at least one more year. She took our advice and returned, changing her major from history to dramatics. That did not do the trick. She remained unhappy about continuing at Bryn Mawr so she applied for a transfer to Berkeley and was accepted.

David's turn to go on the tour of colleges came a year after Janet's. He chose to apply to Swarthmore and Harvard. He was turned down by Swarthmore—presumably because they had too many applicants from the Lab School or from Chicago or whatever. He was accepted by Harvard. I was not very happy about David's going to a large university. He was sixteen years old and not very mature socially. He was still my little boy and I felt he would be better off at a small school. As it turned out, I was wrong. He was very happy at Harvard, where he found a small circle of like-minded friends, some of whom have remained close friends.

From his early years, David was interested in and displayed unusual aptitude for economics. Nonetheless he entered Harvard as a physics and chemistry major. That was largely at our urging. Given that he also displayed interest and talent in mathematics and physics, we felt that he would be better off in a field other than his father's. David was persuaded and not only majored in physics as an undergraduate, but earned a doctorate in physics at the University of Chicago and spent two years at Columbia on a postdoctoral fellowship in physics.

However, his interest in economics was not to be denied. While at Chicago, he was active in the Young Americans for Freedom and wrote columns for their publication, *The New Guard*. While at Columbia, he wrote a book presenting the case for free-market anarchism, *The Machinery of Freedom*, which has become something of a classic in libertarian literature and is now in a revised second edition.[5]

After the two years at Columbia, David decided that he would rather spend his life as an economist than a physicist, and managed to get a fellowship at the University of Pennsylvania to enable him to convert to economics and supplement his dinner table education. He has since come to specialize in the field that his Uncle Aaron pioneered, law and economics.

✢ Chapter Twenty ✢

OUR WANDERJAHR: 1962–63

{ *Rose* } Our twenty-fifth wedding anniversary was reason enough to celebrate the year 1962–63. In addition, as the year began, three books were
nearing completion (*Capitalism and Freedom, Price Theory: A Provisional Text*,
and *A Monetary History of the United States, 1867–1960*) and would be published in the academic year 1962–63. We no longer had children at home:
Janet was finishing her sophomore year at Bryn Mawr and David his freshman
year at Harvard. It seemed an ideal time for a change of scenery, and we had
both an excuse and an opportunity. The excuse was Milton's desire to explore
monetary conditions in countries that had very different monetary arrangements from those of the U.S. or Britain.* The opportunity was a combination
of a Ford Foundation Faculty Fellowship, which relieved Milton from his
teaching obligations, and a supplementary fellowship from the Carnegie Corporation.

Thus it was that we embarked on a year-long trip around the world during
which we stayed for two months or more in each of the five countries that
Milton wished to study in detail: Israel, Yugoslavia, Greece, India, and Japan,
and made briefer visits to sixteen other countries.[1] I had not visited any of

---

* As he wrote to economists in the various countries with whom he wanted to cooperate
or whose assistance he sought: "During the past ten years, I have been conducting a large scale
study of the role of money in economic fluctuations in the United States. This study, which is
now drawing to a close, has produced a considerable number of generalizations about monetary
relations. Although these were derived from experience in the United States, it has seemed to
me that one of the most effective ways of testing them would be to see whether they hold also
for other countries and particularly for countries with a different monetary background. I realize
that it is not feasible for me to make such tests myself because I cannot possibly acquire the
knowledge, background, and mastery of the data of other countries that would be necessary.
What I hope to do is to interest some people in those countries to undertake studies along
these lines."

the five listed countries and Milton had visited only India. In almost every country, former students of Milton or his colleagues were available to help and guide us. The chief exceptions, understandably, were Poland and the Soviet Union.

As it happens, this year is one of our most fully documented years, thanks to collections of letters that I wrote to Dorothy Brady and my sister Becky, and that Milton wrote to Anna Schwartz.

We departed New York on August 29, 1962, on the SS *Queen Elizabeth,* accompanied to the dock by Dorothy Brady, Janet, and David. My mood on leaving is best described in a letter to Becky that I wrote from the ship: "Our second day at sea is almost over, and I am beginning to realize that we are really on our way. Tho' truth to tell, it dawned on me very keenly when I bade my children good-bye. When I saw Jan and David on the other side of the plank from me, I first realized it was I who was going away, and I am afraid I had a strange desire to get off and join them. I know this is silly since if I didn't leave them they would soon leave me." In my notes I comment about the children's reaction: "Jan appears to be very nonchalant about our leaving. I have the feeling she was putting on an act. Not so David—he seems to be anxious to get it over. Seems on the point of tears as was I."

Paris

We disembarked at Cherbourg and made our way to Paris by the crowded boat train. After getting settled at the Hôtel Saint-Simon, a small hotel on the Left Bank that had suited our needs and our pocketbook on earlier trips to Paris, we went for a walk, our favorite pastime in Paris. After spending the first day in Paris at the American Express office attending to the many details of our coming trip, we spent the remaining three days visiting friends: the Rougiers, the de Jouvenels, and our old friends Moe and Carrie Abramovitz, who happened to be spending some time in Paris. In addition, we managed to see the opera *La Dolce* and the Folies Bergères.

From Paris, we went to Knokke, Belgium, to attend a meeting of the Mont Pelerin society. After a week of tours, lectures, receptions and banquets in Belgium, we took off from Amsterdam for Warsaw.

Warsaw

When we arrived in Warsaw, all the leading Polish economists were attending a Polish economic society meeting outside of Warsaw. We had the rewarding experience, however, of meeting Professor Eduard Lupinsky, one of Poland's leading economists, who had retired and therefore was not attending the economic society meeting. I don't remember just how this came about. Professor Lupinsky was a fascinating guide, and we learned a great deal about Poland from him. He told us that he had been a socialist all his life but had come to the conclusion that socialism was possible only when a country was rich enough so that everyone could afford a house and a maid. We asked, "Including the maid?" and he said, "Of course." We met Professor Lupinsky again when we were in Dubrovnik.

{ *Milton* } Some time after we returned to Chicago, I invited Professor Lupinsky, who was on a trip to the U.S., to visit Chicago and lecture to my class and meet with my Money and Banking Workshop. They found his views most interesting, quite different from what they expected.

Warsaw was our first real introduction to communism. A specific incident brought that home most vividly. I had promised to write a piece for the Radio Free Europe station in West Berlin, but completed it only after our arrival in Warsaw. I was not so naive as to believe that I could safely mail the piece to Berlin from Warsaw so I called the U.S. Embassy from our hotel room and asked whether they could get my package from Warsaw to Berlin via diplomatic pouch. The reply was brusque: impossible, against the rules, and then, after a brief pause, where are you staying?

A half hour or so later, a knock on the door, and an American from the embassy came in without saying a word, gave us his card, looked around the room, stationed himself with his back against the wall under a ventilation grille, pointed to it, and conveyed by sign language that it was probably bugged. He then gestured for me to give him what I had. I handed over the addressed package containing my piece, and he left without any of us having said a word during the whole process. A powerful demonstration of how to behave in a totalitarian society. Lupinsky's openness became even more impressive to us. His reputation as a brave and independent person was clearly justified.

Another revealing episode occurred on the roof of the thirty-seven-story Palace of Culture and Science—a recent guide book notes that "with ironic humor, Warsaw citizens will tell you that [that is] the best vantage point from which to admire their rebuilt city . . . because it is the only spot from which you can avoid looking at the Palace of Culture and Science—a wedding-cake-skyscraper gift from Stalin built in 'Stalin-Gothic.'" In the course of his talk, our official guide pointed across the Vistula River to the position where, according to him, the Soviet Union's troops gathered before crossing the river and subduing the Germans. After he finished, we got into an informal conversation with a policeman who spoke English. He pointed to the same place, and with great bitterness said something like: "and waited long enough before crossing the Vistula to give the Germans time to finish destroying Warsaw and killing its inhabitants." He also referred to the Katyn Forest massacre of Polish officers serving with the Russian troops, which was fully confirmed only in recent years. Clearly, there was no love lost between the native Poles and the Soviets.

Soviet Union

{ *Rose* }   Warsaw was a way station to the Soviet Union.[2] We had decided to go to Moscow by bus rather than plane in order to see more of the Soviet Union. We got more than we bargained for. The bus tour that we joined after two days in Warsaw was the last Maupintour trip from Helsinki to Warsaw to Moscow to Leningrad and back to Helsinki. The bus had a Finnish driver, a Finnish guide, a Polish guide on the Polish segment, a Soviet guide on the Soviet segment, a Maupintour representative, and only about eight or ten passengers, including us.

We did not get very far from Warsaw before trouble began. My Christmas letter written at the end of 1962 when this part of our year's travel was still very fresh in my mind tells this part of the story best:

> A three-day trip from Warsaw to Moscow turned into one long hitch as a result of motor trouble. We literally pushed the bus (Finnish with a British motor) across the Polish-Russian border because the truck that had towed us to the Polish border, not having a Russian entry permit, could not cross the border. We barely escaped entering the Soviet Union in the back of a dirty cattle truck and instead made the pilgrimage from the frontier to Brest (formerly Brest-Litovsk, where the treaty was signed that ended the first World War between Germany and the newly emerged Soviet Union) in dignity in our bus which was towed by the cattle truck.

We could not decide whether this series of events was explained by the satisfaction the officials got from humbling the American tourists, or simply by rigid adherence to the rules that no official would consider breaking.

Our hotel in Brest was not an Intourist hotel; it was strictly for local travelers, but our Intourist guide managed to get us rooms. It was by all odds the worst hotel we have ever stayed in—and in the course of a long life of extensive travel, we have stayed at some bad ones. The beds were covered by only a thin sheet, and continuous propaganda came from a loudspeaker in the wall that couldn't be turned off. The floors were dirty. Only one of the rooms had a bathtub. We agreed that it should be occupied by the young ladies traveling with us, but be available to all of us. The bathtub was filthy and was made usable only after the young ladies went out and bought some scouring powder, and scrubbed the tub. The public toilet facilities were unspeakable, and could be located from a distance by the smell. Bad as were the Intourist hotels that we later stayed at in Moscow and Kiev, they were four-star compared to this miserable place.

{ *Milton* } While at dinner, I needed to use the toilet facilities. After walking a long way to find them, I witnessed one of the funniest sights I have ever seen: opening the door to what I thought was an empty cubicle, I saw inside a man perched on top of the Western-style porcelain toilet bowl, with one foot on either side of the bowl going about his business. All his life, he had obviously used only the "oriental" style of toilet, consisting essentially of a hole in the floor, and did not know how to use the new-fangled Western equipment.

{ *Rose* } From Brest-Litovsk, to Minsk, to Smolensk, we made our way from one repair shop to another, never going more than half way on our own steam, always making the last lap behind a tow truck. One principle was definitely established. Russian mechanics could always repair the bus well enough to get us out of range of their shop but never well enough to get us to our next destination—a special version of NIMBY. We finally arrived in Moscow the morning of the fifth day after an all-night ride in a drafty, bumpy local bus provided for us after lengthy telephone calls from Intourist headquarters in Smolensk. From the beginning, we had planned to leave the bus in Moscow and not continue on the tour to its end in Helsinki. So we breathed a sigh of relief when we got to Moscow.

The rural areas that we passed from Warsaw to Moscow showed little change from descriptions of them fifty or a hundred years ago. The same village well and horse-drawn carts, a preponderance of women bent double working in the fields, and an almost complete absence of mechanized equipment. In the main, the villages were dark at night except for an occasional light in the communist headquarters. On one of our many stops because of motor trouble, our driver found that his map showed a side road with a repair garage on it. He persuaded our Soviet Intourist guide, who had joined us at Brest-Litovsk, that we should try it. When we arrived at the side road, we were surprised to find that it was paved—as nearly as we could tell, it was the only paved side road all the way from the border to Moscow. We had not traveled far on this road before an officer on a motorcycle stopped us, and wanted to know what we were doing on that road since it was only for the military. Our guide explained the situation. That officer was not high enough on the military ladder (only one star) to tell us whether, having ventured onto a forbidden road, we were permitted to turn back. We were instructed to stay where we were while he checked with a superior officer. After the arrival of several more officers, we finally were instructed by an officer with four stars that we could turn back and that they would order a tow truck to meet us at the main road and tow us to the next city. We got back to the main road. Needless to say there was no tow truck. So we limped on.

In Moscow, we were impressed by public affluence amidst private squalor. People hurrying along the streets were poorly dressed. Shop windows were drab and the merchandise terribly expensive, both in terms of dollars at the official rate of exchange and in terms of rubles relative to the average income. Much residential building was under way but, to judge from our personal experience at recently constructed hotels in both Minsk and Smolensk, quality was incredibly poor.

On the other hand, the new Palace of the Soviets in the Kremlin was a splendid modern building of aluminum and glass and so was a Pioneer Palace designed for extracurricular activities of the young. The young who attended the palace, we noticed, were brought there in fancy cars driven by chauffeurs. The opera, the ballet, the puppet theater—all were beautiful. All were for the privileged.

Our visit to the Soviet Union was purely as tourists. However, Soviet economists whom we had entertained in Chicago had urged us to see for ourselves what the Soviet Union was like, implying that they would like to show us around. Our Intourist guide telephoned some of these economists at our request. One after another was said to be either ill or out of the country or otherwise indisposed. When we reported our experience at the American Embassy, they told us that relations with the Soviet Union were cyclical, up and down, and that this was a down period.

{ *Milton* } Our guide finally reached a professor of statistics whom we had not met but who knew of some of my work in statistics and expressed a desire to meet us. He invited us to have lunch with him at the faculty club of the University of Moscow. When we arrived at the appointed hour, he was not there. He arrived breathless a bit late and apologized, saying that he had had a flat tire on the way to the club. Not wanting to dirty his clothes by changing the tire himself, he recruited a passerby to change it for him for a few kopecks. According to him, this kind of transaction was ubiquitous. Expanding on the tribulations of a car owner in Moscow, he noted that it was not safe to leave windshield wipers or removable hood ornaments on the car, because they would be stolen when the driver was not there. Everyone kept windshield wipers locked inside the car until it started to rain, and took them off when it stopped raining or they left the car.

The professor, whose name I don't recall, was clearly no enthusiast about the Soviet Union. He referred several times to Stalin though never by name, always saying, "that man," and twirling spikes at the ends of an imaginary mustache. He had apparently never been allowed out of the country, perhaps because, unlike most people we met in any capacity, he spoke very frankly and did not keep looking to see if he was being spied on. The only sign of discretion that he showed was his unwillingness to mention Stalin by name, and it was not even clear whether that was discretion or for effect. He seemed well informed. The questions that he asked us about the U.S. were very different from the naivetés of our guide and other casual contacts. He also seemed well informed about Western contributions to his specialty, statistics.

The meal at the faculty club was very good; indeed, I believe that it was the best meal we had in the Soviet Union. The experience with this one professor, with whom we had no further contact, reinforced a conclusion that I had reached much earlier: despite differences in average incomes in various countries, full professors in major educational institutions have much the same standard of life. The difference in national income is reflected in the relative number of full professors and in the number of jobs from which they get their income.

I did try to accomplish one professional task. I tried to get data on the quantity of money in the Soviet Union, primarily currency and coins issued by the central bank. On inquiring of the economists at the embassy, I was told that the central bank did not publish such figures: they were a state secret. I did not know then nor do I know now of any other country in the world in which such figures are a state secret! The published figures may be highly inaccurate, but at least they are published.

{ *Rose* } I summarized our impression of the Soviet Union in *The Oriental Economist* in October 1976, when the memories were still strong: "It is difficult to put into words the oppressive feeling that we had while in the Soviet Union. There was nothing concrete to which we could attribute our fear. The atmosphere alone made one feel as though one were being watched constantly. The ever-present loudspeakers in every hotel room, the feeling that there were only certain places that one could go or rather be taken to by one or another Intourist guide. . . . The ordinary people that one occasionally met and could talk to seemed fearful of talking to a stranger and were constantly looking around to see who was listening."[3]

Our Intourist guides varied in intelligence and their commitment to communism. Our guide on the bus to Moscow was well indoctrinated but not very bright. She could not believe that we were taken in by what she read about the Soviet Union in the copy of the English-language periodical *Soviet Survey* that we purposely left exposed on our seat on one occasion when we were waiting for our bus to be repaired. She could not resist picking up that or other magazines when she could. On another such occasion when we were waiting in the bus Milton was telling riddles to pass the time. Unlike the passengers, she was at a loss for answers to the simplest riddles. As it turned out, that episode really opened the eyes of several of our young fellow passengers. They had been much impressed by the apparently sophisticated and knowledgeable answers she had given to their questions about the Soviet Union. This episode made them realize that they had been listening to a phonograph record.

Our guide in Moscow on the other hand impressed us as bright and far less committed. We felt that she often asked questions because she was skeptical about what she had been told and wanted to have the information confirmed. However, after many of our answers contradicted what she had been told about the wonders of communism, she broke down in tears. "Why," she said, "do you come here and tell us how bad it is? We have to live here, you don't."

An early experience in Moscow still gives me goose pimples when I recall it. One of the young ladies who was on our bus to Moscow introduced us to a young Russian who she said would like to have any magazines or papers in English. She knew from traveling with us that we had brought some. We were delighted to give him any that we had and suggested that he come to our hotel the following morning. He was hesitant to come to the hotel, suggesting instead that we meet him on a specified corner close to the hotel. When we arrived the next morning, he was on the corner opposite to the one he had indicated. He hurried across, told us that he was being followed, and led us to a metro station close by. He then informed us that a monastery he knew would be the best place to talk and give him the magazines, and that we could get there by metro. A few changes from one train to another brought us to the monastery. Our young man informed us that we were still being followed. At this point, my heart was beginning to beat very rapidly. To the best of my memory, I had never been followed by a mystery man. We had not yet even been to the American Embassy so that no one knew of our existence in the Soviet Union. Milton was beginning to feel the same discomfort and suggested that we take a cab and go back to our hotel. The young man did not disagree but he sent the first cab away so as to confuse his follower, he said, and we took the next one. There was very little conversation in the cab— only, "please hand me the magazines unseen" when we arrived at the metro station that he specified. He got out and disappeared so rapidly we could not even see whether he entered the metro station. Relieved, we went on to our hotel. We were never really sure whether our young man was taking us for a ride or if it was for real. If it was not for real, he should be in Hollywood.

We were encouraged by the friendliness of the people we met—especially when we said we were Americans. Judging from their questions, Soviet propaganda had succeeded in convincing the people that the Americans would start a war. Almost everyone we talked to expressed great anxiety about war and insisted that we convey the message that the Soviet people wanted no war with the Americans. On the other hand, they were not convinced by another propaganda line, one concerning the low standard of living in America. The people we met were always curious about just *how* well an American lived. Their questions were never whether we owned a house but how many we owned. How many cars?

Though our entire visit to the Soviet Union was depressing, two of the most depressing experiences occurred during the Jewish New Year. We had not been to a synagogue for many years, and decided to go in Moscow because we knew that my fluency in Yiddish would enable us to communicate with people there.

The day before the holiday we learned from a woman at a fish market who spoke Yiddish that only two synagogues were left in all of Moscow and only one in Kiev. We took a taxi on our own (a rare event) to the synagogue at sundown on the eve of Rosh Hashana. We got out a block from the synagogue because we knew that riding in cars on high holidays is forbidden by Jewish law. As we approached the synagogue, we saw that the steps and sidewalk were full of the saddest-looking individuals we had ever seen. The men were unshaven and dressed in shabby work clothes. Men and women greeted us with hands extended begging for kopecks. We had been told that begging was permitted only at religious establishments, as part of the Soviet Union's effort to degrade formal religion. The spectacle was particularly depressing because we were accustomed to seeing people, especially women, dressed in their newest outfits on the high holidays. Moreover, carrying money was forbidden.

Since we had no kopecks, we made our way at a slow pace up the steps and inside only to find that the hallway and rear of the synagogue were very crowded and the people there as shabby as those outside. Foreigners were immediately recognized and just about every Russian we saw was eager to talk to us. They were not interested in the religious service and did not hesitate to carry on a conversation while the service was in progress. Like all the Russians we met, they had the same anxiety about war and the same ignorance about anything in the outside world. We finally cut short our visit because, unlike them, we were embarrassed by talking during the service. We did not see a single child or even a young person in the synagogue. What we learned both from this visit and the following one in Kiev was that most Russian Jews who went to synagogue did so not because they were believers but simply because they were permitted to congregate only on high holidays.

{ *Milton* } In the crowded anteroom of the synagogue, a man approached me and asked whether I would change into rubles a U.S. ten-dollar bill that he had apparently been given by an American tourist. It was illegal to hold or exchange foreign currency, which is why he wanted to get rubles instead. Although the black market rate for dollars was much higher than the official rate, all he wanted was the official rate. Engaging in such a transaction in a synagogue on a high holiday was sacrilegious indeed, but his concern with religious conformity was obviously less than his fear of Soviet officialdom.

{ *Rose* } The following morning we flew to Kiev. At the airport, the routine was the same—the Intourist guide and the car were waiting to greet us. I must say we appreciated being met because it was almost impossible to find anyone at the local airports who spoke anything but Russian. Our guide was more relaxed than the ones in Moscow—in fact the whole atmosphere seemed less driven. After a short sight-seeing trip in the afternoon and a ballet in the evening, we mentioned that we would like to be on our own the next day, which was the second day of Rosh Hashana. Our guide had no objection.

Sunday morning was bright and sunny so we decided to walk to the synagogue, which is in the old city. We stopped to rest at a boat station where two women were sitting on a bench. They were mother and daughter. Overhearing Yiddish spoken, I spoke to them. They had come from their village to meet an American relative who was visiting the Soviet Union. He could not come to their village because it was closed to visitors. They did not say why and did not want to talk about it. The atmosphere of fear was pervasive. When the mother began to talk about conditions for Jews in their village, the young woman put her hand on her mother's knee to stop her.

When the relative from the United States arrived, along with relatives from Kiev, he said he had not brought a camera but would like to have a picture of the group, so Milton offered to take it and send it to him when we got home. One man in the group who was not Jewish but married to a Jewess was hesitant to let his picture be taken with the group until Milton assured him that the film would not be developed until after we left the Soviet Union. We never knew whether his fear was from being with an American visitor or with Jews. Our short visit over, we proceeded to the synagogue.

The crowd of people not only filled the sidewalk in front of the synagogue but overflowed across the street. They seemed to us a little better dressed than those in Moscow and there was no begging. But again, there were no young people. As soon as we arrived, one group formed around me and another around Milton with questions. Again, their ignorance and their eagerness to hear about the outside world was impressive. They could not believe that we had no identity cards—only passports for use in foreign travel. One man asked me why American women were so slim. He knew that they had plenty to eat! Many said that they had relatives in the United States and wanted to know how they could get in touch with them. No one appeared to be in touch with relatives outside.

One man said he had an uncle in Philadelphia and asked me if I could locate his uncle if he gave me his name. I said that I thought I could and started to take out my pad to write down the name. His eyes looked over the crowd and he said "never mind." Fear and ignorance were the dominant emotions—fear of the people around them as well as anyone outside. Here as well as everywhere we went, people tried to assure us that the Russian people did not want war. On our part, we kept assuring them that war would not come from our side. All the conversation was in Yiddish.

{ *Milton* } My Yiddish is very much more limited than Rose's since it was not the language at home when I was growing up. However, combined with the one year of German I had taken in college, it was enough to enable me to carry on a halting conversation with the crowd that surrounded me.

{ *Rose* } After about a half hour's questions and answers, a man whispered in my ear, "I think you had better leave or you will get us into trouble," whereupon we left without ever going into the synagogue.

Our final experience in the Soviet Union was getting out. We were scheduled to leave Kiev on a plane that would get us to Moscow in plenty of time to go from the local airport to the international airport from which we were to leave for Belgrade. Our flight from Kiev was canceled, however, and another did not arrive for five hours (we were told this was not unusual). Although we arrived in Moscow three hours before the Belgrade flight was due to depart, we were informed by the guide who met us that he would take us to a hotel because according to the rules we did not have enough time to get to the international airport. We were also informed that the next flight to Belgrade was a week later! However, our guide said that they would look after us.

We had had enough of the Soviet Union and wanted out so insisted that we would take our chances and go on to the international airport. Another Intourist guide was located and we left. On our way our guide explained that he was studying English at Moscow University. When we asked him what he was planning to do after graduating, his answer was instantaneous: "They haven't told me yet." Our guide's home was on the way to the airport and he asked if we would mind if he left us and let the cab driver alone take us to the airport. Of course, we didn't mind. That gave us a chance to talk with the driver—who spoke no English but did speak German. He wanted to know if we had any ballpoint pens. The Russians, he said, didn't make good pens; they leaked. We gave him a pen. However, he said, the Russians made good cars. The car we were riding in was a prewar Plymouth, which bore the same symbol on the radiator cap and the wheel hubs as the ones built in the United States.

We arrived at the airport in ample time to board our plane to Belgrade. The food in the Soviet Union, at least in the restaurants available to us, was so poor that we didn't eat much. As a result, we had many ration coupons left. The only thing we could buy at the airport with our coupons was chocolate bars, which my notes say were a real gyp. After making our purchases we went through customs, which were very superficial. The usual three questions were asked: Did we meet with anyone other than the ones our guide arranged, did we have relatives in the Soviet Union, and were we carrying any letters out?

We were the only Americans on the plane to Belgrade. The other passengers were mostly Ghanaian men who had spent a year in the Soviet Union receiving military training. To judge from the ones we talked to, they did not leave with much love for the Soviet Union. One young man in particular compared his experience unfavorably with that of a cousin who had been sent to the United States.

In later years, we have returned to many of the countries we visited on this trip, but we have never had any desire to return to the Soviet Union (or after the collapse of the USSR, to Russia), despite a number of invitations to do so.

Yugoslavia

We arrived in Belgrade at 4 A.M. The airport was all but deserted. Though also a communist country, Yugoslavia impressed us as much freer than the Soviet Union almost as soon as we stepped off the plane. No Intourist guide greeted us to take us to a hotel that had been chosen for us. Before leaving home, Milton had asked the economist at the Yugoslav Central Bank with whom he would be working (Dimitrije Dimitrijevic) to make a reservation for us. We found a cab and told the driver to take us to the Hotel Moskva. We had no local money with which to pay the cabdriver when we arrived at the hotel, so we asked the man at the desk to advance us enough money to pay the cabdriver, and he did so with no hesitation.

Perhaps it was just our imagination, but the faces of the people did not seem to show the fear that we saw in the Soviet Union. On our part, we felt relaxed and did not feel that we were being watched. No loudspeaker blared in our room. The Yugoslav people we met during our visit could not have been more friendly and helpful. We had some difficulty in communicating but that was more than compensated for by friendliness. Some spoke English, though not fluently, and some spoke some French or German. Whenever we went out, we were impressed by the number of people who were just strolling around. At least in Belgrade, they were, on the whole, well and tastefully dressed. That contrasted strikingly with Moscow, where the women looked shapeless, shabby, and dowdy. Goods, in general, but particularly food, seemed cheap, and again in contrast to the Soviet Union, very good. When we gave the chocolate that we had bought in the Moscow airport to some children in Belgrade, they gave it back after the first bite. We tried it and found that it really did taste like sawdust.

About a week after we arrived in Belgrade, we visited a Belgrade synagogue on Yom Kippur, the Day of Atonement, along with the Stankiewiczes, another Jewish-American couple in Belgrade at the time. The contrast with Russia could not have been greater. The service was well attended and there were no crowds outside. Families were in attendance, parents and children. As at home on such a holiday, all were dressed in their best clothes. Few whom we contacted could speak English, and none Yiddish, as they were Sephardic, not Ashkenazic, Jews, and their counterpart to Yiddish was Ladino. However, many could speak French, so we could communicate, even if only haltingly. The Jews we talked with expressed no fear of anti-Semitism on the part of the non-Jewish Yugoslavs. On the contrary, they were grateful to the Serbs for having tried to protect them from the Germans during the war, even when they were in prison camps together, by not revealing which were Jewish.

As Jews brought up in observant households, we felt at home at the Belgrade synagogue as we had not at those in Moscow and Kiev. The service brought back memories of the services on the high holidays that we had attended as children many years earlier, before we had ceased to attend religious services.

After two weeks in Belgrade, we wanted to see more of Yugoslavia and, being Americans, thought that renting a car and driving to Dubrovnik would be an excellent way to do so. There was no such thing as Hertz, but one of our friends thought he knew someone who would rent us his car. A meeting was arranged but when we told the gentleman where we wanted to go, he turned us down. The road was so bad, he said, that his car would be damaged. Instead, we flew to Sarajevo, where we stayed for a day or two, and then made the trip by bus from Sarajevo to Dubrovnik. The bus carried a mechanic who fixed flats and made other repairs along the way, and we soon came to appreciate the car owner's concerns. Scenically, the trip was hard to surpass. The countryside is hard and poor for the people who have to scratch a living out of the rocks but spectacular to the traveler passing through. Dubrovnik, when we reached it, we found to be truly the glory of the Adriatic. The city itself was fascinating, with its ancient thick walls and cobbled streets one on top of the other with a stone stairway the only entry. I hate to think what is left after the wanton destruction of this loveliest of cities. We are grateful that we had the opportunity of seeing some of the wonderful places that have since been demolished.

{ *Milton* } This visit gave us little hint of the deep hatreds that would lead to the breakup of Yugoslavia and the vicious civil war that is raging in Bosnia as I write these words. We were well aware that Yugoslavia was a communist country and that individual freedom was limited—if only because Yugoslavian friends talked to us more freely in private than when compatriots were present. After all, we were temporary visitors and had neither the incentive nor the opportunity to get them into trouble by reporting any dissident remarks. Their compatriots might be good friends now, but they were there permanently, and relations and incentives might change—as clearly they did. We were also fully aware of the control that the central government exercised over the economy, as well as of the desire for greater autonomy by each of the six republics and two autonomous provinces.[4]

However, as Rose has noted, Yugoslavia was a very different kind of communist society than the Soviet Union and the other totalitarian states. Its dictator, Josip Tito, himself a Montenegrin with a wide following because of his role in leading an underground during World War II, initially aped the

Soviet Union but very quickly came into conflict with Stalin by following an independent national foreign policy. In June 1948, Stalin expelled Yugoslavia from the Cominform and tried to unseat Tito. The attempt failed, though a complete economic boycott by the communist countries caused great hardship. Tito reacted by turning to the West for economic aid, which was given to enable Yugoslavia to remain free of Soviet domination.

As part of its revolt, Yugoslavia rejected the Soviet centrally directed economic system and developed an alternative form of socialism based on a largely private agricultural system, though with some cooperative farms, decentralization of political administration and economic management, and worker ownership of business enterprises, which were to be run by "workers' councils," elected by the workers. For a time, the new system was much admired by Western intellectuals as a feasible alternative to a private-property capitalist system. Workers' cooperatives were clearly a great improvement over a strictly Soviet system, and in the early years, indeed during the period of all our visits, raised substantially the economic output of the country, though not without many problems, including repeated bursts of inflation as the government printed money to finance government activities and bail out unprofitable enterprises. One of our major interests during successive visits was how worker ownership functioned. That led to visits to a number of enterprises and extensive discussion with their managements. More on this in chapter 25.

In the field of my immediate interest, monetary institutions, on the occasion of my first visit the central bank (Narodna Banka) was a centralized institution with branches in the several republics and autonomous provinces. It was later converted into a system on the pattern of our Federal Reserve System, with eight independent banks, one for each of the six republics and the two autonomous provinces.

In sharp contrast to Russia, there was no shortage of data on the quantity of money and other economic magnitudes. The Narodna Banka provided me with an office and with all the help that I could use. Dr. Dimitrijevic, assistant general manager of the Narodna Banka, had done a good deal of work with a student of mine (George Macesich) at Florida State University, and was therefore familiar with my writings on money. He was anxious to work with me and to facilitate my research, so that he could use the results in connection with his functions at the bank. Even our very early analysis of the readily available data revealed that the key relations that we had established for capitalist United States held in communist Yugoslavia. Monetary theory per se is strictly nonideological, though who controls the money supply is something else again.

In addition to the work I did at the bank, I gave a number of talks on monetary theory and policy at the bank, and a talk on the theory of the consumption function at the Planning Board.

I maintained contact with Dimitrijevic and other Yugoslavian economists in later years; several visited my Money and Banking Workshop in Chicago, and Dimitrijevic spent the winter quarter of 1969 as a visiting scholar in the Economics Department, giving a seminar on "Monetary Systems in Countries with Central and Mixed Planning." Dimitrijevic subsequently arranged for the publication in Serbo-Croatian of a collection of my papers on money—the occasion for our trip in 1973.

{ *Rose* } When we left Yugoslavia, particularly Belgrade, we felt that we were leaving good friends behind. We did not expect to see them again and were concerned about what lay ahead for them. We had no such feelings on leaving the Soviet Union.

We Americans take living in a free country for granted. There are degrees of freedom. The Yugoslavs were at least able to criticize their government with relative openness, in contrast to the close-mouthed silence of Soviet citizens. However, we did not feel that we had really come back to freedom and a modern civilization until we arrived in Athens on our way to Turkey. The leaky faucets and smelly toilets were gone, at least temporarily. We spent only two days in Athens on this visit because we were planning to return for a longer stay later. We restricted our sight-seeing to the Acropolis, and saw only George Coutsamaris, a former student, and his wife plus a few people from the Bank of Greece and the Center for Economic Research.

Turkey

Our next extended visit was to be in Israel. Since Turkey was en route we decided to spend three days visiting Istanbul and Ankara, encouraged by the urgings of Oktay Yenal, a former student who had returned to Istanbul, and two former students from the U.S. who were spending some time in Turkey: Michael Bordo and Orvis Schmidt. In addition to the standard tourist attractions like the Blue Mosque, the tomb of Atatürk, and the Topkapi Serai, Oktay arranged for us to visit the university and the Planning Commission.

{ *Milton* } At the university, we had a long visit with the president. He was enormously proud of his accomplishments, and especially of the new buildings he had managed to add to the university. He went on at length about his further plans for expansion. What impressed us was his attitude: it was not that of a civil servant, which presumably is what he was; rather it was that of a private owner of an enterprise: his university, his plans, his achievements. We have come across this attitude before and since, and not only in highly centralized governments, but seldom in so obvious a form.

{ *Rose* } Istanbul is more exciting to visit than Ankara—its location on the Bosporus, almost completely surrounded by water, its mixture of East and West, and masses of humanity milling around. It was our introduction to the bazaars that we had heard so much about. As I wrote in a letter home: "One of the most difficult things for us to get used to was the ever present arm at one's side to pick up this and carry that. Being independent and still vigorous, brought up in a very different environment, we at first resisted, but that was too hard, so we gave in grudgingly. The other sight that was humiliating to us though obviously not to them, was the line outside our room as soon as they heard we were departing. The practice of tipping is always embarrassing to us. But here, it was so direct it took on the air of begging."

One scene fascinated us as we drove through the countryside. A group of women were working in the field and therefore did not have their faces covered as is the custom for Moslem women. As they looked up and saw our car approaching, they quickly picked up their skirts and covered their faces!

Israel

{ *Rose* } After three days, we were off to Israel. Here we had many former students. Don Patinkin, a former student and later visiting professor at the University of Chicago, had emigrated with his family to Israel many years earlier and was a professor at Hebrew University. Michael Michaely, another former student who was teaching at Hebrew University, met us at the airport. On our way to the President Hotel and to pick up the car that Don had arranged for us, Michael told us a little about what we would find in Jerusalem. First of all, as we knew, Hebrew was the language of the country and we knew no Hebrew. I replied that I did not expect that to be a problem because I was fluent in Yiddish. I was taken aback when Michael replied that it would be wise not to use Yiddish. It seemed that the Israelis were trying to live down the world's image of the Jew created in the Diaspora. (On future trips, we found that Yiddish had become more acceptable.)

One reaction that surprised us was our feeling that we were in a foreign country. Though we were not observant Jews, we had expected to feel at home in Israel. Instead we felt less at home than in England or France. The combination of a foreign language of which we were entirely ignorant and the faces of the Oriental Jews, which were so different from the European Jews whom we were familiar with, made Israel seem very foreign.

Since Milton gave two series of seminars at Hebrew University, we generally spent three days of every week in Jerusalem and the other four days on trips to other parts of Israel. The trips were all made by car. Our friends insisted that we take an Israeli with us on all trips to keep us from wandering into hostile country. That suited us very well because we could pick up some of the history of the areas we visited and at the same time visit with our companions. We also did much sight-seeing in Jerusalem itself. There was much to see when Joseph Ben-David took us through old Jerusalem, where he had grown up and knew every nook and cranny.

On our first trip outside of Jerusalem, Ezra and Shule Sadan took us to Kibbutz Moravia. Ezra had two uncles and aunts who had come to Palestine from Poland many years earlier as youngsters of twenty and had been among the original pioneers of the kibbutz. As I wrote to Becky,

> I have never been with such wonderful people—generous, outgoing, kind, and idealistic in the extreme. . . . In addition to the kind of people the older members are (I say older advisedly because the younger are a different breed), the most interesting thing was their drab life. They all eat together in what looks more like a barn than a dining room—on small wooden tables, certainly without a tablecloth and only recently with any sort of paper napkins. I can't really describe the way of serving the food. . . . All I can say is that I lost my appetite when I sat down and it didn't improve when I looked at the food. . . . The children from the time they are born do not live with their parents, but in a communal building. Their parents visit with them for a couple of hours in the afternoon and have them on Saturdays because the people who are in charge of them have to have a day off. . . .
>
> These people came here about 1920, have worked terribly hard, men and women equally, and children somewhat less, from the very beginning and this is what they have achieved. By now, even the old are more than a little disillusioned about their way of organizing things, and the young are definitely displeased. Many of the young, of course, leave, but the old have no choice. If they want to leave, they, of course, are free to do so, but they leave with what they came—nothing, after some forty years of terribly hard work and little comfort. . . .

At the time they started of course, there was much reason for banding together this way, if not for their way of living in detail. And at present, on the whole, the kibbutzim that are starting, have a defense reason. They are strategically located, really as outposts in case of Arab attack, and this aspect of the whole country can really only be appreciated when you see how close are the borders with the enemy.

The kibbutz experience in Israel is of general interest. A communal society was encouraged in Israel via the kibbutz, and to a lesser extent, the moshavim, cooperative farms. Israel is one of the few societies in which communal living is not only freely available but highly regarded. Yet while many of the original citizens and leaders of Israel had their first experience in a kibbutz, they did not remain, presumably because they found it confining and frustrating. They wanted to be free. All told, despite the important security function of the kibbutzim near the border the total kibbutz population never numbered more than about 5 percent of the residents of Israel.

One memorable expedition took us from Jerusalem to Beersheba. From Beersheba, we drove through the Negev Desert—at once beautiful and forbidding—to Eilat, the southernmost city in Israel. En route we stopped at a number of agricultural stations that were experimenting with methods to minimize the amount of water needed for crops, including exploring methods used by residents in biblical times. Eilat was at the time a small village, not the large seaside resort it has become since peace with Egypt. As Milton summarized that trip in a letter to George Stigler:

> This is a wonderful place to spend some time—especially in December. Saturday (today is Tuesday) we went swimming in the Gulf of Eilat, which opens into the Red Sea; Monday, we went swimming in a pool formed by a brook flowing into the Dead Sea. In between, we paid a visit to a Bedouin camp right out of Lawrence's *Seven Pillars,* and then took our departure after much hand-slapping and an exchange of compliments, to drive back to town over the desert in a rattling Dodge open army truck, passing camels, sheep, etc.

I described the Bedouin visit at greater length in a letter to my friend, Dorothy Brady:

> Part of one day in Beersheba we were taken by the military governor to call on a Bedouin camp. They of course had been warned and we were received by the sheik and some other notables. It was one of the most interesting as well as embarrassing experiences we have had.

After shaking the hands of the reception committee outside the tent, . . . we were conducted to some couches along the wall opposite the squatting Bedouin. We were served one, two, three small cups of very bitter coffee, then a glass of very sweet tea. All this time we sat uncomfortably eyeing them and they eyeing us. Occasionally, the governor spoke to the sheik in Arabic and was answered. At one point, five more Arabs arrived, shook hands cordially with the governor, who informed us that they had just been released from prison, where he had sent them for some trespassing charge. They did not appear to bear him any malice. Another big shot Arab arrived, shook our hands, then took his place next to the sheik to drink his three cups of coffee! After the appropriate interval from the last refreshment, the governor told us it was all right to leave. So we left with the appropriate speeches from the sheik in Arabic and Milton in English, all duly translated. Then we went dashing back across the desert . . .— all very much à la Lawrence of Arabia. It was very exciting, though somewhat hard on the bones.

The Dead Sea, which we visited on the same trip, is about thirteen hundred feet below sea level—the lowest sheet of water on the earth. Because it lacks an outlet, and is subject to heavy evaporation, it is a treasure of chemicals, and a major source of income to both Israel and Jordan. The main purpose of going to the Dead Sea was not the sea itself but rather to visit Massada. Some miles north of the beginning of the Dead Sea, Massada is a mountain rising more than fourteen hundred feet, and was "the last stronghold that held out against the Romans during the Jewish Revolt. . . . The fortress was so impregnable that the Romans never overcame its fortifications. At the end of three years of siege the defenders put themselves to death rather than fall into enemy hands. The fall of Massada in 73 A.D. marked the end of Jewish independence."[5]

In 1962 (I do not know whether it is different today), the only way to get to the fortress was by foot up a steep path. (The guide book warns, "Make sure to have sufficient food and water for half a day.") But the climb was well worth it. The ancient fortress had been well restored. Its scope was most impressive—extensive storehouses that enabled the occupants to survive a three-year siege, great water cisterns to collect and store the scarce rain from surrounding heights, living quarters dug out of the rocks, and so on.

After touring Massada, we refreshed ourselves at a delightful place known as David's fountain—a waterfall and a pool with deliciously cool water to which Milton referred in his letter to George. As I wrote to Dorothy, "I kept thinking of you while we were basking in the pool. This was really the most beautiful spot we have ever seen. A beautiful waterfall on four or five levels, rushing over the hills of rock literally covered with maidenhair fern plus a lot of other native plants. It was the maidenhair that I couldn't take my eyes from."

As I wrote to Becky,

Each week-end I think the particular part of the country we are visiting is the most beautiful but the truth is it is all really most attractive. Of course, apart from the scenery you couldn't sell this country to us as a place to live. In some ways, the whole country, or at least the cities in it, is like a small town. Everyone knows everyone else, who he is, what he's doing, even thinking, and all his problems. I think I'd get claustrophobia here. . . . In one sense, as we were saying last night when we were having dinner in a Hungarian restaurant about 30 miles north of Tel Aviv, if we didn't know this was Israel and therefore all the people are Jews, we certainly couldn't tell. They looked like the mixture you would find in a N.Y. restaurant. But this is sort of a dual society. There are the Jews from western Europe and the U.S. (not too many) and the Oriental Jews. The ones who run things and the ones we come in contact with mainly are the western Jews of course. The others we see mainly on the street and you'd never take them for Jews.

One pleasant by-product for me of our visit in Israel was finding some of my maternal relatives who, as I knew from my mother, lived in Israel. They turned out to be delightful people and we see them now whenever we visit Israel.

{ *Milton* } As Rose noted, I gave two seminars at the university, a number of talks in Jerusalem and Tel Aviv, and worked with the Bank of Israel to put together the monetary and other series that I wanted to analyze. Largely because of Don Patinkin, economics students in Israel tended to go to the University of Chicago for their graduate work, and some of our very best students have been Israeli. So we had many former students there who were able to facilitate my research and subsequently carry it further. For the most part, they were also our guides on weekend trips, which covered almost all of what was then a very small but incredibly diversified country, surrounded on all sides by enemies.

Because our guides were generally economists, the tourist trips combined much shop talk as well, enabling us to learn a good deal about the economy of Israel while enjoying its topography and historical sites.

Ever since its origin, the Israeli economy has been largely socialist, and has had in practice two side-by-side socialist governments. One was the official Israeli government which owned or controlled more than 90 percent of the land and decided what it could be used for, owned and operated many industries, imposed heavy taxes, had large government spending not only on the military but also on an expansive welfare state, imposed controls on foreign exchange transactions, granted private monopolies, had tariffs and export subsidies, and so on. The other socialist government was the Histadrut, which originated as a trade union but gradually took over other functions, such as providing medical care, starting business enterprises (which ultimately became some of the largest in the state), owning banks, and functioning as a major player in the political system. The two governments were generally close. The Histadrut was the political mainstay of the Labor Party, and the Labor Party was in control of the government.

There is no doubt in my mind that the socialist policy has slowed Israel's growth. However, its adverse effects were offset to some extent by several factors: first, the inflow of funds from abroad, partly in the form of private contributions from Jews around the world, partly of official development assistance from the United States and other countries; second, the inflow of capital from Jewish entrepreneurs for whom assistance to Israel was a real motivation; and third, the ingenuity of the Israelis in getting around government regulation.

This last factor especially impressed me when I tried to study in some detail the banking industry. I did not know any banking industry in the world that was subject to as much detailed regulation, as many government rules, as the Israeli, and yet the industry was doing quite well. The reason soon became clear. Jews have a well-deserved reputation, established during the Diaspora, for financial shrewdness and ability. Smart Jews were running the banks. Smart Jews were in the government bureaus overseeing the banks. The Jews in the government imposed regulations; the Jews in the banks found ways to get around them; counterparts in the government figured out how to close the loopholes; counterparts in the banks found ways to evade those; and round and round it went to produce the most complex system of banking regulation in the world.

We were able to watch how this system developed in several later trips we made to Israel; but none was as instructive—or I may say as enjoyable—as this, our longest (see chap. 27).

Christmas with Our Children

{ *Rose* } We left Israel the week before Christmas for a long-planned skiing holiday in Austria. Our plan was to have Janet and David join us there for their Christmas vacation.

Sometime before Christmas we learned that Janet had had mononucleosis but was recovering. That made me more impatient than ever to see her. It is sometimes hard for mothers to appreciate that their children are grown up and can take care of themselves.

When I first saw my daughter at the airport in Munich where we met, I was sure she had not taken care of herself. Mono and adjusting to a big campus or perhaps to growing up had taken its toll. Nonetheless we had a pleasant Christmas vacation together. David and his father spent a great deal of time skiing. I spent a considerable amount of time trying to get my daughter back to her usual healthy state. A lot of time sleeping and a little skiing sent her back to California looking and feeling much better than when she arrived but left her mother somewhat anxious and looking forward to our next time together in June. Our Christmas vacation over, we went back to Munich, where Janet and David left for the U.S. and we went on to Arosa to spend two days skiing with our friend Peter Bauer, and then off to Athens, our next stop.

Greece

As at every major stop in our trip, we combined Milton's work, in this case at the central bank of Greece and the Institute for Economic Research, with many delightful hours driving and roaming around the ruins of not only Athens but also Corinth, Delphi, and much more. At one point we wanted a quiet place where Milton could finish an article for the *International Encyclopedia of the Social Sciences* and where I could finish going over the manuscript of the *Monetary History*. A former student of Milton's mentioned that the governor of Rhodes had a degree in political science from the University of Chicago and would be glad to make all arrangements for us on Rhodes. Accordingly, after two weeks in Athens, we interrupted our stay there to spend a week in Rhodes.

The governor more than lived up to our expectations. He not only met us at the airport but entertained us while we were there and saw us off at the airport when we flew back to Athens.

We rented a car and, accompanied by Eleanor Neff, a woman spending some time in Rhodes with whom we became friendly and who served as our guide, visited three ancient cities, Philerimos, Lindos, Kamiros, that made up Rhodes. After having two flat tires and no more spares, we left the car on a mountain, hiked down to the main road circling the island and caught a bus that took us back to the city. The car company was informed where to pick up the car.

"In Greece, as elsewhere before and after," we wrote in our 1963 Christmas letter,

> our happiest experience was the hospitality and friendliness we received from old friends and new. We reflected again on the wonderful dividend from graduate teaching of having intellectual children throughout the world; on the oneness of the academic and scientific community; and on the emotional hold which the University of Chicago has on those who have been there. Russia aside, in every country we visited for any length of time, there were either former students of Milton's or former students of Chicago, or economists we knew by reputation and who knew us. And every place we were made to feel at home and welcome. We came back rich in experience and enormously in debt for the hospitality showered upon us.

{ *Milton* }   In Greece, I worked at the Center for Economic Research run by Andy Papandreou, who had recently returned to Athens from Berkeley. He was not yet fully involved in politics, as he was later, and was still active as an economist, using his center to explore the economic problems of Greece and to devise policies to improve its deplorably low level of income. He was very helpful to me, not only by providing work space but also by getting me entree to the central bank and elsewhere. At the bank, I had a number of long sessions with the governor of the bank, Xenophon Zolotas, and many of his staff. Dr. Zolotas was the long-term head of the Bank of Greece, had an international reputation, and had published extensively on monetary matters, so I knew him by reputation before we met. We got along very well and corresponded for many years, even though (in principle, hardly in practice) he was a hard-money man (in favor of a strict gold standard), and I was not.

One feature of the Greek monetary system that especially interested me was the low level of bank deposits. I quickly found out that the use of bank checks to make payments was very rare, restricted to occasional large payments by large enterprises. Most transactions were by cash, including the payment of wages, rent, etc. At a meeting at the bank, I asked who among those present had a personal checking account, something that in the U.S. we would simply take for granted. It turned out that no one had—including Dr. Zolotas.

This phenomenon so intrigued me that one of the items I always investigated in subsequent travels was how widespread was the use of checks. I learned that countries fell into two groups; those in which checks were rarely used, and those in which they were very common. The difference did not correspond to level of development: checks were rare in Greece and in Japan alike; common in Taiwan as in the U.S. and Britain. The hypothesis I finally came up with was that the difference depended on whether passing a bad check was a civil offense (as it was in Greece and Japan) or a criminal offense, as in the U.S. and Britain. If it is a civil offense, the only recourse of anyone who accepts a bad check is to sue in civil court—an expensive and time-consuming process. Hence, checks are not readily accepted. By contrast, if passing a bad check is a criminal offense, someone who accepts a bad check can turn to the police to help find the welsher and make him or her pay up.

The legal structure has a substantial effect on monetary figures. Among the items I investigated wherever I went was the quantity of money, and also of currency and deposits separately, as a fraction of national income, and also the average denomination of the currency. I had found such data useful in analyzing monetary relations in the U.S., and they proved equally useful elsewhere. In most relatively underdeveloped countries, the amount of money tended to average around 10 percent of the national income, with most of that in currency. (Indeed, I have sometimes felt that multiplying the reported amount of currency, usually a very accurate figure, by 10 gave me a better estimate of national income than the reported national income, a figure subject to a wide margin of error.) In countries in which checks are common, the ratio tends to be somewhat lower; in those where checks are rare, much higher.* There is a greater effect on the average denomination of currency.

---

* In the U.S. currently, the amount of currency outside banks is roughly 6 percent of the national income. Taken at face value, the amount of currency would come to roughly $1,500 per capita, or $6,000 per family of four. Even if one were to suppose that half of that is in the tills of retail and other enterprises, the remaining amount would be unbelievably large. A major explanation is that more than half is not in the United States but is used in countries around the world for legal and (especially) illegal transactions. But even the residual is unreasonably large. That has been the case for decades, and various explanations have been offered, from the use of currency in the black market to its use to store ill-gotten gains from political activity.

For many decades, the most popular denomination, not in terms of number of bills but total value of bills, was the $20 bill, which represented roughly one-third of the total value, with one-third in smaller bills and one-third in larger bills. That situation has changed drastically thanks to postwar inflation. Today, when the largest denomination issued by the Treasury is $100, more than half the value of the currency is in $100 bills. After all, a $100 bill is currently equivalent in purchasing power to that of a $10 bill in the 1930s. In my opinion, it is a mistake for the government not to issue the larger denominations ($500, $1,000, $5,000, $10,000) that are authorized by law. For a further discussion of the same issue, see my comments below on Taiwan.

In check-using countries, it is generally around a day's wages of the average worker; in currency-using countries, around a week's wages.

Lebanon

{ *Rose* } Our next major destination was India, the fourth of the countries where Milton was going to study the monetary system. En route, we planned to visit Lebanon. At the Athens customs, an attendant warned us that we might not get a visa to Lebanon because we had Israel stamped in our passport. We decided to take our chances. If any difficulty arose, we could just go straight on to India. When we arrived at the Beirut airport, we got a porter and asked him to take us to the desk where we could get a visa. He smiled and said that it might be a good idea to remove the El Al stickers that were still on our bags. He removed them and took us to the appropriate desk, where for a few dollars we had no difficulty getting a visa. Despite episodes of violent internal political conflict, Lebanon was relatively peaceful. Beirut, nestled on the Mediterranean, was extremely attractive. Lebanon had turned itself into an entrepot between the Western countries and the Middle East. It had become a major financial and commercial center, and was extremely prosperous.

In addition to Beirut itself, which was an interesting and beautiful city, we wanted to see two places in Lebanon: Baalbek (which had been recommended very highly by Peter Bauer) and the cedars of Lebanon. We rented a car and the next morning set off on a trip to Baalbek that proved very rewarding. As I reported to Becky, "In the course of an hour and a half going straight up, we came from Beirut where we saw at least one man swimming in the Mediterranean to snow and people skiing." In addition to the trip itself, as I reported in a letter to Dorothy, "The temple ruins there are in many ways more impressive even than the Acropolis. So much more remains there, and it is hardly commercialized at all." The next morning we left Baalbek, drove back to Beirut and up again to snow and skiing at the cedars. The drive up—at least the last half hour—was not my idea of fun. It was getting dark and the snow had drifted. However, Milton enjoys this kind of adventure. It was too late to see the trees clearly so we spent the night at a hotel that, as I reported to my sister, "was supposed to be the best hotel up here" though it would have been more accurate to say the only hotel. At any rate, the hotel was a monstrosity—large, rambling, dingy, dark, and mostly empty. We seemed to be the only guests. It had the aura of the kind of haunted house popular in English novels.

In the morning, we were able to see the famous cedars. Alas, after seeing the California redwoods, the cedars of Lebanon were not very impressive. My reaction reminded me of my response to the Riviera on our first trip to Europe.

And so on from Lebanon to India, our next extended sojourn.

India

Our flight from Beirut to Bombay was the longest so far. We flew Pan Am which was in its heyday and offered wonderful service. We flew first to Karachi, arriving there at 4 A.M., were taken to a nice hotel by Pan Am for three hours' rest and breakfast, were then taken back to the airport at 7:45, left for Bombay at 8:00, and arrived at 10:30.

V. V. Bhatt of the Reserve Bank and his little girl met us at the airport. When we arrived at our hotel, the Taj Mahal, a reception committee was waiting with flowers and leis. After all the welcoming speeches, we were escorted to a palatial suite where we went to bed as soon as possible, slept all day, had sandwiches brought in for dinner and went back to bed.

{ *Milton* } Bombay is the financial center of India and is where the Reserve Bank of India is located, which is why we chose it for our first base in India. It also had two organizations favorable to free enterprise, the Council for Economic Education and the Forum for Free Enterprise, among many others of very different persuasion. I gave a number of lectures or seminars at the bank, and two public lectures under the auspices of the Council for Economic Education, arranged by M. R. Pai. They were published by the council under the title *Inflation: Causes and Consequences.*[6]

The bank was very cooperative in providing data and assistance in analyzing monetary relations in India. Because of my earlier visit, I was better prepared to analyze data for India than for any of the other countries we visited.

Our ambassador to India at the time was Kenneth Galbraith, a longtime personal friend despite our sharply different political views. While in Bombay, I dropped him a note saying that we were going to be in New Delhi at a later date, and asking whether we could meet with him. He replied in a friendly note inviting us to have lunch with him at the embassy, and remarked something like, "As you know, I do not agree with your ideas, but they will do less harm in India than anywhere else I can think of."

{ *Rose* } We spent about a month in Bombay at the luxurious Taj Mahal Hotel. We also did a good deal of traveling north to the hill country and south to Madras and environs. Our experiences differed according to the area involved. Much of our travel was by car with, of course, an Indian driver. The dust of the roads plus the generally high temperature made us very thirsty. The only safe way to satisfy our thirst on the road was to buy a coconut and drink the coconut milk. When we stopped for this purpose in rural areas, the local people and especially the children immediately surrounded the car and stared at us as though we were strangers from outer space. Partly of course, this gave them an opportunity to beg but it was also just curiosity.

As I wrote in my first letter to Dorothy from India,

> Here we are in Bombay and what a fascinating place. More foreign than anything we have seen to date—more extreme in both directions of levels of living than anything we have witnessed either in our travels or at home. . . . On our very brief excursions from our hotel and they have been very brief thus far . . . the most distressing experience is being approached or rather followed by the misshapen, malformed human beings asking for alms. I must confess that having children or even an adult here and there, begging in other countries is distressing, but it has never made me physically ill as it does here. The Indians of the class that we meet seem simply to ignore it and advise us to do likewise. And rationally, this is the only solution, as otherwise one would be surrounded by them in no time at all. On the other hand, it is almost impossible to follow this course. I almost dread going out of the hotel. Hardly a solution either.

Or again to Becky: "India and Indians take some getting used to. First, one has to get accustomed to ignore all the little children who either turn somersaults for you and then hold out their hands, plus all the adults who do the same—no somersaults. It's hard enough to ignore all this but it's even worse if one doesn't because then you'd have half of Bombay following you around."

My first impression of the Indians we met at the higher level was summarized in a letter to Becky: "Maybe it's because they are so different from anything we are accustomed to, but I must say I find them on the dull side, no spice, no emotion, no spine, no nothing. But I shouldn't be hasty—so my husband says—though I think he agrees with me."

Similarly to Dorothy: "The other aspect of the people here, the ones we have met at any rate, is their passivity. They don't seem to get aroused by anything." From a later letter:

> Last night we were guests at dinner given by the editor and owner of a weekly newspaper. We were told in advance he was a character

but we weren't told how much of one. He is unmarried—I was one woman, with seven men. When we sat down to dinner and half of the company (these are all university graduates and have been abroad) ate with their right hands [i.e., without utensils], this was a little too much for me. I hope before we leave India to feel close enough to some Indian to get an explanation of this. . . . at the conclusion of the party, we were conducted downstairs by our host with a flashlight and almost stumbled over the sleeping bodies in the hallway.

A high spot in India for me was our visit to Ahmedabad, Amand, and Baroda. Professor Shenoy, whom I believe we had met earlier at one of the Mont Pelerin meetings, was our host and planned our itinerary.

As always, the trips were a combination of lectures by Milton (Professor Shenoy's efforts to educate his people), informal discussions with Indian and occasionally other foreign visitors, and touristic attractions. Another person in the Ahmedabad area whom Milton had met on his earlier trip was H. M. Patel, under whose auspices Milton gave a lecture and at whose house we stayed one night.

From Ahmedabad we drove to Baroda, a lovely town with many monuments and well-cared-for parks. We were impressed that Baroda, which had been a princely state, was in far better condition than those communities that had been ruled directly by the British. We were impressed with this once again when we visited Rajasthan in 1979 while filming the television series *Free to Choose*. Before independence, the rulers of the princely states regarded them as their personal property and took a close interest in seeing that they were maintained. After independence, while the princes transferred their states to India or Pakistan, they mostly remained leading figures in their former states and exercised considerable influence on the local government—and some, of course, on the central government as well. In the other communities, the community facilities belonged to everyone, and accordingly to no one. An interesting example of the power of private property.

Our week in the south of India—Madras, Bangalore, Belur, Halebud and Aurangabad—visiting the famous temples and caves of India was another high spot. Here, again, we had special hosts. Padma, an Indian student whom I had met at the University of Chicago, planned much of our touristic activities. As I wrote to my friend Dorothy,

These caves are unlike anything we have ever seen and for sheer physical achievement, have to be seen to be believed. Though there are many fine pieces of sculpture still standing in almost perfect condition after all these centuries, and the paintings on the walls, almost completely obliterated now, must have been very lovely, I must confess I am much more impressed by the physical achievement of just digging the huge temples out of solid rock, than I am by the artistic achievement. . . . No one really knows how many centuries of labor by underfed, naked people went into these structures. I keep having the feeling that so much of the India of today is to be understood by the India of the Temples and Caves. I know it's very difficult to recognize the superstitions, prejudices and blind spots in one's own culture, but I still feel that I'm not being just chauvinistic when I say that our superstitions are as nothing compared with theirs. . . . In essence, . . . what I'm trying to say is we're talking or behaving in two different languages, we can try to put our words in their mouths but they mean different things. . . . we shouldn't think of introducing our superstructure of what we call the fruits of modern civilization on their structure of mysticism and fatalism.

In another letter to Dorothy I refer to Milton's discouragement whenever he listens to Indian economists but "he gets even sadder when he talks to the Americans on various and assorted missions here. One thing is sure, we may not be helping the Indians but we're certainly creating plenty of plushy job opportunities for lower quality American so-called economists. I didn't know there were so many."

After five days of intensive sight-seeing, we returned to Bombay.

{ *Milton* } Both in Bombay and in our trips north and south, we made a point of visiting as many factories, and talking to as many entrepreneurs, academics, economic journalists, and the like as we could. My major interest was to follow up on the conclusions that I had reached in 1955 about central planning in India and, in particular, the adverse effects of control over foreign exchange. One example will illustrate what I found. A textile factory that we visited in Ahmedabad was highly mechanized, looked as modern as any that I had seen in the United States. That made no sense for India, which is labor rich and capital poor. On investigation, it turned out that the explanation was exchange control and an artificial exchange rate. The owner explained that a government allocation of foreign exchange at the low official exchange rate granted to finance investment made it cheaper for him to mechanize than to hire labor at an artificially high wage rate set by the government—and besides spared him labor union troubles.

Another striking example was the treatment of automobiles. In the name of restricting "luxuries" to "save foreign exchange" the importation of automobiles, whether new or used, is nominally prohibited, though as always there were some loopholes. At the same time, new automobiles, copies of foreign makes, were being produced at high cost in small runs in a few plants in India. The results were most striking in the market for secondhand cars. In wandering through secondhand car lots, we ran across several 1950 Buicks, inferior in condition to one that I sold for $22 before I left the U.S., that were priced at 7,500 to 10,000 rupees, or $1,500 to $2,000 at the official exchange rate, and over $1,000 at the free-market rate.[7] The sensible and cheap way for India to have secured transportation would have been to import secondhand cars and trucks from abroad. In addition to the direct saving from getting the cars cheap, such a policy would have had great indirect advantages by promoting technical literacy, a way of using the abundant manpower available in India, while conserving capital. But India in effect says, "We are too poor to buy secondhand motor vehicles; we must buy new ones." I do not know whether this Indian policy has changed, but I would not be surprised if it has not. It is only in the past few years that India has started to move away from the detailed central control of every detail of the economy that prevailed when I was there in 1955 and again in 1963 and still later when we visited briefly in 1979.

Such policies were and are by no means restricted to India. Many a less developed country that has extensive government planning has followed the same policy. Social policy leads to prohibiting the import of "luxuries"; national pride to having an automobile factory, a local steel mill, and a national airline. The international automobile companies have catered to nationalist tastes by setting up small inefficient plants in separate countries, importing many components. And the international agencies, the IMF and the World Bank, have catered to nationalist tastes by providing funds to subsidize government-supported and approved ventures, thereby strengthening the central governments when what these countries need is precisely the reverse: weaker governments and greater individual freedom.

U.S. policy is tarred with the same foolishness. When the U.S. dominated the world automobile market, and was a net exporter of cars on a large scale, the automobile companies were all ardent free traders. Once Japan started to flood the U.S. with good, low-priced cars, the situation changed. Under industry pressure, President Reagan mistakenly endorsed a so-called "voluntary" import quota on Japanese cars. The trade barrier gave the Japanese an incentive to set up plants in the U.S. Because the U.S. market is so large, the plants could be large enough to take advantage of economies of scale, so it was not as inefficient as the small plants in underdeveloped countries. Nonetheless, if the U.S. had maintained free trade in automobiles, there would be fewer foreign plants in the U.S. today than there currently are. Similarly, Alexander Hamilton's 1791 *Report on Manufactures* led the U.S. to impose tariffs on imported steel to "protect" the "infant" domestic steel industry—yet they are still there two hundred years later.

In Madras, we were able to visit C. Rajagopalachari—fondly known as CR or Rajaji. Then in his eighties, he had been the governor-general of India's interim government from independence in 1948 to 1950, and was still active as head of the Swatantra Party, which he had founded in 1959 and which was the only party in India that supported the free market. Rajaji regularly labeled the Indian economy a permit-license-quota-raj (i.e., a kingdom of licenses, permits, and quotas).[8] He was one of the most impressive Indians I had the privilege of meeting.

In Madras, I published an article in a local newspaper on flexible exchange rates. It probably grew out of meetings that I had with various academic and public policy groups.

{ *Rose* } We left Bombay on March 6 for New Delhi and the Hotel Claridge, which was our base for the next three weeks. In New Delhi, we were able to visit with some of the people Milton had had contact with when he was in India in 1955, as well as with former Indian students, and other former students who were working on Rockefeller and Ford projects designed to help India.

We did accept Ken's invitation and had a delightful lunch with him and his wife, Kitty, at the recently completed Edward Durrell Stone embassy building "with its lacy grilles and an inner water garden, fountains, and islands of plantings," as the *Encyclopaedia Britannica* describes it.

The residence, where we had lunch, was beautiful but I suspect living there would take some getting used to. To achieve the "lacy" effect, it seemed as if a word spoken anywhere could be heard everywhere.

{ *Milton* } I was initially greatly impressed by what seemed like a great improvement in New Delhi since my visit in 1955. However, as I explored New Delhi, I found that the major improvement was in the quality and availability of international class hotels, including the Ashoka Hotel, a luxury hotel constructed by the government, a good example of government conspicuous consumption. The conditions of the masses showed little or no improvement. My visual impression to that effect was reinforced when I looked into what had happened to the amount of food grains per capita (the largest part of the consumption of the ordinary Indian) and cloth per capita. Neither had increased much if any since independence, and indeed both were probably less than the levels reached before World War II.

One episode involving the Ford Foundation is worth noting. Impressed with the absence of any non-governmental institutions of higher education, the Ford Foundation offered to finance an independent university. The government refused to let it do so. Instead of withdrawing from India, as I believe would have been the appropriate response, Ford simply continued to finance "advisers" and projects in India. A good example of how such groups become in effect lackeys of the ruling government and, like foreign aid, serve mostly to strengthen the power of the government.

In New Delhi, I gave public lectures at the Institute of Economic Growth and at the University of New Delhi. The latter was on the subject of monetary theory and policy. In the chair at the meeting was R. K. V. R. Rao (commonly referred to as Alphabet Rao), a Cambridge-educated economist and rabid Keynesian. The usual pattern in India, indeed throughout the former British Empire, is for the chairman to give a flattering introduction to the speaker, and then to move a vote of thanks after the talk. This time was different. Instead of moving a vote of thanks after I finished, Rao launched into an angry attack on the monetarist views I had expressed. As I recall, he said something like, "Professor Friedman is extremely seductive, but I want to warn the students in the audience that if you answer questions in the money exam along Friedman's lines, you will flunk!"

The most encouraging experience during our stay in India was a visit to Ludhiana and Jullundur, two medium-sized towns in the Punjab, north of New Delhi. Ludhiana was becoming a major center for the production of machine tools, bicycles, sewing machines and similar items and had long been a major center for the production of knitted goods. Here was the industrial revolution at its inception—I repeatedly felt that I was seeing in real life the descriptions I had read in economic histories of Manchester and Birmingham at the end of the eighteenth century. There were thousands of small and medium-sized workshops, with extraordinarily detailed specialization of function. A three-man shop was assembling saddles for bicycles from parts that in turn were made by other small enterprises; a bicycle factory with hundreds of employees also purchased many of its parts from smaller firms. One of the owners of the bicycle factory who showed me around was particularly proud of the part that he and his associates had played in helping their employees to establish independent firms. There was no shortage of enterprise or drive or technical skill in Ludhiana. There was rather a self-confident, strident, raw capitalism bursting at the seams.[9]

A major problem of the Ludhiana and Jullundur entrepreneurs was to get enough steel, because steel was being rationed by government planning authorities. The demand for their bicycles and hence the amount of steel required was rising rapidly; their ration was linked to their past output and did not keep pace. We were told that they solved their problem by buying partly finished steel products and melting them down. It would have been illegal for them to buy directly the rations received by other users of steel, but apparently this indirect way of buying them was not illegal.

A foretaste of what a great industrial economy India could be if only the government would release its iron grip on most economic activity. When Indians emigrate to other countries, a disproportionate number become active and successful entrepreneurs. South Africa and the Fiji Islands are good examples. In both, Indians dominate large segments of private business and have been very successful. They could be at home as well, if only they were set free.

David Hopper, a former student at Chicago and at the time employed in New Delhi by the Ford Foundation as an agricultural economist, provided a follow-up on our visit to Ludhiana: "The feeling among several of the Ludhiana businessmen that I have met since you were there was that of all the Western visitors, 'Friedman got the best insight into the workings of this town; of course he asked some of the best questions.' They are still actively debating your devaluation proposition with several prominent persons now supporting the idea, albeit, somewhat fearfully. . . . One certainly has the impression that Friedman managed to 'stir things up' in India's '19th century Manchester' and . . . the discussion around the Rotary Club is still loaded with picturesque Friedmanese."[10]

{ *Rose* } We planned to end our Indian trip at Calcutta. We arrived on March 26, intending to stay until April 6. About two days in Calcutta was more than we could take. As Milton pointed out earlier, nearly a tenth of the population had no home other than the street—they ate, slept, and defecated on the street. The filth and stench were worse than we have ever experienced either before our visit or since and the poverty and begging was even more intensive than in the other places we had visited so we decided that we would move on.

{ *Milton* } The one academic thing we did in Calcutta was to visit the Indian Statistical Institute, headed by P. C. Mahalanobis, whom I had met in 1955, then as in 1963 a member of the Indian Planning Commission (see chap. 18). He was at the time the chairman of a committee appointed by the prime minister (Nehru) to study changes in the distribution of income. The report had not yet been made public when we were in India, but Professor Mahalanobis showed me some of the work that he and his associates at the Indian Statistical Institute had done for the committee.

The sophistication of the statistical work, particularly in conducting sample surveys of urban and rural households, was impressive. These surveys found that the poorest third of the population experienced no increase whatsoever in food consumption per capita during the decade of the fifties—which roughly coincided with the first two five-year plans. This finding had no apparent effect on Mahalanobis's belief in the efficacy of the kind of direct and detailed central planning embodied in the two plans for which he bore major responsibility. Disturbing but not puzzling. Nothing is harder than for anyone, whatever his character, to admit that his plans for a major project were defective; much easier to believe that the plan was fine but that there were defects in its execution and that if those are corrected all will be well. It was irrelevant that the consequences had been predicted in advance by such people as Professor Shenoy and myself.

{ *Rose* } I summed up the Indian portion of our year in a letter to Dorothy as follows:

> We're nearing the end of our Indian installment and I can't honestly say we'll be sorry to have it behind us. It's been most interesting and tantalizing from so many points of view, all intertwined. We are more and more impressed by the existence side by side of two very different societies at completely different levels of economics, culture, education and just about everything else. In a very real sense, altho each is conscious of the other, each ignores the other and takes it as one more manifestation of fate. If one sticks to the main road and good residential areas, this appears to be a very modern, relatively rich country. But just a few paces away, and one is transported back to the 16th or 17th century—the miserable, holy cows wandering around, the stench of urine mixed with garbage, naked children and almost naked adults, lying around on sidewalks or squatting on the edges of the street. How one would go about improving the lot of the masses is difficult to say but two things are certain, the present planning in India does not seem to be succeeding and it will take a long time regardless of the method. In spite of all the evidence, the present governing class seems to be convinced, however, that it has the answer, admitting only that failure thus far is due only to faulty mechanics and thinking to improve things by changing from a relatively short

plan to a longer one. Somehow writing it down seems to them synonymous with achievement. . . .

After a delightful day in Agra, enjoying the Taj Mahal, which is indescribably lovely, we spent two days in Benares, now called Varanasi. Though interesting, this was, on the whole, a very depressing experience. All forms of maimed in body and soul gather here either to benefit from the baksheesh of the rich atoning for their sins at the end of life, or as a result of superstition, hoping to achieve the miracle of recovery from the sacred waters of the Ganges. We took the recommended boat trip along the Ganges early in the morning—fortunately before breakfast, else we might have lost it before we returned. The sight of the masses of people bathing within yards of the inflow of filthy water from the sewers of the city, and practically if not actually touching the diseased of all sorts, and thinking that this will not only make them blessed but also healthy is hard to believe. How can you persuade people with such superstitions of the virtue of inoculations? Where do you begin? When people have so little to eat as so many here do and yet insist on keeping cows for their holiness and are not interested in them for their milk or meat, how does one persuade them of their folly?

Are these prejudices very different from the views of the environmentalists who insist in preserving every living species regardless of the cost?

Going on to Dorothy with my views on India and state planning:

On a very different level, it's so difficult to appreciate the grand style of the universities, with buildings and campuses more than a match for ours, and government buildings that are more than a match for Washington—all this is somehow supposed to improve the lot of the poor. The attitude of the civil servant toward the need and justice of more and more foreign aid, almost as a right, rather than a privilege so that it can be squandered in more public spending, certainly not for the benefit of the poor, doesn't arouse my sympathy. And the Ford Foundation on the whole doesn't seem to be doing much more than enabling the American employees to live at a very high level (perhaps conferring some benefit to the half dozen servants they each employ) and to entertain their Indian equivalents in a style to which they are accustomed.

As you can judge, our visit to India has not changed our fundamental preconceptions about the virtues of state planning—or the welfare state. Some Americans here at least and a few Indians are coming around to our views but by no means enough to make much difference. Most have the same opinion of our preconceptions as we have of theirs. So where are we?

Instead of staying in Calcutta, we made an unplanned trip to Darjeeling, in the foothills of the Himalayas, and a summer station for British civil and military officials during the British occupation. The final stage of the trip to Darjeeling was on a wheezing train going up a very steep slope full of curves—it kept reminding us of "the little engine that could." The people in Darjeeling were altogether different from those in Calcutta: sturdy self-reliant mountain people. No beggars, no vagrants. The views of the Himalayas were spectacular, the sunsets gorgeous, the air clear and cool. A delightful finish to our Indian visit.

{ *Milton* } This visit reinforced the conclusions that I had reached on my earlier visit to India.[11] There were some signs of improvement. The roads in the countryside were notably better, there were many more bicycles and automobiles in both city and country, beggars though still numerous, seemed somewhat less ubiquitous.[12] There were many new buildings, some striking, and more and better hotels; new industrial plants and a few rapidly expanding centers of small industry; there were new universities and evident signs of the expansion of old universities. However, the progress appeared spotty, and some of the appearance of progress is misleading. Many of the most impressive new structures are signs not of progress but of waste, for example factories producing items at far higher cost than that at which they can be purchased abroad. Most important, there was little that was evident to the naked eye in the way of improvement in the conditions of the masses of the people. On every side, there were extremes of unrelieved poverty that are difficult to make credible to someone who has not been to India.

I found that the intellectual climate of opinion about economic policy was almost wholly adverse to any changes in the direction that seemed to me to be required. There was a deadening uniformity of opinion in India, particularly among economists, about issues of economic policy. In talks to and with students and teachers of economics at a number of universities, personnel of the Planning Commission, economists in the Civil Service, financial journalists, and businessmen, I encountered again and again the same stereotyped responses expressed in precisely the same words. It was as if they were repeating a catechism, learned by rote and believed in as a matter of faith. And this was as true when the responses were patently contradicted by empirical evidence as when they were supported by evidence or at least not contradicted.

A few younger and lesser known economists deviated from the dominant position, and many shared the main tenets of the dominant view yet differed on particular elements. Most businessmen grumbled about details but accepted the views of the professional economists as necessarily right in the main. I received a tongue lashing from a prominent and highly successful manufacturer when I made remarks into which he correctly read implicit criticism of India's current economic policies. Of course many of the currently most successful businessmen had a great stake in the existing system.

Bangkok, Angkor Wat, Saigon

{ *Rose* } We spent only two days in Bangkok both because it was very hot and humid but also we had plans to return with our children when they came to join us in Japan for the summer. Bangkok was a pleasant change from India. The people seemed happy and healthy-looking. We took the same trip down the river that Milton took eight years earlier. It was one of the pleasantest mornings we've had. Gethyn Davies and his wife Vivienne introduced us to dim sum, the wonderful Chinese brunch that we have become very familiar with since living in San Francisco but had not experienced up to this time. We were looking forward to returning with our children.

Our next fascinating trip was to Angkor Wat. My recollection is that we flew to Siem Rep from Bangkok, stayed in Siem Rep for three days, spending most of the day at Angkor Wat looking at different sections of the fabulous ruins, then going back to Siem Rep for the night. The temples were quite as impressive as we had been told, and we felt we could easily have spent a week there rather than three days. The Vietnamese war did much more damage to Angkor Wat than tourists ever could.

I remember very little about Saigon, our next stop before Hong Kong, except that it seemed like an American army base which I guess it was on the verge of becoming. The loveliest sight was the Vietnamese women in their *ao dai,* the traditional long tunic and billowing pants. I remember how much I was impressed with their graceful bodies. I could not resist buying an *ao dai* for myself.

Hong Kong

From Vietnam, we moved on to Hong Kong, my first visit there, though Milton had been there briefly in 1955 on his way to India.

Hong Kong was totally different from any of the places we had visited before or would visit after. Then as later, Hong Kong was a shoppers' paradise.

As I wrote to my son shortly after we arrived, "aside from shopping, Hong Kong is one of the most interesting places we've been. A little of S.F., New York and a few other places all thrown together. We took a trip to the new settlements the other day and while the crowding masses and population explosion were very visible, by comparison with Indians, these people look prosperous, though, of course, on an absolute scale, they were very poor." In successive trips to Hong Kong, it was always changing and mostly for the better.

There was still considerable hustle and bustle in Hong Kong when we were last there in 1997, but both the face and the inhabitants of Hong Kong had changed. The Peninsula Hotel no longer held its pride of place. There were more first-class hotels, I suspect, than in any one city in the United States or Europe. The service, while not quite up to the standard of 1963, was still much higher than in a comparable hotel in any city in the world. And the inhabitants, not all of course, but many, impressed us in our recent trips as placing even greater emphasis on financial achievement as the key indicator of success in life than they did earlier, when the bulk of the population were far worse off materially. Much of the atmosphere was a result of the fixation on July 1, 1997, when China instead of Britain would take charge of Hong Kong. That made wealth particularly important because it affected the possibility of emigrating. When we inquired about this, we found that, with hardly an exception, most affluent citizens of Hong Kong had made plans to emigrate if the need should arise.

Returning to 1963, after about a week in this bustling shoppers' paradise, we decided to move to the Repulse Bay Hotel on Hong Kong Island to get some bathing and sun. We felt that we could use a few days of rest and relaxation before moving on to Japan, where we knew the schedule of trips and speeches would be heavy.

{ *Milton* } The hotel, owned by the Peninsula, was something of a phenomenon. It had a central structure in which were the lobby, restaurant, public rooms, etc., and then two enormously long wings on either side containing the guest rooms. I recall pacing out the distance from our room to the front lobby and finding that it was a full quarter of a mile. The hotel was above a lovely bay, and a long bus ride from Victoria, the capital. It must have been easy to get to the beach because one of Rose's letters to her sister speaks of our doing a good deal of swimming.

The two wings are long since gone, the land being much more valuable for residential use than for hotel use in an increasingly populous and wealthy Hong Kong. What was then nearly empty countryside is now a crowded, upscale residential area.

Our extended stay in Hong Kong was mostly R & R, but I did take the opportunity of our visit to look into the Hong Kong economy, particularly to try to get an understanding of monetary arrangements. At the time, the Hong Kong dollar was pegged to the pound sterling: sixteen Hong Kong dollars equal to one pound sterling (or 5.714 Hong Kong dollars for one U.S. dollar). I was interested in the financial mechanism by which the link was maintained. I discussed the issue with economists at the U.S. Consulate General, and a number of both foreign and domestic bankers. None of them had any clear idea of how the system worked, but by the time I had finished checking with them, I thought I did.

I then managed to get an appointment with the financial secretary of Hong Kong, John (now Sir John) Cowperthwaite, a memorable meeting that marked the beginning of a long acquaintance. I told Mr. Cowperthwaite my puzzle. He immediately replied with the answer that I had myself reached. I then said something like, "But the people at the Hong Kong and Shanghai Bank [the principal bank in Hong Kong] don't understand how it works," doubtless listing all the other economists I had discussed the issue with. The financial secretary replied, as I recall, "Better they shouldn't. They would mess it up." With respect to a subsequent query about the paucity of national-income and similar statistics for Hong Kong, Cowperthwaite explained that he had resisted requests from civil servants to provide such data because he was convinced that once the data were published there would be pressure to use them for government intervention in the economy.

Cowperthwaite is the answer to what many have regarded as a paradox: at the very time, shortly after World War II, that Britain was embarking on an extreme socialist policy in the homeland, one of its last remaining colonies, Hong Kong, was embarking on an extreme free-market policy. By some accident of officialdom, John Cowperthwaite of the Colonial Office was assigned to serve as financial secretary of Hong Kong. Although the top person in the Hong Kong government hierarchy was the governor, the financial secretary exercised great power over economic matters. A Scotsman, Cowperthwaite was a disciple of Adam Smith, his ancient countryman, and acted on his beliefs. He is widely credited with the subsequent economic miracle, which led to a phenomenal rise in the average level of living despite a manyfold rise in population.

By following a policy opposite to that of its mother country, a colony thrived, while the mother country did not. In a rating of more than one hundred countries by economic freedom in 1995, Hong Kong is rated first, the United Kingdom sixth. Even more remarkable, per capita gross domestic product in 1994 was a third higher in Hong Kong than in Britain, and only 5 percent less than in the United States.[13] Quite a contrast to what happened in most of the colonies to which Britain gave their freedom after the war.

Japan

{ *Rose* } Japan was our final destination in this wonderful wanderjahr. We arrived the night of May Day, in the midst of a terrible rainstorm. But the overwhelming hospitality of the welcoming group, organized by Professor Chiaki Nishiyama, was more than sufficient to make us forget the rain. As I wrote to Becky, "In true Japanese style, when we were greeted at the airport a huge bunch of flowers was presented not to me, but to my husband. However, the other afternoon when Milton gave a lecture at the university, the girl students presented me with an equally big bunch of flowers. They are really in transition from the traditional man's world to a dual world." I should add that they are still far behind the women's revolution that has taken place in Western Europe and the United States.

We had expected to feel more foreign and less at home in Japan than in most of the countries we had visited because we not only could not speak the language, but could not even read the street signs. But we soon found out how wrong we were. The friendliness and generosity of the Japanese people, those we met casually and especially those we soon came to think of as friends, more than made up for the difficulties of the language. In addition, though culturally very different from the West, in other dimensions Japan seemed to us more nearly like the Western countries we knew. We could drink the water directly from the tap. There was a general aura of cleanliness and civilization that particularly delighted us because we had just come from India and the East. However, when we returned to Chicago and compared notes with a couple (the John Kelloggs) who had also just come back from Japan, our evaluation of the cleanliness was quite different from theirs. We finally decided that the difference reflected our entry to Japan from India; theirs from the West.

{ *Milton* } In India, I was impressed with how little improvement there had been in the condition of the masses since my 1955 visit. In Japan, I was impressed with precisely the opposite. When I wrote to Rose about my one day in Tokyo on the way to India, I stressed the pervasive poverty. The change after eight years was dramatic. No doubt, there was still much poverty, but the pervasive image was of growth and relative prosperity.

{ *Rose* } Chiaki Nishiyama, who made all of our arrangements in Japan, had spent several years at the University of Chicago as a graduate student. He was now a professor at Rikkyo University. He and his wife, Shigeko, who had also been educated in the United States, were excellent hosts. Chiaki had suggested that we make the International House of Japan our residence in Tokyo. This was an excellent choice. It did not have the hustle and bustle of the hotels in the city. Its garden, a famous Japanese garden that had been established several centuries earlier by the family that owned the property then, evoked a feeling of peace and quiet that I appreciated, especially when we first arrived. In addition, the International House, with its beautiful garden, was a favorite place for Japanese weddings, and the month of May seemed to be the favorite month in Japan for getting married. From our windows we were introduced to both the traditional wedding in Oriental dress and style as well as the Western style of wedding. We were impressed with the Japanese formality and bowing even among family members and close friends.

I tried to explain the Japanese special conception of hospitality, which is really unique, in a letter to Becky: "Chiaki (our host) moved into International House for our first week so he would be able to accommodate our needs better—leaving his wife and baby at home. Later on, they are both moving over here for a couple of weeks for the same reason." After seeing more of Tokyo I wrote, "we are still most impressed with this country. . . . Except for the fact that all the signs are in what appears to be an absolutely impossible language, one might be in New York, San Francisco, Paris, or any Western city. . . . I've been through a couple of department stores and they couldn't look more beautiful and thriving." The Japanese really have a sense of artistry that pervades everything they do—from a flower arrangement to a counter or window display in a department store to the wrapping of an inexpensive package. For example, the restaurant displays of the most inexpensive dishes that appear in the windows of modest restaurants always impressed us with their simple beauty:

> On the other hand, some of the customs are most strange. If we can do it without offending, we must get a movie of two Japanese, men or women, or both, greeting one another. They both keep bowing forever, and I don't quite know yet how one decides when to stop. I'm sure that as in so many other things, there is the right protocol on this but I'm not sure just what it is. They are extremely formal, even with one another, and I am sure can't quite understand our informality. But since they are at the same time also extremely polite, they wouldn't think of criticizing.

I was fascinated with Japanese flower arrangements and decided to learn a little about it. I started with a class in a very modern school but was disappointed because it seemed to me they were trying to imitate the Western style of flower arranging and not the traditional Japanese style. I finally found a class that taught the traditional style and was pleased with what I heard and saw. So I continued for one more lesson. As I wrote to Dorothy, "Of course, in typically Friedman style, I am buying the books for all the different schools and can continue my lessons independently when I get home." Unfortunately, the books languish in my bookcase, glanced at only now and then.

The gardens of Japan were one of the high spots for me, an enthusiastic gardener. I tried to explain the effect the Japanese gardens had on me to Dorothy, who spent much time helping me in the gardens at Hideaway and again later at Capitaf. I started my description by comparing Tokyo with Portland where both Dorothy and I grew up:

> Tokyo, as you probably know, is much like Portland in climate and flora. We have already seen more rain in this one week than we have had in the past three months. The difference between Tokyo and Portland is that the Japanese really have an indescribable knack about setting out gardens. . . . It is very hard even to describe just what it is about their gardens that creates the combined impression of beauty, harmony, solitude, peace, and quiet. It's one thing to describe the feeling one gets with adjectives but one is really at a loss about how to convey the impression these gardens make upon one.

We did more traveling in Japan than in any other country we visited. We were undoubtedly introduced to more different customs than in any other country, including India. However, unlike India, even outside the cities, we were never stared at as though we were from outer space, as we were in India. I am somewhat at a loss to explain this difference. The ordinary Japanese people at this time had not traveled much outside of Japan. Was it a reflection of the cosmopolitanism of Japan or of education or just their politeness?

I suspect that Tokyo has more diversity than any other capital in the world. You can eat at a restaurant of almost any cuisine: French, German, Russian, American, Chinese, in addition to all varieties of Japanese cuisine. Almost any evening you can see a Shakespeare play, a Western musical comedy, a Kabuki or No performance; or attend a performance of Japanese music, jazz, or a classical symphony; or see a baseball game or sumo wrestling; and on and on. Yet despite the diversity, the people are extraordinarily homogeneous.

We were introduced not only to all kinds of Japanese foods but also to the different customs and ways of entertaining. I found particularly interesting the Japanese restaurants for small private dinner parties with geisha girls. Such dinner parties are the favorite way to entertain special visitors, whether Japanese or foreign, sometimes by private individuals but more often by business enterprises. For example, Milton has given a number of lectures over the years, beginning with this visit, under the auspices of the *Nihon Keizai Shimbun,* the Japanese equivalent of the *Wall Street Journal.* After each, the president of the paper, until recently Jiro Enjoji, would invite us to a party at such a restaurant. The other guests included editors and writers at the paper and Chiaki Nishiyama, who had interpreted the lecture. The parties were very informal, most enjoyable, and at the same time enabled us to discuss with very knowledgeable people economic and political issues that specially interested them or us.

I was always the only woman at the party, as I generally was at more conventional dinner parties as well. This situation has been changing gradually. However, as late as 1980, when we were in Japan in connection with the Japanese television version of *Free to Choose* and were entertained at a party with geishas, the only woman at the party aside from the geishas and me was the wife of our host. His geisha was also present. This experience plus my own exposure to the geisha assigned to me at one party gave me a very different view of the Japanese geisha than I originally had. My geisha had a daughter about the age of my own daughter and we compared notes. Obviously, like the varieties of restaurants and theaters, I am sure that there are all varieties of geishas—but I am not competent to judge!

I have never forgotten one experience involving such a dinner, which was at Kitchko, a famous Japanese restaurant in Tokyo. A dinner party at Kitchko is a memorable event—and also incredibly expensive. The hostess plus a group of lovely young ladies dressed in Japanese kimonos (the geishas) greet you, your host, and other guests on arrival. They help you take off your shoes and put on slippers and escort you to the private room reserved for your party. There are numerous courses, each very small and each presented in unique containers on a lovely lacquered tray with, of course, sake always in great abundance plus beer for those who like it. One course, a small steak, was presented with individual pottery barbecues for each guest. With help from a geisha, the guest cooks the delicious steak. Finally, the most delicious melon, a variety that we have seen only in Japan, is served as dessert. The geishas then put on an entertainment: songs, dances, skits, etc., all in traditional Japanese style.

On one occasion, within the same week that we were the guests of the *Nihon Keizai Shimbun* at Kitchko, possibly the very next night, we were invited to a second dinner at Kitchko. The behavior of the hostess of Kitchko and all the geishas plus the whole evening's experience gave us a rare insight into the importance of formality and the saving of face to the Japanese. Though the hostess and geishas clearly recognized us, they never let on that they did. For the benefit of our second host, they acted as if this was our first visit. Moreover, though the meal was as delicious and beautifully served as the first one, there was no duplication in the food or the crockery on which it was served. Only the sake and beer were the same.

Another amusing incident occurred when we spent a weekend at a ryokan (a Japanese style inn) with our friend Chiaki as host. This was a typical inn for Japanese people, not tourists. No one spoke English. This did not disturb us since Chiaki could translate. He ordered soft-boiled eggs for breakfast for the morning after we arrived. When our breakfast arrived, the eggs were ice-cold. They had been cooked the night before and refrigerated! We decided that the Japanese did not eat soft-boiled eggs and therefore did not know how they should be served. We had a similar experience with eggs when we traveled overnight by boat to Kyushu. When we came to the table for breakfast, cold fried eggs were already at the table. This time we did not order them, but apparently the cook knew that Americans eat fried eggs, and thought that they should be served cold.

We traveled south to Kyoto, Osaka, Nara, and Kobe, and north to Sendai. In each city, Milton would lecture and we would have private meetings with small groups, usually economists, always all men. In addition, sight-seeing was a big part of every trip. A specially notable trip was to Kyoto, when Nobatani Kiuchi, a prominent Japanese intellectual and head of the Institute of World Economy, was our guide. Kyoto was for centuries the imperial capital of Japan and is full of marvelous temples and other historic sites. Nobatani's learning and deep attachment to Japan's culture added greatly to the visit. He was the first Japanese member of the Mont Pelerin Society and was active in later years in organizing meetings of the society in Japan.

My general impression of the Japanese as expressed in an early letter to Becky has not changed after trips in later years and close association with many Japanese friends. "We will never really understand these people. It's hard to understand any foreign people, but the Japanese are the hardest of all. They are such a mixture of inconsistent complexities, that one always has the feeling that though you understand the words (sometimes) you are never sure of the meaning. As I have said before, they are truly the most hospitable and generous people we have ever known. But you are never quite sure whether they are generous because they really want to be or because their code of behavior tells them to behave that way." We continued to travel to many more areas in Japan on nine trips that we made in following years for a variety of purposes.

Milton was given an honorary degree by Rikkyo University the night before we left for Sendai. The other two people getting degrees were the Archbishop of York and another religious figure, which led Milton to say in his short after-dinner talk that he felt like an egg between two clerical wafers. The university being Episcopal and the archbishop an honoree, the ceremony made us feel that we were in church rather than a university.

{ *Milton* } One way I have described my own conclusion about the Japanese character is to say that any statement about the Japanese that is true has an opposite that is equally true. As Rose says, the Japanese are incredibly kind and hospitable, yet we know from sad experience during World War II that they are also capable of being incredibly cruel. The common impression that the government runs the economy is true. Yet it is equally true that business runs the government. Japan is monopolistic; yet it is also highly competitive.

I have found that one of the best clues to the Japanese is the Japanese language. Before we went to Japan, I read a number of books about the Japanese language. One sentence struck me: "It is literally impossible to write an unambiguous sentence in Japanese." Again and again we found evidence to support that statement. But the ambiguity serves the important function of facilitating the saving of face.

Rose gave one example of the importance of face saving. Let me give another. At that time, all economists in Japan, I had been told, were either Marxists—not necessarily politically communist or socialist, but analyzing the economy on the basis of Marxian economics—or modern economists, which might mean devotees of David Ricardo. The Marxists were at the time in the majority. One of the main tasks I set myself for Japan was to talk to members of both groups and find out what the real difference was. I had no difficulty talking with modern economists at the universities I visited. But when Chiaki tried to set up a series of interviews with Marxists, he received only refusals. His explanation was that if they spoke with me they would have to disagree with me, and it would not be proper to disagree with a foreign visitor!

Only one economist in Japan at the time was not automatically termed a Marxist or a modern economist: Shigetsu Tsuru, who had a Ph.D. from Harvard. As noted in chapter 18, I was his guest at dinner in 1955 on my way to India, and I had no difficulty having a number of long and informative exchanges with him. His American training meant that he had no hesitancy in disagreeing with me. He had a distinguished career, at one point being elected mayor of Tokyo. One other detail: some university departments were all Marxist, some all modern, but most were mixed. In all cases, if a modern economist retired or left for other reasons, he would be replaced by a modern economist, and similarly with a Marxist. As of now, I do not believe that is the case, as modern economists have become dominant.

To return to the Japanese language, I concluded that the method of writing Japanese is a major clue to some of the characteristics of the Japanese. The first written language that the Japanese came in contact with was Chinese. Chinese and Japanese are about as different languages as one can imagine. Chinese is monosyllabic, uninflected, with a very large vocabulary. The method of writing is by ideographs corresponding to the monosyllabic words—no phonetic symbols, which is why people in different parts of China can read the same newspaper but may not be able to understand one another, because different sounds are attached to the same ideographs. By contrast, Japanese is multisyllabic, highly inflected with a relatively small vocabulary. Yet the Japanese managed by the ninth century to adapt the Chinese method of writing to the Japanese language. There are three components of the written language: *kanji,* which are simply the Chinese ideographs, *hiragana,* which is a phonetic alphabet used to provide relevant inflections, and *katakana,* a second phonetic alphabet currently used solely to transliterate foreign names.[14] The basic unit of Japanese speech is a consonant plus a vowel (as in ka ta ka na). There are ten consonants and five vowels, so that each phonetic alphabet has fifty characters, each character representing a consonant plus a vowel. There are 1,850 kanji that postwar law prescribes for general use in publications. Learning to write Japanese therefore requires learning 1,850 kanji and one hundred phonetic symbols. To add to the complexity, every kanji ideograph has at least two sounds: one the Japanese sound for the word it represents, one the original Chinese sound. (For example, the Chinese character for "big" is pronounced "dai" as in the name of the bank Dai-Ichi (the big one) and "O" as the first letter in the name of Osaka.)

The conversion of Chinese calligraphy into a practical way to write Japanese illustrates a leading trait of the Japanese, the ability to adapt as opposed to innovate, illustrated by the development of the VCR, the computer chip, and similar items, all innovated elsewhere. It also helps to explain a tendency to value highly things from abroad. Indeed, I am told that the Japanese word for foreigner is related to the word for superior. The discipline involved in learning to read and write Japanese helps to explain the disciplined character of the Japanese, as well as their generally extremely retentive memory. The common training also intensifies their homogeneity.

On my major mission of studying monetary relations in Japan, I was very successful. In addition to the cooperation of the Bank of Japan, a young economist at the American Embassy, Michael Keran, who had done graduate work at the University of Minnesota, was extremely helpful. He was also sufficiently impressed with our preliminary findings that Japanese monetary relations were very much like those in the United States, and that changes in monetary growth were closely related to subsequent changes in the economy, that he chose to write his doctoral dissertation on that topic. Though his degree is from Minnesota, it was really a product of my Money and Banking Workshop at the University of Chicago, and was published by us in one of our volumes.[15] After Mike returned to the States, he was for many years director of research at the Federal Reserve Bank of San Francisco, and then chief economist of the Prudential Insurance Company.

Another long-term friendship I formed was with a young Englishman who was studying Japanese industrial structure, John Greenwood. He introduced himself to me after one of my *Nihon Keizai Shimbun* public lectures. John had already learned to speak and write Japanese, and had acquired an extensive knowledge of the Japanese economy. He was helpful to me. After leaving Japan, he spent many years in Hong Kong as chief economist at G.T. Management (Asia) Ltd., in which capacity he started a bimonthly magazine, *Asian Monetary Monitor,* which was terminated in 1996 after twenty years. In 1983, when there was an exchange crisis in Hong Kong, John was the architect of the monetary reform that led to the Hong Kong dollar being unified with the U.S. dollar. He was able to play the crucial role he did because he had analyzed the Hong Kong monetary system in a series of articles in the *Asian Monetary Monitor,* pointed out its defects, and sketched possible reforms. During the course of the detailed negotiations that led to the final reform, John was on the phone almost nightly conferring with Alan Walters, then in London serving as an adviser to Margaret Thatcher, and with me in San Francisco, getting our comments and suggestions on the details of the proposed reform. After he had succeeded in getting his reform adopted—which incidentally has been a great success and achieved the results he had intended—he had three small silver ashtrays made recording the event, as mementos for the three of us. John has recently moved to San Francisco where G.T. also has an office.

I also met economists at the Bank of Japan who were helpful at the time and with whom I maintained contact, explaining some of our subsequent trips to Japan. Friendships that we formed with individual Japanese were another dividend that paid off over time. Several subsequently became members of the Mont Pelerin Society, and helped to organize meetings of the society in Japan.

{ *Rose* } About the middle of June, Janet and David arrived in Tokyo for their summer vacation. We spent two weeks in Tokyo, during which they spent a weekend with some young Japanese students at Hakone. The language problem did not prevent them from having a good time: it was solved by communicating in written English. With us they also visited some of our favorite places in and around Tokyo, and helped us to celebrate our twenty-fifth wedding anniversary with a splendid dinner party at International House. Aside from our family, most of the guests were Japanese, some of whom we had known before, others, new friends we had made during our stay. A most enjoyable occasion.

A trip to the Kansai area, a repeat for us which we were delighted to make, took us to Kyoto (still one of our favorite places in Japan), Nara, and on to the top of Mt. Rokko for a weekend with Professor Tanaka and his wife and two children who were about the same ages as ours.

Cruise: Japan to Singapore

We then set sail on the SS *Orsova,* P. and O. Line, to Singapore via Hong Kong and Manila. We found the cruise relaxing after all our activity and it was especially pleasant to have our own little group with our children. Three days on board in Hong Kong gave us the luxury of wandering around Kowloon and then returning to dinner and our air-conditioned quarters on the ship.

We would not have minded missing Manila, where we stayed for a day before going on to Singapore. There we left the ship and did the rest of our traveling by air. We had six days in Singapore, which was really longer than we liked, but we could not get a flight to Bali sooner. That gave us more time than we needed or wanted to see the development area. As I wrote to Becky, "Along with an airline and a steel mill, every underdeveloped country in these parts has its development area. This means a bunch of civil servants who, at the expense of the government, i.e., the poor people, are designing and building an area which is to house and support with industry, etc., 900,000 people. When one looks at these models, plans, etc., it's sort of like something between children playing house and an artist molding a figure." I went on, "It would be interesting to come back in about 20 years and see what happens. My children may, I don't expect to."

As it happened, we did come back to Singapore some seventeen years later to find that my implicit forecast about the results of the development process was radically wrong. In the intervening seventeen years, Singapore, under the highly paternalistic and autocratic guidance of Lee Kuan Yew, had flourished and become a large, bustling city-state.

Bali

From Singapore we flew to Bali, a trip that started as a disaster but turned out to be one of our most delightful weeks. First of all, we arrived in Bali in somewhat depressed spirits after an uncomfortable overnight stop in Djakarta that Sukarno imposed on all travelers to Bali. Djakarta seemed to us a repeat of India with an uncomfortable hotel thrown in. The poverty and unsanitary conditions were most depressing.

Upon arrival in Denpasar, Bali, we proceeded to the hotel (Segara Beach Hotel) which had been reserved by our travel agent in Chicago. Our first sight of the hotel and our rooms left us with the inclination to take the next plane home. The hotel was not only dark but the rooms were dirty and the whole place was depressing, certainly not a place to spend a relaxed vacation. Without unpacking, we went for a walk on the beach and our luck changed. By chance, we met an English lady and as foreigners so often do, we greeted her and she responded. She was also staying at the hotel and she confirmed our first impression. However, she said, this was the only hotel on the island. It used to be very good but had deteriorated badly in recent years.[16]

Seeing our unhappiness she came up with a possible solution. An Indonesian friend who was married to an English woman was putting up a small motel on Bali and she thought that he might accommodate us. So off we went with her directions and our hopes. The motel consisted of four or five little cabins with thatched roofs, most only partly completed, and the house of the owner, Mr. Woworunta. Fortunately, he was at home. When we explained our dilemma, he said he really hadn't opened for business but if we liked, he would accommodate us in one of the cabins and we could take our meals in his house. This turned out be our salvation, not only because the place was clean and bright but because he became our guide—and a splendid one—for the week. He took us on long drives around the island, informed us about the artists in the neighborhood and we and our children bought some of our treasured wood carvings with his help.

{ *Milton* } One of the wood carvings was of a frog. Just a few years ago, a friend of mine, Hugo Van Reijen, a Dutchman who lives in Guernsey, visited us at our apartment in San Francisco. When he saw our frog, he said, "I know the man who carved that frog." It turned out that he had a second home in Bali and one of his neighbors specialized in carving frogs. No way of avoiding the bromide: What a small world.

{ *Rose* } Our host took us to see performances of Balinese dancing and music, and even arranged for us to attend a funeral. He explained that the Balinese custom was to celebrate a death, sometimes long after the actual death, with an elaborate ceremony only some of which we truly understood. All the friends and acquaintances came to the event. The corpse, it seems, was embalmed until the family had enough money for the celebration. At the celebration, the central event was a tug-of-war over a large log containing the corpse. The imagery was that one side was the angels, the other the devils, and that they were competing for the deceased's soul. There was much swaying back and forth but in the end the angels always won. The whole affair was accompanied by much drinking and singing.

One added event of the week was celebrating Milton's birthday with our host. He provided a barbecued piglet, the first we had ever had, and I prepared potato pancakes, one of Milton's favorite dishes, on a kerosene camp stove, all accompanied by much to drink. It was a birthday party never to be forgotten.

{ *Milton* } As part of his move to modernize Indonesia, Sukarno, the postwar dictator and president of Indonesia, outlawed the traditional custom of bared breasts, ruling that brassieres had to be worn. The old naturally are least willing to change practices, the young, the most willing. One amusing result in Bali was the spectacle of old women with bared, mostly pendulous, breasts; the young, nubile females with brassieres covering their firm well-formed breasts. Judged by results, it was a campaign to deprive bared breasts of their usual sexual appeal.

Kuala Lumpur, Hong Kong, Taiwan

{ *Rose* } After a week of snorkeling, swimming, and just loafing on the seashore, thoroughly refreshed, we set out for more vacation and more central banking for Milton in Kuala Lumpur where we were hosted and guided by our good friends the Clifton Whartons, who were wonderful hosts and extremely helpful in enabling us to ship some of our acquired loot back to the United States.[17]

{ *Milton* } Malaysia was interesting as a country divided between the Malays and the Chinese. The Malays were in political control and were dedicated to central planning, which yielded many benefits to the politically well placed. The Chinese were, as in many places, economically enterprising and controlled much of the industry. The result was reasonably rapid economic growth, but growth and level of living well below their potential.

I visited the University of Malaya and gave a public lecture under its auspices. I do not have any records of the lecture, but I remember it very well because of its ending. The chairman was a Malay professor at the university. In my lecture, I contrasted the development of Japan in the early decades after the Meiji restoration, when it was compelled by international agreement to practice free trade (no duties above 5 percent), and did practice nearly complete laissez-faire in economics, and the development of India since it achieved independence and practiced detailed central planning. The contrast is highly favorable to a free-trade policy and unfavorable to central planning. The applicability of my comparison to Malaysia was obvious. At the end of the lecture, the Malay professor in the chair could contain himself no longer and burst out with something like, "If we followed the policy you recommend, the Chinese would dominate the country. We Malays are not going to stand for that."[18]

{ *Rose* } We returned to Bangkok to explore it with our children, then on to Hong Kong, primarily to do some shopping, and then to Taiwan. We spent a few days in Taipai meeting with economists and then we took off on a junket that David had planned with a Chinese friend from a Boston-area college who was spending the summer with her grandparents. She knew the country well and recommended our going to Sun Moon Lake in central Taiwan. She joined us for our trip, which added more spice. I enjoyed the countryside both around Sun Moon Lake as well as on our way there. As I wrote to Dorothy, who also shared my horticultural enthusiasms, "I've decided that rice paddies are really the most beautiful countryside I know. A few tea terraces mixed in, plus banana trees and palms, and what can be lovelier."

{ *Milton* } In Hong Kong, before leaving for Taiwan, we bought some Taiwanese currency in order to have local currency when we arrived. A rather modest sum turned out to be a bulky package. Taiwan had experienced rapid inflation for some years. It was finally getting the inflation under control. However, it had not altered the maximum denomination of its currency, which meant that even the largest bill represented a trivial real amount. At discussions in Taipei at the central bank, I asked why they had not printed larger denomination notes.[19] The answer was one that I had encountered elsewhere under similar circumstances: issuing larger denomination notes would increase the public's fear of further inflation. I argued that, on the contrary, the public's inflation expectations were going to be dominated by the actual inflation and by their knowledge of government's fiscal and monetary policies. By making currency a less attractive way to hold assets, limiting the maximum denomination to a low real value would lead to an increase in velocity and thereby to higher actual inflation. I have no idea whether I convinced anyone since I did not follow closely the future development of Taiwanese denominations.[20]

Another phenomenon that I had come across elsewhere but was especially important at the time in Taiwan was the use of postdated checks as a short-term credit instrument. Small businesses had little access to banks for credit. Equally important, usury legislation limited the interest rate that could be charged on loans, which partly explained the limited access to banks. A favorite device to avoid these problems was for the potential debtor to issue a postdated check to a friend or business acquaintance, who would pay for it not the full amount on the check, but whatever sum was agreed to by the two parties. The creditor might then endorse the check to a third party, who would similarly redeem it for an agreed sum. As the number of endorsements increased, the credit quality of the check increased. In this way postdated checks served as a very flexible and useful credit instrument. I was particularly intrigued by this phenomenon because, as I noted in chapter 3, it so closely resembled the expedient my parents resorted to in their modest retail enterprise when they were short of cash—which was most of the time.

Japan, Then Home via Honolulu

{ *Rose* } After our junket to Taiwan, we returned to Japan for a final fling. We had not been to the southern island of Kyushu but had heard wonderful stories about the hot springs and volcanos there, and our friend Nishiyama recommended strongly that we spend a few days with our children visiting some of the sights in and around Beppu. So, we decided on this last fling and Chiaki as usual contacted friends there who would accompany us on that part of our trip.

We went to Beppu by steamship rather than by railway because we thought it would be more relaxing, and it was. We have no detailed notes on or memories of our visit to Beppu. I have vague recollections of our amazement in seeing the boiling ponds. The overpowering aroma of sulfur mixed with many other minerals is a more distinct recollection.

A few more days in Tokyo saying farewell to the many friends we had made plus a few more trips to favorite gardens brought us to the end of this wonderful year. We had decided to come home by ship, leaving Yokohama on the American President Line's *President Cleveland* for Hawaii. We were hesitant to take the ship all the way to the Pacific Coast because we thought it would become tiresome so decided to get off in Hawaii and fly to the Coast.

However, our voyage was so pleasant that we wondered whether we had made a mistake even though we did enjoy our few days in Hawaii.

Our trip was a never-to-be-forgotten experience but we were also delighted to be back in our own house, visiting with old friends and just getting back to normalcy.

{ *Milton* } Although I never wrote the book that I intended to on the basis of the material I gathered in the countries I studied, I believe that the trip was worthwhile and highly productive scientifically. Aside from my own writing, I did stimulate a good deal of work on monetary issues by other scholars in either all or most of the five countries I studied intensively. More important for me personally, it gave me an insight into the politics as well as economics of monetary matters that I do not believe I could have gained in any other way. It also gave me contacts in other countries, particularly Israel, Hong Kong, and Japan, that led to two-way cooperation in subsequent years. So the trip was a great success for Rose and me both scientifically and personally.

→ *Chapter Twenty-One* ←

PARTICIPATING IN THE PUBLIC-POLICY DEBATE

{ *Milton* } My interest in public policy and political philosophy was rather casual before I joined the faculty of the University of Chicago. Informal discussions with colleagues and friends stimulated a greater interest, which was reinforced by Friedrich Hayek's powerful book *The Road to Serfdom,* by my attendance at the first meeting of the Mont Pelerin Society in 1947, and by discussions with Hayek after he joined the university faculty in 1950. In addition, Hayek attracted an exceptionally able group of students who were dedicated to a libertarian ideology. They started a student publication, The *New Individualist Review,* which was the outstanding libertarian journal of opinion for some years. I served as an adviser to the journal and published a number of articles in it.[1]

The Mont Pelerin Society

The first meeting of the Mont Pelerin Society has been discussed in chapter 13. Following that founding meeting, the society met nearly every year, though I did not attend another meeting until 1957. Some were general meetings, others regional meetings. In the early decades, the society played an important role in enabling individuals who were intellectually isolated in their own countries to spend a week or so with a group of like-minded intellectuals. They could discuss freely their differences, and try out new ideas, without having to watch out for someone waiting for a chance to skewer them. The collegial atmosphere was not so important for those of us from the U.S., because there were more partisans of free markets and free enterprise here than in most other countries. But it was extremely important for Europeans, and later, for Japanese and Latin Americans.

Membership in the society and attendance at the early meetings was relatively small, so it was possible to have vigorous and wide-ranging discussions in which most persons present could participate. However, as the intellectual climate changed and the society became better known, membership and, even more, attendance at the meetings, which included guests, expanded rapidly. The meetings involved less general participation and began to take on the character of presentations to an audience. When I became president of the society in 1971, I concluded that most of Hayek's original objectives had been achieved and that the society had become too large and unwieldy. Insofar as there was still need to bring together isolated supporters of a free society, it seemed to me that the need could best be met by a new society organized by younger people. Accordingly, I arranged for a special meeting of the surviving founding members, plus other members who had held office in the society, to discuss its future. This meeting was held in Montreux, Switzerland, in 1971. The regular biennial meeting was scheduled to be held in Montreux in 1972. I recommended that the society be terminated, with a grand finale meeting in 1972 to celebrate its twenty-fifth anniversary.

The special meeting was extremely pleasant, recreating to some extent the feeling of the first. However, I was completely unsuccessful in converting the other attendees to my view. Most institutions, once established, become perennial, and the Mont Pelerin Society proved no exception. As an alternative, we enacted some measures designed to limit membership and guests.

Those measures have not been very effective. At the twenty-fifth-anniversary meeting in Montreux, attendance numbered 150 members and 60 guests, who with their families totaled more than 320 participants; at the forty-fifth meeting, held in Vancouver in 1992, attendance numbered 415 persons from 33 countries—206 members and 209 guests.

Despite my misgivings about the way the society has developed, I have no doubt that it has contributed substantially to the change that has occurred in the climate of opinion. It has clearly played an important role in our personal life, and continues to do so, though to a much lesser extent.[2]

{ *Rose* } The Saint Moritz meeting in 1957 was the first one that I attended. Milton attended three meetings after that one by himself. Since then we have both attended most of the meetings, beginning with Knokke, Belgium, which was the starting point for our trip around the world. The meetings took us to England, Italy, Scotland, Germany, Switzerland, France, Belgium, Japan, Venezuela, Chile, and Canada. In general the locale for the meetings depended on which members could arrange to underwrite some of the costs, as well as take responsibility for planning the meeting. So far, volunteers have not been a problem. The meetings, of course, vary in the scope and interest of the papers presented. But there has never been a shortage of interesting problems to discuss. And we have always looked forward to visiting with friends.

Particular meetings stand out in our minds for different reasons. We shall never forget the 1972 meeting in Montreux. The topic for Milton's presidential address was "Capitalism and the Jews," which had an unexpected appropriateness because the massacre of Israeli athletes at the Munich Olympics happened to occur during the week of the meeting. And that in turn provided the fuel for one of the most unusual events that has ever occurred at a Mont Pelerin meeting. Gunter Schmolders, past president, was in the chair when the news was passed to him. He interrupted the meeting to report the news and then asked for a moment of silence to express our sadness. At this point, Enoch Powell, a prominent member of the British parliament representing a Northern Ireland constituency arose and, with the appearance of a madman, opposed the moment of silence, screaming something like, "Why do we not have a moment of silence for the people being killed in Ireland?" The audience was horrified at this exhibition and some expressed their feelings vocally. Powell left the room and never appeared at another Mont Pelerin meeting.

The last general meeting that we attended was the 1992 meeting in Vancouver, Canada. Michael Walker, the executive director of the Fraser Institute, hosted that meeting. Since 1992 was also Milton's eightieth birthday, Mike decided to have a special dinner celebrating the occasion. And whatever Mike does, he does with a flourish. So, he gave every guest a copy of Milton's latest book, *Money Mischief,* and arranged for a wonderful ice sculpture on the buffet table. How could one forget such a spectacle?

The Philadelphia Society

{ *Milton* } The Philadelphia Society is something of a domestic offshoot of the Mont Pelerin Society and serves very much the same function: to give the minority of intellectuals in the United States who favor a free economic and political system an opportunity to discuss common concerns in a supportive and sympathetic environment, to meet and to get to know like-minded colleagues, to recharge their batteries for their day-to-day life in frequently hostile surroundings.

It owes its existence, its growth, and its vitality to one person: Don Lipsett. I became acquainted with Don in the early 1960s when he was the Midwest director, later the national field director, of the Intercollegiate Society for Individualists (which has since, regrettably in my opinion, metamorphosed into the Intercollegiate Studies Institute, retaining the initials but concealing the ideological thrust). Don was an extremely active, vigorous, and attractive young man with a wonderful offbeat sense of humor. He organized ISI clubs on campuses, persuaded faculty members to sponsor them, and helped the clubs organize programs to attract students. He became and remained a close friend who brightened my life until his recent untimely death.

Sometime in 1963 or early 1964 he arranged a meeting with Bill Buckley, Ed Feulner (who was and remained throughout the rest of Don's life his closest friend), myself, and perhaps one or two others, to discuss founding a new society that would perform the same function in the United States that the Mont Pelerin Society was seeking to perform on an international level. He persuaded us that such a society was an excellent idea and we formed an organizing committee, originally of twelve persons, later fifteen. Don arranged three initial meetings: at Indianapolis on April 18, 1964; and at Philadelphia and San Francisco on April 25, attended respectively by thirty-six, thirty, and twenty-three persons. About a third of each meeting was devoted to organizational matters, the rest to discussion of presented papers. I spoke at the Indianapolis meeting on "The Role of the Intellectual and the Mont Pelerin Society." All three meetings were highly successful and produced enthusiastic support for Don's project.

The first national meeting of the society, which by then had been incorporated in Illinois, was held in Chicago on February 26–27, 1965, on the topic "The Future of Freedom: The Problem and the Prospects." It attracted about a hundred persons, and the society was well on its way to a long and productive life. I can give the tone of the first meeting and of the times best by quoting from a column, titled "New Torch Burns," that George Crocker published on March 7, 1965, in the *San Francisco Examiner* on his return from Chicago:

> As any college professor knows—and the students too—for many years, on most campuses, to be a conservative hasn't been the "in" thing to do. The pressures of conformity are so pervasive in most faculties that one must be known as a liberal and echo the stereotyped jargon of liberalism or risk being treated as a pariah, which can be not only unpleasant but costly to one's career. . . .
>
> I have just returned from a conclave of the brave, held in Chicago without fanfare. The brave? Yes, there are some eminent professors, and brilliant graduate students who will some day be professors, who have never succumbed to the pressure. They are called conservatives, but with their bent toward individualism they are the true liberals of the academic milieu. . . .
>
> They will call their group the Philadelphia Society, after the city

which is the symbol of our ancient heritage of personal liberty under moral law.

Politics and propaganda they will eschew. Sound scholarship will be their tool, truth their cause. For the dilemma of America today is a philosophical one, in spite of all the political verbiage heard in the land.

They believe the students in our schools are entitled to hear a dialogue, not a monologue of the liberals.

As long as I was in Chicago, I remained active in the Philadelphia Society, serving three terms on its board of trustees, attending most meetings, and speaking at many. Since I have been in California I have continued to participate, but much less actively than earlier. The society did me the honor of naming me a Distinguished Member, thereby relieving me of having to pay dues.

Don Lipsett became the permanent secretary of the society and, in its early years, Ed Feulner served as the continuing treasurer. Both were greatly assisted by Don's wife, Norma, who fully shared Don's enthusiasm for the society. Their devotion to the organization and their willingness to sacrifice time, energy, and money to promote it account for much of the society's continued success and growth. As of now, membership is probably above four hundred. Its meetings have been lively and stimulating, have engendered a considerable number of contributions subsequently published, and have attracted increasing numbers of participants. Most important, it has offered a way of bringing younger scholars into contact with one another and with their elders, as well as of establishing relations between academics, journalists, and businessmen. All in all, I regard it as having been a most successful venture.

The society held its thirtieth annual meeting in October 1994. I was unable to attend but spoke to the meeting by telephone. I ended my comments by saying,

> I believe the Philadelphia Society . . . has had a great deal of influence on the climate of ideas. But we have to keep pecking away to make sure that that change in the intellectual climate is converted into a change in practice.
>
> Finally, I want to end by saluting Don Lipsett who, defying every law of biology, was a true father of the Philadelphia Society, almost a virgin birth. He did a splendid job then and he's been doing a splendid job ever since in tending it, in caring for it with paternal loving care.

Tragically, a year later Don was dead.

CESES

Renato Mieli, a professor at the University of Venice and a member of the Mont Pelerin Society, founded and ran CESES (Centro per studi e ricerche su problemi economico-sociali)—loosely translated, Center for Economic and Social Studies—to promote free-market ideas.³ One of his major projects was to arrange meetings in Europe between economists from the Soviet bloc and from the West. He did so in cooperation with Warren Nutter (the first Chicago Ph.D. whose thesis I supervised), at the time a professor at the University of Virginia, whose specialty was the economics of Russia and the Eastern bloc.

On September 2, 1967, leaving Rose behind in New England, I went with Warren to Italy to attend an East-West meeting from September 12 to 14 at Rapallo, a lovely resort city on the Mediterranean near Genoa.

Western participants at such joint meetings were usually specialists on the Soviet Union, Sovietologists, but not at CESES meetings. According to Mieli and Nutter, the economists in the East with whom they were in contact wanted to meet and exchange views with free-market Western economists, not Western students of the system that they knew only too well. That judgment was certainly confirmed at the conferences I attended: the economists from the Soviet bloc were anxious to learn how a market system works. At one of them we "heard a brilliant talk by a Hungarian Marxist economist. He had rediscovered for himself Adam Smith's invisible hand—a remarkable if somewhat redundant intellectual achievement. He tried, however, to improve on it in order to use the price system to transmit information and organize production efficiently but not to distribute income. Needless to say, he failed in theory, as the communist countries have failed in practice."⁴

In the course of the Rapallo meeting, Renato's wife, Bianca, helped me find and purchase Italian tiles for the kitchen counter in our new house in Vermont, which was then nearing completion. I had a real problem getting them back to Vermont: they were extremely heavy; had I sent them through as baggage, the charge for excess baggage would have more than doubled their total cost. So I took them with me on the plane in two shopping bags as carry-on luggage. That was long before today's terminals, where you walk straight onto the plane at the same level as the door. I remember vividly to this day the strain of carrying the heavy bags up the long flight of steps I had to climb to get on the plane—and since I was returning home alone, Warren was not there to help. In any event when I finally got them to New Hampshire, they were a great delight, and gave us a splendid and colorful kitchen counter in the new house. We still have a few excess tiles that we brought with us to California.

After returning home, I wrote to Renato Mieli, congratulating him on an extremely effective session, and went on to say, "I reported on the conference briefly to the Mont Pelerin Society at Vichy. In doing so I felt that I had come from the Mont Pelerin Society of the East to the Mont Pelerin Society of the West." But I went on to say that "I have often felt at the Mont Pelerin Society of the West that people on the rostrum were preaching free markets while proposing measures of intervention. By contrast, at Rapallo I found that people were preaching socialism, while recommending measures that would promote free markets. The preaching is not without importance but practice may ultimately be more important."

Mieli arranged for a meeting to be held in 1968 in Budapest, which I agreed to attend, and Rose planned to accompany me. That meeting was canceled as part of the Western protest against the Russian invasion of Czechoslovakia earlier that year. Since we were coming to Europe for a Mont Pelerin meeting at Aviemore, Scotland, we spent the time saved partly in Britain, including participating in an American Bankers Association Conference of University Professors at Ditchley Park; and partly in visiting Trygve Hoff and his son Ole-Jakob in Norway. Rose and I attended two later CESES meetings, one in Milan in 1970, and one in Ermonville, near Paris in 1972.

After the 1970 meeting, we spent some days in Venice, where the Mielis had an apartment, and they greatly added to our enjoyment of that wonderful city. In particular, Renato introduced us to a glass blower at one corner of the Ghetto Nuovo Square who made beautiful miniatures of traditional Jewish figures. We bought a set and they are still among our prized possessions, on display in our entry hall. Again, in 1973, we spent a pleasant few days in Venice, where Renato was holding a seminar for Italian participants, at which I lectured. Later that year, Renato and Bianca paid us a visit in Vermont.

Capitalism and Freedom

The Volker Foundation financed a series of summer programs beginning in 1956, designed to present an overview of the history, philosophy, and economics of a liberal (in the original sense) world view. Each program had three or four expositors and twenty or thirty young academics. The first was held in June 1956 at Wabash College and was directed by John Van Sickle and Benjamin Rogge. I gave a sequence of lectures at this program and at similar programs in subsequent years. In each case, one or two lectures covered basic principles of economic liberalism, and additional lectures applied these principles to special problems.[5]

Capitalism and Freedom, described in the Preface as "a long-delayed product" of these lectures, was published by the University of Chicago Press in 1962. Rose was mainly responsible for putting the lectures in publishable form. As the Preface says, "She pieced together the scraps of the various lectures, coalesced different versions, translated lectures into something more closely approaching written English, and has throughout been the driving force in getting the book finished."[6] As I also said in the Preface, "this series of conferences stands out as among the most stimulating intellectual experiences of my life": the stimulation was provided partly by the talented young academics who attended and participated actively in vigorous discussions both at the lectures and during free time, partly by my getting to know and to learn from my distinguished fellow commentators.

I have already referred to the intellectual climate at the time of the Mont Pelerin Society's founding. Even fifteen years later "when *Capitalism and Freedom* was first published," I wrote in a new preface for a paperback edition published in 1982, "its views were so far out of the mainstream that it was not reviewed by any major national publication, . . . though it was reviewed by the London *Economist* and by the major professional journals. And this for a book directed at the general public, written by a professor at a major U.S. university, and destined to sell more than 400,000 copies in the next eighteen years. It is inconceivable that such a publication by an economist of comparable professional standing but favorable to the welfare state or socialism or communism would have received a similar silent treatment."[7]

By now the book has sold well over half a million copies in English, and has been translated into eighteen other languages. A Russian translation was published in 1982 in the United States. We have been told that it was smuggled into the Soviet Union and served as the basis for an underground edition. We know that an underground Polish version was published sometime in the early eighties. Since the fall of the Berlin wall, the book has been translated into Serbo-Croatian, Chinese, Polish, and Estonian, and still other translations are pending. We are much impressed by numerous letters from residents in the former Soviet Union and Soviet satellites maintaining that *Capitalism and Freedom,* along with books and writings by Ludwig von Mises and Friedrich Hayek, played a major role in spreading and keeping alive an understanding of the meaning of a free society.

Lecturing in a Hostile Intellectual Climate

I was at odds with the reining orthodoxy about both public policy and economic theory: about welfare-state and socialist views in public policy, and

Keynesianism in economic theory. I recall well the Harvard graduate student who came to visit me, saying something like, "I had to see for myself what that black magician from the Middle West was like."

On the same theme, in 1989, I received a letter from Mark Rollinson, who had been a student at Duke University thirty years earlier: "My days at Duke," he wrote,

> were not happy ones. . . . To make matters worse, most of my fellow students and all of my professors held my views on several subjects in overt disdain.
>
> One day after particularly severe ridicule in an economics class I went to the professor after the session and told him that I was quite certain that I was not stupid and I asked him if there were not at least some economists who shared my views. "Oh, yes," he said, "as a matter of fact we've discussed you frequently here at the faculty level. You're nearly a clone of some chap in Chicago named Milton Friedman. It's truly amazing."
>
> Well, I went running over to the library with your name in hand, only to find that you were not in the name catalogue. On consulting with my professor later, he explained that Duke had a system of screening new material by the appropriate department and the Economics Department did not consider your work worthy of carrying.
>
> Whereupon I went to the Dean of Men . . . and made an offer: put Friedman into the library or take Marx out; otherwise I would write a letter to the editor of every newspaper I could find.
>
> They opted to add you and keep Marx.
>
> When you received the Nobel Prize, I was prouder probably even than you, as you might imagine.

My maverick status did not keep me from receiving more requests than I could accommodate for talks from universities, colleges, and nonacademic groups.[8]

Despite having views that were not "politically correct," to use a term that has come into wide use only recently, I do not recall any significant unpleasantness in those years (that was to come later over Chile; see chap. 24). That is not surprising for technical talks, where the very concept of PC has little relevance. But on general issues also, I have always gotten along very well with student audiences, even when they were initially hostile to my views.

In the 1960s, when controversy on campuses was rife, I gave a number of talks to audiences of students allied with the SDS (Students for a Democratic

Society), then the dominant radical student organization. I introduced those talks by saying something like, "Your objective is the same as mine—greater individual freedom. The difference is that I know how to achieve that objective and you do not." That seemed to make it clear that we were differing not about ends but about means, and it produced a responsive audience. Two other episodes are of interest.

In 1961, Haverford College, which had started a program of inviting visiting professors to give a few days of instruction in advanced subjects that they did not offer, asked me if I would provide instruction in mathematical economics. At the time, Janet was at Bryn Mawr College, which is in the neighborhood of Haverford, so I agreed. Subsequently, the president of Haverford asked me whether I would give a talk in their chapel service to the entire college. I agreed, giving a title that had the word "Freedom" in it (I have not been able to locate the exact title, and this, like what follows, is entirely from memory). I then discovered that chapel was compulsory at Haverford. Accordingly, I wrote to the president asking him to make an exception for my talk since it seemed hypocritical to give a talk on freedom to a captive audience. He replied that it was not possible to make an exception for my talk, but that I shouldn't be concerned because students had a generous allowance of cuts from chapel.

Nothing further happened until the president and I were walking over to the chapel. On the way, I asked him how attendance was taken. He said that proctors in the balcony registered the absentees early in the session. I asked whether he would object if I asked the proctors to let me know when the tally was complete. He obviously did not like the idea but he could hardly forbid me to do so.

When I started to talk, I asked the proctors to let me know when they had finished taking attendance. I explained my problem about talking to a captive audience about freedom, and invited anyone who wanted to leave to do so after the tally was complete. After the tally was complete, I announced a recess during which those who wanted to leave could do so. About two persons got up to leave and they were roundly booed by the rest. Never have I had an audience in my hands the way I had that one.

I should explain that this was no mean feat. In today's language, the Haverford faculty and students were as PC as they come. In the 1960 presidential election, Haverford wanted to stage an election debate between proponents of Kennedy and Nixon. They could not find anyone on the campus willing to support Nixon. They had to bring in an outsider.

Some years later I engaged in a debate at the University of Wisconsin with Leon Keyserling, a lawyer who had been chairman of the Council of

Economic Advisers under Truman. He was a committed left-wing ideologue, and a rather unpleasant character. His debating technique was to make fun of my views as utterly reactionary, deserving only ridicule. He chose as his example a list of items from chapter 2 of *Capitalism and Freedom* that, I said, "cannot, so far as I can see, validly be justified in terms of the principles outlined above." He was doing very well with the audience of students as he went through my castigation of price supports, tariffs, and so on. Then he came to point 11, "Conscription to man the military service in peacetime." That expression of my opposition to the draft brought ardent applause and lost him the audience and the debate.[9]

American Enterprise Institute

The kind of policy-oriented think tanks that are common today were few and far between in the fifties. They were to come later along with the cold war and the ideological competition between capitalism and socialism. Such prominent academic nonteaching institutions as the National Bureau of Economic Research and the Hoover Institution were engaged in scientific long-range studies of a generally nonideological character, and devoted little if any attention to short-range policy issues.[10] The major think tank in Washington was the Brookings Institution, widely regarded as left-wing and a home away from home for out-of-office Democrats. Almost the only significant free-market think tank was the Foundation for Economic Education, founded by Leonard Read in 1946.[11]

The American Enterprise Association was founded in 1943 but was largely inactive until it was reenergized by two remarkable individuals: William J. Baroody and W. Glenn Campbell. Baroody became president in 1954. He recruited Campbell to serve as research director, a position he held until 1960, when he left to become director of the Hoover Institution. In 1962 the American Enterprise Association was renamed the American Enterprise Institute for Public Policy Research (all future references will use AEI to refer to the whole period). Baroody and Campbell wanted to present the free-market point of view on public policy and thereby provide an alternative to the Brookings Institution. One key element of their strategy was to present alternative, not monistic, points of view while maintaining the highest scholarly standards.

They began with a series of analyses of important legislative proposals that presented the arguments for and against each proposal in a strictly objective and nonpartisan way. They offered to send these to any legislator who requested them. It did not take long before a large fraction of the legislators of both parties asked to be put on the mailing list. Baroody justified the policy by saying that the non–free-market view was available regardless of what AEI did, and that the only way to expose unsympathetic legislators to the free-market view was to make both views available to them. The analyses were thorough, well written, and earned a great deal of respect.

The AEI also staged a series of debates on important issues, and published the edited transcripts. Finally, the AEI began publishing a steady flow of pamphlets and books on important public policy issues and continues to do so today.

I entered the Washington political scene through association with the American Enterprise Institute. To assure the quality of the AEI's publications, Baroody and Campbell early on established an Academic Advisory Board, later renamed Council of Academic Advisers. I served as a member of this board from 1956 to 1979. During the period that I served, the academic advisers typically met several times a year, went over all manuscripts submitted for publication, and reviewed proposed studies. I felt that I was performing a useful service, and that as a result of our joint efforts the publications of AEI were kept to an exacting academic standard. After we moved to California, I decided that I could no longer continue to be as active as I had been. Accordingly I resigned, saying in my letter of resignation, "I have always followed the principle of not serving on boards, lending my name to committees, or the like, no matter how much I was in sympathy with the objectives and activities of the group, unless I was able to devote enough time to it to be more than a name on a letterhead or on the cover of a book."

I also participated in two of their debates, one in 1967 with Robert Roosa on the balance of payments, the second in 1971 with Wilbur Cohen on Social Security.[12] I personally benefited from these debates by being forced to refine my own analysis in discussions with able and worthy opponents, and by being given a significant forum for expressing my views.*

Sometime in the early 1960s, Bill Baroody arranged for me to serve as an adviser for a small group of Republican congressmen who were trying to develop a philosophy and legislative program for the Republican party. The

---

* I particularly benefited from Wilbur Cohen. Although we disagreed about policy, we had similar patterns of thought, and I found many of his arguments extremely perceptive and relevant to issues other than Social Security. In particular, when I contended that Social Security transferred income from relatively low to middle and upper incomes, he did not disagree but went on to say: "I am convinced that, in the United States, a program that deals only with the poor will end up being a poor program." I do not regard that as a valid argument for Social Security in its present form, but it is an extremely perceptive remark that has been repeatedly confirmed before and since by the numerous "poverty programs," whether AFDC, public housing, or whatnot.

group included Melvin Laird, Gerald Ford, Tom Curtis, Don Rumsfeld, and perhaps one or two others. I met with them from time to time for a few years. One product was a book entitled *The Conservative Papers,* to which I contributed an article "Can a Controlled Economy Work?"[13] An unanticipated benefit was an intensive education in politics in action and acquaintance with some of the leading figures in the Republican party. I was impressed with their intelligence, their willingness to put aside narrow partisan concerns and look at policies in terms of the broad public interest. They may have been exceptional, but I am sure that there are such politicians on both sides of the aisle today.

{ *Rose* } In his State of the Union Message in 1964, President Johnson announced that his administration was "declaring unconditional war on poverty." In their 1964 annual report, his Council of Economic Advisers proposed to define poverty as a money income of $3,000 per family, regardless of size of family, and went on to use this crude estimate to construct detailed tables of the number of poor persons and families.[14]

During my work on the Consumer Purchases Study in the 1930s, and my subsequent work on consumption, I had become interested in the concept of "poverty"—its meaning and the varying definitions that have been used at different times. I wasn't working on anything in particular in 1964 so when Tom Johnson, the research director of AEI, asked if I would write an essay on poverty and how to measure it, I was interested. The resulting pamphlet was published by the AEI in February 1965 under the title *Poverty: Definition and Perspective.*

I began the essay by pointing out how the concept of poverty has changed over time. According to an eminent French economic historian, as late as the eighteenth century in France, an income that allowed the purchase of three pounds of wheat per capita per day "did not represent a realizable possibility but *an ideal* whose attainment would solve every social problem."

The council's crude estimate of $3,000 per family was derived by much the same logic, updated. It tried to define an income that would enable a family to purchase a "nutritively adequate diet," basing its estimate on data on the nutritive adequacy of diets actually consumed by families with different incomes. It assumed that a family at the poverty level would spend about a third of its income on food, that $1,000 would suffice to purchase a "nutritively adequate diet," and so three times that figure could be used to define the poverty level.

In the major part of my essay, I tried to use the concept of nutritive adequacy in a more sophisticated way. I concluded that the council's estimate of poverty income was seriously defective and a gross overestimate judged by its own criterion.

The council recognized in its 1964 report that "No measure of poverty as simple as the one used here would be suitable for determining eligibility for particular benefits or participation in particular programs."[15] Yet that is precisely what has happened over time. The measure has been updated and improved by allowing for size of family and adjusting for inflation, yet the resulting measures, now used to determine eligibility for an increasing number of federal and state programs, have not corrected the major flaw that I pointed out—reliance on current money income. Over time, fringe benefits, the imputed rent from an owned home, and other nonmoney sources of income have become considerably more important. Estimates of the effect of allowing for such income roughly halve the estimated number of "poor."

I concluded:

> The past century and more has seen an unprecedented improvement in the material conditions of the ordinary man in this country. Central heating, electricity, running water, telephones, and automobiles have become so much a part of our environment that they are taken for granted. Yet, less than a century ago, these commonplaces of today either did not exist at all or were the prize only of the rich. . . .
>
> Nutrition, the first need of man, has improved markedly even since the 1930's—which is as far back as we have satisfactory measurements. In 1936, a third of American families had diets that were classified as "poor"; in 1955, only an eighth had such diets, according to the same standards. . . .
>
> The many separate individuals and organizations, each working in its own area and its own field of interest to relieve distress and alleviate misery, need no comprehensive statistical blueprint to guide them. Voluntary cooperation in charity, no less than in economic production, can be and is guided by an invisible hand. But if a centralized governmental program is to be directed at anything like the right problems, let alone succeed in mastering them, it must be guided by a far more sophisticated and extensive study of just who are the poor and how poor they are than any that is now available.[16]

More than three decades later, that comment is no less relevant. Numerous more sophisticated studies have been made; tens of billions of dollars have been spent; there has been continued "improvement in the material conditions of the ordinary man in this country"; yet by the still crude official measure, the fraction of families below the poverty line is currently higher than it was in 1970!

Would anyone today subscribe to the utopian hopes expressed in the Council of Economic Advisers 1964 report? "There will always be some Americans who are better off than others. But it need not follow that 'the poor are always with us.' In the United States today we can see on the horizon a society of abundance. . . . It is high time to redouble our efforts to eliminate poverty."

Educational Vouchers

{ *Milton* } In 1955, I published "The Role of Government in Education," an article I had written during the year that we spent in Cambridge (1953– 54).[17] (That article, slightly revised, appears as chapter 6 in *Capitalism and Freedom.*)

I distinguished among three levels of government involvement in schooling: requiring schooling, financing schooling, and administering schools. I argued that a case could be made for "both the imposition of a minimum required level of schooling and the financing of this schooling by the state." However, I went on, a "third step, namely the actual administration of educational institutions by the government, the 'nationalization,' as it were, of the bulk of the 'education industry'" is difficult to justify on any grounds.[18] "Governments could require a minimum level of schooling financed by giving parents vouchers redeemable for a specified maximum sum per child per year if spent on 'approved' educational services. Parents would then be free to spend this sum and any additional sum they themselves provided on purchasing educational services."[19]

Given the existence of government schools, I suggested that "Parents who choose to send their children to private schools would be paid a sum equal to the estimated costs of educating a child in a public school, provided that at least this sum was spent on education in an approved school."[20]

This proposal attracted a good deal of attention at the time and has continued to do so ever since. During the more than forty years since my first article was published, Rose and I have been repeatedly involved in movements to use a voucher system to enable parents to choose the schools to which their children go—in New Hampshire, Connecticut, Michigan, Colorado, Oregon, California, among other places. We have discussed the issue in our subsequent books and have cooperated with a variety of interested parties in designing detailed proposals for a particular community. I have written many articles and op-ed columns on the subject; have given numerous talks on the general issue or in connection with a particular movement to adopt a voucher system, and have engaged in extensive correspondence and controversy on the subject.[21] Monetary policy aside, no subject of public policy has commanded so much of our attention over so long a period.

The experience has been both rewarding and frustrating. It has been rewarding because we have encountered so many public-spirited citizens who have been willing to dedicate themselves to trying to improve the schooling available to children and because the public support for radical reform in our school system has continued to grow, and has begun to produce concrete results. It has been frustrating because we have had so little success, nearly every effort being derailed by the special interests of the educational establishment, notably the teachers' unions. The more we have learned about our educational system the greater has become our confidence that an unrestricted voucher system would lead to enormous improvement in the schooling available to our children, especially those in the most disadvantaged families.

The National Education Association and the American Federation of Teachers, the two major teachers' unions, and their local affiliates are widely recognized as the most potent lobbying group in the country. President Clinton's change of position on school choice provides a recent example of its potency. As governor of Arkansas he supported free parental choice among both public and private schools. At least an eighth and perhaps as many as a quarter of the delegates to the 1992 Democratic convention were from the teachers' unions. As president he has favored free choice among public schools but has strongly opposed any extension to private schools, despite sending his own daughter to a private school.

The performance of our school system, the character of our society, and the functions assigned to the school system have all changed greatly since 1955 when my initial article on education was published. The tendency toward centralization that had been proceeding since the beginning of the century has continued apace. The number of school districts went from 150,000 in 1928 to 55,000 in 1956 to 15,000 in 1996 despite a doubling of population since 1928. From 1960 on, centralization was accompanied by increasing unionization, leading to effective monopoly control of government elementary and secondary schools by the National Education Association and the American Federation of Teachers and their local affiliates. Centralization and unionization have also been accompanied by increasing dissatisfaction with the performance of the school system and one ever-more-ambitious effort after another to "reform" the school system, all without any significant success. The breakdown of central cities and the changing character and role of the family have imposed greater burdens on the school system. Finally, the technical revolution of recent decades and the increasing importance of international trade have raised the levels of cognitive skills required by industry, while the level attained by students has declined.

Free parental choice of schools would promote both equity and efficiency—equity by eliminating the present situation in which parents who choose to send their children to private schools must pay twice for schooling, once through taxes, once through tuition; and efficiency, by establishing an incentive for private enterprise to compete with the present government and private schools, almost all nonprofit. While my initial article mentioned both equity and efficiency, the major emphasis was on equity. Since then, the changes summarized in the preceding paragraph have led us to put greater stress on efficiency.

The tendency for our society to become increasingly stratified—to simplify, the skilled and highly schooled haves versus the unskilled and poorly skilled have-nots—threatens the social stability of our society. Radical improvement in the quality of schooling is the only major force that seems currently available to offset the tendency to stratification. We believe that the possibilities are very great. Schooling is one of the technically most backward of our major industries. It is backward because it is a socialist enterprise controlled by a monopoly that has every incentive to serve its leaders and membership and none to serve the students. Like every socialist enterprise it is highly inefficient. Privatization of schools through unrestricted vouchers would provide the opportunity for a new private-for-profit industry that would have the right incentive—to serve the students who would be its customers. Innovation and greater efficiency would follow as it has in telecommunications after the AT&T monopoly was broken up, in message and parcel delivery when the post office monopoly was challenged, and in many other industries. Competition would force the government schools to shape up or close down.

Public dissatisfaction with the present school system is growing rapidly. Sooner or later pressure for free parental choice will succeed in breaking the hold of the union monopoly. Initially, the unions opposed any element of choice. The first break was their acceptance of some measure of choice within the government school system. Since then, they have been forced to give ground to the charter school movement, though reluctantly and resisting every step of the way. Charter schools are a step in the right direction, but a highly limited one. The schools are and will be limited in number and are still part of the government system. Those so far established enjoy somewhat more autonomy than other government schools. However, they are kept on a tight leash by the educational establishment. Most important of all, they rule out the opportunity for the dynamic force of private-for-profit enterprise to offer competition to the government system.

Rose and I feel so strongly about the importance of privatizing the school system that we have established the Milton and Rose D. Friedman Foundation with the sole mission of promoting public understanding and support of the measures necessary to achieve that objective.[22]

Instructional Dynamics

From 1969 to 1978, I recorded a biweekly commentary on current economic events, under the auspices of Instructional Dynamics Inc. (IDI). When we were in Chicago, William Clark, moonlighting from his regular job with the *Chicago Tribune,* would come to our apartment and record an interview. For the six months that we were in Vermont, Rose took the place of Bill Clark and did the interviewing. Only recently, a friend, who had been a subscriber to the tapes long before he met us, recalled his pleasure at getting acquainted with Rose in this way. All told, over nearly ten years, we taped 215 interviews. This project fit in very well with my *Newsweek* column. Both gave me an incentive to keep current with what was going on and to think about the implications of those events.

In the late seventies, IDI got into financial difficulties. For a time, I agreed to take shares of stock in IDI in payment for my services in place of cash. When it became clear that the difficulties were more than temporary, we ended the series.

This story is worth telling because of the aftermath. We transferred the then worthless shares to the trust fund that we had set up for our grandson Rick, Janet's son, and thought no more about it. Several years later IDI was taken over and the shares of stock suddenly became valuable. Our grandson reaped a substantial windfall, and we were paid the outstanding debt for which we had not agreed to take stock. To our pleasure, our grandson did a great deal better than we did!

International Monetary Market

In late 1971, Leo Melamed, the imaginative and innovative chairman of the Chicago Mercantile Exchange, telephoned me to explore the possibility of our meeting to discuss tentative plans that he had been developing for a public market in currency futures.[23] My name had come to his attention thanks to a news story in the *Wall Street Journal* which noted my longtime advocacy of floating exchange rates, my expectation that the Bretton Woods system of fixed exchange rates was bound to break down, and my belief in the desirability of a public futures market in foreign exchange. That belief was based partly on a personal experience. In November 1967, it became clear to me and other observers that Britain was going to be forced to devalue the pound. I called all the major banks in Chicago attempting to sell the pound short. No bank would take my order, insisting that they dealt in futures only with their regular customers and only in connection with commercial activities. When I pressed them, I received the answer that "the Federal Reserve [or perhaps the Bank of England] would not like it." In subsequent *Newsweek* columns, I laid out the case for eliminating government restrictions on trading in foreign currencies and argued for the adoption of a system of floating exchange rates.

So long as the Bretton Woods system of fixed exchange rates guided by the International Monetary Fund was in effective operation, a broad, resilient public futures market in currencies was not feasible. Many changes in exchange rates did occur during the era of the Bretton Woods system. However, they were large changes—like the British devaluation in 1967—occurring at widely separated points of time. Between such changes, exchange rates were held within narrow limits by central bank manipulation. Under such circumstances, there is little for a public futures market to do most of the time, and hence it cannot attract traders.

The Bretton Woods system came to an end on August 15, 1971, when President Nixon announced that the U.S. would no longer live up to its commitment to sell gold to central banks on demand at $35 an ounce. That announcement induced Leo and his associates to move to implement the tentative plans they had developed to initiate trading in currency futures. His phone call to me was one result.

I met with Leo and Everette B. Harris, the president of the Chicago Mercantile Exchange, in New York on Saturday morning, November 13, 1971. Leo and Everette, as best I can recall a quarter of a century later, arrived with a fully fleshed out plan for establishing what was to become the International Monetary Market (IMM). They had done their homework. I had little to contribute on that level. However, establishing such a market was clearly a costly and risky enterprise. My role turned out to be to assure them that Bretton Woods was dead for good and that any arrangements that replaced the Bretton Woods system of fixed rates subject to occasional change would involve the kind of wider and more continuous fluctuations in exchange rates that were necessary to make a public market in currency futures viable.

They contracted with me to write a memorandum explaining the need for such a market that they could use in presenting their proposals to the authorities in Washington. The memorandum was completed in late December and issued in printed form under the title "The Need for Futures Markets in Currencies" in early 1972.

With his usual generosity, Leo has publicly given me much more credit for the establishment of the IMM than I deserve.[24] Over a long life, I have learned repeatedly how large a gap separates the giving of advice from the taking of advice, and how seldom that gap is bridged. I am more than willing to take credit for foreseeing, along with other economists, the weakness of the Bretton Woods system and for recommending the adoption of floating exchange rates as a substitute—I did that first in a paper written in 1950 and published in 1953, and again in a memorandum to President-elect Richard Nixon in December 1968.

Leo Melamed deserves the greatest share of credit for recognizing the importance of taking prompt advantage of the opportunity offered by Nixon's closing the gold window, and having the courage to do so, despite the risks. It took real persistence and diplomacy to get a prompt go-ahead from government officials much more prone to delay than to act. In retrospect, it is remarkable that the IMM opened for business less than ten months after President Nixon closed the gold window. That was possible only because of advance planning that long preceded the president's action.

The rest is history: Chicago is today the world's most important center of futures trading thanks to Leo's initiative and his subsequent role in guiding the Chicago Mercantile Exchange on its expansionary path.

National Tax Limitation Committee

The National Tax Limitation Committee (NTLC) was an outgrowth of Governor Reagan's unsuccessful 1973 attempt to pass a constitutional amendment in California that would limit state spending and taxes (see chap. 23, p. 389). Lew Uhler, who had been in charge of drafting Governor Reagan's Proposition 1, was unhappy about the result and believed strongly that pressure to limit government spending was of the highest importance. After discussions with a number of other like-minded individuals, he and Bill Rickenbacker, along with ten other founding members, of whom I was one, started NTLC in late 1975. Its aim was to encourage the adoption by individual states and the federal government of constitutional provisions limiting the taxing and spending power of the states and federal government. It proposed to do so by creating a national membership base, encouraging the development of strong state tax-limitation organizations, providing educational and other materials to its members and other interested parties, and working with the state legislatures and the U.S. Congress promoting tax limitation.

During the more than two decades since the NTLC's founding, Lew Uhler has been president and CEO and has done a magnificent job of keeping NTLC concentrated on its central purpose. He has worked with every state in the country and with the federal government. I have nothing but admiration for his steadfastness of purpose and the complete integrity with which he pursued that purpose. Other groups and organizations have of course also been active in seeking a constitutional amendment, and NTLC has consistently cooperated with them.

The obvious question is why seek a constitutional amendment. The legislature and the chief executive vote to spend and tax. They are elected by the public and in principle are ruled by the will of the public. Every survey shows that a large majority of U.S. voters believes that their government is spending too much of their money, that the government budget should be balanced, and that the balancing should be done by cutting spending, not by raising taxes. Yet government spending continues to rise, deficits are large and persistent, and Congress tends to prefer tax increases to spending cuts. The so-called Republican revolution of 1994 raised hopes that at long last a Congress had been elected that would cut government down to size. Those hopes have not been realized, and by no means solely because of the opposition of President Clinton and the Democrats.

How is it that a government of the majority produces results that the majority opposes? The reason is that we are ruled by a majority, but it is a majority composed of a coalition of minorities representing special interests. Each minority may lose more from measures benefiting other minorities than it gains from measures benefiting itself. Yet no minority has any incentive to be concerned about the *cumulative* effect of the measures passed. Even if it were willing to give up its own special measures as part of a package deal eliminating all such measures, there is currently no way that it can express that preference.

The result is a major defect in the legislative procedure. Each measure is considered separately, and the final budget is the sum of the separate items, subject to no predetermined total.

A constitutional amendment is a way, and apparently the only way, to make a package deal of the kind that is needed. Hence our emphasis on promoting a constitutional amendment.

But what kind of an amendment? Our first major activity, after the initial organizing stage of attracting membership and putting out leaflets and information on the importance of limiting government spending, was to convene in early 1979 a Federal Amendment Drafting Committee of twenty-eight knowledgeable and concerned scholars, lawyers, legislators, and activists to draft a specific amendment.

The amendment as initially drafted was directed entirely at limiting government spending. It did not require a balanced budget. It was our view that what was important was cutting government spending, however spending was financed. A so-called deficit is a disguised and hidden form of taxation, and so a bad form of taxation. The real burden on the public is what government spends (and mandates others to spend), not that part of its spending that is financed by open taxes. As I have said repeatedly, I would rather have government spend one trillion dollars with a deficit of a half a trillion than have government spend two trillion dollars with no deficit.

An excellent analysis of the fiscal consequences of adopting the proposed amendment was made by Professor Craig Stubblebine of Claremont McKenna College, who has throughout served as director of research studies for NTLC.

In trying to promote the proposed amendment with members of Congress it quickly became apparent that political support would be greatly enhanced by including provision for a balanced budget. To combine budget balance and spending limitation, the proposed amendment was changed from a spending limitation amendment to a "balanced-budget tax-limitation" amendment. (With a balanced budget, limiting taxes is equivalent to limiting spending.)

In that form, it was approved by the Senate Judiciary Committee in 1981 as S.J. Res. 58. Under pressure from President Reagan, it passed the Senate by the necessary two-thirds vote near the end of the 1982 session. The Democratic leadership in the House tried to keep the amendment from coming to a vote. They failed, thanks to a clever parliamentary maneuver by the proponents of the amendment. A vote was held a few days before adjournment. The amendment was approved by a majority of the members of the House, but not by the necessary two-thirds. That was the high point of our effort. We have never since come so close to getting a good amendment passed.

I was actively involved in this process: testifying before Congress, writing *Newsweek* columns and articles in popular magazines, participating in press conferences, conferring with the senators who were most active.[25] Aside from the military draft, I believe that this is the only issue on which I have done extensive lobbying in Congress.

Prior to the 1982 defeat, Lew and his associates were pursuing a parallel course of working in the individual states both to get limits placed on state spending, with a good deal of success spurred by the passage of Proposition 13 (property tax relief) in California, and to get state legislatures to request the Congress to call a constitutional convention to adopt a balanced-budget tax-limitation amendment. According to Article V of the Constitution, the Congress must call a convention if two-thirds of the states request it to do so. No such convention has ever been called since the founding convention and it is not likely to be. If two-thirds of the states are on the verge of requesting a convention, the Congress itself would pass the desired amendment in order not to be upstaged by the convention. But calling for a convention is the most effective way to get Congress to act. By the time the Senate Judiciary Committee had approved S.J. Res. 58 in 1981, thirty states out of the necessary thirty-four had called for a convention. Since then, the number has risen and fallen, reaching a high of thirty-two.

Since our near success in 1982, a number of proposed amendments have been introduced in Congress. Our main task in connection with those has been to assure that the proposed amendments would have teeth, in particular that they would contain an effective tax-limitation provision. Several members of Congress, recognizing the popularity of the symbol of a balanced budget have sought to achieve the symbol without the substance of effective limitation. The most egregious offender was ex-Senator Paul Simon of Illinois who proposed an amendment requiring an annual balanced budget, with no limitation on either spending or taxation and no enforcement mechanism. He was able to get a number of Republicans to join him to present a bipartisan proposal that would have been ineffective. We consistently opposed his proposal and can claim some credit, I believe, for showing up its emptiness.

The climax came in 1994, when a balanced-budget amendment including a provision requiring a super-majority vote to raise taxes was included in the Republican's Contract with America that contributed to their gaining control of both houses of Congress. The amendment passed the House by the necessary two-thirds vote. When it got to the Senate, past history was repeated. In the hope of getting a two-thirds vote in the Senate, the Republicans in charge compromised with Simon and other Democrats by omitting the requirement for a super-majority vote for a tax increase. The much publicized struggle that followed ended with one vote short of the two-thirds vote necessary—Senator Dole was unable to get a fellow Republican, Senator Hatfield of Oregon, to vote for the amendment. In my opinion Senator Hatfield did his country a great favor, whether for the right reason or not. The amendment in the form in which it was voted on would have been worse than no amendment because it would have prevented a truly effective amendment from being passed. A narrow escape.

NTLC is increasingly joining its forces with U.S. Term Limits, which has been effective in recent years in bringing to public attention the case for limiting the terms of state and federal legislators. It looks very much as if a call by the states for a constitutional convention is the most likely way to persuade Congress to propose amendments providing for effective term limits and effective limitation of government spending—amendments both of which are against the immediate self-interest of many members of Congress.

Newsweek

{ *Rose* } I described Milton's emergence as a columnist in the *Oriental Economist:*

In the summer of 1966, the editor of *Newsweek* magazine telephoned to ask whether my husband would consider becoming a columnist for *Newsweek.* Their idea was to have a troika of economists contribute columns, one each week in a regular rotation, and to select the economists in such a way as to present a variety of views. They approached Paul Samuelson, as a representative of the "new economics" or "new deal liberal" wing of the profession; Henry Wallich, as a representative of the live center; and my husband, as a representative of the "old liberal" or "free enterprise" wing.

Though agreeing that this was a worthwhile project, my husband was very reluctant to undertake the assignment. He thought he would have difficulty finding enough issues which he could discuss clearly in the space allotted to a column. He had other similar objections which I no longer remember but most of all he felt that it would take too much time and thus interfere with his research which was, along with his teaching, his main task. I agreed, of course, that his research came first. I did not believe, however, that writing a column every three weeks would interfere very much with his research. I also felt that research findings were barren if they were not communicated to the public. In general, these two tasks have been performed by different people. This has not always been true, however. John Maynard Keynes, for example, did both. For whatever reason, the task of explaining the relationship between political freedom, for example, and a free market economy or the consequences of the spread of government into more and more areas of our lives, has not been performed very well. I felt that my husband's special abilities and knowledge put him in a particularly good position to do so. The debate between myself and our son, who agreed with me, on the one side and my husband on the other, continued for some days. We succeeded in persuading him without too much pressure, however, because he found the assignment a challenging one and could not resist trying it.[26]

{ *Milton* } To satisfy myself, I compiled a list of possible topics, and wrote a couple of sample columns. I sent both to George Stigler, asking his judgment. George encouraged me to go ahead, like Rose, pooh-poohing the idea that I would be stuck for ideas to write on. I also had a long phone conversation with Paul Samuelson, who strongly urged me to agree. I should note that though Paul and I have often differed sharply on issues of public policy, we have been good personal friends and have respected each other's competence and contributions to economics.*

Finally, I checked with Henry Hazlitt. Henry had been associated with *Newsweek* from its start in 1934. For many years he had written a column "Business Tides," which appeared on the last page of *Newsweek,* where George Will and Meg Greenfield now appear on alternate weeks. Our troika was to replace Henry. Since Henry and I had essentially the same ideological views, I wanted to make sure that he had no hard feelings about his termination by *Newsweek.* He assured me that nothing of the kind was involved and urged me to accept the offer.

{ *Rose* } Again from the *Oriental Economist:*

> The fear of not having enough subjects to write about has turned out to be a problem in reverse. There is almost always more than one issue that it seems urgent to explore and the problem is one of choosing the one that calls for enlightenment most urgently. Though the issues dealt with are typically suggested by the news of the day, my husband has used current issues to develop themes that seemed important to him. Like all of my husband's work, the columns fall into two categories: positive economics and normative economics. The first group deal with the purely scientific question of the effects that can be expected from specific stimuli. Most of these have been concerned with inflation, monetary policy, and fiscal policy. . . . My husband's views in this area have sometimes differed from the views

---

* Paul described the situation very well in a comment in a letter of December 8, 1995: "I hope it will be said of us that, though we disagreed on much, we understood wherein our logical and empirical differences were based and that we were pretty good at preserving amiability, friendship, and respect throughout."

of other economists. The most important single question of this kind is the role of monetary vs. fiscal policy in affecting the course of events. The *Newsweek* columns have, I believe, played a major role in changing the views of the lay public on this issue. . . .

The *Newsweek* columns, much to our surprise, have been read by professional economists and have often been referred to in articles in professional journals and technical economic books. However, they were aimed at, and have mostly influenced a very different audience—the intelligent and concerned citizen layman. My husband's determination to be technically rigorous and yet to write simply about difficult subjects has, I believe, been one of the most important factors in his popularity as a columnist and his ability to get his views across. . . .

The second general class of columns that my husband has contributed includes columns about specific issues or problems that apply his general philosophy as set forth in *Capitalism and Freedom,* i.e., his fervent belief that the promotion of individual freedom should be the prime objective of social arrangements. These columns cover such topics as a volunteer army, which my husband was very active in promoting and which was finally instituted, social security and welfare, which in addition to other defects are he feels an intrusion on one's personal freedom, schooling which everyone agrees is abominable and which he feels could be much improved by the injection of competition through the voucher plan; the post office which like schooling, is exceedingly poor and would benefit greatly from an injection of free competition if the prohibition on the private carrying of mail were removed, and many others. [All told, Milton wrote more than three hundred columns over eighteen years.]

Along with the spread of his philosophy through *Newsweek* columns has come a great increase in the number of invitations to lecture. Here, too, the audiences have been extremely varied extending from businessmen who value his judgments about economic prospects to the general public who come to hear his general philosophy and how it applies to the problems that society faces. Here, as in the *Newsweek* columns, I believe that my husband's tremendous success comes from his ability to say things, however complicated, in simple terms. He has always insisted that if one really understands his subject, it is not necessary to use technical and complicated language. A reviewer of *There's No Such Thing as a Free Lunch,* a second collection of *Newsweek* columns, put it this way: "The nice thing about Friedman is his empathy for the ignorant. No man, I am given to understand is more at home in the abtrusities of his science; yet he is a lucid and perceptive apostle to the ignorant."[27]

{ *Milton* } One condition that Paul, Henry, and I insisted on was that we have final say over the content of our columns, though we welcomed editing suggestions. That condition was severely tested a little over a year later when I wrote a column (December 11, 1967) severely criticizing a 22-page *Newsweek* article "The Negro in America," using the same title for my column. "*Newsweek's* remarkable cover story on the Negro in America," I wrote,

> is depressing for what it reveals about the present position and attitudes of the Negro minority in these United States. It is more depressing for what it reveals about the views of well-intentioned liberals. . . .
>
> Many of the problems that the Negro faces in America today were produced or aggravated by governmental measures proposed, supported and executed by liberals holding the views that dominate the *Newsweek* story.

Replying to a letter that Oz Elliott, the editor of *Newsweek,* wrote dealing with other matters in which he also commented on my column, I replied, "I honor, admire, and appreciate your tolerance in publishing my attack without question or hesitation" (letter dated December 12, 1967). That tolerance continued.

In 1974, Wallich left Yale to accept an appointment as a member of the Federal Reserve Board, which ruled out his writing a regular column. *Newsweek* did not replace him. In 1981, for reasons that I do not know, Paul stopped writing his column. *Newsweek* replaced him with Lester Thurow, also of MIT.

In the Preface to the first edition of *An Economist's Protest,* which consists primarily of columns in *Newsweek* for the first six years, I reflected on my *Newsweek* experience: "The task has been challenging and highly rewarding. It has forced me to try . . . to express technical economics in language accessible to all. It has forced me also to stick my neck out in public without the usual qualifications and reservations that make the professional journals so otiose. Best of all, it has produced a stream of reactions from readers—sometimes flattering, sometimes abusive, but always instructive. I have learned in the process how easy it is to be misunderstood or—to say the same thing—how hard it is to be crystal clear. I have learned also how numerous are the perspectives from which any issue can be viewed. There is no such thing as a purely economic issue."

In early 1984, two weeks after he had taken over as editor-in-chief, Richard M. Smith decided to terminate both Thurow's column and mine, explaining the decision in a friendly letter by saying, "I think it is time to redirect our business columns. I am eager to steer them away from economic analysis and toward a form that would include both analysis and reportage. We have enlisted Robert Samuelson to do a column of this sort every other week, alternating with Jane Quinn" (January 18, 1984).

I had mixed feelings about the termination of my column. On the one hand, as I wrote to Mr. Smith, "I have enjoyed and benefited from my long association with *Newsweek* and I must candidly say I regret its termination" (January 26, 1984). At the same time, I was glad to be relieved of having to face a triweekly deadline. I was subsequently approached by a number of papers to write a regular column (the *Wall Street Journal* and Rupert Murdoch for his papers in Australia, Britain, and the U.S.) and refused to do so—perhaps a better indication of revealed preference than my comment to Mr. Smith.

I never regretted letting Rose and George talk me into accepting *Newsweek*'s offer. (I later returned the favor to George by encouraging him to write a regular column for *Dun's Review*.) My writing style improved not only in the columns but in everything I wrote, and so did my coherence in stating a position. The need to write a column forced me to keep up to date on what was going on, particularly in the area of monetary and fiscal policy, a popular topic (well over one-third of all columns). That was particularly valuable in connection with my ongoing research in money. The column enabled me to play a role in current affairs that would have been hard to duplicate in any other way.

Readers who disagreed with me were understandably far more likely to write than those who agreed—except on those occasions where I was hailed by readers with strong convictions on special issues for, as they would say, "having the courage to express an unpopular position." A column that generated about twenty-five uniformly negative responses was one titled "How to Ration Water" (March 21, 1977) that I wrote shortly after we had moved to San Francisco from Chicago. It was about the drought from which the West, and particularly California, was suffering. I used the scheme of a fixed ration per person that had been adopted in Marin County as typical and suggested that a market two-price system would make everyone better off. (The specific plan that I suggested was "Let the water authorities set a supplemental price per gallon of water; let them charge this price for all gallons used in excess of the current limit; and let them pay this price to families using less than their limit.") I asked why that scheme had not been adopted and suggested that a "plausible answer is the general aversion to using a price system in any form, for any purpose, even by the executives in Marin who owe their affluence to the effective operation of a price system. They, too, have become corrupted by the collectivist sentiment of our time, which reveals by its actions that it prefers orders by bureaucrats to voluntary exchanges by free individuals." Sure enough, most of the negative replies, only a quarter from California, reflected that theme: "an insensitivity to the unrich"—though I had been careful to point out that both the poor and rich would benefit, "short-sighted logic," "Friedman is still stuck in the nineteenth century," "water is priceless," "Milton Friedman's mumbo-jumbo about pricing conceals his real proposal: the rich shouldn't have to suffer," "to disperse the available water supply via a price system is greedy, irresponsible." As these excerpts suggest, few of the negative letters offered reasoned arguments; most simply consisted of diatribe and questioning of my motives. As I have often said, it is frequently easier to question an opponent's motives than to meet his arguments.

One column that generated mostly favorable comments was titled "Laws that Do Harm" (October 25, 1982) with the theme "Government social programs have achieved the opposite of the results promised by their proponents." The reason for the favorable response was undoubtedly the challenge in the last paragraph: "The amazing thing to me is the continued gullibility of intellectuals and the public. I wish someone would explain that to me. Is it simply because no one has given this widely documented generalization a catchy name—like (suggestions welcome)?" I received over forty suggestions from somewhat fewer than forty people, since a number offered several suggestions. The one that struck me as clearly the best was "The Invisible Foot of Government," suggested by Richard Armey, at the time the chairman of the Department of Economics at North Texas State University, later a Republican member of Congress, and, as I write this, majority leader of the House of Representatives. Two others that I rather liked, for different reasons, were "Egonomics," and "Milton's Theory of Paradise Lost." Most of them were rather clever and on target.

One column that generated many abusive letters but more letters of support than I expected was titled "An Open Letter on Grants" (May 18, 1981). It recommended the abolition of the National Science Foundation. It was addressed to Philip Handler, president of the National Academy of Sciences. He wrote me a long personal letter in reply, and also one that *Newsweek* published, in defense of the NSF. Understandably, I got little support from fellow academics, but I was surprised how much support I got from a number of independent scientists associated with nonacademic research groups.

A column published in the issue of May 1, 1972, "Prohibition and Drugs," set out the case for legalizing drugs. It was occasioned by President Nixon's announcement of a war on drugs. That column, which has been reprinted several times since, produced a strong reaction, most of it abusive and negative. However, there were more favorable letters than I, or their authors, expected to be the case, since they nearly uniformly commended me for having the courage to take so unpopular a position. I believe that people are unduly deterred by the prospect of publicly taking an unpopular position. As someone who has repeatedly done so over a very long period, I believe that doing so seldom involves high costs.

There was a similar reaction to a column titled "Frustrating Drug Advancement" (January 8, 1973) in which I castigated the Food and Drug Administration and recommended its abolition. As evidence I cited a careful study that had been made by a colleague, Professor Sam Peltzman. I was surprised to get only a few abusive letters, swamped by a much larger number of supporting letters, some from the pharmaceutical industry, others from persons with medical problems or with children with medical problems, all reciting horror stories about the FDA. Their replies led me to write a follow-up column titled "Barking Cats" (February 19, 1973) which I regard as one of the best columns I have written, in both substance and form. To quote:

> The column ["Frustrating Drug Advancement"] evoked letters from a number of persons in pharmaceutical work offering tales of woe to confirm my allegation. . . . But most also said something like, "In contrast to your opinion, I do not believe that the FDA should be abolished, but I do believe that its power should be changed" in such and such a way. . . .
>
> I replied as follows: What would you think of someone who said I would like to have a cat, provided it barked? Yet your statement that you favor an FDA provided it behaves as you believe desirable is precisely equivalent. The biological laws that specify the characteristics of cats are no more rigid than the political laws that specify the behavior of governmental agencies once they are established. The way the FDA now behaves, and the adverse consequences, are not an accident, not a result of an easily corrected human mistake, but a consequence of its constitution in precisely the same way that a meow is related to the constitution of a cat. As a natural scientist, you recognize that you cannot assign characteristics at will to chemical and biological entities, cannot demand that cats bark or water burn. Why do you

suppose that the situation is different in the social sciences? [© 1973, Newsweek, Inc. All rights reserved. Reprinted by permission.]

The first of these two columns created quite a stir in Washington. The head of the FDA replied in a letter to *Newsweek,* to which I rejoined; the *Washington Post* wrote several long articles on the issue, not surprisingly, defending the FDA. A congressional committee under Senator Gaylord Nelson held hearings. I was invited to appear—though only at a late session—but the date specified was one when I was to be in Europe, so I sent a written statement instead. I believe that Sam Peltzman did testify. (As an aside, I long ago decided it was a waste of time to testify before congressional committees. In most cases, those are occasions when congressmen use most of the time to advertise themselves, and the witness gets only a few words on the side. But even when that is not the case, I believe that spending the same time writing an op-ed piece or its equivalent or giving a talk is a more efficient use of time for the purpose of influencing policy. For example, my column got a much fuller hearing than my testimony would have.)

Five years later I came back to the FDA in a column "Standards of Morality" (December 18, 1978) in which I sharply criticized Dr. Donald Kennedy, then head of the FDA, and an eminent biologist, later president of Stanford University, for an article he wrote in the *Journal of the American Medical Association* defending the FDA against the charge of a "drug lag," i.e., the slower rate of approval of drugs in the U.S. than in Britain and other countries. "Kennedy's counterattack," I wrote, "is a lawyer's brief not an objective analysis. . . . His textual comments seem clearly intended to put the best possible face on FDA performance." And my subheads were "Using Statistical Data . . . for Support, Not Light." My final paragraph reads, "Let me emphasize that my purpose is not personal criticism of Kennedy, whom I have never met. His article simply happens to be a convenient example of a widely prevailing double standard. He published the article as part of what he conceived to be his duty as head of the FDA. He would almost surely not have been willing to submit the same article to a responsible professional journal in his personal scientific capacity."

Kennedy replied in a letter to *Newsweek.* I met him for the first time after he became president of Stanford. Our relations were cordial, never close, and I am sure he still resents what he doubtless regarded as a public attack on his character.

Something of a fun column was titled "A Family Matter" (April 10, 1972), and started "How would you like to get a letter from your married daughter suggesting that you and your wife of 30 years' standing get a divorce? That is what happened to us recently." Our daughter, a lawyer, had written to point out the marriage penalty in the income tax, noting that if we were legally divorced we could continue to live together and enjoy a lower tax. I mention this partly because the marriage penalty is once again in the headlines as I write. I may add, perhaps to demonstrate that we are not driven solely by pecuniary motives, that we did not follow our daughter's advice. At any rate it was fun to publish a table listing the "Saving from Living in Sin" for various income levels.

I have published one column in *Newsweek* since my regular column was terminated. That was in a regular "My Turn" column, chosen each week from those submitted. My column, titled "Right at Last, an Expert's Dream" (March 10, 1986), was an "I told you so" with respect to columns I had published on the oil crisis in 1974 and 1983. In the 1974 column, I had predicted that "the Arabs . . . could not for long keep the world price of crude at $10 a barrel." As I wrote in the final column, "For that prediction, I was awarded the booby prize by the Association for the Promotion of Humour in International Affairs. . . . The price of crude oil has finally dropped to a level that, adjusted for inflation, is below the $10 limit of my 1974 column. Hence my title. But I hasten to add, I am far from fully vindicated. Timing, as well as direction, is important." I had expected the price of oil to come down far sooner than it did.

Since ending my regular *Newsweek* column, I have, when the spirit moved me, written occasional op-ed pieces that I have submitted to a number of newspapers. My favorite outlet for op-ed pieces, and also letters to the editor, has been the *Wall Street Journal,* but I have also published such items in the *New York Times,* the *Washington Post,* the *San Francisco Chronicle,* and a few other papers. It will come as no surprise that the *New York Times* and the *Washington Post* have been less hospitable to my submissions than the *Wall Street Journal,* but they have accepted more items than they have rejected. I send items to them only when I believe that their readers are a better target for my purposes than the readers of the *WSJ.* On checking the detailed bibliography that Gloria Valentine, my longtime indispensable secretary, compiles, I am surprised to find that she lists 103 op-eds and letters to the editor, of which twenty-one were published prior to the termination of my regular column in 1984, eighty-two after. These items appeared originally in a total of twelve different publications, and many have been reprinted in other places as well.

In addition to columns and letters to the editor in newspapers and popular magazines, I also wrote a number of more substantial articles which were published in popular magazines such as *Harper's, National Review, Reader's Digest, New York Times Magazine,* and the like. One that has probably been reprinted more frequently than any other of my articles, scientific or popular, is "Social Responsibility of Business," published in the *New York Times Magazine,* September 13, 1970. I argued there, as I had in *Capitalism and Freedom,* that "there is one and only one social responsibility of business—to use its resources and engage in activities designed to increase its profits so long as it stays within the rules of the game, which is to say, engages in open and free competition without deception and fraud."

I was originally paid around $1,000 for the article. Even though it is a quarter of a century since its publication, hardly a year goes by that we do not receive more than that for permission fees to reprint the article. The reason is simple. "Social responsibility of business" has become a standard item in business and law school courses on ethics. Teachers want to assign readings on "both sides." Few other economists have been willing to take so extreme (I would say, straightforward) a position, hence my article is in demand to present a defense of what most of the instructors doubtless regard as an indefensible position.

Conclusion

This chapter omits my participation in public policy by serving as an informal adviser to a presidential candidate and two presidents. That story is told in the next two chapters.

It also omits what is undoubtedly our most direct, extensive, and time-consuming foray into the debate over public policy, namely the production of two television programs plus a follow up and the accompanying books: *Free to Choose* and *Tyranny of the Status Quo.* The story of these programs is told in chapters 28 and 29.

THE GOLDWATER CAMPAIGN, AND NEW YORK, 1963–65

{ *Rose* } After our trip around the world, we had every intention of remaining in Chicago for the next few years. We were more than ready to settle down in our own home, in our accustomed ways, and with our old friends. Our children were both away from home: Janet in her final year at the University of California at Berkeley, and David in his third year at Harvard. We expected no unusual events.

Janet graduated in June 1964, and announced that she had attended her last class and had no intention of continuing her education. We were not pleased with that announcement but decided that Janet had to make her own decision and we would wait patiently. We knew that her Berkeley classes had not been challenging and that she had resorted to playing bridge for mental stimulation. Milton wisecracked that Janet had become a master—bridge master—before she became a bachelor.

We did not go out for her graduation because she said she was not attending it herself. There was no point, she said, because the class was so large that unnamed diplomas were handed out and individual names were added later.

In the course of her studies, Janet had repeatedly changed her intended major, but whatever her current major was, her fondness for math had led her to continue taking math courses. As a result, it turned out when it was time to graduate that the only field in which she had enough courses to qualify as a major was math. In the process she had taken a course or two in programming. As a result, she had no difficulty getting a job as a programmer with Matson Steamship Co. in San Francisco. Of course, she was excited about starting to work but she soon concluded that programming had little promise as a future for her. So, without saying anything to us, she took the law boards and applied to Boalt, the law school at Berkeley. She was accepted because her board scores were very good and offset the poor grades she had gotten at Berkeley.

Janet entered Boalt in September 1965. In a conversation with her uncle Aaron about law school, he told her a little about how strenuous the first year would be and that she would have to give up bridge. She said she would, and did. After her second year, on the recommendation of a professor whom she had done some work for, she was hired for the summer by Morrison and Foerster, a leading San Francisco law firm, the first female they had ever hired. At the end of the summer they offered her a position to begin after she got her degree. She turned it down because she wanted to clerk for a judge for a year first. They offered to hold the position for her and did. She graduated at the top of her class and was accepted as a clerk by Roger Traynor, chief justice of the California Supreme Court. After her year as a clerk, she went to work for Morrison, still the only woman.

Our expectation of a quiet period came to an end when Columbia University invited Milton to come to the university for the 1964–65 academic year as the Wesley Clair Mitchell Visiting Professor in Economics. Our many friends in New York, and nostalgia for the happy years we had spent there some twenty-five years earlier, induced us to start packing again. Our life was further complicated by Barry Goldwater's decision to run for president and Milton's participation in the campaign.

In 1964, before we left for the summer in New Hampshire and then a year in New York, we sold our house on Kenwood Avenue. The children having flown the coop, we rattled around in the large house and decided that we would be better off in an apartment.

The Goldwater Campaign

{ *Milton* } Though long interested in the role of government and how it functions, neither Rose nor I had ever been active in politics. The closest either of us came to it was when Rose served as a Republican election judge at the local polling place. Our precinct in Hyde Park, the area contiguous to the University of Chicago, was the most solidly Democratic precinct in a Democratic city. It was hard put to it to find people willing to serve as Republican judges, which explains why Rose was drafted.

Bill Baroody, who played a major role in inducing Barry Goldwater to seek the 1964 Republican nomination for president, was responsible for my participation in the Goldwater campaign. In late 1963, after we got back from our wanderjahr, Bill persuaded me to help him produce a platform for Gold-water, and sometime in 1963 or 1964, I became Goldwater's economic adviser on the understanding that it would not involve any active campaigning.

I had met Senator Goldwater, probably at Bill's house, in 1961 or 1962, had corresponded with him, and had established a good rapport with him. He had firm opinions, but was open-minded and open to persuasion. Like so many of those who worked for his nomination and election, I was impressed with Goldwater's firm adherence to basic principles, his courage in taking unpopular positions, his willingness to sacrifice what seemed like political ex-pediency to stand up for what he thought was right, and, not least, his quick wit.

The Republican convention at the San Francisco Cow Palace in early July 1964 was a raucous fight with no holds barred between the Eastern liberal-establishment Republicans who initially backed Nelson Rockefeller for the nomination, and then William Scranton, and the maverick conservative Re-publicans who organized the pro-Goldwater movement. Rose and I did not go to the convention. Instead, we remained glued to the radio at our summer home in New Hampshire listening to what was going on. I thought Goldwa-ter's acceptance speech, crafted by Goldwater himself, with the help of a bril-liant group of wordsmiths, was splendid. I recall particularly relishing the sen-tence that came back to haunt Goldwater: "Extremism in the defense of liberty is no vice. And . . . moderation in the pursuit of justice is no virtue." This statement was used to label Goldwater an extremist, which was very damaging. In a 1988 autobiography, Goldwater explained that "The reference came from Harry Jaffa, a professor of political science at Claremont Men's College in California. As was explained to me at the time, the words were first used by Marcus Tullius Cicero in the Roman Senate."[1] How different the press reac-tion might have been if Goldwater had introduced the statement by, "as Cicero said more than two thousand years ago." However, given the bias of the press and the intelligentsia against Goldwater, that might have made little differ-ence. They would probably have misconstrued some other sentence. Nonethe-less, that episode impressed me greatly with how much difference the right choice of words can make.

As it happened, Goldwater had been on good personal terms with John Kennedy while he thoroughly disliked and distrusted Lyndon Johnson. I have always believed that if Kennedy had not been assassinated, and had been the opposing candidate in 1964, the character of the campaign, both Democratic and Republican, would have been entirely different. There surely would have been far less of the meanness, the attacks on personal character, the ques-tioning of motives, the negative advertising that made the campaign so repellent. In books published long after the event, Goldwater makes a similar state-ment, and stresses his great reluctance to be a candidate after Kennedy's assassination.[2]

I doubt that Kennedy would have resorted to picturing Goldwater as an irresponsible warmonger, highlighted by the infamous commercial that "showed a little girl in a sunny field of daisies. She begins plucking petals from a daisy. As she plucks the flower, a male voice in the background starts a countdown . . . ten . . . nine . . . eight . . . becoming constantly stronger. The screen suddenly explodes and the child disappears in a mushroom cloud." As Goldwater said in his autobiography, "There was no doubt as to the mean-ing: Barry Goldwater would blow up the world if he became president of the United States."[3]

While neither candidate was a warmonger, they differed sharply on the means that would be most effective in bringing the Vietnam war to a rapid end. In hindsight, it seems clear that Goldwater's approach of using concen-trated force on Hanoi would have been more effective than Johnson's failed gradualist approach which prolonged the misery without a victory.

Despite the subsequent election results, the defeat of the hitherto domi-nant Rockefeller Republicans was a crucial step in the gradual shift of public opinion away from liberalism as popularly understood and toward free-market conservatism, a shift that crested first when Ronald Reagan was elected presi-dent in 1980 and then in the 1994 election, which gave Republicans control of the House for the first time in forty years.

The Goldwater campaign "launched Ronald Reagan . . . as a national political figure" after he gave "the best speech of the campaign . . . called 'A Time for Choosing.'"[4] Rose and I well remember that extraordinary speech. It was our first exposure to Reagan, whom I did not meet personally until seven years later.

After Kennedy's assassination, Goldwater's personal inclination was to withdraw as a candidate because of his dislike and distrust of Johnson. Bill Baroody played a major role in persuading Goldwater not to withdraw and served as head of Goldwater's informal brain trust during the campaign. Most of my involvement in the campaign was through Bill. Denison Kitchel, a friend of Barry's from Arizona, became national campaign director. Denny was a talented lawyer and a splendid human being who had never before been involved in national politics. We became good friends in the course of the campaign, and have remained so ever since. One of the benefits of later trips to Phoenix was the opportunity to see the Kitchels and to play tennis with Denny and his wife Naomi.

The kickoff of the campaign took place in Prescott, Arizona, on September 3, 1964. We did not have a television set in New Hampshire, so we went to a neighbor's house to watch the evening news report on the speech. The reporter gave excerpts from the talk that made Goldwater appear a racist and extremist, even to us, his supporters. On returning home, I immediately phoned Bill Baroody to warn him about the way the talk was reported and to urge him to keep any statements that could be used in that way out of the talk. Bill was very reassuring, saying there was only one sentence in the speech that could be interpreted in this way and that it had been taken out of context. In preparation for writing this section, I have reread the text of that speech, and I must say I cannot find even one sentence that justifies the kind of concern that we expressed. I was surprised to find that some sentences and paragraphs had a very familiar ring—until I realized that they had come from memos or drafts of possible speeches that I had written myself.

My main contribution to the campaign during the summer was writing such memoranda and discussing over the telephone various issues of policy as they came up. Rose and I were dismayed by the many distortions about Goldwater's views that appeared in the media. In a vain effort to counter these distortions, I wrote an article on "The Goldwater View of Economics" that was published by the *New York Times* in its Sunday magazine section.[5]

Then as now, the overwhelming majority of the academic and, more broadly, the intellectual community favored big government, were hostile to the market, and voted Democratic. Academic precincts are among the most reliable Democratic constituencies in the nation. The opposition to Goldwater was particularly strong in New York City because of his bitter fight for the nomination with New York's own Nelson Rockefeller, the liberals' favorite Republican. It was hard to find any respectable intellectual in New York who was willing to defend Goldwater.

As a result, I was very much in demand to present the Goldwater point of view after we got to New York in September to begin my visiting professorship at Columbia. The next six weeks up to the election were a blur of one meeting or interview or talk after another, leaving barely enough time for me to meet my professorial obligations.

I referred to this experience in a talk I gave a decade later at the fifty-fourth annual dinner for faculty given by the board of trustees of the University of Chicago:

> I talked to and argued with groups from academia, from the media, from the financial community, from the foundation world, from you name it. I was appalled at what I found. There was an unbelievable degree of intellectual homogeneity, of acceptance of a standard set of

views complete with cliché answers to every objection, of smug self-satisfaction at belonging to an in-group. The closest similar experience I have ever had was at Cambridge, England, and even that was a distant second.

The homogeneity and provincialism of the New York intellectual community made them pushovers in discussions about Goldwater's views. They had cliché answers but only to their self-created straw-men. To exaggerate only slightly, they had never talked to anyone who really believed, and had thought deeply about, views drastically different from their own. As a result, when they heard real arguments instead of caricatures, they had no answers, only amazement that such views could be expressed by someone who had the external character-istics of being a member of the intellectual community, and that such views could be defended with apparent cogency.[6]

I doubt that I made many converts at those meetings. But I may have instilled a few doubts in hitherto closed minds. I have always said that anyone who is converted in an evening isn't worth converting. The next person of opposite views with whom he spends an evening will unconvert him. And I do know that many of the people who seemingly turned deaf ears to my arguments at the time have since come a long way toward accepting the views I was defending.

{ *Rose* }   One more example of the attitude about Goldwater. At Harvard, while David majored in physics and chemistry, he also took courses in philoso-phy and, since he always enjoyed writing poetry, in poetry.[7] He was enrolled in a course in poetry at the time of the Goldwater campaign. An avid Goldwater supporter, he was devastated when Goldwater lost the election. As often hap-pened, David expressed his feelings in a poem. He submitted it as part of his work in the poetry class:

> Ten A.M., November Fourth, 1964
>
> The end at last has come seen from afar.
> Did we follow a falling star?
> Is it truly the twilight glow
> Fading slowly but soon to go
> That shines on the world where I was born?
> I know not what the coming years will show
> I only know that this defeat is shorn
> Of half its bitterness by long defeat;

The sea has left its wreckage on the beach,
The self same sea that now may find it meet
To nibble at our sandy ramparts, reach
Its silver tendrils through the growing breach
and drown our lights.

And drown our lights like the mirage that lured
Was there some ill we might have cured
Or is it only age that kills,
Eating the state as the sea the hills,
Turning our labor to ashes and dust?
I know not what my dearest friends, who kill
Our freedom blindly, when and if they must
Answer my questions in a ruined world
Will tell me. Does it matter? They have won
And we have lost, our tattered banners furled.
And all our fight is wasted; it is done.
The votes are cast, the people had their fun.
The night will fall.

The night will fall; all must from free decline
Cannot the sun forever shine?
Or if in time the sun must fall
Why must my time be that, of all
The times I might have chanced in? Must I face
The rising tide that drowns our dikes deep, call
My challenge to the screaming winds that race
To our destruction, to lie broken, pinned,
Beneath the wreck where freedom is a lie?
I know that all of this is empty wind.
As empty as the wind that sweeps the sky
Of Arizona, where our dreams will die.

When the poem was returned, the professor attached a note compliment-ing David on the "characteristics" of the poem and then followed this with: "How can anyone feel this way?"

David graduated from Harvard in June 1965. Unlike the graduation exer-cises at Berkeley when Janet graduated, which we did not attend, we attended David's graduation exercises. They were held out-of-doors in the Harvard Yard and were very impressive. The exercises were followed by a social hour at Lowell house, the house in which David had lived.

Photo by Kenneth Yimm

Milton at his seventy-fifth birthday party with Janet, Rose, David, Betty, and Aaron, 1987

David and Milton at a Hoover Conference on the occasion of Milton's seventy-fifth birthday, 1987

Rose and Milton with Edwin Feulner and President Reagan at the Heritage Foundation's tenth-anniversary dinner, 1982

Photo by Steven N. S. Cheung

Milton and Rose at Tiananmen Square, 1988

Dinner in Ecuador with family on golden wedding anniversary, 1988

Rose with grandson William Friedman, 1993

Granddaughter Rebecca Friedman at age five, 1994

Milton and Rose with Edward Teller and Margaret Thatcher at the Hoover Institution, 1995

{ *Milton* } An amusing footnote to the election campaign. Sometime in 1964, I was asked whether I would be willing to stand for election for a four-year term as a policy-holder representative to the board of CREF (College Retirement Equity Foundation). I agreed, firm in the belief that I would not be elected, since I was widely known as an adviser to Goldwater, and the academic community was overwhelmingly opposed to him. To my surprise, I was elected. I concluded that the liberal professors did not want a conservative as president of the country, but when it came to looking after their retirement funds, that was something else again.

New York, 1964–65

{ *Rose* } Before we came to New York, we had arranged to sublet a furnished apartment. Like Chicago, New York had rent control, one provision of which was that it was almost impossible to eject a tenant when his lease expired; the tenant was legally entitled to extend the lease and to sublet it at an uncontrolled price.[8] We paid market rent to the prior tenants who received a handsome income from the excess of the market rent over the controlled rent they paid. The leaseholders (really owners in fact; we have no idea how long it was since they had actually occupied the apartment) had little incentive to invest any money in the apartment, and the original owners even less.

The location of the apartment was ideal—on the corner of Riverside Drive and 116th Street. The apartment itself left much to be desired. The equipment and furnishings dated from the late thirties or early forties. The kitchen in particular showed its age. Rent control had worked its mischief. Nonetheless, the apartment was acceptable as a temporary home. Other features of New York troubled us much more.

We were introduced to one such feature the first night we occupied the apartment. We had driven our Buick convertible down from New Hampshire and parked it in front of our apartment on Riverside Drive, a major, much-traveled artery. Innocents abroad, we assumed that it would be safe to leave it there overnight. In the morning, we found that vandals had cut the convertible top to get entry into the car. Their total loot was one flashlight, worth at most a dollar at the time. After getting the top replaced, we arranged with Milton's sister Tillie in Rahway, N.J., to store our car, and depended thereafter entirely on public transportation and taxicabs to get around New York City.

In this respect, too, New York had gone downhill since we left in 1945. Then, as later in Chicago, we had been able to have cabs pick us up at our apartment. No longer. To get a cab, we had to walk to Broadway and hail a passing cab. It was not a long walk, but during most of the winter a very unpleasant one. Chicago is always referred to as the windy city, yet I have never experienced a winter in Chicago that was as windy, and as uniformly gray, as the winter we spent in New York. Similarly, riding the subways was less attractive than it had been. A wave of subway crime had led to the stationing of police on the trains. They conveyed some feeling of safety, but at the same time were a visible reminder of how much New York City had changed.

After the hectic period preceding the election, we were able to resume our accustomed ivory-tower life. The rest of the year at Columbia was both pleasant and largely uneventful, offering compensation for the less pleasant aspects of New York life. We were able to renew our relations with longtime friends in New York; Milton enjoyed teaching a rather different group of graduate students, and interacting with the Columbia faculty, most of whom we already knew and several of whom had been fellow students at Chicago or Columbia; and we were able to enjoy a fair number of Broadway plays and other New York attractions. Moreover, David was not far away, at Harvard, so we enjoyed frequent visits from him.

{ *Milton* } One exciting event of the year was a wholly unexpected and very attractive offer of a professorship at Stanford. Rose has for the whole of our married life wanted to live on the West Coast, and preferably in the Bay Area, so she was very favorably inclined. My emotions were much more mixed. I agonized for several days and at one point tentatively decided to accept. After sleeping on that decision, I could not really face deserting the intellectual climate at Chicago in which I felt something of a proprietary interest and that I found so stimulating, and finally refused, much to Rose's disappointment.[9]

As usual, we spent the summer in New Hampshire except that we left earlier than usual to attend a meeting of the Mont Pelerin Society in early September at Stresa, Italy, and a meeting of the first world conference of the Econometric Society in Rome, for which I organized a session on money. I was also able to make arrangements with an Italian professor to send several of his most promising students to spend a year in my Money and Banking Workshop. We then returned to Chicago and moved into the Shoreland Hotel—a former luxury hotel on the shore of Lake Michigan that had been acquired by the University of Chicago to provide housing for faculty and graduate students. We stayed at the Shoreland for two years while we were awaiting the completion of a new apartment house at 5825 Dorchester Avenue, to which we moved in 1967.

ADVISER TO PRESIDENTS NIXON AND REAGAN

Richard M. Nixon

{ *Milton* } During the final years of the Eisenhower administration, Allen Wallis was a special assistant to the president to work with the Cabinet Committee on Price Stability for Economic Growth, chaired by Vice-President Nixon. Allen arranged for me to have a long visit with Nixon. I no longer remember what the occasion or the subject of our discussion was. I do remember that I was very favorably impressed with Nixon. He was highly intelligent, an intellectual in the sense that he was interested in discussing abstract ideas, extremely knowledgeable, and enjoyed engaging in discussion with someone who had different ideas, whether he initially agreed or did not. He was also personally pleasant.

While vice-president, Nixon developed a high opinion of Arthur Burns, who served as Eisenhower's chairman of the Council of Economic Advisers. Early in the 1968 election campaign, Nixon asked Arthur to serve as chairman of a "Nixon advisory group on the economy" during the election campaign. Arthur recruited me to join the committee.[1]

Our advisory committee organized a series of some twenty or so task forces on different topics, with a total of some 150 members, many from the academy. The task forces were not organized to promote the campaign, but rather to engage in advance planning for the administration after the election. They were nonpartisan, though most participants were Republicans. The various task forces took their assignments seriously and produced reports that were extremely helpful to the new administration. After the election we had a one-day meeting of all task force members with Nixon at which each chairman presented the conclusions of his group.

In retrospect, perhaps the most important positive effect of the task force process was to bring George Shultz to Nixon's notice and launch him on his extraordinary career of public service. We asked George, at the time dean of the School of Business of the University of Chicago and longtime labor negotiator, who happened to be spending the academic year at the Center for Advanced Study in Stanford, to chair the labor task force. His group did such an outstanding job, and George presented their conclusions so effectively, that Nixon offered him the secretaryship of labor, which George accepted. A year later Nixon persuaded him to come to the White House and serve as director of the Office of Management and Budget. He served there for two years and then in 1972 was named secretary of the treasury and assistant to the president. He left in 1974 after Nixon resigned. He was one of the few high Nixon officials who left office without any mark on his character. After a spell in private industry, he served as a leading adviser to Ronald Reagan and as secretary of state from 1982 to 1989, all in all a remarkable career. I have long thought that he would have made a splendid president, if a noncareer politician could conceivably get the nomination and win the election. I have always been proud of having had a small part in launching his public career. I shall have many occasions to refer to him again.

After the election, I met with Nixon at his Pierre Hotel interim headquarters in New York and gave him a memorandum dated October 15, 1968, titled "A Proposal for Resolving U.S. Balance of Payments Problem," saying that "the first few weeks of the new administration . . . will offer a unique opportunity to set the dollar free and thereby eliminate for years to come balance of payments restraints on U.S. economic policy." I went on to say that "if they [the measures I proposed] are not taken at once, the new president, or members of his administration, will inevitably make statements and commitments about gold and exchange rates that will make it very difficult to take such measures except in conditions of great crisis. Never again will the range of options be so wide." That is surely one of the best predictions I ever made.[2] I believe that the reason Nixon did not follow my advice was that Arthur Burns, a much more senior adviser whom Nixon planned to appoint as chairman of the Federal Reserve System, did not agree. In many long discussions with Arthur about floating versus fixed exchange rates, I had failed to persuade him of my view.

The major specific measures recommended in the memorandum were to abolish all restrictions on foreign investment by U.S. corporations and all restrictions on foreign lending by commercial banks and to announce that the "U.S. will engage in no further gold transactions." Finally, and most important, "The U.S. will engage in no exchange transactions in order to affect the rate of exchange between the U.S. dollar and other currencies—neither to peg the rates of exchange at fixed levels nor to manipulate them." As I had predicted, the pressure of events forced the president to take essentially the same measures on August 15, 1971, under much more adverse conditions.

In mid-1970, when I met with the newly appointed secretary of the treasury, John Connally, I handed him a copy of the memo, saying, "Here is a memo I wrote for you two years ago."

Nixon wanted to appoint Arthur Burns chairman of the Fed. Bill Martin still had one year left of his term as chairman and refused to resign. Accordingly, Nixon appointed Arthur counselor to the president as a temporary post until he could appoint him chairman the next year. Martin Anderson served as an assistant to Arthur. Also Daniel Patrick Moynihan, currently Democratic senator from New York, though a longtime Democrat, was brought into the White House in an advisory capacity. I mention all this because the three of them played a crucial role in two different Nixon initiatives in which I became involved, one, highly successful, the second, a failure.

All-Volunteer Armed Force

The first was ending the draft, a measure that I had publicly favored for many years, beginning with the Wabash lectures and *Capitalism and Freedom*. In 1966, Sol Tax, an anthropologist at Chicago, and a number of other colleagues organized a four-day conference at the University of Chicago on the draft (December 4–7, 1966). The seventy-four invited participants included essentially everyone who had written or spoken at all extensively on either side of the controversy about the draft, as well as a number of students. The proceedings were held on the University of Chicago campus. They were open to the public, limited only by the availability of seats. As Sol Tax wrote in the Preface to the edited proceedings: "With the Selective Service System under fire, at least on the campuses, and under scrutiny by Congress and the Administration, it was a strategic time for a conference; interest was intense and widespread. . . . The conference itself was an exciting event, with 'We won't go' student meetings outside, and a variety of political machinations inside."[3]

Walter Oi, a California Nisei who graduated from UCLA and earned a Ph.D. in economics at Chicago, gave what I believe was the most effective paper at the conference. Walter suffered from a degenerative eye disease so that he had gradually lost his sight. By the end of his graduate school days, he was blind and had to resort to a guide dog. Nonetheless he carved out a remarkable career as an economist and econometrician and outstanding teacher. He became interested in and did a good deal of research on military manpower recruitment. A convinced libertarian, he strongly opposed the draft. At the conference he gave an eloquent paper presenting the case for ending the draft on grounds of both principle and expediency. The impact was dramatic. Here was a blind man, enormously impressive simply for his capacity to prepare and deliver a cogent, closely argued, and fully documented paper. He conveyed a clear sense of moral outrage on an issue about which he had no conceivable personal ax to grind. To me, it was the high point of the conference.

I have attended many conferences. I have never attended any other that had so dramatic an effect on the participants. A straw poll taken at the outset of the conference recorded two-thirds of the participants in favor of the draft; a similar poll at the end, two-thirds opposed. I believe that this conference was the key event that started the ball rolling decisively toward ending the draft.

Nixon had long supported the draft. Martin Anderson, one of an informal group of close Nixon associates and sympathizers who were developing policies for an as yet unannounced run for the presidency, wrote

> a seventeen-page policy memorandum for Nixon that spelled out the essential arguments, pro and con, for ending the draft and setting up an all-volunteer force.
>
> Nixon read it, indicated that he found it "very interesting," and said he wanted to think further about it. . . .
>
> On November 17, 1967, Nixon was returning to New York City from Washington on the Eastern Airline shuttle. . . . he was accompanied by a . . . reporter . . . from the *New York Times.* . . . As [the interview] was winding down, [the reporter] suddenly changed the subject. "What would you do about the military draft?" he asked, knowing that Nixon had openly and consistently supported . . . the draft. . . .
>
> Nixon smiled and replied evenly, "I think we should eliminate the draft and move to an all-volunteer force."[4]

Much later in the campaign, Nixon issued a position paper on the issue and gave a major campaign speech setting forth his support for an all-volunteer army.

President Nixon's policy was by no means the dominant view of his fellow Republicans. All that he could get in the 1968 Republican party platform was, "When military manpower needs can be appreciably reduced, we will place the Selective Service System on standby and substitute a voluntary force obtained through adequate pay and career incentives."[5]

On March 27, 1969, less than three months after he had been inaugurated, President Nixon announced the creation of a fifteen-member "Advisory Commission on an All-Volunteer Armed Force under the Chairmanship of the Honorable Thomas S. Gates, Jr., former Secretary of Defense," and chairman of the executive committee of Morgan Guaranty Trust Co. As a special assistant to the president assigned to follow through on the all-volunteer army, Marty Anderson played a key role in suggesting members. Of the fifteen members, five were declared proponents of the draft, five, declared opponents, and five, uncommitted.[6]

Most presidential and congressional commissions are named to dispose of an issue that is politically troublesome. They hold hearings, prepare reports, and are never heard of again. This one was destined to be an exception. It was named to provide the support—intellectual, moral, and political—that was necessary to get a policy favored by the president enacted. And it performed its function, submitting its final report on February 20, 1970. Conscription was ended on January 27, 1973.

The first step was the appointment of a staff to gather evidence, organize hearings, and conduct such studies of special issues as the commission desired. Allen Wallis, who, like me, was a member of the commission, recruited William Meckling, a Chicago Ph.D. and dean of the University of Rochester School of Business, as executive director, and he in turn recruited an able staff, of whom Walter Oi was one of the most productive.

As Tom Gates said in transmitting our final report to the president, we had "numerous official meetings, totaling more than 100 hours, usually over weekends in Washington. In addition, Commission members worked diligently on their own time in order to review the hundreds of pages of staff memoranda devoted to the study and review of this vital subject."[7] Tom Gates was a splendid, open-minded, even-handed chairman, who gradually shifted his position to become a convinced supporter of an all-volunteer army. The same thing happened to the other two men from the military, Al Gruenther and Lauris Norstad. Though evenly split at the outset, we ended by submitting a unanimous report, save only for Roy Wilkins, who was prevented by illness from participating in the last three months of our proceedings and therefore decided to abstain. In his letter of transmittal, Gates wrote:

> We unanimously believe that the nation's interests will be better served by an all-volunteer force, supported by an effective standby draft, than by a mixed force of volunteers and conscripts; that steps should be taken promptly to move in this direction; and that the first

indispensable step is to remove the present inequity in the pay of men serving their first term in the armed forces.

We have satisfied ourselves that a volunteer force will not jeopardize national security, and we believe it will have a beneficial effect on the military as well as the rest of society.[8]

Our final report was published as a book by a commercial publisher as well as by the Government Printing Office.

The shift of opinion from an even split at the outset to unanimity at the end was produced by the weight of the evidence: a series of highly competent reports produced by the staff, the testimony by proponents and opponents at hearings, and the discussion among ourselves. In many years of discussions about a draft for the U.S., I have never known someone who initially opposed the draft reverse his or her opinion on the basis of evidence; I have known many who initially favored the draft do so.

As Chairman Gates said in his letter of transmittal to the president, "We consulted a wide range of representatives of the public, interested organizations, and experts as well as the Service Secretaries, the Joint Chiefs of Staff and other high officials in the Department of Defense and armed forces."

The most dramatic episode for me in the course of these consultations occurred when General Westmoreland, top commander of our troops in Vietnam, testified. "He was then, I believe, Chief of Staff of the Army, and he was testifying in that capacity. Like almost all military men who testified, he testified against a volunteer armed force. In the course of his testimony, he made the statement that he did not want to command an army of mercenaries. I stopped him and said, 'General, would you rather command an army of slaves?' He drew himself up and said, 'I don't like to hear our patriotic draftees referred to as slaves.' I replied, 'I don't like to hear our patriotic volunteers referred to as mercenaries.' But I went on to say, 'If they are mercenaries, then I, sir, am a mercenary professor, and you, sir, are a mercenary general; we are served by mercenary physicians, we use a mercenary lawyer, and we get our meat from a mercenary butcher.'" That was the last that we heard from the general about mercenaries.[9]

During the course of our deliberations, we commissioners became very friendly with one another. I formed a specially close friendship with three of my fellow commissioners whom I had not previously known: Al Gruenther, Crawford Greenewalt, and Steve Herbits. Gruenther had a fine mind and an outgoing personality; he was interested in a wide range of issues, and had the ability to explore them in depth and weigh sensitively opposing considerations.

A delightful companion, he and I carried on a correspondence for many years after the commission had completed its task.

Crawford was trained as a chemist and was clearly an unusual business-man. I believe he was the first person without Du Pont blood to head the company, though he did marry into the family. His great passion was taking beautiful pictures of hummingbirds. He traveled all over the world to take the pictures and produced highly regarded picture books from his slides. He too had wide interests and for years was president of the American Philosophi-cal Society, the meetings of which in Philadelphia we often attended.

Steve Herbits was a young law student in his late twenties who had spent several years as a congressional staff person, had become very much interested in the issue of the draft, and active in groups opposing it. He was named to the commission to represent the young people. He was an extremely valuable and effective member of the commission. After the report had been completed he spent several years in the Defense Department helping to facilitate the transition. He later was employed by the Seagram Company, where he rapidly rose to a high executive post. We have remained in touch ever since.

No public-policy activity that I have ever engaged in has given me as much satisfaction as the All-Volunteer Commission. I regarded the draft as a major stain on our free society. I had talked and written against it for more than a decade. Membership in the commission enabled me to contribute to ending the draft far more directly, and in addition was intellectually stimulat-ing and personally rewarding. To cap it all, it was crowned with success, not only in the sense that legislation was enacted to terminate the draft, but more important, that by general consent the all-volunteer army has displayed in practice for more than two decades the advantages that we claimed for it in our report. Clearly, the timing was propitious; public sentiment was shifting against the draft. Yet without the force of the commission's report and its marshaling of evidence, I doubt that the draft would have been ended as soon as it was.

Family Assistance Program

A second Nixon initiative I participated in to a much lesser extent was a version of the negative income tax that I had proposed in *Capitalism and Freedom.* Pat Moynihan did the major drafting of the proposal that went to Congress, though Marty Anderson and Arthur Burns and of course Nixon himself partic-ipated. I consulted with Pat, Arthur, and Marty on the proposal but I did not play a major role. I did endorse the initial version of what was labeled the "Family Assistance Program." However, as it went through the political process, I became disenchanted. As I wrote in a *Newsweek* column of May 18, 1970,

> I have long supported and worked for the general principles of the welfare-reform bill that is now making its way through Congress. Yet I would vote against the bill in the form in which it passed the House. . . . The key idea of the proposed reform is to give people on welfare both the opportunity and the incentive to become self-supporting. . . . The trouble is the bill proposed by the Administration and passed by the House does not conform to this design. On the contrary, it gives most people on relief even less incentive than they have under the existing system of welfare. . . . This is a travesty on the original intention.

The original design would have eliminated food stamps, and reduced the amount received at the margin by fifty cents for each additional dollar earned. By the time it passed Congress, food stamps were back in, and each additional dollar earned would have reduced the amount received at the margin by increasingly more than fifty cents. Indeed, in the final bracket, a recipient would have lost more than a dollar for each additional dollar earned so that "many families would be better off to earn less rather than to earn more." Now, more than a quarter-century later, as welfare reform is back in the headlines, the final paragraph of my column is prophetic: "It is long past time that we reversed the relentless climb of the welfare rolls, that we gave the unfortunate people on welfare a chance to work themselves off welfare and to become independent and responsible citizens. It will be a tragedy if the present opportunity is wasted by either administrative incompetence or political log-rolling."

An amusing note is that in the course of a television interview during the campaign, Nixon was asked whether he thought my proposal of a negative income tax was

> an effective alternative to these welfare programs that you have been so critical of. . . .
>
> Mr. Nixon: No, I don't. I wish it were, and I have great respect, incidentally, for Milton Friedman.

After his election, Nixon supported a version of the negative income tax that I came to oppose!

Commission on White House Fellows

In early 1971, President Nixon appointed me to the Commission on White House Fellows, a program that had been established by President Johnson and still continues. Each year a competition is held open to men and women aged 23 to 35 to select fifteen to twenty young persons for one-year fellowships, to serve as assistants to the president, vice-president and cabinet-level officials. Competition for the fellowships attracts persons from all walks of life. Regional committees select a pool of about thirty-five finalists who then meet for a weekend with the fifteen members of the commission, and those of their spouses who choose to attend, at a government-owned estate in Airlie, Virginia. The commission selects the final Fellows from the finalists. A permanent staff arranges for an extensive program of meetings and travel to supplement the Fellows' service with cabinet-level officials. It is a prize well worth competing for.

During the three years that I served, the finalists were an extremely impressive group of young men and women from every walk of life—business, professions, education, military, and other governmental agencies. As I wrote to President Nixon when I resigned in October 1973, after having participated in three selection sessions, "The opportunity that you gave to me to serve on this Commission has been a richly rewarding experience. It has renewed my faith in the quality, the character, and the energy of the young men and women of this country."

I was particularly impressed with the quality of the candidates from the military services. I had completely forgotten that Colin Powell was one whom we had chosen to be a White House Fellow until he reminded me of it at a session in the White House at which President Reagan awarded me the Presidential Medal of Freedom. Henry Cisneros, later mayor of San Antonio and secretary of housing and urban development, is another name that comes back to me from one of those selection sessions. Almost all of the White House Fellows have enjoyed rewarding careers.

The finalists were all so well qualified that I concluded that our intensive selection process was little if any better than selecting half of them by pure lottery. That was the reason I resigned when I did.

Wage and Price Control

In my opinion, Nixon's imposition of wage and price control on August 15, 1971 did far more harm to the country than any of the later actions that led to his resignation. It was also a policy that Nixon had long opposed, beginning with his experience as a lawyer with the Office of Price Administration during World War II. In his memoirs he writes, "What did America reap from its brief fling with economic controls? The August 15, 1971, decision to impose them was politically necessary and immensely popular in the short run. But in the long run I believe that it was wrong. The piper must always be paid, and there was an unquestionably high price for tampering with the orthodox economic mechanisms."[10]

Whence the political necessity, as Nixon viewed it? A demand by the British for the conversion of U.S. dollars into gold at the legally fixed price of $35 an ounce "forced us to accelerate dramatically our economic time-table."[11] The obvious answer was to close the gold window and float the dollar, the action I had recommended nearly three years earlier.

However, simply closing the gold window would have been regarded by the public and media as a negative, reactionary step. Headlines would have emphasized that "Nixon Takes U.S. Off Gold Standard." To avoid that outcome—and here I am giving my own interpretation, not Nixon's—the president decided to adopt a bold program that had earlier been recommended by Secretary of the Treasury John Connally to deal with the domestic economy: "total war on all economic fronts, including across-the-board wage and price controls," even though, just six weeks earlier, Connally had briefed the White House Press corps "that there would be . . . no mandatory wage and price controls."

Agreement to adopt this program was reached at a Camp David meeting on the weekend of August 13–15. Nixon reports that

> While there was relatively strong, though skeptical, support among those present for the freeze and other domestic actions, there was substantial disagreement on . . . suspending the convertibility of the dollar into gold.
>
> The strongest opposition came from Arthur Burns, Chairman of the Federal Reserve Board. He wanted us to wait. . . .
>
> I always gave great weight to Burns's opinions because of my respect for his superior intellect and because he always followed the practice he once described to me of "telling the President what he *needs* to hear, not just what he *wants* to hear." This was to be one of the few cases in which I did not follow his recommendations. I decided to close the gold window and let the dollar float. As events unfolded, this decision turned out to be the best thing that came out of the whole economic program I announced on August 15, 1971.[12]

Arthur was consistent on exchange rates, but this time Nixon disregarded his advice. A more interesting point is that Nixon did not record Arthur as opposing the wage and price freeze, even though Arthur had been one of the strongest and most outspoken critics of wage and price controls over the prior decade and more. However, not long after his accession to the chairmanship of the Fed, he started moderating his position and, in the spring of 1971, gave an influential talk suggesting that voluntary controls might sometimes be desirable. That talk did much to free businessmen to recommend openly control of wages and prices, no doubt in the expectation that wages would be more effectively controlled than prices, probably the reverse of what actually happened. A striking example of the old saying, "Where a person stands depends on where he sits."

My first *Newsweek* column after August 15 was entitled "Why the Freeze is a Mistake" (August 30, 1971). I devoted three more columns that year to criticizing the controls, and a number of later columns.

Selling Government Securities

On October 30, 1959 in testimony before the Joint Economic Committee, chaired by Sen. Paul Douglas, I criticized the current method of auctioning [government securities], indicating that it lent itself to collusion, and suggested an alternative that has come to be known as a "Dutch auction." While my initial proposal produced a brief but lively discussion in professional journals, it had no effect on Treasury policy. However, in 1972, when George Shultz was Secretary of the Treasury and Jack Bennett was Undersecretary for Monetary Affairs, I was able to persuade them to experiment with Dutch auctions for some issues of long-term securities. The experiments ended in 1974, when William Simon became Secretary. For all his admirable qualities, Bill Simon was too recently a bond trader on Wall Street to welcome an experiment vigorously opposed by professional government bond dealers.

Two economists at the Treasury subsequently evaluated the performance of comparable bond issues sold by Dutch auction and by the standard procedure. The results were unambiguous. The Treasury got a better deal under the Dutch auction. . . .

The authors submitted their article to a professional journal, which accepted it for publication. However, for more than two years the Treasury refused to authorize its publication. The veto was withdrawn in 1979 [but the paper has still not been published].

When he left the Treasury, Jack Bennett returned to Exxon, where he introduced Dutch auctions for at least some Exxon debt issues. Since then the practice has been spreading, so that it is no longer simply a theoretical possibility.[13]

In 1991, Salomon Brothers was accused of manipulating a Treasury auction of securities and later admitted to doing so. That awakened fresh interest in my ancient proposal and led me to publish the op-ed article in the *Wall Street Journal* just quoted. Under great pressure, the Treasury has since modified its method of auctioning securities in the direction of a Dutch auction, though I do not know how far it has gone.

All in all a minor episode, yet most instructive. Personalities do matter. If George Shultz had remained treasury secretary, I am persuaded that the method of auctioning securities would long ago have been drastically reformed. Good ideas may be neglected, but they seldom die. Also, the episode sharply illustrates the rigidity of government even on a purely technical matter that has no ideological overtones.

Oval Office Meetings

The four times during 1970 and 1971 that I met with Nixon in the Oval Office, he was in full command of the factual economic situation and of the available alternative policies. I had no reason to question my earlier high opinion of his intelligence and knowledge. In particular, at no time did he ever use the profane and scatological language that his enemies described as his usual mode of expression.

Two meetings stand out in my memory because they reinforced an impression that I formed at a meeting at Mission Bay, California, during the Nixon campaign in 1968 of his readiness to put his own political interests above the public interest. At a session with his advisory committee on that occasion, he indicated that he had reluctantly decided to support a protectionist measure for textiles. His reason was entirely political: he believed that his position on textile protection would determine whether he won or lost one or two crucial southern states. He did not ask our advice; he knew that economically it was the wrong thing to do. At my meeting in the Oval Office in June 1971, he wanted me to urge Arthur to have the Fed increase the money supply more rapidly. I protested, saying that faster monetary growth was not desirable because it would lead to later inflation. Nixon agreed but said that it would first promote economic growth and assure that the economy was expanding before the 1972 election. I replied that it might not be worth winning the election at the cost of a major inflation subsequently. Nixon said something like, "We'll worry about that when it happens."

In September 1971, after Nixon had imposed wage and price controls, George Shultz and I discussed a range of issues with him. As I was getting ready to leave, Nixon said something about wage and price controls being a monstrosity that they would get rid of as soon as they could, and then went on to say, "Don't blame George [then serving as administrator of price and wage controls] for this monstrosity." As I remember it, I replied something like, "I don't blame George. I blame you, Mr. President." (In an attempt to see whether my memory is reasonably accurate or I had inadvertently polished this episode to my advantage, I inquired of the National Archives whether it would be possible to get a transcript of that segment of the infamous "Nixon tapes." A courteous reply listed the dates that I had met with the president, but stated that that part of the tapes "have not yet been processed for release.")

Another item that I remember from the 1968 Mission Bay meeting was the demonstration of Nixon's schizophrenic character. In our meeting with him during the day, he was low-keyed and unemotional. Our session with him had all the characteristics of a back-and-forth seminar among a group of college professors. In late afternoon there was a barbecue, or its equivalent, for the press corps. The Nixon who came out for that was a different human being: hail-fellow-well-met, arms waving, emotional, the farthest thing from the intellectual you might have taken him for earlier in the day. Naturally, we thought this artificial, that the Nixon we had met with earlier that day, or whom I had met with nearly a decade earlier, was the *real* Nixon. But who is to say?

I was a strong supporter of Nixon in 1968, less so in 1972, though I still voted for him. In retrospect, I must confess that I question whether the support was justified. Few presidents have come closer to expressing a philosophy compatible with my own; and few if any have had a higher IQ; yet performance belied the rhetoric and the ability. The most extreme, but by no means the only, example is wage and price controls. Though Nixon supposedly was for a smaller and less intrusive government, federal-government spending came to about the same percentage of national income at the end of his term as at the beginning. On reexamining the evidence, I was shocked to find that the explosion in federal regulatory activity had its start in the Nixon administration. Though he supposedly was for free markets, the Environmental Protection Agency (EPA) and a number of other regulatory authorities were established during his presidency, among them the Occupational Safety and Health Administration (OSHA), the Consumer Product Safety Commission (CPSC), the Legal Services Commission (LSC), and the Department of Energy; in addition, the Economic Employment Opportunity Commission (EEOC) replaced an earlier and less powerful agency established by President Johnson. The number of pages in the Federal Register, a record of all government regulations, went from 20,000 in 1968 to 46,000 in 1974, the year Nixon resigned.

On the plus side, Nixon had an imaginative, and on the whole effective, foreign policy, and he was responsible for ending the draft. His record is as complex and mixed as his personality. He was an intensely private, I would say even shy, person, yet he lived most of his life in the glare of publicity. He was intensely ambitious, and seemingly ready to jettison his professed principles at the slightest sign of political advantage, yet this was far less so in foreign policy. As a final illustration of his complexity, despite my public attacks on his price and wage controls, when I was scheduled to have a by-pass operation at the Mayo Clinic in December 1972, Nixon took the trouble to telephone personally Dr. Wallace, my surgeon, to express his interest and concern in my welfare. On a personal level, I am indebted to President Nixon for the opportunities he gave me and for the personal kindness he showed. I have never been able to join the numerous band of Nixon-haters. Rather, I regret that his talents were never effectively used and sympathize with the extraordinary ordeal he brought on himself by an excess of hubris and ambition.

Ronald Reagan

I first met Ronald Reagan in 1967, when I was a visiting professor at the University of California at Los Angeles and he was beginning his tenure as governor of the state. As noted in chapter 15, I was taken to visit him at his Los Angeles home by Henry Salvatori, one of the group of close associates of Reagan who had taken a leading role in promoting his candidacy for governor. We had a pleasant meeting and I was very favorably impressed. We discussed at some length the financing of education at all levels. He had, as governor, recently made a stir by recommending higher tuition for state universities. The chattering classes naturally objected, but I was glad to learn that Reagan had thought the issue through and was fully aware of the inequity of taxing those who did not go to state universities for the benefit of those who did. He was also fully aware of the case for greater choice of school for parents of students attending elementary and secondary schools.

I learned years later from my friend Sam Husbands, who was at the time engaged in Republican politics, that there was another link between Reagan and myself. Sam's story was that Reagan arrived a little early for a lunch that Sam was having in the course of building support for Reagan's run for governor. When Sam came out to usher him in for lunch, he found him reading a paperback that he quickly stuffed into his pocket. Sam reports that the book was *Capitalism and Freedom.*

Sometime later, Reagan decided that he wanted to propose an amendment to the state constitution that would limit the total amount that the state of California was authorized to spend in any year. He assigned Lew Uhler of his staff to develop a proposition to that effect that could be put on the state ballot. Lew, in turn, organized a group to design the project and asked me to cooperate. That was the beginning of my involvement in the movement to get spending-limitation amendments adopted by the states and by the federal government.

Proposition 1, the result of that effort, was on the ballot in California in 1973. I was in California when Governor Reagan wanted to start his campaign to promote the proposition. After my by-pass operation at the Mayo Clinic in December 1972, I spent most of the next two months convalescing at Palm Springs, California. Lew visited me there to inquire whether I would be sufficiently recovered by mid-February to accompany Reagan on a barnstorming tour of California promoting the proposition. As it turned out, I was sufficiently recovered and I did accompany Reagan for an unforgettable experience. We flew in a small private plane from place to place, and at each had a press conference on the proposition. Between stops Reagan talked freely about both his life and his views, and I got to know him more intimately than I had before. We finished the day with a big press conference in Los Angeles at which one of the questions I was asked was whether I would support Reagan for the presidency in 1976, to which I answered that I would.

The proposition was narrowly defeated in the subsequent election, but it started a movement that is still going strong (see chap. 21, p. 352).

Reagan opposed Gerald Ford for the 1976 presidential nomination but started rather late and failed in his attempt. In November 1977 I received the Scopus Award at a Friends of the Hebrew University dinner at which Ronald and Nancy Reagan were guests and he spoke. As we went up to be seated at the head table behind a brass band in typical Hollywood extravagance, I commented to the Reagans: "It should be playing 'Hail to the Chief.'" Ronald reacted with a smile; Nancy, by contrast, had a look of extreme disappointment that made both Rose and me realize for the first time how strong her ambition for the presidency was.

In 1980, when Reagan started early and ran a very successful campaign, first for the nomination and then for the presidency, Reagan's chief research person was Martin Anderson, with whom I was in frequent touch. Also, sometime in 1980 Reagan named the Economic Policy Coordinating Committee to develop a program for action once he was elected. He asked George Shultz to chair the committee and me to be one of the thirteen members.[14] He also named advisory groups for other policy areas, but I had no contact with them.

Appointing such a group to draw up advance plans has become something of a common practice. I have been impressed over the years how important it is for the success of a new administration. Such an administration has only a limited honeymoon, and it is likely to make its main impact in the first year, even few months, of its term. That was true for Reagan, as it was also for Margaret Thatcher, to name perhaps the two most eventful initial terms. By contrast, when Begin unexpectedly was elected prime minister of Israel in 1977 in a major upset, he had no advance plans and, as a result, he accomplished very little.

Our coordinating committee met occasionally during the rest of the period prior to the election, exchanged drafts on various aspects of policy, and on November 16, early in the transition period, met with the newly elected president to pass on to him, and discuss with him, a final report titled "Economic Strategy for the Reagan Administration." Once in office, Reagan acted very much along the lines that we recommended. It is not possible, however, to know whether this was because of our recommendations or because he had chosen as advisers persons who shared his views on policy. To give one particularly clear example: we recommended that "you promptly exercise the discretion granted to the president to remove the price controls on crude oil and petroleum products," and that was indeed one of his first acts after the inauguration.

On election eve, Rose and I had dinner at the Shultzes both to listen to the election returns and to enable George and me to put the finishing touches on a draft of the final report. Needless to say, we were overjoyed at the landslide victory that emerged early in the evening. By prearrangement, a BBC radio station called me at the Shultzes late that evening California time (in the middle of the night British time) to participate in a taped discussion of the election returns, "Countdown to the White House." Edward Heath, the former Conservative prime minister who had been ousted from the leadership of the Conservative party by Margaret Thatcher, was supposed to participate in the discussion. He was not there at the outset, but wandered in about halfway through the session. I had met Heath twice before, once when Rose and I went to our first and last White House dinner,[15] which was in honor of Heath, a second time when we were in Britain during his term as prime minister. On both occasions he had been very friendly and interested in talking about policy issues. This time was very different. It was quickly evident that he had come from a lively party and was very much under the influence. He seemed as upset about Reagan's rise as he had been about Thatcher's. He launched into a vitriolic and libelous attack on Thatcher and her advisers, including me—utterly unrestrained and totally lacking in civility. I no longer recall how I responded except that I was taken aback. The moderator of the program of course tried his best to stifle and offset Heath but had little success. He later apologized to me. Heath never did and I never had any other contact with him.

Unpleasant though it was to hear myself castigated in public a continent away, it was most instructive in revealing the kind of emotions that a political struggle can unleash. The same kind of emotional reaction emerged in the attacks on Reagan and his advisers in the United States in later years. Indeed, I suspect that Bush had a similar though milder reaction, and that it helps to explain why as president, he deliberately cut himself off from all Reaganite influences.

I believe that Reagan made a mistake when he chose Bush as his vice-presidential candidate—indeed, I regard it as the worst decision not only of his campaign but of his presidency. My favorite candidate was Donald Rumsfeld. Had he been chosen, I believe he would have succeeded Reagan as president, and the sorry Bush-Clinton period would never have occurred. One amusing incident in that connection. When Rumsfeld left government, he became the CEO of Searle Pharmaceuticals. One day in Chicago, prior to the convention, I happened to ride up in an elevator with Mr. Searle. I mentioned to him my high opinion of Don Rumsfeld, and expressed the wish that Reagan would name him as the vice-presidential candidate. Mr. Searle protested vigorously: he said that he could not afford to lose him.

After the election, President Reagan, at the suggestion of Martin Anderson, by then his domestic policy adviser, appointed a President's Economic Policy Advisory Board, PEPAB for short, on which he asked me to serve.[16] It consisted of twelve economists, all of whom were outside the government, although most of them had served in the government at one time or another. All of us shared a general free-market orientation, though we occasionally differed widely on specific issues and had a reputation as independent thinkers who could be counted on to express our opinion whether we agreed with or differed from the president. In short we were not "yes" persons.

George Shultz was the initial chairman of the group. After he was appointed secretary of state in 1982, Walter Wriston, chairman of Citibank, served as chairman until the end of Reagan's term.* Martin Anderson, who

---

* The other members included Arthur F. Burns, Paul McCracken, and Herbert Stein, all former chairmen of the Council of Economic Advisers; Alan Greenspan, Arthur Laffer, James Lynn, William Simon, Thomas Sowell, and Charls E. Walker. As Anderson writes,

served for two years as a special assistant to the President for policy analysis, organized PEPAB, and then was in charge of arrangements for our meetings until he left the White House. He then became a member of PEPAB. Only one other change in membership occurred during Reagan's eight-year presidency.[17]

"During the critical first year, PEPAB met six times with President Reagan, every time strongly reinforcing his long-held views of economic policy."[18] Before each scheduled meeting, George Shultz, when he was chairman, or Walt Wriston subsequently, would notify us about the key issues that the president would like to discuss, and would ask selected members to prepare a brief analysis of each issue, to be circulated in advance of the meeting. We would then meet at the White House, generally at ten o'clock, to give the members coming by air from New York time to get there, and spend an hour or so discussing the issues among ourselves, seeking to reach a consensus or to clarify differences. We would then be joined by the president and his entourage, consisting of Vice-President Bush, the chief of staff (James Baker during the first term; Don Regan during the second), and especially in the first term, Ed Meese and James Deaver. Our meetings were often attended by other officials with a special interest in the subject under discussion, occasionally to brief us, usually to listen.[19]

While Vice-President George Bush was almost always one of the entourage that accompanied Reagan to meetings, I do not recall his ever making a comment of substance at the meetings. My only contact with him was to say hello and good-bye. I realize that his behavior is in line with conventional expectations about the proper behavior of vice-presidents. But it was not in line with Reagan's pleasure in a spirited discussion. In any event, it meant that I had no direct evidence of his beliefs, so I was not prepared for his prompt reversal of Reaganomics when he became president.[20]

"The twelve charter members were an elite group, unmatched in their collective reputation. . . .

"The . . . members, with one exception, had advised Reagan throughout the presidential campaign and the transition. . . . They were truly the board of directors for the development of Reaganomics. . . .

"The one exceptional member was Herbert Stein [member and chairman of President Nixon's Council of Economic Advisers from 1969 to 1974].

"Stein had nothing to do with the development of Reaganomics during the campaign or the transition. He made no effort to support Reagan during the campaign. . . . Stein rarely saw a tax he didn't like. But while I was putting together the proposed membership list of PEPAB I noticed that we had virtually every former holder of key economic policy posts in past Republican administrations—with one obvious exception. So in order to have a clean sweep, I recommended Stein. He never disappointed us, recommending tax increases (in vain) at almost every meeting of the board." Anderson, *Revolution*, pp. 266–67.

After the president joined us, the chairman would summarize the conclusions the group had reached on the issues discussed, and then turn the session over to the president. We then had a rather free, open discussion for another hour or so, followed by an informal sandwich lunch, for which the president might or might not stay, and on a few occasions a more formal lunch for which the president did stay.

> Reagan loved meeting with [PEPAB]. . . . Many of the members were old friends and his eyes would twinkle and his face would beam when he joined them in the Roosevelt Room or the Cabinet Room. What they did for him more than anything else was to reassure him that the course he was following was right. It was they who pressed him to resist any tax increases, it was they who strongly urged more and more cuts in federal spending, it was they who pushed for more deregulation. And most importantly, it was they who praised him, to his face, for his consistent, determined effort to restore the economic health of the United States. . . .
>
> The counsel of these economic gurus was taken with great respect. . . . Their presence was especially important toward the end of that first year when many of Reagan's senior advisers, including Stockman, Baker and Regan, were buckling under the pressures of the increasing budget deficit and began pressing the president to change his adamant opposition to tax increases. PEPAB was summoned as quickly as possible and they personally reassured the president that he, and not his advisers who wanted to boost taxes, was right. Milton Friedman and William Simon, two of Reagan's favorites, were very eloquent and persuasive on this point.[21]

The president was always well informed on the issues he had asked us to discuss, generally though not always had definite views about them, but was anxious to hear other views and to be informed of additional evidence. During the first several years, inflation, monetary policy, and tax policy were understandably frequent topics. Reagan was very knowledgeable about monetary policy, recognized the key role of monetary growth, and was fully aware that the initial impact of a disinflationary policy would be a recession, and perhaps a fairly serious one, as indeed it was. He was prepared to take the heat on that for the long-term advantage of bringing down inflation. Our group was essentially unanimous on this issue though there were some differences about the appropriate severity of monetary restraint.

I doubt that any other president since FDR would have behaved the way Reagan did. The standard experience was for the White House to pressure the Fed to ease at almost the first signs of rising unemployment, rather than to take the longer view (witness my own experience with Nixon). Reagan refused to behave that way and instead encouraged Paul Volcker to stick with restraint until he broke the back of inflation. The results were as we all predicted: the initial effect was a severe recession in 1981 and 1982, during which Reagan's favorable ratings in public-opinion polls plummeted. Inflation started to drop. When the Fed eased in late 1982, the economy expanded. Inflation, which had been cut in half, rose mildly and then resumed its decline. Public-opinion polls reversed and Reagan was on the way to his landslide victory in 1984. Sounds simple in the telling, but it was not simple in the doing. Reagan went not only against the dictates of political expediency but also against the widespread Keynesian views of the time. Our group was nearly unanimous on the general direction of monetary policy—though I and a number of others were highly critical of the erratic way that the Fed operated, letting monetary growth vary widely in brief periods. I believe that all of us regarded it worth suffering a recession to make possible monetary restraint sufficient to reverse inflation. I have no doubt that our support encouraged Reagan. However, given his strong principles, and his willingness to adhere to them, I doubt that it had any actual effect on the policy that he followed.

The so-called "voluntary" export quota on Japanese cars was one major matter on which he went against our advice and against his own basic principled belief in free trade. The automobile producers had been fervent defenders of free trade so long as they were major exporters and dominated the domestic markets. But when high-quality, relatively low-priced Japanese imports became a serious threat to their domestic markets, the automobile producers, or most of them, changed their tune and appealed to Washington for assistance. Malcolm Baldrige, the secretary of commerce, suggested and, I believe, negotiated an agreement with the Japanese government agreeing to set a limit on exports of cars to the U.S.

Every member of PEPAB as well as every economist in the administration, including all members of the Council of Economic Advisers, was opposed to such an agreement. I was both surprised and disappointed at the time that Reagan was willing to go along. His political advisers, and Secretary Baldridge, argued that the "voluntary" quota was the lesser of evils, that if it was not approved, Congress would pass an even more outrageous bill, setting a minimum to the "domestic content" in vehicles sold in the U.S., and that support would be strong enough to override a veto. I have always been persuaded that Reagan agreed not primarily for this reason but because of his strong sense of loyalty to the subordinates he had appointed, in this case Secretary Baldridge. My view was, as I wrote in a *Newsweek* column on this and other protectionist measures, "The Reagan administration has paid a very high price for very dubious short-term political gains."[22]

One of the ancillary advantages of the PEPAB meetings was the opportunity to influence the persons attending, in my case in the early years, particularly Don Regan. Over and over again in the meetings, and in casual discussion before or after, I tried unsuccessfully to persuade him to have the Treasury issue purchasing-power securities, i.e., bonds in which both the coupon and the redemption value are adjusted for inflation. Many countries then and now issue such bonds. My major argument with Regan at that time was in terms of the administration's commitment to bring inflation down. I pointed out that the high interest rates on the bonds that the Treasury was selling to the public provided compensation for a much higher inflation rate than the administration was committed to, that its actions were inconsistent with its talk. By issuing only purchasing-power bonds, the administration would be suiting its actions to its words, and would, besides, reap the short-term benefit of lower interest costs, thereby reducing the recorded deficit. Unfortunately, I was never able to persuade Regan to act.

More recently, purchasing-power bonds have been discussed, this time as an aid to monetary policy, and the Treasury has begun to issue such bonds. Robert Hetzel, a former student of mine and an economist at the Federal Reserve Bank of Richmond, suggested that the Treasury issue matching nominal and purchasing-power bonds. The difference in the yields on the two would then provide a market estimate of the anticipated rate of inflation, which, he argued, would be of great value to the Fed in conducting monetary policy. Alan Greenspan supported such action in testimony to Congress. I have gone farther and suggested that the Congress instruct the Fed to keep the anticipated rate of inflation less than, say, 3 percent, and that any failure to do so lead to automatic sanctions on the Board members (e.g., a halving of their salary).

The view that, as a matter of equity, the Treasury should issue purchasing-power bonds is a very old one, and has been widely supported by professional economists.

When Don Regan shifted places with James Baker at the end of the first term, and became chief of staff, he tried to terminate PEPAB and almost did. However, when Reagan learned what was going on, he reversed Regan and insisted that PEPAB be continued.[23] However, the second term was preoccupied or, should I say, bedeviled, by noneconomic issues, notably Iran-Contra. As a result, PEPAB met less frequently.

I have always believed that one reason why the second term was so much less productive than the first was that Reagan chose to run the 1984 campaign on a "feel-good" platform with no specific commitments for actions. That was in sharp contrast to the 1980 campaign, when he stated very specifically the actions he intended to take if elected, particularly, cutting marginal income-tax rates. As a result, he had a specific mandate when elected. He did not have one when he was reelected.

Concluding Comment on Reagan

I have no such mixed feelings about the Reagan administration as I do about the Nixon administration. My high hopes that 1980 would mark a decisive turn toward smaller government were frustrated, but not because of the Reagan years. During those years, inflation and unemployment were brought down, thanks to Reagan's willingness to support a restrictive monetary policy, and there was a significant reduction in regulation and controls. Thanks to the continued control of the House by the Democrats, government spending and taxing was reduced much less than Reagan hoped, but there was a start that would have accelerated with the end of the cold war, if Bush had not reversed Reaganomics. Robert Bartley's *The Seven Fat Years* is a far more accurate depiction of the consequences of Reaganomics than the distorted picture that has been churned out by Reagan's ideological enemies. And, of course, outside of the economy, the firmness, persistence, and insight that guided his policy toward the Soviet Union was a major factor in producing the collapse of communism.

We have hanging on our wall a poster produced by the Young Americans for Freedom which quotes from Reagan speeches in 1961 and 1962 in which he says,

> We'll dismiss it [communism] as a sad, bizarre chapter in human history whose last pages are even now being written. . . .
> What we see here [in the Soviet Union] is a political structure that no longer corresponds to its economic base.

These prescient predictions are in sharp contrast to the favorable comments on the Soviet Union at about the same time by such prominent intellectuals as John Kenneth Galbraith and Paul Samuelson.

No other president in my lifetime comes close to Reagan in adherence to clearly specified principles dedicated to promoting and maintaining a free society.

Chapter Twenty-Four

CHILE

{ *Milton* } From 1955 to 1964, the University of Chicago Department of Economics had an agreement with the Catholic University of Chile, financed by the U.S. Agency for International Development, to provide scholarships for Chileans to study at Chicago and to send personnel to Chile to help them improve their Department of Economics. Having our people in Chile to interview the candidates for scholarships resulted in a steady flow of high-quality graduate students from Chile. Professor Arnold Harberger was the faculty member most actively involved in this project. He spoke Spanish fluently, made many trips to Chile from 1955 on, married a Chilean, and served very much as the mentor of the Chilean, and incidentally other Latin American, students.

My involvement in this program was as a professor teaching the basic course in economic theory at the University of Chicago taken by all graduate students and running the Workshop in Money and Banking, in which some Chilean students participated.

From Allende to Pinochet

In 1970, Salvador Allende, backed by the combined left parties, was one of three candidates for the presidency of Chile. He received 36.8 percent of the vote, more than either of the other candidates but not a majority, so, under the Chilean constitution, the senate had to select the winner. In accordance with long tradition, and after extensive negotiations among the parties, Allende was named president. Once in power, he used every device to convert Chile into a communist state.[1]

The communist, i.e., Soviet, leaders welcomed the Allende regime as especially noteworthy because it was achieved through a legal democratic process. As a result, "Chile became a focal point of international interest from 1970 to 1973 not because it had a Marxist government . . . but because it had a *freely elected* Marxist government."[2]

In September 1973, after extensive public unrest and protest, the military under the leadership of General Augusto Pinochet staged a coup, in the course of which Allende was murdered (or by some accounts, committed suicide).

In response, the

> worldwide Communist movement, under the direction of Moscow, . . . launched a major propaganda campaign aimed at toppling the military junta currently ruling Chile and restoring the kind of Marxist-Leninist leadership which brought the nation to the brink of chaos.
>
> As usual, the Communists have allies in the so called "progressive forces" in the Western world ranging from kneejerk liberals in the media to influential members of the United States Congress.[3]

The "Chicago Boys"

The students who returned to Chile from Chicago began "promoting free-market economics . . . as a way out of the economic stagnation that plagued the Chilean economy. In late 1972, when it seemed likely that Allende's policies would push the economy to the breaking point, . . . [they] began putting together a plan for economic recovery. By the time of the coup, . . . they had assembled a 189-page draft of diagnosis and proposals, which they gave to the generals."[4] (It is worth noting that, thanks to their training, our students were almost the only economists in Chile who had not been involved with or favorable to the Allende government.)

For the first year and a half, the generals did little with the proposals. Instead, they put the military in charge of undoing the damage that Allende had done. Not surprisingly, the military were largely ineffective. In 1975, when inflation still raged and a world recession triggered a depression in Chile, General Pinochet turned to the "Chicago Boys"—as the group of economists later became known—and appointed several of them to powerful positions in the government.

My only direct involvement in Chile came at this point when Al Harberger asked me to accompany him to Chile under the auspices of the Banco Hipotecario to participate with him and Carlos Langoni, one of our Ph.D.s who had been actively involved in economic reform in Brazil, in a week of seminars and public talks.

Six Days in Chile

The seminars were planned as a way both to inform us of the actual situation and to enable us to pass on our initial reactions. They were to be held with government officials, representatives of the public, and members of the military. The talks were planned to enable us to inform the public about our interpretation of the situation and our recommendations for action. All in all, the result was, as I wrote in my notes on the visit, "a hectic and continuous schedule."[5]

It soon became even clearer than it had been before we came that the key problem was inflation. As I noted about a discussion with representatives of the private sector, "one of the major themes that emerged was the extraordinary difficulties that inflation imposed on the operations of the private sector. Over and over again . . . I kept asking people what fraction of time they were required to spend on problems directly related to the extremely high and variable rate of inflation. Undoubtedly many people overestimated this, but the answers never ranged to less than 20 percent and sometimes came to 90 percent."

One of our meetings was with General Pinochet—which gave an iota of substance to later charges that I was a personal adviser to the general. As I wrote in my notes, "in a session that lasted perhaps three-quarters of an hour or so and in which we had to communicate through interpreters, it is very hard to get much of an idea of the character of the man. He was very much interested in getting our reaction to the situation in Chile. He reacted from time to time. . . . He was sympathetically attracted to the idea of a shock treatment but was clearly distressed at the possible temporary unemployment that might be caused. Beyond this, he indicated very little indeed about his own or the government's feelings, but he did stress and urge that I write him my judgment after the end of my visit to Chile." This I did after we got back to Chicago (reprinted as item 1 in appendix A).[6]

I believe that the "Chicago Boys" had already reached the conclusion that a shock treatment was required to end the inflation and establish the basis for economic recovery and growth; and that the key to both ending inflation and economic recovery was a drastic cut in government spending, since the inflation was clearly being driven by the need to print money to finance a major government deficit.* Our role was to check their conclusion, give it, as it were, the stamp of approval, and help to sell it to the public and the military junta.

All three of us were involved in many seminar-like meetings, and each of us gave public talks. At talks for students at the Catholic University and Chile University, "I departed from the main theme of all the other talks which had to do with inflation and talked on the fragility of freedom, emphasizing the rareness of free societies . . . and the role in the destruction of a free society that was played by the emergence of the welfare state. The general line I was taking—which was that their present difficulties were due almost entirely to the forty-year trend toward collectivism, socialism, and the welfare state, that this was a course which would hurt people not help them, and that it was a course that would lead to coercion rather than freedom—was, from their reaction, obviously almost completely new to them. There was an attitude of shock that pervaded both groups of students at hearing such talk."[7]

That six-day visit plus my prior role as a professor turned out to have consequences that we never anticipated and that we had to deal with for the next decade, including organized protests against me almost wherever I went, the largest being in Stockholm at the 1976 Nobel award ceremonies, when some five thousand or so protested. At speaking engagements, Rose and I became used to being ushered in to the head table via the kitchen or some other indirect route in order to avoid the small bands of protesters massed in front. My crime was that I was allegedly "the intellectual architect and unofficial adviser for the team of economists . . . running the Chilean economy."[8] I never could decide whether to be more amused or more annoyed by the charge that I was running the Chilean economy from my office in Chicago.

Reaction

Two nearly simultaneous events marked the start of the active campaign against me:

---

* In simplest terms, government spending was over 40 percent of national income, tax receipts about 20 percent, and the creation of money the only recourse for financing the deficit. After years of inflation, the public had learned how to economize on the holding of money so the outstanding stock of money had declined to a small fraction of national income, giving a small base on which to levy an inflation tax. That was clearly not a sustainable situation, since it would take increasingly high rates of inflation to finance the deficit, leading ultimately to runaway inflation. Moreover, given the magnitude of the problem, a gradualist approach, if even possible, was not at all attractive.

1. A *New York Times* article of September 21, 1975, reporting that I was "the guiding light of the junta's economic policy" was followed by an October 2, 1975 column in the *New York Times* by Anthony Lewis, in which he wrote that an interesting area of American responsibility

> is economic. The Chilean junta's economic policy is based on the ideas of Milton Friedman, the conservative American economist, and his Chicago School. Friedman himself has visited Santiago and is believed to have suggested the junta's draconian policy to end inflation.
>
> The policy, in keeping with the Chicago School's theories, is to cut public expenditure, curb monetary expansion and sell off publicly owned facilities. If there is a growing disparity between the incomes of rich and poor, that would in the Friedman view have the desirable effect of increasing investment and eventual economic growth.
>
> Of course, any political or economic theory can be perverted from what its framers intended. But if the pure Chicago economic theory can be carried out in Chile only at the price of repression, should its authors feel some responsibility? There are troubling questions here about the social role of academics. [The implicit assumption is that there was some other economic theory that could have been carried out that would have avoided the repression. Should journalists not feel some responsibility to state what the alternative was?]

2. In its issue of October 3, 1975, the *Chicago Maroon,* the student paper, reported on its front page under the heading, "Radicals Plan Friedman Protest; Harberger Also Accused of Role," that

> Left-wing campus and area organizations, at the initiative of the University branch of the Spartacus Youth League, have formed a united front to protest the involvement of University professors Milton Friedman and Arnold Harberger in policy making for the ruling military junta in Chile.
>
> The united front, officially titled the "Committee against Friedman/Harberger Collaboration with the Chilean Junta" has called for a protest demonstration today on the quadrangles in front of the Administration Building.

Attractively printed posters carried the message, "Drive Friedman Off Campus through Protest and Exposure."

The *Maroon* asked me to respond to the charge by the Spartacus Youth League. I did so by permitting them to publish, in the same issue of October 3, a response that I had written in July to a highly critical letter from an unnamed professor. (My letter was reprinted in the *Wall Street Journal* on October 27, 1975 and is reprinted as item 2 in appendix A.)

Some ten days later Student Government rejected a proposed condemnation of Al and me. Still later, on October 27, Student Government created a "Commission of Inquiry on the Friedman/Harberger Issue," which was promptly condemned by the then president of the University of Chicago, John Wilson, and gradually fizzled out.

The protests organized by the united front were annoying, especially when they included pickets marching up and down with signs in front of the apartment house in which we lived, but they were not very serious. However, they were the first of many during the next five or so years.

Articles that appeared in newspapers and periodicals were at least as annoying as the organized protests. For example, in January 1976, *Business Week* had a long article on Chile titled "A Draconian Cure for Chile's Economic Ills," which was generally highly critical of Al and me and included the utterly fallacious allegation that we had "uncomfortably close ties" with the Central Intelligence Agency. In August 1976, Orlando Letelier, who had served as Chilean ambassador to the United States and minister of foreign affairs in the Allende government, published an article in *The Nation* titled "Economic Freedom's Awful Toll." Not long after the article was published, he was assassinated in Washington, creating a great furor and scandal, and he promptly became a martyr. His article was reprinted in the *Guardian* and no doubt many other places.

He at least was willing to present an alternative in the form of the centralized planned economy that the Allende regime had tried to create. The similar articles and editorials that appeared in Britain, France, Germany, Canada, and no doubt many other countries, had no such saving grace. What we were doing was, according to them, deliberately mean, nasty, inhuman—not stated explicitly but implied because we were said to support a fascist military junta that allegedly took delight in torturing people. It was taken for granted that there was an obvious preferable alternative that sensitive human beings could have recommended—but no writer ever spelled out what it was.

The cookie-cutter character of the published attacks was matched by the protests. After one protest when I gave a talk at the San Francisco Commonwealth Club, we picked up in the street a crumpled call to attend a protest against me that had a blank space to be filled in with the particular place and date! (Reprinted as item 7 in appendix A.) At other protests, we came to recognize not only the identically worded placards but also a few faces common to Cornell, Chicago, and San Diego. We rapidly came to the conclusion that we were part of a worldwide organized protest against the Pinochet regime in Chile.

What annoyed me more than anything else was the pusillanimity of so many academics. The dedicated socialists and communists were one thing; other academics a very different thing. There were some notable exceptions— one that especially pleased me was Zvi Griliches at Harvard, a former student and teacher at Chicago, who wrote several excellent letters to the *Crimson*, the student paper at Harvard. But for the most part, academics waffled, wanting to be on the "right," i.e., "progressive" side, even when they did not condemn me outright.

Some years later, on returning from a trip to China, I wrote a letter, out of sheer deviltry, to the *Stanford Daily* noting that I had just returned from China, clearly a more repressive state than Chile, that I had given the same advice as I had in Chile, and asking whether I should expect the same protests as were directed at me after I returned from Chile, and, if not, why not (the full text of the letter is reprinted as item 8 in appendix A.)

Al had his bellyful of protests, but they were less frequent than those against me, especially after I was awarded the Nobel Prize. And this was true even though as Claudia Rosett wrote, "The 'Chicago Boys' . . . are often described as disciples of Milton Friedman, but Friedman did not know any of them well, and had little direct impact on what the Chicago Boys did in Chile. Their real mentor was Arnold Harberger, . . . who has visited Chile frequently since 1955."[9] That is entirely accurate. Most of them took my classes and a few were in my Money and Banking Workshop, but there is no doubt that Al was far closer to them than I.

The reason that I was chosen for special attention is obvious. My connection with Goldwater and Nixon, my *Newsweek* column, and my being awarded the Nobel Prize made me better known to the general public and hence a more useful target.

The announcement of the Nobel award on October 14, 1976, raised the controversy to a new level. The catalyst was two letters criticizing the award that were published in the *New York Times* on October 24, both dated October 14 and both from Cambridge, Massachusetts, each signed by two Nobel laureates: one, by David Baltimore and S. E. Luria, who had received Nobel prizes for medicine; the other, by George Wald, who had received his prize in medicine, and Linus Pauling, who had received two prizes in chemistry and peace. The image of four busy scientists reacting within hours of the announcement and independently pairing up and deciding to write letters to the *Times* baffles the imagination—an invisible hand indeed (the texts of the letters are reprinted as item 4 in appendix A).

On the day that I accepted the prize in Stockholm (December 10, 1976), the *Wall Street Journal* concluded an editorial, titled "Nobels and Smears," as follows: "Given any remote chance to gun down an effective spokesman for conservative economics as a secret fascist and torturer, even Nobel laureates can, we see, succumb to an itchy trigger finger. With so powerful a compulsion at work, the myth about Mr. Friedman is no doubt indelible in a good many minds. But anyone who takes the time to learn the facts should recognize the smear as McCarthyism of the left."

The Nobel ceremonies themselves were marred by an individual protest at the award ceremonies and the largest demonstration during the whole of the period (see chapter 26 for a fuller discussion).

As a nonreader of the *New York Times,* I did not see the letters from the Nobel laureates when they first appeared—but they were very quickly called to my attention by both friends and opponents. Months later, on May 22, 1977, the *New York Times* published a follow-up under the title "Milton Friedman, the Chilean Junta, and the Matter of Their Association," consisting of a letter I had written to the four signers, the reply by two of them, and my response (item 6 in appendix A). In the interim, the *Times* had published letters on both sides of the dispute, the *Wall Street Journal* had come to my defense (item 5 in appendix A), and I had received a steady stream of letters, including both hate mail and expressions of support, though weighted more heavily to hate mail.

The protests did not stop with the Nobel ceremonies. In September 1977, there was a particularly vigorous protest by the Spartacus Youth League at a lecture that I gave at Cornell, matched by a simultaneous counterprotest by the Young Americans for Freedom. In November 1977, I gave a talk for the Commonwealth Club of San Francisco titled "Liberal McCarthyism" in which I discussed my own experience in terms of the double standard that was being employed with respect to right-wing and left-wing dictatorships. As usual there was a small protest.

Similarly, in December 1977, at the annual meeting of the American Economic Association, there was a protest outside the dining room in which a lunch was being held to honor me for receiving the Nobel Prize. That was one session that Rose and I entered via the kitchen.

The Nobel demonstration excepted, all the rest were small, consisting of at most a few dozen fanatics. At all of them the audience greatly outnumbered the protesters, and the audience was uniformly on my side. A quotation from a newspaper story about a talk that I gave at Stanford will give the flavor of such occasions. "While about a dozen peaceful protesters carried signs and chanted outside and a handful hissed his speech indoors, Friedman spoke Thursday evening to an overflow and largely enthusiastic crowd of more than 1,100 on the Stanford campus."[10]

Results of "Shock Treatment"

As almost invariably occurs in stopping an inflation, and as we had predicted in our talks in Chile, the initial effect of slowing monetary growth in Chile was a recession—as in the United States in 1981–82, when the Fed under Paul Volcker with the support of President Reagan undertook to stop the stagflation of the 1970s. Then, as expectations adjust to a slower rate of price rise, growth can resume. In Chile, 1975 was a year of severe recession, with gross domestic product falling at the annual rate of 13 percent. By the end of 1975, the rate of price rise had already been halved and the economy turned around, with gross domestic product growing at the rate of 3 percent. The next five years were years of rapid improvement, with growth in gross domestic product averaging 7.5 percent per year.

The diversity of reaction to these events was phenomenal. In 1978, one observer, just returned from a visit to Chile wrote, "During the days of Allende, I received a letter from Chile saying, 'We are like Humpty Dumpty— who can ever put us together again?' What we saw in Chile gives us great confidence in the private enterprise system. Under the direction of what are sometimes called 'The Chicago Kids, or Friedman's Boys,' the economy of Chile has made a fantastic return from utter chaos." Almost simultaneously, a columnist in the *Detroit Free Press,* just returned from a visit to Chile, wrote, "The consequences [of the economic philosophy operating in Chile] are the devastation of public education, health and social programs and the removal of government controls over the economy. The human cost is one of mounting illiteracy, health problems, retardation and repression."[11] Talk about a glass being half full or half empty!

By 1981, the negative commentary had largely disappeared; Chile was widely being acclaimed as an economic miracle. In Chile itself, the public expressed its approval by giving the Pinochet government a decisive majority in a constitutional referendum.

That was shortly to change. In the euphoria of the rapid decline in inflation and rise in economic growth, the authorities decided in 1979 to peg the exchange rate of the Chilean peso to the U.S. dollar.* The rate of inflation in the U.S. at the time was in the low double digits—high for the United States but lower than inflation in Chile. By pegging, the Chilean authorities

---

* I am doubtful that there is ever a good time for a country like Chile that has a central bank to peg its currency. I have consistently taken the position that a country like Chile with a central bank should let its exchange rate float. The alternative is to abolish the central bank and unify its currency with that of its major trading partner, i.e., establish a currency board system.

hoped to bring the Chilean rate of inflation to the U.S. rate. They got more than they bargained for, thanks to the economic policy introduced by President Reagan in 1981, which brought inflation down sharply in the U.S. and led to a sharp appreciation in the U.S. dollar. The peg imposed strong deflationary pressure on Chile, resulting in severe recession. Gross domestic product fell by 13 percent in 1982 and by 3.5 percent in 1983. The architect of the peg, Finance Minister Sergio de Castro, was relieved of his post in April 1982, and the peg was abandoned in August 1982.

The commentary on Chile quickly reacted to these developments. Instead of articles extolling the economic miracle, articles appeared under the heading, "An Aborted Economic Test," "Friedmanism is exonerated in Chilean debacle," "What Went Wrong in Chile."[12]

Once the peg was dropped and the exchange rate allowed to adjust, rapid real growth resumed. The sharp recession left its mark and undoubtedly was one reason why a plebiscite in October 1988 on the Pinochet government yielded a different result than that in 1980. This time, the public rejected the Pinochet dictatorship. To the surprise of many of Chile's critics, General Pinochet accepted the verdict of the people and arranged for presidential elections in December 1989, at which Patricio Alwyn was elected president. The new government has largely continued the free-market economic policies introduced by the Pinochet government.

A Final Evaluation

In January 1982, I wrote a *Newsweek* column under the title "Free Markets and the Generals," in which I summarized my views on the developments in Chile. I wrote:

> The adoption of free-market policies by Chile with the blessing and support of the military junta headed by General Pinochet has given rise to the myth that only an authoritarian regime can successfully implement a free-market policy.
>
> The facts are very different. Chile is an exception, not the rule. The military is hierarchical and its personnel are imbued with the tradition that some give and some obey orders: it is organized from the top down. A free market is the reverse. It is voluntaristic, authority is dispersed; bargaining, not submission to orders, is its watchword; it is organized from the bottom up.
>
> Military juntas in other South American countries have been

as authoritarian in the economic sphere as they have been in politics. . . .

Miracles: Chile is an economic miracle. Inflation has been cut from 700 percent a year in mid-1974 to less than 10 percent a year. After a difficult transition, the economy boomed, growing an average of about 8 percent a year from 1976 to 1980. Real wages and employment rose rapidly and unemployment fell. Imports and exports surged after export subsidies were eliminated and tariffs were slashed to a flat 10 percent (except for temporarily higher rates for most automobiles). Many state enterprises have been denationalized and motor transport and other areas deregulated. A voucher system has been put into effect in elementary and secondary education. Most remarkable of all, a social-security reform has been adopted that permits individuals to choose between participating in the government system or providing for their own retirement privately.

Chile is an even more amazing political miracle. A military regime has supported reforms that reduce sharply the role of the state and replace control from the top with control from the bottom. This political miracle is the product of an unusual set of circumstances. The chaos produced by the Allende regime that precipitated the military takeover in 1973 discredited central economic control. In an attempt to rectify the situation, the military drew on a comprehensive plan for a free-market economy that had been prepared by a group of young Chilean economists. . . .

Chile is currently having serious difficulties—along with much of the rest of the world. And the opposition to the free-market policies that had been largely silenced by success is being given full voice—from both inside and outside the military.

This temporary setback will likely be surmounted. But I predict that the free-market policy will not last unless the military government is replaced by a civilian government dedicated to political liberty—as the junta has announced is its intention. Otherwise, sooner or later—and probably sooner rather than later—economic freedom will succumb to the authoritarian character of the military. [© 1982, Newsweek, Inc. All rights reserved. Reprinted by permission.]

Fortunately for Chile, the military dictatorship has been replaced by a civilian government.

Gumersindo Ruiz concluded a highly critical 1977 article on Chile published in the Spanish paper *Vanguardia,* "The real proof that the Chicago economists could show in defense of their theories, applied to Chile, would be the economy's recovery and, at the same time, authentic political freedom (unions and political parties) with respect for human rights. That would be the only proof: the sound operation of a free-market economy in a free society."[13]

As I write, more than twenty years after the Chicago Boys were given authority, that proof is now available for all to see. From 1973 to 1995, real income per capita multiplied more than two-and-a-half-fold, inflation fell from 500 percent per year to 8 percent, the infant mortality rate per 1,000 live births fell from 66 to 13, and life expectancy at birth rose from 64 years to 73 years.[14] And authentic political freedom has been restored with the turnover of power by the junta to a freely elected government. Truly, "the sound operation of a free-market economy in a free society."

→ *Chapter Twenty-Five* ←

TRAVELS AND TRAVAILS

{ *Rose* } Our life together has seen high spots and low spots but rarely dull spots. In general, the low spots came early, the high spots later.

Three things came together to produce an active and exciting period between 1966 and 1976, capped by the Nobel award in 1976. One year in particular, 1972, went from highs to lows.

1966–71

Milton's monetary research (*Monetary History* was published in 1963) generated many invitations to appear at business conferences and monetary conferences, both at home and abroad. Also, his association with the early years of the Nixon administration, especially his advocacy of reforms like the volunteer army and negative income tax, which President Nixon backed, brought extensive press and TV coverage. Finally, his joining *Newsweek* as a columnist generated invitations to appear on TV shows, such as *Meet the Press, Face the Nation,* and *The Donahue Show,* as well as to visit foreign countries. His popularity as a defender of the free-enterprise system (*Capitalism and Freedom* was published in 1962) generated many invitations to give public lectures. What had been a steady stream of invitations became for a time a veritable flood, which was in the course of dying down when it was revived by the award of the Nobel Prize in 1976.

This activity was accompanied by extensive and favorable press and TV coverage. A *Time* cover story (December 19, 1969) was followed by one in the *New York Times Magazine* (January 25, 1970). Both stories included cartoons of Milton. I have the *Time* cover and the original of the cartoon that was on the cover of the *New York Times Magazine.*

409

I described our introduction to the *Time* story in the *Oriental Economist:* "In December, 1969, when we returned from a brief visit to New York, we found our neighbors in Vermont very excited. It seemed some people from *Time* magazine had been inquiring of them about our whereabouts and whether they had any knowledge about when we were returning. Of course, they knew about neither. The day after we returned, the *Time* people appeared at our door with photographers to interview and take pictures for a cover story."[1]

The stories report Milton's scholarly accomplishments and also give a glimpse of the person. A small sample from *Time:* "Friedman is a man totally devoted to ideas—isolating them in pure form, expressing them in uncompromising terms and following them wherever they may lead. His basic philosophy is simple and unoriginal: personal freedom is the supreme good—in economic, political and social relations. What is unusual is his consistency in applying this principle to any and all problems, regardless of whom he dismays or pleases, and even regardless of the practical difficulties of putting them into effect. He alternately delights and infuriates conservatives, New Left radicals and almost every group in the crowded middle road."

Milton Viorst, a New York liberal, wrote an equally flattering profile of Milton in the *New York Times Magazine.* In his words:

> Because he has championed economic freedom in an age when the left has put its faith in Government intercession . . . Milton Friedman has inevitably been considered a "right-wing" economist, an impression seemingly confirmed by his association with Goldwater in 1964.
>
> But if the term "right-wing" implies an inordinate sympathy for the vested interests of society, along with a high degree of indulgence for existing social institutions, then nothing could be further from the truth. Friedman is no Chamber of Commerce economist, and surely no Bircher. Whatever the classical foundations of his thinking, he professes ideas that are warmly social and espouses programs that are, within the framework of our time, genuinely radical. Friedman may not be a pure egalitarian but he has no tolerance for a system of government that proclaims programs to help the poor but winds up with a structure that enriches the rich.

Milton was taken by surprise when *Playboy* magazine approached him for an interview about his views. He did not think that he was a proper subject for *Playboy.* Much to our surprise, we discovered that the magazine had a serious intellectual section. Judging from the number of people who mentioned seeing the interview and the letters that *Playboy* received in response to it, the number of serious people who read the magazine was much larger than we expected. (For example, in connection with "Free to Choose," we discovered that Antony Jay's first exposure to Milton's ideas was through the *Playboy* interview.)

The encomiums heaped on Milton by the press in this period are more than matched by the vilification that came with the Chile experience, which reached a peak in the seventies (see chap. 24).

The opportunities for visits abroad fit in with our own situation, especially mine. My role as mother was largely over, leaving me free to join Milton in foreign travel that combined professional activity—mostly lecturing and attending professional conferences—with tourism and sight-seeing.

David was back in Chicago beginning graduate work in physics at the University of Chicago but living in his own apartment. Janet, who was attending Boalt Law School, became engaged to Lew Stansby, whom she had met in the course of playing bridge at Berkeley. Lew was a talented mathematician who was working as a computer programmer, and was also a top-rated bridge player. Their friends were mostly in the Bay Area, so it was the obvious place for the wedding. By happy chance, the annual meeting of the American Economic Association, traditionally held between Christmas and New Year's, was in San Francisco in 1966, which assured that many of our friends would be there also. Accordingly, the wedding took place at that time.

Japan

In 1966, we made the first of eight trips to Japan after our long stay in 1963. Some were trips to Japan only; others were in connection with trips elsewhere. Whatever the length or occasion for the trip, Milton gave at least one lecture under the auspices of the *Nihon Keizai Shimbun* (Japanese Economic Journal), which sponsored an annual series of lectures on economic issues.[2] Jiro Enjoji, the president of the paper for most of the period, always arranged a dinner party the evening of the lecture. Chiaki Nishiyama, who generally was Milton's translator, and some of Mr. Enjoji's associates were always part of the group. Enjoji's parties were always held at a Japanese geisha house, usually Kitchko. The dinners combined excellent food and typical Japanese entertainment with interesting talk.

Whenever the period was long enough, Chiaki, our guide and companion on almost every trip, made sure that we saw just a little more of Japan each time.

{ *Milton* } Our trip in 1966 was for the purpose of consulting with Chiaki about a Rikkyo project he was directing on postwar economic growth.[3] His project was financed by the Ford Foundation, which also financed our trip.[4] This time we visited Kyoto again where, in addition to sight-seeing, I conducted a symposium on monetary matters.

We then went to Kurashiki, a small town on the Inland Sea. Chiaki thought we ought to visit Kurashiki because it is a very traditional Japanese town where the Ohara textile mills are located. The most interesting attraction in Kurashiki, however, turned out to be an art museum that Mr. Ohara, the founder of the textile mills, had erected around the turn of the century. Set among a number of typical Japanese structures, one of which houses a collection of Japanese textiles, the art museum was a reproduction of a small Greek temple and of course looked completely out of place. Inside was a collection of just about the worst impressionist paintings we have ever seen. Many were signed by famous impressionist painters: Cézanne, Dufy, Manet, Renoir, and on and on, but were clearly not the best works of these artists. The explanation we got for the Greek temple and its contents was that Mr. Ohara wanted to help acquaint the Japanese people with the best European art of the time. He collected the art by providing aspiring Japanese art students in France with a fixed sum of money with which to purchase paintings for exhibition in his museum. Quantity took precedence over quality.

{ *Rose* } Japan was hosting an international exposition in Osaka in 1970 (Expo '70) on the theme of "Progress and Harmony for Mankind." Milton was asked to give a lecture as one of a series on that theme. His title was "The Role of Free Markets in Promoting Progress and Harmony for Mankind."

The hospitality offered us was superb. We were always accompanied by guides from the exposition and in addition had a full-time guide, a young lady who spoke excellent English. We corresponded with her for some years, and met with her more than a decade later when she visited the U.S.

The U.S. pavilion was noteworthy for its "elliptical translucent domed roof" that was the "largest and lightest clear-span, air-supported roof ever built," according to the official guidebook. The enormous area without a pillar was indeed most impressive, as were many of the specific exhibits.

{ *Milton* } The Bank of Korea invited me to give a talk under their auspices and since we had not been to Korea we decided to spend a day in Seoul at the end of our visit. Despite the brevity of the trip, it did give us something of a feel of an East Asian country very different from Japan. Unfortunately, we never found it possible in later years to take advantage of opportunities for longer visits.

Two later trips to Japan, in 1983 and 1985, were made to attend international monetary conferences organized by the Institute for Monetary and Economic Research of the Bank of Japan. The institute was established in 1982 to commemorate the centennial of the establishment of the Bank of Japan. The arrangements for the initial international conference were made by Hidekasu Eguchi, who had been a participant in my Money and Banking Workshop. I was asked to serve as an overseas special adviser to the institute and in that capacity gave a keynote address at each conference.[5] Yoshio Suzuki, who was director of the institute in 1985, made arrangements for the second conference. I had gotten to know him well on earlier trips and have continued to stay in touch with him. He is one of the most sophisticated and informed analysts of the Japanese economy, a member of the Mont Pelerin Society. He has recently gone into politics and is now a member of the Japanese legislature.

Arthur Andersen and Co. was in the process of establishing a "Financial Futures Center—Japan" in 1985. They timed the inauguration of the center so that it just preceded the conference and I agreed to give a talk at the inauguration. The other outside speaker was Leo Melamed, who is responsible for my involvement in financial futures issues (see chap. 21, p. 350). We enjoyed being in Tokyo at the same time as Leo and Betty Melamed.

Our latest trip to Japan was in 1988 to attend a Mont Pelerin meeting organized by Chiaki Nishiyama. It was unusual in that it was split between one day in Tokyo and the rest of the time in Kyoto. The opportunity to visit our Japanese friends was an added attraction of this meeting. From Japan we went on to make our second visit to China (see chap. 30).

Grand Cordon. Our connection with Japan was capped when I was awarded a decoration in 1986 by the Japanese emperor, "Grand Cordon of the First Class Order of the Sacred Treasure." According to the rules, the emperor is supposed to confer the decoration in Tokyo. However, I was not willing to make a special trip for the purpose. Accordingly, the San Francisco consul arranged for an exception to the rule. He made the award in the San Francisco consulate, interpreting it as subject to extraterritoriality and therefore technically Japanese soil. After an impressive formal ceremony, we and some of our friends enjoyed a delicious dinner. The decoration is a cherished possession. It reminds me of nothing so much as a famous picture of Eugen Böhm-Bawerk, a noted Austrian economist, with a wide ribbon across his chest and jewelled medals attached.

Over the course of our many trips to Japan, we have seen a tremendous change in the country. On my first visit, in 1955 en route to India, Japan was a very poor country. Scars of war were very evident in Tokyo. Even eight years later, when we had our longest stay in Japan, I could remark that Japan was my favorite country because it was the only country in which I, at 5′ 2″, felt like a tall man. Though the scars of war had not yet been eradicated, they were far less visible, the increase in the standard of life was clear to the naked eye, and the statistical data confirmed what the naked eye suggested: amazingly rapid progress. Each subsequent trip left the same impression. My remark about height obsolesced before my very eyes as the younger generation seemed to grow by inches between trips. Our final trip, in 1988, came during what later came to be called the bubble economy—a period when prices of stocks and land ballooned to untenable heights, leading to a major stock-market crash in 1990, followed by years of serious recession or depression, from which Japan has not yet (1997) emerged.[6]

Iran

In September 1970 we spent a week in Iran at the invitation of the Bank Markazi Iran (the central bank of Iran). I gave a lecture at the bank on "Monetary Policy for a Developing Society." The bank subsequently published the lecture in its bulletin.[7] In addition, I had a few seminar discussions with civil servants on monetary policy and plans for economic development. However, we spent most of the week touring the country.

The shah was still in power, perhaps at the height of his power. On the surface, certainly to the short-time visitor, all was peaceful and orderly. A foreign consortium managed Iran's most important resource, oil, in conjunction with a government company, under an agreement by which Iran received 50 percent of the profits. The state controlled much of the rest of the economy, though private markets flourished in small-scale industry and in retail trade.

{ *Rose* } In Teheran we stayed at the Hilton Hotel, where we consumed so much caviar and became so sated by week's end that we had no interest in caviar for years. The famed bazaar impressed by its extensiveness and variety. I could not resist buying a delicately wrought gold chain for my sister and another for myself along with a gold medallion with the shah's portrait.

From Teheran we were driven to Isfahan, a famous center of rugs and carpets. Like most tourists, we visited a rug factory and were shocked by what we saw. Large looms were erected vertically to a height of perhaps six or eight feet or more. Perched at the very top of a scaffolding were young girls, not yet in their teens and to our eyes as young as 8. We were told that they excelled at making the delicate knots required, and that they stayed at their task hours at a time. At the time we visited, they were working on a huge rug for a church.

From Isfahan we went on to Shiraz, the jumping-off place for the Persepolis ruins. When Milton asked the driver of the ancient but well preserved Mercedes taxicab that we hired to get to the ruins what the market price for his cab would be, he cited a price that was enough to purchase a new Mercedes in Germany—another example of the phenomenon we observed in India (see chap. 20, p. 309). In order to develop a domestic auto industry, Iran had put a prohibitive tariff on the import of foreign cars and restricted sharply the import of used cars.

A vast extent of ruins dating back to the fifth century B.C., when its construction was started by King Darius the Great to serve as the capital of his extensive empire, Persepolis was discovered and excavated in the 1930s by archaeologists from the Oriental Institute of the University of Chicago. Further excavation and restoration was later undertaken by Iran.

Though extensive and in places well preserved, the ruins gave only a glimmer of the original magnificent structures. Isolated columns stood some fifty feet high, bearing as capitals large statues, generally a double-headed bull or a lion or an eagle. Those statues weighed many tons, yet they had been raised to the top of the high columns and placed stably enough to last for more than two millennia. Like so many ancient ruins that we have visited, these generated humility about the achievements of our own times compared with the past.

When we inquired how a statue could have been raised to the top of a column, our guide explained that sand was piled around the column, presumably as it was erected, and the statue then hauled up the inclined plane by the usual hordes of human, or perhaps animal, power. We are not competent to judge the correctness of this explanation. What is clear is that primitive methods can achieve results we marvel at provided only that there are enough human laborers (slaves) and enough time at the disposal of an absolute ruler. The marvelous results remain; the record of the suffering that made them possible disappears in the mists of time.

A frieze on the eastern staircase of the Apadana Palace shows representatives of the countries under the suzerainty of the Persian emperor bringing gifts and offerings and the produce of their countries for presentation to the king. As we approached the frieze, we were impressed with how clear and sharp the images were, and one of us remarked to the other, "Do you suppose these are reproductions? They look too good to be two thousand years old." Another tourist carefully examining the frieze overheard us and said superciliously, "Of course they are original. They fell face down in the sand, and thus were protected until they were rediscovered in the twenties." I seem to remember we later read this in the guidebook.

Southern Spain, 1971

{ *Milton* } After the special meeting of the Mont Pelerin Society at Montreux in September 1971 (see chap. 21), we participated in a seminar on economic policy organized by *Mundo*, a weekly review published in Barcelona. The announced subject for the seminar was "Development without Inflation: Monetary Policy versus Fiscal Policy." However, I remember the extracurricular activities better than I do the substance of the discussion, a result foreshadowed in the letter of invitation, which said: "the 13–16th days [of September] are scheduled for work and papers, while from the 17th to the 19th foreign professors are invited to a trip through Spain so that they may know our country, even though in a sort of 'bird's-flight.' "

Several visits planned for us on this trip are still very vivid in our memory. Sebastian Auger, president of *Mundo* and an influential Catholic layman, arranged a visit for Richard Musgrave, another participant in the conference and a leading authority on public finance, and me with Prince Juan Carlos, who had been designated by Franco as the future king and head of state. He was sworn in as king in 1975 after the death of Franco. The Prince had studied at Harvard, where he had taken a course from Musgrave. He proved to be a highly intelligent and extremely pleasant young man.

{ *Rose* } When a trip to a farm that had a private bullring was suggested we hesitated before accepting. We had been to a bullfight in Madrid in 1953 because our good friend and colleague Earl Hamilton said "You must see a bullfight when you're in Spain." We went, and vowed never to go to another. The performance at the private farm, however, was very different. The host staged bullfights with several bulls, entirely professional except that there was no final fatal sword thrust. Guests were invited to play the part of the bullfighter. Milton did not take up that invitation. We were told that despite the lack of blood at the mock bullfights, the bulls involved would be slaughtered the next day. The experience they had gained would make them too dangerous to use again.

We visited a number of bodegas in Jerez de la Frontera, observing the complex and lengthy process by which wine from many vintage years were blended to make the final sherry while maintaining the homogeneity of the product. We had a more extended visit to a splendid bodega at Sanlúcar when we paid a visit to our friend Gerarda de Orleans-Borbón at her home in Sanlúcar. We first met Gerarda in Peru in 1981 when she was the wife of Hernando de Soto. Mr. Mauricio González-Gordon Diez, the proprietor of the bodega that we visited with Gerarda, collects signatures of guests on barrels of sherry—a rather unusual autograph collection. At his request, Milton and I autographed a barrel for his collection. At this bodega, we observed the ritual of tasting maturing sherry to determine whether it is ready to be bottled. We were impressed by the grace with which the taster in one motion swoops the long dipper out of the barrel and over his head, and pours it into the glass in his other hand, all without spilling a drop.

Our visit to Barcelona included the Picasso museum, devoted to Pablo Picasso's early years, spent in Barcelona (the "blue" period). The museum was filled with traditional landscapes, portraits, and the like, to our eyes more impressive than the later more radical paintings.

Heights and Depths, 1972

Nineteen seventy-two was truly a year of extremes for us. Some of the happiest events of our life occurred; also, some of the most trying. Our first grandson, Richard Kyle Stansby, was born on July 4, the same month and year that his grandfather attained the ripe age of sixty. We added another member to our family when our son married Diana Forwalter in September. We celebrated Milton's sixtieth birthday belatedly at a wonderful gathering in Charlottesville attended by many of his students and professional associates. These were three of the happiest events of the year. At the other end of the scale, the final weeks of the year were anxious ones. Milton, who up to this time had enjoyed excellent health, spent about two weeks in the hospital in Chicago for observation and treatment for a coronary problem, and when the treatment proved unsuccessful, had open-heart surgery at the Mayo Clinic.

The year began in Los Angeles where Milton took part in a TV program on conservatism with Clare Booth Luce, William F. Buckley, Jr., and James Buckley. The Buckley brothers were on their way to Antarctica, we to Hawaii where Milton was scheduled to teach the winter quarter, and Clare was going to her home in Hawaii. So, after the program, we flew to Hawaii together. It was a memorable trip. The lively discussion begun on the program continued. In addition, I enjoyed discussing what it means to be a Catholic with Clare and Jim while Milton talked to Bill. When we arrived in Hawaii, we all went to Clare's home for breakfast with Bill Buckley serving as chef. This was a wonderful beginning to four months in Hawaii (see chap. 15).

Fortunately our home away from home in Hawaii was a short distance from Clare's beautiful home, which was full of extraordinary artifacts from all corners of the world—a museum combined with a home. We spent many pleasant hours with her after our first meeting. She was a wonderful conversationalist, and with many interests in common there was always much to discuss. In addition, she and I had recently had cataract surgery, and since this was before the days of lens implants, we were both having problems with the contact lenses that were then available. So we could compare notes and console each other.

Milton had a commitment to give two lectures in the David Horowitz lecture series in Israel (see chap. 27). When planning our itinerary after Hawaii we found that going to Israel from Hawaii rather than Chicago would give us a few days to spend in Japan on the way there. Since we always enjoyed our visits in Japan, however brief, we took advantage of the opportunity and spent four days in Tokyo. While there, Milton met with Prime Minister Sato and discussed exchange arrangements, as well as economic policy. We went on to Hong Kong, and then to Israel. Our stay in Israel was brief as we had been away for some months and were anxious to get home. We flew home to Boston en route to Vermont, and had what for us was a unique and very annoying experience clearing customs in Boston. Believing that we were free to go, we were calling for a porter when an official tapped Milton on the shoulder and asked us to accompany him and a female official to a side office. Once inside, they curtly demanded to see Milton's wallet and my handbag, and proceeded to search them thoroughly without telling us what they were looking for. In the course of examining Milton's wallet, the male official came across one of his business cards and his demeanor changed instantly. Now respectful rather than overbearing, he said something like, "You should probably be questioning me, not the other way around" and immediately let us go. We were as annoyed by his change in demeanor on recognizing Milton's name as by being singled out for close examination without being informed what if anything we were suspected of. As it happened, we had nothing special to declare, but innocence is no defense against bureaucracy.

Sometime later when we saw George Shultz, who as secretary of the treasury at the time was in charge of the customs service, I told him our story and complained of both aspects. George just said it had happened to him and was probably simply a part of a policy of selecting some passengers at random to provide evidence on the effectiveness of the customs procedures.

Except for a trip to California in July to welcome into the world on July 4 our first grandson, we spent the summer "quietly" in Vermont working until September when we went to Montreux, Switzerland, for one week to attend the twenty-fifth anniversary of the Mont Pelerin Society (see chap. 21).

Charlottesville

Sometime during the summer of 1970, Richard Selden, a former student of Milton's, then teaching at the University of Virginia, approached me for ideas about celebrating Milton's sixtieth birthday. A number of Milton's former students, he said, were searching for a suitable way to express their gratitude for the many contributions that Milton had made to their own development as economists, as well as to economic science generally. He wanted to know any suggestions I had about such a celebration and what I thought about the conventional festschrift. I had not given the matter any thought up to this point but I did know from past experience that Milton was not very enthusiastic about festschrifts in general.

The final decision was to hold a conference on October 20 and 21, 1972 in Charlottesville, Virginia. Selden, by then chairman of the Department of Economics at the University of Virginia, was the primary organizer. He also edited the book, *Capitalism and Freedom: Problems and Prospects,* that contains the papers presented at the conference and the discussions that followed. As Selden wrote in the preface to the book, one "may wonder why a conference in honor of a University of Chicago faculty member, and attended by a large number of his University of Chicago colleagues, happened to be held at the University of Virginia, under the sponsorship of that University's James Wilson Department of Economics. The explanation is simple. . . . The James Wilson Department of Economics has long had close ties to Milton Friedman and the University of Chicago's Department of Economics. Five current faculty members . . . did their graduate work at Chicago . . . and Friedman served as principal thesis supervisor" for three of these five. One of the five was Selden himself. Another was Warren Nutter, who wrote the first dissertation that Milton supervised.

Having decided on a conference, the problem remained of narrowing the scope to manageable proportions. Selden wrote: "Milton Friedman's contributions to the field of economics have been so enormous and far-ranging—encompassing such diverse areas as price theory, monetary theory, methodology, economic theory, business cycles, public finance, statistics, monetary policy, labor economics, and international finance—that a dozen conferences would be needed to properly assess his impact." He goes on: the group decided that "the time was ripe for a reappraisal of the broad package of economic reforms set forth by Friedman in his *Capitalism and Freedom* ten years earlier. . . ." The conference was planned to accomplish that task. It covered such economic policy topics as: "The Pathology of Politics," "The Franchise in the Welfare State," "Property Rights," "Pollution and Power,"

"Urban Problems," "Law Enforcement," and finally "A Flexible Monetary Policy."

The occasion was memorable for both Milton and me. We were touched by the many friends who came from distant parts of the country to share in this celebration. Both of our children were there and even our three-month old grandson came. I must confess, however, that contrary to his grandfather's basic principles, he had no voice in deciding whether he wished to attend or not! The conference itself was interesting and lively. In addition to our very vivid recollections of the occasion, we have as souvenirs two albums of photographs taken during the conference.

Open-Heart Surgery

{ *Milton* } Sometime during the summer of 1972, I experienced what I thought were angina pains during the night. My father died from angina pectoris at the age of 49, and I had vivid memories of his suffering and his reliance on tiny nitroglycerine pills, so I have always been concerned about my heart. When we returned to Chicago I saw Dr. Leon Resnekov, a cardiologist at the University of Chicago Hospitals and Clinics. He attempted to control the angina with medication. That proved unsuccessful so he suggested an angiogram, a procedure that shows in great detail pictures of the circulation of the blood through the arteries and thus where any obstructions appear. Chicago did not then have the facilities for doing angiograms so Dr. Resnekov suggested that I go to the Mayo Clinic in Rochester, Minnesota.

A visit to the Mayo Clinic was unlike any annual checkup I had ever had up to that point. After seeing the physician assigned to me on the basis of the particular medical problem involved (Dr. Robert O. Brandenburg, a skilled cardiologist, was my physician), I spent the day going from one clinic to another having every possible test. The next morning I again saw Dr. Brandenburg to get the results of the tests. The angiogram showed one serious blockage. Dr. Brandenburg's judgment was that a heart attack was not imminent but was a likely possibility in the near future. Open-heart surgery to remove the blockage was the only way to avoid a heart attack. We spent a weekend in Rochester pondering whether to go ahead with the surgery then or postpone it for a while.

{ *Rose* } Milton decided that he did not want to live with the uncertainty about a possible heart attack at any time. He preferred to get it over with.

We intended to say nothing about the coming surgery except to our children and closest friends until it was over. However, Milton made the mistake of giving an interview about the economic situation to the local press when we first arrived in Rochester. As a result the media learned about the coming surgery and it was reported by newspapers throughout the country as well as on a number of television programs. The result was a flood of telephone calls from far and near. One reward was a strengthening of our belief that, though Milton had professional foes—people who do not see the world as he does—he had no personal enemies.

By now, bypass surgery has become routine. It was not in 1972. The first successful bypass had been done only six years earlier (at the Cleveland Clinic). The Mayo Clinic had very quickly followed suit.

The care and concern at the Mayo Clinic was impressive. During Milton's surgery, I was monitored for the entire period of the operation. If I left the waiting room, I had to inform the attendant about my whereabouts. They also knew where I could be reached for the entire period of his hospitalization. As it happened, this turned out to be important the first night after surgery. Milton was bleeding slowly internally. At first, the surgeon (Dr. Wallace) thought it would stop in the course of the day. However, when it didn't, he decided to take Milton back to surgery. Close to midnight, I got a call at the motel where I was staying across the street from the hospital. The caller wanted me to come to the hospital because they were taking Milton back to surgery. As it happened, I was on the phone with our good friend Arthur Burns when the call from the hospital came through. This caused anxiety among our friends in Washington as well as at Mayo's. When I got across the street, Milton had already been taken to surgery so I settled down in the nurses' quarters for an anxious wait. Like everyone at the Mayo Clinic throughout our stay, the nurses on duty couldn't have been more solicitous. They provided me with blankets and pillow and when I couldn't relax, they provided me with coffee and cigarettes (I was still smoking). I was touched when Dr. Wallace, after finishing his work in the surgery, came in to assure me that all would be well. He was apologetic about the necessity of having to take Milton back to surgery but he did not know why it happened. Very soon, I was able to go up to intensive care and see Milton. To see him was a relief, but the sight was also painful.

The week or ten days in the hospital went slowly. After the first two or three days in intensive care, when I could only see him for short periods during the day, he was moved to a private room where there were no restrictions on my visits. There were good days and not so good days, such as the one when he was not quite rational and insisted that I could grade the prelim in economic theory that the candidates for the Ph.D. had just taken. Only when, in desperation and fatigue, I broke into tears did he agree that one of his graduate students could do the grading. But gradually, the days got better and he behaved more normally.

The response from friends and strangers, people who wrote "You don't know me but I'm praying for your recovery," was most gratifying. The hospital room looked more like a greenhouse before the week was over and we were delighted to be able to pass some flowers on to others who were less fortunate. While the experience was traumatic for both of us, we have pleasant memories as well as painful ones. We have always felt that we were blessed with many good friends but we didn't realize how many.

We planned to go to Palm Springs for Milton's convalescence. This being the Christmas season, flights out of Minneapolis were booked solid. But, as was true during this whole episode, friends came through. George Shultz somehow made it possible for us to get reservations. The stop in Chicago was facilitated by George Stigler's meeting us at the airport and visiting until our plane took off. When we arrived in Palm Springs we went to the house that Armen Alchian had rented for us. When I went into the garage, I found a car waiting. Troy Allen had arranged that. We spent about two months in Palm Springs. The first few weeks Milton did little but convalesce, but by the end of January he was ready for more activity. A group of aides from Governor Reagan's office came to Palm Springs to discuss a plan for an initiative to limit state expenditures by constitutional amendment, and before we left, he barnstormed the state with the governor in support of the amendment (see chap. 23, p. 389). On February 17, we left Palm Springs and Milton's period of convalescence was at an end. From then on, the physicians imposed no limitations on his activities.

We were so pleased with Mayo's that Milton and I decided to go to the clinic for annual checkups. The report on Milton's condition one year after surgery was so satisfactory that Dr. Brandenburg decided that it was not necessary to do an angiogram to see if all was well. Our visit the second year proved that our confidence in the Mayo staff was justified. My physician felt a small lump in my right breast during the annual physical. A mammogram that he ordered showed no evidence of possible malignancy but he was not satisfied. He brought in the surgeon and between them they decided that the lump was suspicious enough to justify a biopsy regardless of the mammogram. The biopsy was positive. It was agreed that if the biopsy was positive, the surgeon would proceed with a mastectomy. And this is what was done.

I do not recall any discussion about just what kind of a mastectomy was to be performed. We trusted the surgeon to do what he thought best. After I recovered from surgery, the question of further treatment was raised. The physician I talked to was very frank. The clinic was conducting a study but the benefits resulting from either radiation or chemotherapy were at the time very uncertain. He offered me the opportunity to participate in the study if I wished but he made no effort to persuade me. When we returned to Chicago, we talked to several physician friends about how to proceed, and the general feeling was that doing nothing further was probably the best. Since that was our feeling as well, we did nothing more than go in for annual check-ups. Fortunately, there has been no recurrence since then. Though we no longer make our annual visits to the Mayo Clinic, I still get a form every year to fill out about my physical condition. Their statistical survey must be continuing.

Further Travels

Yugoslavia

On March 17, 1973, we left for Europe. Our first visit was to Yugoslavia. The Institute of Investment Analysis had translated a collection of Milton's essays into Serbo-Croatian and invited us to visit Yugoslavia as their guests. Dimitrije Dimitrijevic made the arrangements for our trip. Milton had corresponded with Dimitrije about the monetary studies that he was conducting at the central bank, had visited with Dimitrije when he visited Yugoslavia with Warren Nutter before a CESES meeting in 1967, and Dimitrije then spent a quarter as a visitor in Milton's Money and Banking Workshop in Chicago in 1969.

Aside from visiting the central banks of most of the component states of Yugoslavia and discussing their problems, we were interested in the changes we saw in the country's economic situation since 1962, when we had last been there together. There were many more automobiles in Belgrade in 1973 than in 1962. The ratio of automobiles to people turned out to be one to five— a ratio higher than that in Rome. If salaries were as low as they were said to be, we wondered how so many people could afford automobiles. We were told that individuals could supplement their income in many ways.

{ *Milton* } We became aware of striking differences in levels of living in the several parts of Yugoslavia. Croatia and Slovenia were clearly more developed and economically more advanced than the other areas of Yugoslavia. Montenegro, to take one example, was less developed. We were also well aware of the existence of separate nationalities and the rivalry among them. But these differences almost never surfaced in our contacts. In the many discussions I had in the various parts of Yugoslavia, I was seldom aware whether the person

I was talking with was a Serb, Croat, Bosnian, Muslim, Slovene, Macedonian, or Albanian.

The role of communism impressed us more than the role of regional rivalry. On each of my trips, I was well aware of who was and who was not a member of the Communist party and that it made a great deal of difference in people's position and power. Though many bureaucrats were not members of the party, essentially all top policy people were. Some people would speak as if Yugoslavia were a completely free country in which nobody had to be afraid of saying anything and in which everybody was safe in his job and his activities. Others would make clear that the Central Committee of the Communist party had an extremely powerful influence; that everybody with any sense was extremely careful about what he said, watched his step, was likely to be fired if he did not, and had to know how to play the game in order not to get into trouble.

In visits to industrial enterprises, both in 1967 and during our 1973 trip, my major interest was in the system of worker ownership and self-management. It clearly seemed to be a more productive system than the kind of detailed central control that it superseded and that was practiced in the Soviet Union. But was it a satisfactory alternative to capitalist enterprise? One thing that impressed me in observing such enterprises was the deference paid to the manager by the employees as we walked through the shop floor. The relation was the same as in a capitalist enterprise, even though in principle the manager was hired by the workers rather than the other way around. In practice, the manager was chosen by a managing committee selected by the workers for a term of some years. It was in the workers' self-interest to choose a competent manager.

The key problems at the firm level are different: how to distribute the annual profits of the firm between investment in more or improved capital and wages or wage supplements (e.g., housing). The workers had little incentive to make investments for the future, since they retained no rights to subsequent earnings if they left the enterprise. Several managers told us that they encourage nepotism to counter this problem, giving preference in employment to spouses and children in order to give the workers a greater interest in the future of the company.

Another problem is that existing workers tend to object to the addition of new workers since that reduces per capita profits. Raising external capital was a major problem since only worker enterprises were permitted to hold capital in or lend money to other worker enterprises. The central government repeatedly pressured regional commercial banks (which were also worker enterprises) to provide such capital, and made it possible by infusions from the central bank, a major source of the repeated inflations that plagued the country.

I concluded that the basic defect was the absence of any satisfactory mechanism for financing risky enterprises. Suppose a manager has an idea that he believes has one chance in ten of yielding fifty times its cost. With private enterprise, self-interest will lead to that gamble being taken. In the Yugoslav (or Soviet) system, there is no incentive to do so. If it fails, and nine times out of ten it will, the manager is likely to lose his job. If it comes off, at most he will get a pat on the back and perhaps a minor raise in pay. The only way to finance the venture would be by government subsidy, but any government bureaucrat or political official would have the same disincentive to approve its financing.

Another item that interested us and that we inquired about everywhere we went was the level of income differentials. The communist philosophy that Yugoslavia supposedly followed included Marx's dictum "from each according to his abilities, to each according to his needs." The practical counterpart is near equality of incomes, so in factories, banks, and universities we would inquire about the ratio of the highest income paid to the lowest. In these terms the difference seemed very narrow. For example, at a highly successful electronics plant in Zagreb with some four thousand employees and gross annual sales of about $30 million, the general manager received a salary only seven times as large as the lowest paid employee—a much narrower ratio than in a comparable U.S. plant.

However, the salary does not tell the whole story. There are also very considerable perks. For example, the Narodna Bank in Belgrade provided its key employees with housing, in many cases excellent modern apartments at absurdly low rentals and with the prospect of ownership after a specified number of years. We found that the provision of housing by employers, whether in government or in the self-management enterprises, was very widespread. Furthermore, as elsewhere, the distribution of income is very much affected by how many members of a family work, by moonlighting and other undercover ways of making money. It was impossible for us to reconcile the large number of expensive cars we saw in Belgrade with the supposed egalitarianism. Most of the figures that are readily available exclude the truly privileged: the upper echelons of the Communist party. Their real income was a very much larger multiple of the average income than the income of a factory manager.

{ *Rose* } After two weeks of sight-seeing and visiting with various groups throughout Yugoslavia, the National Bank of Slovenia, where we were visiting, provided a car and driver to take us to Venice, the next stop on our itinerary.

After a stop in Venice for some lectures to a group of students and professors involved in a seminar on economic history, we went on to our final week, which was pure holiday. After brief stops in Siena and Florence we went on to Castel Gondolfo (the locus of the Pope's summer home) where we were the guests of Guido Zerilli-Merimò, an Italian businessman whom we had never met but who had corresponded with Milton on various issues. He had been urging us for some time to pay him a visit at his home. He was a most generous and congenial host, with a fantastic home and garden.

Brazil

Because of Milton's heart surgery, we postponed to December 1973 a trip to Brazil initially scheduled for December 1972. Upon arriving in São Paulo, we were impressed with the tremendous building boom in the city. In the main, new buildings were in the construction stage, indicating that the boom was recent. We wondered whether Brazil, like Spain and the Soviet Union when we were there, would end up with half-finished buildings that years later would be undergoing repairs without ever having been finished.

{ *Milton* } Brazil had been through a period of large deficits financed by a rapid increase in the quantity of money in the late 1950s and early 1960s. This produced an inflation that reached a rate of more than 100 percent and was headed for hyperinflation. Government attempts to suppress the inflation by measures such as fixing prices and wages, controlling foreign-exchange transactions and introducing multiple exchange rates, as always, produced waste, inefficiency, and black markets. A "tight" money policy reduced the rate of inflation to about 30 percent in three years and was accompanied by recession and increased unemployment. After the initial shock had been absorbed, the widespread introduction of escalator clauses, termed "monetary correction" in Brazil, plus the freeing of markets and a period of political stability unleashed unsuspected dynamic forces. The result, as I wrote in a *Newsweek* column (January 21, 1974) on our return from Brazil, was "a period of growth so rapid as to justify the term 'economic miracle.' The explosion is obvious even to the casual visitor. The cars that jam the streets of São Paulo and Rio are almost all new; multistory buildings, both new and still under construction, dot the sky; cranes are almost as numerous as TV antennas, and the air of bustle and hustle is unmistakably different from the pre-Christmas shopping rush. . . . 'Will it really last?' is a question that no one asks yet that all seem to have at the back of their minds."

Unfortunately, it did not last, and Brazil was fated to experience several episodes of near hyperinflation in the following decades. New currencies were introduced in a vain attempt to achieve by name changes what required a real commitment to checking monetary growth.

My many trips around the globe, to countries differing in political and economic organization, stage of development, culture, and many other factors, have taught me how uniform are the economic problems that affect them and how few are the economic principles that are required to explain apparently diverse phenomena. In each country, the problem appears to the participants to be unique and to demand detailed knowledge of local circumstances. Yet, whether the issue is inflation or deflation; scarcity or surplus; balance of payments; boom or recession; economic growth or stagnation, the same principles apply to all and the special circumstances are as likely to distract from as contribute to an understanding of what is going on. Of course, the magnitudes and the details of policy depend on local circumstances and institutional arrangements. The cures must be specific to the particular country, but the ills that afflict the body politic, like those that afflict human beings, are more often generic than specific.

We were taken to Brasilia, the nominal capital of Brazil, a city constructed, beginning in 1957, on a remote plateau 580 miles from Rio de Janeiro. The Brazilians were very proud of their capital. Its description as an "epoch-making event of contemporary architecture" is appropriate. It struck us, however, as a museum full of impressive and attractive buildings meant for show, not use. Our impression was that it was used chiefly for major formal occasions, such as the inauguration of a new president, and for carrying on the more routine business of government, while important political activity took place in Rio. The major government buildings were inspiring as art objects; the planned living quarters conjured up images of Orwell's *1984*: block after block of identical large apartment buildings, laid out in identical patterns, with only a number plate to distinguish one apartment from another, which reminded me of Moscow in 1962. The impression as we left Brasilia was that it was a dead capital.

While in Brazil, we spent a few days in Salvador in the northern state of Bahia. It was a sharp, and pleasant, contrast to the hectic activity in São Paulo and Rio—an older, calmer, more traditional community—one of the very picturesque parts of the country. The people we met in Salvador, as well as in São Paulo and in Rio, were all most hospitable.

Australia

After our trip to Chile (see chap. 24) we went on to Australia on March 30, 1975. Both this trip and a later one in 1981 were arranged by Maurice Newman, then a partner in Constable and Bain, a leading stockbrokerage firm in Australia. Maury is a convinced libertarian, a member of the Mont Pelerin Society, and over the years has become a close friend. On both of our trips to Australia, he spared us all the detailed arrangements and was with us during most of our visit.

We arrived in Sydney on a holiday. We were taken to the big event of the week, the Royal Easter Show, which is run by the Royal Agricultural Society. Many of the features of the show were familiar to us from our visits to county fairs in New England, but the big parade of all the prize cattle was impressive. After that there were the usual parties interspersed between lectures and press conferences. We were entertained on a cruise of Sydney Harbor so as to view the Opera House from the water before being taken to view it at close hand, and eventually, attending a symphony concert there before leaving Sydney.

When Maurice Newman inquired whether we would be interested in crossing the country by train to Durbin, we replied that there were undoubtedly more interesting ways to spend three days in Australia. Instead, we visited, among other places: a large sheep and cattle property; several open-cut, i.e., strip-mining, coal operations; Queensland Alumina, the largest alumina refinery in the world; the wonderful parks, and the Great Barrier Reef. On a later trip, we visited a nineteenth-century gold-mining village that had been preserved as a museum.

Although we have seen many sheep grazing in the fields in northern California, we had never seen the sheep sheared. We were impressed by the highly efficient process by which the sheep is relieved of his coat of wool with a few skilled passes of the electrically powered shears.

The trip to the strip mines took us over wide expanses of country and gave us for the first time an idea of the extraordinary dimensions of Australia. Its land area is roughly equal to that of the United States, but its population is only about 6 percent of ours. Part of the explanation is that the whole central area of the continent is a desert. Even the area we were flying over, used for grazing and for growing some crops, was rather arid in appearance. One result is that what we would call ranches—and they call "stations" or "properties"—are enormous in extent, so people will speak quite casually of having a station of four, five, six, or seven thousand acres.

The coal operation exemplified the benefit accruing from international investment. It was an activity of the Utah Development Corporation, as the name suggests, an American corporation. Dr. Radmanovich, who was in charge of the mine and served as our guide, pointed out that "if the Australians had had to go it on their own, they would be nowhere near as far along and it would have been many years before they would have been effective in the open-cut mining operation."

We were very much impressed by the magnitude of the operation and particularly of the machines. There were two sizes of diggers with baskets, one capable of picking up something like twenty to twenty-four tons of earth or coal at a time and one capable of picking up forty-six tons of coal, both on self-propelled vehicles (I say vehicles but they look more like battleships), which can gradually creep out on the land. They strip away the upper layer of earth, leaving open a rich seam of pure coal. They then strip away the coal, which is loaded, taken away, cleaned, and so on, before being shipped out. Before moving to the next strip, they put the spoil back in the trench from which the coal has been removed, and so keep on moving, strip by strip.

The manpower requirements are much lower than in underground coal mining. According to Dr. Radmanovich the ratio is one to ten for a given amount of coal. The economy of labor is a powerful counter to the environmental objections to strip mining, especially in view of how hard and dangerous underground mining of coal is as an occupation.

{ *Rose* } After seeing another, less profitable mine, we left Blackwater and flew to Gladstone, leaving the following morning by helicopter for Heron Island, a small coral island on the Great Barrier Reef. Our weekend on Heron Island was the high spot of our trip. Flying from the mainland to the island by helicopter gave us a foretaste of what was ahead. Large black flat rays were clearly visible in the waters below. Just as we emerged from the helicopter on Heron Island, we were lucky enough to encounter another remarkable sight: a batch of turtle eggs hatching. The turtles come ashore to lay their eggs in the sand. When the eggs hatch, they all hatch simultaneously since apparently, because of the clouds of gulls and other avian predators, no one baby turtle alone would ever make it across the sand to the water. There is a veritable explosion, in which hundreds of baby turtles come out of the sand and immediately start to make their way, flapping their flippers, to the sea. They are apparently led to the sea by its lighter color, which causes difficulty at night when the lights are on at the resort and some head to the resort instead of the sea. Helpful people with pails pick them up and make sure they get to the right destination.

Heron Island is a small island, some forty or fifty acres in extent, of pure coral. It has a lovely sand beach ringing it and a pleasant resort establishment. We were fortunate to have an introduction to Dr. Rohde, a parasitologist working with a research group based on the island. He was very helpful and informative, taking us in the research station's boat to a reef a mile or two from the island where we could do some snorkeling among extraordinarily beautiful corals and fish. He also took us for a walk on the reef at low tide, giving us an informed tour of the various animals and plants indigenous to the reef. We also enjoyed a trip on a glass-bottom boat and a great deal of swimming in pleasantly warm salt water. All in all, an extremely enjoyable weekend.

The weekend over, we returned from Heron Island as we came, by helicopter to Gladstone, from Gladstone to Brisbane to Sydney, where we met Maurice Newman and left with him on a flight to Canberra, which on first sight reminded us of Brasilia.

Like Brasilia, Canberra too is a planned city. It is a beautiful town which like the Brazilian capital is full of monuments of architecture and has an artificial air as a place for a sheltered population rather than where ordinary life is lived. On the other hand, it is far more human than Brasilia because it is in fact the true capital of the country. The embassies are actually all here. In addition, people live in private houses spread throughout the town. It has one of the highest, if not the highest, average income of any city in Australia. Perhaps even more important, it is much closer to the financial and population centers, Sydney, Melbourne, and Brisbane, than Brasilia is to Rio and São Paolo.

{ *Milton* }   In Australia, as in Brazil, we had numerous meetings with businessmen, central bankers, government officials, especially those concerned with economic policy, and faculty and students at universities. Some were discussions of subjects of common interest; others were occasions for me to give talks on a variety of subjects. In both countries, as in so many others then and since, a major issue was controlling inflation, and consequently, many of the meetings and many of the talks dealt with the sources of inflation and proposed cures. For example, in Sydney, I gave a talk on the topic "Can Inflation Be Cured before It Ends a Free Society" at a dinner attended by some five hundred people. Few other of my audiences in Australia were that large.

In Canberra, we were supposed to have a meeting with Prime Minister Whitlam but his office called it off on the grounds that he was very engaged and had been canceling all his appointments. We heard rumors later that he had canceled for very different reasons. He had read newspaper accounts of the lectures and talks I had given the previous week in which I had put the blame for the inflation strictly on the government, and consequently preferred not to meet with me.

Instead, Maurice managed to wangle tickets for us to get in the back seats of the parliament chamber for the question period, when, as in Britain, the members can ask direct questions of ministers.

Mr. Whitlam showed himself to be a clever debater. He was asked by a member of the opposition whether he had read the comments that I had been making about inflation being caused by money and government expenditures, and whether he was still inclined to believe that the major source of inflation had been the rising wage rates; and if it was the latter, whether he had gotten in touch with Robert Hawke (the president of the Australian Council of Trade Unions). Mr. Whitlam's answer was that the questioner had referred to two eminent authorities, that he thought the second of the two was rather more familiar with this particular situation in Australia than the first, and that therefore he was inclined to accept his views.

In Australia, the immediate problem was inflation at a rate of 15 to 20 percent along with much greater increases in wages resulting in recession and unemployment. The source, as of all inflations in modern times, was rapid growth in the quantity of money, in this case as in most others, to finance rapid growth in government spending. The particular consequences, particularly the rapid rise in wages, did depend on local institutional arrangements and political developments, notably the universal character of legal wage regulation and the election of a Labor government a few years earlier.

A 1981 trip to Australia duplicated many of the activities of the 1975 trip, including meetings and discussions with many of the same people; talks, radio, and TV appearances, and a visit to Canberra. We also had a most enjoyable repeat weekend on Heron Island.

One notable feature of the many public sessions we participated in was the almost invariable question from the floor from a Henry Georgite persuaded that land-value taxation was the panacea for all of Australia's difficulties. Over the years, I have had many contacts with Georgites, who are on the whole very sensible, except for overstating the uniqueness of land, underestimating the difficulty of distinguishing the "original and indestructible" qualities of the soil from those imparted by investment, and overestimating the revenues and favorable effects from their pet single tax. I have generally compromised with Georgites by agreeing that a pure land tax is one of the least bad taxes that is possible.

On our first visit to Canberra, the Labor party was in power, and, as noted above, an appointment to meet with Prime Minister Whitlam was canceled. Now the Liberal party was in power, and again we had an appointment to meet with the prime minister, Malcolm Fraser.* This time it was honored, though we were astounded at the amount of red tape involved; getting through

---

* "Liberal" in this context retains its original nineteenth-century meaning of support for limited government and free markets.

into the prime minister's section and office was much more trouble than I have ever had getting into the White House in Washington. In general, Canberra gives the impression that it is overgrown and much too big for Australia. Australia has a population of about fourteen million, roughly comparable to the population of the state of Illinois. Canberra and the Parliament House ought to be comparable to Springfield, whereas they put on all the pretensions of equality with Washington, D.C.

The discussion with Mr. Fraser was not among the most friendly discussions we have ever engaged in. He was very cold, arrogant, quite uninterested in hearing anything other than an echo of what he himself said. He began by asking questions about the situation in the United States, especially about President Reagan's budget. His initial tendency was to derogate the size of the budget cuts and make unfavorable comparisons between what Reagan was setting out to do and what he himself had succeeded in doing in Australia. Fortunately, I knew what the figures were for Australia and I also knew what the figures were for the United States. That was the first point of less than harmonious feelings.

This discussion continued for something like an hour. In general we (Maurice as well as Rose and I) did not go away with anything like a warm feeling toward Mr. Fraser or a high opinion of his intellect. It is a puzzle that he was able to retain the political position that he did, because, entirely aside from his merits, he gave the impression of being an ineffective political leader. As it turned out, he did not long retain his leadership. Two years later, the Liberal party was out of power and the Labor party back in, this time headed by Robert Hawke.

After the visit with the prime minister, we met a group of Liberal and Country (conservative) party members of Parliament. From there we met with the leader of the Labor opposition, Bill Hayden, mostly for a social chat before going off with him to a dinner with a group of Labor party members. This was by all odds the most acrimonious and least cordial session we had during either of our visits to Australia. Some Labor party members were unreconstructed socialists, not merely left-wingers but real socialists. They reacted as socialists generally do by emphasizing objectives rather than means—how can you be so lacking in compassion; you really want to send these people out into the cold to die; how long a period of unemployment would you be willing to accept, and so on. Hayden himself said hardly a word. Bob Hawke, whom we had met on the earlier trip when he was president of the Australian Council of Trade Unions, a post that he had given up to be a member of Parliament, made a long and involved statement out of which I could make neither hide nor hair.

The most memorable tourist trip on this visit was one that I had occasion to refer to in my book *Money Mischief.* It was to Sovereign Hill Historical Park, a reconstruction of an important Australian gold-mining town dating from the gold rush of the 1850s. One display included an advertisement for ice from Thoreau's Walden Pond. Cut in the Massachusetts winter, the ice was packed in sawdust and carried as cargo in the holds of ships sailing around the tip of South America and across the Pacific to Melbourne, where it was unloaded and hauled by horse-drawn wagons a hundred or more miles to the mining community—a trip of some fifteen thousand miles. All this to satisfy the desire of a handful of newly rich gold miners for cold drinks! (I wonder what Thoreau thought of the ice of "his" pond being used for this purpose?)

I used this incident in my book to illustrate how a gold find can have very different effects on individuals than on the community at large: "The lucky persons who first extracted the gold were clearly enriched. But what about the community at large? At the end of the process, the community was worse off." As the new gold spread throughout the world, its main effect was simply to raise the price level in countries adhering to the gold standard. Everyone who held wealth in nominal money units in those countries suffered a capital loss—the equivalent of a wealth tax. This loss financed the activities involved in extracting and distributing the new gold, including the cost of dragging ice from Massachusetts to Australia.[8]

New Zealand

During the year prior to our second trip to Australia, I had received several inquiries from New Zealand about the possibility of a visit. One was from Don Brash, at the time general manager of Broadbank, a large merchant bank, and was stimulated by his reading *Free to Choose.* Another inquiry came from a producer of Television New Zealand following their screening of the "Free to Choose" TV program. So we asked Maurice Newman to include a visit to New Zealand in the itinerary he was planning for us. With his usual efficiency he did so by arranging for John McDowell of a New Zealand brokerage house linked with Bain and Co. (formerly Constable and Bain) to serve as our host in New Zealand. After our visit in Australia Maurice accompanied us to New Zealand for an extremely pleasant ten-day visit, including the usual discussions with economists, businessmen, and politicians, public talks, and radio and television appearances. Our visit came not long after New Zealand Television had screened "Free to Choose," so I experienced a greater degree of public recognition than I otherwise would have had.

As Maurice had done in Australia, our New Zealand hosts made our trip especially pleasurable by accompanying us on tourist expeditions, enabling us to combine sight-seeing with economic inquiry.

{ *Rose* } Donald Brash and his wife accompanied us on a trip to Wellington, the political capital of New Zealand, and to Christchurch, an industrial and educational center. The tourist feature that we found most interesting in Christchurch was the location of the windows in a Christchurch College dormitory. Built in the nineteenth century, the plans were drawn up by architects from Cambridge, England. Following the common practice they located all the windows on the south side of the building to get the benefit of the sun. But New Zealand is in the Southern Hemisphere, where the sun traverses the northern half of the sky during the day, not the south. Yet here stands the dormitory, built according to the architects' specifications with all the windows facing the sunless south!

Don was running for a seat in Parliament at the time. He was defeated but remained very much involved in government. We were very favorably impressed by his understanding of monetary and economic issues, and by his general ability.

John and Julie McDowell accompanied us on a visit to Taupo, a lovely lake on North Island, and to Queenstown, a favorite tourist spot far south on South Island on Lake Wakatipu, famous for its trout fishing. One charter company was headed by a well-known Olympic athlete, who advertised that he would guarantee a catch to anyone hiring his services. John hired him and his boat for our fishing expedition. Milton had long regarded himself as a jinx to any fishing party. We set out one morning on a fine boat with rods and lines out equal to the number in our party. Hours passed; we had an excellent luncheon and turned our attention back to serious fishing. No bites, no catches for hours on end. The shadows lengthened and other boats were starting to return to dock, but we kept trying. Finally, just as our guide was deciding that we too would have to return, a bite, and that rod was hastily handed to Milton. With some help, he succeeded in landing a large trout and our guide's boast was vindicated.

{ *Milton* } When we were in New Zealand in 1981, the government, controlled by the conservative National party, with Robert Muldoon as prime minister, was pegging the exchange rate by imposing extensive foreign-exchange control, maintaining wage and price control, intervening extensively in the economy, and presiding over a rising inflation.

In 1984 the conservative government was replaced by a Labor party headed by David Lange. Under the impetus of its minister of finance, Roger Douglas, the Labor government did a U-turn to free-market policies, eliminating exchange controls, freeing the exchange rate, prices, and wages, and privatizing government enterprises. A major step was converting the central bank to a quasi-private entity under contract to the government and charged with the specific task of eliminating inflation. Don Brash was named governor. His contract with the government commits the bank to contain the inflation rate between limits (currently, 0 to 4 percent) jointly agreed on by himself and the government. If he fails, his contract can be terminated. Don has been extremely successful. The rate of inflation has come down from nearly 20 percent when the bank was established to the neighborhood of 2 percent currently. This is part of the remarkable transformation that has been produced in the New Zealand economy by the transformation of one of the most collectivist welfare states in the West into one of its freest economies.

The short-term effect was as usual a period of difficult readjustment, which did lead to the reforming Labor party's being turned out in a subsequent election. However, its policies were continued. As the changes have been absorbed, New Zealand has achieved rapid growth without inflation and has become another example of the long-term benefits of free markets.

One final pastoral note. In New Zealand, deer had traditionally been a nuisance, difficult to keep out of gardens and voracious in their appetite. They roamed wild and were shot on sight—very similar to the situation at our second home in California where, despite every effort to fence the deer out, they continue to make inroads and are a menace to Rose's garden. The difference is that we do not shoot them and there are severe limitations on hunting deer.

In New Zealand, the situation was transformed when it was discovered that the powder that forms on a deer's antlers is regarded as an aphrodisiac in the Orient and is much in demand. Deer rapidly became valuable animals cultivated to produce a marketable product and are now fenced in rather than out.

South Africa

In early 1976, we spent almost three weeks in South Africa and Rhodesia (now Zimbabwe) at the invitation of Meyer Feldberg, then dean of the Graduate School of Business of the University of Cape Town.

Like many other white South Africans, our host, Meyer Feldberg, emigrated not long after our visit, initially to a teaching position at Northwestern, then successively became dean of the business schools at Tulane, where he again served as our host in 1984, the Illinois Institute of Technology, and currently Columbia University.

I gave the usual talks at universities, public forums, and dinners arranged by business groups, met with officials at the Reserve Bank, the Ministry of Finance, and other government agencies to discuss economic problems of special significance. The chief economic issues in South Africa included inflation, monetary policy, exchange control, and exchange rate policy. The problems, the consequences of the attempted solutions, and the possible cures were the same as in the other countries we had visited. Our major reward from the trip was exposure to a complex society very different from any that we had encountered, one that was in the early stages of working out its fundamental contradictions. Our visit only reinforced abhorrence of the apartheid policies imposed by the Nationalist government. Yet it made us recognize, as we had not before, how complex the actual situation was.

The most interesting, and informative, day of our visit was spent with Gatsha Buthelezi, a hereditary chief of the Zulus and the equivalent of the prime minister of Kwa Zulu, the second most advanced of the homelands that the Nationalists had established. Buthelezi was and remains a leading figure in South Africa.

Kwa Zulu consisted of twenty-eight bits and pieces, some large, some small, resulting from gerrymandering to assure that whites were not dispossessed. We met at a hotel in one of the white enclaves that had been created in this process. The end of apartheid has changed the political situation but has not produced a situation that is satisfactory to Buthelezi and the Zulu nation.

The day was divided into two parts. In the morning we attended a meeting that Buthelezi had with white advisers from the Nationalist government to discuss highly detailed and specific plans for industrial and commercial development in the independent Zulu homeland that was supposedly coming. Buthelezi was cooperative and spoke as if he agreed with the white advisers that an independent homeland would in fact be established and become an independent state along the lines of the Transkei—that is, as if the Nationalist vision of apartheid was capable of being realized.

After lunch with Buthelezi and the white advisers, we retired to a much more private conversation with Buthelezi, his black economic adviser, Feldberg, and myself. The women went off on a sight-seeing expedition in town. Now the discussion changed character altogether. Buthelezi stressed that he was going along with what the South African government was doing because the most important thing for his people was to get them more jobs and more opportunities, and this was a way of doing so. At the same time, he had no illusions whatsoever about the long run. He thought that the idea of a separate Kwa Zulu state broken up into bits was utterly impractical.

His discussion of the attitude of his people and the pressure for violence—with young radicals asking him why on his return from foreign trips he did not bring guns rather than books—brought home to us more than anything else how untenable the current situation was and the likelihood of a bloodbath in the course of its transformation. We have not yet seen the final results of the end of apartheid. However, a bloodbath has so far been averted.

Buthelezi, whom we saw again some years later when he visited San Francisco, made a very favorable impression on us. I still use a lovely carved olive walking stick he gave me as a memento.

We had lunch with Helen Suzman at her home in Johannesburg. She had been the most prominent and outspoken opponent of apartheid, and for some fifteen years the lone representative in Parliament of the Progressive Reform party, whose aim was to end apartheid. A large part of the discussion was devoted to the theme that the only way a multiracial community could develop was through a laissez-faire economic policy that would make it possible for people to cooperate economically without legislative action and without necessarily mixing socially. Mrs. Suzman was very graphic in describing the situation in Soweto and obviously knew a great deal about the problems and difficulties of the black community. We were much impressed at this lunch, as we had been on many occasions, by the sharp difference between the English-speaking, and in particular the Jews, and the Afrikaners in their attitude to future prospects. "There is no sign," I wrote in my notes on the trip, "among the Afrikaners of . . . any real contemplation of the possibility of emigrating. . . . But we met hardly any English-speaking person who did not have somewhere under the surface the possibility of providing a second line of defense for himself or his children. In Helen Suzman's case, although she is obviously deeply involved in the politics of South Africa and has no intention of leaving or getting out, the Suzmans' children are all abroad, one daughter in London and one daughter in Cambridge, Massachusetts. And this was the pattern."

A lunch hosted by the Afrikaner chairman of the Mobil Oil South Africa Company, at which all the guests were Afrikaners, brought this difference out most sharply. As I wrote in my notes, "they felt themselves very strongly in control of the situation, expressed a very strong degree of confidence in the stability of the situation in South Africa and in its permanence, talked in terms of themselves and their ancestors having been there for hundreds of years and were going to be there for hundreds of years more." Ultimately, of course, it was an Afrikaner, Frederik De Klerk who, in cooperation with Nelson Mandela, presided over the end of apartheid.

We were reminded again and again of the emphasis on ethnic purity which tends to foster the closeness of every separate group. At the time of our visit to South Africa, President Carter could be berated for using the term ethnic purity in the United States but by now it has become commonplace. Our own increasing emphasis on ethnic purity—i.e., multiculturalism—threatens a similar balkanization of the United States.

One memorable incident was a visit to the Western Deep Gold Mine, at the time and perhaps still the largest and deepest gold mine in the world. The trip began with a change of costume to miner's dress, consisting of white coveralls, miner's boots (which are very heavy), and a cap to which could be attached a safety light. We were then taken to the pit of the mine where we went down something like two miles underground. We went down in a succession of three elevators, each one taking us to a lower level.

When we got down to ten thousand feet and started walking through the passages, it was like a science-fiction movie, with enormous rooms filled with machinery and equipment. In order to make work possible underground, air conditioning is necessary, because for every hundred feet or so that you go down the temperature tends to go up 1°F. That means that at ten thousand feet below ground the temperature is a hundred degrees warmer than at the surface, much too hot to permit working without air conditioning.

The extraordinary thing is that all this engineering is required to bring out gold that tends to run in a very narrow strip, perhaps the width of a pencil. On the average, we were told, two tons of rock must be brought to the surface and processed in order to get one ounce of gold.

Back at the surface we were briefed on some of the mine's labor problems and how they handled the completely unskilled, illiterate people whom they bring in for work in the mines from both South Africa and neighboring countries. Because the workers speak many different dialects, a completely artificial language has been developed to use in the mines. It is a very simple language, can be taught readily, and is a kind of lingua franca to enable the miners to communicate with one another. Although wages might seem low by comparison with urban wages, they are very high by comparison with the alternative income that the miners can get, which explains the inflow from other countries.

A helicopter flight over the waters that surround Cape Town was unforgettable. One island is the favorite home of sea lions and was literally covered with them. As the helicopter passed over it, the noise frightened the sea lions, which produced the spectacle of literally hundreds of sea lions simultaneously diving from the rock into the ocean.

Rhodesia

{ *Rose* } From South Africa we went to Rhodesia (now Zimbabwe), where we spent two and a half days in Salisbury making the rounds, visiting with officials of various private groups, the government, and the Reserve Bank, and then spent three days at a game park and visiting Victoria Falls before leaving to return home.

Rhodesia and South Africa display both similarities and differences. The most striking difference derives from the relative number of whites: in South Africa, one-fifth of the population; in Rhodesia, one-twentieth. Apartheid could appear viable in South Africa, not in Rhodesia. To our eyes, race relations in Rhodesia appeared to be far better than in South Africa. We saw no evidence of that petty apartheid—separate post office entrances, toilets, and the like—that was our shame in the American South and that we found so galling in South Africa. The education of blacks had been proceeding by leaps and bounds. Half or more of the students at the University of Rhodesia were black.

The streets of Salisbury gave a visual impression of a black sea with occasional white faces, bringing to life the twenty-to-one population ratio. It is very difficult to reconcile that visual impression with any widespread oppression of, or feelings of oppression by, blacks. If it existed, Rhodesia could not easily maintain such internal harmony or so prosperous an economy. That was then.

One episode at Victoria Falls brought home the excellent relations between blacks and at least some whites in Rhodesia. When we arrived at Victoria Falls we were met by Miss Dee Gilpin, a courier for the tourist agency handling our trip. When she drove up to the park to take us to see the falls, she threw the keys to a black attendant and asked him, speaking in Shona, his native language, to park and watch the car for us. We expressed surprise at her casualness in relying on him. She replied that the natives were extremely reliable and made light of the matter. Whenever she talked with police or park officials, as well as with waiters at lunch, there was a palpable change in their attitude toward her because she spoke their language. Their faces lit up with recognition and with a feeling of comradeship. Similarly there was no element of condescension in her attitude toward them.

It turned out that her parents had come to Rhodesia some forty-five years earlier and had been very successful farmers. She and her two brothers had been born in Rhodesia. As I wrote in my notes, "she was extremely, virulently, and chauvinistically patriotic about Rhodesia, and had nothing but contempt for the attitudes of the British and Americans who had been opposed to it.

439

. . . She was about as one-sided as anybody we came across in Rhodesia. But then it was also true that she and her parents, and one of her brothers at least, were planning to spend the rest of their lives in Rhodesia, and were very glad to be able to do so."

1976 at Home

{ *Rose* } Nineteen seventy-six was Milton's final year of teaching at the university. As usual, he taught in the winter and autumn quarters and we spent the spring and summer quarters in Vermont.

Before leaving Chicago for Vermont, we turned over our apartment on Dorchester Avenue to George Stigler and rented a furnished apartment for the fall quarter.

That summer, on July 29, our second grandson, David and Diana's son Patri, was born in Blacksburg, Virginia, where they had just moved and where David was scheduled to begin teaching at the Virginia Polytechnic Institute in the fall.

On our way from Vermont to Chicago later that summer, we stopped at Blacksburg to be introduced to our new grandson, only to find that David and Diana were having marital problems. These came to a head not long after, when Diana took Patri and went to live with her parents in Chicago.

Like his father, David loves children, and was devastated at the breakup of his marriage and the prospect of being a part-time father. The separation, however traumatic, was amicable. Diana would have custody, with the understanding that David could visit Patri, which he did frequently, and have custody during the summers as soon as that was feasible. Diana subsequently remarried and moved to Pennsylvania, on the Main Line out of Philadelphia. Patri was schooled there and spent every summer with David, to their mutual satisfaction.

Chapter Twenty-Six

THE NOBEL AWARD*

Announcement of the Award

{ *Milton* } I left Chicago about seven o'clock on the morning of October 14, 1976 for Detroit to spend the day in Michigan campaigning for a proposed amendment to the Michigan constitution, Proposal C, designed to set an upper limit to spending by the state government—the counterpart to Proposition 1 that then Governor Reagan had proposed in California three years earlier. Lew Uhler and several local people involved in the campaign met me at the airport in Detroit. We drove to the Press Center in Detroit, where arrangements had been made for a press conference. On the way, we did not turn on the radio because we were talking about our plans.

When we got to the Press Center, I was surprised by the number of photographers and reporters in the parking lot. I knew that Proposal C was important but didn't think my campaigning for it deserved that much attention. As I got out of the car a reporter came up to me and said, "Tell me, what is your reaction to the award?" "What award?" I said. He handed me a press release, a Teletype sheet, which contained an announcement about the Nobel award. That was my first knowledge of it. It was a marvelous coincidence because, although Proposal C ultimately lost, the attention I received in campaigning for it increased exposure to it manyfold.[1] From that point on, I was repeatedly impressed with the attention devoted to this award.

*Milton's part of this chapter is mostly adapted from Milton Friedman, *The Nobel Prize in Economics, 1976,* a talk given at the Hoover Institution on January 29, 1977 (Stanford, Calif.: Hoover Institution, 1977). Rose's part is mostly adapted from Rose D. Friedman, "Milton Friedman: Husband and Colleague—(10)," *Oriental Economist,* February 1977.

{ *Rose* } In his first reaction to the news of the award, Milton responded to journalists' questions by saying that the award was "not the pinnacle of my career" and that he would not himself "choose the particular seven people who make these awards as the jury to which I would want to submit my scientific work." This was quoted without the rest of his statement and provided some journalists with the opportunity for their usual colorful comments, such as that he reacted with "characteristic gall," "brutally candid," and "pure Friedman, arrogant to the last where many other men would have tried to be humble." As I wrote in the *Oriental Economist*, "No one would ever call my husband humble, but only someone who did not know him or deliberately wished to misrepresent him would describe him either as 'arrogant' or with 'characteristic gall.' I should perhaps add parenthetically that the journalists who described him in this fashion have always been unsympathetic to his political views."

Few reported Milton's explanation of what he considered the pinnacle of his career, and what jury he would select to judge his work. However, one week later when he appeared on the TV program *Meet the Press* and a panelist asked these questions, Milton replied: "I believe the true test of a scholar's work is the judgment that is made not at the time his work is being done, but twenty-five or fifty years later. . . . The jury I would like to have judge my work is the economics profession not today, primarily, but twenty-five or fifty years from now, and the real pinnacle of the work would be the embodying in the whole body of economic analysis of some of the work I have done."

Not all editorial comment after the press conference was negative. An Associated Press business analyst who was present called the particular press conference in the parking lot of the Detroit Athletic Club "a setting that was perfectly fitting." Milton's activity in this connection "was typically Friedman. . . . He expressed his true feelings, honestly and without guile, and he offended many people. . . . The philosophy . . . and the practical activities that emanate from it, are based in his unshakable belief in free men and markets, unencumbered by government. . . . His influence has been pervasive and on many levels. While never forsaking the intellectual quality of his work, he has become a columnist, debater, commentator, consultant, and popular teacher." Or again, Steven Rattner, in an editorial in the *New York Times*, "Economist in the Public Cause," after listing the many areas of public policy that Milton had influenced, pointed out that, "Throughout the long years of advocating laissez-faire principles and monetary economics, even his critics agreed that he never sacrificed his intellectual integrity. He turned down a number of government posts partly because he did not believe that he would be able to maintain his principles."

{ *Milton* } In a talk at the Hoover Institution in January 1977, I elaborated further on my reaction to the awards. I noted that however much I may have personally benefited from the award, the whole system of Nobel awards may well do more harm than good in two different ways. In the first place, it causes the public at large to attribute to the opinion of people who receive this particular award an importance that is utterly unjustified. It converted Linus Pauling into an expert on Vitamin C, William Shockley into an expert on genetics, and George Wald into an expert on Chile. That's one effect, but I don't believe that it is the major problem.

The major problem is suggested by the remark Rose has quoted that I made in Detroit in the parking lot when I was asked whether I regarded the award as the pinnacle of my career. My statement was interpreted as a criticism directed at the members of the committee personally—something that I never intended. The particular people who made the choice are eminent, able scholars who did their best. But is it desirable in any discipline that a few scholars who have made their mark in that discipline should have the power to decide the kind of work that is prestigious, on which other scholars ought to concentrate if they want their work to be recognized as important? Is it desirable to have that much centralization of power effectively directing the course of research in basic fields? The effect is not restricted to economics; it is the same for physics, chemistry, or any other area. A friend of mine highlighted the essential point when he wrote that he agreed with my statement, and went on to say, suppose that only one person made the choice.

I hadn't quite realized until we were in Stockholm how much the Nobel Prizes mean to Sweden. Wrap together the World Series in baseball, the Super Bowl in football, and the presidential election, and you have a rough idea of what the Nobel Prizes mean there. The award ceremony is the great event of the year. I remarked to someone in Stockholm, "I understand that the Nobel Prizes and the spring breaking up of the ice are the two great events in Sweden." With utter seriousness, he said, "Oh, the breaking up of the ice doesn't hold a candle to the Nobel Prizes!"

{ *Rose* } I received the news of the award in Chicago after some difficulty. On our return from Vermont in October, we had moved to a temporary apartment. This was to be our last quarter at the University before Milton's retirement and we were moving to San Francisco at the beginning of the next year. By then George Stigler was occupying our apartment, so he got the first message from the Nobel Committee and gave them our new telephone number. Milton had already left for the airport when the call came. I not only got the news first, but also was besieged by calls from news media. Like Milton, but for a different reason, I disappointed reporters who asked me whether I was proud of my husband—the implication being now that he had received the Nobel Prize. My answer was "I have always been proud of my husband; it didn't take the Nobel Prize to persuade me."

As I said in the *Oriental Economist,* "The mountain of editorial comment both in the United States and abroad as well as the personal messages which we are still receiving . . . are not only laudatory but many capture my husband's personality as well as his achievements. The overwhelming sentiment is that the prize is not only well deserved, but long overdue. . . . The *Wall Street Journal* started its editorial of congratulations with 'We offer our greatest congratulations to the Swedish Academy of Science which has just awarded the Nobel Prize in Economics to Milton Friedman. The academy's selection is a credit to its members.' Like the *Wall Street Journal,* the *Financial Times* of London begins its editorial 'The Timeliness of Milton Friedman' with 'Congratulations are surely due to the committee concerned rather than to Professor Friedman on this Nobel Prize in economics; it is overdue. Friedman is unquestionably the most influential economist of our day, and events now seem to be conspiring to give a harsh demonstration of the truth of some of his most important insights.'"

The reaction that it was overdue raises two different questions: (1) why did people expect it to come sooner and (2) why *did* it take so long? I tried to answer these questions at the time in the *Oriental Economist,* by giving a little of the history of the economic award:

> The Nobel Memorial Prize in Economics is a late comer. It was not established by Alfred Nobel. It was established by the Central Bank of Sweden to commemorate its tercentenary. The first prize was awarded in 1969.
>
> The first year that the Nobel Prize in Economics was to be awarded there was a great deal of guessing among economists and economic journalists about who would be the first winner. Two names appeared in every newspaper story or conversation about the coming award—Paul Samuelson and Milton Friedman. Of course, the lists included other names as well but I believe that I am correct in saying that all lists were headed by these two names. When the first year's prize went to Ragnar Frisch of Norway and Jan Tinbergen of the Netherlands, the guessing people were taken somewhat aback but quickly recovered because it seemed rather fitting that the first prize should go to two Europeans.
>
> The second year there was somewhat less speculation about the

possible winners but the two names most often mentioned remained the same. Paul Samuelson won the prize that year and as my husband wrote in his *Newsweek* column on Paul Samuelson "The Award to Professor Samuelson is a well-deserved honor for scientific work over many years."

When my husband was passed over for the next five years, it seemed obvious to me as it did to many colleagues, that there was something in addition to contribution to economic science that was being weighed in the scale. And I, at least, was no longer excited about "who would win the prize." In this sense, when the word came on October 14, I was taken by surprise.

A colleague of my husband's in his letter of congratulations, sent from France, expressed my feelings at the time better than I can myself. "I must confess to being surprised. Not that I doubted that one day you would be awarded the Nobel Prize. It would be a scandal if you were not. But I had thought they would postpone making the award as long as possible. Which momentarily caused me to think that you must have been taken seriously ill."

To the best of my recollection, no one suggested that Milton was unworthy of the prize because he had not made a significant contribution to the science of economics. The one source of negative comment when the prize was announced was that he was "the intellectual architect and unofficial adviser for the team of economists now running the Chilean economy" (see appendix A).

The second question is: Why *did* it take so long? Two of the commentators explained it thus:

Larry Martz, assistant managing editor of *Newsweek* at the time, in a column "A Nobel for Friedman": "If his peers were voting, Friedman would long since have had the prize—and by all accounts, Sweden's Royal Academy has delayed the honor only because of his penchant for controversy and right-wing political activism."

Louis Rukeyser: "If Milton Friedman had been more committed to academic glory and less committed to human freedom, he would have had his Nobel Prize in economics years ago." Rukeyser then refers to the "unprecedented and heated debate" that preceded his selection. As I commented in the *Oriental Economist* at the time: "What is not clear from this and other reports of 'unprecedented and heated debate' is that the debate took place not among the professional economists who made the recommendation for the award but among the broader committee of the Swedish Academy of Science, mostly non-economists, that had to approve the recommendation. Ordinarily, approval by the broader committee is a mere formality—but this time it apparently was not. Professional economists in Sweden and elsewhere are fully aware that my husband's contributions to positive economics have been accepted and acknowledged by economists of every political view, from the extreme right to the extreme left. The non-economists on the committee knew only of his more publicized role as a political gadfly out of sympathy with the dominant socialist philosophy of our time."

The Preliminaries

{ *Milton* } Alfred Nobel was a remarkable Swede, an ingenious inventor, responsible for dynamite in its present form. An extraordinary businessman, he created a multinational firm. The term wasn't used in those days, but the Nobel organization was a multinational firm with companies in many countries throughout Europe. He died on December 10, 1896, and left specific instructions in his will for the awards. He specified five awards, the order in which they were to be awarded, and which institutions should be responsible for selecting the recipients. Because he mentioned physics first, chemistry second, medicine third, and literature fourth, whatever the ceremony, the recipient of the physics award is first, the chemistry award second, and so forth. The fifth prize is a peace prize and is awarded in Oslo by a committee from the Norwegian parliament. It was not awarded in 1976.

As Rose has noted, the economics award was established by the Central Bank of Sweden to celebrate its tercentenary as a central bank. However, the procedures mimic precisely those for the original Nobel award.

Nineteen seventy-six was an extraordinary year for the United States and for the University of Chicago. All seven recipients were Americans (seven because the medicine prize and the physics prize were each divided between two people). Two recipients, Saul Bellow for literature and I for economics were from the University of Chicago. As a result, Chicago went all out. The *Chicago Tribune* sent a reporter and a photographer to Stockholm and each of the local TV stations—ABC, CBS, and NBC—sent a crew to film the ceremony. It was not the first such great year for the university. Exactly a decade earlier, in 1966, the University of Chicago also had two Nobel Laureates, Professor Robert Mulliken in chemistry and Dr. Charles Huggins in medicine.

{ *Rose* } We arrived in Stockholm on Monday, December 6, one day before the calendar of events began in order to give ourselves twenty-four hours to recover from jet lag. Our arrival at Stockholm airport was, I suspect, a new experience for the Nobel Committee and for Stockholm—and most certainly for us. We expected to be met at the airport by a representative from the committee. We did not expect the number of people who were in the reception room to welcome us or the tight security that surrounded us from the moment we arrived until we departed from the same airport.

Every laureate is assigned an attendant from the Swedish foreign office to be at his service for the duration of the week. They take the laureates to the appointed places, arrange their schedules, see that they get to the right places and do little errands for them. Johan Lillehöök was our attendant and certainly enhanced the pleasure of our stay. He was of course at the airport to greet us but he made himself known only at the end of the receiving committee.

Things happened so quickly that I am not at all sure of the order of events. This much I do remember. We were taken to a special VIP room where Professor Carl Bernhard, secretary of the Swedish Academy of Sciences, Professor Erik Lundberg, chairman of the Nobel Economic Committee, representatives from the American Embassy, plus a few other people were waiting for us. Entry formalities were attended to and our luggage magically appeared.

After a most friendly welcome, we were told that no representatives from the press had been permitted at the airport because of the fear of demonstrations. Also, we were to have twenty-four-hour a day police protection for the entire time that we were in Stockholm. There had been demonstrations and newspaper attacks, sponsored by an organization called the Chilean Committee, against Professor Lundberg and the Nobel Committee protesting the award of the economics prize to Milton. As we left the airport for the trip to the Grand Hotel where all the laureates were housed, the official car assigned to us for the week was preceded and followed by police cars. From that moment until we left, we were never without our two bodyguards, two delightful young men to whom we became very attached. In addition, our room was under surveillance day and night by other police. Not even a maid, we discovered, was permitted to enter our room without a police escort! Though we did not feel that we were in any personal danger, we were of course grateful to the Swedish government and the Nobel Committee for taking such precautions.

A press conference had originally been scheduled for the afternoon of our arrival, but Milton asked that it be postponed to the next afternoon. And so it was. This was probably the largest press conference that any laureate had ever had—with the exception of Solzhenitsyn—not because reporters and others from the media had a burning desire to hear Milton's views on economic matters or anything related to his receiving the prize. Questions about economics were conspicuous by their absence. All interest and all questions centered around Milton's alleged participation as an adviser to the Chilean Junta. With a few exceptions, the questions were not particularly hostile. I was impressed by how hard it is to disabuse people of notions that they have formed on the basis of erroneous information. In anticipation, Professor Arnold Harberger, who had arranged Milton's one six-day trip to Chile, had written a detailed letter to Baron Stig Ramel, president of the Nobel Foundation, setting forth the facts about his and Milton's involvement with Chile. This letter was given wide circulation, both in the U.S. where it was published by the *Wall Street Journal* and in Sweden (reprinted as item 5 in appendix A). Yet it did not prevent continuing attacks on Milton based on wholly false information.

Though the journalists in the room were not hostile, we were told that a crowd of demonstrators both in the lobby of the Swedish Academy and on the street were very agitated. After the conference, Professor Bernhard, who had done an excellent job of moderating the press conference, escorted us to the library of the academy. We stayed in the library visiting and admiring the various pieces of furniture and memorabilia until our bodyguards together with other police had arranged for us to leave. Our official car was hemmed in by demonstrators or other cars, we never found out which, so we were taken by a side door to a side street where a police car was waiting. Even with all this precaution, there were still a few demonstrators in our path who managed to get a couple of pictures—nothing more.

We spent the evening of the press conference quietly at an informal dinner hosted for us by Professor and Mrs. Lundberg. Our police guard kept an eye on us from the outside but everything was quiet. Among other things, we reminisced about our visit with our children to the Lundberg home when we visited Sweden in 1954.

Unlike some other laureates, we were not accompanied to Stockholm by our family. Our children were both adults, had their own families, and were busy with their own work. While delighted with the honor given their father, they did not feel it necessary to witness the ceremony. However, we were not alone in Stockholm. Our good friends, Dr. and Mrs. Trygve Hoff (the Scandinavian actress Asa Bye) came to Stockholm from Oslo, Norway, for the occasion. The friendship with Trygve dating from the first Mont Pelerin meeting in 1947 had strengthened and widened over the years to include both our families.

Professor Bernhard hosted the first official affair of the Nobel week, a reception and dinner at the academy. Most of the people who came through the receiving line on this occasion were new to us, as were the other laureates and their wives—except for Saul Bellow and his wife whom we knew from Chicago.

At the dinner after the reception, when we were seated at small tables for about ten people, we began to recognize names and faces. By the end of the week, the faces became very familiar and we were often even able to match names and faces! At the close of the dinner, Professor Bernhard used the occasion to explain in some detail how the Nobel laureates are selected. I don't know whether the secretary of the Nobel Committee makes this explanation every year or whether Professor Bernhard made it this year because of the reports of controversy about the prize in economics.

On Thursday, December 9, the American ambassador, David Smith, and his wife hosted a luncheon at the embassy for the laureates and their wives, some of the members of the Nobel Foundation, and a few Americans who happened to be in Stockholm. Since this year's prizes were all awarded to Americans, the United States was the only country outside of Sweden that played an active part in the festivities.

We went almost directly from the embassy to a reception by the Nobel Foundation. Here, again, we saw many of the same people whom we had been seeing plus, of course, a few new ones. An added feature of this reception for the laureates and their families was a film that the Nobel Foundation had made of the presentation of the awards at an earlier festival ceremony. This was, of course, very interesting to all of us because it gave us some idea of what the ceremony would be like. As it happened, the film we saw was for the year Alexander Solzhenitsyn received the Nobel Prize.

That evening the Stockholm Club of Economics hosted a dinner in our honor. Milton had been asked to give a brief talk after the dinner. When I asked him what he was going to talk about, he said: "In 1954, I gave a talk in Stockholm on 'Why the American Economy is Depression Proof.' So far the predictions in that talk have held up remarkably well and the forces I discussed then are just as relevant now. So I'll give them the 1976 model of the same talk." The talk was followed by questions and some controversy from the older academic people present—many of the same objections that were raised in 1954. Milton later received a letter from a young academic who had been present, asking him not to judge the present state of economics in Sweden on the basis of the discussion at the club!

The Award Ceremony

The three most impressive and memorable events of the week were the ceremony itself, the banquet at the City Hall immediately after the ceremony, and the king's banquet. However, the continuing sequence of TV interviews, press conferences, receptions, dinners and the like kept us quite busy for the eight days we were in Stockholm.

Friday, December 10, 1976 marked the eightieth anniversary of Alfred Nobel's death and the seventy-fifth awards ceremony. Stockholm is not a cheerful city at this time of year. Daylight lasts only four or five hours, and the sun rarely shines. This year, Friday was gloomier than the previous days because it was rainy as well as dark. However, the gaily lit and flower-bedecked Concert Hall where the presentation is made was anything but gloomy. The colorful dresses of the ladies in the audience stood out against the black and white of the men's formal wear.

{ *Milton* } A digression on white tie and tails. The information from the Nobel Committee about the required costume includes a statement that, at your request, they will arrange for you to rent the formal wear, provided you send your measurements. I was preparing to send them my measurements when my tailor in Chicago called and said, "I hear you are going to need white tie and tails in Stockholm. I have a friend who is in the business of renting out formal costumes, and he just told me that he would be delighted to provide you with white tie and tails that I could fix up to your measurements, and that you could use there, provided that you would pay the counterpart of his rental fee to a charity at the University of Chicago that he is interested in." So I had a very well-fitting suit.

{ *Rose* } We were told before we left our hotel that there was to be a demonstration outside the Concert Hall by the same group that had been demonstrating before we arrived in Stockholm. There was much activity among our police guard but we and the Hoffs, who accompanied us to the hall in our car, were never aware of any demonstration. I do not know whether that was because we entered the hall through a door unknown to the demonstrators or whether we were so well surrounded by plain-clothes police that we did not see the demonstrators. The police around us were always in plain clothes, never in uniform. For this occasion, our special bodyguards, like Milton, were in white tie and tails.

Soon after we entered the Concert Hall, Milton left to join the other laureates; the Hoffs and I went to the seats reserved for us. While the hall was filling, the orchestra played a selection of tunes from *West Side Story*, familiar to all Americans. The hall quickly filled so that by 4:50, the appointed time, all seats seemed to be occupied. A blare of trumpets at exactly five o'clock, and King Carl followed by Queen Sylvia, with Prince Bertil and his wife, Princess Lillian, came out to the platform from a door at the left to the music of the "King's Song" played by the Stockholm Philharmonic Orchestra. From a door on the right side of the platform, the laureates, each escorted by a representative of the Nobel Committee, then entered. Their arrival, as usual in the order specified by Alfred Nobel, was also heralded by a blare of trumpets. The laureates took their places on the right side of the platform, their escorts on the left. Already seated on the platform before the arrival of the king and his party were the laureates of previous years, who sat behind the laureates of the current year, and members of the Nobel Foundation who sat at the center rear. The entire audience stood from the time that the trumpets heralded the arrival of the king until the laureates were seated. Music was played between all events on the program.

The actual presentation began after a welcoming oration in Swedish by Professor Sune Bergstrom, chairman of the Nobel Foundation. The representative from the Nobel Physics Committee rose and gave a fairly lengthy speech in Swedish (we were provided with English translations beforehand) justifying the award to the physics laureate or, as in this case, two laureates. At the conclusion of the speech, the escort addressed the laureate, who in the meantime had stood up, in the latter's language. (This year since all laureates were American, English was the only other language used.) This speech was short and ended with an invitation to the laureate to receive the Nobel gold medal, the diploma, and a draft for the monetary prize, from the hand of His Majesty.

At this point, according to custom, there is a blare of trumpets and the laureate from his side and the king from his walk to center stage, the laureate receives the medal and certificates from the king, shakes hands, some words which no one remembers pass between the king and the laureate, and the king returns to his place while the laureate faces the audience, bowing to the applause.

Each laureate was presented in this fashion, chemistry following physics, then medicine and literature. Up to this point, the ceremony proceeded in its time-honored pattern. But then the pattern changed. Professor Lundberg, the representative from the Nobel Economics Committee, gave his speech in Swedish justifying the award. Milton rose from his seat as Professor Lundberg gave the short speech in English ending with the usual invitation to receive the diploma, etc., from the king. At this point, a figure in tails stood up in the far rear of the balcony, hands outstretched, shouting in English "Down with capitalism, freedom for Chile." The moment was short but very tense. Ushers or police, I don't know which, quickly removed the demonstrator from the hall. Professor Lundberg in a low voice apologized to Milton for the interruption, ending with "It might have been worse." Since demonstrators were not a new phenomenon for Milton and me, we felt that it might indeed have been worse. Milton and the king proceeded to center stage and after receiving his medal and certificates and shaking the king's hand, Milton stood for a longer ovation than had been received by any of the preceding six laureates.

The audience, overwhelmingly Swedish, was clearly not in sympathy with the demonstrator. Wherever we went during the next few days, we were met with apologies for the occurrence. The Nobel Foundation was embarrassed and immediately set in motion an investigation to determine how the young man got into the hall. Tickets for the Nobel ceremony are distributed in February for the following December. Receiving a ticket is prized very highly. We learned later that the young demonstrator's father received two tickets in his capacity as headmaster of one of the Swedish schools. Late in the afternoon of the festival, the son prevailed upon his father to give him a ticket and took advantage of his father's generosity to make an exhibition of himself.

{ *Milton* } As so often happens, such a demonstration tends to backfire. The immediate result of this one was partly that the young man was grabbed by the marshals and pulled out of the room. In addition, I ended up with twice as long an ovation as anybody else.

{ *Rose* } After presentation of the last prize, the royal family, followed by the laureates and others on the platform, left the stage. One of our bodyguards suddenly appeared and escorted the Hoffs and me to an anteroom where the laureates were waiting to join their wives and families. We then proceeded in our respective cars from the Concert Hall to the City Hall where the Nobel banquet is held.

The Nobel Banquet

We were told that a large demonstration was being staged outside the Concert Hall. Newspapers reported anywhere from two to six thousand people marching up and down with banners protesting Milton's involvement with Chile. Our attendants protected us by using a somewhat roundabout route to take us from the Concert Hall to the City Hall. As a result, we saw the demonstration only in the distance from the windows of our car. The mass demonstration inconvenienced many of the guests much more seriously, both when they initially entered the Concert Hall and later when they made their way on foot from the Concert Hall to the City Hall. The experience did nothing to increase their sympathy for the demonstrators.

Upon arriving at the City Hall, we, along with the other laureates and their wives, were ushered into a large room called the Prince's Gallery for a ceremony at which the foreign minister of the relevant country presents the laureates and their wives to the royal family. This year Ambassador Smith was the only foreign minister in attendance. Like all other Nobel affairs, this one was carefully planned to give the impression of being casual. The laureates and their wives took their places along one side of the gallery. The king followed by the queen and other members of the royal family entered the gallery and moved at a leisurely pace along the receiving line, the ambassador making the introductions. Conversations were brief, informal, and friendly.

This little ceremony completed, the king and queen led the party, in pairs, down a beautiful stairway to the Gold Room. Escorts had of course all been settled beforehand so that there was no confusion. The Gold Room, in which the banquet is always held, was ablaze with light and the scene dazzled the eye. The crosswise tables were already occupied by the other guests before the king's party entered the hall.

The main events during the banquet were toasts, first to the king by the president of the Nobel Foundation and then by the king to Alfred Nobel. At the end of the dinner, a representative of the Nobel Foundation gave a brief talk in English to the laureates and invited the laureates one by one to answer. Each laureate then delivered a brief talk that he had prepared in advance. Since Milton's talk, unlike his scientific Nobel lecture, has not been published anywhere else, I record it here.

> It is a great honor and privilege for me to be here tonight, sharing in the reflected glory from my distinguished colleagues, not only the six fellow members of the class of 1976, but the many more who, over the past seventy-five years, have made the term "Nobel laureate" the highest mark of distinction to which a scholar can aspire.
>
> My science is a late comer, the Prize in Economic Science in Memory of Alfred Nobel having been established only in 1968 by the Central Bank of Sweden to celebrate its tercentenary. That circumstance does, I admit, leave me with something of a conflict of interest. As some of you may know, my monetary studies have led me to the conclusion that central banks could profitably be replaced by computers geared to provide a steady rate of growth in the quantity

of money. Fortunately for me personally, and for a select group of fellow economists, that conclusion has had no practical impact—else there would have been no central bank of Sweden to have established the award I am honored to receive. Should I draw the moral that sometimes to fail is to succeed? Whether I do or not, I suspect some economists may.

Delighted as I am with the award, I must confess that the past eight weeks have impressed on me that not only is there no free lunch, there is no free prize. It is a tribute to the worldwide repute of the Nobel awards that the announcement of an award converts its recipient into an instant expert on all and sundry, and unleashes hordes of ravenous newsmen and photographers from journals and TV stations around the world. I myself have been asked my opinion on everything from a cure for the common cold to the market value of a letter signed by John F. Kennedy. Needless to say the attention is flattering, but also corrupting. Somehow we badly need an antidote for both the inflated attention granted a Nobel laureate in areas outside his competence and the inflated ego each of us is in danger of acquiring. My own field suggests one obvious antidote: competition through the establishment of many more awards. But a product that has been so successful is not easy to displace. Hence, I suspect that our inflated egos are safe for a good long time to come.

I am deeply grateful to you not only for the honor you have conferred on me, but equally for your unfailing Swedish hospitality and friendship.

The banquet came to a close with a most impressive performance by students of Stockholm, come to greet the laureates. Singing was first heard before the students actually appeared. Then we saw them entering the balcony above the banquet hall. First came a student walking slowly bearing the flag of Sweden. Then the student chorus—all moving from the end of the balcony to the open staircase. Small groups of students bearing banners of various student societies followed the chorus and then came students, male and female— hundreds of them—or so it seemed. All were in white tie and tails or long dresses, and the young men all wore the standard student cap—a billed nautical cap made of white soft material.

The singing stopped and one student stepped forward, removed his cap and addressed the laureates in perfect English. The student selected this year to greet the laureates was Lars Wijkman and his talk was a delight for us to hear.

{ *Milton* } Wijkman presented an extremely effective statement of his belief in freedom, of the danger to freedom that arose from government controls and the expansion of government, and of the importance of maintaining a free society that would enable individuals to pursue their own objectives. Well-worded, well-said, and in English, the talk gave us hope that such sentiments were developing among the younger people in Sweden. Wijkman's ringing call for a free society was a welcome contrast to the parrotlike conformity of the demonstrators, a contrast that I suspect was drawn with malice aforethought.

{ *Rose* } The departure of the students, singing as they went, concluded the banquet but not the evening's celebrations. We made our way, following the students, to the so-called Blue Room. Here the students were already dancing. We too did our share of dancing but found it more interesting to talk with groups of students gathered around. Before the evening was over, Milton was presented with a student cap by one of the students and the next day received a Stockholm University tie to go with it. Whether these gestures on the part of the students were their way of apologizing for the one among them who performed so disrespectfully at the presentation of the awards or whether they was just a result of the usual affinity that Milton has with students of all lands, and vice versa, I cannot say, but we were touched.

For us the party broke up at midnight because we knew that there was more ahead.

St. Lucia

We had been told earlier of the St. Lucia tradition—that the morning after the festival banquet a modern St. Lucia, not the Christian martyr who died in Syracuse in the year 304, but a young candle-crowned girl playing the St. Lucia role, and her friends would come to our room to serenade us and bring coffee and "St. Lucia buns." However, in the excitement, we had completely forgotten this bit of local lore.

{ *Milton* } About seven o'clock that morning someone knocked on our door, which of course was locked. I went to unlock it and looked out, and an enterprising photographer took my picture in pajamas with the lovely young girls in their white dresses and the crown of candles. I must say that I got more exposure (in both senses) through that picture than through any other picture that's ever been taken of me. The girls came in, served us coffee and St. Lucia cookies, and sang some songs. It's a lovely custom.

King's Banquet

{ *Rose* } The night following the festival banquet, we went to the king's banquet for the laureates given in the Royal Palace. At the appointed time, our car was announced and we came down to the lobby. We were driven across a bridge, through the narrow streets of the old town with its street markets, to the island on which the palace is situated. Passing through the palace gates with its guards, the car finally pulled up at the canopied entrance to the palace. Since neither our bodyguards nor our foreign office attendant was invited to the king's banquet, we were on our own once we entered the palace. On our own that is, if account is not taken of palace guards on all sides. We had no difficulty finding our way up the broad carpeted stairway, going from one level to another, at the end of which was a cloakroom where we left our outer garments. One more flight of stairs brought us to the salon where the other laureates and their wives along with a number of men and a very few women were gathered. Somehow or other, a receiving line was formed just before the royal family entered the room with very little fanfare and leisurely made their way through the receiving line. Conversation was brief but we were welcomed graciously to the palace.

After this brief ceremony, the king led the way into the banquet hall. As at the festival banquet, finding one's escort or lady to be escorted offered no difficulty—all had been arranged. Men outnumbered women at this banquet because, as we were informed, many men from the Nobel Foundation and former laureates were invited without their wives.

Many toasts, but fortunately no speeches, punctuated an elegantly served dinner. At its conclusion, the king led the way into the grand salon where people visited in groups until very inconspicuously a young lady (from the royal household, I assume) approached and invited us to go over to talk with Prince Bertil and his wife. We followed her and joined the prince and princess. We found Prince Bertil a most engaging person—straightforward, with no pretense whatsoever.

{ *Milton* } As the younger son of King Gustav, Bertil was the heir to the throne until King Gustav's grandson matured. However, King Gustav had ruled that Bertil couldn't succeed to the throne if he married a commoner. Out of a sense of duty, therefore, Prince Bertil did not marry the commoner whom today we would call his "significant other." Instead they led a happy life without benefit of clergy. When King Gustav died, his grandson, King Carl, was more liberal and permitted the prince to retain his royal position even if he did marry a commoner. The king could hardly have done less since he himself had married a commoner. As a result, the prince had been married only a week or two before—a great event in Sweden. When I told Bertil that we had been married for thirty-eight years, he said that he had been unmarried for thirty-three.

{ *Rose* } We were enjoying our visit when, at the appropriate time, another member of the royal household, this time a male, approached and said that the king and queen would like the pleasure of talking with us. As in all other respects, this way of giving each guest an opportunity to visit with the king and queen is well planned, but all is very casual and informal. As it happened, the king had visited the University of Chicago the previous spring. Milton attended the luncheon given by the university for the king and met him then. We talked about that visit and other things. After the king and queen had visited with all the laureates, they left the hall and the party was over.

The festivities of the Nobel week ended with the king's banquet. However, the Nobel week was not over for us. Our foreign service attendant had planned a leisurely day for us on Sunday. We first drove around the countryside and then ended up at a delightful Swedish country-inn type of restaurant for a delectable smorgasbord.

On the last day, after a pleasant lunch at the Stockholm School of Economics and another St. Lucia visit, this time with the honored guest fully clothed, Milton gave his Nobel lecture.

The Nobel Lecture

There was a good deal of apprehension beforehand about the possibility of another demonstration. Though our bodyguards and other security men were constantly around us, I must confess that for the first time I myself felt some apprehension. Universities are not adapted to tight security and, at least in recent years, have been a popular place for demonstrations of all kinds. We were all relieved when our fears proved unfounded. For the most part, only economists attended the lecture, which was expected to be, and was, technical in nature. The room was full but all who came were there because they wanted to hear what Milton had to say.

{ *Milton* } The establishment of a Nobel Prize in economics has frequently been criticized on the ground that economics is not a scientific discipline like physics or chemistry or medicine, but rather a part of philosophy or politics or current affairs, so enmeshed with values that objective judgment of scientific work is impossible. I do not myself believe that there is an iota of difference in these respects between economics and the other disciplines. Politics enters into the other disciplines at least as much as it does in economics. Edward Teller is an excellent example. His failure to get a Nobel award in physics is not unrelated to the political positions that he has taken. It is ironic in the extreme that an award named for Alfred Nobel, whose great contribution was to develop high explosives, should be denied to someone because he developed an even higher explosive.

I wrote my lecture primarily to make the point that economics was or could be a positive science like physics and chemistry. Instead of discussing the methodological issue explicitly, I tried to illustrate it by example. The example I chose was the change in professional views on the relation between inflation and unemployment. Those views had changed drastically over the previous thirty years. And they changed, not because of any change in values, not because of any political considerations, but because the facts made it impossible to continue to hold certain hypotheses that had originally been accepted. The initial so-called Phillips-curve hypothesis, that there was a stable negative relation between inflation and unemployment, became untenable because the facts contradicted it—in exactly the same way that in any other discipline a scientific hypothesis is rejected because the facts have contradicted it.

An alternative hypothesis—that what mattered was not inflation per se, but the difference between actual and anticipated inflation—came to rule the roost not because of political values or beliefs, but because it fitted the facts better; it explained phenomena that the other hypothesis didn't explain. In citing the evidence that this was not a political matter but a scientific matter, I said that thinking on this issue had gone through three stages: the first stage was the simple Phillips-curve stage, the second was the expectations-adjusted Phillips curve, and the third stage was the new stage that we were coming to, in which people were wondering whether there wasn't a positively sloped Phillips curve. In introducing the third stage I quoted from James Callaghan, the Labour prime minister of Britain, and from a white paper to the Canadian government explaining that the facts did not conform to the beliefs that people had had. Although that was intended to be the main thrust of the talk, most of the newspaper commentary left that out and went to something else.

That was our final day in Stockholm. We left that night. It was a great week, and Rose and I were reminded of an old TV program entitled *That Was the Week That Was.*

A final amusing note. President-elect Carter decided to call all Nobel laureates of 1976 to congratulate them. When he told his secretary to call me, she called another Milton Friedman, who had been serving as a speech writer for President Ford, on leave from his permanent position in the Department of Agriculture. That Milton Friedman, when told that President-elect Carter was calling him, thought lightning had struck, that he was going to be offered a job in the new administration. Unfortunately, it was only mistaken identity. Carter's secretary finally reached me in Vermont, where we were at the time, and I had a pleasant talk with Carter, the only direct contact I have had with him from that time to this.

→ *Chapter Twenty-Seven* ←

ISRAEL

{ *Milton* } We have made four trips to Israel since our first extended stay in 1962: in 1969, as guests of the Israeli government; in 1972, to deliver the Horowitz Lectures; in 1977, to receive an honorary degree from the Hebrew University—which by coincidence coincided with the unexpected election victory of Menachem Begin and his Likud party; and in 1990, to participate in a conference on Israeli economic policy organized by Daniel Doron and his Israeli Center for Social and Economic Progress (since renamed the Israel Center for Free Enterprise).

The 1969 Trip

The 1969 invitation was sparked by the election of Richard Nixon to the presidency. As an informal adviser of the president, a Jew sympathetic to Israel, and a *Newsweek* columnist, the Israeli government must have listed me as someone worth cultivating. That may have been a poor call, since my role as informal adviser came to a sudden end in 1971 after the president imposed price and wage controls. We welcomed the opportunity of seeing the new Israel less than two years after the end of the six-day war and finding out how Israel was coping with its new role as an occupying power.

The detailed itinerary prepared by the Division for Official Guests, Ministry for Foreign Affairs, for our twelve-day stay included visits, at our suggestion, with friends and, at theirs, with numerous government officials. By far the most notable feature of the trip was meeting the military officials in charge of the West Bank and touring the West Bank. On returning from Israel, I summarized my impressions in the following *Newsweek* column (May 5, 1969), titled "Invisible Occupation":

On a recent visit to Israel, I toured the west-bank territory occupied during the 1967 six-day war. Much to my surprise, there was almost no sign of a military presence. Israeli soldiers were conspicuous only by their absence. The Jordanian Arabs were peacefully going about their business. I had no feeling whatsoever of being in occupied territory.

We crossed and recrossed the frontier between Israel and the west bank without encountering any soldiers and without noticing any obvious barriers to free movement. Traffic in Jenin, one of the major cities in the west-bank territory, was being directed by a Jordanian policeman wearing a gun on his hip. Even Israeli civilian administrators were few and far between. Governmental functions were being carried out by the prewar Jordanian civil servants.

The Dayan policy. The absence of a military presence and the continuity of administration are deliberate. At the outset of the occupation, Moshe Dayan, the charismatic general and Minister of Defense, laid down a policy of laissez-faire—if I may appropriate that much abused economic term to describe a related political phenomenon. Intervention by Israeli authorities was to he held to a minimum—and even that minimum was to be exercised as far as possible by consultation with the appropriate local groups rather than by order.

This wise policy involved almost literal laissez-faire in the economic sphere—and is possible only because it did. Jordanian money is permitted to circulate alongside Israeli money. West-bank farmers may grow whatever they wish and may sell their produce at any price they can command not only in the west bank but also in Jordan itself, so there is active trade across the Jordan River. An agricultural extension service manned by several hundred Jordanian civil servants, plus a literal handful of Israeli experts added after the war, has been galvanized into greater activity and has been extremely effective, so that agricultural output is growing rapidly. To a casual observer, the area appears to be prospering.

The major interferences with economic laissez-faire are restrictions on the export of farm products to Israel and on the movement of labor. Restrictions on exports have been imposed because Israel has adopted a governmental policy of supporting the prices of some farm products (we are by no means the only country that goes in for such foolishness). The importation of these products into Israel from the west bank would tend to force down the fixed prices or require the accumulation of additional surpluses. Restrictions on the movement of labor partly have a similar rationale—preservation of union wage rates—and partly the valid justification of reducing social tension and the danger of disruptive activity.

Trade and aid. These restrictions encourage the west bank to sell to Jordan rather than to Israel. As a result, Israel exports more to the west bank than it imports from the west bank and the west bank exports more to Jordan than it imports from Jordan. Jordan thereby gets foodstuffs and other items partly in return for pieces of paper (Jordanian currency) hoarded by west-bank residents. In effect, Israel is indirectly giving the equivalent of foreign aid to Jordan!

Another surprising consequence is that the military, who generally favor running things by direct orders coming down a chain of command, are in Israel the strongest supporters of free markets and nonintervention. They see by example that the anonymous market frees them from burdensome tasks and eliminates much potential conflict. They see that the elimination of barriers to the movement of goods, men and capital would foster the economic integration of the west bank with Israel without requiring political integration.

Here, on a scale sufficiently small to be readily comprehensible, is a striking illustration of the general principle that the free market enables people to cooperate in some areas to their joint benefit while permitting them to go their own way in other areas of their life. This principle explains why the nineteenth century, when laissez-faire was the ruling philosophy, was an era of international peace and economic cooperation while the twentieth century, when the key words are central planning and government intervention, has been marred by recurrent international strife and discord. Marx to the contrary notwithstanding, trade unites and politics divides. [© 1969, Newsweek, Inc. All rights reserved. Reprinted by permission.]

Unfortunately, the happy situation described in the *Newsweek* column was short-lived. The six-day war was followed by the Yom Kippur war in 1973. Palestinian guerrillas launched terrorist attacks on Israeli civilians, and the rest of the dreary record of violence of the ensuing years unfolded. In addition, the Dayan policy of laissez-faire was largely abandoned, in line with growing government control of the Israeli economy.

I believe that the increased socialization of the Israeli economy was a tragedy for both the internal economy and external relations. If Israel had followed a more laissez-faire policy internally, it would have been more prosperous and could have followed more nearly a Dayan policy with the occupied territories. That would have provided greater economic opportunities for the Palestinians and greatly eased political relations.

The 1972 Trip

Our 1972 trip was for the purpose of delivering lectures in honor of David Horowitz, the former head of the Bank of Israel, whom I had met on our 1969 visit.[1] The rest of the visit was purely social.

The 1977 Trip

The 1977 trip was in many ways the most memorable of our trips to Israel, partly because of its coinciding with Menachem Begin's election victory.

The occasion of the trip was to accept an honorary degree from the Hebrew University in Jerusalem—an offer that had been generated by my friend Don Patinkin, chairman of the Economics Department at the Hebrew University, supported by the other members of the department. Thanks to my close personal contacts in Israel, plus the close relations between our department and Don and his associates, the offer pleased me greatly and I was honored to accept.

Arrangements for the trip were made before the election that resulted in the unexpected victory of Menachem Begin and his Likud party. However, that event only briefly preceded my visit and led to our extending our stay in order to consult with the new government. As I wrote in a *Newsweek* column on my return:

> Prime Minister Begin and his government have proclaimed their intention to cut government down to size and to give greater scope to the free market. Much as I approve of those objectives, their attainment will not be easy. Too many groups have a vested interest in government subsidies, including many supporters of the Likud. In a discussion that I had in Israel with a group of private businessmen,

private farmers and private bankers, the business leaders expressed support for eliminating government subsidies—provided the process started with agriculture. The leaders of agriculture expressed support for eliminating government subsidies—provided the process started with business. Ditto the bankers.

It will be a triumph of leadership and idealism if Prime Minister Begin and his government can untangle the snarl they inherited from the 29-year rule of their socialist opponents. Their success is vital both for Israel and for free men everywhere. I wish them well.[2]

While my hopes were high, my expectations were low that Begin would succeed, for two reasons that reinforced the pressure of the special interests (incidentally, I opened my session with them by saying something like, "You people are the major obstacle to effective reform"). First, as Rose and I stated in *The Tyranny of the Status Quo,* "a new administration has some six to nine months in which to achieve major changes; if it does not seize the opportunity to act decisively during that period, it will not have another such opportunity."[3] Second, as I discovered in a long and very friendly meeting with Mr. Begin— during which he kept referring to me as "Professor Milton," his heart and mind were in military and political strategy. He knew economics was important and needed attention, but he had no real interest in, or feel for, economics. Combined with the unexpectedness of his victory, that meant that he came into office with no detailed economic policy. It was the strength of both Margaret Thatcher and Ronald Reagan that they recognized the need to have a detailed plan for action in advance, and hence were able to make effective use of their honeymoon. In Begin's case, the honeymoon was squandered in bickering among private interests and newly appointed policy officials about what should be done, with the end result that nothing was done.

The actual outcome was a major expansion rather than contraction in the role of government in the economy. That expansion laid the seeds for an accelerating inflation that was finally checked by a major monetary reform in 1985.[4] The reform was highly successful in bringing inflation down, but did nothing to reduce government control over, and intervention into, every aspect of economic activity.

As I write these words (July 1996), history may be repeating itself. As in 1977, a controversial leader of the Likud party has become prime minister and is proclaiming his "intention to cut government down to size and to give greater scope to the free market." The new prime minister, Benjamin Netanyahu, has demonstrated greater interest in economic matters and greater determination to reduce the role of the state than Begin ever did. There is wider recognition in Israel of the importance of expanding the role of free markets, and at least two think tanks have been both promoting free markets and preparing programs for privatization. On the other hand, he faces a more difficult task. The role of the government has expanded greatly since 1977. Government spending is higher relative to national income now than then; government regulations are more numerous and detailed; and special government privileges of all kinds more widespread. I do not know whether Mr. Netanyahu came into office with a detailed program for action in the economic sphere, but, as in 1977, there are many able free-market economists in Israel who would have been able and willing to advise on such a program.

As it happened, the role of socialism and free markets in Israel was a central theme of the talk I gave at the Hebrew University commencement on July 4, 1977, when I was asked to respond on behalf of all the recipients of honorary degrees. Herewith some excerpts from that talk which, so far as I know, has never been published.

> I first visited Israel fifteen years ago, when I spent several months as a visiting professor at this university. I summarized my impressions by saying that two Jewish traditions seemed to be at war in Israel: a hundred-year-old tradition of belief in paternalistic socialist government and rejection of capitalism and free markets; and a two-thousand-year-old tradition, developed out of the necessities of the Diaspora, of self-reliance and voluntary cooperation, of ingenuity in getting around government controls, of using every device of Jewish ingenuity to take advantage of such market opportunities as escaped the clumsy grasp of government officials. I concluded that, fortunately for Israel, the older tradition was also proving the stronger.
>
> This conflict between traditions has been critical for Israel since its birth and remains critical for its future. Socialism appeals to generous and unselfish instincts. It has captivated many fine, warm, and idealistic persons. It may well be that the early kibbutz movement, the idealism, self-sacrifice, and sense of community that played so large a part in the early days of a Jewish homeland and still plays so large a part in today's Israel, might not have been possible without the ideals and hopes that so many of the participants vested in socialism.[5] And certainly throughout the history of Israel, the needs of de-

fense have mandated a large role for government. Yet even a good thing can be carried too far. Even the noblest of ideals can rest on false foundations.

The ideal of socialism is one thing. The reality, if carried very far, quite another. State socialism, in practice as contrasted with the idealistic vision, is not and never has been in the interest of Jews individually or of Israel collectively. State socialism, I believe, violates the most basic Jewish values: an individual's responsibility before God for his own actions; personal charity; voluntary community; respect for diversity of opinion; an abiding faith in reason. These basic Jewish values are perverted in a system that—carried to its logical extreme—substitutes collective authority for individual conscience, antiseptic welfare administered by an impersonal bureaucracy for personal charity, compulsory conformity for voluntary cooperation, rule by either a majority or a governing elite for individual rights.

Socialism as an ideal has captivated not only Jewish intellectuals but intellectuals around the world. The resulting growth in the size and power of governments is a major reason, I believe, why freedom around the world has been declining. Fortunately, the practical working of socialism is producing increasing skepticism about the ideal. That is a major reason for hope for the future.

But whether this be true or not on the global scale, the conflict between socialism in practice and Israel's interest is crystal-clear. If state socialism had swept the world in the twentieth century, there would be no State of Israel today. That is a sentence worth repeating, because it is at once so patently true, indeed, nearly self-evident, and yet so strikingly at variance with beliefs voiced by so many Jews around the world. *If state socialism had swept the world in the twentieth century, there would be no State of Israel today.* Under state socialism, government controls the resources of a country. But did governments help or hinder the original Zionist development? Did the initial support for a Jewish homeland come from the government of Great Britain or from individuals in Britain and elsewhere who were able to contribute funds and to work for a Jewish homeland only because of the existence of capitalism and free markets and of the political freedom which accompanied these economic arrangements? What has made possible the successive aliyot [return of Jews to Palestine]—both before and after Israel's establishment? Assistance from governments, whether socialist or not, or from individual Jews? From Jews in the state socialist countries or in the bastions of capitalism? From the Jews in Russia and its satellites, or from the Jews in the United States, Great Britain, South Africa, Western Europe? The state socialist countries have been the source of some immigrants—but only after those countries were bribed with funds from the capitalist countries to let some of their Jewish citizens go!

Or take a longer view. If state socialism had dominated the past two thousand years, the Jews would never have survived the Diaspora. Israel, in every sense, would have perished. How did the Jews survive? Occasionally a monarch or a despot protected the Jews—but typically only because elements of a capitalist market economy enabled a few Jews to put the monarchs in their debt, a less romantic but also more reliable and less bloody recourse than the stratagem of Mordecai and Esther. For the most part, Jews were able to survive the Diaspora despite, not because of, the actions of governments. Where did they not only survive but prosper? Only in those countries that gave wide scope to competitive capitalism and free markets. Equally striking, within those countries, they prospered most in those areas where competition was freest.

A personal experience will illustrate this vital point. Some years ago I participated in an International Monetary Conference, organized by bankers, and attended by the two top officials of each of the leading banks of the world, plus a group of invited "experts" such as myself. Fewer than 2 percent of the assembled bankers were Jewish. More than 25 percent of the invited "experts" were Jewish. Why? Because banking is a monopolistic industry in which a government franchise is needed to operate, while intellectual activity is a highly competitive industry.

The true hope of Israel—and of freedom everywhere—is the enterprise, initiative, ingenuity, drive, and courage of the individual citizens, cooperating voluntarily with one another, producing that miracle of progress in every sphere that comes only from the achievements of the individual. The threat from your neighbors unfortunately imposes a large military effort on Israel. That effort must be coordinated and administered by government. You cannot escape having a sizable socialist sector. But that sector can remain, as it has been, relatively efficient, only so long as it is supported by a free people and a strong, productive, private economy.

The miracle of Israel has been achieved by free men and women fighting against incredible odds. This occasion symbolizes the contin-

467

ual passing of the torch of freedom to the young. May you who will carry it on the next lap recognize how rare your heritage is. May you guard and cherish it, so that you too may pass it on, still burning, to future generations.

The 1990 Trip

In the mid-1980s, Daniel Doron, a fourth-generation Israeli native, at the time an art dealer in New York and Israel, founded the Israel Center for Social and Economic Progress to serve as a free-market think tank that could both explore the policy changes necessary to reduce the role of the government in the economy and develop public support for those policies. Daniel early on enlisted our support, both intellectual and financial, for his venture, as he did that of many other persons in the U.S. In Israel, he enlisted David Levhari, professor of economics at the Hebrew University and one of Israel's leading academic economists, as director of research and organized and encouraged leading economists and jurists to analyze Israel's economic problems from a free-market perspective.

The center was successful in producing policy options for a wide range of issues, and organizing conferences and seminars to develop and spread information on those policy options. It has performed an important educational function, and deserves much credit for a major change in public attitudes of the same kind as has occurred in the U.S., away from an unreasoning acceptance of a statist ideology and toward a widespread support for free markets. Unfortunately, as elsewhere, the change in the accepted rhetoric has so far had little effect on actual socialist practice.

The center arranged for the broadcast in Israel in early 1989 of our *Free to Choose* TV program and for the publication of a Hebrew translation of the book of the same title. In 1990, it organized a major international conference ostensibly to celebrate its fifth anniversary. We made our 1990 trip in order to participate in this conference. The conference, as a leading Israeli journalist, Pinhas Landau, wrote, brought "to Israel a most intelligent and interesting group of people from the United States and the Soviet Union, from England and from Hungary, and even from distant New Zealand to give lectures and hold discussions on the painful and important subject of changing the face of the economy." It also attracted as participants and audience most of the movers and shakers in the Israeli government, quasi-governmental organizations, and business sector. At its conclusion it broke up into several workshops to make recommendations on reforming the Israeli economy. Enactment of the list of recommendations that emerged would have gone a long way to transforming the Israeli economy.

The president of Israel, Chaim Herzog, opened the conference at a gala dinner in Tel Aviv. I followed, giving the keynote address, in which I emphasized the lack of progress in the thirteen years since my earlier visit in 1977. Pinhas Landau reported on my speech in these words:

> What has changed is the entire world around him, which has come a long way toward his concepts of a free economy, minimum government intervention in economic life, and maximum free choice by its citizens as consumers. . . .
>
> He begged his listeners not to learn from the United States of the twentieth century, which has embarked on a path of increasing government intervention. The model to be copied, he said, is the United States of the nineteenth century, when the economy grew very quickly in the absence of government intervention, and even welfare services, which were then in private, voluntary hands, functioned better than they do today."

I also gave a talk at the closing dinner in Jerusalem, in which I said that "the free market system's main justification is, in my opinion, its moral strength, not its superior efficiency, though that is now proven. Governments have expanded into areas they have no business to be in and as a result they are failing to carry out properly the tasks they are supposed to do."

As part of my talk, I contrasted the experience of Israel with that of Hong Kong, a surprisingly well-matched pair for a controlled experiment on the relative merits of free markets and socialism. Israel adopted socialist economic policies; Hong Kong adopted near-complete laissez-faire. Both were small, not very important entities just after World War II. In 1948, when Israel was established, it had a population of 720,000; in 1945, at the end of the war, Hong Kong had a population of 600,000. Both experienced a tremendous influx of refugees during the next decade—Jews from Europe, Yemen, Iraq, Egypt, and northern Africa into Israel; Chinese from mainland China into Hong Kong. Both had a good record in maintaining civil liberties and personal freedom. And both Chinese and Jews had the reputation of possessing outstanding entrepreneurial skills.

Israel's one disadvantage was the continual military threat that forced it to devote a sizable fraction of its income to defense. However, the economic effect was largely offset by the far greater foreign assistance it received—from the United States alone, Israel received nearly $14 billion of official assistance from 1946 to 1988; Hong Kong, $44 million. And that doesn't count the private assistance Israel received from around the world. In economic terms, defense was an export industry. When I was in Israel in 1977, I made a careful analysis of the net cost to Israel of defense and, as I recall, I concluded that it came to something under 15 percent of the national income—high compared to other countries, but not an unacceptable burden.

Hong Kong's disadvantage was the complete lack of resources, other than a great harbor, and its small size. Israel was far richer in natural resources. In 1994, the population density in Hong Kong was twenty-two times that in Israel.

The results are clear. Per-capita gross national product, expressed in dollars, was more than 50 percent higher in Israel than in Hong Kong in 1950; by 1965, it was 7 percent lower and by 1994, 44 percent lower. And this despite a more rapid growth in the population of Hong Kong: from 600,000 in 1945 to 6 million in 1994, compared to Israel's growth from 720,000 in 1945 to 5.3 million in 1994.

If Israel had adopted the same policy as Hong Kong, I believe that by now its population would probably be twice what it is and its gross national product four times as large. Its political position would be vastly stronger and, in the process, there would have been far less friction with its Arab neighbors, and they too would be far better off.

That is of course water over the dam, but it suggests the potential rewards if Prime Minister Netanyahu can achieve the economic reforms he has stated to be his goal.

After the conference, we remained in Israel for several days to visit with Rose's relatives and to meet some government officials. The most notable was a long meeting with Shimon Peres, at the time finance minister. It was a very unsatisfactory meeting. There was no language problem, since Peres speaks English fluently, and he is clearly very knowledgeable and intelligent. But there was no real meeting of the minds. Socialist to the core, yet anxious to appease the growing sentiment for free-market reform expressed at the conference, he was very friendly and conciliatory, yet I had the feeling that he was trying to make debating points, rather than seriously discuss the issues, that the meeting was for show, not substance. I have no record of the conversation, and recall few of the details, so what I am recording here is simply the general impression of the man that I carried away.

FREE TO CHOOSE

{ *Rose* } We arrived in San Francisco in early January 1977. Milton had arranged to spend the first three months as a visiting scholar at the Federal Reserve Bank of San Francisco. More important, he had accepted an offer from Glenn Campbell, director of the Hoover Institution at Stanford, to join the Hoover staff on a permanent basis (see chap. 31).

The Preliminaries

A few days after we arrived, we received a telephone call that launched us on the most exciting venture of our lives. It was a follow-up of an earlier conversation with our friend Allen Wallis, who told us to expect a call from Robert Chitester. He explained that Chitester was a most unusual chief executive officer of a PBS television station (WQLN in Erie, Pennsylvania), a libertarian rather than a socialist, who was interested in using television to spread free-market ideas.[1] Chitester's call was followed by a visit on January 14.

After our first meeting, Bob sent us a detailed prospectus of his proposed project. Extremely ambitious, it included

> A lecture series
> Audio and video cassettes of lectures
> A television series
> A college-credit course
> High school resource material
> Publication of a book which he suggested might be an expanded
>   edition of *Capitalism and Freedom*

Bob included a proposed timetable and budget for the television series component. He envisioned starting work on the documentary in April 1977 and
having the final product ready for PBS to broadcast in February 1979. At this
point, Bob estimated that the documentary would cost two and a half million
dollars. Remarkably, nearly every element of his ambitious program has in
fact been realized in one form or another, including his estimate of cost, except
only that the documentary aired a year later than he foresaw.

Bob's next visit in February was longer than the first—this time, several
days. We had much to discuss about the various items in his prospectus. One
suggestion, a weekly discussion program on television, while a good idea in
the abstract, did not appeal to Milton. The lecture series and television documentary did. Milton and I have spent much of our life trying to persuade
our fellow men and women of the dangers of an intrusive government and
the key role that a free competitive economy plays in making a free society
possible. Bringing these ideas to the large audience that a TV documentary
could attract excited us.

Peter Bernstein described the origin of the series in an article published
while the series was appearing on TV:

> Chitester became a convert to Friedmanism almost as soon as he
> found out what it was. In the fall of 1976, pursuing one of his
> ideas, he drove to the University of Rochester to meet W. Allen
> Wallis, an economist who was chancellor of the university and
> chairman of the Corporation for Public Broadcasting. Over lunch,
> the two men started talking about Friedman, a former colleague of
> Wallis's at the University of Chicago. Wallis gave him a copy of *Capi-
> talism and Freedom,* which Friedman and wife Rose, also an econo-
> mist, published in 1962. Now Chitester can sometimes be seen car-
> rying his dog-eared copy around with him. "It has been my Bible
> since 1976." . . .
>
> Overwhelmed by Friedman's ideas, Chitester quite naturally
> wanted to bring them to television. Friedman . . . greeted the proposi-
> tion without enthusiasm, "I have always believed that influence is
> exerted much more by the written word . . . My own role was persuad-
> ing economists, not the public at large." . . .
>
> Luckily for Chitester, Rose Friedman was on his side. "I have
> always been more optimistic about reaching out to the general pub-
> lic," she says. After four meetings at the Friedmans' apartment,
> Chitester had a commitment from them to do the series.[2]

{ *Milton* } Although we verbally committed ourselves to proceed with the project in February, it was not until July 26 that I "put on paper what we have agreed to verbally," writing to Bob, "Provided that the funding is assured, I am prepared to devote a large part of my time and energies during the next year to eighteen months to a TV series designed to present my personal social, economic, and political philosophy." In the event, it turned out to be more like three to four years.

In April, Bob arranged a meeting in New York to brainstorm the project with a larger group, including Leo Rosten and Ben Rogge, longtime friends who shared our views, had skills in communication, and experience in participating in television programs,[3] and Dick Ellison, Tony Machi, Bill Frazer, and Barbara Reeves, whom Bob knew from the world of television. The meeting was held at the New York Athletic Club, thanks to Frank O'Connell, at the time vice-president of the Olin Corporation and very sympathetic to our project.

As of this time, the plan was that I would give a series of lectures covering the major issues relevant to understanding free markets and their relation to a free society. Bob would film the lectures and associated question-and-answer sessions. The films would be used to guide the production of the final television series. Initially, I naively thought that the final programs, or at least some of them, could be constructed by linking together clips from the televised lectures. I was quickly disabused of that idea.

In preparation for the meeting, I drew up a list of eighteen possible topics for lectures and developed detailed outlines for five of them (item 1 in appendix B, which refers to this chapter). Not surprisingly, the list includes essentially all of the subjects covered in the final documentary series. The discussion at the meeting concentrated on the lectures, partly on their content, partly on the priority for inclusion in the final product, partly on problems of exposition. In addition, we discussed how to use the lectures in the final documentary and the form that the final programs should take.

Bob visited us at Capitaf in early May to assess the outcome of the New York session. That led to my visiting Erie over the Memorial Day weekend to produce a sample of the kind of documentary we proposed. Bob arranged for his crew to film me in a tomato garden and a hardware store, discussing some of my ideas, using the tomato plants and the hardware as props. The purpose was primarily to provide him with a piece that he could use in fund raising. He found it very effective in giving potential funders a sample of content and also assuring them of my ability as a presenter.

Meeting with PBS

In the interim between our committing ourselves to undertake the project and the New York meeting, Bob Chitester had been very active. An essential prerequisite for raising funds was a commitment to funders that the final series would be seen nationally on a major TV network. PBS seemed the obvious outlet. As president of a local PBS TV station, Bob could determine what Station WQLN showed, but not what PBS included in its core program. From past experience Bob knew that he could not take it for granted that PBS would include a documentary that he sponsored in their core program.

Though the Corporation for Public Broadcasting is the conduit through which taxpayer funds are funneled to operations of the Public Broadcasting System, it does not make decisions about programs. The permanent bureaucrats at PBS have the final say over what programs they encourage, help to finance, and include in their core program. And those bureaucrats, then and now, are very left-biased. They were delighted to join the British Broadcasting Corporation to foster and help finance Kenneth Galbraith's *Age of Uncertainty,* which was shown in 1977. A program on the opposite side of the fence was a very different thing. As Laurence Jarvik writes, "While Galbraith was seen as a moderate by PBS, Friedman, who called himself a liberal and who advocated laissez-faire free-market policies, was viewed as an extremist." He quotes Allen Wallis as saying "The public broadcasting people regarded Friedman as a fascist, an extreme right-winger. They didn't want to have anything to do with him."[4]

In early March 1977, Bob met with the top officials at PBS. He did not get a firm commitment from them. However, he concluded, and as it proved, correctly, that the pressure to provide some balance to Galbraith's clearly ideological series would make it impossible for them to refuse to broadcast a program originated by one of PBS's own member stations, which presented the other side, especially a program by a Nobel laureate.

Typically, PBS contributes to the financing of the major miniseries that it shows, as it did for Galbraith's series. However, Bob realized that he could not expect any financial assistance from PBS. Though obviously a handicap, that decision fit in with Rose's and my preference for private financing. I had long been opposed to government financing and operation of television stations. Moreover, we wanted to exercise complete independence in determining the content of the series, and only unrestricted private financing would ensure that. Aside from our suggesting possible donors, Bob undertook complete responsibility for raising the sizable funds that would be required. By dint of great effort and persistence, and unusual persuasive powers, he did a remarkable job, raising more than three million dollars from fifteen major donors (item 2, appendix B).[5]

Finding a Producer

At the same time that Bob was raising funds, he was also exploring possible producers for the series. Bob had neither the staff nor the experience to produce the kind of major documentary miniseries that we were planning. He contacted a number of experienced producers, including Adrian Malone, who had produced Galbraith's series. Malone took himself out of the running because of his lack of sympathy with our philosophy. Bob, Rose, and I met with a number of promising potential producers in the United States. Their technical competence was impressive, but none had any real sympathy with our philosophy. No doubt, as professionals they would have tried their best to help us present our views, but we felt that it was essential that the producer have his heart and not merely his technical skills in the project. In an effort to find such a producer, I called my friend Ralph Harris, the director and one of the founders of the Institute of Economic Affairs, the preeminent free-market think tank in Britain.[6] He suggested several possible names and promised to explore these and other possibilities.

Bob had been planning a trip to London to talk to the BBC about its interest in acquiring the program when it was completed and to talk with possible producers. The extra stimulus from Ralph's encouraging reaction led Bob to take off for London on August 10.* He spent a very busy two days in London: visiting the BBC, interviewing potential producers who had come to his notice, and meeting Samuel Brittan, one of my tutees the year that I spent at Cambridge, who had become the chief columnist of the *Financial Times* and who I was sure would be sympathetic to our project. By far the most important interview was with Antony Jay, recommended by Ralph Harris as "a Friedman fan" (initially from reading my *Playboy* interview). Jay was a partner in Video Arts, a television production company formed by ex-BBC employees who had wanted to escape bureaucracy.[7]

On Bob's return with an enthusiastic report on Jay, I telephoned Jay. We

---

* { *Rose* }   Two days after Bob left for London it so happened that the Galbraiths, Buckleys, and Banfields came to Capitaf for lunch. After lunch, when Milton offered to take our guests to the pond for a swim, Ken decided he would rather take a nap. I stayed at the house to clean up after lunch. When Ken woke, I took the opportunity to ask him what advice he could offer us for our project on the basis of his experience with *The Age of Uncertainty*. His advice was, "Get a good contract for your book." That was not the advice I was looking for though it was doubtless good financial advice.

had a long conversation about our project that was sufficiently encouraging to persuade me to undertake a trip to London for a face-to-face meeting with Jay and his partners. Prior commitments necessitated a lapse of over a month before Bob and I took off on September 20 for London, where we had extensive discussions with Antony Jay and two of his partners who were to be the most closely involved in the production of *Free to Choose,* Michael Peacock, managing director, and Robert Reid, chairman. In addition, Peacock arranged for us to interview Michael Latham as a potential producer.[8] Unlike the producers we had interviewed in the United States, both the Video Arts trio and Michael Latham were sympathetic to our philosophy and enthusiastic about producing a documentary to present it. (Interesting that Britain, the fatherland of the welfare state and the home of a major avowedly socialist party, should be where we would find producers sympathetic to free markets.)

The discussion at Video Arts dealt mostly with two issues: the proposed contents and the specific form of the documentary—essentially covering the same issues that we had discussed at our April meeting in New York. This time, however, the talk was with experts on producing television documentaries and hence was on a more concrete and specific level. Bob, Rose, and I had mostly contemplated a series consisting of one-hour documentaries like those in Galbraith's series. Antony Jay suggested the alternative of "a thirty-minute program, shot on film and for the most part on 'location' followed by a separate program which would be some variation of a discussion program."[9] The suggestion had the great merit of being much less costly than hour-long documentaries, since discussions filmed at a single location are far cheaper to produce than documentaries shot at different locations. It also had the virtue of being more flexible. As the suggestion worked out in practice, it enabled us to give our opponents a chance to express their criticisms. Antony also believed that the combination of documentary and discussion would give greater scope to my own particular skills.

Though we did not reach a formal agreement on the spot, we returned from London persuaded that Video Arts would be an excellent choice. A final agreement with Video Arts was reached about a month later, while Michael Peacock was in the United States on a business trip.

Rose met Michael for the first time when he visited us in San Francisco on October 19. I have no very clear recollection of that visit. However, a letter from Michael makes it plain that we discussed a production schedule and arranged that I would send him as promptly as possible transcripts of the lectures I gave that they could use for detailed planning. At about the same time, he reached an agreement with Bob that the participants from both sides of the Atlantic would meet in Boston over the Thanksgiving weekend for a full planning session.

The search for a producer was over.

The Lectures

{ *Rose* } William Jovanovich, CEO of Harcourt Brace Jovanovich, played a key role in enabling us to finance videotaping of the proposed lecture series. (Videotaping aside, no funds were needed, since the sponsors always paid the travel and other expenses connected with the lectures, and frequently an honorarium as well.) On September 14, 1977, Bill Jovanovich advanced $100,000 to finance videotapes and transcripts of the lecture series in return for the right to sell them and to have first call on publishing the book that was expected to emerge from the series (item 3, appendix B).[10] Bill had more than a passing interest in our venture. His heart was in the promotion of our ideas. HBJ published the book *Free to Choose* which appeared simultaneously with the TV program. HBJ also published *Tyranny of the Status Quo,* which followed in 1984, and Bill personally edited it when we spent a week at his home in Canada.

The Nobel award to Milton in December 1976 had unleashed a flood of invitations to give lectures. He had simply acknowledged most of them without commitment. On returning to Capitaf in early April, we proceeded to select among the invitations those that seemed most promising for our purpose. That involved making sure that we could cover the subjects we wanted to cover, at locations and on dates that fit in with our personal loca-tions—Vermont and San Francisco—and our travels to and from these two homes, and then confirming the arrangements. In addition, we were anxious to include as wide a range of audiences as possible. Little time was spent on content—Milton had been giving lectures on the subjects we wanted to cover for a long time. In addition, he always spoke from very brief notes.

While we were still at our home in Vermont, Milton gave the first two lectures, both in New York. The first was delivered on September 12 under the auspices of Pfizer, the pharmaceutical company, in the nearby Ford Foundation Auditorium on the topic "Who Protects the Consumer?"; the second on September 15 in Harlem before an organization named Harlem Parents on the topic "Putting Learning Back in the Classroom." Each of these lectures, and all later ones, was followed by an extensive question-and-answer session. These two lectures were the "prior commitments" that delayed Milton and Bob in going to London to meet with Video Arts.

The next four lectures—at Cornell University, at a college in Erie, Pennsylvania, where the lecture was sponsored by WQLN, at the University of Chicago, and at Utah State University in Ogden—were delivered in the course of driving from Capitaf to San Francisco. This was a sixteen-day trip that also included saying good-bye to our friends in Chicago, arranging for the furniture from our Chicago apartment to be shipped to San Francisco, having our annual medical check-up at the Mayo Clinic, and visiting my sister and brother-in-law in Reno, and ended by our moving into a literally empty apartment that we had bought the previous spring but had not occupied. The Cornell lecture was the most notable, not for content but for the sizable demonstration against Milton for his association with Chile (see chap. 24), which evoked a counterdemonstration by Young Americans for Freedom. Though the protest continued inside the auditorium, the bulk of the audience wanted to hear the lecture and shouted down the protesters, preventing them from seriously interfering with either the talk or the question-and-answer session. All in all, Milton gave fifteen lectures, the final one on May 19, 1978, at the Mayo Clinic on "The Economics of Medical Care." Nine were given at universities, the others to widely varied audiences.

The Boston Meeting

In the interim between Michael Peacock's U.S. visit and the November 22–26 meeting in Boston, Video Arts recruited Michael Latham, whom Milton and Bob had interviewed briefly in London, to serve as producer. Latham was the producer of one of BBC's most popular programs, a weekly program entitled *The Man Alive Report.* He had also produced a series of ten one-hour films, *Ten Who Dared,* that won two British Academy Awards. The selection and recruitment of Latham by Video Arts was a major contribution to the success of the program. Thoroughly sympathetic with our objective, he wholeheartedly devoted his imagination and television expertise to conveying our message. In addition, he was a wonderful companion throughout some very hectic days. He was always there to entertain us and relax us with his tales of earlier experiences in television, many of which were hard to believe (like his tale of the African chief who had his mother-in-law's heart in his refrigerator for future consumption, as a mark of respect for her memory). He displayed extraordinary organizational skills, a talent that is rarely combined with so imaginative and original a mind.

During this interim, at Peacock's request, Milton sent Video Arts a list of the proposed lecture topics, transcripts of lectures already given, and taped comments on the contents of the remaining lectures. On the basis of this material, Peacock, Jay, and Reid began making detailed plans for the series. A key result was four pages of "Notes from Tony Jay on proposed topics for discussion at Boston" in which, among other items, Jay asked Milton to propose his "top ten" topics for a series of ten programs, and to provide "opening and closing statements of the series," which Jay said, "should be designed for our own personal guidance, not as script for speaking to camera. Their purpose is to focus all of our minds on where we are starting from and where we are going to." This searching document, covering such items as "the overall framework and progression of the series," "the order of subjects," "what should be the principal locations for each film," "what should be our production style and conventions," was our real entry into the new and unfamiliar world of TV production.

Milton responded to Jay's memo by providing a list of ten TV topics and key ideas and possible opening and closing statements (item 4, appendix B). Along with Jay's memo, these provided the agenda for our meeting in Boston.

Michael Latham accompanied Peacock, Jay, and Reid to the Boston meeting. It was my first exposure to the man who was going to run a large part of our lives for the next two years. It was also my first exposure to Jay and Reid. Ben Rogge and our son David attended this meeting in addition to Bob Chitester, Milton and me, and the four from Video Arts, making a total of nine, just about the right size for an effective working group.

The session proceeded on the basis of Jay's earlier proposal of ten programs, each consisting of a half-hour documentary followed by a half-hour discussion. We provisionally chose the ten topics, discussing at length how the ideas that they were intended to convey could best be translated into television. We chose a proposed program on "protecting the consumer" as the first program to film in response to Jay's suggestion in his memo that "It is of central importance that we should have one program sufficiently complete for all of us to view and discuss before we set out on the main filming. Only an actual completed film will identify the pitfalls, and reveal the opportunities in a way that we can all understand and agree on."

About two weeks after the Boston meeting we received from Antony Jay a proposed outline for the pilot program. Milton was very much troubled by the outline. I urged him to be completely frank in replying. That set a pattern of complete openness on both sides that prevailed throughout our relationship with Video Arts. I do not remember any occasion from the first day to the last when there was any unpleasantness as a result of our frankness.

Milton did not mince words in replying to Antony. "I am very much puzzled," he wrote, "by the role and function of this outline of argument. It seems to me primarily a restatement and a condensation of many of the arguments in the lecture. What I do not see is that it has really changed the structure of the argument or indeed improved it or made it more accessible to television treatment." Having said that the outline was no improvement over the lecture, Milton went on even less tactfully with "The introduction will not I think do because I think the point that is made is fundamentally wrong."

In responding a few days later (December 18, 1977) to the receipt of outlines for three other programs, Milton wrote,

> I remain puzzled about the purpose of the outlines, but much more important, I fear that they are going off in a direction that diverges sharply from my own conception of the thrust that is desirable. . . .
>
> Perhaps I can indicate the source of my uneasiness best by stating what seem to me four essential requirements for the series:
> 1. No gimmicks.
> 2. This is an intellectual program, openly and unashamedly so.
> 3. There shall be no talking down to the audience. More than willing to sacrifice numbers for thoughtfulness.
> 4. I am going to speak my own words and no one else's."

{ *Milton* } On rereading these words long after the series was completed and broadcast, I am impressed with how closely these requirements were adhered to. Re point 4, I insisted from the beginning that I was not going to read from a script, and I never did. We had a shooting script, which indicated when and where we were going to film and what point the filming was intended to make, but never a textual script giving the words to be spoken. That requirement reflected my own judgment about my capacities.

{ *Rose* } Milton was so disturbed that he phoned Antony to transmit his apprehensions to him promptly. In a lengthy reply to Milton's letter, Antony wrote, "I hope that our telephone conversation . . . helped to set your mind at rest on some of the points" and went on to say, "The purpose of this letter is to allay your fears and resolve your bafflement, and I would therefore like to start with an apology. I should have prefaced these outlines with a covering letter explaining what they are, and—even more important—what they are not." And then Antony went on for four pages explaining to Milton how producing a television program differs from delivering a lecture. After this explanation of the difference he assured Milton, "I do not think there is any real problem in your making the transition from writing and lecturing to broadcasting: your unique gift for vivid, lucid, and jargon-free exposition of the fundamental economic truths will convert easily from one to the other.

But it may be helpful to be aware of what is the transition that has to be made." Along with this letter came a little book *Effective Presentation* that Antony had written earlier to deal with some of the differences between broadcasting and writing for the printed page.

The penultimate paragraph of Jay's letter also persuaded us, if we needed persuasion at this point, that he had fully grasped our purpose in producing this documentary:

> It also means, I think, aiming at changing attitudes rather than explaining principles. Of course the central point of each program is a principle. But you have said yourself that anyone who can be convinced in half an hour isn't worth convincing. The effect of these programs, I suggest, is to make a whole new audience, hundreds of thousands—perhaps millions—of reasonably intelligent laymen, suddenly think in a new way about their old assumptions. They can go on to read your books and articles and grasp the facts and the logical arguments that you build on them and the conclusions you reach, and be genuinely convinced and converted. But the programs in themselves and of themselves will serve rather to state the important questions than to supply the fully documented and substantiated answers.

Antony's long and fascinating letter then concludes,

> all the programs will be built up of visual sequences, and our joint task in structuring them is to marry the intellectual development of the argument with the narrative progress of the story. The outlines I have written are my first and fumbling attempt to do this. What is important, as we go forward, is that we should—obviously—not lose sight of the point of the series, which is the exposition of your vision, your arguments, and your conclusions; but also that we should develop as far as we can an interesting, intriguing program structure that holds the viewer's attention at the narrative level while the intellectual argument proceeds; and to find ways of making that narrative not merely carry the argument, but illustrate and reinforce it as well.

Rereading this letter some eighteen years later reminds me how fully our television team not only adhered to the four requirements Milton had set forth but also performed all of the purposes of the documentary that Antony detailed. As the saying goes, "the proof of the pudding is in the eating." The documentary was shown in every major country except France and in many smaller countries. Friends around the world wrote to tell us how much they enjoyed it.

The outlines for the ten programs were developed during the rest of January in correspondence between Jay and Milton. At the end of the month Bob Reid and Michael Latham, who had been working with Jay in London, came to San Francisco to make final plans about the structure and schedule for filming the pilot program. After three days they returned to London and we to our various activities.

The Pilot Program

The filming for the pilot program, finally titled "Who Protects the Consumer?" was done in San Francisco, Sacramento, and Washington in March 1978.

Michael Latham arrived on March 11, Bob Chitester on the twelfth, the entire crew assembled and the filming for the pilot started in our apartment on the thirteenth. Though I had long had a flat rule that our home was out of bounds for TV filming, this was special. It was our own program. Mike was extraordinarily persuasive, and the view from our balcony was breathtaking. The crew was very careful not to make too much mess and I was more tolerant than usual.

Not having been involved in this kind of filming before, we were surprised at the size of the crew, consisting of two groups—the Video Arts contingent (Mike Latham; Graham Massey, film director; Eben Wilson, associate producer and principal researcher; Margaret Young, assistant to the film director and production secretary; and Jackie Warner, production manager); and the film crew (a cameraman, assistant cameraman, sound man, and grip). The five from Video Arts accompanied us on all the shoots and became our temporary family—people on whom we could depend and to whom we became very attached.

The film crew was generally hired at each new location, with some exceptions for the United States. (By chance, Gil Hubbs, who served as lighting director and cameraman for all the U.S. scenes and did an outstanding job, had been a classmate of our daughter Janet at the University of Chicago Laboratory School!) One of Mike's unanticipated virtues was that, thanks to his extensive international experience and longtime connection with the BBC, he was extremely knowledgeable about the availability of professional film crews at all the places around the world where we filmed. As a result, we had excellent film crews everywhere. We discovered the existence of a worldwide industry of free-lance film crews. And we learned that the crew was none too large. The actual filming was, in a way, the least of it. Exploring alternative sites at which to film, getting permission to film, making the detailed arrangements of when and how to film—all of these activities went on behind the scene, as it were, but were essential preliminaries whether for a thirty-second segment or a five-minute or longer one.

We were not the only ones for whom this project was a new experience. Making a documentary with Milton was undoubtedly a new experience for the crew as well. Unlike most documentaries, there was no written script for this one. All talks to camera and all voice-overs were planned on the spot. While the TV people were setting up for shooting, Milton and I, and generally Mike, would find a quiet spot to talk about what Milton would cover in his comments. He would try it out and then he would talk to camera. This was the way he had always run his classes and lectures, and he was comfortable with this way of performing. But it was not what the crew was used to. We, on the other side, especially Milton, learned a lot about performing on television from Mike. While Milton has done a great deal of lecturing to live audiences, and has been extremely effective in presenting his ideas—as I have been told over the years by people who have attended his lectures—and while he had appeared frequently on television, he had not up to this time found himself in the capacity of a presenter. Under Mike's tutelage he became effective at it.

{ *Milton* } Mike reinforced Antony's message about the difference between lecturing and talking on television, explaining that the aim in a lecture is to project; on television, the presenter is a guest in a living room, and the aim is to converse. More important, he monitored my performance, told me when I did well and when badly, and did not hesitate to make me repeat a statement when he judged that it had not been effective. I welcomed such repetitions, but not those that were caused by extraneous disturbances, such as noise from a car horn or the like. Mike's tutelage has stood me in good stead ever since. I have frequently been on television since *Free to Choose*, and on each occasion, Mike is looking over my shoulder whether he knows it or not.

{ *Rose* } Another fascinating feature of the filming was the interest that the crews took in what Milton was saying. They were mostly hearing ideas that were new to them, unorthodox and yet appealing to them as free-lancers and independent individuals naturally attracted to the free market. Hardly a shoot ended without an informal seminar following. Ever the teacher, Milton enjoyed the discussions, as the crews clearly did also. No doubt, PBS and BBC bigwigs would never have approved this subversive activity on our part. (Interestingly, of the Video Arts contingent recruited from the BBC, only Graham

Massey returned to the BBC. The rest found the competitive market more attractive.)

To return to the pilot program, the filming in our apartment was just one part of three days of filming in San Francisco at various locations, which included Macy's Department Store, Merrill's Drug Store, and a number of others. Milton was involved in most but not all of the filming. From San Francisco, we went to Barstow, near Sacramento, where there is a railroad exhibit, including a very well-preserved, well-maintained, and extremely elegant private railroad car that had been owned by Lucius Beebe, a colorful figure of the railroad age. It was a highly appropriate location for a discussion of the Interstate Commerce Commission.

We then all moved to Washington, D.C., for six more days of filming—this time in and around Washington, some involving our presence and some, like a sequence about a Corvair performing on a race track, without us. One episode was particularly memorable. As it happened, a longtime colleague and friend from Chicago, Daniel Boorstin, was librarian of Congress at the time, and he arranged for us to film in the main rotunda of the Library of Congress and to withdraw from the stacks all the volumes of the Federal Register since its inception in the 1930s. The crew stacked them in piles by date around the circumference of the rotunda, the stacks getting higher and higher and then one stack not being enough for a session of Congress. The result was a striking and dramatic picture of the exponential growth of regulation. I no longer recall whose idea it was, but it was a splendid one.

The innocuous phrase, "The crew stacked them in piles," conceals more than it reveals, as Eben Wilson, of the Video Arts group, made clear in a recent letter giving his "view from the trenches." "What you don't know is that it took me and a wonderful black gentleman two hours to haul the damn things off the shelves, dust them off, load them on a trolley, wheel them up to the front hall, get them in year order and pile them up. In addition, while we were doing that we were both having explosive sneezing fits because of the dust. I was covered in it too, black with dust from my hair to my toes. I had to go back to the hotel to shower and change."[11]

Mike took the footage back to London to assemble the numerous clips into a program, and we went back to San Francisco marveling at his confidence that he could do so.

One month later, we flew to London to view Mike's work. After viewing his preliminary program, we, including Bob Chitester, spent several hours in the "cutting room," with Mike and Graham and the technicians making minor changes in response to our suggestions. We were extremely pleased with the result—it seemed nothing less than magic for Mike and his associates to have woven the seemingly disconnected shots into a coherent and entertaining film.

The rest of the two days that we spent with Video Arts were devoted to detailed discussion, in light of the lessons from the pilot program, of the remaining programs, the order in which they should appear in the final series, their content, and film ideas. We learned that although each final program covered one subject and included material filmed at different locations, each filming location generated bits for a number of programs, which meant that by contrast with what we had done for the pilot program, we had to shift from one topic to another at each location. For example, the first program ("The Power of the Market") used film from Hong Kong, Glasgow, the New York Stock Exchange, Britain, India, Rochester (New York), Ellis Island, New York streets, San Francisco, and probably a few other locations that I have forgotten. The other side of the coin was that film shot in Washington was used in nearly every program. This meant that the filming for all ten programs had to be planned before any substantial shooting took place, in order to minimize travel. I believe it was during these sessions that Michael produced a schedule for shooting at different locations and for the discussions at the end. Remarkably, his schedule was fulfilled to the day, with only one change that I will explain later, and that was entirely out of his control.

Filming on Location

In the United States

The crew began filming again in June in California, getting footage that would be used to illustrate points in several of the programs: wafer inspection at Intel, responding to a medical emergency at Rancho Santa Fe Ambulance Station, border patrol capturing illegal immigrants, migrant labor picking grapes, and on and on, all scenes that had been suggested as relevant to one or another program by the fertile imagination of Mike or Eben or Graham or in the course of Milton's and my discussions with Video Arts in London. As we learned, the trick was to film far more than could ever be used. Once a location was decided upon, the cost of extra filming was small and it was not possible to know in advance which images would make the relevant point best.

We joined the crew in Washington in July, Milton having delivered the final three lectures of the series in the interim. We continued filming in the U.S. until the end of August. Starting in Washington, we filmed at the Lincoln and Jefferson memorials and in and outside various government buildings: the capability of the production team to get permission for us to film continued to surprise us.

{ *Milton* } In Washington, the two most notable examples were filming in the rotunda of the Library of Congress, already referred to, and filming in the Bureau of Engraving and Printing, where I probably did as much to slow inflation as in any of my writing. To illustrate the crucial role of money in inflation, I wanted to stop in its tracks the press from which freshly printed currency was flowing, and, to my surprise, we were given permission for me to press a button that did so. I got a real kick out of that.

I also enjoyed a scene filmed in the gold vaults of the Federal Reserve Bank of New York, a scene that was made possible by Paul Volcker, at the time president of the Federal Reserve Bank of New York, whom I had known for many years. I wrote Paul after Graham reported having difficulty getting permission to film in the board room and the gold vault. In his friendly reply he said, "We don't ordinarily permit film makers into the Bank generally, much less the gold vault, and this will mark, to my knowledge, the first time that television cameras have been permitted into the board room for this type of filming."

In thanking Paul Volcker later for his help, I wrote, "I am tremendously grateful to you for your assistance in connection with our filming ventures at the Federal Reserve Bank of New York. Our crew was absolutely delighted with the cooperation and assistance they got, and I must say I enjoyed the session greatly, especially giving a little bit of a talk while seated on a bench of solid gold. For someone who could hardly be called a partisan of gold, it was real fun."

One vivid memory of the filming in Washington was of trying to talk to camera in front of the building housing the Social Security Administration. One take after another would start off fine and then be spoiled by an airplane flying overhead, or trucks driving by. As I recall, we gave up after some fifteen or so attempts, changed our plans, and moved into an office inside the building to shoot the planned statement.

{ *Rose* } Two interesting places at which we filmed in the United States were Monticello and historic Philadelphia. Although Milton and I had visited these spots earlier as tourists, being there for filming was quite different. First of all, we discovered early on that, like so many other activities, filming meant hurry up and wait so we had a considerable amount of time to wander around. For example, at Monticello, we had a very pleasant chat with the resident historian who brought out Jefferson's account books to demonstrate his extravagance. Jefferson died owing a great deal of money that his son-in law, we were told, spent the rest of his life paying off.

We criss-crossed the country more often than ever before. When we filmed in the eastern part of the United States, we went to Vermont to rest whenever there were a few days between shoots. When we filmed in the West, we returned to San Francisco. It proved very convenient having homes at both ends of the country.

We were able to spend a weekend in San Francisco before setting out for the last week of filming in the U.S. at the end of August. The week started in Salt Lake City, where we filmed a discussion with George Eccles about the experience of his family's banking firm during the banking crisis in 1933, as well as scenes in the bank. From there, we went to Las Vegas to film a late-night gambling session at the roulette table that provided some of the most entertaining film of the series. Milton and I had been to the casinos of Reno and Monte Carlo but never to those in Las Vegas. We were observers, not participants, on this occasion. However, the gambling provided a splendid image to illustrate the important role of risk-taking in a free market. As an aside, I was amazed at how many parents spent their vacations at Las Vegas gambling while their young children were presumably occupied in other activities.

From Las Vegas, we went to Bodie, an old gold-mining town that had been restored as a tourist attraction. Eben had discovered this spot in a book called *Ghost Towns of the West*. Mike was so entranced with it that he and Gil Hubbs spent the night outside in sleeping bags so that they could film the sunrise. Bodie completed our part of the filming in the United States.

The crew went on to Los Angeles, to film at UCLA, where they got wonderful scenes of parking lots full of automobiles and of students asleep in the classroom in contrast to their activity at the swimming pool. We used those scenes to contrast with others filmed earlier at Dartmouth College to show the difference between a private and public university.

Filming Abroad

After four days in San Francisco to relax and pack, we left for Hong Kong to attend a meeting of the Mont Pelerin Society. To coordinate with our plans, Mike had scheduled foreign filming to start in Hong Kong at the end of our meeting.

We spent about a week filming in Hong Kong, getting some of the most outstanding scenes of the series. Hong Kong gave Milton an opportunity to illustrate the benefits of free markets even under the most adverse circumstances, since Hong Kong was at the time as close to a complete free-market economy as any place in the world.

From Hong Kong we went to Japan, where we had many friends. We did our best to see as many as we could between filming. Milton even gave a lecture for *Nihon Keizai Shimbun,* something he did on almost all of our trips to Japan. The crew did a good deal of filming without us for background in Japan. The aim was to contrast Japan's successful industrialization after the Meiji restoration with India's lack of success after receiving independence from Britain. One particularly interesting contrast was how differently the two countries treated their weaving industries.

After our visit to India in 1963, I had no desire to return there ever. Begging children and people eating and sleeping on the curb were too depressing. However, it was an important part of our television story, so we had no choice. In the main, we filmed in places that were not the most depressing spots, and I had little time to wander about without the crew. We filmed a wonderful dancing performance in one of the palaces of the former maharaja of Jaipur. It was very colorful since the dancers were all in lovely saris, and the guests were also in colorful costumes. This was the best part of the Indian trip. As on our earlier visit, we found that the former princely states were much cleaner and apparently more prosperous than the others even after they had become independent. The maharaja in whose palace we filmed had turned some of his original palaces into hotels; we stayed in one while filming. We also filmed in and around Madras. We did not film in Calcutta, which is at the opposite end of the scale, economically and scenically.

From Asia we went to Europe, first to Cos, a Greek island that Milton and I had never visited. Cos is the island where the famous Greek physician Hippocrates had his hospital, and where the Hippocratic oath supposedly originated. According to Mike and Eben's research, Hippocrates' hospital had stood at the spot where we filmed. Here we learned something new about filming. We had decided what Milton was to say, the cameras were rolling, and Milton was talking when we heard the loud mooing of a cow. Mike immediately stopped the cameras. When we asked why, Mike's answer was that if the cow had been in the camera's vision, it would have been all right to leave the mooing but to have the sound and not see the cow was bad television. So we started over again, hoping the cow would be quiet, and it was. The same problem had occurred often in earlier filming when a plane would fly overhead and the cameras were stopped. We had assumed it was because of the disturbing noise but learned by the experience with the cow that that was not the main reason.

{ *Milton* } "Just one more take" became a refrain that I both expected and feared. Generally, the first take was the most spontaneous, though the second frequently proved preferable because I was able to correct something I did not like about my first attempt. But from there on, I felt that it was all down-hill. Instead of spontaneously making my point, I inevitably was trying to remember and reproduce what I had said before. Professional actors deliver a memorized script and have trained themselves to repeat it as many times as necessary with the same intonation and emphasis. I was not a professional actor.

One technical point led to a larger number of repeated takes. Our pro-grams were all shot on film, whereas today they would all be shot on videotape. At the time we were filming, the use of tape was in its infancy and, in Mike's judgement, yielded lower-quality pictures than film. With tape, it is possible to have an instantaneous replay before deciding whether another take is desir-able. With film, the exposed film had to be developed, often at a distant lab, so that it was generally not available to view until after we had moved to a different location. As a result, it was sensible to resolve any doubt about whether a particular take would prove satisfactory by "just one more take."

{ *Rose* } Our next stop was Germany. Our shooting schedule included film-ing in West Berlin first and then in East Berlin. Mike thought that he had an agreement with the authorities in East Berlin to film there without our films being censored. In the event, however, the East Berlin authorities changed their minds before we got there and agreed to our filming only on the condition that the East German authorities would have final say on what could be broadcast. We all agreed that we would not film under those condi-tions. Instead we included a scene in the filming in West Berlin in which the cameraman and Milton stood on a raised platform alongside the Wall from which parts of East Berlin were visible and Milton explained why we were showing East Berlin in this way. (Milton and I did go across to East Berlin as tourists simply to look around.)

The cancellation of the filming in East Berlin (the change in schedule referred to earlier) left us with a few days before our next scheduled filming. Milton and I were given the option of going to London for rest and recreation or a quick trip to Vermont. We chose Vermont, where we stayed on European time and told no one that we were there. While in some ways an eerie experi-ence, making day into night and vice versa, it was delightful. We arrived fresh and relaxed in London about one week after leaving the crew in Germany. They used the extra time to set up the filming in the U.K.

Back to work, we filmed first in Cambridge. For one sequence, we very much wanted to film in Keynes's rooms in King's College. However, all of Mike's persuasive capacities did not succeed in getting us permission. As an alternative, we filmed in a room in Gonville and Caius College, after putting in books and pictures that would make it look as authentic as possible.

After filming in London, we went to Manchester and then to Scotland to film at Glasgow University, where Adam Smith once taught. Our European filming completed, we returned to Vermont, but not for long. We joined Mike and the crew for one more week of filming in the United States, primarily in Washington, filling in gaps that Mike found when he reviewed the twenty-six miles of film and audiotape that had accumulated. Our final filming was on November 20 in Ottumwa, Iowa, which had been named the "All-American City of 1978." The authorities of Ottumwa were so delighted to be included that when we finished filming they threw a wonderful farewell party for all of us.

Editing and Voice-overs

We returned to San Francisco to resume our normal life for a few months while Mike and his fellow professionals worked to produce coherent programs out of the mass of film—most of which of course ended up on the cutting-room floor. We returned to London for our longest stay, more than three weeks, on March 17, 1979 when Mike was ready for us to view the end product of their work and for Milton to dub the voice-overs.

{ *Milton* } A word about voice-overs. Many of the pieces of film that ultimately constitute a program have words linked directly with them, as when I was filmed on location commenting on something or other, or someone else was commenting or being interviewed. But many pieces of film consist simply of pictures, as for example a scene of the Border Patrol chasing Mexicans crossing the border illegally. To integrate them into the story requires an accompanying commentary, a voice-over. The role and importance of voice-overs and the technical problem of dubbing them on the film was completely new to me, but it was my major function during this stay.

In the preliminary programs that Mike and the others had put together, they had dubbed in tentative voice-overs to provide continuity, to be replaced by both my voice and my words.

{ *Rose* } Our first week was spent mainly viewing the preliminary programs. We were most favorably impressed by what they had done, but we still had problems with many details. That led to a good deal of editing, recutting and the like. We learned in the process how drastically the impact of pictures can be affected by the voice-overs that accompany them, which made us realize how crucial that step was.

In addition, Milton did some promotional films that Bob Chitester wanted for each program. We also did some additional filming in London to fill in a few lacunae that had shown up in the editing. I have a wonderful recollection of some filming at St. Catherine's Dock because Graham Massey took some pictures of me to try out a camera that he had bought in Hong Kong. One shot pleased us so much that we used it on the dust jacket of *Free to Choose*.

{ *Milton* } Mike warned me in advance that the dubbing was a nerve-wracking process because the words spoken not only had to tell the right story but had to be of precisely the right length to match the film it referred to. The procedure is carried out in a special room with a large screen on which the film is shown, and a soundproof box in which the commentator sits with a microphone. Ordinarily, the commentator has a script from which he reads as the film is shown on the screen, a script that has already been calibrated to be of roughly the right length. In our case, however, Mike wrote, "It still seems best that we ask you to 'speak' rather than 'read' the commentary. In essence it will follow the pattern of the filming itself, in that you may do as many 'takes' as you wish. The real difference is that you will not have to work in public: this time you'll do it in private in a dimly lit padded cell!"[12] On location, I only had to be sure I got my statement right, without worrying about the precise length. Here, ensconced in my monkish cell, I not only had to emit the right words, I had to have them precisely match in length the pictures that were unfolding before my eyes. I found it a real challenge, both exhausting and exhilarating. Most days, I was so drained that I could hardly wait to get back to our hotel apartment and sink into an easy chair with a drink in my hand. Rose helped by picking up food on our way home from the studio so we could eat at home.

{ *Rose* } The schedule for the dubbing was one program a day plus a certain amount of rerecording after Mike had seen the film. Mike felt it was essential that Milton relax between the dubbing sessions, so he had thoughtfully obtained tickets for every play in London he thought we might enjoy. I think we saw more theater productions in the three weeks we spent in London working than we have ever seen when on holiday. In addition, we were able to see many of our London friends. My memory, as well as my appointment book, tells me that we had a very active and pleasant three weeks in London.

After Mike saw the complete series, he decided there were one or two spots he wanted to change and items he wanted to add, and so we came back to the U.S. to do a bit more filming, this time in Salem, Massachusetts.

The Discussions

{ *Milton* }   The initial contract with Video Arts covered only the documentaries. But early on, we insisted that Mike Latham should also produce the discussion sessions, and Bob Chitester made a deal to that effect with Video Arts, differing from the initial arrangement in that WQLN took responsibility for much of the equipment and the film crew, though all were to be under Mike's control.

Planning for the discussion sessions began in mid-1978, and continued until they were filmed in September 1979. The issues that we were involved in were first, the location; second, whether to have a moderator and if so, who; third, the participants in the discussion. We started discussing possible participants with Mike and Eben in March 1979, when we were in London for the dubbing, and from June on, Mike and Eben spent three months interviewing possible participants. In July, Mike set up a temporary office in a hotel in Chicago staffed by Jackie Warner and Maggie Young.

Location

Rose and I wanted the discussions to be held at the University of Chicago. After all, that was my intellectual home and the major academic center at which there was strong support for free-market ideas. Mike reported to Bob Chitester on December 14, 1978 that after looking at some two dozen possible locations at the university, "We favour the North Reading Room of Harper Library for the post-film discussions. It is about the right size; though modern, it is clearly set in an old, established university; it requires minimum art direction to make it work well; the floor and wall coverings are rich; it will look good." That suited us fine. The North Reading Room had been the Law School Library before the Law School moved to new quarters. It was in a building adjacent to the Social Science building where I had had my office for thirty years, and I had frequently used it when I was in residence. In 1979, it was in a building occupied by the Business School.

Studio discussions were planned for the first nine programs. The plan for the tenth was to close with a twenty-minute interview with an interlocutor in which I could summarize the major themes of the series. Mike proposed to have that interview in Robie House, a famous Frank Lloyd Wright residence that had been purchased by the university and housed the alumni office.

The Harper reading room had to be converted into a film studio for our purposes. I hadn't realized how much was involved until, in going over material that Mike Latham sent us, I came across a four-page single-spaced set of notes on a meeting of ten participants on July 27, 1979, to plan the actions that were required to adapt the reading room. The memo was accompanied by several detailed sketches of the room and the changes.

Moderator and Choice of Participants

{ *Rose* } Milton was initially dubious that we needed a moderator for the discussions, believing that he could serve as his own moderator. But we were easily persuaded that it would be better to have a separate moderator. Bob or Mike sounded out a number of well known U.S. radio and television personalities but none was available. Michael Peacock suggested Robert McKenzie, professor of sociology at the University of London, who had frequently served as a moderator on BBC programs, and of whom Michael thought well. A Canadian resident of Britain, he did not seem the right person for the interview that was to end the series. For that, we ultimately settled on Lawrence Spivak, the originator and producer of *Meet the Press*.

We first met McKenzie at a meeting Bob arranged early in July at Lake Morey Inn in Fairlee, Vermont, close to Capitaf. That meeting had a dual purpose: first, to enable us to meet McKenzie and to discuss the role he would play; second, for us, Bob, and Michael Peacock to discuss with Mike and Eben the preliminary results of their exploration of possible participants. By this time, they had already spent a month on the search.

We were most anxious that the discussions be as wide-ranging and as open as possible, and that the participants include the most effective defenders of various points of view. In addition, Mike wanted to be sure that the participants were also good performers on television. For each program, we tried to suggest the names of the persons we thought would present the best case against Milton's position, as well as names of persons who would share our views. In their search, Eben and Mike interviewed every potential participant, to explore both the person's views on the issues and also his or her capacities on TV. In the process, they added names to those we had suggested. The plan was to have four discussants on each program, two more or less pro; two, definitely con. As it happened, for one program we ended up with only three. Also, two discussants (Peter Jay and Thomas Sowell) each served on two programs. In all, thirty-three separate persons took part in the discussion segments (item 5, appendix B). I have no idea how many people Mike and Eben contacted in the search for the final thirty-three, but it was several times that number.

The thirty-three participants covered a wide range. A plurality of ten were university professors, followed by five each of bureaucrats and representatives of nonprofit groups, three each of bankers, businessmen, and labor union representatives, two members of Congress, one journalist, and one ambassador—all told, not only varied but also distinguished. In eight of the nine programs, the discussants who differed with Milton generally outnumbered those who agreed, which in my view was appropriate since Milton was there to defend himself. The one exception was the program on inflation, a more technical subject on which Milton's views had become conventional wisdom among both academics and central bankers. Two of the discussants on that program were central bankers, Otmar Emminger, the president of the German central bank, and William McChesney Martin, former chairman of the U.S. Federal Reserve System.

Production

We arrived in Chicago on September 3 for the final stage, the actual filming of the discussions. We hardly recognized the library reading room after it had been converted into a film studio. A large circular area in the center accommodated the moderator, Milton, and the discussants for the session; the audience sat around this circle at a higher level. Four lighting towers had been carefully placed to provide proper lighting. Three cameras were in place to film the discussion, one on a crane, the others on pedestals, and an artificial bookcase had been built in back of the area reserved for the discussion in order to hide one camera that would shoot from the back and to conceal the technicians who would monitor and mix the sound. Dressing rooms were prepared outside the studio, and also a room outside the studio equipped with monitors where Mike, Bob, Michael Peacock, and I could watch the discussion (in television parlance, a "green room"). We could call Mike's attention to a possible problem and Mike could communicate with the film director on the floor. In addition, there was a remote van containing much of the recording equipment.

The first two days were spent constructing the set; the third day, meeting with the technical crew to discuss the schedule, where the cameras would be set and other technicalities, and finally, a rehearsal. Additional rehearsals were held during the morning and early afternoon of the fourth day. Sometime in the afternoon, the audience and principal speakers arrived and were briefed.

About 3 o'clock on the fourth day, the audience and principal speakers viewed the half-hour documentary film for "Who Protects the Consumer," Bob McKenzie made an opening statement, and the discussion of the program began. After the first day, since the pattern was set and the problems solved, we did two discussion programs a day for the next week—one in the morning and one in the afternoon. As novices in live television production, we were most impressed with the amount of preparation required and the precision of the timing.

{ *Milton* } All participants had been informed that the film of the discussion would not be edited for content, though some editing might be necessary to remove noise, eliminate pauses, etc. The aim was to assure that there would be no censoring of opinion. But that also meant that the discussion had to last just a trifle longer than one-half hour, to allow for the editing out of pauses. There was no room for second thoughts.

That week compares with the week of dubbing as one of the most stressful weeks that I have ever experienced. By the end of the second program of the day, I was emotionally exhausted. I had not anticipated in advance that two half-hour sessions would have that effect. However, the knowledge that this was it, no second takes, no editing of what I said, the need to concentrate on what the discussants said, all combined to make it a very demanding half hour. We ended each day by returning to a suite we were occupying at the Drake Hotel, having a drink, and then dinner via room service. The filming of the nine discussions ended on Friday, September 14. On Saturday, we filmed my discussion with Lawrence Spivak at Robie House. That was more relaxed. For one thing, there was no audience. For another, it was one on one, not one on three or four.

At the conclusion of the filming of all the discussions, we had dinner with the crew at Maxim's to celebrate not only the ending of the filming but also Michael Peacock's fiftieth birthday.

Naming the Series and the Separate Programs

What to call the series and what names to give to the separate programs was the subject of much discussion among all participants, both in person and by correspondence. It began not long after the Boston meeting over the 1977 Thanksgiving weekend and did not reach a final conclusion until some time in 1979.

A memo on the "Milton Friedman Series," of February 13, 1978, lists titles and the proposed running order for the ten programs that we had agreed on. Only one interim title corresponds to the title finally used ("Who Protects the Worker?"). Similarly, we went back and forth for about a year before we finally settled on a title for the series. Rose and I originally suggested "The Invisible Hand," but were informed by Michael Peacock, in a note dated February 23, 1978, that "None of us like 'The Invisible Hand' as a title." Michael closes a memo to his associates on the series title dated October 30, 1978, "More ideas, please. A bottle of Champagne awaits anyone who comes up with a winner."

A memo from Mike Latham to Michael Peacock of January 1, 1979, reads, "This is to confirm that . . . [we] all agree that the series will be called 'Free to Choose.' I invented the title. I hereby claim my case (or was it two cases?) of French Champagne!"

The story behind that claim is that Mike suggested "Free to Choose" as a title for the program finally labeled "Who Protects the Consumer?" Rose and I, as I recall, at once realized that it was the perfect title for the series as a whole, and so it proved to be.

Titles for the separate programs and the order in which they were to be shown was not finally settled until the end of July 1979.

The Book Free to Choose

The book *Free to Choose,* which we wrote to accompany the video, is special in a number of ways. It is the only book that either Rose or I have ever written to a deadline. It took the least time to write. It is the only book that is based almost entirely on spoken rather than written English. Partly for that reason, it has sold many more copies than any other book that we have written.

These special features all reflect the origin of the book. It was not written originally from scratch but was based on the transcripts of the TV programs that we brought back from London in April after the end of the dubbing sessions. We started to write the book as soon as we returned from that visit. We delivered a completed manuscript to Harcourt Brace Jovanovich on Labor Day. The transcripts needed a great deal of editing, and we added much additional material. Yet the text clearly reflects its origin in spoken English.

The speed with which we delivered the manuscript to HBJ was matched by the speed with which Bill Jovanovich got the book to the market. He made sure that it was in the bookstores before Christmas. It was reviewed widely and was number one on the nonfiction bestseller list for many weeks. It was the best-selling nonfiction book in the United States for the year 1980 as a whole. The original hardback version has sold roughly four hundred thousand copies since its publication in 1980; a popular paperback version was published by Avon in 1981, and a quality paperback by HBJ in 1990. We do not have accurate figures on how many copies Avon has sold, but we believe that sales of the various U.S. editions total more than a million copies.

Free to Choose has been translated into at least seventeen languages—every major language and many minor ones. Before the fall of the Berlin wall, it was translated sub rosa in the Soviet Union, Poland, and several other communist countries. By now, there are authorized translations in both mainland China and Taiwan, as well as Russia, Poland, the Czech Republic, Estonia, Croatia, and Hungary.

We do not have data on how many copies have been sold abroad. We do know that the book was a bestseller in Japan, where the original hardback translation sold around two hundred thousand copies, which equals or tops American sales per capita.

"I would hope it's Keynesian economics, but it's probably Milton Friedman's 'Free to Choose'."

BERRY'S WORLD © United Feature Syndicate. Reprinted by permission.

The U.S. Broadcast

The initial pay-off for three years of effort by so many people came in the second week of January 1980, when 196 PBS stations in the United States, 72 percent of all PBS stations, broadcast the first episode of *Free to Choose,* most at the scheduled time, others at times of their own choosing. Stations sympathetic to the program sought to show it at times that were attractive to their viewers and scheduled repeat broadcasts of each episode; others chose unfavorable times but even they generally repeated the program at other times. The most egregious example was in New York City—the hotspot of American liberalism. WNET, the major PBS station in New York City, scheduled the initial program opposite the Super Bowl. Some of the station's financial supporters who shared our ideological view were outraged and brought enough pressure on the station so that it repeated the broadcast at a better time.

Taken as a whole, the reaction was extremely favorable. According to the standard ratings, the program attracted an average of three million viewers, a very good audience, we were told, for PBS, higher, for example, than the number attracted to *Masterpiece Theater,* one of PBS's most popular programs. Reviews in newspapers and magazines were generally favorable, even when the writer expressed disagreement with our free-market position.

Letters from viewers were one of the most rewarding products of the series. One source was from responses to an offer by WQLN of a viewer guide for one dollar. Barbara Praetzel, project coordinator for WQLN, sent us "a sampling of the letters we receive here daily. We have been averaging between 200 and 300 a day. One negative letter has been enclosed because we have, in fact, received some, but no more than six to date." The one negative letter she included started, "The first installment of professor Friedman's soap opera on economics was a sorry spectacle, all the more so because a bevy of prestigious discussants failed to point out the fallacy of it" and then continued for three long paragraphs of diatribe on what is wrong with a free economic marketplace. Most favorable comments were much briefer. Herewith some excerpts.

> Thoroughly enjoyed the series, even though my political and economic thinking sharply differs with that of Mr. Friedman.

> Our family is so excited by your show. As far as I am concerned there hasn't been a more important show in the history of TV. . . . your shows come on three or four times a week here and I watch it each time.

> Currently the *best* program on TV.

I enjoyed this program thoroughly. I hope you will continue this fine line of programming. P.S. I am fourteen years old.

This is the finest public service program that I have ever witnessed.

Tell Milty I think he's great if you get a chance.

Comments on the discussion session covered the waterfront. At one extreme, "After the first three segments of the series, I have decided to listen only to Dr. Friedman's presentation. . . . With few exceptions . . . the people that 'discuss' their ideas with Dr. Friedman tend to make the hour end up on a cloudy, confusing and unsatisfying note." At the other extreme: "The discussion in the Harper Library, one of the best discussions I've seen on television, vividly illustrated contrasting viewpoints. I only wish it could have been longer."

In addition to the letters accompanying requests for viewer guides, we received nearly two thousand letters addressed to me personally or to Rose and me commenting on the TV series and the book. Though I have always tried to answer every personal letter that I receive, I was driven on this occasion to use a form letter, explicitly so described, to reply to most of the correspondence (item 6, appendix B). Most, though not all, of the letters were favorable. Some commented on specific points, either to add information or to criticize our statements. I tried to answer all of those individually.

I referred earlier to "the initial pay-off." Subsequent pay-offs included (a) broadcasts in other countries, (b) use of films and later videotapes in high school and college courses and special educational programs, (c) reprinting of excerpts from the book in many different publications.

Broadcasts in Other Countries

Video Arts was responsible for marketing the program in other countries. By now the original program has been shown, often without the discussion sessions, in more than a dozen countries, sometimes in English with subtitles, sometimes with dubbing in the native language.

I participated in two of the most important foreign broadcasts: in Britain and in Japan.

BBC bought the rights to show six of the programs, and arranged for me to film five new discussions with British participants. Peter Jay served as moderator. I have been unable to unearth a list of the British participants in the program, but I do recall that BBC recruited a distinguished group, including at least one minister in the Conservative government and one former minister of the prior Labour government. The new discussions were recorded on five successive days in mid-February 1980, and the programs were broadcast for six successive weeks beginning the middle of February (the first program broadcast, "The Power of the Market," was not accompanied by a discussion session). In Britain, as in the United States, the program was very successful, almost certainly reaching a larger fraction of the potential audience than in the United States, thanks to the more limited alternatives to BBC than to PBS.

In Japan, Suntory, a major producer of alcoholic beverages, purchased the rights to broadcast the series on a commercial network. Their advertising agency, Dentsu, arranged for a producer, a film crew, and Chiaki Nishiyama as interpreter to come to Capitaf at the end of May to film an interview with me as well as some introductory comments for the various programs. They also managed to work some wonderful film of Capitaf into the broadcast. In September, we spent about ten days in Japan under the auspices of Suntory, filming a number of discussion sessions with Japanese guests, and attending a seminar organized by Suntory at which I gave a talk, all as part of their publicizing of the series. One or more of the episodes was on the air during our stay, which is when we saw the film that they had shot in Vermont. It was quite an experience to hear myself speaking fluent Japanese on the little screen and not to understand a word that I was saying!

In the Japanese tradition of extraordinary hospitality to which we had become accustomed, Dentsu not only wined and dined us but also arranged a very special touristic treat.

The Moss Temple is one of the leading attractions in Kyoto. A beautiful Japanese garden, the ground cover consists exclusively of more than fifty varieties of moss.[13] At the time we were there, it had been closed for months to visitors to enable the moss to recover from the effect of too many visitors. Dentsu arranged a special guided tour of the nearly fully recovered Moss Temple for us. Not only was it an unusual pleasure to have the whole garden to ourselves, but our guide was the Buddhist abbot in charge of the temple and head of the monastic community. Highly intelligent, well informed, and fluent in English, he was a splendid guide, and the garden, almost ready for reopening to visitors, was at the very peak of its extraordinary beauty.

In Germany, the federal government channel, leftist-oriented like most government TV systems, at first refused to broadcast the series. However, Isabel Mühlfenzl, a producer and presenter on Bavarian regional television and a libertarian member of the Mont Pelerin Society, persuaded the regional channel to air the series. It proved to be so popular that the federal channel was shamed into showing it nationwide.

In Italy, France, and Switzerland, a strong supporter and fellow Mont Pelerin member, Mr. Zerilli-Merimò made great efforts to have the series shown. A wealthy industrialist, his major outside interest was television. His writings played an important role in what he described as the "de facto" liberalization of broadcasting in Italy. As he wrote, "As to Italy, I consider practically impossible to have any hope in national State Television." However, he did suceed in inducing a major private television station, "Telé Milano," to air the series in Italy.

In France, he ran into a stone wall, even though French television had shown all thirteen episodes of Galbraith's *Age of Uncertainty,* itself paying for the rights. In response to a letter from Zerilli-Merimò urging the airing of the series, Maurice Ulrich, the president of Société Nationale de Télévision en Couleur, wrote "Il s'avère que les thèmes abordés par ces émissions ont déjà été largement traités dans des productions d'ANTENNE 2."[14] Zerilli-Merimò immediately wrote back, saying that he was soon going to be in Paris, would like to see some of the programs presenting the same issues, and asking Mr. Ulrich to have someone assemble the relevant cassettes for him to view. The answer was a gem: "Il se trouve, en effet, que les responsables des programmes d'ANTENNE 2, et notamment la Direction de l'Information, ont choisi, afin d'intéresser le public aux problèmes économiques et sociaux, de traiter ces questions directement dans les journaux et magazines d'information, plutôt que de diffuser des séries d'émissions dont la longueur et le caractère 'technique' peuvent décourager a priori les téléspectateurs."[15] Somehow, that did not discourage them from broadcasting the even longer Galbraith series.

After similar responses by regional stations, Zerilli-Merimò, despairingly concluded, "We are perhaps deluded and naive enough to believe that, after all, the citizens would actually like to learn the truth. . . . But evidently we are wrong because these wonderful State televisions deem that their task and their function is that of simply entertaining the by-standers, of cultivating . . . the worst parts of the public tastes." I believe that France is the only European country in which the program was never aired.

Educational Use

Bob arranged a contract with Encyclopaedia Britannica Educational Corporation to produce and distribute 16 mm film prints. These were expensive, priced at $300 a print, or $3,000 for a complete set of the ten programs. I do not know how many copies were sold. I do know that the Americanism Educational League, a southern California tax-exempt foundation, managed to accumulate more than a dozen sets, which they loaned without charge to educational institutions for limited periods on a rotating basis. All in all, the league reported that it had made the films available to hundreds of schools and colleges.

We were very anxious to make the program available to individuals and schools at a lower cost, and the development of VCRs made that increasingly possible. However, Penn Communications, Inc., a subsidiary of Station WQLN, owned the rights to the film, and Encyclopaedia Britannica had the exclusive right to market the program. When the contract with Encyclopaedia Britannica was up for renewal in 1987, Rose and I wanted to buy the rights to distribute *Free to Choose,* in order to make possible an inexpensive videocassette version. The obstacle to doing so was that the National Federation of Independent Business had helped finance the original production by a substantial non-interest-bearing loan, supposedly to be paid back out of future profits that Penn Communications would make from the series. However, those profits never came close to being enough to repay the loan. Buying the rights meant assuming the liability for the loan, which we were not able or willing to do. The NFIB shared our interest in as wide a distribution of the series as possible, so Bob negotiated an agreement with them to cancel the loan in return for a brief statement by them introducing the videocassette version of the original series. That is why a brief statement by John Sloan, President of the NFIB at the time, introduces each tape.

The upshot was that we bought all rights for $25,000, and set up, jointly with Bob, Free to Choose Enterprise, with Bob and us as joint owners, to handle distribution of the original and later programs. Videocassettes of the entire series were priced initially at $110 a set, making it feasible for many more schools and colleges to use the series as part of a course. In addition, many individuals have acquired sets for their own use.

One of the real rewards for us from the program is the number of people who have come up to us at public events that we attend, or for that matter, on the street or in restaurants, to tell us how much they enjoyed seeing our series in one of their courses.

More recently, the Foundation for Teaching Economics has been conducting intensive summer sessions in economics for student leaders and for teachers of economics in secondary schools not only in the United States, but also in the Czech Republic, Poland, Hungary, and perhaps some other foreign countries. *Free to Choose* serves as a centerpiece of their presentations.[16] It has served the same function in many similar programs conducted by other organizations.

Tyranny of the Status Quo

{ *Rose* } Our second venture into television three years later was much more modest, much less expensive, and much less effective. It was filmed at the Hoover Institution, and produced by Bob Chitester. Milton discussed a series of topics with seven students.[17] We called the program *Tyranny of the Status Quo* and wrote a book by that title to accompany the program. Bob was unable to persuade PBS to include the series in its core program. So it was delivered by satellite to any stations that wanted to pick it up.

Milton raised a series of questions concerning such issues as higher education, agricultural subsidies, crime, and drugs, and then moderated a discussion among the students and spoke on the topic himself. We were not very happy about this program when we viewed it. Our reaction was that it was too much like Milton giving a lecture to the students. It would have been much better to have someone more nearly at their level conduct the discussion.

In retrospect, the book was the biggest dividend from this venture. It never achieved the best-seller status of *Free to Choose,* but it sold a respectable number of copies, received good reviews, and is still in print.

Conclusion

Since it is more than seventeen years since we produced *Free to Choose,* we decided to look at the videos to refresh our memory. I had two reactions. First, the problems that we explored still plague the country, and in many cases have gotten worse. Second, our views have clearly gained ground in the world of ideas, yet there is no shortage of critics who offer the same objections and solutions today as the participants on the program did then.

As we look back at the events chronicled in this chapter, it all seems like something of a fairy tale. Who would have dreamed that after retiring from teaching, Milton would be able to preach the doctrine of human freedom to many millions of people in countries around the globe through television, millions more through our book based on the television program, and countless others through videocassettes.

However important the initial telecast, the educational use of the series may well be its most important product. People form their opinions when young. It is the rare person who changes his or her basic opinion after the late teens or early twenties. Hence the educational use reaches youngsters at a favorable time.

The fairy tale was made possible by our incredible good fortune in the cast of characters that were involved in the production of *Free to Choose:* Bob Chitester, the first crucial member of that cast; Bill Jovanovich, who provided a generous advance at a key point; Antony Jay, Robert Reid, and Michael Peacock from Video Arts, who converted the lectures into a program for television; Michael Latham, who proved to be the ideal producer for our purposes, and Eben Wilson, Graham Massey, Margaret Young, and Jackie Warner, four other TV professionals to whom we are indebted for their unstinting cooperation and above all, friendship.

{ *Milton* } One other person needs to be added to that cast of characters: Rose. Her title as associate producer was far more than a formality. She played an indispensable role: she participated in every planning session and every editing session; she was on every shoot and involved in every discussion about the content of my statements to the camera; she was the best critic of my performance, and perhaps most important, the only one willing to be blunt in criticizing me, and the most helpful in setting me on the right track.

⤳ *Chapter Twenty-Nine* ⤶

FILMING IN EASTERN EUROPE

{ *Rose* } One more experience completes our venture into television production. For some time Bob Chitester and other enthusiastic friends had been suggesting an update of *Free to Choose*. The fall of the Berlin Wall and the subsequent changes in Eastern Europe seemed to be the logical time. We agreed to an update that would include a new documentary filmed in Eastern Europe plus four of the original documentaries, and new discussion sessions for all five. Once again, Bob Chitester arranged the funding, was the executive producer for the documentary in Eastern Europe, and producer of the discussions. We persuaded Michael Latham to produce the Eastern European program and Eben Wilson to assist.

Czechoslovakia

We planned to attend the 1990 Mont Pelerin meeting in Munich and then go on to Czechoslovakia to begin the filming in Eastern Europe. By chance, Shirley Temple Black, the U.S. Ambassador to Czechoslovakia, was a fellow passenger on our plane to Munich. We had met her earlier in California. This good fortune enabled Milton to get a thorough briefing on Czechoslovakia from a very knowledgeable source.

As usual, the Mont Pelerin meeting was very pleasant. When it was over, Eben met us in Munich and we drove with him to Regensburg, West Germany, where we stayed overnight in a Ramada Motor Inn, one of the many American motels and hotels that we encountered in Central and Eastern Europe. The next morning we drove from the German border to Prague, witnessing en route graphic evidence of the effect of communism on a formerly prosperous area. The factories looked as if they were ready to fall apart. So did much of the housing—large, extremely standardized apartment complexes, almost always in the neighborhood of a factory. Pilsen, a center of heavy industry, was particularly depressing. As we were to see during the rest of our trip, communism was a disaster not only for the human spirit and human well-being but also for the environment.

We arrived in Prague Sunday afternoon. The city was very beautiful, but that beauty derived from the distant past: palaces, churches, bridges, constructed centuries earlier. We stayed at the Diplomat Hotel, which had just been opened, an elegant, luxurious, Western-style hotel run by a Viennese hotel group. All meals were buffet-style, presumably because of a shortage of competent English-speaking waiters. The few waiters available all spoke English.

Mike arrived early Sunday afternoon and we all went to Wenceslaus Square, the site of the famous series of demonstrations that led to the overthrow of communism—the velvet revolution. Mike planned to film a statement on that episode at that location. However, a heavy rain ended that possibility. As we had learned during our earlier filming experience, a producer like Michael Latham can always improvise. The segment that appears on the finished film as if it had been filmed at the square was actually filmed in Hungary. Unable to film, we went instead to a cafe to get out of the rain. It was of pre-1939 vintage, strictly Viennese, with music from the same period, and it was jammed. Old Vienna was clearly popular. The crew did some filming in order to get a sample of Prague before the war.

The next morning we filmed an interview with Václav Klaus, the finance minister (later, prime minister) and a convinced believer in free markets. We had met him earlier at the Mont Pelerin meeting in Munich. During the communist period, he had been employed at a research institute that was compiling an economic encyclopedia. By chance, one of his assignments was to write an article on Milton's contributions. As a result, he reported that he had been much influenced by Milton and shared many of his views.

Arriving at the filming session straight from parliament, Klaus complained bitterly about the problem he was having with liberals (in the American sense) in parliament. For the interview, he discussed his views about the best way to privatize the economy. Like Milton, he believed it should be done rapidly. He had his plans well worked out, but they had to be passed by the legislature. As he explained to us, many legislators did not agree with his approach. They wanted to move much more slowly. We met some of these people later in our visit, and had no difficulty in understanding Klaus's frustration.

By contrast, his staff included able young people who shared his outlook and were committed to moving as rapidly as possible toward a strictly privatized economy. They succeeded remarkably well in the next few years, outpacing all the other former Soviet satellites. They also succeeded in enforcing a monetary and fiscal policy that kept inflation relatively low. The pay-off has been rapid economic expansion, low unemployment, rising living standards.

That afternoon we filmed some footage on a communist millionaire, a man who had started accumulating wealth well before the revolution. As he explained to us, he was a popular rock singer and composer. That gave him advantages not available to others. He was allowed to go abroad—to the United States and to Western Europe. He used the foreign currency he earned to buy equipment required to produce audiotapes and videocassette tapes, for which there was a ready market in communist Czechoslovakia. He expressed the belief that the changes brought about by the revolution would open up tremendous additional opportunities for him and many others. His home, which was also his business location, was extraordinarily luxurious, not only by communist but by Western standards. For example, he had a swimming pool inside his house.

Mike, Eben, and the crew left the following morning to drive to Budapest, which would take them most of the day. They planned to film en route and also the following day without us, as well as to make arrangements for filming when we got to Budapest. This gave us two days as tourists in Prague. The first day we spent partly doing the usual tourist things: visiting castles, churches, and so forth; and partly redressing the oversight of not having visas to either Hungary or Poland. Getting visas for Hungary was simple and straightforward. We went to the Hungarian Embassy, filled out the forms, paid a certain amount of money, and came back twenty-five minutes later to pick up our visas. The Polish experience was very different. First of all, the woman who was in charge of visas was very unpleasant. In a nasty tone, as though we were interfering with whatever it was she was supposed to be doing, she said she couldn't tell us when we could get the visas, that it was going to take time. But, she went on, if we were willing to pay double the regular price ($50 instead of $25) she would make it express. That was more than I could take from this bureaucrat so, as Milton reported in his notes, I said "To hell with it. We'll do it in Budapest," and we walked out. Since someone working with the crew got our Polish visas for us when we were in Budapest, I don't know how the Polish bureaucrat there behaved. The different experiences in the two embassies may have been simply a difference in personalities or may have reflected Hungary's earlier move to a freer economy. My guess is that it was the first.

After this experience, we tried out a state-run restaurant accompanied by our interpreter, Jana Slamova, and a state-run subway on our own. The restaurant was very bad, the subway very good. It was a remarkable structure. We went down a very long escalator to get to the tracks. It was all very clean—no graffiti anywhere. The cars also were meticulously clean. The cost to us was essentially zero. Milton figured that at the Czechoslovak rate of exchange at the time, it came to one U.S. cent. And the trains seemed to run on time. We had had the same experience in Moscow some thirty years earlier. Apparently one thing that a collectivist society can do is construct and run a subway.

At the Mont Pelerin meeting, a friend had given us the names of some libertarians in Prague. Jana, who was a very bright young lady, found the telephone numbers after much difficulty and we got in touch with the vice-rector of the Prague School of Economics. He persuaded Milton to visit the school and talk to what he said would be a few of his students. The few turned out to be several hundred and were mostly teachers, not students, since this was the vacation period. Since no interpreter had been arranged for this meeting and the teachers' knowledge of English was very poor, there was some difficulty in communicating but what the teachers lacked in language ability they made up in enthusiasm. That has been our general experience whenever we have traveled in communist or ex-communist countries.

The rector of the school, whom we met at lunch, had been one of the group associated with Dubcek in 1968. He had served as general secretary of the Communist party when Dubcek was being held in Moscow for a month before the Soviets invaded. After the Russians came, he went into opposition but somehow managed to stay alive. He struck us as a decent human being who was seriously trying to think his way through the issues. However, he felt that Klaus wanted to go too fast. He still believed that a better way was the kind of socialism with a human face that the Dubcek group wanted to introduce when the Soviet invasion crushed their plans. He now dubbed it capitalism with a human face. Klaus had mentioned at our meeting two days before that those who shared the rector's views were his most serious domestic opponents. They were looking, he said, for a third way between a real market economy and a socialist economy. He felt that was neither feasible nor desirable—as he put it, there is no third way.

The vice-rector was very different. He was a confirmed libertarian, as were the group of young people around him. They were very optimistic about where Czechoslovakia was going. Jiri Schwartz had taken the lead in founding the Liberalni Institut to promote libertarian ideas. Since then, the institute has prospered. Gary Walton, president of the Foundation for Teaching Economics, has cooperated with the institute to offer teachers and students short, intensive courses in economics, like those the foundation conducts in the summer in the United States. In addition, the institute sponsored a regional meeting of the Mont Pelerin Society in 1995, followed by a series of lectures and discussions by Gary Becker. Milton participated in a similar series of lectures and discussions two years later and received an enthusiastic reception.

After another afternoon of sight-seeing—this time on our own and through the old Jewish ghetto, including a Jewish museum, a synagogue, a cemetery and so on, we left for the airport and a plane for Budapest. The plane was a Czechoslovak Airlines plane of Russian make, a Tupelo. The seats were so close together that we could hardly move. The attendants did a remarkable job of serving what was supposed to be dinner in a flight of about an hour.

Hungary

Budapest was humming with foreign entrepreneurs who were busy making deals with the Hungarian bureaucrats. The tourists and the businessmen had occupied all the hotels, and the only arrangement that Mike could make for us was in a hotel that was literally a boat anchored on the bank of the Danube with a view of the cathedral from the window. It was probably the least satisfactory hotel that we stayed in on the whole trip—and also one of the most expensive. A new hotel, we were told that it had been financed by Koreans but was being run by an Austrian group. The front half of the boat consisted of the original cabins that had been redone with new furniture. There was a small bathroom with a shower. Beds were couches with very thin mattresses. Advertisements describing it as a first-class luxury hotel were hardly an example of truth in advertising. It did have a good dining room and the food was good. Our crew was worse off. They had to spend one night in one hotel and move to another hotel the second night.

Like Prague, Budapest is beautiful and, again, the beauty comes from the old monuments and the old buildings. While the crew spent the morning filming background around Budapest, we met with Mike to plan the pieces to film that Milton would be doing in the afternoon. Then we spent the afternoon filming those pieces, including the one that was used as if it had been filmed in Wenceslaus Square.

On short notice, Mike had managed to have us invited as special guests to a reception that Price Waterhouse representatives were giving for a group of American businessmen. The Americans were not very interesting. For the most part, they were single-minded businessmen concerned only with their own businesses. They were consulting in the main on behalf of very large enterprises. There was a representative from DHL Worldwide Express, several from General Electric, and others. The crew did film an argument that Milton had with some of them on whether they were doing more to promote or retard the conversion of Hungary from communism to free markets.

{ *Milton* } The most remunerative course for them was to deal with the government and seek special concessions for assisting or taking over government corporations. I don't blame them. At the time, the government consisted mostly of ex-communist bureaucrats, who followed a policy of giving special treatment to ventures by foreign enterprises. However, the business representatives were not only taking advantage of the policy but defending it as desirable, whereas I believe it is a serious mistake.

{ *Rose* } The next day we started our drive to Cracow, Poland. We were now a convoy of three cars. Bert Hopeman, a board member of Bob Chitester's foundation who was doing some touring in Central Europe and wanted to see how a film was made, joined us in Hungary. We drove to Cracow in his car. Eben, Mike, and the crew had two cars.

We encountered our first problem when we arrived at the border. It turned out that to get from Hungary to Poland, we had to go through Czechoslovakia. Bert, Milton and I had no problem because Americans do not need visas for Czechoslovakia, but British and other nationals do. Mike and Eben had no problem because both had multiple entry visas. However, whoever made the travel arrangements for the crew in London got visas for only one entry to Czechoslovakia. They had used their one entry when they went to Prague. When the crew did not follow us across the border, we returned and learned that the border guard was threatening to send them back to Budapest for visas. That would have meant a two-day delay. When Milton asked whether he could call Václav Klaus for help, our bureaucrat decided he had to get help from someone higher up. Bureaucrats, communist or not, are almost never willing to make a decision on their own. They always have to get approval from someone higher up. Eventually he called his boss in Prague and was told that it was possible to buy visas at the last exit point from Czechoslovakia to Poland. He then called that exit point, told them about the situation and authorized the crew to go through without visas. They could buy their visas at the last exit point. However, there was still one more problem; in order to get visas they needed pictures and while they undoubtedly could get their pictures when they got their visas, this exit point also had facilities for making pictures and, of course, wanted the business at the high price that they charged. Pictures taken, we moved on.

Poland

Thanks to the delay at the border and a wrong turn, we got separated from the crew. However, despite taking a much longer, very scenic route, we ended up before they did at a comfortable Holiday Inn in Cracow at ten o'clock that night. We had a good dinner that was incredibly cheap, thanks to an artificial exchange rate and the recovery from hyperinflation. A drink of Scotch cost $1.30 and no dish on the menu cost more than two or three dollars. The crew were not so fortunate. They did not arrive until after midnight when the restaurant was closed, but they were happy that at least they were not stuck in Hungary.

The next day, which was Saturday, we spent filming in the market. This was fascinating. The large public market consisted of two parts. One resembled our farmers' markets. It was well organized, with beautiful vegetables, fruits, and flowers—all remarkably cheap in terms of dollars. The other part looked like what we call a flea market. We were told that the market had existed under the communists but had exploded since the new government had taken over, eased price controls, and reduced restrictions on people going into business. The spirit of entrepreneurship was everywhere.

We were fascinated by a seventeen-year-old entrepreneur who was in the market with a stock of about four pairs of jeans, a TV antenna, a hair curler and a couple of other odds and ends. When we talked to him through our interpreter, he told us that he had to go to school on weekdays. Saturday, his only day off, he bought his goods at a discount store somewhere and sold them in the market to make a bit of money. We were amused by his reply when Milton asked him what he was studying in school. He said he was studying to be a gardener but that his ambition was to be a businessman. Mike thought the jeans were so cheap that he bought a pair for about twelve dollars. He said they were the same kind of faded jeans that sold in the United States with designer labels for a multiple of that price. I imagine Mike bought them in order to help the young man, as well as to give us more time to talk to him.

In the afternoon, the crew went to film Novahuta, the big steel mill not far from Crakow that has been one of the monstrous catastrophes of Poland because of its pollution. The crew didn't want us to go with them because of the pollution. When they returned they said that sometimes one couldn't see the smokestacks from a few hundred feet away because of the cloud of black smoke and soot obscuring them.

The next day was our last day of filming. The crew left for the airport and we rented a car from Budget Rent a Car to drive to Warsaw. The young lady who brought the rental car to our hotel said that an American from New York owned and ran the business. It was strictly private, the government had nothing to do with it, and she was delighted to be working in a private enterprise.

Auschwitz, the notorious Nazi concentration camp, was not far from Cracow and only a minor detour on our way to Warsaw so we decided to visit it. As we expected, it was a most depressing experience. What we had not been aware of and what struck us particularly was the enormous extent of the place. Building after building had been devoted to stockpiling people before murdering them either in the gas chambers, or by hanging or shooting them. The exhibits were simultaneously impressive and repellent. Thoroughly depressed, we continued on our drive to Warsaw.

In Warsaw, we met with two groups that demonstrated the same split we had seen in Czechoslovakia between the proponents of a socialist market economy and proponents of a truly free, private-market economy. The United States Information Agency in Washington had made arrangements with the one group and Guy Sorman, a French economist friend, with the other. The USIA described the group with which it arranged a meeting as "the country's most prestigious gathering of politicians and intellectuals, Club Europa." They proposed that Milton give a talk followed by an extensive question-and-answer period. Guy Sorman suggested a conference in Parliament House hosted by several parties and foundations.

Most of the first group had been members of Solidarity's intellectual faction and had participated actively in the anticommunist campaign. Many were currently serving in the government of Tadeus Mazowiecki. Like the group in Prague that opposed Václav Klaus's free-market program, most Club Europa members favored a "third way," neither capitalist nor socialist. The second group were mostly libertarians in favor of free-market capitalism.

Although sponsored by the USIA, Milton chose as his topic for the Club Europa meeting, "Why the United States Is Not the Right Model for Poland." The point of his lecture was that during the century and more preceding extensive government involvement in the economy, the United States had become wealthy enough so that we could now afford to support a large and wasteful government. He went on to describe briefly the wasteful measures: the 42 percent of our income that the government was spending plus the regulations and controls that were distorting the economy. The right model for Poland, he argued, was Hong Kong or the U.S. of a century ago.

The dominant sentiments of the audience quickly became evident with the first question: "How do you justify having served as consultant to General Pinochet when he was dictator of Chile?" Milton and I were immediately transported back to the seventies when he was under attack for allegedly having been an adviser to Augusto Pinochet. By 1990, Chile had turned into a success story, and attacks on Milton on this issue had long since disappeared at home.

The question about Chile was followed by more substantive ones that made it clear that most of the intellectuals present, while strongly anticommunist, were still socialist. They were bending to the current fashion by talking about the need to resort to the market but their concept of the market was strongly influenced by the Lange-Lerner vision of a socialist market economy—i.e., one run by them. They did not trust the people; they knew better what was good for them. One or two people in the audience did support free enterprise but their voices were lost in this crowd.

The day before our meeting with Club Europa, at Guy Sorman's suggestion, Janusz Korwin-Mikke, who headed a libertarian group in Warsaw called the Union of Real Policy, had arranged for us to meet with a group of legislators at the parliament. The atmosphere was hospitable, not hostile, and was directed at promoting greater understanding of what a free private market

BY DANZIGER FOR THE CHRISTIAN SCIENCE MONITOR

© 1990 Christian Science Monitor News Service. Distributed by Los Angeles Times Syndicate.

513

required and how it worked, not at making debating points and questioning motives. The one meeting left us very optimistic, the other pessimistic.

{ *Milton* } Janusz Korwin-Mikke, with whom I had corresponded, had been active before liberation as an underground publisher, bringing out a translation of *Capitalism and Freedom* and Hayek's *Road to Serfdom,* as well as other libertarian literature. Subsequently, he ran for president on a strict libertarian platform. At the time we were in Warsaw, his Union of Real Policy was housed in a former dwelling that was a literal maze of small offices, all occupied by young people actively working on spreading the libertarian gospel. We had very good, lively discussions with them.

We also met with Lech Walesa, but I don't remember anything about it except that most of the conversation was with his very intelligent interpreter.

Our ambassador to Poland, Thomas Simons, had a lunch for us, to which he invited some of the high officials of the Polish government, including the deputy prime minister and finance minister, the head of the central bank, three other ministers, several professors, and deputies in the parliament. At the time, Poland was trying to peg the exchange rate, and I made my usual case for floating the rate. More interesting than the technical discussion was observing the same split among the officials present that we had found between the Club Europa and the libertarian legislators. The head of the central bank, in particular, impressed me as an unrepentant collectivist, who may have changed his label but not his mind. The minister of finance and several of the other officials present, on the other hand, seemed much more sympathetic to free markets.

{ *Rose* } We were impressed with the many examples of free enterprise, whether in the subway, the train station, or just around town. Everywhere there were stands, some selling flowers, some books and knick-knacks, some food items or, it seemed, anything for which there was a market. The people were free and seemed to me to be making the most of their freedom.

{ *Milton* } The day before we left Warsaw happened to be Rosh Hashana, the Jewish New Year, one of the holiest days of the year. We took the occasion to visit what I believe was the only synagogue still active in Warsaw. A fair number of people were present, mostly very old, the last native survivors of the Holocaust, but there were also a number of relatively young people and some children taking part in the religious ceremony. Our surprise was eliminated when we found that they were from the Israeli Embassy, not the local population. The freedom of the remaining few Jews to worship was a bright sign; the age and condition of the remnant of observers, distressing.

Back Home

{ *Rose* } Soon after we arrived home, we began to select the discussants for the updated version of *Free to Choose*. We did a much less careful search than Mike and Eben had done the first time, partly because we had fewer to select, partly because we relied more heavily on our own knowledge of potential participants. In the main, Bob Chitester and Milton and I selected the discussants, without interviews, from people we knew. Again, our main effort was to get a balanced discussion.[1] Though some of our choices turned out very well, I must confess that, judging by the results, we were not as uniformly successful as Mike and Eben had been.

Linda Chavez did an excellent job of moderating the discussions, and Bob arranged to have each program introduced by a strong supporter of free market ideas.[2]

Bob Chitester was not able to get Public Television to show the updated *Free to Choose* series even with the new program on Eastern Europe. He made arrangements instead with CNBC. The individual who was in charge when Bob made the arrangements was interested in the program and promised to give it a good time slot and promote it heavily.

Unfortunately, by the time the program was ready for distribution, that man had left CNBC. His successor had little interest in the ideas we were presenting, yet was committed to distributing the program. At the same time CNBC was going through a reorganization. The end result was that there was little promotion of the program. It was shown at various viewing times, and those times were not advertised. As it happened, we were in Hawaii when the program was shown there. It did not appear on the television schedule but we happened to turn on the TV one evening and it was on the screen.

As with the earlier program, videocassettes are available at a moderate price for the 1990 version, and many have been sold.[3]

⇀ *Chapter Thirty* ↼

CHINA

{ *Milton* } The three visits to China that we have made over a thirteen-year period—the first, as a guest of the Chinese government, the other two under predominantly private auspices—together constitute one of the most fascinating experiences of our life. By chance, the visits were so dated that they gave us the opportunity to observe an unprecedented natural experiment—the introduction of free-market elements into a communist command society. Fortunately, the arrangements for our visits enabled us to travel widely, and equally important, to speak—mostly through interpreters—with Chinese from the top of the ruling hierarchy to the bottom of the social scale. We are not China experts but we have had a unique opportunity to observe in practice what we have long preached in theory—the efficacy of free-market arrangements in promoting both prosperity and freedom.

Fortunately, we have detailed notes on our three trips, written or dictated at the time or shortly thereafter. The contemporaneous notes have a freshness and accuracy that our faulty memories do not, so I shall rely on them as much as possible.*

At the time of our first visit, no communist country had ever made a transition to a relatively free society. Even today, the only ones that have come close to doing so are countries that had communism forced on them from outside.[1] China was the first communist country to take timid steps, after the death of Mao and the takeover by Deng Xiaoping, to expand the role of the free market. After the fall of the Berlin Wall in 1989 and the breakup of the Soviet Union, another set of similar experiments began. Comparison of

---

* To avoid cluttering up the text, I am suppressing my prejudice as a scholar and not indicating by quotation marks when I am quoting rather than paraphrasing the notes.

the several experiments will provide fodder for the research of students of economic and social development for decades.

At the time of our first visit, 1980, the Chinese experiment had barely gotten started, yet some results were already beginning to emerge. More important for us personally, it provided a base for judging future developments. Our second visit, in 1988, came at perhaps the most hopeful period of the Chinese experiment, before the political strains exploded on Tiananmen Square. Rereading my notes on these two visits brings home sharply how different China was in 1988 from what it was in 1980. The Central Committee still ruled, speech and press were closely controlled, and most of the economy was controlled directly by government. Yet the limited economic freedom permitted had changed the face of China, strikingly confirming our faith in the power of free markets.

There was no longer the old dull drabness, sameness of dress, uniform dinginess and decrepitude that impressed—and depressed—us in 1980. The color and variety in the clothing of the crowds on the street was matched by an air of hope and expectation, by obvious signs of economic enterprise and expansion. The initial changes by Deng Xiaoping affected mainly agriculture, where they had remarkable results, both increasing agricultural output and releasing manpower for a burst of rural industry. By 1988, the reform had started to affect the cities, though not to any substantial extent the state-owned enterprises.

The small free markets of 1980 had dealt almost entirely in food products. By 1988, free markets dealt not only in food but also in items like clothes and small appliances. In Shanghai, a wholesale market was selling things like bundles of buttons to small private enterprises that manufactured clothing. Similarly, many villages had converted from complete dependence on agriculture to getting much of their income from small local manufacturing enterprises.

Intellectual freedom had also expanded. Comments at lectures were wider ranging. However, the willingness of people to speak freely was by no means complete. A professor we had met in 1980 in Shanghai, with whom I had corresponded in the interim, was unwilling to come to our hotel room in 1988 because he was sure that the room was bugged. Yet, all in all, a remarkable change from 1980.

Then came Tiananmen Square, and a real setback. By 1993, on our third visit, China had overcome the initial effects of Tiananmen Square and the economy was again expanding rapidly. However, the political situation was uncertain, awaiting the transition of power destined to follow the expected death of Deng, then in his nineties. If anything, there seemed less willingness to speak openly than in 1988, and even the economic expansion had elements of a Potemkin village.

The recent takeover of Hong Kong marks the next, highly important, stage in China's transition. Much depends on how that proceeds.

The 1980 Trip

Our first trip was initiated by an inquiry from the Committee on Scholarly Communication with the People's Republic of China informing me that I had been nominated, presumably by their Chinese counterpart, "to participate in the first lecture exchange program between our two countries. . . . Should you be interested in pursuing this endeavor," the letter went on, "you will receive an invitation from the Institute of World Economy of the Chinese Academy of Social Sciences where you would spend the majority of your time."[2]

On expressing an interest, about six weeks later I received two letters from China: one, in Chinese, an official letter from Qian Junrui inviting me to lecture on inflation, the world economics of the 1980s, and using the market in a planned society; the second, in English, from Chengxi Lo, who wrote, "I am your former student . . . I am now a research fellow in the Institute of World Economy . . . asked to do the liaison work for your visit."[3] I remembered Lo very favorably from his time in Chicago, and we looked forward to having him as our guide in China. Unfortunately, he wrote in June saying that he had to be part of a delegation going to the United States during the time that we had agreed on for our visit, and asking whether we could change our plans to come earlier. Unfortunately, that was not possible, because we had arranged the visit to China to follow a week that we had agreed to spend in Japan on activities connected with the showing of the Japanese version of *Free to Choose*. (We finally visited with Lo three years later, thanks to a fortunate coincidence. After a stint as a visiting scholar on the East Coast, he, his wife, and a son returned to China via Vancouver at just the time that we were attending a Mont Pelerin Society meeting in Vancouver.)

Beijing

We spent one day short of three weeks in China, arriving in Beijing on Monday, September 22, 1980, and leaving Canton on October 12. We were met at the airport by Professor Luo Yuanzhen, deputy director of the Institute of World Economy, who was in charge of our visit. He and an interpreter, Xiao-ling, accompanied us everywhere in China. Because of scheduling conflicts, we arrived a day later than we had initially planned. Although we cabled the Foreign Affairs Bureau about the change, they neglected to pass the information on to Professor Luo in time so he had gone to the airport the day before. Also, copies of the lectures I was to give had been airmailed to the institute ten days earlier but had not been received—and so far as I knew had still not arrived when we left China three weeks later. Fortunately I had an extra set that I could give Professor Luo to transmit to the interpreter. This was typical: immense personal good will, great efficiency in small things, tremendous bureaucracy and inefficiency in the large.

{ *Rose* } Upon arrival, Professor Luo informed us that although we had been told that we would be staying at the Beijing Hotel, the premier hotel in the city, we were going to stay at a newly built hotel in a suburb ten miles from town. Professor Luo explained that they had decided to put us there because the Beijing Hotel was so noisy and crowded. We discovered very soon that that was a flimsy excuse, since the suburban hotel was not only second-rate but also so noisy that we found it hard to sleep. Moreover, staying there necessitated spending an inordinate amount of time going back and forth from the hotel to town after each lecture in a rickety car that could not travel over fifteen or twenty miles an hour, partly because of the condition of the car and partly because of the congestion created by bicycles. When we met Professor Luo the next day, we told him that unless the academy could find us housing in the city we would have to cut our trip short and return to the U.S. We then discovered the reason for the change of hotels. There was a waiting list for rooms at the Beijing Hotel and the academy apparently did not have enough clout to get us a room.

The threat of having an invited guest leave because of poor housing arrangements roused them to great efforts. After two days, they got us a room in the Beijing Hotel by posting a person full-time at the hotel to act as soon as a guest was seen to leave. We were at a morning discussion session when we were told that they had a room at the Beijing Hotel for us. We lost no time. In the middle of the discussion, Xiao-ling and I went off in a taxi to our hotel in the suburb, packed our bags, and brought them to the Beijing Hotel. After the discussion, Professor Luo and Milton were driven from the Academy of Social Sciences to the hotel. By chance, we all arrived at the hotel at the same time. And then ensued a rather interesting episode that was typical of service in Beijing. Porters were standing around inside the door, but no one came out to get the bags. Professor Luo and Milton took the bags out, some of them quite heavy, and carried them inside. Once the bags were inside the anteroom to the lobby, the porters condescended to pick them up, put them on a trolley, and take them to our room. My first impression upon entering our room was, "It reminds me of Russia." The bathroom looked as though it hadn't been cleaned for some time.

{ *Milton* } I had earlier asked Professor Luo whether tipping was permitted, and he said, "Oh, no, no, no." Here was a good example of the resulting standard of service.

{ *Rose* } Our activities in China were of three kinds: lectures by Milton, sight-seeing, and going to banquets and artistic performances. Our first touristic experience in Beijing occurred the first or second evening after we arrived. The occasion was a New Moon Festival. Professor Luo took us to a park with a small mountain that was *the* place to view the moon that evening. Professor Luo knew his way and led us toward the slope, making our way through increasingly dense crowds of people who had come to celebrate the occasion. We were much relieved when Professor Luo decided it was too crowded to go to the top. The next morning we learned that later that evening several people had been crushed to death in the mob.

{ *Milton* } During our first three days in Beijing I gave three lectures: "The Mystery of Money," "Money and Inflation," and "The Western World in the Eighties." I held two discussion sessions: one at the Academy of Social Sciences on inflation and one at the People's Bank of China. The session at the People's Bank was attended by more persons than the other session: employees from four banks plus officials from the Ministry of Finance and perhaps other ministries.

The lectures in Beijing and later in Shanghai were attended by about 250 persons. All were invited guests, who had to show a ticket of invitation to attend. They consisted of officials at various institutes and government ministries and teachers at universities. Essentially all, we gathered, were professional economists or bureaucrats concerned with economics. We were struck by the age distribution: the great majority appeared to be fifty and older (the pre–Cultural Revolution generation); a small minority, thirty-five or younger (the post–Cultural Revolution generation); almost none in between, a clear sign of the devastating effect of the Cultural Revolution. The lectures were translated sentence by sentence, partly by an interpreter from the Bank of China whose English was fluent but economics nonexistent, and much more satisfactorily by Professor M. T. Teng of Anhui University, who had studied economics in England in the late 1930s.

Changchun

After three days in Beijing, we went to Changchun where I gave one lecture and held one discussion session. Changchun was the capital of Japanese Manchuria from 1931 to 1945, and the home of the last emperor of China after he had been deposed in China and the Japanese had installed him as the puppet ruler of Manchukuo. The Chinese have converted it into a major center for heavy industry. Changchun also has Jilin University, a continuation of one started by the Japanese, and a branch of the Academy of Social Sciences, which is why it was on our lecture schedule.

The hotel we stayed at had been built some twenty years earlier, ostensibly to hold conferences, though my conjecture is that it was mostly to serve as a retreat or vacation resort for the leaders of communist China. An imposing stone structure in the Stalinist style, the hotel was set in a large park, nicely landscaped, with many walks and trees, and dotted with a number of elaborate villas that had been built for party leaders but were locked up when we were there. The whole area is enclosed in a sturdy fence and the entrance has large iron gates manned by several guards—clearly it can all be closed off.

Both the accommodations and, especially, the food were decidedly better than at the Beijing Hotel, confirming the comment by Simon Leys in his book, *Chinese Shadows,* that in general you eat better in the provinces than in Beijing.

The room in which I lectured the next morning was in the same building as our accommodations. Large and elegant with an even larger anteroom, it featured an enormous painting showing a radiant, benign, genial Chairman Mao standing up larger than anybody else and surrounded by a host of admiring, good-looking, attractive and well-dressed citizens in different costumes representative of various parts of China.

We were struck by the contrast between the luxurious room and the people who occupied the chairs. The first impression was of a group of workers who had just come off the night shift, dead-tired and still in their work clothes. All, men and women, wore much the same uniform—pants and a Mao jacket. Most looked as if they had slept in their ill-fitting clothes for days without changing them. Many of the men wore caps that they kept on during the whole of the session. A minority wore good, well-pressed, well-fitting clothes. To judge from our experience driving in from the airport, the best dressed were not necessarily the top people. Of the group from the Academy of Social Sciences that met us at the airport, two presumably senior men drove with us to the hotel, one who had a terrible body odor and was dressed as a worker,

the other, in well-cut-business clothes. The worker type was the deputy director of the institute, that is, the top man; the other was an assistant director.

The audience, as in Beijing, consisted of two widely separated age groups;
the larger, old, the smaller, quite young. The older ones look older than their
years, as if they had led a brutally hard life, as indeed most of them had,
thanks to the Cultural Revolution. Professor Luo spent more than two years
at manual labor in the country and the two professors from the local university
who hosted a banquet for us that evening, more than three years. That story
was repeated wherever we went.

After lunch we had a discussion session, mostly with academics, about
inflation, monetary theory, and related topics. When one of the academics
raised a question about the internal contradictions of capitalism, I was very
undiplomatic, stating firmly that I didn't believe there were any such contradictions. I should have stopped there but in the heat of the discussion went
on to point out how wrong Marx's predictions about capitalist development
had been, and how much better ordinary people lived in capitalist than in
communist countries.

The result, a day later, was a polite attempt to show me the error of my
ways. Professor Luo had us come to his room to be briefed for several hours
by an expert from the Academy of Social Sciences on the history of the communist revolution and the role that intellectuals like him had played. It was
clear that the expert had initially been a democrat, not a communist. However,
he maintained that Chiang Kai-shek, after he took over from Sun Yat-sen,
had subverted the aims of the Sun Yat-sen regime and governed China as a
fascist and dictator, in the process persecuting the intellectuals who had nowhere else to go but to the communists. In those days, he maintained, the
communists were only seeking to be partners in a coalition government; they
were prepared to compromise by accepting a combination of an essentially
liberal democratic market system plus communist elements. (Note the enter-
ing-wedge technique that much later examples, e.g., Chile, demonstrated.)
The expert blamed all failures to achieve a coalition government on Chiang's
perfidy.

He then proceeded to sketch the early history of communist China,
maintaining that for the first five or six years everything went swimmingly,
that the communists invited the smaller capitalists—not the big four families
who had gone to Taiwan with Chiang—to cooperate, resulting in an economic boom for some six or seven years. Then, he argued, progress went to
the heads of the communist leaders and they became convinced that they
could organize the economy centrally. They expropriated most of the capitalists' property, giving them paper shares of some kind. He then sketched the

rigidity of central planning, the subsequent Cultural Revolution and the aftermath. He maintained that under Deng some of the expropriated capitalists were being rehabilitated and compensated for the property taken from them.

All in all, it was a fascinating talk, well-informed, and entirely sincere. The purpose was clear: to correct our demonstrated ignorance about the history of communist China so that we would view it more favorably.

Some of the places we visited in Changchun were the locomotive and carriage works, an embroidery factory, a jade factory, and a department store.

{ *Rose* } We had lunch one day with a couple of young Americans who were teaching English in Changchun. They were enjoying their stay. Their only complaint was that they had so little opportunity to meet the Chinese students on a person-to-person basis. They were not permitted to eat with their pupils or to meet them outside the classroom. We were disturbed by the same practice. Except for official "banquets" and other official meals, we were consistently returned to our hotel after a morning session, there to have lunch by ourselves. If there was an afternoon session, we were transported back to the appropriate location. Even when we were traveling and staying at the same hotel as Professor Luo and Xiao-ling, they ate in one dining room, we in another. We departed from that pattern only twice: once in Hangchow because we arrived very late, after the dining rooms had closed. To keep us from starving, the hotel people managed to hustle up some noodles which they served to the four of us. The second time was at an airport stopover on our way to Guilin. Professor Luo rationalized the practice by saying that prices in the dining rooms for foreigners were several times higher than those in the dining rooms for Chinese. But that was a thin excuse in our case. Their expenses as well as ours were being paid by the government, and essentially all of the dining rooms involved were government-owned and operated, so it was all just a matter of bookkeeping. We did not observe this practice on our later trips, which were not government-sponsored.

Beijing

{ *Milton* } We returned to Beijing from Changchun for a few more days, which included one more lecture, "The Use of Market Mechanisms in Centrally Planned Economies," sight-seeing in Beijing, especially tourist attractions like the Palace Museum, the park and the water fountain in the Forbidden City, as well as the Great Wall. We were taken to a dance performance by Madame Wang. She is the widow of Liu Shaoch'i (the first president of China, who was imprisoned, disgraced, and driven to his death by Mao). She was lively, intelligent, and clearly, enormously popular. We enjoyed visiting with her. The top people of the Academy of Social Sciences entertained us at a "banquet" dinner, as such meals were always referred to, and the deputy minister of materials distribution at a lunch.

FRANK AND ERNEST

WOW, CHINA REALLY <u>IS</u> LOOSENING UP! MY FORTUNE COOKIE MESSAGE IS A QUOTE FROM MILTON FRIEDMAN.

THAVES 11-12

FRANK & ERNEST © United Feature Syndicate. Reprinted by permission.

If we needed convincing about the gulf of misunderstanding that separates people immersed in different economic institutions, this lunch did the job. The deputy minister was going to the United States soon to observe the American economy. He wanted help on whom to see. His first question was, "Who in the United States is in charge of materials distribution?" That question took Rose and me aback. I doubt that any resident of the United States, however unsophisticated about economics, would even think of asking such a question. Yet it was entirely natural for a citizen of a command economy to ask it. He is accustomed to a situation in which somebody decides who gets what from whom: who gets what wages from whom, who gets what materials from whom, etc. My initial answer was to suggest that he visit the floor of the Chicago Mercantile Exchange where commodities such as wheat, cotton, silver, gold, etc., are traded. This answer understandably baffled our host, so I went on to elaborate. There was no single person—or even committee of persons—"in charge of materials distribution." There is a Department of Commerce and a Department of the Interior that are concerned with materials production and distribution in a wholly different way. But no single person or political body "is in charge of materials distribution" in the sense in which there is or has been such a person or political body in China or Russia.

{ *Rose* } We had one visit in Beijing before we left that I will never forget—dinner at the home of Professor Luo. This was the only occasion on which we visited in a Chinese home. Mrs. Luo is a physician. Though we had not met before, she was so warm and friendly that I felt that I had known her for years. Her children and their spouses were also at the dinner, and Mrs.

Luo insisted that they take many pictures of us with her and Professor Luo. Departing from Mrs. Luo was like leaving an old friend. I have never seen her again.

{ *Milton* } Of two former students whom I had contact with, I have already mentioned Lo Chengxi, whom I corresponded with in making arrangements for the trip. The other, Li Zhi-wei, had been much closer to me than Lo since Lo was a master's student while Li wrote a doctoral dissertation under my supervision. He first came to my attention in a course on economic theory in which he did very poorly on exams but wrote an outstanding paper, far and away the best in the class, when I happened to assign a take-home problem. It was that experience that led me to adopt the practice of always judging students on both take-home problems as well as standard classroom exams (see chap. 15). When he was writing his dissertation, he spent some time with us at our then summer home in New Hampshire—as a bonus teaching Rose how to make Lobster Cantonese, a skill from which I have greatly benefited.

Li was from Macau, not mainland China. Yet, like almost all overseas Chinese, he was extremely faithful to China. He got his degree in 1951, a time when relations were disturbed between Red China and the United States over Taiwan. We had lengthy discussions about what he should do. He recognized that his professional opportunities would be greater if he stayed in the United States. But if he became a citizen, he might be drafted, and if hostilities developed between the U.S. and China, he doubted that he could bring himself to fight against China as his obligations to the United States would require. He finally concluded he could not do that and decided to return to China. For a time, he was employed by a Chinese agency in Hong Kong, and I kept in touch with him. Then he moved to mainland China and I lost touch.

I saw Li again for the first time in thirty years when he came up after one of my lectures. We subsequently had several fascinating private meetings. After some other activities, he had ended up as a teacher. However, he was not permitted to teach economics. He was a non-Marxist Western economist and only Marxist economics could be taught. Instead he taught English. Like so many other intellectuals, he had suffered during the Cultural Revolution, being forced to spend years as a manual laborer in the country separated from his family. He was rehabilitated after the revolution. When we saw him he was teaching statistics—still not economics—at an institution of higher learning. After he received his doctorate at Chicago, his parents had generously sent me an ancient Chinese scroll as a token of appreciation. When we left Beijing, Li gave me a modern Chinese scroll. We have had both of them hanging on the wall of our apartment as a striking demonstration of the decline of culture under the communists: the ancient scroll, subtle and low key, a work of true beauty; the modern scroll, bright and garish, of a different genus.

{ *Rose* } I have had some problems understanding Li's behavior. On the one hand, he had brothers in the United States during his difficult years in China, and had come back to see them at some time or other. Why did he not stay? He was vague about this. His parents were still in Macau. Also, we never met his wife or his children when we were in Beijing. Somehow, to me, his stories were not entirely convincing. He didn't seem the straightforward young man that I remembered from his visit with us in New Hampshire.

One small incident in the lobby of the Beijing Hotel surprised us and impressed our hosts. A number of Chinese who were visiting from Hong Kong or Singapore came up to Milton to say how much they enjoyed our documentary, *Free to Choose*. Milton's role as a television performer seemed to impress our hosts more than his academic accomplishments.

Shanghai

{ *Milton* } We left Beijing on October 3 for Shanghai, where I gave one lecture and had one discussion session. We spent a day visiting Soochow, coming back to Shanghai for dinner with the deputy mayor of Shanghai. We then visited Hangchow and then went to Guilin (Kweilin).

One high spot in Shanghai was the evening we were taken to a theater around the corner from our hotel, the Shanghai Art Theater, to enjoy a performance of acrobatics. It was stunning. We had had a foretaste of that sort of thing on a TV program in the U.S., but the skill, facility, daring, and agility of the acrobats here was incredible. We were led to remark that the one place in China where you could see elegance, cleanliness, precision, and brightness was on the stage. It's an artificial world and that shows up in all sorts of ways. The lighting is bright, where almost everywhere else it is dim; the stage itself and the settings are beautiful and well-designed; the performers are dressed in colorful costumes that seemed just to have been cleaned and pressed or, for that matter, to be brand-new. That goes even for the clothing worn by the people who are not in costume. For example, at each of two performances we went to, there was a woman who announced before each act what the act was going to be. She was dressed completely in Western clothes, with Western jewelry, earrings, cosmetics and makeup—something we did not see on anybody in the street. In one act, two men gave a remarkable performance of tricks with the mouth; that is to say, by using a loudspeaker and their own mouth, they imitated all sorts of noises from airplanes to motorboats to cannons firing to a baby crying. They were remarkably good. They too were dressed in Western suits, with Western shirts and ties. The conclusion we came to is that the theater is artifice, the Western world is artifice, and therefore it is all right to imitate the Western world in the theater.

We witnessed another remarkable acrobatic performance at the end of a boat trip on the Hwang Pu river. During the boat trip, we had been in a first-class section at the top of the boat, which was like all the first-class sections we had been herded into throughout our trip, quiet and empty. But at the end we were taken to a crowded hall on a lower deck to witness a theatrical performance that was extraordinary, especially on a boat that was far from stable. The performance consisted in part of some of the same kind of juggling and balancing tricks that we had seen the night before in the acrobatics show at the Shanghai Art Theater. However, one of the balancing tricks was even more elaborate and impressive: a young man balanced an incredible number of glasses and other objects, one on top of the other, all in turn on a small round ball which was on top of a chopstick that he held in his mouth.

On returning to Shanghai after our side trip to Soochow, we had the best dinner of our stay in China. The banquet was given by the deputy mayor of Shanghai, Wang Dachan, who impressed us not only by his gastronomic acumen but also by his intellectual ability and his openness to new ideas. We saw him again on both of our later trips to China—each time in a new capacity—and he visited us in San Francisco between our later two trips, bearing not crabs but a bottle of Mai-tai.

The banquet was at a very nice place called the Eastlake Hotel, which we suspected was reserved for the upper echelons of the party and was not available for foreign guests. David Hess, an extremely well-informed staff member of the U.S. consulate, had never heard of it. We were ushered into a pleasant, clean, well-painted, well-lighted room, where we sat and talked for a while before going to another room to eat. The high spot of the dinner was a special kind of crab from a freshwater lake that I believe is in the neighborhood of Shanghai. Such crabs are available only for a brief time in the fall. They were very different from our West Coast Dungeness crabs, much smaller, extremely sweet and very good.

Wang reminded us of Chicago's Mayor Daley (the father, not the son). He had the same kind of big, open-hearted, expansive personality, very friendly, jovial. He obviously liked both his drink and his meal. At the time, he had been deputy mayor of Shanghai for only about three months, having apparently been sent down from Beijing to see that Shanghai conformed to the new economic policy. He was a strong supporter of the reforms and was much interested in how to introduce greater competition and more reliance on market forces into the economy. When we saw him in 1988 he was still in Shanghai, no longer deputy mayor, but clearly a person of great influence. Then in 1993 he was in Beijing, heading a research institute, and still a person of great influence. All in all, a fascinating character.

{ *Rose* } One of our most bizarre experiences occurred on one of the few times that we took a walk in Shanghai unaccompanied by either Professor Luo or Xiao-ling. Two young men approached us, saying that they wanted to practice their English. It was soon obvious that they were trying to find some way in which they could get us to help them get out of the country. The older of the two said that he had studied to be a chemist and was working as a chemist. He said that during the Cultural Revolution he had hidden out and had done no work in order to avoid being sent to the country. The younger one came out bluntly and asked me whether I wouldn't like to have him as a son. We finally had to put them off with some excuse and make our way back to the hotel.

Guilin

{ *Milton* } Guilin (Kweilin in the earlier transliteration) was on our itinerary at our own request because we had heard such high praise of its beauty. It was indeed as lovely as we had heard. And, as one would expect in a popular tourist spot, the accommodations were the most luxurious that we encountered in China—a villa attached to a large hotel. We were told that President Nixon and Dr. Kissinger stayed there on their visit to Guilin.

It was luxurious by any standards in terms of space and service. In addition, it was air-conditioned, which for Guilin with an outside temperature of 65 to 95 degrees and high humidity was a great blessing. However, beyond space, service, and air-conditioning, the quality of the accommodations was far below that of a typical Holiday Inn. Our suite consisted of a large living room, a bedroom, and a bathroom. The beds were the hardest we have ever slept on. Instead of springs, there was a firm bamboo woven base, topped by a pad not more than an inch thick, and a mattress pad rather than a mattress. The basin in the bathroom was satisfactory but the bathtub was discolored and cracked, the fittings leaked, and one of the towel racks fell off the wall while we were there.

We also had a large private dining room across from our suite. We and our Chinese guides were the only occupants of the villa at the time. Nevertheless, Rose and I ate alone in the dining room in solitary splendor and were served special meals. Luo and Xiao-ling ate in another dining room. The dining room was nicely decorated, convenient, and air-conditioned, and an attractive and accommodating young lady served us. Unfortunately, she could speak only about four words of English so we communicated mostly by sign language. Our Guilin interpreter and guide, of whom more later, was a great help. When she asked us what we wanted for breakfast, we suggested soft-boiled eggs. She had difficulty explaining this exotic dish to the dining-room waitress. When she finally understood, she did bring us two-minute eggs, and they were excellent. Initially, however, she brought them on a flat saucer without anything you could break them into. By sign language, we managed to convey that we wanted two empty cups. There was no shortage of willingness or friendliness or energy, only of understanding.

The high point of our visit to Guilin was a day-long boat trip down the scenic Liang river. The rocky hills on both sides are said to have inspired some of the most famous of the ancient—and modern—Chinese scroll paintings. Equally interesting is the native life on the river and alongside it: peasants working in the fields, others on the small reed rafts that are used for fishing or transporting things from place to place; occasional ferries taking people with bicycles across the river; people crossing the shallow river afoot—all of the active life of people in the countryside anywhere. The boat goes downstream some seventy kilometers, the guests disembark, spend a little time at a local market, and then return by car because it takes the boat twice as long to return against the current.

For the return to Guilin, we had two cars as usual, because the regulations do not allow more than four people in one car and we were five. So our Guilin interpreter, Rose and I, and a driver were in one car; Luo, Xiao-ling, and a driver in the other. The same thing happened again later on. The two occasions allowed us to have long and interesting conversations with our Guilin interpreter. (There had been a few other occasions on our trip to talk frankly and freely with individual people but, except for our conversations in Beijing with my former student Li, none was as interesting.) She was very free-thinking and very much interested in the ideas of strict capitalism. I made it perfectly clear that I was what they called in China a "capitalist roader" and did not believe in communism. She was interested in hearing about all of this and very frank in expressing her own opinion.

We learned her story over the two days that we spent with her. She was married in Canton in 1966, where she was teaching English. Immediately after their marriage her husband had been spirited off for reeducation in the countryside and spent a year there before he was able to return. In 1976, toward the end of the Cultural Revolution, she had been transferred to Guilin to serve as an interpreter. Under the pressure of the campaign against intellectuals, however, and the argument that the educated class should learn from the peasants, she herself was sent off to spend eleven months at a commune. The experience was clearly an unhappy one. The intellectuals had to do hard physical work, exactly the same as the peasants. She was very frank that the addition to the work force of these highly educated young people had probably reduced rather than increased the total output of the peasant community. The peasants accepted them because they had to, but in actuality they resented them and had no use for their help.

The "young girls' team," as she called it, tried to set up a night school and a nursery for the peasants but the peasants weren't interested. They preferred to have their children taken care of by grandma at home, and had little or no interest in what the night school offered. She and her husband had had misgivings at the time about the reeducation program, but the propaganda was so universal that they found themselves more or less persuaded that this was the right thing to do. In retrospect, she has no doubt that it was a serious mistake. From us she quickly learned the phrase "free to choose" and began to use it on every possible occasion. In general, she used it in a way that showed a comprehension of its significance and meaning.

Canton

From Guilin we went to Canton, where we spent three days before leaving for Singapore. We were entertained at one banquet and visited factories and an agricultural commune not far from Canton. In all our visits, in Canton and elsewhere, we were always briefed by an official assigned primarily to public relations, sometimes quite knowledgeable about the economic details and operation of the enterprise, sometimes only superficially so.

Some General Conclusions about China in 1980

The intellectual atmosphere. We were at first rather surprised at what seemed an extraordinarily open intellectual atmosphere, with wide-ranging questions, willingness to accept and to voice criticisms of socialist performance, etc. But we soon discovered that the appearances were somewhat deceptive. No doubt there was a vastly freer atmosphere and more open discussion than was possible during the Cultural Revolution. However, it remained true that there was a greater tendency to ask questions than to express opinions. Moreover, after reading Hua Guofeng's speech at the third session of the Fifth National People's Congress on September 7, 1980, I discovered that any criticisms of internal affairs that were expressed were almost entirely confined to those that had been officially voiced—which means that all criticism, no matter how harsh, of policies followed during the Cultural Revolution was acceptable and that discussion of proposals for reform were largely confined to the items covered in Hua's speech.

I started to test this atmosphere by commenting, with feigned naiveté, that the Cultural Revolution had been pursued by millions of people and had been widely praised and applauded by many intellectuals. Surely, some of the proponents of the Cultural Revolution must be of the same opinion still. How was it, I asked, that I had met no one in China who had a good word to say for the Cultural Revolution? My question was invariably met by embarrassed silence and a quick change of subject.

State of economic understanding. The key bureaucrats had essentially all been educated, and begun their careers, in a closed society in which economic activity had been rigidly directed and controlled from the center. Few spoke or read any language other than Chinese or Russian, and few had visited any Western country. Even those who had, had experienced the West only superficially. They had been well briefed on the external political and economic conditions in the rest of the world, informed about major events, etc., but were unbelievably ignorant about how a market or capitalist system works.

The professional economists were in a different situation. Some of the older ones, like my interpreter, Professor Teng, had been educated in Britain or the U.S. either in the late 1930s or in the immediate postwar period. They were knowledgeable about economic theory up to that point. However, most of them were regarded with suspicion by younger economists. As noted above, one of my own students who had returned to China had been assigned primarily to teaching English for most of the past three decades. And even those who had managed to pursue a professional career in economics (aside, of course, from the nearly universal two to four years in the countryside during the Cultural Revolution) knew little or nothing about the developments in economics in recent decades.

Most economists had never been abroad and had been trained in China (a few in Japan) on a heavy dose of Marxist economics. They had only the vaguest, and most ill informed, understanding of "bourgeois" or "capitalist" economics. Because of the switch in government policy and the attempt to give market mechanisms a greater role, they were now eager to learn more about how the market worked. More important, perhaps, the rapid opening of relations with Western countries, the possibility of gaining access to foreign scientists and professional literature, and contact with overseas Chinese had awakened a brutally suppressed natural curiosity. The curiosity was reinforced by the obvious contrast between the prosperity of overseas Chinese (and of

Taiwan, about which it had become permissible to speak) and the poverty and backwardness of the People's Republic.

The mixture of ignorance and interest led to curious results. For example, I was astounded to find great interest in the work of Friedrich Hayek, including articles about him in Chinese publications for economists and translations of some of his works. Equally, we were astounded to find copies of the Japanese translation of our book *Free to Choose* (published in Japan only a few months earlier) in the hands of some Chinese economists who had studied in Japan, and even more astounded to learn that plans were underway to publish a Chinese translation of our book in the People's Republic.

Differences among Beijing, Shanghai, and Canton. There was a perceptible change in the qualities and interest of the participants in discussion sessions in the several cities. The atmosphere was more bureaucratic, less academic, in Beijing, less open and less informed (except for the bankers) about conditions in the West. The fraction of persons who spoke or understood English was decidedly higher in Shanghai than in Beijing, and even higher in Canton—as is to be expected in passing from the political capital to commercial and mercantile centers. The same differences existed before the revolution.

In part, our impression of a difference in sophistication between those cities was produced by a few quite old, and clearly retired, professors at the Shanghai session who had spent much time in the West, spoke English fluently, and appeared to be much franker and freer in their comments than most of the others. The most interesting was Dr. Chin-hsiang Hsia, who had been secretary to the minister of finance under Chiang Kai-shek before the revolution, spoke English fluently, and seemed entirely uninhibited in his comments. I corresponded with him subsequently, and we saw him again on our second China trip in 1988.

The state of the economy and its prospects. In a report that I submitted to the sponsoring committee on my return, I summarized my judgment about the current state of the Chinese economy and its prospects. I quote here from that report, in order to assure that contemporary judgment is not tainted by hindsight.[4]

> On an absolute level, China is a very backward economy. The great bulk of its enormous population is engaged in agriculture (of which we saw only one commune plus markets in the cities), and the level of productivity in industry is extremely low. As in all communist countries we have visited, the level of maintenance of structures is deplorable—even fairly new buildings seem decrepit and in a poor state of repair. . . .

Although we were repeatedly reminded of India, there were some important differences. The most obvious is that you do not see beggars on the streets of the cities in China as you do on the streets in India. Also you see few or no people in rags or looking as if they were starving. The Chinese boast that they have established a minimum level is justified, at least for the larger cities which we saw. We were told the situation was different in many outlying and backward areas, and clearly it had been different during some past years.

With respect to change, as opposed to level, the situation is more complex. There clearly has been a decided improvement in the economy over the past three years or so. The Chinese attribute this to the new "pragmatic" policies adopted under Vice-Premier Deng, who is clearly the person in charge.

My own impression is somewhat different. It is a common observation that the restoration of order in a society that has been in a state of turmoil is capable of producing a rapid improvement in the economy. The rapid recovery of Germany and Japan after World War II is a case in point. Similarly, the termination of the Civil War in China with the victory of Mao, and even more, the ending of hyperinflation, was followed by a few years of rapid progress and a jump up in the economic level. This did not last.

Subsequently, the Mao experiments—the Great Leap Forward and the Cultural Revolution—again introduced turmoil and a period of incredible disorder. The mere restoration of order on the death of Mao and the gaining of power by Deng was bound to permit a rapid recovery and a jump up in economic level. I believe that is a far more fundamental explanation than the Deng reforms, most of which are so far only on paper.

The reforms—the attempt to introduce market elements, the opening up of contacts with the West, the encouragement of foreign investment, and so on—are in a desirable direction. But the test of whether they will be carried out and what their effects will be is still for the future, and some of the initial euphoria over them is now evaporating, as some of the plans—particularly for joint projects with foreigners—have had to be scaled down. The potential is enormous. The present level is extremely low. That cannot be attributed to either the character of the people or the lack of natural resources—after all, to disprove such explanations it is only necessary to look at the achievements of the Chinese in Singapore, Hong Kong, and Taiwan, which are if anything less well-endowed in resources than mainland

China. Why should the Chinese be able to do so well everywhere except in their native land? The explanation must be the method of organization and control of the economy—and that explanation is supported by the low level of economic well-being in other communist societies. Hence, a change in the method of organization and control is potentially capable of achieving an economic miracle comparable to that attained in Japan and Germany and, more recently, in Chile.

My own conjecture is that there will be considerable progress in the next few years as some of the newly announced policies work themselves through the system. At the same time, I am pessimistic that the progress will be long continued. Opening up the system involves dispersing power and responsibility and that will produce threats to the security of the centralized political apparatus. It is likely to respond by closing down again.

After all, the communist period has been characterized by such swings from relative flexibility to renewed rigidity. The extreme excesses of the Cultural Revolution are unlikely to be repeated. But power struggles will remain. It cannot be that all the wounds are healed, and, in any event, ambition remains and the only effective outlet is political.[5]

From China to Singapore

From China, we went to Singapore. What a pleasant shock to walk into an air-conditioned airport that was clean, where everything worked, and waiting was minimal, after three weeks in China. The hotel where we stayed, the Shangri-La, was an even bigger contrast. We were back in civilization.

Two items stand out from the few days that we spent in Singapore. One was having dinner with Lee Kuan Yew, his wife, and some younger officials at Lee's official residence. In the conversation at dinner and after dinner, Lee and his wife were the only ones other than Rose and me who ever initiated discussion. The others spoke up only when called on by Lee or his wife. No question who was in charge. Both the Lees were clearly highly intelligent and thoroughly in command of every detail in Singapore. I asked Lee why he did not permit a free press but continued to impose strict censorship. His answer started with a lengthy summary of how difficult it had been for him and his party to overcome communist resistance when they first acquired control shortly after Singapore had become a separate nation. He still regarded communist subversion as a problem and felt that censorship was justified to prevent it. We were in no position to dispute his judgment, but it seemed to us a pretty weak defense—though perhaps not unexpected from a benevolent dictator.

The other was connected with my reason for being in Singapore—to inaugurate a lecture series sponsored by the Institute of Southeast Asian Studies. My topic was "The Invisible Hand in Economics and Politics." In my lecture, I compared the progress of Singapore and Hong Kong. I pointed out that, while both had done extraordinarily well, Singapore enjoyed much more favorable conditions than Hong Kong, yet had averaged roughly the same rate of growth in per capita income. I attributed the relatively better performance of Hong Kong to its more complete reliance on the market. Some high Singapore officials were outraged at my remarks and accused me of a bias against Singapore.

From Singapore to France

Our plans called for flying from Singapore to London on the Concorde, then catching a connecting flight to Paris, where I was scheduled to lecture. The trip proved a comedy of errors—with a most serendipitous outcome.

Because of the outbreak of the Iran-Iraq war, the Concorde had to change its usual route to avoid overflying the battle area. The new route involved flying more over land, which meant that it had to fly subsonic for a greater distance, putting a greater drain on its fuel supply. Consequently, instead of flying nonstop from Singapore to London, the plane stopped in Bahrain to take on more fuel, guaranteeing that we would be several hours late in arriving in London, which in turn meant that we would not be able to get to Paris that night. We asked Singapore Airlines to wire Robert Heller-Lozada, our friend in Paris who was supposed to pick us up, explaining the situation.

Despite the extra stop, the plane began running short on fuel when it was over Europe and the pilot decided that it was not safe to try to get to London. Instead, he made an unscheduled landing at Orly Airport in Paris. We were not the only passengers whose ultimate destination was Paris, and there were enough of us to persuade the pilot to let us off on the tarmac and to unload the baggage so that we could each get our own. We then went up to the concourse and there waiting for us was Robert, who had never received the telegram!

The 1988 Trip

A chance falling together of events led to our second trip to China. In 1987 I received an invitation from President Xie Xide of Fudan University in

Shanghai to visit there as a guest of the university. At the same time, the Cato Institute was planning a conference, "Economic Reform in China: Problems and Prospects," to be held in Shanghai, cosponsored by Fudan University. Ed Crane, president of Cato, invited me to participate. Finally a regular Mont Pelerin meeting was scheduled to be held in Japan at about the same time.

Learning that Steve Cheung, a friend and former student, now a professor at Hong Kong University, was also to attend the Cato conference, I asked him to arrange the schedule for Fudan. He agreed to do so and in addition suggested that he would like to arrange and accompany us on an extended trip in China after the conference. Steve keeps in close contact with people in China and is extremely knowledgeable about what is going on there. He arranged a most informative and fascinating trip.

We arrived in Shanghai from Osaka on Saturday afternoon, September 10, 1988 and left Xian for Hong Kong on Thursday, September 22. We then stayed seven days in Hong Kong before leaving for San Francisco on September 29. The nineteen days between arrival and departure left few idle moments.

We were met on arrival by Chen Guan Lie, a Fudan professor and Shu Yuan, an assistant dean, as well as someone from Cato. The Fudan representatives gave us the proposed schedule for the next two days until the Cato-Fudan conference convened. It involved lunches, a dinner, a talk by me at the university, and various other events.

We stayed at the Hilton International Hotel, the headquarters for the conference. It is a typical high-rise, U.S.-style, Hilton hotel, brand-new and very clean—a type of hotel of which we had observed none when we visited China in 1980 and a foretaste of the major changes we were to observe during our trip. One caveat: as we had earlier observed in India, international hotels, mostly for foreigners, seem to form the leading edge of economic development; judging from them gives an exaggerated measure of progress.

On arriving at the hotel, we called Dr. Hsia, the elderly, learned, and open-minded gentleman who had participated in the 1980 Shanghai discussion and with whom I had corresponded since. He agreed to join us for dinner. When he called from the lobby, we suggested that he come up to our room. He was hesitant to do so, and asked us to come to the lobby. It turned out that his hesitancy reflected his fear that our room was bugged—shades of our experience in Warsaw in 1962. At dinner in the hotel restaurant, he was apprehensive and kept looking around. "Don't speak too loud," he whispered, "we don't know about these waiters." On comparing notes about our correspondence, it turned out that he had written several letters to me that I had not received. On the other hand, he had received all of my letters. Apparently, the authorities may have read or examined incoming mail but they did not stop it, as they did outgoing mail. Professor Hsia was well informed about the state of the Chinese economy and was frank to talk about the problems, particularly as concerned inflation, a hot issue at the time. Dr. Hsia attended the Cato conference and was one of the few Chinese participants who made comments from the floor that were not fully consistent with the official position. He refused to let the interpreter translate for him. Instead, he made his comments first in Chinese and then in English.

Our first engagement, on Sunday, September 11, assumes greater importance in retrospect than it did at the time. It was a meeting followed by a lunch co-hosted by Xie Xide, president of Fudan University, and Jiang Zemin, then party secretary of the Shanghai Committee. It was clear to us at the time that Jiang was a top communist leader, but of course we had no idea that he was destined to become the general secretary of the Communist party and the president of the People's Republic of China.

Xie Xide is a physicist. She studied in the United States, has a master's degree from Smith and a doctor's from MIT. We were very much impressed by her. She did not speak a great deal. By contrast, Jiang Zemin was outspoken and clearly felt himself to be a very important person. Though he spoke some English, most of the discussion was conducted through an interpreter. A number of other people were there, some from Fudan University. Not surprisingly, in the presence of Xie Xide and Jiang Zemin they were not willing to discuss sensitive issues freely. As a result, the discussion was largely a two-way discussion between Jiang and me. I emphasized the importance of privatization and free markets, and of liberalizing at one fell stroke. He repeatedly referred to the political difficulties, all of which, though he didn't put it that way, came down to his own personal position, which would be threatened by real liberalization. (In view of our later contact with Jiang Zemin, it is perhaps worth recording that this paragraph is based entirely on the notes dictated at the time, with only minor verbal changes to adjust from spoken to written style.)

In the afternoon, a young student with whom I had corresponded was waiting for us when we returned to the hotel. I will let Steve Cheung tell the rest of that story:

> I arrived in Shanghai on September 11. After checking in at the Hilton, I gave Friedman a call. The first thing he said was: "Steve, could you come over to my room right away? I need your help to make arrangements for a young lady.". . . In the room was a Chinese girl, about twenty years old. I hardly had time to wonder whence she came before Friedman said, "She wants to attend tomorrow's lecture, but

she does not have an admission ticket. Can you help to arrange that?"
I answered that . . . she didn't have to worry.

After a few moments I learned from the young lady that she was
a student at Xiamen University, and was translating Friedman's works
into Chinese. With total savings of about a hundred yuan, she was
brave enough to travel all the way alone by train from Xiamen to
Shanghai. A youth with such an enterprising spirit and determined
mind was China's hope. How could I not help her? I arranged for
her to take a photograph with Friedman. I also insisted that she accept
my offer to pay for her trip home.[6]

That night we went to a dinner hosted by the *World Economic Herald*.
One of their journalists, who was at the time a visiting scholar at Hoover, had
made the arrangements with us earlier in San Francisco. Qian Benli, editor-in-
chief of the *Herald,* told us how he had started the weekly newspaper in 1980
with some assistance from a government insurance group that paid him in
advance for advertising, enabling him to bring out an issue or two without
having to charge for it. Apparently he started the paper with the idea of making
it something of a mouthpiece for economic reform. In 1980, the paper had
a circulation of 20,000; by 1988, of 300,000. He told us that he had often
been in trouble with the authorities. On one occasion, they tried to get him
to give up control of his paper, and he had a hard fight to hang onto it. He
and the group he had gathered around him were very favorable to free-market
reforms and had been influential in promoting the movement to economic
reform. All in all, we had a wide-ranging discussion about the problems relating to the achievement of greater freedom in China.

(As things turned out later, the crackdown that followed Tiananmen
Square ended the *Herald* and led to the incarceration or flight of a number
of those associated with it. The hopeful feelings that characterized this and
later meetings during the 1988 trip were dashed, and, despite some recovery,
had not been fully restored by 1993, when we made our third trip.)

Fudan University

The next day, Monday, we spent at Fudan University. At the entrance stands
an enormous statue of Mao. After being inducted as an honorary professor
of Fudan University, I lectured to some four hundred students crowded into
an auditorium that had a capacity of at most three hundred. I lectured in
English without translation, yet the students apparently understood what I
said, to judge from their attentiveness during the lecture and the intelligent
questions they asked afterward. Some of the questions sounded as if they were

phrased to be acceptable to those in power, yet to elicit from me replies that would not be.

I started my lecture by discussing the problems facing China in its attempt to transform the economy, and the opportunities open to it. I went on to consider how to get from where they are to where they want to be, pointing out that Hong Kong, South Korea, and Taiwan had demonstrated that it was possible to achieve in thirty years what it had taken the U.S. and other Western countries two hundred years to achieve, thanks to the ability to draw on the experience of those countries and to benefit from their capital markets and technology. I stressed the importance of drawing on the knowledge and initiative of individuals and the efficacy of voluntary cooperation through the market as a way to do so. Both in the lecture and in answering questions, I discussed the problem then uppermost in China: how to halt the accelerating inflation.

After the formal session was over, I was besieged by students who jammed the platform to ask further questions and to get my autograph. Many had copies of books of mine in Chinese and a few, in English, though most were asking for autographs on slips of paper. They impressed us as a livelier and better-informed group of youngsters than any we had met in 1980. Their command of English was especially impressive—clearly, there is a strong incentive to learn English.

We took the opportunity of the drive to and from Fudan to query the professor who was driving us about how university professors lived, their salaries, fringe benefits and the like. As usual, he complained that intellectual workers were underpaid—a standard complaint of every class in every country. Our impression, based on our observations and his detailed replies, was that the intellectuals were a sheltered group who had little contact with the rest of society, lived in their own world, and were not well informed on what was going on outside that world.

The Cato Conference

The Cato conference started that evening with an opening banquet. Before the banquet we had a meeting with Wang Dachan, the former deputy mayor of Shanghai. It was a small meeting with about a dozen people, including people from Cato as well as Chinese accompanying Wang. Although no longer deputy mayor, it was clear that Wang was still a powerful person. Later in the week, he hosted a banquet for us at which the culinary feature was the freshwater crabs that we had enjoyed so much in 1980.

The conference was wide-ranging, featuring about equal numbers of

Western and Chinese speakers and commentators. It attracted a large audience and received extensive coverage in the Chinese press. The proceedings were published in English in 1990 and in Chinese in 1994.

I gave the first talk, titled "Using the Market for Social Development." This was a variant of the title of my fourth Beijing lecture in 1980. Rather than repeat that lecture, I distributed copies of it and added to it by discussing a number of related topics, concluding, "There are better and worse ways to privatize a command economy, but there is no magic formula for shifting painlessly from a command to a voluntary-exchange economy. Nonetheless, the potential rewards are so great that, if the shift can be achieved, transitional costs will pale into insignificance. It is a tribute to the current leaders of China that they recognize that the potential gains dwarf the transitional costs and that they are engaged in a serious effort to make the transition. The Chinese people would be the main but by no means the only beneficiaries of the success of this effort. All the people of the world would benefit. Peace and widely shared prosperity are the ultimate prizes of the worldwide use of voluntary cooperation as the major means of organizing economic activity."

The commentator on my talk was Pu Shan, director of the Institute of World Economics and Politics, Chinese Academy of Social Sciences. A graduate of MIT who spoke fluent English, he was intelligent and thoughtful, but also very careful not to say anything that was not politically correct.

One afternoon, Cato arranged a tour of Shanghai for the Western participants. The most interesting feature was a tour of a shopping area containing government stores, private stores, and a crowded alley lined with private shopping stalls. It was in this alley that we observed proprietors of stalls selling things like bundles of buttons to small private enterprises that manufactured clothing. Many stalls also sold toys, as well as a wide variety of other goods. While impressive, this free market was less extensive than some we saw later in other cities. We visited some of the stores and I asked our guide how we could tell the private from the governmental stores. Her answer was simple: "In the private stores, they are really trying to sell you something. In the state stores, they don't care; the clerks just stand around."

Later, at a reception staged by the U.S. consulate, I met a young American woman who had started a private import-export business in Hong Kong. While she thought that the opportunities in China for foreign firms were excellent, she was critical of the way the Chinese conducted business and the extent to which it was necessary to bribe and use influence to do business. The Chinese officials did not take money, because that was too obvious and would get them into trouble. However, though no one in her office smoked, she spent $200 a month on cigarettes as gifts to the Chinese officials with whom she had to deal. She reported that on a larger scale the most useful inducement was for an American firm to offer officials scholarship support for their children to study in the United States. The money would be disbursed in the United States and never recorded as money received under the table, so the officials would be pretty sure not to get into trouble. She also explained more clearly something that had puzzled me: the effective multiple exchange rate system. There was an official exchange rate of not quite four Chinese yuan to the dollar. That was the rate that tourists would receive in the state stores. There was also a semiofficial rate varying from six to eight yuan to the dollar that government trade officials could grant in negotiations with individual enterprises. Finally, there was an unofficial black market on which the rate might be nine or ten yuan to the dollar. Later discussions fully confirmed her description.

Shanghai to Beijing

Steve organized and accompanied us on the rest of our trip. We went from Shanghai to Suzhou and Wuxi by car, to Nanjing by train, to Beijing and Xian and then back to Hong Kong by plane. Steve had arranged for Lucy Ma to accompany us from Shanghai to Nanjing. Lucy's mother is a major participant in Hong Kong–Chinese trade in that area, and Steve had consulted her in planning our trip. From Nanjing to Beijing to Xian, Andrew Chow accompanied us. Andrew is a Hong Kong businessman who had been active for a decade in trade with China and investing in hotels, including the Bell Tower Hotel where we stayed in Xian. Lucy and Andrew were extremely pleasant, well informed, and highly efficient. They arranged for us to meet the mayors and local business people in each of the cities. We ended up having banquets noon and night given by the mayor or the head of the planning authority or some other official. The banquets were an opportunity for the mayors and their henchman to get a good meal at the expense of the community, so they were delighted to host banquets for visiting firemen.

We were very much impressed by the scope of the free market in all of the cities, but especially in Wuxi where, in addition to stalls selling agricultural products, there were stalls offering a wide variety of clothing, others with a cobbler putting heels on shoes, and on and on. Each stall contained an identical sign that clearly was a permit. When I asked our interpreter how to get a permit, he explained that technically you were supposed to get permission from your employer but in fact the way to get a permit was to bribe the official in charge.

In Wuxi we had an outstanding luncheon banquet at a recently developed restaurant owned partly by the community and partly by private individuals. Unlike the sloppy service and indifferent food at state-managed restaurants, both the service and the food were excellent. All the serving dishes were silverplate polished so that they gleamed. The cook came in to show us the large duck they were about to serve us, and there was real pride in his attitude toward his work. Similarly, the people who served us took pride in what they were doing. It was a striking demonstration of how much difference incentives can make.

Before leaving Shanghai, Steve learned that his friends in Beijing who had arranged for us to meet with Zhao Ziyang, the general secretary of the Communist party, would like me to give Zhao a written memo. Zhao was at the time one of the three most important officials in China: Deng Xiaoping at the top, Zhao as general secretary, and Li Peng as prime minister. Preparing the memo led to a highly productive running seminar on Chinese economic reform conducted as we were traveling between cities. Rose, Steve, and I, and anyone else who happened to be riding with us discussed successive drafts. Though I did the actual writing, and my name is attached to the final memo, it was really a joint product.

We were met at the Beijing airport by Mrs. Wong, a nice woman from Zhao's office who handled our arrangements in Beijing. She and a number of other government officials accompanied us to the Diaoyutai Guest House where we stayed while in Beijing. It is a magnificent estate reserved for top government officials and distinguished guests. The estate has many villas and was originally constructed by an emperor who was fond of fishing, so it has many ponds and some villas bordering on the water so that the emperor could fish while remaining indoors. The villas, judging from the one we were in, are modern and well maintained.

We had dinner the evening of our arrival with members of the Development Research Council, the think tank for Zhao. We discussed the same topics that we were to discuss the following day with Zhao. The next morning, I gave a talk to more than two hundred selected officials, many of whom had been brought to Beijing from outlying areas to attend the talk. I stressed the importance of free private markets, and then discussed at greater length two problems currently important in China, inflation and a dual price system. Here, unlike Fudan, my talk was translated into Chinese. Andrew Chow served as the interpreter, with occasional help from Steve. The questions were all written and had to be translated for me. I was encouraged by the session, since the questions seemed to me more far-reaching, bolder, and more inquiring than those I remembered receiving in Beijing eight years earlier.

Rose noted that the audience seemed to fall into three groups: relatively old, middle-aged, and very young. The relatively old and the very young seemed to understand much of the English, while the middle group, presumably thanks to the Cultural Revolution, got nothing whatever from it.

Meeting with Zhao Ziyang

That afternoon we had our meeting with Zhao Ziyang—certainly the high spot of our two weeks in China. We discovered later that our meeting had been highly unusual in several ways. First, while his sessions with visitors generally lasted half an hour, ours lasted a full two hours; second, in addition to our group and people from Zhao's staff, a reporter from the *People's Daily*, the major Chinese newspaper, attended; third, after our session, Zhao accompanied us out to the driveway to see us off and allowed pictures to be taken. We were told this was almost unprecedented. The meeting itself was fascinating. Only Zhao and I spoke, except for the translator. (The memo that I gave Zhao when we met him as well as a transcript of the discussion are reproduced in appendix C.)

I have long believed that a feeling for economics is something people are born with rather than acquire through education. Many highly intelligent and even highly trained professional economists know the words but don't get the music. On the other hand, people with little or no training in economics may have an intuitive feeling for it.[7] Zhao impressed me as in the latter class. He displayed a sophisticated understanding of the economic situation and of how a market operated. Equally important, Zhao recognized that major changes were needed and evidenced an openness to change.

He began our meeting by giving a long, clearly organized, and very lucid account of the economic situation in China as he viewed it, the problems that China faced, and the solutions he proposed to undertake. The key sentence was: "at the Thirteenth Party Congress, it was decided that the governing mechanism of our economic activity would be for the state to regulate and control the market, while the market controls the economy." (This is impossible. The state is organized from the top down; the market, from the bottom up. The two principles are incompatible. The state can control part of the economy, and the market, part; but the combination Zhao described is not feasible.) We heard essentially the same words from Jiang Zemin when we saw him in Shanghai, and five years later when we saw him in Beijing, when he was a successor to Zhao. But there was a big difference. Zhao's subsequent comments and his replies to my comment showed that he understood the inherent inconsistency of the two parts of the statement; whereas Jiang Zemin did not. Zhao displayed a real understanding of what it means to free the market; Jiang Zemin did not.

None of this contradicts the fact that Zhao is a communist and that, to paraphrase Winston Churchill, he did not become secretary general to preside over the destruction of the party. He is entirely serious in believing that promoting economic growth by making greater use of market mechanisms will increase the power and stability of the party, not by enabling it to control in detail economic developments but by promoting prosperity and the welfare of the citizens. I do not share his belief but I do not doubt his sincerity.

I decided later that part of the reason for our meeting and its special features was that Zhao was in deep trouble. He was the prime proponent during the previous eight years of freeing prices from control. He also was an enthusiastic supporter of a major program of economic expansion. Zhao was blamed for the inflation that resulted when financing the expansion led the People's Bank to issue too much money. He was also severely criticized for going too far in market reform—though in fact that reduced rather than increased inflationary pressure. At a long meeting of the party's top brass in the summer, two factions had emerged: one, headed by Zhao in favor of proceeding full speed ahead in reform; the other, headed by Li Peng, in favor of calling a halt, at least for the time being, to reform. The gossip had it that Zhao had lost out.

Our meeting with Zhao, in the presence of a *People's Daily* reporter, gave Zhao an opportunity to publicize his views and to give the impression that he was really still in charge. He prepared his opening statement at our discussion carefully not primarily for my benefit but for both the broader public and as a warm up for another summit meeting that was shortly to be held dealing with the same problems. Some comments at the end of the statement sounded very much like whistling in the dark: "our direction will not change" and "the newspapers in Hong Kong have . . . suggested that there is a split within China's top leadership. . . . That is not the truth."

Our meeting received a great deal of publicity in the Chinese papers, and even more, I understand, in Hong Kong. The shot of Zhao seeing us off was featured. Moreover, the next day, I was interviewed by the reporter who had been present at the meeting. I learned that he was the foreign news editor of the *People's Daily*. He did not interview me about the meeting, but rather about a much wider range of issues.

Matters did not come to a head until the Tiananmen Square protest some eight months later, though it may well be that Zhao was losing power to Li during the interim. At any rate, Zhao refused to go along with the forcible repression of the demonstrators, knowing full well that not doing so would mean the loss of power. When he and Li went to talk directly to the students on Tiananmen Square, he closed his highly emotional talk by saying that he would not see them again. Chinese friends who heard his final statement told me that many of the listeners ended up in tears. And after the leadership approved the use of force to repress the demonstration, Zhao was put under house arrest, where I understand he still remains.

The leadership tried to blame the developments that led to Tiananmen Square on Zhao's policy of freeing markets and promoting a greater degree of openness. In that connection, I was frequently mentioned in the news stories as having had a bad influence on him. That did not affect me, but people in Zhao's entourage were less fortunate. To mention one, Sun Qinghai, who was the active head of Zhao's Development Research Center, left China for the United States. He is still in the United States on a temporary visa as I write, and is desperate to have his visa extended because he is sure that he will be in trouble if he returns. (His visa was indeed extended not long after I wrote this.) It was he who conducted the discussion I had with members of the center. As to Zhao himself, I am told by my friends that he has suffered nothing more severe than house arrest only because of his still great popularity, particularly in southern China.

The day after my meeting with Zhao, we (Rose, Steve, and I) had lunch at a small dining house set in a lovely garden with many such buildings surrounded by ponds and gardens—a park that was maintained as a duplicate of an emperor's favorite park. The lunch was arranged by Mrs. Wong to continue the discussion with economists from the Development Research Center plus other economists, mostly academic.

(The lunch is memorable because five years later when we were again in Beijing, the System Research Institute, either the successor to or the hierarchical parent of the Development Research Center, hosted a duplicate lunch with many of the same people who had been at the lunch in 1988. It was a moving occasion, with a great deal of back and forth discussion and everybody full of recollections and nostalgia for the period when Zhao Ziyang was running things.)

Xian

While the meeting with Zhao was the intellectual high point of our trip, Xian was the touristic high point. We had no official business in Xian, although we did have one dinner with the celebrities of the town—the mayor, deputy mayor, etc. We especially enjoyed talking with the Austrian manager of the Bell Tower Hotel, an employee of the Holiday Inn chain, about the benefits and costs for an Austrian running a hotel in China. However, the most notable feature of the dinner was that it confirmed our suspicion that the excess of food at all the official banquets we attended was for the benefit of the participants. On this occasion it was abundantly clear, because they all left with doggie bags. I suspect there was still some left over for the help.

Xian is famous for the recent discovery of an army of terra cotta soldiers buried by an emperor more than two thousand years ago to protect him in the afterlife. At the time we were there, they had uncovered only about one-seventh of the relevant area, and in that part alone there were about a thousand soldiers, all life size, arrayed in orderly ranks, looking as if they were ready to march off. Each soldier is made in three pieces: the feet, legs, and thighs are solid cast, the torso hollow cast, and the head individually sculptured. Facial features and uniforms differ from soldier to soldier. There are terra cotta horses to accompany them and to pull the wooden wagons carrying supplies that were in the tomb originally but have decomposed. The terra cotta figures have not. Certainly, one of the most remarkable and memorable sights that we have ever seen.

Hong Kong

From Xian we flew to Hong Kong, where we spent a very active week, mainly socializing and shopping, seeing our old friends, making many new ones, and enjoying the culinary richness of Hong Kong.

One high spot for us was a talk that I gave at the Performance Arts Center on my impressions of China. The talk was arranged by Richard Wong for the benefit of the recently organized Hong Kong Centre for Economic Research. Wong and the center did such a good job of publicizing the talk that we had a full house of people who had bought tickets at what I was told was an exorbitant price. The entire proceeds went to establish an endowment for the center. The lecture was followed by a full hour and a half of questions and answers—understandably, since Hong Kong was destined at the time that I spoke to revert to China in less than a decade.

Another high spot was a day devoted to the Chinese University of Hong Kong. I had agreed before leaving San Francisco to give a lecture as part of a celebration of their twenty-fifth anniversary. The university, which is in the New Territories, almost as far north on the Kowloon side as Hong Kong goes, impressed us as an active and vigorous enterprise. It is organized to some extent along the English pattern of colleges. At the time we were there, it had four colleges and a total of around seven thousand students. We had lunch with faculty members of the economics and other social science departments.

A surprising number had been trained at the University of Chicago. The vice-chancellor, Charles Kao, had made a substantial fortune as a pioneer in fiber optics. He then shifted to serving as vice-chancellor. A highly intelligent and thoughtful person, he impressed us as a strong proponent of free markets and, like most people in Hong Kong, very much concerned about Hong Kong's future.

The lecture was held in a large hall, holding some two thousand people. A supplementary lecture hall, where the proceedings were shown on closed-circuit TV, held an overflow of about a thousand. I had planned to give a talk of around half an hour and answer questions for another half hour. However, just before going in to the lecture hall, the vice-chancellor told me that regrettably it was not possible to arrange for a question-and-answer session and that he expected me to give a full hour-long lecture. With some difficulty, I managed to stretch out my planned remarks to forty-five or fifty minutes. My title was "Free Markets and Free Men," and I discussed the interrelations of economic freedom, civil freedom, and political freedom. An edited version was later published by the Chinese University in its *Bulletin*.[8]

The Chinese University has something of a sister relationship with Fudan University. That causes a rather odd problem. When professors at the Chinese University go to Fudan as part of the arrangement, their Fudan colleagues insist on entertaining them lavishly, because that is one way the Fudan professors can get a good meal at the government's expense. The Hong Kong professors would much prefer to keep the visit short. But when the Fudan professors come to the Chinese University, they want to stay as long as possible and expect their colleagues there to treat them as lavishly as they were treated at Fudan. The professors at the Chinese University, however, have only a small appropriation for entertainment, and if they treated their Fudan colleagues in lavish style, the money would have to come out of their own pockets. As a result, many Fudan University professors return home disgruntled, feeling they have been treated as second-class citizens.

At a well-attended news conference in Hong Kong and a long interview with a magazine editor, the chief subject was the phrase used by the Chinese government in reassuring Hong Kong: "one country, two systems." I created a good deal of controversy by asserting that such a combination was impossible, that only one system would survive. The real question, I argued, was not whether there would be two systems, but which of the existing two systems would be dominant: the free-market system of Hong Kong or the mixture of central control and market mechanisms of China. In particular, I expressed the view that, whatever the intention of the Chinese government, they would not for long tolerate the coexistence of two currencies circulating at a free-market exchange rate: one, the Hong Kong dollar, linked to the U.S. dollar; the other, the Chinese yuan.

While in Hong Kong, we spent one afternoon—the day that Steve had a fancy dinner for us—at a photographic studio with him. We discovered that Steve, who is incredibly talented in many directions, is among other things a world-class photographer, who as a young man made a career of photography. As a result of that afternoon, we treasure some photographs of Rose and me that are the best of the many that have been taken of us. Some years later, Steve organized in Hong Kong an exhibition of photographs taken by himself and three other Hong Kong photographers, and produced an illustrated volume containing the photographs exhibited, including several of those he took of us. Like most things Steve tries, the exhibit was a great success, and, along with sales of the book, was even financially successful.

Shenzen

The day before we left for home, we drove to Shenzen, a city on the Chinese side of the border with Hong Kong. Even though the officials in Shenzen had sent two people to expedite our trip through customs, it was slow going because a long line of trucks was waiting to get through customs.

Shenzen is an extreme example of the changes that had occurred in China since our earlier visit. In 1982 its population was six thousand. When we visited it in 1988, its population was 500,000. It was really an extension of Hong Kong except that it was on Chinese soil and populated by citizens of China. It was also one of the new economic zones established by the government in which there were specially favorable rules for entrepreneurs, such as a lower tax rate on corporate income, and a relatively free market in foreign exchange.

Our first view of the town was from a revolving restaurant at the top of what we were told was the tallest building in all of China. Looking down, we could see about four square blocks with a number of old shacks that we were told comprised the original town. That area was surrounded by high rises, a striking example of the influence of Hong Kong, which was responsible for the more rapid progress in the southern provinces of China than in the rest of the country.

The development was not without its critics. The vice-mayor of Shenzen, who hosted a dinner for us, was a hard-liner. He expressed the view that market-opening had gone too far and should not go farther. He used the analogy of two hands: one, the private market; the other, the government. The two, he said, had to work together. It was clear that he was part of the government hand and had no intention of giving up the privileges which that status had brought him.

The 1993 Trip

Hong Kong

We arrived in Hong Kong on October 15, left for China on October 19, returned to Hong Kong on October 27, and returned home on October 31, so all told, we divided our time fairly evenly between Hong Kong and China.

The first notable event upon our arrival in Hong Kong was a dinner on Sunday, October 17, at the fabulous home of a very wealthy Hong Kong resident, Heung Chit Kau. Mr. Heung and his wife had invited about fifty other guests, some of whom were to accompany us to China. Thereby hangs a tale. Some years earlier, I received a letter from an acquaintance in Hong Kong, George Shen, chief editor of the *Hong Kong Economic Journal,* saying that "an admirer of yours," Mr. Heung Chit Kau, "wonders if he could have your autograph with the words 'Free to Choose' preceding your signature."[9] I sent him the paper he asked for.

{ *Rose* } Some months later I received a telephone call from a representative of Lalique Crystal in New York. She said that they had a Lalique dining room table for us. The base could be sent out immediately but the top was not ready since it was a special size and was not yet finished. I was sure she had the wrong number, probably the wrong Friedman as well, and told her so, and also said that I had not ordered any table from Lalique. She went to check the order and came back with the information that a Mr. Heung in Hong Kong had ordered it sent to us. All she wanted to know from me was did I want her to send the base immediately and the top when it was ready or would I prefer to receive them both at the same time. I told her I was in no hurry. The mystery was solved a day or so later by a letter from Sally Lam, chairman of the *Hong Kong Economic Journal,* saying, "To express his appreciation and gratitude, Mr. Heung has asked me to forward to you on his behalf a 'Cactus' table from Crystal Lalique."[10]

The table finally arrived in three or four crates. Fortunately, there are some strong men who work in our apartment house and they brought the crates up and helped us unpack them. The table arrived entirely disassembled, each piece had a number engraved on it with a comparable number for where it should go. The instructions were very definite. I believe that it took us at least one evening to assemble the base. The top was another problem. We could not lift it. The strong men came up the next day and three of them managed to lift it and put it on the base. The table is a piece of art, but it is also a splendid and functional table. A friend who had seen it in our dining room and then priced it at Harrod's in London wrote me the following note: "Do you really think it is wise to have such an expensive table in a city that is prone to earthquakes?"

{ *Milton* } Calligraphy is a major art form in China, which explains Mr. Heung's use of my signature: he had it reproduced in Italy in mosaic and put it on the living room wall of the multimillion dollar house that he was in the process of building. The dinner was partly to let us see how my calligraphic art had been used.

The house is fantastic: a showplace. I cannot call it a home. It is not for living but for showing off: big pots of artificial flowers, electrified closets in which hundreds of suits or dresses are hung and can be commanded to come down in orderly rows; a living room with a twenty- or thirty-foot ceiling, and windows covered by draperies in sections that can be separately controlled by an elaborate array of switches; a dining room that does not seem crowded with fifty-some guests seated at a round table; and on and on. Veblen's conspicuous consumption to the nth degree.

On Monday, October 18, I gave a luncheon talk at a conference the Hong Kong Monetary Authority was holding on monetary problems, and in the afternoon I lectured at the University of Hong Kong.

This trip to China differed from our two earlier trips in several respects. First, it was arranged entirely by Steve. Second, we were part of a group of about twenty, which included some of Steve's relatives and associates; an editor of a leading Hong Kong magazine; and Hong Kong businessmen with interests in China. Some of the men were with their wives, some alone, including Andrew Chow, who had been our host for part of the 1988 trip. An interesting and varied group from whom we learned as much about China as we did from the officials and others whom we met in China itself. The two most interesting of those whom we had not met before were Jimmy Lai and Yeung Wai Hong.

Jimmy was born in poverty in China. Despite a minimal education, he made his way to Hong Kong as a boy. Perhaps after many other enterprises of which I am unaware, he started a clothing store carrying jeans, t-shirts, belts, and similar items which was very successful and which he franchised under the name Giordano, with many stores in mainland China. More re- markable, on his own, he acquired a liberal education and became a confirmed libertarian, absorbing all the classic literature from Adam Smith to Ludwig von Mises and Friedrich Hayek. He acted on his principles by starting first a monthly magazine and then a daily newspaper to popularize them. Both were highly successful and more recently have brought him into conflict with the powers that be in China. One result of this activity was that he was forced to divest himself of control of Giordano in order for the stores under that name to continue operating in China.

Yeung Wai Hong is a pure intellectual, extraordinarily well-informed who edits *Next,* the magazine that Jimmy established. Under his editorship, it became the best-selling magazine in Hong Kong. Like Jimmy, he is a confirmed libertarian. Both are stimulating people with whom to discuss issues as well as fine companions for long trips.

Chengdu

Our first stop in China was in Chengdu, the capital of Sichuan province, the most densely populated province in China.

The provincial governor, whom we met along with other high officials, turned out to have been a follower of Zhao Ziyang, was clearly sympathetic to reform, and seemed to have some understanding of how a market system worked. However, I had the same experience with him that I had had in earlier trips to China: he impressed me as speaking freely and openly about problems of reform only because he was the first one from whom I heard the official line, in this case, concerning plans for monetary reform.

The Chengdu Tianzuo Shopping City, an underground mall in what had been a bomb shelter built during Mao's regime, was most impressive. Less than a year before our visit, a group had undertaken to convert the shelter into a shopping mall. Xie Yunfu, the chairman of the board, told us about the difficulty he had in raising the money to build the mall—a mixture of private and government funds and of loan and equity instruments amounting to a total of about $200 million. It was a remarkable structure, built in a short time. Shops of all kinds, some government-owned, but mostly private, sold clothing, food, and electronic equipment. Though the fashionable name brands from the West were well represented, they did not dominate the shopping mall; most of the stores sold goods for, if not the masses, the immediately next higher class.

The shops were open cells with no doors. Owners or employees stood ready to serve customers. Many shops were franchises of Hong Kong enterprises—indeed, Jimmy Lai believed that he had a franchisee in the mall though we did not run across it. Similarly, some of the money to build the center came from Hong Kong. Yet the mall was a product primarily of local talent and enterprise. It provided impressive evidence of the strides that private enterprise was making, certainly in marketing. Escalators linked the several floors.

The shopping center also had an entertainment center that included a night club. We were there during the daytime hours, when the night club was closed, but Xie Yunfu arranged for a show solely for our benefit. It was not the usual night club entertainment but performances by some of the best artists in the province.

The outdoor market that we visited that evening after dinner was the working-class counterpart of the upscale underground shopping mall. It was extensive, stretching on and on, with booths and stores selling the usual variety of items, from belts and clothes and shoes to food; there was even a cobbler repairing shoes on the spot. We were impressed at how low prices were, even at the official exchange rate: shoes for something like four or five dollars a pair, jeans for a couple of dollars, and other items in proportion. Prices seemed to us decidedly lower than those we sampled later in Shanghai and Beijing.

Chungking

Our next stop was Chungking, where we stayed just one night. We spent what seemed half of the day of our arrival getting from the airport to our Holiday Inn hotel, thanks to horrendous traffic. Arrangements had been made for a boat ride on the Yangtze River but the weather was so cold and overcast that Rose and I decided not to go. Those who went congratulated us on our foresight when they returned. They reported that the river was so filthy that the boat ride was like navigating in a garbage dump. In addition, the river is at the bottom of a gorge. To get to it requires going down a very long flight of stairs. Going down was easy, going up, something else again. Wong Sum-chuyen, an elderly gentleman who was one of our group and who had worked off and on for Steve for many years, was unable to make it back up. Jimmie Lai, as usual, found the solution, which requires a digression. We have all seen, in the flesh or in pictures, Chinese peasants or workers carrying two buckets slung over a pole across their shoulders. During the nonagricultural season, many farm laborers come to the cities looking for work. One category is called "pole people" because they bring their long poles with them and get odd jobs carrying buckets or other objects. Jimmy went to the top of the stairs, recruited a pole man, who carried Wong up the rest of the way.

After dinner with various local notables, we were scheduled to visit a recently established futures exchange—a real curiosity in a provincial city. It was opened late, to allow for the difference in time between Chungking and the United States markets. Owing to confusion about the time of opening, unfortunately, we never managed to get to the exchange. Despite a rather interesting tour the next day of a park and an art museum, the visit to Chungking was pretty much a fiasco, and we were glad to leave for Shanghai.

Shanghai

We were met in Shanghai by representatives of the Shanghai municipal government. After a very long drive from the airport partly on a recently completed throughway, we ended at the Garden Hotel, as impressive a hotel as we have ever stayed in. The Garden Hotel was financed and is run by the Okura Hotel group of Japan. It is comparable to the Tokyo Okura, which has long been our favorite hotel in Japan. We were met by the manager, a Japanese who had spent thirty-three years at the Tokyo Okura, and the assistant manager, a Dutchman who had spent nineteen years there. The hotel was clearly planned as a home away from home for Japanese businessmen who were in Shanghai on business. In any event, we had an extraordinarily luxurious suite on a very high floor, with a living room about the same size as our living room in San Francisco.

The evening we arrived our group drove in a minibus through the newly developed shopping streets of Shanghai—almost all developed since we were in Shanghai five years earlier. The streets glittered with neon signs of all kind, reminding us of the Ginza in Tokyo. The famous designers of the world all had shops there. Department stores had extensive display windows. The streets were not only brightly lit but also crowded. People were streaming in and out of the stores carrying packages.

Andrew arranged for nine people representing a variety of activities to join us for breakfast in our suite the next morning. Some were from state-owned enterprises, others from private joint ventures. In the course of our intensive discussion, it became clear that, while there was a good deal of private enterprise, the process of privatizing state-owned enterprises was not going well. One participant who specially impressed us represented a large state-owned enterprise that was trying to follow the course Zhao had commended in our 1988 discussion, corporatizing without privatizing. Not surprisingly, the managers of state-owned enterprises are not at all willing to give up their powers.

In the course of this discussion and others that I had later with officials and private entrepreneurs in Beijing, it emerged that the much publicized stream of foreign investment was a mixed blessing. Foreign investment is a good thing if it competes on equal terms with domestic investment. However, foreign investment that is attracted primarily by special privileges offered by the government is not a good thing. It has to be paid for. In China's case, local entrepreners have learned how to take advantage of the special privileges that the government extends to foreign ventures, such as a tax holiday for three years, half-rate taxes for the next three years.

One young entrepreneur whom we talked to in Beijing was particularly frank in telling us that the joint venture he was involved in with a Hong Kong partner was undertaken solely to get special treatment. His venture manufactured blazers, parkas, and the like, partly for export, mostly for domestic sale. He explained in detail the devices he used to overstate the fraction of his output that he exported in order to qualify for the foreign exchange he needed to buy materials from abroad. Another young entrepreneur was on his own without a foreign partner. He explained that he was willing to give up the advantages of a joint venture to have complete independence. Both of these young men were very optimistic about the prospects for China and the opportunities available to persons like themselves.

Once again, we visited with Wang Dachan, the former deputy mayor of Shanghai, who this time was heading a quasi-private organization called the Council of Policy and Strategy. Despite the brochures that we were given and the long talk that we had with Wang and his associates, we never could figure out precisely what his council was, or how it was financed. I conjecture that it is set up to be a middleman between foreign and local enterprises and individuals, on the one hand, and the government on the other, and was being paid (bribed) to get favorable treatment from the government, possible because of the clout (quanxi) that Wang had as someone high up in the communist hierarchy.

The only talk I gave in Shanghai was at a Modern Market Economic Forum, a recently organized group of Shanghai businessmen and government officials that met for dinner once a month—much like Rotary and similar organizations.

Our most interesting activity in Shanghai was a tour of the Pudong Development District, across the Hwang Pu river from the main part of Shanghai. A major aspect of the project, which had been underway for some years, was a bridge connecting Pudong with Shanghai. It had just been completed and an elaborate ribbon-cutting ceremony had been held the day before. (It enabled us to have a talk with Li Tieying, a member of the State Council, who had come from Beijing to participate in the bridge opening ceremonies.) The bridge was extremely impressive—either the second- or third-longest suspension bridge in the world. However, according to Richard Wong, head of the Hong Kong Centre for Economic Research, who was one of our group, it was really an example of an expensive government showpiece. Transportation experts whom he had consulted believed that tunnels under the river would have been very much cheaper to construct than the bridge. Equally important, the bridge approach occupied a good deal more of the densely occupied, valuable land on the Shanghai side than a tunnel would have, raising sharply the total cost. Yet it is easy to see why government officials preferred the bridge to the tunnel. The bridge is visible, lends itself to pictures and boasts about the nth-longest suspension bridge in the world. A tunnel, once dedicated, is out of sight. The money spent on the bridge is all included in the investment component of gross national product; yet the extra money spent on the bridge rather than a tunnel is pure waste for economic development, money spent on building a monument, not on productive activity. An example of the kind of activity that justifies discounting governmental claims about rate of growth.

Deng had visited the Pudong Development on his southern tour a year earlier and had expressed disappointment that the development seemed to be going rather slowly. The officials in charge are reported to have told him, "Come back in a year and we will show you real progress." They stepped up their efforts and, with the aid of much subsidization, developed, outwardly at least, the one long street that we drove along: neon signs everywhere, stores of all kinds lining the street, crowds shopping. In a talk I gave later in Hong Kong, I described it as a Potemkin village built for a reigning emperor.

Beijing

We were met at the airport by representatives of the Chinese Society for Research on Restructuring the Economic System, which had sent me a formal invitation to "visit Beijing . . . and exchange our opinions on China's economic reform and development."

We stayed at the Grand Hotel, which was simply a connected addition to the Beijing Hotel where we had stayed in 1980. So far as we could tell from walking through the Beijing Hotel, it had not changed one iota since 1980, though of course we could not tell whether the rooms were cleaner or the service better. At the Grand, there was some service: our luggage was taken out of the car in which we arrived and was taken to our room. The small suite we had was reasonably satisfactory but a sharp comedown from the Garden Hotel in Shanghai.

We had meetings, lunches, and dinners with a number of private entrepreneurs and officials, and Steve and I gave talks to various groups of bureaucrats and academic economists.

The most notable meeting was with Jiang Zemin, general secretary of the Communist party and president of the Peoples' Republic of China, whom we had met in Shanghai in 1988. This meeting was different in every respect from our meeting with Zhao in 1988. Jiang first asked me to comment and I spoke for perhaps ten minutes, expressing my usual views about monetary problems, multiple exchange rates, and excessive benefits offered to foreign ventures. Jiang then launched into a rambling talk of about forty-five minutes that used up almost all the available time (the meeting, which started at five o'clock had to be terminated at exactly six because he was welcoming the visiting president of an African republic). I conjecture that Jiang did not really want to hear what we had to say.

Several things became clear in the course of his talk. His image of what he repeatedly referred to as a socialist market economy was very different from Zhao's or ours. He viewed the market strictly as a mechanism to be controlled closely from the center. He referred to both Japan and Singapore as models, under the mistaken impression that detailed guidance by the Japanese Ministry of International Trade and Industry (MITI) was responsible for Japan's successful postwar development, and by Lee Kuan Yew for Singapore's success. Those models appealed to Jiang because they would enable the central government to play the leading role and retain its power and importance while using market mechanisms to achieve growth and prosperity.

Before leaving San Francisco, we had learned that C. B. and Beulah Sung, venture-capitalist friends of ours in San Francisco, were going to be in Beijing at the same time as we were. C. B., a graduate of MIT and a highly successful and intelligent businessman, had for some years been active, along with his wife, in establishing joint ventures in China. His command of Chinese gave him an advantage over many of his competitors who spoke only Western languages. He had a larger pool of partners and managerial employees to choose from, was in a better position to judge them, and could communicate with them via fax more easily. When we reached Beijing we got in touch with C. B. and he invited us to join them for lunch at the Great Wall Hotel, of which he is part owner. By coincidence, his other guest was the wife of Li Tieying, the member of the State Council whom we had been able to meet in Shanghai because he had come from Beijing to participate in the opening of the bridge to Pudong. His wife, Dr. Quing Xin Hua, was deputy director of the Department of Sciences and Technology at the Ministry of Public Health. She and C. B. were discussing a possible joint venture to produce fruit juice for school children, a venture that did not pan out.

The evening before we left China, we had dinner at a restaurant that no one in our group was later willing to take responsibility for choosing. We drove what seemed an inordinate distance to reach the restaurant. We went through a room that was crowded and noisy to a private room that had been reserved for our party. The first dish served was puppy. It was cut up but it was laid out with what looked like a little tail coming out of one end and ears out of the other. The second dish was a camel's hoof, followed by a snake. They were a most exotic and unusual assortment of dishes that we and most of our group had the good sense not to eat. Jimmy Lai, undoubtedly the most adventurous among us, sampled everything and ended by throwing up after we returned to the hotel. We were told that these animal dishes were not unusual in China, but they were a little extreme for us.

Hong Kong

The day after we returned to Hong Kong, I gave a talk about my impressions of China at a large fund-raising dinner for the Hong Kong Centre for Economic Research, a summary of which was published in the *Far Eastern Economic Review*.

We also met for lunch with a much smaller group of about fifteen movers and shakers which Richard Wong had arranged as part of his fund-raising effort. They all were active in the Hong Kong economy and very well informed, so we had a most interesting discussion, centering of course on the future of Hong Kong after the coming takeover by China. I asked the participants whether they had arrangements that would enable them to exit Hong Kong if that proved necessary after China took over. All but one did. The one who did not was Joseph Yam, the head of the Hong Kong Monetary Authority. He expressed complete confidence that Beijing would live up to every detail of its agreement with Britain and in particular would not interfere with the maintenance of a Hong Kong dollar unified with the U.S. dollar and trading at a floating exchange rate with the Chinese yuan and would not impose exchange or capital controls. That is the politically correct position for him to take, but I have a high enough opinion of his ability to suspect that he has private doubts. At any rate, I expressed grave doubt that China would be willing to tolerate two independent national monies trading at a floating exchange rate. The only precedent in monetary history that I recall was during the Civil War period in the United States when gold and greenbacks both served as money and traded at a market rate. Perhaps there are others.

I do not doubt that when the Chinese take over they will want to maintain Hong Kong as a thriving, innovative financial and economic center that can continue to provide capital and entrepreneurial leadership to the mainland. But with the best intent in the world, will they be able to do so? I very much doubt it. The officials who are sent to Hong Kong will mouth all the right words, but it is parrot talk, not a key part of their understanding, experience, or background. Hong Kong will continue to be a high-income enclave, providing financial and technological expertise. But unless the hardly conceivable happens, and China simultaneously adopts the Hong Kong system of civil and economic freedom, Hong Kong may remain an important financial and commercial entrepot but will no longer serve as a major international financial center, and will gradually lose much of the dynamic, innovative character that has been produced by personal liberty, free trade, low taxes, and minimal government intervention. China has made great progress since Deng's 1976 reforms in moving from centralized authoritarian control toward greater economic and civil freedom. But the progress is great only because there was so far to go, and it has only come a short way toward the kind of civil and economic freedom that Hong Kong has taken for granted. The hope must be that Hong Kong, though it suffers in the process, can provide an additional stimulus for further and more rapid movement of the whole of China toward a free, private, market society.

We stayed for another day or so in Hong Kong, spent mostly in socializing with our by now many friends, and returned to San Francisco on October 31.

→ *Chapter Thirty-One* ←

LIFE AFTER RETIREMENT

{ *Milton* } Moving to San Francisco in 1977 realized a dream of Rose's that dated back to her first visit to San Francisco more than four decades earlier. Occasional visits to California, and a year's stay at the Center for Advanced Study in Stanford, had simply sharpened her desire for such a move. Accordingly, when I retired from teaching at the University of Chicago at what used to be the mandatory retirement age of sixty-five, we moved to San Francisco. Glen Campbell added icing on the cake when he invited me to join the Hoover staff.

My secretary in Chicago, Gloria Valentine, made the transition to Hoover easy when she volunteered, "have typewriter, will travel." Like Rose, Gloria had long dreamed of living in California. She arranged for transferring all our papers from Chicago to Hoover, and for getting the offices assigned to us all fixed up before I ever set foot in them. More important, she decided to live in San Francisco, rather than in Stanford or Palo Alto, preferring the large city to the small, and accepting the cost of commuting. I have been able to continue to do most of my work at home, going to Hoover only to meet people, attend seminars, and the like. When we are in San Francisco, Gloria brings the mail to me when she comes home; I dictate answers on a tape; she transcribes them; I check them; and out they go. An extremely satisfactory arrangement, for which I am indebted to Gloria's flexibility and ready cooperation. I have now benefited from her helpful support for a quarter of a century!

We made the move to California in two steps. I accepted an invitation from Mike Keran, director of research at the Federal Reserve Bank of San Francisco, to serve as a visiting scholar for the first three months of 1977. During that period we lived in a rented apartment that Janet had found for us on Nob Hill, within walking distance of the bank, and looked for a permanent home. We were fortunate to find a fine apartment with a spectacular view that would be available in the fall at the Royal Towers, a cooperative apartment house at 1750 Taylor Street. That apartment was home until 1987, when we shifted to a larger apartment in the same building that has been home ever since. Our 270-degree view covers the bay from the Golden Gate Bridge to the Bay Bridge and down to the financial sector.

{ *Rose* }   When a journalist recently asked Milton for the best and worst forecast he had ever made, he said that he was not sure what the best one was but he had no question about the worst one. He predicted that retiring from teaching at the University of Chicago and moving to sunny California would mean a relaxed life with plenty of time to do scholarly research. Looking back over the years since retirement, we have decided that retirement *has* been exciting, but it has been anything but relaxing.

Our first quarter in San Francisco provided a foretaste of what was to come. Aside from Milton's activities as a visiting economist at the Federal Reserve Bank, we got acquainted with Rick, Janet's son and our first grandson, set out on the *Free to Choose* project, attended a conference of the Institute for Contemporary Studies in Monterey (a lovely spot that we have since visited many times), made a trip to Mexico in February that ended less happily than it began, and another in early April to New Orleans without mishap. The trip to Mexico was planned as usual with some work (Milton gave talks in Monterrey and Mexico City) and recreation for both of us. The recreation was supposed to be a trip to the south to explore the Mayan ruins. Unfortunately, we never got there because I came down with a strep throat in Mexico City. We were also uneasy about the seeming necessity for tight security, so we decided to postpone our excursion and go home. It was almost fifteen years before we finally toured the Mexican ruins.

In the spring, we followed our usual pattern of spending the six months from April to October at our second home in Vermont. However, the early stages of our activities on *Free to Choose* plus a month-long trip to Alaska and Europe from mid-June to mid-July made it very different from our usual summer of largely uninterrupted scholarly activity. Later, *Free to Choose* activities had the same effect on our stays at Capitaf in 1978 and 1979. By that time, we had decided that instead of trying to maintain Capitaf while living in California, it made more sense to get a second home in California that we could use year-round. Consequently, 1980 was the last summer we spent at Capitaf.

{ *Milton* } The occasion for going to Alaska was a conference at the Alaska Pacific Bank. However, a visit to the Prudhoe Bay oil operations on the north slope and a cruise in Prince William Sound with Walter Hickel and his wife were far more memorable.

We flew to Prudhoe Bay in an oil company plane that was used to ferry workers back and forth from Anchorage, flying past the magnificent Mount McKinley. Prudhoe Bay itself was a revelation. Here in the Arctic on frozen tundra three thousand feet thick were structures to house workers that were the equivalent of a Hilton hotel: an indoor garden area, a theater, and comfortable bedrooms, all put together from components built in Seattle and towed to Prudhoe on rafts during the six weeks a year that the harbor was navigable. The mechanical equipment needed to drill, extract oil, separate the oil from the water, store it, and then send it through a pipeline, itself an engineering feat specially designed not to interfere with the migration route of the caribou, had had to be conveyed to this remote spot in the same brief interval. We were there in the summer, the warmest time of the year, when the daytime temperature was well above freezing, though the ground remained frozen and covered with snow. We could hardly imagine how the complex operation was carried out in the winter, with perpetual darkness, subzero temperatures, and much deep snow.

After our return to Anchorage, we had a wonderful weekend as guests of Walter Hickel and his wife on his boat cruising Prince William Sound. The former interior secretary and governor is a man of many parts. He not only captained his boat, he was also chief cook. Along with spectacular scenery and excellent food, we enjoyed interesting and wide-ranging conversation.

From Alaska, we flew to Europe, where in quick succession we visited Switzerland, Denmark, Sweden, and Norway, in each of which I gave one or more talks, as well as enjoying visits with friends and viewing the sights. We then went on to Israel for a longer stay, discussed in chapter 27.

The most unusual part of this trip was its end. From Israel we stopped briefly in France then sailed from Cherbourg July 9 on the *QE2*, courtesy of Cunard, a most agreeable arrangement that we had enjoyed on several earlier occasions—I paid for our trip by giving a number of lectures en route.* This time, when we arrived in New York on July 14, the city was closed down by an electric blackout. There was no electricity on the pier to run the equipment used to unload the luggage. The captain announced that passengers would have to postpone disembarkation.

---

* An amusing incident on one such voyage occurred when I inquired about our dining room table. The attendant couldn't find our name on the passenger list until I told him that I was giving lectures, at which point he remarked, "Oh, you're one of the entertainers."

{ *Rose* } Milton was scheduled to give a talk to an Oppenheimer group that same morning, and a car had been sent to pick us up. Thanks to the ingenuity of the young driver, we, and our luggage, did manage to get ashore. Without lights, however, there was no way to have a meeting at the Harvard Club, where the event was to take place, so we went directly to the airport instead. Planes were flying, and there was no blackout in Vermont.

{ *Milton* } We first occupied our new apartment in San Francisco on October 13, 1977, at the end of the long drive across the country referred to in chapter 28. Despite the demands of the *Free to Choose* project, we managed during the next three years to establish an agreeable pattern for our life in California. On the professional side, I enjoyed the great advantages of Hoover as a place to do my research and writing on public-policy issues: its excellent facilities, talented and stimulating colleagues, frequent seminars, access to Stanford faculty, libraries, and other facilities. I also became acquainted with people and groups in San Francisco who had similar interests. On the personal side, we got to know San Francisco as only residents can, and, most important, were able to acquire a second home to replace Capitaf.

Earlier chapters have chronicled many of the activities that have filled our years in California. It remains for this chapter to cover a few items of interest that have fallen between the cracks of the partly chronological, partly topical organization we have adopted. I start with the acquisition of a second home.

Sea Ranch

In the spring of 1979, after visiting several developments on the coast, we fell in love with the Sea Ranch, a community about 110 miles north of San Francisco, which had been developed by Castle and Cook in the 1960s, and is some two and a half hours by car from our San Francisco apartment. Originally a sheep ranch, Sea Ranch runs roughly ten miles north and south along the Pacific Ocean, and extends between one and two miles inland. A planned community, half of the area is to be kept as commons, not to be built on, and buyers of lots are subject to restrictions about design and the like, intended to assure that "people would join the natural environment with minimal impact," or in a favorite phrase, "live lightly on the land."[1] It is a beautiful area, with meadows and pines in the area between the ocean and Route 1, which more or less bisects the community, and mostly lush redwood forests on rising hills to the east of Route 1. One of the many hiking trails runs some eight miles along the coastal bluff; others go through the redwoods. There are two recreation areas with tennis courts and swimming pools, a golf course, a lodge with a restaurant, postal substation, and all the other amenities of a planned community, including a security force.

We originally planned to buy a lot and build as nearly as possible a duplicate of Capitaf. As we soon found out, that was not feasible. Not long after Sea Ranch began operation, the citizens of California passed a proposition establishing a Coastal Commission to oversee development on the coast. Although the developers had planned Sea Ranch as a model ecologically sensitive community, and had given part of its original land to the county for a park to assure public access to the sea, the commission demanded that Sea Ranch grant additional public access. The resulting dispute between Sea Ranch and the commission dragged on for years, and was finally settled only by a special enactment by the state legislature. In 1979, when we were looking for a second home, the Coastal Commission was refusing to grant permits to build. All building at Sea Ranch was at a halt and there was little prospect that the logjam would be broken for some years (as in fact it was not). Accordingly, in July 1979, we bought a house that had been built before the halt in the issuance of permits. Its location was ideal: on a lot of roughly an acre directly on the coastal bluff, about seventy-five or so feet above the water with a splendid view over the Pacific. The house itself was less than ideal. We remedied that by rebuilding it, roughly doubling the usable space and adding a greenhouse. We were very fortunate in having Bill Turnbull, one of the original Sea Ranch designers, as our architect, and Matt Sylvia as our builder.

Since 1981, after the rebuilding was completed, we have spent about half of our time at Sea Ranch, in intervals of a week or more spread throughout the year rather than in the solid six-month stretch that we formerly spent at Capitaf. It has proved an excellent arrangement for both work and recreation. Rose has converted a half acre of brush into a literal fairyland of flowers, with color at all seasons of the year, as well as a source of fresh vegetables. To make that possible, we had to put a solid six-foot fence all around the property to keep the deer out. On the few occasions when the deer have breached the fence they have devastated the garden. Both of us have enjoyed and continue to enjoy the trails and the beaches, and I have used the tennis courts and the swimming pools. While I still use a swimming pool, I have had to give up tennis. For some years we joined other residents in a most enjoyable annual canoe trip up a river just south of Mendocino. All in all, while I sometimes still miss Vermont in the summer time, Sea Ranch has proved a splendid substitute for Capitaf, and on a year-round basis.

Guatemala

We had a most enjoyable trip in March 1978 to Guatemala, where I lectured at, and received an honorary degree from, a remarkable institution, Francisco Marroquin University. The institution was founded in 1971 by a group of private businessmen who were very much disturbed by the Marxist orientation of existing higher-educational institutions in Guatemala. The founders had become strong proponents of the free-market vision offered by Von Mises and Hayek and set out to create a private institution that would combine instruction in the theory of a free society with the usual curriculum of a university.

The results have been little short of spectacular. Starting small, with privately contributed capital of $40,000 and an initial student body of 125, it offered degrees in law, economics, business administration, and theology. The university attracted students from the very beginning, and has expanded steadily, adding graduate schools in business, medicine, architecture, and other disciplines. It now has a total enrollment of more than six thousand at its modern campus and an additional five thousand in "distance education." Francisco Marroquin has become one of the leading universities in Central America, one of very few strictly private universities, supported by neither the church nor the government.

Manuel Ayau (Muso to his friends and enemies) was the leading figure in the group that started the university. He served as president of the university and dean of the School of Economics in its early years while at the same time continuing to conduct his regular business. Muso was politically active, serving as a member of the legislature, and years later running unsuccessfully for president and for vice-president. He became an extremely controversial figure and told us harrowing tales of the lengths to which he had to go to protect himself from assassination.[2]

Muso became a member of the Mont Pelerin Society sometime in the 1960s, as did Ulysses Dent, the other member of the founding group whom I got to know well. Both were extraordinary individuals: successful businessmen and also intellectuals, self-taught scholars with a profound understanding of economics and political philosophy.[3]

In addition to the activities at the university in 1978, we spent a few days with Muso and his wife, Olga, in the Guatemala highlands, populated mostly by Indians—the locus of the fierce guerrilla war that raged for so many years and that, we hope, has finally been brought to an end. For us, it was more interesting as the locale on which Sol Tax based his influential monograph, *Penny Capitalism,* in which he described a society that achieved a higher living standard than its neighbors by laissez-faire capitalism, but was stagnant and unprogressive.

Skiing

Rose and I, and Janet and David, had all started skiing at Arosa, Switzerland, during our year in Cambridge (chap. 17), but I was the only one of the four who kept it up at all regularly. When Rose visited her sister Becky in Reno, often in the winter, I would take the opportunity to ski at one of the many areas not far from Reno. I was also able to ski occasionally in New Hampshire and Vermont, whenever we were at Capitaf in snow season.

When we moved to San Francisco, I became acquainted with Lawry Chickering, one of the founders of the Institute for Contemporary Studies and its research director for many years. He became one of my closest friends, and also tennis opponent, despite being a far better tennis player than I. Lawry's parents had been among the original founders of Sugar Bowl, a splendid ski area in the Sierra Nevada not far from Lake Tahoe, and had a house at Sugar Bowl. Lawry was an expert skier, and I enjoyed a number of visits with him at Sugar Bowl. On at least one of these occasions we were joined by Bill Buckley, whom I knew by virtue of having been with him on a number of television programs, including his *Firing Line,* and whom Lawry was close to, having worked with him at the *National Review* shortly after finishing law school.

In 1980, we shifted locale and initiated an annual event that was to be one of the high spots of the year for me: a skiing expedition in the second week of January with Lawry and Bill Buckley at the Alta Lodge in Alta, Utah. The snow was wonderful, the accommodations excellent, and the company superb. In addition, Lawry's ski instructor at Sugar Bowl, Junior Bounouse, had become the head of the ski school at a nearby area and was persuaded to spend a day skiing with us. He is a marvelous instructor and did wonders for my mediocre skiing. Both Lawry and Bill are better skiers than I, but that didn't keep us from enjoying our joint expeditions on the slopes. And a day on the slopes was followed by a relaxing spell in a hot tub, and then in due time by talk over drinks and food—in many ways the best part of the day.

We did not miss a year for sixteen years until, in 1994, I developed physical problems that led to an operation on my back, and left me in a condition where I could get around only with the aid of a walker, so I could not join them in 1995. In the fall of 1995, I had another operation that improved my mobility but still not enough to enable me to ski so I was out for 1996 and

1997. I still have high hopes of joining them in 1998, if not for very limited skiing, at least for unlimited talking.

Villa Cypress

Nineteen eighty saw the initiation of another event that, after an interruption, became a high spot of our year. This one included both Rose and me. George Shultz was at the time president and director of Bechtel Group, Inc., which owned Villa Cypress, a lovely house on the Seventeen-Mile Drive in Monterey. George arranged for a weekend get-together at Villa Cypress in February for close friends interested in national issues. The regular attendees, in addition to George and, until her untimely death in 1995, O'bie Shultz, included Bill and Carol Simon, Walt and Kathie Wriston, Ed and Jeannik Littlefield, and, until his untimely death in 1991, George Stigler. At times members of the Bechtel family and the Bechtel organization attend, occasionally others, and more recently, Gary and Guity Becker and Gerhard and Regina Casper.

The first two sessions were in 1980 and 1981. They were suspended during George's tenure as secretary of state. I write this not long after returning from the latest, in 1997. A lovely house, beautiful location, ample facilities for golf, tennis, walking, and visiting Monterey, and, as at Alta, most important, leisurely evenings for talk, guided by George, who has a true genius for keeping a conversation among prima donnas on track.

Downing Street

During our visit to London in February 1980 to film the discussions for the British version of *Free to Choose*, Margaret Thatcher invited us to meet with her and some of her ministers at 10 Downing Street. The meeting generated an interesting and spirited discussion, especially after Mrs. Thatcher left, asking me to instruct some of the "wets" in her cabinet. As on earlier and later meetings with Mrs. Thatcher, it was impossible not to be impressed with her intellect, character, and force of personality.

Fraser Institute; Economic Freedom Conferences

During our years in California, we have had much contact with Michael Walker, executive director of the Fraser Institute in Vancouver, Canada, since it was founded in 1974. Mike has done a remarkable job of developing Fraser into one of the leading free-market think tanks in North America and by far the most influential such group in Canada.

At a Fraser conference that we attended, the idea emerged of constructing a quantitative measure of economic freedom, comparable to the index of political freedom published annually by Freedom House. That turned out to be more difficult than we initially supposed. It led to a series of conferences spanning thirteen years, for most of which Rose and I served with Mike as co-chairs, though Mike and his associates at Fraser did all the work. The conferences brought together a small group of economists and political scientists who had a special interest in the subject.[4] Fraser published four books based on these conferences. The latest product is a book by James Gwartney, Robert Lawson, and Walter Block, *Economic Freedom of the World, 1975–1995*.

As I wrote in a foreword to that book,

> Freedom is a big word, and economic freedom not much smaller. To talk about economic freedom is easy; to measure it, to make fine distinctions, assign numbers to its attributes, and combine them into one overall magnitude—that is a very different and much more difficult task, as we found out after we started on this quest some thirteen years ago. . . .
>
> For many of us, freedom—economic, political, civil—is an end in itself, not a means to other ends—it is what makes life worthwhile. We would prefer to live in a free country even if it did not provide us and our fellow citizens with a higher standard of life than an alternative regime. But I am firmly persuaded that a free society could never exist under such circumstances. A free society is a delicate balance, constantly under attack, even by many who profess to be its partisans. I believe that free societies have arisen and persisted only because economic freedom is so much more productive economically than other methods of controlling economic activity.
>
> It did not require the construction of an index of economic freedom for it to be widely believed that there is a close relation between economic freedom and the level and rate of economic growth. Theoretical considerations gave reason to expect such a relation, and little more than casual observation sufficed to show that what theory suggested, experience documented. We have not in a sense learned any *big* thing from this book that we did not know before. What we have done is to acquire a set of data that can be used to explore just how the relation works, and what are the essential connections, and that will enable skeptics to test their views objectively.[5]

The Heritage Foundation launched a somewhat parallel effort in 1989, which resulted in a series of volumes (beginning in 1994) presenting an index of economic freedom. There is considerable overlap but also significant differences between the Fraser and Heritage volumes, reflecting different objectives. The Fraser project is directed to academic students of development; the Heritage project, to governmental dispensers of foreign aid and business leaders contemplating investment abroad. There was also some collaboration: Heritage scholars attended and contributed to some of the Fraser conferences.[6]

Second Marriages

{ *Rose* } Our children were not as fortunate in their first marriages as we were. We have already told the story of the breakup of David's first marriage. Janet's lasted longer than David's. She had a child after six years and continued with Lew for some eight years more. I never felt that it was a good marriage, but did not express my feelings to Janet until she announced that she was getting a divorce.

Charles Martel, a graduate student at Berkeley working toward a doctorate in computer science and another avid bridge player, fell in love with Janet. Fortunately, that converted her unhappiness about her marriage into action. She and Chip were married on June 25, 1982. Janet said she chose to be married on the same date that we were because she thought it would be a good omen. It has been but because she chose the right man this time rather than because of the date.

Chip's father was a professor of mathematics and his mother a librarian. They were divorced when Chip was a teenager. They were observant Jews so Chip and Janet had a Jewish marriage ceremony, just as we did for the sake of our parents. The marriage took place in the party room of our apartment house. In addition to Chip's parents and sister, many of his relatives and friends came, as well as Janet's friends and our relatives and friends, and it was a very festive and joyous occasion. Chip has been a wonderful husband and equally important, from a grandmother's point of view, a wonderful father to Rick.

Chip is now a professor of computer science at the University of California at Davis. When he received his appointment, they moved to Davis, and Janet opened a law practice. She also did some part-time teaching at a nearby law school.

Lew also remarried and the two families have remained on good terms. Lew and Chip have remained frequent bridge partners, the two of them winning many national and international titles. Janet has also continued to be a top bridge player, sometimes with Chip as partner. At one of the bridge tournaments at which Rick served as a helper, he wore a t-shirt with the slogan, "My Fathers are Bridge Partners."

David too has had a second marriage. Sometime after Diana left Blacksburg, David became acquainted with Elizabeth Cook, a graduate student in geology. Though they were in different professions, they had many extracurricular activities in common—including participating in the Society for Creative Anachronism, medieval cookery, and science fiction. They were married on June 4, 1983, in Cleveland Heights, Ohio, where her parents live. My brother Aaron and sister Becky went to the wedding with us.

David's second marriage has been very successful and fruitful. We now have two more grandchildren, Becca, born in 1990, and William, born in 1993. In 1995, David accepted a position at Santa Clara University to teach in the Economics Department and the Law School, so David and Betty now live in California, and this gives us the added pleasure of seeing them all more frequently. Patri is a student at Harvey Mudd College. He too has been a delight.

Dinner with the Queen

In March 1983, Queen Elizabeth II visited San Francisco in the course of a world trip on her yacht, *Britannia*. President and Mrs. Reagan invited us to attend a dinner that they hosted in honor of Queen Elizabeth and Prince Philip at the De Young Art Museum in San Francisco. And the queen in turn invited us to a party on her yacht the next night.

When it came Milton's turn to be introduced to the queen while going through the receiving line, she remarked, "I know you. Philip is always watching you on the telly"—a tribute to the reach of *Free to Choose*.

The dinner itself was a glittering affair, attended by the leading citizens of California and many from the rest of the country.

Milton made a real faux pas as he boarded the yacht the next night, remarking in an audible voice, "Some boat," only to be politely corrected by a much bestriped officer, "This is a ship, sir." Once on the yacht, the arrangements were very informal, with the queen and Prince Philip circulating freely among the guests. David Packard had given the queen a Hewlett-Packard computer and Milton was able to advise her on how she could use it to keep track of her race horses. Prince Philip was very interested in social policy and well informed on the issues we talked about.

In this age of democracy, Elizabeth and Philip, like the king and queen of Sweden, were very friendly, unpretentious, attractive people. "Regal" is not a word that springs to mind to describe their behavior.

From Iceland to Cap d'Antibes, 1984

{ *Milton* } En route to a Mont Pelerin meeting at Cambridge, England, we spent several fascinating days in Iceland. Reykjavik turned out to be a lovely city, shining clean with clear air, thanks to the availability of ample water from hot springs to heat the houses.

Our host was Hannes Gissurarson, at the time a rather lonely, and highly effective, defender of free markets and limited government in Iceland. The ostensible occasion for our visit was for me to give a public lecture. Our reason for accepting the invitation was to see something of Iceland, a small country that has a long history, notable especially for the Icelandic sagas, dating from the thirteenth and fourteenth century. Our interest was stimulated by our son, David, a great admirer of the sagas, whose article, "Private Creation and Enforcement of Law: A Historical Case," examines the "legal and political institutions of Iceland from the tenth to the thirteenth centuries" and has become something of a classic of libertarian literature.[7]

Hannes arranged for us to meet with President Finnbogadottir and other officials, arranged a discussion with academics, and gave us a most rewarding tour of the points of interest in Iceland. The ancient history that we had heard from David was supplemented by discussion of current problems and disputes. Continuity over a millennium.

From the Mont Pelerin meeting, we went on to a two-week vacation, mostly in southern France. Nineteen eighty-four was near the peak of the appreciation of the dollar in the first Reagan term, so the exchange rate for the franc was exceptionally favorable—something like ten francs to the dollar, if my memory serves me right. That made a luxurious vacation affordable to us, starting with a week at the Hôtel du Cap d'Antibes, a truly splendid hotel and idyllic location, followed by a drive in a rented car up the famous Napoleonic highway, the route Napoleon took on his "hundred days" return from exile in 1815. We spent four days getting to Paris, stopping en route at every accessible three-star restaurant. We particularly enjoyed the Auberge du Père Bisc, in Talloires, close to the Swiss border. In Paris, we stayed at the famous Ritz, paying something like $100 a night, thanks to the favorable exchange rate. The occasion for our visit to Paris was the publication of a French translation of our book, *Tyranny of the Status Quo.* We returned to New York on the *QE2*, again as an "entertainer." All in all, a memorable vacation, which may, however, have paved the way for the heart attack that I had later that year.

Second Bypass Operation

In late 1984, we were visiting our son David in New Orleans, where he was teaching at Tulane. As usual, combining business with pleasure, I was scheduled to give a lecture under the auspices of my friend Meyer Feldberg, dean of the Tulane Business School. The lecture was to be part of the ceremonies inaugurating a new building. Over the weekend before the scheduled talk, I developed severe angina and then had a minor heart attack. Again we were fortunate. The Tulane Hospital proved extremely competent when we showed up there early Monday morning, after I had spent most of the night in agonizing pain. I will never forget the intense relief and indeed sense of utter comfort that flowed through me as the first shot of morphine took effect. The experience for the first time gave me some emotional understanding of drug addiction.

{ *Rose* } Milton spent the next two weeks in intensive care at Tulane Hospital. And I spent two weeks as a guest of the hospital. Unlike the patients, I was not bothered with temperature-taking and all the other tests that they are kept busy with. Instead, I had a lovely private room, with three delicious meals delivered daily on a small table covered with a gleaming white tablecloth. When Milton was well enough to leave the intensive-care unit, we were both moved to a suite so we could be together. From the head of the hospital down, we benefited from true southern hospitality.

Because of Milton's earlier experience, I decided to call Dr. Brandenburg for advice about how to proceed after we left Tulane, in particular, whether we should consider returning to the Mayo Clinic. I called the clinic and was told that Dr. Brandenburg had retired and was living in Arizona. So I called him at his home and told him our story. He was very kind and interested. He said that the cardiology department at Stanford was excellent and we would do well to go there.

After two weeks at Tulane, Milton was well enough to leave, although the hospital insisted that the nurse who had taken care of him accompany us on the trip. She was delighted to go to San Francisco. Bill Jovanovich, with his usual generosity, sent his private jet to take us to San Francisco. Milton then spent a few more days convalescing at the Stanford Hospital before coming home. Five weeks later, after an angiogram, Dr. Norman Shumway performed a second bypass. That one, I am glad to say, has so far lasted Milton twelve years.

Dr. Rose

{ *Milton* } Rose had frequently been embarrassed by being addressed as "Dr." She had satisfied all requirements for the degree at Chicago except for the thesis, which she never managed to complete. In December 1984, Pepperdine University removed the embarrassment by conferring an honorary doctorate on Rose at its convocation. Executive Vice-President (subsequently President) David Davenport of Pepperdine made it into a very nice occasion. The degree was both well deserved and much appreciated.

Seventy-Fifth Birthday

Hoover did me the great honor of convening a day-long seminar and hosting a dinner on July 15, 1987, to celebrate my seventy-fifth birthday. Among others, our son David participated in the seminar, and one of our favorite pictures is of him and me side by side on the platform—a testament to the influence of genes. A number of my former students participated in the seminar. A real intellectual treat.

The dinner was a festive affair. We were greatly touched by the number of friends who came from far away to attend the dinner—the distance record was set by Maurice Newman, who flew from Australia to attend, returning home the next day. Hanging on a wall in our apartment is a memento from the occasion signed by most of the people present.

New England Revisited

We spent the first two weeks of October 1987 revisiting the various places in New England that had played a role in our lives. We chose that period because it is the peak time for viewing the fall color, a New England miracle that we have not been able to match in California. We started in Hanover, seeing friends and visiting familiar locales.

We returned to our first summer home in Orford, New Hampshire, for the first time since we sold it and met its current owners They were very friendly and let us explore as we would. The studio, in which I spent so much time so fruitfully and in which we all enjoyed playing Ping-Pong, had burned down and was not replaced. The cottage had been winterized and added to and was the year-round home of its occupants. The living room and its splendid stone fireplace remained largely as it had been. But for the rest, the place had largely lost its charm.

We visited Capitaf, to find that no one was at home. Externally, the saddest change for Rose was the disappearance of the flower garden and the landscaping that had been her pride and joy—and the product of much sweat and hard work. Another change was a tennis court that Bob Aliber had constructed, something I had long contemplated but never succeeded in achieving.

We next had a most enjoyable visit with Laura and Ed Banfield in Montpelier, driving through an unusually early snowstorm to get there.

After returning to New York for two days to participate in a seminar in honor of Anna Schwartz, we resumed our New England tour, driving to the Mount Washington area to visit Dick and Beverly Ware, who had moved permanently to what had long been a second home for them. Dick was still climbing mountains, and we had a pleasant time recalling the many mountains that we had climbed together, as well as discussing the state of the nation. Through the Earhart and Relm foundations, Dick, in his quiet, unobtrusive way, had played a major role in the revival of intellectual understanding of, and support for, a free-market society. An impressive fraction of current classical liberal scholars have been Earhart Fellows, a program Dick introduced and ran.

The rest of our trip was pure nostalgia: driving through Maine to Lake Kezar. We drove around the lake but were unable on our own to find the cottage where we had spent our honeymoon forty-nine years earlier. In desperation, we drove to the North Lovell post office seeking information. The postmistress, who clearly had not been born when we occupied the cottage, did not recognize the name of the woman, Mrs. Paisley, from whom we had rented the cottage. However, she suggested that we might get some help from a father and son realty firm just down the street from the post office. There we hit pay dirt. When we knocked at the door, the father answered, explaining that he was retired but his son would be back shortly. However, our business was with him. It turned out that he knew Mrs. Paisley and the property very well. He gave us precise directions that enabled us to find the cottage without difficulty. The lake and the surrounding area were as we remembered it, but not the cottage. It apparently had not been occupied for some time, and looked badly neglected. It was no longer the "stone cottage in the woods" of nostalgic memory—and perhaps never had been.

Our goal of revisiting our past completed, we returned to San Francisco.

Golden Wedding Celebration

June 25, 1988, was the fiftieth anniversary of our marriage, as well as the sixth anniversary of Janet's marriage to Chip. To celebrate, we decided on a family excursion to Ecuador and the Galapagos Islands. Janet made the detailed arrangements, and we converged on Quito from different directions on June 24—eight in all: Rose and I; Janet, Chip, and Rick; David, Betty, and Patri. We spent a day or two in Quito, and the rest of the first week touring the highlands and the monumental ruins of the Inca empire.

We then flew to the Galapagos Islands, where we boarded a chartered boat with a capacity for twelve persons and a crew of five: captain, assistant captain, cook, handyman, and, most important, a naturalist. The arrangements were ideal. There was ample room for us, the food was excellent, and the crew and the naturalist scheduled our daytime stops at various islands so as not to coincide with large groups from the big tourist ships and covered the long distances between islands at night as we slept. The large turtles, iguanas, and other unusual animals fully lived up to their reputation, and all of us, young and old, very much enjoyed our nature walks.

Equally enjoyable were our water excursions. We swam in the waters alongside friendly seals, who seemed amused by our amateur thrashing around in the water and gave every appearance of trying to show us how to do it right. A high point for Patri, our twelve-year-old grandson, who had become an enthusiastic fisherman, was trips in the dinghy to waters where fish were plentiful, and where Patri could pull up one after another, almost as fast as he could bait the hook and drop it overboard. Most were thrown back because inedible, but there were enough edible ones to provide several splendid meals. Patri was in seventh heaven.

All of us enjoyed the spectacle at night, as we were sailing through the water, of being accompanied by dolphins, swimming ahead and around the ship, leaving fluorescent trails as they went. Natural fireworks.

Medals of Science and Freedom

During 1988, I was awarded two medals: the National Medal of Science and the Presidential Medal of Freedom.

The National Medal of Science was awarded in 1988 to twenty scientists. The recipients are generally natural scientists, but occasionally, as in my case, social scientists. The medals are awarded by the president in the White House. Unfortunately, I was unable to go to Washington for the occasion, so I arranged for David to accept the medal on my behalf.

The nation's highest civilian award, the Presidential Medal of Freedom, is awarded each year to recipients designated by the president. President Reagan awarded it to eight people at a ceremony on October 17, 1988, only a few months before he was to leave the White House. Rose and I were able to attend the event, and we arranged invitations for my two nephews, Jerry and Allen Porter, and their wives, and for David Meiselman and his wife, and, most important, for our grandson Patri, who unquestionably got the biggest kick out of meeting Ronald Reagan as well as the other civilian and military dignitaries present on the occasion.[8]

A Wedding in Seattle

In 1989, Steve Cheung asked me to officiate at his forthcoming marriage to Linda Su. When Steve taught at the University of Washington, he had also dabbled in real estate. One venture involved developing a shopping center on a substantial piece of land in Mill Creek, near Seattle, part of which was too marshy to be part of the center. Steve converted the marshy area into a beautiful Oriental garden as part of a Chinese restaurant complex, Imperial Gardens. He planned the wedding ceremony and feast to take place at his restaurant, which was being managed by his bride-to-be.

I protested that I was not a minister or a justice of the peace. He explained that the legal marriage would be performed before the public ceremony, and my presiding at the latter had no legal significance. It would simply be part of the party.

I could not resist the unusual opportunity. At the wedding, I bedecked myself in my academic robe and cap; Steve, Linda, and I stood on a typical red Oriental bridge spanning a waterfall, with all the guests below us, and I went through the proper procedure, asking the usual questions of bride and groom, prefaced, however, with something like this: "This is a truly international and intercultural event: here we are in the United States, with a Chinese Buddhist living in Hong Kong being married to a Chinese Christian living in the United States, and the marriage being performed by a Jew." It was a fine party, followed by a marvelous Chinese feast.

Surviving an Earthquake

I was in our apartment on the nineteenth floor of 1750 Taylor Street, a building sitting on solid rock, when the October 17, 1989, earthquake hit San

Francisco. The shock was severe and shook the building enough so that I had to grab at a piece of furniture to keep from falling down. But it was brief and did no structural damage to the building. Though we had many glasses and other breakable objects on open shelves, only one object fell down and broke. However, electricity was immediately cut off, which meant not only no lights but, more important, no elevator service.

{ *Rose* } My experience was very different from Milton's. I have always had poor teeth, and Dean Kirkpatrick, my dentist, who is always learning about new dental practices, had persuaded me some six months earlier to have my upper teeth implanted. The surgery had all been completed and I was in the final stage of having impressions prepared for my new teeth. I was in the dentist's chair waiting for one more set of impressions to be prepared when suddenly the lights went out and everything started to shake and fall from the shelves, including my unfinished impressions. I was so stunned that I don't remember the dentist's chair I was sitting in shaking, but I assume it did. Dean pulled me from the chair and led me to the fire escape door. He explained later that that was the only place where there was a metal support of some kind and therefore was relatively safe. Standing on the fire escape, we watched bricks falling from the building across the street. When Dean decided it was safe for us to leave, we walked down the two flights of stairs and went our separate ways. Dean's office was in an old building in the financial district, which was one of the two areas in San Francisco that were most heavily damaged. The building we were in was later condemned and torn down.

As I think back, I must have reacted as though in a dream and behaved automatically. I had always walked to and from Dean's office, so I walked home. It seemed strange that the stores and beauty parlors along the way were dark but I didn't give that much thought. It was only when I reached the Royal Towers and walked up the four flights of stairs to the lobby floor and found Milton and a number of other tenants nervously waiting that I realized something important had occurred. As of that moment, I believe that I had suffered less than Milton.

However, the next two or three weeks were different. Without an upper set of teeth I could only eat mush until Dean, using the office of the surgeon he worked with, finished what he had been working on. Fortunately, he had some of the impressions he had taken before the earthquake. He never told me how he retrieved them. In any case, he made me a temporary set until he could really get back to work in a new office. Dean never misses the opportunity of telling whoever is in his office when I am there about our experience.

{ *Milton* } In my safety, I was obviously very concerned about Rose. I tried telephoning Dean's office, to no avail. I walked down to the first floor, where I joined other occupants of the building milling around. I then decided that I would drive to Dean's office along the route that I thought Rose would take walking home, to see if I could find her.

It was an eerie experience. Traffic lights were out, along with all other lights. There was little automobile traffic, though many pedestrians were in the streets. Drivers were very much aware that there were no traffic lights to depend on, and self-regulation worked very well. I was disappointed not to see Rose en route, but had no difficulty getting down to Dean's office building, and even parking across the street from it. The door to the building was open, but when I went up to Dean's office, I encountered only a locked door. My worst time was after I returned to 1750 Taylor without sighting Rose en route and found that she had not returned while I was gone. It was an enormous relief when she turned up some time later—it seemed a very long time but was probably only fifteen minutes or so.

We climbed the nineteen flights back to our apartment. From our living room window, we watched the fire that had broken out in the Marina, observed the break in the Bay Bridge, listened on a battery radio to accounts of the damage and loss of life, and congratulated ourselves on having suffered so little harm—though two weeks without upper teeth was hardly a picnic for Rose.

Aaron's Ninetieth-Birthday Party

In the summer of 1991, George Stigler suggested a surprise party to mark Aaron's ninetieth birthday on September 21, 1991. He talked to Rose and also to Priscilla (Sunny) Scott, who had become a close friend of Aaron's through her husband, Kenneth, a professor in the Stanford Law School and a Fellow at Hoover. Sunny and Ken live in the Stanford area and offered to host the party. George, Rose, and Sunny drew up a list of people to be invited, and George sent out invitations from Chicago, cautioning everyone that it was to be a surprise.

Rose and I drove Aaron to the party on the pretext that the three of us had been invited to have dinner at the Scotts. I shall never forget the look of complete surprise on Aaron's face as we entered the Scott's yard to find it occupied by so many former colleagues, former students, relatives, and friends from all over the country who burst out with "Happy Birthday to you." It was a wonderful party.

Nobel Foundation's Ninetieth-Birthday Party

Nineteen ninety-one was the ninetieth year in which Nobel prizes were awarded. The Nobel Foundation decided to celebrate by inviting all living Nobel laureates and their spouses to the 1991 Nobel ceremonies. Rose and I were delighted to accept the invitation. We decided to overcome jet lag and get warmed up for cold Stockholm by first vacationing at Marbella, in southern Spain, and visiting Morocco, a country we had never previously visited.

We were at a hotel in Marrakech when Gloria reached us with the sad news that George Stigler had died. As we later learned, he had been in the hospital with pneumonia, had recovered, and was about to be released. In a phone conversation with Aaron on the morning of his death, he seemed in excellent spirits and was exulting in the prospect of having good food again. Before he could be released, he had a massive heart attack. The news was devastating. Hard to believe that we would never again enjoy the company of our vital, brilliant, witty friend of so many years, who only three months earlier had been with us to celebrate Aaron's ninetieth birthday.

{ *Rose* } News of George's sudden death cast a pall over the rest of our trip, and events cooperated, our luggage failing to accompany us to Stockholm. The day after our arrival, Milton was scheduled to give a talk at Gothenburg, and he had to appear there in his casual traveling clothes, as did I. It was only after three days, when our luggage at last turned up, that we began to enjoy the Nobel ceremonies. Indeed, the absence of protesters dogging our steps enabled us to enjoy to the full the ninetieth-birthday party, as we had not been able to enjoy the ceremonies in 1976.

Mexico

{ *Milton* } In May 1992, the Cato Institute organized a conference in Mexico City titled "Liberating the Hemisphere: Free Trade and Beyond" in cooperation with several Mexican organizations. I gave the keynote address at the opening dinner and participated in several discussion panels. I also met with economists at the Bank of Mexico and with a group of economists who had studied at the University of Chicago. The most amusing highlight of the busy and productive week were cartoons in Spanish language newspapers lampooning me for my stand on the decriminalization of drugs. A framed duplicate of one of those cartoons hangs on a wall of our Sea Ranch home.

After the conference, Carolina de Bolívar and her husband Simón enabled us to achieve the trip to the Mayan ruins that we had aborted fifteen years earlier. They were marvelous hosts and tour guides. We flew to Villahermosa, where they had arranged to have a van waiting to take us to all the important sites: Palenque, Uxmal, Chichén Itzá, and ending up at Cancún. The ancient monuments fully lived up to their billing, and as I wrote to Ed Crane, "We had a splendid week in the Yucatan. We could not have had better hosts than Simón and Carolina Bolívar. Moreover, we spent a whole week without seeing a single newspaper. What bliss."

Traveling for Old Folks

Greece

A letter from the Travel/Study programs of the Stanford Alumni Association introduced us to a new form of recreational traveling, the cruise. Our only foretaste had been trips across the Atlantic, most recently on the *QE2*. But they had simply been good ways to get home. We had never before been on a cruise as a form of recreation.

The letter asked whether I would be willing to serve as one of the lecturers on a cruise to the Greek islands in September 1993. I gladly accepted, pleased at the opportunity to revisit an area that we had visited earlier. The cruise was on the *Royal Viking Queen,* a splendid ship with an efficient and courteous crew.

We first had to get to Athens to embark on the cruise, and that proved the one bad part of the experience, being stranded at the Frankfurt airport for something like ten to twelve hours, owing to missing a connection through no fault of our own.

After two days in Athens, mostly recovering from jet lag, we boarded the *Queen* and were off to the Greek islands. We soon discovered that visiting an island meant running the gauntlet of purveyors of souvenirs lined up on both sides of the road leading from the dock into the town or village. The laws of economics are inexorable: as mass tourism has brought a flood of potential customers to places worth seeing, purveyors of souvenirs have followed as the night the day. Our biggest shock was in Rhodes, the one island that we had visited before. Our recollection was of a lazy, peaceful, traditional island. This time, before we could see the island, we had to pass through what seemed a mile of hucksters. We soon discovered that we enjoyed the cruising and the amenities aboard the ship, but had much less interest in the tourist stops.

The *Royal Viking Queen* proceeded from the Greek waters through the Mediterranean, stopping among other places at the Isle of Capri. Once again we were frustrated, as we had been many years earlier, in our desire to enter the Blue Grotto. Once again, the sea was unpropitious. The cruise ended at Monte Carlo, from where we flew back home after a very enjoyable experience.

San Francisco to New Zealand

Our second cruise in November 1994 was strictly recreational: a three-week cruise to New Zealand on the *Royal Viking Sun,* a sister ship of the *Royal Viking Queen.* We embarked in San Francisco along with Sam Husbands and Dorian and John Adams, so we had very good company. We had planned the cruise before I developed the physical problems that led to my having a spinal laminectomy on September 14, 1994. My physician and the surgeon who did the operation both encouraged us to go ahead with the cruise, expecting that I would fully recover within six weeks. Unfortunately, that was unduly optimistic. Though the operation was not supposed to affect my lower body, I was able to walk onto the ship only with the aid of a walker, and had to use it throughout the cruise. That did not prevent us from enjoying our time aboard ship. Nonetheless, my condition did limit our activities, and made it necessary for us to cancel the longer visits in New Zealand and Australia that we had planned. We stayed one night in New Zealand and another in Australia, in both cases able to visit with friends, and then flew back to San Francisco.

San Francisco to Hong Kong

In January 1997, by which time, after another operation and the expert attention of Dr. Joel Saal, my physical condition was much better and I had dispensed with both walker and cane, we took another *Royal Viking Sun* cruise, this time a four-week cruise from San Francisco to Hong Kong. This was partly a working trip: we took with us a laptop and draft copy of most of this book, planning to revise it during the course of the voyage. The working conditions were ideal: no phones, no meetings, no papers, no interruptions, and a most comfortable cabin, with an outside balcony, in which to work. We managed to put in reasonably complete form all but two chapters (including this one), for which we did not have a good initial draft.

In Honolulu, we were joined by Sam Husbands and Margaretha af Ugglas, a wonderful Swedish lady and longtime friend of Sam's who had served as foreign minister of Sweden from 1991 to 1994 when the Moderaten (conservative) Party was in power. They were wonderful company, and we did not get as much work done after they joined us as we had on the week's sail to Honolulu.

Once again, the ship and the amenities on board were the best part of the cruise. We did stop at the Marshall Islands, Guam, and the Philippines, all interesting but none exciting.

We spent the better part of a week in Hong Kong. We arrived just at the time of the Chinese New Year, which meant that everything was closed for three days. However, that did not prevent Steve Cheung from arranging activities and dinners with friends from our earlier trips. The most interesting and innovative activity that Steve arranged was a seminar at the University of Hong Kong devoted entirely to my academic work—a real exception, since almost all the talks that I have given in Hong Kong have been about issues of policy, not science. He and a colleague took turns questioning me about successive topics that I had worked on and to which I had made contributions—professional incomes, the theory of consumption, methodology of positive economics, flexible exchange rates, and monetary theory, history, and policy. I had never previously taken part in that kind of discourse. The discussion of my early work brought back memories and details that I had had no reason to recall for many years.

From Hong Kong we went to Bali to visit Hugo van Reijen, who has a lovely house and grounds in Ubud, the artistic center of Bali. As with Rhodes, the character of Bali had changed since we had visited it a third of a century earlier. Tourism had overwhelmed it. We had brought back beautiful carvings from Bali on our 1963 visit. This time, everything seemed to be mass-produced. Hugo took us to the best current carvers and craftsmen, but we were unable to find any small-scale carvings that seemed to us to match in quality the ones we already had. No doubt they exist, but they account for a much smaller fraction of the market.

Throughout history, the major benefits of economic progress have accrued to the masses not the classes. What has happened to tourism in recent decades is a clear example. Technological advances in transportation, particularly air travel, have lowered the real cost of travel at the same time that real incomes have risen. The result has brought foreign tourism into the reach of lower and lower income classes. The market has responded, to the detriment of the formerly privileged.

Celebration of the Fiftieth Anniversary of Mont Pelerin

We have just returned (June 1997) from our first trip to Europe since 1990. The occasion was a special meeting of the Mont Pelerin Society to commemorate the fiftieth anniversary of its founding. The special meeting was held at Mont Pelerin, Switzerland, where the initial meeting took place fifty years ago and from which it took its name.

In an attempt to reproduce the spirit of the initial meeting, the number of attendees was limited, though to a number beyond the capacity of the Hotel du Parc where we stayed in 1947. Instead, the meeting was held at Le Mirador, a splendid resort hotel.

Of the thirty-nine people who participated in the first meeting, only three are still alive: Aaron Director, Maurice Allais, and myself. I was the only one of the three present at the memorial meeting.

It was a well planned and conducted meeting. The agenda duplicated that of the original meeting.[9] The world has changed, yet the issues discussed fifty years earlier seemed entirely topical. The spirit came close to that of the original meeting, thanks to the limited size of the group, and its composition, consisting predominantly of members of long standing. The sessions were substantive and involved spirited discussion of serious intellectual issues. There was much informal discussion stimulated by the formal sessions.

The final session was devoted to retrospect and prospect. In my talk, I noted that those of us at the initial meeting regarded the spread of central planning and nationalization as the key threat to freedom. Britain had just elected an explicitly socialist Labour government; France was going in for what it termed "indicative planning"; wartime government planning in the United States had conferred prestige on detailed government intervention; and Russia, with its centralized authoritarian system, was in high repute among Western intellectuals.

That threat, in its original form, had disappeared. Central planning proved a failure in every nation that had preserved a large measure of civil freedom. The left soon shifted from trying to control production directly to controlling it indirectly through regulation and to using the tax system to redistribute the output of industry. The regulatory and welfare state, not the socialist state, became, and remains, the main threat to freedom.

To judge from the climate of opinion, we have won the war of ideas. Everyone—left or right—talks about the virtues of markets, private property, competition, and limited government. No doubt the Mont Pelerin Society and its many associates around the world deserve some credit for that change in the climate of opinion, but it derives much more from the sheer force of reality: the fall of the Berlin Wall; the tremendous success of the Far Eastern tigers—Hong Kong, Singapore, Taiwan, Korea—and, more recently, Chile.

However, I went on, appearances are deceptive. In the realm of practice, our economies are less free than they were when the society was founded. Government spending has gone in the United States from 20 percent to 40 percent of national income; and much the same has happened in other Western countries. Equally important, the range and extent of regulation, both of industry and of personal conduct, has increased in even greater measure. We have gained on the level of rhetoric, lost on the level of practice.

As an innate optimist, I believe that we are witnessing the usual lag of several decades between ideas and action, that the growth in government has largely come to a halt and is starting, however slowly, to shift direction.

After our wonderful stay at Mont Pelerin, we spent a few days in Prague, where I gave a number of lectures, had extensive discussions with leaders of business and government, enjoyed a cocktail party in our honor given by our lovely ambassadress, Jenonne Walker, and was awarded an honorary degree by the Economics University.

From Prague, we went to London for a few days, our primary purpose being to host a twentieth-anniversary reunion for those who had participated in the filming of *Free to Choose.* We had a splendid party attended by all but one of the wonderful group to which we owe so much, and most of their spouses. It was by all odds the high point of our stay in London.

And then, back to Paradise.

Surviving a Forest Fire

Paradise, alas, threatened to turn into Inferno a few weeks later. It was 4:40 P.M., Friday, July 11, 1997. Our son David, his wife Betty, and their two young children, Bill, four, and Becca, seven, had spent the previous three days with us at Sea Ranch and were preparing to leave. The car packed, they started off. But when they got to the top of the driveway, they saw heavy smoke a quarter of a mile away at the north end of Yardarm Drive (the inner drive on which our house is located). They came back to warn us. In the short time it took us to rush up the driveway, flames as well as smoke were visible. The exit from Yardarm Drive to Route 1 had already been closed by a raging wall of fire that was being driven by a strong wind from the north and was consuming the brush and the trees in the space between Yardarm and Route 1.

A flying spark had already started a fire on the grounds of our neighbor to the north. We were sure that we would lose our house. The only question was how to save our family.

While we were considering our next move a deputy sheriff arrived and urged us to make our way south along the ocean bluff until we could get to the shore, where we would be protected if a grass fire should sweep west. We left quickly with only the clothes on our backs (shorts and short-sleeve shirts) without a thought about rescuing anything from the house, or even closing the doors or windows.

Since there is no easy way to get to the ocean shore from our house, we took off south, tearing out pieces of a fence to get to our neighbor's property, which is bordered on the south by a large open field covered with blackberry bushes and other low vegetation. The going was tough, especially for Betty with four-year-old Bill, and for us with our bare legs. About a half-mile down the coast, the field runs down to the ocean. David was the first to reach a small stone-covered beach, where he figured we would be safe if a grass fire should sweep west. As we waited on the beach, helicopters were flying over the ocean alongside us, picking up water in hanging buckets and proceeding inland to drop the water on the fire.

Fortunately, the wind drove the fire east to the forest so a grass fire to the west did not develop. After half an hour or so, a four-wheel-drive ambulance made its way across the open field to where we were, picked us up and took us to Stewart's Point, a hamlet two miles south of the Sea Ranch, where we could wait for news of the fire.

Stewart's Point has a small general store and a telephone. Fire engines from neighboring communities were rapidly assembling there. About thirty fire companies, some professional but mostly volunteer, were engaged before the fire was finally put out the next day. A contingent from the Sea Ranch Volunteer Fire Department was at Stewart's Point coordinating the activities of the firefighters. As is usual in an emergency, the information about the situation at Yardarm was vague, often contradictory. We were assured that volunteer firemen were protecting the houses on Yardarm Drive and that our house had not been damaged, but we could get no definite word about when we could return.

The situation was so uncertain that we began thinking about where the family could spend the night. We had no car and in any case could not drive north to the Sea Ranch Lodge, where we might get rooms, because the road was closed. One place we thought of was Timber Hill Ranch, a splendid resort in the hills twelve miles or so from Stewart's Point, where we had occasionally dined and had established a friendship with the two couples who ran the resort. Rose phoned and was told that every cottage was occupied. However, sensing our desperation, they said they would take care of us somehow. In about half an hour, Frank, one of the proprietors, arrived at Stewart's Point. The six of us plus Frank crowded into his car and off to the ranch we went. When we arrived, Tarran, another proprietor, greeted us and took us to the activities room while Frank parked the car. It was now after 7 o'clock, so she suggested dinner. Seeing Rose's hesitancy about appearing in the main dining room in our disheveled state, she asked whether we would be more comfortable eating in the activities room, where they could set up a table. After a wonderful dinner served to us on spotless linen and the elegant crystal that was standard at the ranch, while Bill slept peacefully on the floor, mattresses and bedding appeared and we proceeded to make our beds and try to sleep.

After a restless night, we called the number we had been given the night before for information about getting into our house and were told we could return. Barbara, another of the proprietors, volunteered to drive us home. After some backing and filling, and delays due to crossed orders, we did indeed find ourselves back at Sea Ranch in our own home. David and his family started back to the city immediately, and we turned to the task of dealing with a house lacking electricity and telephone.

We learned later that the fire had started opposite the house of our friends the Caygills at the north end of Yardarm. It was caused by a branch falling on a high-voltage electric line, which fell to the ground and set the undergrowth on fire. Only one house suffered severe fire damage. Our house was unscathed. Burnt spots in the garden not twenty feet from the house were evidence of how real the danger had been and how much we owed to the volunteers, who were on the alert and promptly doused any possible fires.

The destruction in the area was extensive but mostly in open land or forests—a terrible sight but not a threat to life or limb. Electricity was not restored until Sunday night, and telephone service not until Monday night. When all was back in order, we left for San Francisco on Tuesday. Hereafter, we shall view those frequent television pictures of raging forest fires very differently.

→ Epilogue ←

{ *Milton and Rose* } As each new wonder came along, Rose's mother would greet it with the remark, "America gonif"—literally, America the thief, figuratively, America the magician.* The example we remember best is the look on Rose's father's face as he heard for the first time his own voice coming from a tape recorder. That is the way we feel as we look back on a long and fruitful life. America—by which Rose's mother meant the United States— has been good to us as it has to so many of its residents. It has given us the opportunity to make the most of our abilities, to earn a comfortable income through Milton's doing for pay the teaching and research that he would have wanted to do on his own if he had had an independent income, to raise two children and enjoy four grandchildren, and, far from least, to participate in and, we hope, contribute to the public affairs of our nation.

The world at the end of our life is very different from the world in which we grew up—in some ways enormously better, in other ways, worse. Materi- ally, the wonders of science and enterprise have greatly enriched the world— though some products of science, like atomic energy, have been a mixed blessing. Few monarchs of ancient times could have lived as well as we have. In the course of our own lifetime, we have been treated to automatic washing machines, dryers, and dishwashers, microwave ovens; radio, television, computers, cellular phones; passenger airlines, first prop, then jet; and so on and on.

---

* Leo Rosten on *gonif:* "In that phrase was (and is) wrapped admiration, awe, gratitude, and a declaration of possibilities beyond belief and without limit. To say 'America *gonif*' was to say 'Anything is possible in this wonderful land.' 'America is a miracle!' 'America? Inventiveness, resourcefulness, ingenuity—and that's what it rewards.' 'Where but in America could such a thing happen?' " The Joys of Yiddish (New York: McGraw-Hill, 1969), p. 139.

Biologically, advances in medicine have lengthened life spans. Milton has lived decades longer than his father, thanks to such advances. Life expectancy in the United States is almost 50 percent higher now than when we were born. Equally important, medical advances have lessened pain and suffering, and improved the quality of life at all ages.

The situation is far less clear-cut in the social realm. Perhaps it is simply nostalgia, but we recall our youth as a period when there was far less concern for personal safety and safety of property. It was not unusual to leave home without locking doors; people worried less about walking in the streets at night. One indication that this is more than nostalgia is that the fraction of the population in prison today is three times as large as it was in 1928, though that was the age of prohibition and Al Capone and other notorious gangsters.

Physicians and hospitals did not have the amazing array of medications, tests, techniques, and equipment that they have now, but there is little doubt that there was a healthier relation among patient, physician, and hospital. The first question a patient faced was not, "What insurance do you have?" but "What is wrong?"

The income tax did not apply to most people, and was a page or two in length for those who had to file. Governments at all levels were controlling the spending of 10 to 15 percent of the national income.

In one sense, we are freer now than then—there is far more tolerance for unconventional behavior (though recall that the twenties were the era of the flapper and "companionate marriage"), less anti-Semitism, and less prejudice against blacks and Catholics. In another sense, we are less free. We are close to being enmeshed in that "network of petty, complicated rules that are both minute and uniform" that Tocqueville conjectured might be the inevitable effect of an excessive drive to equality.[1] There doubtless are many causes for the loss of freedom, but surely a major cause has been the growth of government and its increasing control of our lives. Today, government, directly or indirectly, controls the spending of as much as half our national income.

Our central theme in public advocacy has been the promotion of human freedom. That was encouraged by our participation in the Mont Pelerin and Philadelphia societies. It is the theme of our books, *Capitalism and Freedom* and *Free to Choose;* it underlies our opposition to rent control and general wage and price controls, our support for educational choice, privatizing radio and television channels, an all-volunteer army, limitation of government spending, legalization of drugs, privatizing social security, free trade, and the deregulation of industry and private life to the fullest extent possible.

Judged by practice, we have been, despite some successes, mostly on the losing side. Judged by ideas, we have been on the winning side. The public in the United States has increasingly recognized that government is not the universal cure for all ills, that governmental measures taken with good intentions and for good purposes often, if not typically, go astray and do harm instead of good. The growth of government has come to a halt, and seems on the verge of declining as a fraction of the economy. We are in the mainstream of thought, not, as we were fifty years ago, members of a derided minority.

So we close this book full of optimism for the future, in the belief that those ideas will prevail and that our children and grandchildren will live in a country that continues to advance rapidly in material and biological well-being and gives its citizens ever wider freedom to follow their own values and tastes, so long as they do not interfere with the ability of others to do the same.

→ *Appendix A* ←

CHAPTER 24 (CHILE): DOCUMENTS

*1. Letter to General Pinochet on Our Return from Chile and His Reply**

April 21, 1975

Personal
Excmo Sr. Augusto Pinochet Ugarte
El Presidente
Edificio Diego Portales
Santiago, Chile

Dear Mr. President:

During our visit with you on Friday, March 21, to discuss the economic situation in Chile, you asked me to convey to you my opinions about Chile's economic situation and policies after I had completed my visit. This letter is in response to that request.

May I first say how grateful my wife and I are for the warm hospitality that was showered on us by so many Chileans during our brief visit. We were made to feel very much at home. The Chileans we met were all aware of the serious problems your country faces; all realized that the immediate future was going to be difficult; but all displayed a determination to surmount those difficulties and a dedication to work for a happier future.

The key economic problems of Chile are clearly twofold: inflation, and the promotion of a healthy social market economy. The two problems are related—the more effectively you can invigorate the free private market, the lower will be the transitional costs of ending inflation. But they are also distinct: strengthening the free market will not end inflation; ending inflation will not automatically produce a vigorous, innovative free market.

The source of inflation in Chile is crystal clear: government spending is roughly 40 per cent of the national income; roughly one-quarter of this spending is not matched by explicit taxes; it must therefore be financed by creating new money, which is to say, by the hidden tax of inflation. The inflation tax which is currently called on to raise an amount equal to 10 per cent of the national income is therefore extremely heavy—a tax rate of 300 to 400 per cent

---

* This letter and General Pinochet's reply have not heretofore been published.

(i.e., the rate of inflation)—levied on a narrow tax base—3 to 4 per cent of the national income (i.e., the value of the quantity of money in Chile in the form of currency and demand deposits).

This inflation tax does enormous harm by inducing people to devote great effort to hold down their cash. That is why the base is so narrow. In most countries, developed and underdeveloped, the quantity of money is more like 30 per cent of the national income than 3 to 4 per cent. In terms of total spending, which is a multiple of income, the money in Chile amounts to only about three days' spending, which forces hand-to-mouth operation on the business system and strangles the capital market.

There is only one way to end the inflation: by reducing drastically the rate of increase in the quantity of money. In Chile's situation the only way to reduce the rate of increase in the quantity of money is to reduce the fiscal deficit. In principle, the fiscal deficit can be reduced by cutting government spending, by raising taxes, or by borrowing at home or abroad. Except for borrowing abroad, the other three methods will have the same temporary effects on employment, though affecting different people—cutting government spending will initially affect government employees; raising taxes will initially affect persons employed by taxpayers; raising borrowing will initially affect persons employed by the lenders or the persons who would otherwise have borrowed the funds.

In practice, cutting government spending is by far and away the most desirable way to reduce the fiscal deficit because it simultaneously contributes to strengthening the private sector and thereby laying the foundation for healthy economic growth. It will therefore involve the least transitional unemployment.

A cut in the fiscal deficit is the indispensable prerequisite for ending inflation. A less clear question is how rapidly inflation should be ended. For a country like the U.S., where inflation is around 10 per cent a year, I favor a gradual policy of ending it in two or three years. But for Chile, where inflation is raging at 10 to 20 per cent a *month,* I believe gradualism is not feasible. It would involve so painful an operation over so long a period that I fear the patient would not survive.

There is no way to end the inflation that will not involve a temporary transitional period of severe difficulty, including unemployment. But unfortunately, Chile only faces a choice between evils: a brief period of high unemployment or a long period of high—though slightly less high—unemployment. I believe that the experience of Germany and Japan after World War II, of Brazil more recently, of the post-war readjustment in the U.S. when government spending was slashed drastically and rapidly, all argue for shock treatment. All suggest that the period of severe transitional difficulties would be brief—measured in months—and that subsequent recovery would be rapid.

To ease the transition and facilitate the recovery, I believe that the fiscal and monetary measures should be part of a package including measures to eliminate obstacles to private enterprise and to relieve acute distress.

For definiteness, let me sketch the contents of a specific package proposal. My knowledge of Chile is too limited to enable me to be either precise or comprehensive, so these measures are to be taken as illustrative.

If this shock approach were adopted, I believe that it should be announced publicly in great detail, to take effect at a very close date. The more fully the public is informed, the more will its reactions facilitate the adjustment. Herewith the sample proposal:

1. A monetary reform replacing the escudo by the peso, with 1 peso = 10,000 escudos (or, perhaps 1,000). By itself, this measure accomplishes nothing substantive; but does have a valuable psychological role.

2. A commitment by the government to reduce government spending by 25 per cent within six months, the reduction to take the form of an across-the-board reduction of every separate budget by 25 per cent, the personnel separations to take place as soon as possible, but the spending reductions to be spread over a six-month period to allow for the payment of generous separation allowances. [Any attempt to be selective is likely to be defeated by the machinations of each agency to have the cut bear on someone else. It is desirable first to cut across the board, then redirect the lower total.]

3. A national stabilization loan from the public to supplement the reduction of spending during the first six months in order to permit a faster reduction in money creation than in spending. The terms should include provision for inflation readjustment to give the public confidence in the government's determination to end inflation.

4. If possible, a stabilization loan from abroad for the same purpose.

5. A flat commitment by the government that after six months it will no longer finance any government spending by creating money. [As economic recovery occurs, the desired quantity of money in real terms, i.e., the quantity consistent with stable prices, will rise, but this increase should serve as the base for the expansion of a private capital market rather than be used to finance government spending.]

6. A continuation of your present policy of an exchange rate designed to approximate a free-market rate.

7. The removal of as many obstacles as possible that now hinder the private market. For example, suspend, with respect to newly employed persons, the present law against discharging employees. That law now causes unemployment. Remove the obstacles to establishing new financial enterprises. Eliminate as many controls over prices and wages as possible. Wage and price controls are not measures to cure inflation. They are one of the worst parts of the disease. [Remove obstacles, but do *not* substitute subsidies. Private enterprise is entitled to receive the rewards of success only if it also bears the penalties of failure. Every businessman believes in free enterprise for everyone else, but for special favors for himself. No obstacles, no subsidies should be the rule.]

8. Provide for the relief of any cases of real hardship and severe distress among the poorest classes. Note that the measures taken will not of themselves harm this group. The discharge of present government employees will not reduce output but simply eliminate waste—their discharge will not mean the production of one fewer pair of shoes, or one fewer loaf of bread. But indirectly, some of the poorest classes will be affected and whether they are or not, the program will be blamed for their distress. Hence it would be well to make some provision of this kind in the program. Here, especially, my ignorance of the present situation and arrangements in Chile makes it impossible for me to be specific.

Such a shock program could end inflation in months, and would set the stage for the solution of your second major problem—promoting an effective social market economy.

This problem is not of recent origin. It arises from trends toward socialism that started forty years ago, and reached their logical—and terrible—climax in the Allende regime. You have been extremely wise in adopting the many measures you have already taken to reverse this trend.

The end of inflation will lead to a rapid expansion of the capital market, which will greatly facilitate the transfer of enterprises and activities still in the hands of the government to the private sector.

In addition, the most important step is to free international trade so as to provide effective competition to Chilean enterprises and to promote the expansion of both exports and imports. This will not only improve the well-being of the ordinary Chilean by enabling him to obtain all items at the lowest cost; it will also lessen the dependence of Chile on a single major export, copper. Perhaps the greatest gain in this area would be obtained by the freeing of the importation of motor vehicles.

I know that your administration has already taken important steps and plans further ones to reduce trade barriers and to liberalize trade, and that as a result Chile's true competitive advantage is better reflected in its trade today than for decades past. This is a great achievement. I recognize also that in this area, a strong case can be made for gradualism in order to give Chilean producers an opportunity to adjust to the new conditions. However, gradualism should not mean standing still. Personally, I believe Chile would be well advised to move toward liberalization of trade more rapidly and to a far greater extent than has so far been proposed. Complete free trade is the desirable final goal, even if it cannot be achieved in the very near future.

May I close by saying that I am persuaded that Chile has great potential. It has an able, literate, inventive, and energetic people; it has a long history and tradition of an orderly, peaceful society. Some forty years ago Chile, like many another country, including my own, got off on the wrong track—for good reasons, not bad, because of the mistakes of good men not bad. The major error, in my opinion, was to envision government as the solver of all problems, to believe that it is possible to do good with other people's money.

If Chile now takes the right track, I believe it can achieve another economic miracle, that it can take off into sustained economic growth that will provide a widely shared prosperity. But to benefit from this opportunity Chile must first surmount a very difficult transitional period.

Sincerely yours,
Milton Friedman

Santiago, Chile May 16, 1975

Distinguished Mr. Friedman:

I am pleased to acknowledge receipt of your courteous letter of this past April 21 in which you gave me the opinion you formed about the situation and economic policy of Chile after your visit to our country.

On this matter I appreciate your concern, a concern which is transmitted through your interesting letter.

The valuable approaches and appraisals drawn from an analysis of the text of your letter coincide for the most part with the National Recovery Plan proposed by the Secretary of the Treasury, Mr. Jorge Cauas. The Plan is being fully applied at the present time—a plan for which we have high expectations of advancing the Chilean economy.

For the undersigned President of the Republic it was very pleasant to be able to receive you during your stay in Chile and also to know that you as well as your wife enjoyed the hospitality of those who had an opportunity to become acquainted with both of you.

Along with reiterating my gratitude for your personal contribution to an analysis of the economic situation of my country, I am also taking this occasion to express my highest and most respectful regard for you.

Courteously yours,
Augusto Pinochet Ugarte
General of Army
President of the Republic

(Translation by Gloria Valentine.—M.F.)

2. Response to Letter from Unnamed Professor Printed in Chicago Maroon
October 3, 1975

Milton Friedman submitted the following letter to the Maroon, *in response to the article concerning him which appears in today's issue. The letter is addressed to an anonymous professor and is dated July 16 1975. Mr. Friedman made no other comment.*

Dear (Professor————):

I hesitate to reply to your hysterical letter of June 16, 1975, because it is difficult to do so without descending to your level of diatribe and invective.

Everything else aside, you display a curious double standard. Some years back, I spent two weeks in the Soviet Union. I have more recently made a number of trips to Yugoslavia, where I worked at and with their Central Bank and have given lectures under the sponsorship of the Central Bank. Yet I have never heard complaints from you about giving aid and comfort to these totalitarian regimes with their millions of innocent victims. I approve of none of these authoritarian regimes—neither the Communist regimes of Russia and Yugoslavia nor the military juntas of Chile and Brazil. But I believe I can learn from observing them and that, insofar as my personal analysis of their economic situation enables them to improve their economic performance, that is likely to promote not retard a movement toward greater liberalism and freedom.

Your remarks on Chile display the same double standard. My impression is that the Allende regime offered Chile only bad choices: either communist totalitarianism or a military junta. Neither is desirable and had I been a Chilean citizen, I would if possible have opposed both—or alternatively have emigrated as you and others did faced with the Nazi threat. The institution of a communist totalitarian state would have meant, and in its preliminary stages clearly presaged, the elimination of thousands and perhaps mass starvation, as it has elsewhere. It too would have meant torture and unjust imprisonment, as it has elsewhere.

As between the two evils, there is at least one thing to be said for the military junta—there is more chance of a return to a democratic society. There is no example so far as I know of a communist totalitarianism developing into a liberal democratic society. I had hopes that Yugoslavia might be the exception, but recent developments there have been in the opposite direction. There are examples—most recently, Greece—of military juntas being replaced and reverting to democracy. Developments in Brazil are in the same direction, though still far from complete or certain.

The reason for the difference is not the superior merit or demerit of the generals versus the commissars. It is rather the difference between a totalitarian philosophy and society and a dictatorial one. Despicable though the latter is, it at least leaves more room for individual initiative and for a private sphere of life.

To return to Chile, my brief visit there persuaded me of one thing. The likelihood that the junta will be or can be temporary and that it will be possible to restore democracy hinges critically on the success of the regime in improving the economic situation and eliminating inflation. Failure will mean a tightening of control by this or a successor government. Only success will make this liberalization possible, as it has done to some extent in Brazil. This is a special case of the general point I made earlier. Insofar as we were able to give good economic advice, I believe that we contributed to strengthening the forces for freedom, not the reverse.

Incidentally, on the atmosphere in Chile, it is perhaps not irrelevant that at two universities, the Catholic University and the University of Chile, I gave talks on "The Fragility of Freedom," in which I explicitly characterized the existing regime as unfree, talked about the difficulty of maintaining a free society, the role of free markets and free enterprise in doing so, and the urgency of establishing those preconditions for freedom. There was no advance or ex post censorship, the audiences were large and enthusiastic, and I received no subsequent criticism. Could I have done that in the Soviet Union? Or, more to the point, in the communist regime Allende was seeking, or Castro's Cuba?

Let me stress again. I do not approve or condone the regimes in Chile, Brazil, Yugoslavia, or Russia. I had nothing to do with their establishment. I would fervently wish their replacement by free democratic societies. I do not regard visiting any of them as an endorsement. I do not regard learning from their experience as immoral. I do not regard giving advice on economic policy as immoral if the conditions seem to me to be such that economic improvement would contribute both to the well-being of the ordinary people and to the chance of movement toward a politically free society.

Sincerely yours,
Milton Friedman

3. Letter to Newsweek and Reply, June 14, 1976

Advising Chile

Our committee wishes to express shock and dismay on learning Milton Friedman has been serving as an economic adviser to the Pinochet Chilean junta. It is extremely difficult to reconcile his being permitted to so act while providing regular columns on the U.S. economy for your highly regarded magazine.

Kathryn J. Anderson
Mary Grabow
Florence Heist
Citizens' Committee on Human Rights and Foreign
  Policy
Minneapolis, Minn.

Milton Friedman replies:

I am not now, and never have been, an economic adviser to the Pinochet Chilean junta. I spent six days at the end of March 1975 in Chile under the auspices of a private Chilean bank. I gave public lectures and seminars on inflation, talked to many citizens from different walks of life and met with many government officials, including General Pinochet. That was my first and only visit to Chile, and my only contact with Chilean governmental officials.

Having set the facts straight, let me add that, despite my sharp disagreement with the authoritarian political system in Chile, I do not regard it as evil for an economist to render technical economic advice to the Chilean government to help end the plague of inflation, any more than I would regard it as evil for a physician to give technical medical advice to the Chilean government to help end a medical plague.

4. Letters from Laureates in New York Times, October 24, 1976

The Laureate

In a deplorable exhibition of insensitivity, the Nobel Memorial Committee on economics has awarded the prize this year to Milton Friedman. That comes just after the assassination in

596

Washington of the young Chilean economist, Orlando Letelier, formerly director of the loan division of the Inter-American Development bank, later Chilean Ambassador to the United States from the Allende government and still later its Minister of Foreign Affairs.

On Aug. 28, Letelier published in The Nation a critique of the Chilean economy as managed under the present dictator, General Pinochet. Perhaps in retaliation for that article, the Chilean Government withdrew Letelier's citizenship just two weeks before his assassination. In that article Letelier characterized Milton Friedman as "the intellectual architect and unofficial adviser for the team of economists now running the Chilean economy."

Friedman had earlier stated, "In spite my profound disagreement with the authoritarian political system of Chile, I do not consider it as evil for an economist to render technical economic advice to the Chilean government, any more than I would regard it as evil for a physician to give technical medical advice to the Chilean government to help end a medical plague."

Yes, indeed, a proper physician would treat a wounded criminal, but he must not help him to commit the crime.

It should be understood that the Government's operations, aside from blatant violations of human rights and the torture of political prisoners, include the suppression of political parties, the destruction of labor unions and church organizations, and the terror maintained at home and abroad by the notorious DINA, the secret police.

These are the circumstances within which Milton Friedman performs his "technical" functions. Presumably the Nobel committee in awarding him the prize took a similarly "technical" attitude. The Chilean people and the friends of Chilean democracy cannot afford that degree of abstraction.

George Wald, Linus Pauling
Cambridge, Mass., October 14, 1976
Professor Wald won a Nobel prize in physiology or medicine in 1967; Professor Pauling won two Nobel prizes (chemistry, 1954; peace, 1962)

At this time, when the issue of the responsibility of scientists to be concerned with the social consequences of their work is being raised forcibly and effectively, it is very disturbing that a Nobel prize for economics should be awarded to Prof. Milton Friedman.

According to reports in the Times and elsewhere, Professor Friedman has been a major economic adviser and supporter of the Chilean junta, an oppressive anti-democratic government that our Congress has recently excluded from economic credits. That the Swedish committee should have chosen to honor Professor Friedman at this time is an insult to the people of Chile, burdened by the reactionary economic measures sponsored by Professor Friedman, and especially to those Chileans who are in jail or in exile as a result of the policies of the military government.

The fact that the junta came to power in Chile with the blessing of our Government and the help of the C.I.A. does not diminish the responsibility of Professor Friedman as a supporter of the enemies of democracy.

David Baltimore, S. E. Luria
Cambridge, Mass., October 14, 1976
The writers won Nobel prizes for medicine in 1975 and 1969, respectively.

(The award of the Nobel prize to me was announced on October 14, 1976; these letters are dated the same day.—M.F.)

5. Letter from Arnold Harberger to Stig Ramel, as Reprinted in the Wall Street
Journal, *December 10, 1976*

Setting the Record Straight on Chile

*The following is a letter from Arnold C. Harberger, chairman of the Economics Department
of the University of Chicago, to Stig Ramel, president of the Nobel Foundation, concerning criticism
of the foundation's award of the Nobel Prize in Economics to Milton Friedman. An editorial concerning this subject appears elsewhere on this page today.*

The publicity generated by this year's Nobel Prize in Economics contains frequent mention of an alleged "association" of Milton Friedman with the present government of Chile.
Mr. Friedman went to Chile largely on my urging, and I was with him during his six-day visit
to Chile in March 1975—the only visit he has ever made to Chile. Further, my name has
been linked with his in many of the statements—and misstatements—arising out of that visit.
Accordingly, I would like to try to set the record straight.

We went to Chile under the auspices of a private Chilean foundation, to give public
lectures on our assessment of Chile's critical economic situation. We were not there as consultants to the government and neither of us has ever had any official connection with the present
government of Chile.

Our visit to Chile did not and does not in any way connote approval of the present
Chilean government, much less of its repression of individual liberty and its imposition of
restraint on free and open discussion and debate.

Mr. Friedman made his position very clear at the time by turning down two offers of
honorary degrees from Chilean universities, precisely because he felt that acceptance of such
honors from universities receiving government funds could be interpreted as implying political
approval.

Mr. Friedman also showed his concern by delivering a lecture on "The Fragility of Freedom" at both the Catholic University of Chile and the (National) University of Chile. He
characterized the present government of Chile as one which was denying and curtailing freedom
in many important ways, and expressed the hope that in the near future Chileans would once
again enjoy a full measure of political and intellectual liberty.

In short, Mr. Friedman, the long-time libertarian, behaved in a fashion fully consistent
with his stated ideals and philosophy, both in his actions and pronouncements in Chile, and
in his subsequent remarks on the subject. My own role has received less public attention, but
I have made no secret of my refusal to work as a consultant for the present government of
Chile, as I had freely and willingly done in earlier periods (1959, 1965–69) for other Chilean
governments.

Like many others, Mr. Friedman and I are deeply disturbed by the breakdown of Chile's
long tradition of democracy and freedom. We profoundly oppose authoritarian regimes,
whether from the right or the left. That is why we have consistently maintained a distance
between ourselves and the government of Chile and have repeatedly condemned, publicly and
privately, its repressive measures.

At the same time, we have no apologies for our activities in Chile. We believe now, as
we did when we visited Chile, that the restoration of political freedom is impossible without
a restoration of economic health. As we said in our public lectures, there is no easy road to
that result, but there are better and worse roads, and scientific economic analysis has much to
contribute to a wise choice.

Our own connection with Chile derives from a contract between the University of Chicago
and the Catholic University of Chile for the years 1956 to 1964, financed by AID, under which
many Chilean students studied at Chicago, and Chicago faculty visited Chile. As it happens,

Mr. Friedman had no active part in that program, although of course the Chilean students, like the rest of our students, took his courses. The complexity of the Chilean issue is reflected in the different ways in which our former students have reacted to the events of the past few years. Some (including some who had also served earlier Chilean governments) accepted positions of responsibility in the present government. Others (also including some officials of former governments) have not been willing to do so. Some of these support, some oppose the present regime. One, who was a former high official of the Allende government, is in political exile; others simply choose to remain outside of Chile without ascribing any political motivation to their decision.

These different reactions are part of a tragic chain of events that has riven and polarized Chilean society and has broken that country's long tradition of constitutional government. As has so often occurred under similar conditions in other countries, the process has reached down into the personal lives of the people—producing broken friendships, ruptured family ties, and many other manifestations of the passion and conviction with which different persons hold totally contradictory views. Each individual has faced, not just once but on many occasions and in many ways, unpleasant necessities of choice.

Mr. Friedman and I, while firmly maintaining our own position vis-à-vis the Chilean government, have great sympathy for our former students. We know them to be honorable and compassionate men and women. We respect their individual choices and judgments even when they differ from our own. We are not willing to turn our backs on them. On the contrary, we shall continue to do our best to help them surmount the problems and dilemmas they face in these difficult and troubled times, regardless of their individual persuasions and views.

6. My Reply to Letters in the New York Times *from Laureates, May 22, 1977*

An Exchange Among Nobel Laureates

Milton Friedman, the Chilean Junta and the Matter of Their Association

The following exchange of correspondence was initiated by two letters published in The Times on Oct. 24, 1976, shortly after the public announcement of the award to me of the 1976 Nobel Prize in Economic Sciences. Each letter was signed by two Nobel laureates: one by George Wald and Linus Pauling, the other by David Baltimore and S. E. Luria. Both letters objected to my selection for the award on the ground of my alleged involvement with the Chilean junta. My reply of Jan. 18, 1977, was addressed to each of the four men individually. Wald and Pauling have never replied. Baltimore and Luria did on Feb. 18, 1977, but they have not replied to my response of March 14, 1977.—Milton Friedman

Friedman's Letter

I am enclosing three items dealing with my activities in connection with Chile: (1) a letter by me to a colleague, published in the Wall Street Journal on Oct. 27, 1975 [replying to his criticism of my trip to Chile, expressing dismay at the double standard it reflected, neither he nor anyone else ever having criticized me for earlier trips to the Soviet Union and Yugoslavia, and stressing that giving lectures in a country by no means connoted approval of that countries policies]; (2) a statement by me in Newsweek in response to a subscriber's letter [explaining that I was not then and never have been an economic adviser to the Chilean junta, that my only personal contact had been a six-day visit in Chile in March 1975 under the auspices of a private foundation]; (3) a letter by Prof. Arnold C. Harberger to Stig Ramel of the Nobel Foundation [which was also published in the Wall Street Journal, in December 1976, setting out in detail the circumstances of our joint trip to Chile, describing our activities there, including the public lectures that I gave, and summarizing the background, particularly a cooperative project between the University of Chicago and the Catholic University of Chile from 1956 to 1964, sponsored and financed by the U.S. Agency for International Development].

The first two items were available to you before you wrote your letter to The New York Times dated Oct. 14 and published on Oct. 24, 1976. The third was not. Perusal of all three will demonstrate that your letter was based on a lack of knowledge about the true situation. As a result you did an injustice to me personally and to the Nobel Memorial Committee on Economics and contributed to misinforming the public at large.

As an eminent scientist who is ready to revise his tentative hypotheses when additional evidence contradicts them, you will no doubt wish to correct, to the limited extent that is possible, the harm you have done. The least that is called for is a public apology to me and a retraction of your criticism of the Nobel authorities, published in the same place, namely The New York Times, as your original letter.

I look forward to receiving a copy of such a letter to The New York Times.

Baltimore and Luria's Reply

Our letter to The New York Times, in which we expressed our disturbed feeling at the award of the Nobel Prize for Economics to you, regretted that the Committee had been insensitive to your identification with the economic policies imposed as a "shock treatment" by the Chilean junta and administered in Chile by your students and disciples. In our minds, your identification with the shock treatment policies, reinforced by your trip to Chile, associated you with the economic policies and repressive action, that are inseparable aspects of the Chilean junta regime. Your disclaimers of having been a formal supporter of that regime do not remove our belief that the award of the prize evidenced a regrettable insensitivity to the significance of your association, however indirect, with the political and economic policies of the Chilean government.

Friedman's Response

The turgid and convoluted language of your letter of Feb. 18, 1977 matches perfectly its content. Do consider the implications of what you write.

1. You implicitly condemn the economic policies of Chile. Are you competent to do so? The fact is that the economic policy adopted by the Chilean government has been well adapted to the problems it inherited from the Allende regime and has been working: inflation has been drastically reduced, depleted international reserves have been replenished, debts have been paid off, agricultural output has been rising, and industry and employment are recovering. The critics of this policy have offered no effective alternative—unless you consider a totalitarian state as an alternative. The economic policy, which I commend, can be separated from the political situation, which I deplore. Every country, regardless of its politics, which has faced Chile's problems and which has not succumbed to totalitarianism, has had to adopt similar economic measures—Portugal is perhaps an example that will surprise you.

2. Do you seriously suggest that we should not accept or teach students who come from countries that may have repressive regimes at some future date? Do you apply that political test to your students?

3. Do you seriously suggest that a scholar should not travel or give lectures in countries of whose political regimes you disapprove? Should one refuse to visit or lecture in Yugoslavia, China, Russia, Bulgaria, and on and on? Should no scholar have been willing to visit or lecture in Greece during the Colonels' regime? How else are we to break down barriers between countries? Are you seriously recommending intellectual isolation?

4. Finally, and most important, your support of a political test for recognition of scientific

achievement flies counter to the traditions of freedom of speech, freedom of thought, and academic freedom that the intellectual community has defended for many centuries. Do you really favor a political test for appointment to your faculty? Do you truly want your Nobel awards to be regarded as awards for "correct" political views rather than for scientific achievements?

I said in Stockholm that "the stench of Nazism is in the air." I cannot believe that on reflection you will really want to add to that stench—as your letter so clearly does.

7. Crumpled Call to Attend Demonstration Found After Protest

CHICAGO'S ECONOMICS: CHILE'S POVERTY

Since the overthrow of Salvador Allende in September, 1973 and the institution of a fascist military junta in Chile, the people of Chile have been subjected to severe political repression, tortures, and draconian economic policies. To carry out these measures the junta has relied upon the "expertise" of such varied groups as ex-Nazi officers, the C.I.A., and economists associated with the University of Chicago.

In March, 1975 Professors Milton Friedman and Arnold Harberger visited their former students—known in Chile as "the Chicago boys"—who hold key positions in the government and provide the expertise needed by the junta to carry out its so-called "shock treatment" against the working class in Chile. Friedman's role in developing this program has been crucial. The shock program has resulted in massive unemployment, monopolization of the economy, a transfer of wealth from poor to rich, and massive cutbacks in spending on health, education and nutrition.

Milton Friedman is speaking in *S.F. today* and we urge you to demonstrate with us in solidarity with the Chilean people against the junta and its supporters.

(*The italicized words were inserted by hand into a blank space in the document.*—M.F.)

8. Letter to Stanford Daily, October 27, 1988

Any Reaction to Friedman's Travels?

In 1975, I spent five days in Chile, on my way to Australia, as a guest of a private organization.

I gave a series of talks and met with many proponents and opponents of the Pinochet regime.

In addition, I had one meeting with General Pinochet and his fellow junta members. A month or so after I returned to the United States, I became the object of organized protests whenever and wherever I spoke, on campus and off campus, including the Nobel ceremonies in Stockholm in December 1976. The protesters accused me of unspeakable crimes for having been willing to give advice to so evil a government.

I have just returned from a 12-day stay in Communist China, where I was mostly the guest of governmental entities.

I gave a series of talks and met with many proponents and a very few opponents of the Communist regime. One talk in Beijing was to a group of 200 civil servants, some stationed in Beijing, others brought in for the occasion from other cities.

In addition, I had a two-hour private meeting with Zhao Ziyang, the General Secretary of the Chinese Communist Party.

Incidentally, I gave precisely the same advice to both Chile and China—stop inflation by controlling the quantity of money, free individual prices from control, privatize governmental activities, eliminate exchange control.

I doubt that anyone will deny that, in every relevant sense, the Chinese Communist regime has been and still is more repressive than the Chilean military junta, or that there is less chance that real democracy will emerge in China than in Chile.

Under the circumstances, should I prepare myself for an avalanche of protests for having been willing to give advice to so evil a government? If not, why not?

Milton Friedman
Senior research fellow, Hoover Institution

→ *Appendix B* ←

CHAPTER 28 (*FREE TO CHOOSE*): DOCUMENTS

1. *Topics Proposed at the New York Meeting*

The Free Market: The Secret of American Success
Myth and Reality in Contemporary Public Opinion
Moral Values and Free Enterprise
Capitalism and the Jews (with a notation "highly uncertain about whether to include this one")
How to Put Learning Back in the School Room
Needed Consumer Advocates
Money and Inflation
International Trade and Finance
What Is Wrong with the Welfare State
National Health Insurance
The Tax Mess
Regulation of Industry and Unions
Pollution
Energy
Discrimination
How Limit Government
The Future of Freedom
Democracy vs. Bureaucracy

2. *Donors*

Sarah Scaife Foundation
Getty Oil Co.
Readers Digest Association
John M. Olin Foundation
Firestone Tire & Rubber Co.
FMC Foundation
W. R. Grace and Co.
Lilly Endowment

Pepsico Foundation
General Motors Foundation
National Federation
   of Independent Business
Whittaker Corporation
General Mills Foundation
Bechtel Foundation
L. E. Phillips Charities

→ *Appendix B* ←

3. Titles of Lectures

The lectures are listed in the order in which they appear in *Milton Friedman Speaks,* not the order in which they were delivered.

Title	Date	Sponsor
1. What is America?	Oct. 3, 1977	University of Chicago
2. Myths that Conceal Reality	Oct. 13, 1977	Utah State University
3. Is Capitalism Humane?	Sept. 27, 1977	Cornell University
4. The Role of Government in a Free Society	Feb. 9, 1978	Stanford University
5. What is Wrong with the Welfare State?	Feb. 23, 1978	University of Rochester
6. Money and Inflation	Nov. 7, 1977	University of San Diego
7. Is Tax Reform Possible?	Feb. 6, 1978	Americanism Educational League, Pasadena
8. Free Trade: Producer vs. Consumer	April 27, 1978	University of Kansas
9. The Energy Crisis: A Humane Solution	Feb. 10, 1978	Bank of America
10. The Economics of Medical Care	May 19, 1978	Mayo Clinic
11. Putting Learning Back in the Classroom	Sept. 15, 1977	Harlem Parents
12. Who Protects the Consumer?	Sept. 12, 1977	Pfizer, Inc.
13. Who Protects the Worker?	Sept. 29, 1977	WQLN, Erie, Pa.
14. Equality and Freedom in the Free-Enterprise System	May 1, 1978	College of William and Mary
15. The Future of Our Free Society	Feb. 21, 1978	National Association of Manufacturers

4. Drafts of Opening and Closing Statements, Dated November 21, 1977

Possible Opening Statement

We, the citizens of the free world, are at a vital stage of decision. For the past half century, we have been moving toward a centralized, collectivized state—while at the same time preserving a large measure of the vitality, diversity, and independence that are the proudest products of a free society. We have been able to do both because we have been living on the heritage of the past. The free institutions that had developed in the West over the prior two centuries provided a structure of values and an economic base for a generally beneficent extension of government to ever wider areas of our lives.

That heritage is not inexhaustible. The widespread erosion of moral values, the decline in respect for the law, the loss of individual autonomy to the leviathan state, the economic problems of inflation, stagnation, and unemployment—these are all symptoms that we are reaching a new stage.

If we continue down the path we have been going, the pace toward Orwell's 1984 will quicken and we shall soon pass the point of no return. But we need not continue. Our basic values, our basic institutions, our basic beliefs remain fundamentally sound. We are rich and powerful peoples. We can be masters of our own destiny.

A turn away from the path we have been following will require reinforcing our heritage rather than simply living on it. It will require reining in the ambitions of our political authorities and setting limits to their power and scope. It will require once again widening the field within which the individual, the family, the voluntary organization can exercise initiative and ingenuity free from control by political authorities. It will require dismantling many of the shackles with which we have bound the economic activities of our citizens, so that enterprise can regain its vigor and fecundity. That is how the great achievements of the modern age were attained. It is how we can achieve a fresh renaissance of culture, humanity, and wealth.

Possible Closing Statement

Freedom is a rare and delicate plant. Today, most of the inhabitants of the earth live in misery and under tyranny. At any point on the earth's surface, tyranny and misery have been the lot of its inhabitants for the greater part of human history. We in the West have been living in a rare golden age—a golden age that has combined freedom with prosperity. Is that golden age coming to an end—or can we, by taking thought, make possible a new rebirth of freedom?

Our golden age was made possible only by the accidental development of institutions and traditions that narrowly limited the scope of government. Political and civil freedom have flourished only where voluntary cooperation through free-market capitalism has been the major reliance for organizing our economic activities.

Our golden age is threatened by the spread of government power and control, always for good purposes, always extravagant in its promises, always disappointing in its results, always eating away at our substance and undermining our liberties.

Economic freedom is a necessary condition for political and civil freedom. It is also a major component of freedom. Property rights are not in conflict with human rights. On the contrary, they are themselves the most basic of human rights and an essential foundation for other human rights.

We want a world in which people of many races, many creeds, many colors, many opinions, many cultures can live harmoniously together, cooperating in ways in which they can mutually benefit while respecting the right of each individual or family or clan to march to its own drummer insofar as it wishes so long as it does not interfere with the rights of others to do the same. There is widespread agreement on that objective. To attain it, we need to achieve an equally widespread recognition that the appropriate means consist of a limited government plus free-market competitive capitalism.

5. Discussants on the Programs

The Power of the Market (1)

Barber B. Conable, congressman, ranking minority member of Ways and Means Committee
Robert Galvin, chairman of Motorola
Michael Harrington, Democratic Socialist Organizing Committee
Russell Peterson, former governor of Delaware

The Tyranny of Control (2)

Jagdish Bhagwati, professor of economics, MIT
Richard Deason, International Brotherhood of Electric Workers
Helen Hughes, director of economic studies, World Bank
Don Rumsfeld, president, G. D. Searle & Co.

The Anatomy of Crisis (3)

Nicholas von Hoffman, syndicated columnist
Peter Jay, British ambassador to the U.S.

Robert Lekachman, professor of economics, CUNY
Peter Temin, professor of economics, MIT

Cradle to Grave (4)
James R. Dumpson, former administrator of human resources, administration of New York City, currently Fordham School of Social Sciences
Robert Lampman, professor of economics, University of Wisconsin
Helen O'Bannon, secretary of welfare, State of Pennsylvania
Thomas Sowell, professor of economics, UCLA

Created Equal (5)
Peter Jay, British ambassador to the U.S.
Frances Fox Piven, professor of political science, Boston University
Thomas Sowell, professor of economics, UCLA

What's Wrong with Our Schools? (6)
Gregory Anrig, commissioner of education, State of Massachusetts
John Coons, professor of law, University of California at Berkeley
Albert Shanker, president, American Federation of Teachers
Thomas A. Shannon, executive director, National School Board Association

Who Protects the Consumer? (7)
Joan Claybrook, administrator, National Highway Traffic Safety Administration
Robert Crandall, economist, Brookings Institution
Richard Landau, professor of medicine, University of Chicago
Kathleen O'Reilly, president, Consumers Federation of America

Who Protects the Worker? (8)
William H. Brady, president, W. H. Brady & Co.
Ernest Green, assistant secretary of labor
Lynn Williams, international secretary, United Steel Workers of America
Walter Williams, professor of economics, Temple University

How to Cure Inflation (9)
Clarence Brown, congressman and member, Joint Economic Committee of the U.S. Congress
Ottmar Emminger, president, Bundesbank (German Central Bank)
William McChesney Martin, former chairman, Board of Governors, Federal Reserve System
Beryl Sprinkel, executive vice-president, Harris Bank.

6. Form Letter Responding to Comments on Free to Choose

Please pardon this form letter. The volume of mail generated by the "Free to Choose" TV series and book has become so great that, for the first time in my life, I have had to abandon any attempt to reply personally to every correspondent.

I appreciate very much your writing, and I know I shall benefit from your comments. Perhaps things will settle down again to the point at which I can resume my former practice.

The mail persuades me that our series and book have touched a sensitive chord: the response has been overwhelmingly favorable to the views expressed—though there have of course been a small fraction of highly negative and even abusive reactions.

For those of you who objected to some of the statements made on TV, may I note that you will find a fuller discussion of all the issues in our book.

I am delighted to find that there are more of us who favor cutting government down to size than I had supposed.

✣ *Appendix C* ✦

CHAPTER 30 (CHINA): DOCUMENTS

Memorandum from Milton Friedman to Zhao Ziyang

Mr. Zhao Ziyang
General Secretary
Re: Some Comments on Chinese Economic Reform

Dear Mr. General Secretary,

In making some suggestions about the key steps that I believe to be essential at this stage of Chinese economic reform, I should emphasize that I am not an expert on China and am not familiar with the detailed structure of the Chinese economy. However, I have studied the process of economic development in many countries, both as a scholar of history and, for more recent decades, as an observer. Every country always believes that its circumstances are special. Yet it turns out that there are elements common to a wide range of circumstances. These common elements suggest a few key lessons that have broad applicability. For brevity, I state these lessons, as I believe they apply to China, rather dogmatically, fully recognizing that others are far more competent than I to judge how they can be best carried out in practice.

1. *End exchange control, establish a free market in foreign exchange, and permit the exchange rate to be determined by the market.*

I first became persuaded of the importance of such a policy more than thirty years ago when I served for some months as an economic adviser to the finance minister of India. My advice to end exchange controls and free the exchange rate was not followed. Continued observation of India in the decades since indicates that much of the subsequent corruption and inefficiency in India, as well as the lack of any significant improvement in the living standards of the ordinary people, derives directly from the continued existence of exchange controls and multiple exchange rates. A major contributor to Hong Kong's development has been the complete absence of exchange controls, from the very earliest postwar period to today. On the other hand, the maintenance of exchange controls was an important factor in the failure of development in such countries as Brazil, Argentina, and Mexico.

2. *End inflation.*

There is one and only one way to end inflation, and to avoid its recurrence: control the rate of growth of the quantity of money, which in China at present means primarily the quantity of currency. In China's present circumstances, controlling monetary growth requires limiting (a) the government deficit financed by money creation; (b) the amount of credits granted by the branches of the People's Bank to enterprises, whether state, collective, or private. Controlling inflation would be greatly facilitated by making sure that the interest rate paid to savers and paid by borrowers is higher than the rate of inflation. The present situation in which the interest rate is much lower than the rate of inflation discourages savings and encourages wasteful investments.

3. *Decontrol individual prices and wages as rapidly and as fully as possible.*

Many countries have believed that they could control inflation by controlling individual prices and wages. I do not know a single case in which such a policy has succeeded. On the other hand, many countries have ended inflation through monetary restraint without imposing price control.

One example in Asia is Japan, which in 1973, when both inflation and monetary growth had reached over 25 percent per year, ended inflation rather rapidly by sharply lowering the rate of monetary growth.

Ending or at least moderating inflation is essential for successful decontrol of prices and wages. Free-market prices are necessary to provide information on demand and supply, to encourage production of goods in short supply and high demand, and discourage production of goods in the opposite situation. They are also necessary to assure that supplies go to those who can make the best use of them.

A once-and-for-all rise in reported prices as a result of the end of price and wage control is *not* inflation and will contribute to reducing inflation, provided monetary restraint is maintained. The reported price rises, but the actual price paid, whether in money, wasted time, or doing without, goes down. A dramatic example was provided by Germany in 1948, when Ludwig Erhard ended all price and wage controls on a Sunday. He did it on Sunday because the offices of the American, British, and French occupation authorities were closed and hence they could not countermand his order, as he was sure they would have done if they could have. At the same time, he maintained monetary restraint. The results were dramatic. Prices and wages rose overnight, but money became worth something. The black market disappeared, the use of such substitute currencies as cigarettes and cognac ended, and the postwar economic miracle of Germany began.

It should be emphasized that while price and wage controls were ended suddenly, the favorable effects of that step occurred gradually over time.

The present dual price system in many products in China is an open invitation to corruption and waste. Artificially low prices for raw materials inevitably lead to shortage and rationing by favoritism and bribery. The result is their inefficient use. Similarly, artificially low prices for final products discourage their production and generate the need for state subsidies. Freeing prices and wages would end all this at one bold stroke.

4. *Replace centralized government controls of the economy and state enterprises by decentralization and private control.*

China has been moving in this direction to good effect. The more promptly and more extensively it can replace centralized bureaucratic control by decentralized market control the greater the rewards it will reap. The essential element is to privatize the costs and rewards of economic activities. This is the most effective way to take advantage of the uniform effort of private individuals to improve their condition for the purpose of promoting the growth, prosperity and peace of society as a whole. That is clearly the objective of the Chinese responsibility system, which has been producing excellent results in some areas and can and should be carried much farther.

Seventy years ago, before the Russian Revolution, even forty years ago, before the Chinese Liberation, able and well-informed people could reasonably believe that centralized planning by able officials dedicated to promoting the welfare of their people could produce better results than the apparently chaotic and unplanned market economies coordinated by the actions of individuals, each seeking to promote his interests and the interests of his family. It was possible to believe that the visible hand of government could produce better results than the invisible hand of the marketplace.

Today, few if any people any longer hold fast to that belief. The reason is clear: no country that has relied primarily on detailed central planning has been able to achieve a high level of prosperity for the masses of its people. On the other hand, every country that has achieved a high level of prosperity for the masses of its people has relied primarily on *free private markets* to coordinate economic activities.

The use of markets alone is not enough. Privatization alone is not enough—as is demonstrated by India, Bangladesh, Mexico, and many African and Latin American countries. What is needed is *free private markets,* where "free" means open to competition, from both abroad and domestic sources. In particular, individuals or groups should be free to establish any enterprise producing or selling any good that is legal to buy and sell without requiring permission from any official. If a license is required, it should be granted automatically on payment of a modest fee. That is, licensing, if any, should be treated as a tax, not as a means of determining who may do what.

The example of India again demonstrates how important this step is. Favoritism in granting permits to set up plants, operate hotels, trade in foreign markets, and so on, has produced many wealthy businessmen and officials and also many poor people.

The experience of Hong Kong, Singapore, Taiwan, Japan, and South Korea—to stick to the Far East—demonstrates that extensive use of free private markets has enabled these countries to achieve in thirty years what took the United States two hundred years. The Asian countries have been able to benefit from the Western experience, have been able to borrow technology, benefit from foreign skills and investment, and so to shorten the development process. China could do the same.

Finally, a word of caution. Beware of getting stuck part way through the process. The example of Yugoslavia comes to mind. Its initial rejection of the Russian planning model and substitution of worker ownership of enterprises and limited elements of private markets enabled it to jump rapidly to a substantially higher economic level. However, it got stuck at that level because it did not go further with privatization; in particular, it did not make ownership rights transferable (salable). The result has been repeated bouts of inflation, unrest, and economic difficulties.

China's initial steps of reform have been dramatically successful. China can make further dramatic progress by placing still further reliance on *free private markets.*

Respectfully yours,
Milton Friedman

2. A Dialogue with General Secretary Zhao Ziyang*

General Secretary Zhao Ziyang (hereafter, Zhao): I warmly welcome Professor and Mrs. Friedman. Today is a rare opportunity, and I would like mainly to listen to your suggestions.

---

* The meeting chronicled here took place between 4:30 p.m. and 6:30 p.m. on September 19, 1988, at Zhong Nan Hai in Beijing. The transcription of it was translated by Ronald W. C. Teng and Na Liu from the Chinese version edited by Steven N. S. Cheung, which was published in the *Hong Kong Economic Times,* January 26, 1989. The English version was published in Milton Friedman, *Friedman in China* (Hong Kong: The Chinese University of Hong Kong Press, for the Hong Kong Centre for Economic Research, 1990), pp. 127–40. Reprinted by permission.

→ Appendix C ←

You are concerned about our reforms. You are a professor and I am just a pupil. You have come from afar. You should do more talking and I more listening.

Professor Milton Friedman (hereafter, Friedman): Eight years ago, in 1980, I came to China and visited Beijing, Hangzhou, Guilin, Shanghai, and Guangzhou, at the invitation of the Chinese Academy of Social Sciences. This is my second visit. I have come from Shanghai, Suzhou, Wuxi, and Nanjing to Beijing. Compared with what I saw last time, China has changed a great deal. The reform has made great progress. I am amazed and also delighted.

Zhao: Why don't you go to Xian and have a look?

Friedman: We are going there tomorrow.

Zhao: Before I listen to Mr. Friedman, I want to give you a brief introduction to our situation. From the third plenum of the Eleventh Party Congress up till now, China's reform has been proceeding for ten years. In comparison with your last visit[in 1980], there are changes. These mainly show economic vibrancy. However, there are also many problems. Generally speaking, China is a developing country, and many complicated problems arise in changing her from her previous economic mode into a new one.

The resolution taken at the Plenary Session in 1984 says that China will set up a planned commodity economy. Last year, at the Thirteenth Party Congress, it was decided that the governing mechanism of our economic activity would be for the state to regulate and control the market, while the market controls the economy. Having decided to go in this direction, we have done a great deal during the past ten years. We feel now that if we want to carry the reform further, we must reform the price system. Of course, we have already done a lot. But now price reform should be an important item on our agenda for reform. Price reform does not involve simply a readjustment of prices, but more importantly the formation of a mechanism under which prices are determined by the market.

China's present situation is basically that 50 percent of the commodity prices are determined freely according to market supply and demand. These are mainly daily consumer goods, mechanical and electrical products, and agricultural produce except grain, cotton, and edible oil. Prices of some other commodities, like major raw materials and agricultural products, are regulated according to a dual-track price system. That is, the prices are partly set by the state and partly determined in the market. These commodities include steel, nonferrous metals, grain, etc. Another set of prices, for example, air services, power supply, and transportation are completely set by the state. This is our present situation. What we intend to do in carrying the reform further is to reduce the number of prices that are under the dual-track system and state control.

However, just as we are ready to go a step further toward price reform, we are faced with difficult problems, especially sizable inflation. Therefore, from now on, we must deal with price reform while curbing inflation at the same time. Of course, inflation is not something that happened just this year. It has accumulated over several years. We feel, however, the phenomenon of inflation has become more acute this year. If we do not take action to curb inflation, it will not be possible to free prices without precipitating a rise in prices. A rapid rise in prices raises a practical problem. Can the people take such a shock, both economically and psychologically? For twenty-six years, from 1950 to 1976, prices were frozen in China. The Chinese people had no experience of price changes for twenty-six years. Therefore, the psychological tolerance of the Chinese people toward a price rise is very low. From 1980 to 1988, the perception of our people toward prices had undergone a great transformation. But, psychologically they still find it intolerable. That is a problem.

Another major problem is that for a long time the Chinese people have been in the habit of saving their money. They put much of their savings in the bank. If prices rise too rapidly, it is hard to avoid a substantial decline in bank deposits. This again is another shock which

610

the Chinese economy cannot take. If prices rise substantially, and bank interest rates also rise to very high levels, enterprises would not be able to survive. In that case, many enterprises would close down and go bankrupt. I am all for the idea that bankruptcy is a good thing. It allows the new to supersede the old. But if a large number of enterprises go bankrupt all at once, massive unemployment may result and social stability will be threatened. China's price reform must give due consideration to these problems, especially the problem of shock tolerance. China's price reform and inflation control should be pursued at the same time.

At this point we have to answer a question. Why did inflation occur in China? As you know, in the past, our country followed the traditional socialist model. This model has a common disease called shortage economy in which demand exceeds supply. That is contrary to the situation in countries based on a market economy. In the West, supply exceeds demand. We have been carrying out our reforms for ten years, but we still have not solved the problem of self-regulation in enterprises and local departments; I should say, we have not solved it completely. Of course, this does not mean that our situation is worse now than what it was before the reform, but that the reform has not reached the stage where enterprises and local departments have become self-regulating. As a consequence, in recent years, we over-invested in capital construction; local consumption funds grew too fast. For these reasons, there has been an excess supply of money. Therefore, while we continue with price reform, we are going to reduce the scale of fixed investment and the growth of consumption funds, so that we can create those conditions that will allow us to continue with our price reform, free the prices of more products, and further the reform of the enterprise mechanism.

Whether it is price reform or inflation control, the essential issue is to solve the problem of the enterprise mechanism, so as to improve the internal economic efficiency of enterprises. With improved efficiency and lower costs, price reform should be able to offset the negative effect of a rise in the price of raw materials, and to prevent it from spilling over into a rise in commodity prices. We have, therefore, decided to control the scale of our investment in fixed assets and the excessive growth of consumption funds. At the same time, we should strengthen the capability of the enterprises for self-regulation by reforming the enterprises to enable them to take full responsibility for their own profits and losses.

That raises another problem. How can we strengthen the capability of state-owned enterprises for self-regulation and for taking full responsibility for their own profits and losses? The road we plan to take involves two things. First, we plan to implement the separation of the two rights: ownership rights and enterprise management rights. This will allow the manager of an enterprise the right to manage, utilize, possess, and dispose of its assets. To use a metaphor, the owner of an asset is like the owner of a musical instrument in an orchestra, and the manager is the conductor of the orchestra. At present, the separation of the two rights is achieved primarily through the managerial responsibility system; that is, the state contracts an agent to assume responsibility for managing an enterprise. Second, we also plan to introduce a shareholding system so that ownership rights in state enterprises will be clearly defined.

At present, property rights are not clearly defined. To whom do the state enterprises belong? To me? Or to him? Or to the Ministry of Finance? Or to the State Planning Commission? It is not clear. Property rights should not be left ambiguous; they should be made clear. For instance, how many shares does a certain ministry own, how many shares does a local government own, how many shares do the employees of an enterprise own? Of course, how many shares does a foreign company own? The ambiguous property rights in state property should be divided into shares that belong to different ministries, localities, companies, and enterprises. That is to say, from now on enterprise reform will be, first, to implement the separation of the two rights and, second, to introduce a shareholding system so that property rights can be clearly defined. In this matter we have been inspired by the success of the village and township enterprises. In recent years, these rural enterprises have grown rapidly; their economic vibrancy is the greatest in China. If Mr. Friedman is interested, I suggest that you go to Suzhou and Wuxi and visit one or two village or township enterprises.

Friedman: I have already done so.

Zhao: Their property is not privately owned, but it is clear who owns the property. It belongs to the village or township government. Of course, I cannot say which has more vibrancy, their system of ownership or the system of private enterprise in the West, but I am sure that their system has more vibrancy than the state enterprises. That is why I think if we introduce a shareholding system in China, so that property rights can be clearly defined, it would be a tremendous reform of the state enterprises. This question has been discussed in China for nearly three years. The opinions within the academic circle have by and large converged. So I can say that the conditions for introducing a shareholding system in China are ready. Naturally, on this point I was inspired by the West, for example, the case of the Federal Republic of Germany. Mr. Friedman probably knows a lot more about this than I do. In the Federal Republic of Germany, many enterprises belong to the trade unions, but they are well managed; much better managed than the nationalized enterprises.

In the future, China's major task in reform is to solve the following three main problems: first, price reform; second, curbing inflation; third, implementing a shareholding system for enterprises. China, of course, does not have much experience of controlling inflation. We may encounter many difficulties in solving this problem. Implementing the shareholding system is another new problem. The degree of difficulty in solving these three problems is quite great. However, there is one thing I would like to say to Mr. Friedman. The direction of the reform will not change. We will go firmly step by step in that direction. Of course, some problems will need further exploration, but our direction will not change, although the concrete measures and methods that will be adopted may be continuously changed and adjusted to fit China's situation.

Recently, the newspapers in Hong Kong have published many reports on China's reform. They suggested that there is a split within China's top leadership. They say who and who have split. That is not the truth. Our leaders, including myself, should keep studying and discussing the concrete situation in China. China has a saying:

Judge the hour and size up the situation,

Apply the proper degree of leniency and strictness.

They come from a pair of couplets which are hung inside the Zhuge Wu Hou Shrine in Chengdu.

To govern a country, one has to "judge the hour and size up the situation," one also has to "apply the proper degree of leniency and strictness." This may sound a bit like the "rule of man." In any undertaking it is very important to first set the direction. Suppose we are going to America. We should study how to get there, because there are mountains and oceans in the way. This is to "judge the hour and size up the situation." Nothing remains the same forever. We have to keep analyzing the changing situation. China's problem is not that there are different opinions among the leaders, but that we need to keep discussing the new situations and the new problems. For instance, in our meeting today, if it were not now but three months earlier, I could not talk this way. If we meet next year, I am going to say something different. I have been talking for too long. Now I would like to listen to Mr. Friedman's opinion.

Friedman: I appreciate the information the General Secretary gave us. What you said is very clear and complete. Just now you said that I am the professor, you are the pupil. But on hearing your analysis of China's economic situation, I believe that you are a professor by nature.

Zhao (laugh): I only went to high school.

Friedman: The length of time that one spends in school and the amount of knowledge that one has are very different things. Some people spend many years in school yet do not have much knowledge. Some people do not spend much time in school but have much knowledge.

Zhao: We, too, have these two kinds of people in China. There is an old saying in China describing some people as competent without being learned: some people are "learned but incompetent," and some others are "not learned but competent."

Friedman: I do not know much about the concrete situation in China, and I am not an expert. You gentlemen here understand the Chinese situation far better than I do, so I will not go into the specific situations. For many years I have done research on a good number of countries working on reform. The circumstances of each of them were not entirely the same, and each regarded its own situation as special. But this is not true in some cases, for there are common elements applicable to all despite their different circumstances. For example, the principles of physics apply in all nations; by the same token, the basic principles of economics are applicable in all nations too. The most essential one among these is the relationship between economic prosperity and private property rights. One simple yet crucial law in economics which you know and agree with is that people are more prudent at spending their own money than somebody else's money. This explains why rural enterprises are more efficient than state enterprises, and private enterprises are the most efficient of all. Thus, decentralization of power is a key issue, the more decentralized the better.

I want to talk about three issues: inflation, price reform, and enterprise vibrancy. I am not going to discuss them in detail. You know the details better than I do. The phenomenon of inflation has existed for centuries and has appeared in many nations. We cannot curb inflation by controlling individual prices; many nations tried, and they all failed. Sixteen hundred years ago it was tried in the Roman Empire. The Roman emperor wanted to control inflation this way, but he failed.

Zhao: We also used this method in the past.

Friedman: To give another example, the United States. In 1971, the inflation rate was 4.5 percent. President Nixon believed then that 4.5 percent was too high, so he adopted a wage-price control scheme and froze individual prices and wages. He had to give it up three years later because such a control scheme made it difficult for the American economy to grow. By then, the inflation rate had already reached 8 percent. This was the beginning of the American inflation in the 1970s.

The most important lesson regarding inflation is to separate price inflation in general from the rise of individual prices. Many countries did not choose to control individual prices; they curbed inflation by controlling the quantity of money. Japan is a good example. From 1971 to 1973, the Japanese inflation rate was 25 percent, so was the rate of increase in money. The Japanese government decided to slow down the growth of the money supply and soon, inflation was under control. The inflation rate began to take a downward trend, which laid the foundation for Japan's subsequent economic development.

The problem of controlling the money supply to avoid inflation is an important issue and is related to the question of economic reform. This is because once inflation sets in, its social impact will be serious. There is only one way to deal with it and that is to limit the quantity of money supplied. In China, this means you print less currency. Banks in China are not like banks in the West where money supply can be decreased through some established mechanism; the Chinese banks print money by order of the central authorities to provide capital and loans to industries. I think the inflation problem in China comes not so much from investment or consumption but from an oversupply of money. Of course, society needs investment and consumption, but the money should come from savings and production.

To free prices is good for controlling inflation, because it will allow resources to be used more efficiently, encourage savings, and prevent wasteful investment. The example you gave is a good one. You said that if the interest rate on savings is lower than the rate of inflation, people will not save, and various enterprises will strive to borrow money from the banks because of the low interest rate. But this type of investment which ignores economic efficiency is in fact wasteful. If the interest rate is freed and determined completely by the market, people will be encouraged to save and wasteful investment will be avoided. There is a lot more to talk about on this first (inflation) problem, but, I fear that would occupy too much of your time, so I now turn to the second problem.

Just now I was talking about freeing prices, but we did not touch upon the most critical issue of exchange rates. I first started to appreciate this problem thirty years ago. I was then an economic adviser to the Indian Minister of Finance. Back then, there were a number of exchange rates in India, and the simplest way to get rich was to obtain an import license through some connections. Thus, a few became millionaires but a lot more became poor. Moreover, the system could easily lead to corruption. I suggested to the Indian government that foreign exchange control should be removed, and that the exchange rates should be decontrolled, but they rejected that advice. Their doing so is a major reason why there is not much change between now and thirty years ago in the standard of life of the ordinary people.

I believe that an important reason for the failure of the Indian economy is that they granted import licenses and maintained multiple exchange rates. I once paid a visit to an Indian textile mill. I discovered that their facilities were very modern. It was all imported and labor saving equipment. On the other hand, there were many people in India waiting for employment. So I asked the plant manager the reason for importing such advanced equipment. He replied that it was worth it because the government allowed them to buy machines at the official exchange rate. This was certainly beneficial to the factory owner, but not to the country.

As I understand it, there are several exchange rates in China too; the lowest is the official rate, the semi-official rate is in the middle, and the market (black-market) rate is the highest. If you get rid of the dual-track price system, the high rate will drop and the low rate will rise.

I believe that it would not be inflationary to free prices and carry out price reform. If you have a low official price but cannot buy things, then the price is in effect not low. If you spend five hours in a queue to purchase something, that price is not low either. My wife has told me an old story. There are two butcher shops on opposite sides of a street, each facing the other. A housewife goes to one of them to buy mutton and complains about the high price. The shopkeeper then says, if you think our mutton is expensive, go across the street—it is cheap there. But there is no mutton in the other shop! So what is the use of cheap prices? That is why I say the dual-track price system is making prices more expensive, not less.

Now, the third problem is about decentralizing power. I have already touched upon it, but I like to approach it from a different angle. If we want an enterprise to have vibrancy, the main thing is to create a competitive environment. Again, I will talk about the case of India. I have visited India many times in the past thirty years. In India, you need a permit to build a factory. When someone is given a permit, he has power. This is just as bad as state monopoly. The important thing is for everyone to be able to open a shop or an enterprise freely. Of course, an appropriate tax can be collected from them. If there were more private individuals who are free to establish their enterprises and be responsible for their own profits and losses, that would force the state enterprises to either raise their production efficiency or go bankrupt. The government-owned U.S. Post Office is a good example. The U.S. Post Office used to have a monopoly in carrying express mail, and it was legal. Now other companies also have the right to carry express mail. They have literally slaughtered the U.S. Post Office in the express mail business. If America's government-owned post office had no monopoly in other types of mail, I can surely predict that the U.S. Post Office would go bankrupt. So I suggest that China should do away with permits. I believe that if you wish the enterprises to be full of vibrancy, you had better provide them with more opportunities to compete. It makes no difference whether they be rural enterprises or private enterprises. Let them compete.

Finally, let me make one simple point. The most critical issue of reform is not to "get stuck" in the middle. Yugoslavia is a precedent. I have visited Yugoslavia a number of times. The first time I went there from Russia. Going from an economically backward country to a more developed one, I was deeply impressed. Later on, I went to Yugoslavia from Austria, and had a different feeling. At that time Yugoslavia adopted a workers-cooperative system, and the Soviet Union was a collectivistic, state-planned economy. Yugoslavia, however, proceeded only half-way—she did not hand over the property rights to the workers. The factory workers had the right to profit-sharing, but they could not sell or transfer their right. To make money, these enterprises did not want to hire more workers, or make more investment. Workers found it difficult to move ahead or change jobs. If the workers in Yugoslavia had been able to transfer property rights, the situation would have been different. I choose this example not to illustrate how good a workers-cooperative system is, but to show how reform should not "get stuck" in the middle. I admire very much what the General Secretary was saying a while ago, that China's reform would continue, and that the direction would not change. Now I would be very glad to answer any questions the General Secretary might have.

Zhao: Thank you very much, Mr. Friedman, for giving us many excellent suggestions. On the question of prices, we do not intend to control individual prices. Rather, we want to keep inflation down through managing our currency circulation. As Mr. Friedman has said, we have to make use of the banking mechanism. However, the reform of the Chinese banking system has only begun, so it is very difficult for the banks to follow the Western practice where you can control inflation by tightening up the money supply. The state banks must coordinate their activities with the state's macro control and regulatory plans. To tighten up the money supply now may squeeze the agricultural sector, but may not reduce duplications in capital construction.

Friedman: This is because power is vested on top, and the top level totally controls all power.

Zhao: Both problems exist. On the one hand, it is local government control; on the other hand, the bank's own structure is not rational.

Friedman: I understand, that is why I recommend the establishment of a system of mutual competition. Right now, China is like what the West was a hundred and fifty years ago. Back then, when banks were being set up in small cities and towns in the West, their interest rates were determined by the market. These little banks served their purpose. China can also have banks in small towns to coordinate affairs.

Zhao: We touched upon private enterprise a moment ago. At the People's Congress held in March this year, we discussed, amended, and adopted a law allowing the development of private enterprises; it made no special limitation on private enterprises.

Friedman: Two days ago, I visited a self-employed businessman in Wuxi. He told me that to open a shop he had to get a permit, he had to apply to the appropriate government department, and he even had to entertain them. It was quite troublesome. Was he pointing to difficulties that existed before March this year, or after?

Zhao: The law is one thing, but reality is another. The phenomena you described are still present in abundance. It will take some time before they can all be eliminated. It cannot be said that once the law is in place, all the problems are solved.

Friedman: Please allow me to make another point. China's neighboring areas such as Hong Kong, South Korea, Taiwan, and Singapore have developed very rapidly. In thirty years, they have achieved what took the West two centuries to accomplish. The most successful example is Hong Kong. She has the most remarkable record despite the fact that she had to overcome more difficulties. Hong Kong also has the least interference from the central authorities. China is a big country; naturally she will encounter many big problems. But I think China, too, can, in thirty years, have the same achievement as the Western countries have accomplished in two hundred years. China's neighbors all drew lessons from the West, including learning their technology and skills. I hope the Chinese people can become strong and prosperous. I wish to see China's reform succeed so that she can contribute more to the progress of mankind. The development of areas like South Korea and Hong Kong has brought great benefits to the United States. The development of the Chinese economy is also beneficial to the United States. This is friendly competition, not a conflict of economic interests.

Zhao: Let us talk about the problem of exchange rates. Two years ago, a Chinese-American professor named Zhou Zhizhuang* suggested to me the idea of floating exchange rates.

Friedman: He was my student.

Zhao: He told me he had made this recommendation to Chiang Chingkuo many times, but Chiang did not take his advice at first. He hoped that China would take up the idea of floating exchange rates.

Friedman: Even Taiwan has not completely floated her exchange rate. The government frequently interferes with the foreign exchange market.

Zhao: Quite a number of our people have raised the same issue. The head of China International Trust and Investment Corporation, Rong Yiren, has raised the question of freeing the exchange rate many times. But we have a difficulty. China is in the process of reforming her prices, but our present price structure is not linked to the international market. Our cost of earning foreign exchange is not high, about four dollars Renminbi in exchange for one U.S. dollar. Of course, the situation varies with each commodity. Given the irrational domestic price structure, freeing the foreign exchange rate may result in an irrational exchange rate, which, in turn, could drastically push up the cost of raw materials.

Friedman: But the greatest benefit of freeing the exchange rate is precisely to solve the problem of the irrational price system, prevent resources from being wasted, and facilitate the reform.

Zhao: Price reform and the freeing of the exchange rate have to go together. The two should by and large be in phase with each other.

Friedman: Certainly it is very desirable if both can be considered together. Nevertheless, if there are political obstacles and the two cannot be tackled at the same time, then freeing the control over the exchange rate is more important.

Zhao: I want to express again our gratitude to you for your constructive suggestions. My colleagues and I will study your recommendations very carefully. The last thing I want to say is that China's reform will not change. I completely agree with you that China's development is entirely in keeping with the interest of the people of the United States of America.

Let us stop here for today.

* Editor's note: Professor Gregory C. Chow of Princeton University.

❖ Notes ❖

Chapter Two
1. Jozef Statkowski, *Poland—Old and New* (Warsaw: M. Arct, 1938).

Chapter Three
1. As Rutgers has been converted into a mega-state university, a class of competitive scholarships for financially needy students which go not to those who score highest in the exams but to underachievers is a nice illustration of how our standards have been corrupted over the years.

2. "Arthur Burns," in *In Memoriam: Arthur Burns, 1904–1987* (Washington, D.C.: Board of Governors of the Federal Reserve System, 1987), pp. 7–8, 10–11.

3. The preceding paragraphs draw on my paper, "Homer Jones: A Personal Reminiscence," *Journal of Monetary Economics* 2 (1976): 433–34.

Chapter Four
1. In my contribution to *Lives of the Laureates: Seven Nobel Economists,* ed. William Breit and Roger W. Spencer (Cambridge: MIT Press, 1986), pp. 77–92.

2. Ibid., pp. 82–83.

3. We are still in touch with one another. He is now retired from medical practice.

4. Jacob Viner, "Cost Curves and Supply Curves," *Zeitschrift für Nationalökonomie* 3 (1931): 23–46; reprinted in American Economic Association, *Readings in Price Theory* (Chicago: Richard D. Irwin, 1952), pp. 198–232, with a supplementary note in which Viner acknowledges his error.

5. Though never formally published, the lecture, according to a footnote in George J. Stigler, *Memoirs of an Unregulated Economist* (New York: Basic Books, 1988), p. 23, is available in Warren J. Samuels, ed., *Research in the History of Economic Thought and Methodology,* Archival Supplement 2 (Greenwich, Conn.: JAI Press, 1991).

6. *How Collective Bargaining Works: A Survey of Experience in Leading American Industries* (New York: The Twentieth Century Fund, 1942).

7. Milton Friedman, "Comments on the Critics," in *Milton Friedman's Monetary Framework,* ed. Robert J. Gordon (Chicago: University of Chicago Press, 1974), pp. 162–63; reprinted from *Journal of Political Economy* 80 (September–October 1972): 906–50.

8. Milton Friedman, "My Evolution as an Economist," in *Lives of the Laureates,* p. 84.

9. Y. H. Farzin, "The Time Path of Scarcity Rent in the Theory of Exhaustible Resources," *Economic Journal* 102 (July 1992): 813. The Hotelling article referred to is "The Economics of Exhaustible Resources," *Journal of Political Economy* 39 (September 1931): 256–71.

10. One of my fellow students in Hotelling's classes was Susanna P. Edmondson from Alabama, formerly an instructor in French, who had decided to change careers and study economics. After one of the first class sessions, Susanna emerged from class and remarked to a fellow female student, "I'm going to marry that man." And so she did. Hotelling, who had studied statistics with R. A. Fisher in Britain, had become a disciple of Fisher's not only in statistics but also in genetics. He was persuaded by Fisher that the higher birth rate of lower socioeconomic classes than of the higher classes would inevitably produce a decline in the quality of the human race. The response both of Fisher, of whom more in a later chapter, and Hotelling was to father large families—Fisher, eight; Hotelling, two by his first wife and six by Susanna.

Susanna, with her Southern upbringing, played a major role in persuading Hotelling in 1946 to leave Columbia and establish an Institute of Mathematical Statistics at the University of North Carolina at Chapel Hill. He remained there until his death in 1973.

A few years ago at a meeting of the American Economic Association, I had a real shock when I saw a youthful Harold Hotelling walking toward me in the corridor. It was Harold Hotelling, Jr., the spitting image of his father at Junior's age.

11. Wesley C. Mitchell, *Lecture Notes on Types of Economic Theory* (New York: Augustus M. Kelley, 1949).

12. Alvin Johnson, "Obituary, John Bates Clark," *Economic Journal* 48 (September 1938): 572.

13. See F. A. Hayek, *Hayek on Hayek,* ed. Stephen Kresge and Leif Wenar (Chicago: University of Chicago Press, 1994).

14. Stigler, *Memoirs,* p. 26.

15. Eugen Slutsky, "The Summation of Random Causes as the Source of Cyclic Processes" (in Russian), *Problems of Economic Conditions,* vol. 3, no. 1 (Moscow: The Conjucture Institute). Revised English version in *Econometrica* 5 (April 1937): 105–46.

16. Although in the course of moving I lost or destroyed the drafts that I had completed, I learned recently that copies of my drafts still exist among Knight's papers at the University of Chicago's Regenstein Library.

17. "For a general check on the argument and aid in connection with references, I have relied upon an able graduate assistant, Miss Rose Director, who has lately been working over the material intensively in connection with a more specialized study in the history of the theory of capital." Frank Knight, "The Ricardian Theory of Production and Distribution," *Canadian Journal of Economics and Political Science* 1 (May 1935): 171.

18. In the Preface, "Milton Friedman, a former graduate student of mine, came to my rescue and for a year continued to render valuable assistance" (p. xiii). In a footnote to the title of chapter 18, "I am profoundly grateful to Mr. Milton Friedman for invaluable assistance in the preparation and writing of these chapters and for permission to summarize a part of his unpublished paper on indifference curves" (p. 569). Henry Schultz, *The Theory and Measurement of Demand* (Chicago: University of Chicago Press, 1938).

19. The English title of the paper Professor Tsujimura sent to me was: Kotaro Tsujimura and Sakiko Tsuzuki, "The Fisher-Friedman Definition of Complementarity Restated in Relation to the Slutsky Decomposition—A Pragmatic Point of View."

20. Milton Friedman, "Lange on Price Flexibility and Employment," *American Economic Review* 36 (September 1946): 613–31, reprinted in *Essays in Positive Economics* (Chicago: University of Chicago Press, 1953), pp. 277–300.

21. We have discussed this issue at length in *Free to Choose: A Personal Statement* (New York: Harcourt Brace Jovanovich, 1980), pp. 20–24.

22. Hildegarde Kneeland and others, *Consumer Incomes in the United States; Consumer Expenditures in the United States,* both volumes prepared for the National Resources Committee (Washington, D.C.: Government Printing Office, 1938 and 1939). I was listed as one of the authors of the second but not of the first, though my contribution was acknowledged in the preface.

23. *Theory of the Consumption Function* (Princeton: Princeton University Press for the National Bureau of Economic Research, 1957).

24. Quoted from a statement included as a frontispiece in every book published by the National Bureau for nearly two decades, later replaced by a resolution describing the function and aims of the Bureau. I have taken the quote from Simon Kuznets, *Seasonal Variations in Industry and Trade* (New York: National Bureau of Economic Research, 1933), a book that, as it happens, I reviewed in the *Journal of Political Economy* in 1935 while I was still at Chicago.

25. The exact reference is U.S. Congress, Senate, 73rd Cong., 2d sess., S. Doc. 124.

26. "The Use of Ranks to Avoid the Assumption of Normality Implicit in the Analysis of Variance," *Journal of the American Statistical Association* 32 (December 1937): 675–701. I published a follow-up article, "A Comparison of Alternative Tests of Significance for the Problem of m Rankings," in the *Annals of Mathematical Statistics* 11 (March 1940): 86–92.

27. Conference on Research in National Income and Wealth, *Studies in Income and Wealth* (New York: National Bureau of Economic Research), vol. 1 (1937); vol. 2 (1938); vol. 3 (1939).

28. *Fifty Years of Economic Measurement: The Jubilee of the Conference on Research in Income and Wealth,* Studies in Income and Wealth, vol. 54, ed. Ernst R. Berndt and Jack E. Triplett (Chicago and London: University of Chicago Press, 1990).

An amusing sidelight: in their introduction, the editors write, "despite the availability of modern computerized technology, the present editors have failed to duplicate Milton Friedman's editorial feat of bringing into publication the first three volumes of the Studies in Income and Wealth series in the same year in which the conference was held. Future historians may determine whether this is evidence of a decline in efficiency, of increased consumption on the job, of substitution of capital (quality) for labor (quality), or of some as yet undetermined measurement error" (p. 1).

29. *Delaware Income Statistics Compiled from Income Tax Returns for 1936, 1937, and 1938,* vol. 1 (Newark: Bureau of Economic and Business Research, University of Delaware, 1941).

30. Frank A. Hanna, Joseph A. Pechman, and Sidney M. Lerner, *Analysis of Wisconsin Income* (New York: National Bureau of Economic Research, 1948).

31. Part of the book was accepted at Columbia as my dissertation for the Ph.D.

32. Steven J. Davis and John Haltwanger, "Gross Job Creation, Gross Job Destruction, and Employment Reallocation," *Quarterly Journal of Economics* 107 (August 1992): 819–63.

Chapter Six

1. *Encyclopaedia Britannica,* 1970 edition, 6:165.

2. Leonard Silk, *The Economists* (New York: Basic Books, 1976), p. 58.

3. Published as Milton Friedman and Walter Heller, *Monetary vs. Fiscal Policy* (New York: W. W. Norton & Co., 1969).

4. I have drawn on this report without specific acknowledgment in much that follows. A much abbreviated version of the report that Bob Lampman sent us appears as "Essay 2, The Milton Friedman Affair at Wisconsin, 1940–1941," in *Economists at Wisconsin, 1892–*

1992, ed. Robert J. Lampman (Madison: Department of Economics, University of Wisconsin-Madison, 1993), pp. 118–21.

5. "The Teaching of Statistics," *Annals of Mathematical Statistics* 19 (March 1948): 95–115.

6. Mark Perlman, "Jews and Contributions to Economics: A Bicentennial Review," *Judaism* 25 (1976): 301–11.

Chapter Seven

1. Standard metropolitan areas were first defined in the 1950 Census, when the population of the Washington-Virginia-Maryland metropolitan area was 1.5 million.

2. Dorothy S. Brady and Rose D. Friedman, "Savings and the Income Distribution," *Studies in Income and Wealth*, no. 10 (New York: National Bureau of Economic Research, 1947), pp. 247–65.

3. Walter Salant gave the paper in December 1941 at a meeting of the Econometric Society and it, along with my comment, were published in the *American Economic Review* 32 (June 1942): 308–20.

4. Milton Friedman, *Essays in Positive Economics* (Chicago: University of Chicago Press, 1953), pp. 251, 253.

5. A member of the board has a fourteen-year term, a chairman, only a four-year term. Eccles remained a member for more than fourteen years, because he was first appointed in November 1934 to complete the term of Eugene Black who had resigned in June 1934, and then to a full term in February 1944. See Marriner Eccles, *Beckoning Frontiers: Public and Personal Recollections*, ed. Sidney Hyman (New York: Knopf, 1951), pp. 165, 175, 384, 434.

6. One by-product was my article, "The Spendings Tax as a Wartime Fiscal Measure," *American Economic Review* 33 (March 1943): 50–62.

7. J. M. Keynes, *How to Pay for the War: A Radical Plan for the Chancellor of the Exchequer* (London: Macmillan & Co., February 1940).

8. Whittaker Chambers, *Witness* (New York: Random House, 1952), pp. 383, 384.

9. As it happened, current payment was first imposed on 1943 income, but at the time of the main discussion of the Ruml Plan, the objective was to impose current payment for 1942 income.

10. Passage of the Revenue Act of 1942 on October 21, 1942, and the Current Tax Payment Act of 1943 on June 9, 1943, completed the major reconstruction of the tax system on which I had worked.

Chapter Eight

1. The Statistical Research Group (SRG) was one component of the Applied Mathematical Panel, which in turn was a component of the National Defense Research Council (NDRC), itself a subsidiary of the Office of Scientific Research and Development (OSRD), the lead organization set up to mobilize scientists for war work.

2. See Allen Wallis, "The Statistical Research Group, 1942–1945," *Journal of the American Statistical Association* 70, no. 370 (June 1980): 322.

3. Wallis, "The Statistical Research Group," pp. 322–23.

4. The books are: Abraham Wald, *Sequential Analysis* (New York: John Wiley Sons, 1947); Statistical Research Group, *Sequential Analysis of Statistical Data: Applications*, ed. Harold A. Freeman, M. A. Girschik, and W. Allen Wallis (New York: Columbia University Press, 1945); Statistical Research Group, *Selected Techniques of Statistical Analysis for Scientific and Industrial Research and Production and Management Engineering*, ed. Churchill Eisenhart, Millard Hastay, and W. Allen Wallis (New York and London: McGraw Hill Book Co., 1947); Statistical Research Group, *Sampling Inspection: Principles, Procedures, and Tables for Single,*

Double, and Sequential Sampling in Acceptance Inspection and Quality Control Based on Percent Defective, ed. Harold A. Freeman, Milton Friedman, Frederick Mosteller, and W. Allen Wallis (New York and London: McGraw Hill Book Co., 1948).

5. Wallis, "The Statistical Research Group," p. 320. In writing about the work of the Statistical Research Group, I have drawn heavily on Allen's article referred to above and also on "Final Report of the Statistical Research Group, Columbia University," submitted by Allen to Dr. Warren Weaver on September 29, 1945. At the time the 131-page final report was classified secret because it had to have the highest classification assigned to any of the numerous studies that it summarized. By now, all of the material has been declassified.

6. Wallis, "The Statistical Research Group," p. 329.

7. Milton Friedman, *Journal of Political Economy* 61 (August 1953): 277–90.

8. Wallis, "The Statistical Research Group," pp. 325–26.

9. Ibid., p. 328.

10. I was introduced to Willard Gibbs, the most famous U.S. scientist of the nineteenth century, among whose students, I later discovered, were E. B. Wilson, a mathematical economist with whom I had much correspondence, and Irving Fisher, undoubtedly the greatest economist the U.S. has yet produced. A poet, Muriel Rukeyser, has written a fascinating biography of Gibbs: *Willard Gibbs* (1942; paperback ed., New York: E. F. Dutton Co., 1964).

11. "Final Report of the Statistical Research Group, Columbia University," September 29, 1945, p. 48.

Chapter Nine

1. An interesting footnote to this conflict is contained in the recently published *Letters of Ayn Rand,* ed. Michael S. Berliner (New York: Dutton, 1995). In a letter of September 12, 1946, to Leonard Read she wrote:

"I offered you my services without charge, to protect your publications from internal treachery.

"You chose not to take advantage of the offer. And you have published a booklet (*Roofs or Ceilings?*) which is, without exception, the most pernicious thing ever issued by an avowedly conservative organization.

"I presume you do not know what your booklet actually advocates. So I had better tell you: it advocates the nationalization of private homes" (p. 320). She really did have quite an imagination!

In a later letter (October 25, 1946) to Rose Wilder Lane she wrote, "I didn't accuse them [FEE] of being Communists. I accused them of publishing a Communist booklet, which it is" (p. 335).

I am indebted to Mark Skousen for calling my attention to these comments by Rand.

Chapter Ten

1. Rose Friedman, *Oriental Economist,* August 1976, p. 21. Reprinted by permission.

2. John A. Davenport, "Reflections on Mont Pelerin," *The Mont Pelerin Society Newsletter,* special supplement, July 1981, p. 1.

3. Ibid., p. 2.

4. The exception was Maurice Allais, the Nobel Prize–winning French economist, who had concluded from an elaborate theoretical analysis that the optimum interest rate for a society was zero. However, a zero interest rate would mean that any permanent appropriable economic good, of which land is the only significant example, would have an infinite value. On this basis, Allais, following Henry George, favored government ownership of land and hence objected to the inclusion in the "Statement" of the words, "The group holds that . . . without the diffused

power and initiative associated with these institutions [private property and the competitive market] it is difficult to imagine a society in which freedom may be effectively preserved."

Allais later modified his views and rejoined the society, so even his disagreement was temporary.

5. The Volker Fund was a pioneer in promoting activities that fostered an understanding of the foundations of a free society. It not only helped finance the first and later meetings of the Mont Pelerin Society, it also helped finance bringing Hayek to the University of Chicago as a professor in the Committee on Social Thought. For many years it financed summer meetings at Wabash College, Claremont College, and elsewhere to which young academics were invited to hear lectures by leading free-market intellectuals. My book *Capitalism and Freedom* is based on lectures that I gave in 1956 at one of those meetings at Wabash. Mr. Harold W. Luhnow, the founder of the Volker Fund, had the foresight to specify that the capital of the fund should be dispersed in a specified number of years. The final grant that exhausted the fund in accordance with those terms was to the Hoover Institution.

Chapter Twelve

1. The formal title of the office that invited me was Economic Cooperation Administration, Special Representative in Europe, Trade and Finance Division.

2. I should emphasize that I favored NAFTA, but as the lesser of evils, not as the greatest of goods. It would have been far preferable if we could simply have reduced trade barriers against all the rest of the world and have induced other countries to do the same. But that seemed outside the realm of political feasibility.

3. From a memorandum by Milton Friedman to Hubert F. Havlik re "Flexible Exchange Rates as a Solution to the German Exchange Crisis," December 19, 1950.

4. First published in Milton Friedman, *Essays in Positive Economics* (Chicago: University of Chicago Press, 1953), pp. 157–203.

Chapter Thirteen

1. Edward Shils, "Robert Maynard Hutchins," in *Remembering the University of Chicago* (Chicago: University of Chicago Press, 1991), pp. 194, 196.

2. The rumor was that most of these sums came from Hutchins himself.

3. From letter to Professor Quincy Wright of January 21, 1947, in reply to a request for comments on the 4E contract. I went on to say, "There seems to me no excuse for the exploitation of universities by individuals who use their faculty position primarily as a means of obtaining income from other activities. Actual experience under the 4E contract has brought to light a number of difficulties that I had not foreseen in advance."

4. I have a copy of Number 457 of the Round Table series, for a program titled "Can World-wide Income Inequalities Be Lessened?" broadcast on December 22, 1946, in which I participated along with Theodore Schultz and Louis Wirth of the Sociology Department. It was undoubtedly the first of the many Round Table programs in which I took part.

Chapter Fourteen

1. *Journal of Political Economy* 42 (February 1934): 2.

2. Paul H. Douglas and Aaron Director, *The Problem of Unemployment* (New York: Macmillan Company, 1931).

3. On the relation between Knight and Douglas, and the part played by Henry Simons and Aaron, see Stigler, *Memoirs,* pp. 181–90.

4. *American Economic Review* 38 (March 1948): 1–41.

5. L. R. Klein, *Economic Fluctuations in the United States, 1921–41* (New York: Wiley, 1950).

6. Milton Friedman and L. J. Savage, "The Utility Analysis of Choices Involving Risk," *Journal of Political Economy* 56 (August 1948): 270–304, and "The Expected Utility Hypothesis and the Measurability of Utility," *ibid.*, 60 (December 1952): 463–74.

Chapter Fifteen

1. Alfred Marshall, "The Present Position of Economics" (1885), reprinted in *Memorials of Alfred Marshall*, ed. A. C. Pigou (London: Macmillan & Co., 1925), p. 159.

2. Stigler, *Memoirs*, p. 162.
I first discussed the distinction between what I came to call Marshallian and Walrasian economics in "The Marshallian Demand Curve," *Journal of Political Economy* 57 (December 1949): 463–95 (reprinted in my *Essays in Positive Economics*).

3. My subsequent experience with this student is discussed in chap. 30, pp. 525–26.

4. Quotations in this and preceding paragraph from Friedman, *Price Theory*, pp. ix and vii.

5. Milton Friedman (ed.), *Studies in the Quantity Theory of Money* (Chicago: University of Chicago Press, 1956); A. James Meigs, *Free Reserves and the Money Supply* (Chicago: University of Chicago Press, 1962); George Morrison, *Liquidity Preferences of Commercial Banks* (Chicago: University of Chicago Press, 1966); David Meiselman (ed.), *Varieties of Monetary Experience* (Chicago: University of Chicago Press, 1970).

6. Salvatori later financed the Henry Salvatori Center at Claremont devoted to the study of freedom.

Chapter Sixteen

1. Especially Phillip Cagan's chapter, "The Monetary Dynamics of Hyperinflation."

2. In addition to the articles and books by Anna and me, Phillip Cagan's *Determinants and Effect of Changes in the Money Stock, 1875–1960* (New York: National Bureau of Economic Research, 1965) was also a product of the Bureau study.

3. *Journal of Monetary Economics* 34, no. 1 (August 1994). The three reviewers are Robert E. Lucas, Jr., Jeffrey A. Miron, and Bruce D. Smith.

4. J. Daniel Hammond, "Early Drafts of Friedman's Methodology Essay," paper presented at the History of Economics Society meeting, College Park, Maryland, June 1991, p. 1.

5. Thomas Mayer, "Friedman's Methodology of Positive Economics: A Soft Reading," *Economic Inquiry* 31 (April 1993): 213.

6. Ibid.

7. Milton Friedman, "The Methodology of Positive Economics," in *Essays in Positive Economics*, p. 15. A note attached to this quotation lists seven articles on this controversy by five different authors in the *American Economic Review* from 1946 to 1948.

8. Ibid., p. 3.

9. Milton Friedman, "Lange on Price Flexibility and Employment: A Methodological Criticism," in *Essays in Positive Economics*, p. 300. The title of one of Popper's books, *Conjectures and Refutations*, suggests the affinity between my approach and his.

10. Rose D. Friedman, "Milton Friedman: Husband and Colleague—(2) The Beginning of a Career," *The Oriental Economist*, June 1976, pp. 21–22. Reprinted by permission.

11. In 1967, for example, I engaged in a public debate under the auspices of the American Enterprise Institute that was published as Milton Friedman and Robert V. Roosa, *The Balance of Payments: Free versus Fixed Exchange Rates* (Washington, D.C.: American Enterprise Institute for Public Policy Research, 1967).

12. I summarized some of these episodes in a *Wall Street Journal* piece, "Déjà Vu in Currency Markets," September 22, 1992.

13. Milton Friedman, *Money Mischief* (New York, San Diego and London: Harcourt Brace Jovanovich, 1992), p. 248.

14. Alan Walters, *The New Palgrave: A Dictionary of Economics,* ed. John Eatwell, Murray Milgate and Peter Newman (New York: Stockton Press, and London: Macmillan Press Limited, 1987), s.v. "Friedman, Milton" (vol. 2, p. 426).

15. J. M. Keynes, *The General Theory of Employment, Interest and Money* (New York and London: Harcourt Brace and Co., 1936), p. 97.

16. Dorothy S. Brady and Rose D. Friedman, "Savings and the Income Distribution," *Studies in Income and Wealth,* vol. 10 (New York: National Bureau of Economic Research, 1947), pp. 247–65.

17. H. S. Houthakker, "The Permanent Income Hypothesis," *American Economic Review* 48 (June 1958): 396–404; quotation from p. 404.

18. Robert Eisner, "The Permanent Income Hypothesis: Comment," *American Economic Review* 48 (December 1958): 972–90. The reply by Houthakker follows after a brief comment by me, the quoted statement being on p. 993.

19. John Maynard Keynes's book, *The General Theory of Employment, Interest, and Money,* had been published in 1936 and rapidly became the orthodox view among most economists.

20. Letter from Gaylord A. Freeman, Jr., dated October 22, 1976. The occasion for the letter was to congratulate me on the award of the Nobel Prize in Economics.

21. Included in *Stabilization Policies,* a series of research studies prepared for the Commission on Money and Credit (Englewood Cliffs, New Jersey: Prentice-Hall, 1963), pp. 165–286.

The paper was essentially complete when the CMC offered to finance a research project (a preliminary version was presented in the workshop in October 1959). I was taking a leaf from a conversation I had with Leo Szilard, the famous atomic scientist. He told me that whenever he submitted a request for funds, he proposed research that he had already completed, in order to be sure to satisfy the terms of the grant. On one occasion, he was turned down on the grounds that the project was not feasible!

22. The three major critical articles were Ando and Modigliani, "The Relative Stability of Monetary Velocity and the Investment Multiplier," Michael De Prano and Thomas Mayer, "Testing the Relative Importance of Autonomous Expenditures and Money," both in the *American Economic Review* 55 (September 1965): 693–728 and 729–52, respectively, and Donald D. Hester, "Keynes and the Quantity Theory: A Comment on the Friedman-Meiselman CMC Paper," *Review of Economics and Statistics* 46 (November 1964): 364–68. In both journals, our reply and the critics' rejoinder were in the same issue as the critical articles.

23. "The Report of the Commission on Money and Credit: An Essay in *Petitio Principii,*" *American Economic Review* 52 (May 1962): 291–301.

Incidentally, one comment in my paper illustrates very well the practice described in the preceding paragraph of the text: "I cannot leave the Commission's section on monetary policy without commenting on one subsection beginning, 'Some experts have argued that monetary policy works so slowly that its effects become perverse because the effects of a restrictive policy are not felt until after the start of the ensuing downswing and the effects of monetary expansion until the next boom.' . . . I suspect that I know intimately at least one of the 'experts' the Commission believes itself to be referring to. He assures me that the statement grossly oversimplifies his views and in the process converts his objection into a straw man. . . . Let me set the record straight by quoting from a recent publication of the expert: 'I have never argued that policy actions are necessarily or on the average perverse, though, in fact, monetary actions have been perverse on many occasions, but only that they are largely random relative to the actions that in retrospect would have been appropriate. The result is to convert actions taken for countercyclical purposes into additional and unnecessary random disturbances.'" The reference is, as you would expect, to an article of mine.

24. James Tobin, "The Monetary Interpretation of History: A Review Article," *American Economic Review* 55 (June 1965): 464–85.

25. Milton Friedman, "The Role of Monetary Policy," *American Economic Review* 58 (March 1968): 1–17.

26. The same basic idea was presented about the same time by Edmund S. Phelps, "Phillips Curves, Expectations of Inflation and Optimal Unemployment Over Time," *Economica,* n.s., 34 (August 1967): 254–81.

27. Many Keynesians, unwilling to accept my terminology in fear that "natural" would be interpreted as "desirable," though I went out of my way to scotch that notion, renamed the natural rate of unemployment, the nonaccelerating inflation rate of unemployment, or NAIRU.

28. James Tobin, "The Natural Rate as New Classical Macroeconomics," in *The Natural Rate of Unemployment: Reflections on 25 Years of the Hypothesis,* ed. Rod Cross (Cambridge and New York: Cambridge University Press, 1995), p. 40.

29. *Milton Friedman's Monetary Framework: A Debate with His Critics,* edited by Robert J. Gordon (Chicago: University of Chicago Press, 1974); quotations in this paragraph from his Introduction, pp. ix and x.

30. Robert E. Lucas, Jr., "Tobin and Monetarism: A Review Article," *Journal of Economic Literature* 19 (June 1981): 560.

31. Wesley C. Mitchell, *Business Cycles,* vol. 1: *The Problem and Its Setting* (New York: National Bureau of Economic Research, 1927); Wesley C. Mitchell and Arthur F. Burns, *Measuring Business Cycles* (New York: National Bureau of Economic Research, 1945), a volume dealing with the techniques developed at the National Bureau for analyzing the cyclical characteristics of time series, and Wesley C. Mitchell, *What Happens during Business Cycles: A Progress Report* (New York: National Bureau of Economic Research, 1951).

32. Michael D. Bordo (ed.), *Money, History, and International Finance: Essays in Honor of Anna J. Schwartz* (Chicago and London: University of Chicago Press, 1989), pp. 247, 249.

33. In addition to the three major volumes by Anna and me that we produced as part of the monetary study, we also published an article that bore more directly on the original assignment to study the role of money in the business cycle: Milton Friedman and Anna J. Schwartz, "Money and Business Cycles," *Review of Economics and Statistics* 45, part 2, supplement (February 1963): 32–64, reprinted in Friedman, *The Optimum Quantity of Money and Other Essays,* pp. 189–235.

34. The annual meeting of the American Economic Association was traditionally held between Christmas and New Year's Day. The date has more recently been changed to the first weekend in January. In 1965, the meeting was held in New York.

35. Amusingly, the session at which his talk was given was on methodology, and nearly every paper and comment by a discussant, including Papandreou's, was partly or wholly, an attack on my article "The Methodology of Positive Economics."

Chapter Seventeen

1. See D. E. Moggridge, *Maynard Keynes: An Economist's Biography* (London and New York: Routledge, 1992), pp. 597–603.

2. Much of the preceding three paragraphs is taken verbatim from my introduction to "A Milton Friedman–Sir Dennis Robertson Correspondence," *Journal of Political Economy* 81 (July/August, 1973): 1033–39.

Chapter Eighteen

1. Because I went on my own, leaving Rose and the children in Chicago, this is one of the best documented of my trips: long plane rides are conducive to letter writing. I continued

the pattern after I got to New Delhi, and Rose kept all of my letters. Unfortunately, I seem not to have kept hers. All quotations in my part of this chapter, unless otherwise designated, are from my letters to Rose.

2. Adam Smith, *The Theory of Moral Sentiments* (first published in 1759; New Rochelle, N.Y.: Arlington House, 1969), pp. 342–43.

3. In 1957, reported forcible rapes were 8 per 100,000 inhabitants, and aggravated assaults were 65 per 100,000; by 1989, the corresponding figures were 38.1 and 383, or roughly five times as frequent.

4. "The Indian Alternative," *Encounter* 8, no. 1 (January 1957): 71–73.

5. Subroto Roy and William E. James (eds.), *Foundations of India's Political Economy* (New Delhi, Newbury Park, and London: Sage Publications, 1992), pp. 19–20.

6. John Kenneth Galbraith, *A Life in Our Times* (Boston: Houghton Mifflin Co., 1981), pp. 323–24.

Chapter Nineteen

1. Brainard Currie, law; David Easton, political science; Benson Ginsberg, biology; Louis Gottschalk, history; and Milton Singer, anthropology.

2. T. W. Anderson and Milton Friedman, "A Limitation of the Optimum Property of the Sequential Probability Ratio Test," in *Contributions to Probability and Statistics,* ed. I. Oklin et al. (Stanford: Stanford University Press, 1960), pp. 57–69.

3. The members of the panel in addition to me were Barbara Ward Jackson, Leo Cherne, J. Kenneth Galbraith, Robert L. Heilbroner, Neil H. Jacoby, and Leon Keyserling.

4. George tells the story in Stigler, *Memoirs,* p. 157.

5. *The Machinery of Freedom: Guide to a Radical Capitalism* (New York: Harper & Row, 1973; 2d ed., LaSalle, Ill.: Open Court, 1989).

Chapter Twenty

1. France, Belgium, Poland, Russia, Turkey, Austria, Lebanon, Pakistan, Cambodia, Vietnam, Hong Kong, Taiwan, Philippines, Singapore, Malaya, Thailand.

2. When we went to the Soviet Union, we had to pay in advance a fixed sum per diem for all expenses, including hotels and food. Intourist chose the hotels for us and paid for them directly. We received ration coupons for meals.

3. Rose Friedman, *Oriental Economist,* October 1976, p. 25.

4. Bosnia and Herzegovina, Croatia, Macedonia, Montenegro, Serbia, including the autonomous provinces of Vojvodina and Kosovo, and Slovenia.

5. Zev Vilnay, *The Guide to Israel,* 5th ed. (Jerusalem, 1962), p. 287.

6. The short book was subsequently reprinted in my *Dollars and Deficits* (Englewood Cliffs, N.J.: Prentice-Hall, 1968).

7. This car was one that George Stigler and I had purchased jointly for $300 in 1958 when we were at the Center for Advanced Study. When we decided to get rid of it before setting off on our round-the-world trip, the most we could get for it was $22, and that only because it had several good tires!

8. As in the U.S., businessmen cannot afford to oppose visibly and vigorously the government authorities that have privileges to give and penalties to be imposed. As example, a leading businessman who was a strong backer of the Swatantra party cited as a sign of his courage and independence that he had given as much money to Swatantra as to Nehru's Congress party.

9. This paragraph is based on a first draft of an article titled "Indian Economic Planning," dated May 6, 1963, that I wrote shortly after we arrived in Japan. The article was intended for publication in the United States but was never published.

10. W. David Hopper, personal letter, June 21, 1965.

11. This and the following paragraphs are based on the draft referred to in footnote 9.

12. In comments on my draft, Professor Shenoy wrote, "The increase in the number of bicycles and automobiles is not evidence of 'improvement.' It is evidence of income transfers."

13. James Gwartney, Robert Lawson, and Walter Block, *Economic Freedom of the World, 1975–1995* (Vancouver, B.C.: Fraser Institute, 1995), Exhibits S-1B and 4-1A.

14. The number of kanji was initially limited only by the number of Chinese ideograms, and an educated Japanese before World War II was expected to know five thousand or so kanji. In the interest of simplicity, the postwar government limited the number of usable kanji to 1,850, so that an educated Japanese today may not be able to read Japanese books written in the 1930s. Many a Japanese scholar educated before the war must use an assistant to check any manuscript he writes to single out the kanji that are no longer usable.

15. Michael Keran, "Monetary Policy and the Business Cycle in Postwar Japan," in David Meiselman (ed.), *Varieties of Monetary Experience* (Chicago: University of Chicago Press, 1970), pp. 163–248.

16. The *Encyclopaedia Britannica*, 1970, vol. 3, p. 5, comments on Bali, "Important items in Bali's balance of trade are the sale of craft articles and the tourist trade. The latter could be much larger, were it not for the discouraging hotel facilities and the cumbersome controls by the central government." We can vouch for the accuracy of both of these statements. The hotel situation has changed drastically but that has also changed the atmosphere of the island.

17. Clif had received his Ph.D. from our department and was directing an agricultural research project in Malaya. He has since been a university president, CEO of TIAA-CREF, and deputy secretary of state.

18. The contrast between Japan and India is discussed in some detail in our *Free to Choose*, chap. 2, pp. 57–64 (hardcover edition).

19. Taiwan at the time had two overlapping central banks, which is why I use the ambiguous language. Pretending to be the government of all of China, there was a Bank of China; but then there was also a Bank of Taiwan, both in practice providing central bank services for the same area. This duplication extended to other parts of government as well.

20. This phenomenon is equally relevant in the United States today. See footnote p. 303 above.

Chapter Twenty-One

1. The Liberty Fund has republished the articles that appeared in the *New Individualist Review in New Individualist Review:* A Periodical Reprint (Indianapolis: Liberty Press, 1981), to which I contributed an introduction.

2. R. M. Hartwell, *A History of the Mont Pelerin Society* (Indianapolis: Liberty Fund, 1995).

3. Renato Mieli was responsible for arranging for an Italian translation of *Capitalism and Freedom.*

4. Quoted from *Free to Choose*, p. 24.

5. All the conferences were held in June, and lasted a week to ten days. I participated in a second one at the University of North Carolina in 1957; a third at Claremont College in 1958; a fourth, again at Wabash, in 1959; and a fifth at Oklahoma State University in 1961. The expositors at the various conferences included Peter Bauer, Trygve Hoff, Joseph Wood Krutch, Bruno Leoni, Fritz Machlup, Don Paarlberg, Jacques Rueff, and Jacob Viner.

6. Milton Friedman with the assistance of Rose D. Friedman, *Capitalism and Freedom* (Chicago: University of Chicago Press, 1962), pp. x and xi.

7. Ibid., 1982 reprint, p. v.

8. In my file of notes on talks given, which is far from complete, I have notes for forty-nine talks given from 1949 to 1961, twenty-nine to academic audiences, twenty to nonaca-

demic. Most of the academic talks were on technical economics, dealing with such topics as monetary theory, history and policy, the theory of consumption, and methodology, and were delivered to graduate students and faculty in economics departments. About a third of the academic talks were to undergraduate student groups about issues of general social policy. Most of the nonacademic talks were about economic policy and prospects. In addition, I have notes for sixteen talks given during the year 1953–54 that we spent in Britain. They were given in Denmark, Spain, Sweden, and Switzerland, as well as Britain, and ranged very widely, from a talk on U.S. foreign policy in Britain to a talk in Sweden on "Why the American Economy is Depression Proof," in which I predicted that a major depression would not occur, though a major inflation might. The depression prediction has been correct for more than forty years as I write, and I see no reason today to alter it. As to inflation, the 1970s were marked by a substantial inflation but not what I would call a major inflation. That is still possible, but I believe increasingly unlikely.

9. Paraphrased from the Preface to the 1982 reprinting of *Capitalism and Freedom,* p. ix.

10. An excerpt from a statement published in every National Bureau book for many years gives the flavor: "The object of the National Bureau of Economic Research is to ascertain and present to the public important economic facts and their interpretation in a scientific and impartial manner."

11. George Stigler's and my *Roofs or Ceilings* was one of their earliest publications. I met Leonard Read personally for the first time at the initial Mont Pelerin Society meeting.

12. With Robert V. Roosa, *The Balance of Payments: Free versus Fixed Exchange Rates,* Rational Debate Seminar (Washington, D.C.: American Enterprise Institute, 1967); with Wilbur J. Cohen, *Social Security: Universal or Selective?* Rational Debate Seminar (Washington, D.C.: American Enterprise Institute, 1972).

13. In *The Conservative Papers,* Introduction by Melvin R. Laird (Garden City: N.Y.: Doubleday & Co., Anchor Books, 1964), pp. 162–74.

14. *Economic Report of the President,* January 20, 1964, pp. 14 and 55–84.

15. Ibid., p. 58.

16. *Poverty: Definition and Perspective* (Washington, D.C.: American Enterprise Institute for Public Policy Research, February 1965), pp. 43, 44, 46.

17. Robert A. Solo (ed.), *Economics and the Public Interest* (New Brunswick, N.J.: Rutgers University Press, 1955).

18. *Capitalism and Freedom,* p. 89. I hasten to add that while a case can be made for both compulsory schooling and financing, it is by no means a conclusive case. Indeed, we have since been persuaded by the empirical evidence on the extensiveness of schooling in the absence of government involvement that neither is justified. The advantages of leaving it to parents to provide for and finance the schooling of their children, where feasible, are stated in *Capitalism and Freedom,* p. 87.

19. Ibid., p. 89.

20. Ibid., p. 93.

21. In addition to my initial article and the discussion in *Capitalism and Freedom* and *Free to Choose,* I have published the following: Communication on "A Free Market in Education," *The Public Interest,* no. 3 (Spring 1966), p. 107; "The Higher Schooling in America," *The Public Interest,* no. 11 (Spring 1968), pp. 108–12; "Decentralizing Schools," *Newsweek,* November 18, 1968; "Homogenized Schools," *Newsweek,* February 28, 1972; "Busing: The Real Issue," *Newsweek,* August 14, 1972; "The Voucher Idea," *New York Times Magazine,* September 23, 1973; "Comment: 'Are Externalities Relevant?'" in *Nonpublic School Aid: The Law, Economics, and Politics of American Education,* by E. G. West (Lexington, Mass.: D. C. Heath & Co., Lexington Books, 1976), pp. 92–93; "Busting the School Monopoly," *Newsweek,* December 5, 1983; "Vouchers No Threat to Church-State Split," letter to the editor, *Wall Street*

Journal, December 31, 1991; "Parental Choice: The Effective Way to Improve Schooling," *The Commonwealth,* August 31, 1992, pp. 514–16, 521–23 (excerpts of an address before the Commonwealth Club of California on August 7, 1992); "Parental Choice: An 'Evil' Proposal?" *Liberty & Law 2,* no. 1 (Winter 1993): 1, 3, and 8; "The Case for Choice," in *Voices on Choice: The Education Reform Debate,* ed. K. L. Billingsley (San Francisco: Pacific Research Institute for Public Policy, 1994), pp. 91–101; "Public Schools: Make Them Private," *Washington Post,* February 19, 1995; "Voucher Wars Revisited," *National Review West,* September 11, 1995. My correspondence file on vouchers extends for a packed ten inches.

22. The president and chief operating officer of the foundation is Gordon St. Angelo, a friend of many years standing. Its office is in Indianapolis: One American Square, Suite 2440, P.O. Box 82078, Indianapolis, Indiana 46282.

23. This section is largely drawn from my Introduction to Leo Melamed, *The Merits of Flexible Exchange Rates* (Fairfax, Va.: George Mason University Press, 1988).

24. See ibid., pp. 418–22; Leo Melamed, *Escape to the Futures* (New York: John Wiley & Sons, 1996), pp. 173–79.

25. I testified on May 17, 1979, at Hearings before the Subcommittee on Monopolies and Commercial Law of the Committee of the Judiciary, House of Representatives, 96th Congress (serial no. 67). I wrote six *Newsweek* columns: "After the Election," November 15, 1976; "A Progress Report," April 10, 1978; "The Message from California," June 19, 1978; "Implementing Humphrey-Hawkins," March 5, 1979; "Jerry Brown's Kiss of Death," March 26, 1979; "Why Deficits are Bad," January 2, 1984. I published at least two articles: "Less Red Ink," *Atlantic,* February 1983, pp. 18–26; "The Limitations of Tax Limitation," *Policy Review,* Summer 1978, pp. 7–14.

26. *Oriental Economist,* November 1976, pp. 17–18. Reprinted by permission.

27. Ibid., pp. 18–19. Reprinted by permission.

Chapter Twenty-Two

1. Barry M. Goldwater, with Jack Casserly, *Goldwater* (New York: Doubleday, 1988), p. 186.

2. Barry M. Goldwater, *With No Apologies* (New York: William Morrow, 1979), pp. 160, 163; *Goldwater,* pp. 139, 149–54.

3. Both quotes from *Goldwater,* p. 198.

4. Ibid., p. 209.

5. *New York Times Magazine,* October 11, 1964.

6. "Schools at Chicago," *The University of Chicago Record,* 1974, p. 6.

7. For his twenty-first birthday, I had a collection of his poetry printed and bound.

8. We are informed by Bruce Caldwell that subsequent legislation has limited the price that can be charged for a sublet, giving rise to the widespread practice of "key fees" as a way of evading the law.

9. One reason for my hesitancy was undoubtedly that the offer was stimulated by a local donor who was prepared to finance a professorship for a free-market economist and specifically named me as the kind of economist he had in mind. Accepting it would involve moving to a department that had never before tried to attract me and that I considered somewhat hostile, even though several of its members were longtime personal friends.

Chapter Twenty-Three

1. Other members were Pierre Rinfret, an investment adviser and friend of Nixon; Alan Greenspan, who, along with Martin Anderson, was in charge of domestic research for the campaign; Maury Stans, who had been director of the budget under Eisenhower and was serving as financial chairman of the Nixon for President Committee; Don Paarlberg, an agricultural

economist at Purdue; Peter Flanagan, who was serving as deputy campaign manager and later served as a presidential assistant; and Paul McCracken, University of Michigan.

2. Though written in 1968, my memo was not published until 1988 when Leo Melamed included it in *The Merits of Flexible Exchange Rates: An Anthology* (Fairfax, Va.: George Mason University Press, 1988), pp. 429–38; quotation is from pp. 431–32.

3. The edited proceedings were published in *The Draft: A Handbook of Facts and Alternatives,* ed. Sol Tax (Chicago: University of Chicago Press, 1967), to which I contributed an article, "Why Not a Voluntary Army?" (pp. 200–207). The quotation is from pp. viii and ix.

4. Martin Anderson, "The Making of the All-Volunteer Armed Force," in *Richard Nixon: Cold War Patriot and Statesman,* ed. Leon Friedman and William Levantrosser (Westport, Conn.: Greenwood Press, 1991), pp. 173–74.

5. I am indebted to Martin Anderson for calling this to my attention.

6. The members were: Chairman Gates; General Alfred Gruenther, former supreme Allied commander, Europe, and longtime favorite bridge partner of Dwight Eisenhower; Lauris Norstad, former supreme Allied commander, Europe, and chairman of the board, Owens-Corning Fiberglass Corporation; Allen Wallis; Alan Greenspan; Milton Friedman; Thomas Curtis, vice-president and general counsel, Encyclopaedia Britannica and former congressman from Missouri, whom I had come to know and respect in that capacity; Frederick Dent, president, Mayfair Mills; Crawford Greenewalt, chairman, finance committee, E. I. DuPont de Nemours and Co.; Stephen Herbits, student, Georgetown University Law Center; Theodore Hesburgh, president, University of Notre Dame, chairman, U.S. Commission on Civil Rights; Jerome Holland, president, Hampton Institute; John Kemper, headmaster, Phillips Academy; Jeanne Noble, professor, New York University and vice-president, National Council of Negro Women; and Roy Wilkins, executive director, NAACP.

7. *The Report of the President's Commission on an All-Volunteer Armed Force* (New York: Collier Books/Macmillan Co., 1970), unnumbered second page of letter of transmittal.

8. Ibid., first page of letter of transmittal.

9. Quoted from Milton Friedman, *The Meaning of Freedom.* The twelfth Sol Feinstone Lecture delivered at the United States Military Academy, West Point, September 26, 1984 (West Point, N.Y.: United States Military Academy, 1985). I had no transcript of the hearings, so I cannot vouch for the precise wording of the quoted testimony, but there is no doubt about its general accuracy.

10. Richard M. Nixon, *The Memoirs of Richard Nixon* (New York: Grosset and Dunlap, 1978), p. 521.

11. Ibid., p. 518.

12. Ibid., pp. 518, 519–20.

13. Milton Friedman, "How to Sell Government Securities," *Wall Street Journal,* August 28, 1991. Under the traditional method of auctioning government securities, bidders pay the price they bid, so different purchasers pay different prices. Under a Dutch auction, all bidders pay the same price, that being the highest price at which the whole amount offered can be sold. The advantage of the Dutch auction is that it encourages a wider range of potential purchasers to bid.

14. The other members were Arthur Burns, Alan Greenspan, Michael Halbouty (an independent oil producer from Texas), Jack Kemp, James T. Lynn (head of OMB under Nixon), Paul McCracken, William Simon, Charls E. Walker, Murray Wiedenbaum, Casper Weinberger, and Walter Wriston.

15. Not because we had no other invitations, but because we found such formal dinners unappealing, full of Beltway types trying to demonstrate their importance.

16. See Martin Anderson, *Revolution: The Reagan Legacy* (Stanford, Calif.: Hoover Institu-

tion Press, 1990), pp. 261–71, for an explanation of the origin and subsequent history of PEPAB.

17. Tom Sowell resigned for health reasons and was replaced by Rita Ricardo-Campbell of the Hoover Institution.

18. Anderson, *Revolution,* p. 267.

19. The names that come to mind are Don Regan, secretary of the treasury during the first term; Murray Wiedenbaum, Martin Feldstein, and Beryl Sprinkel, during their successive stints as chairmen of the Council of Economic Advisers; George Shultz, secretary of state, and Allen Wallis, undersecretary of state for economic affairs.

20. See my op-ed piece, "Oodoov Economics," *New York Times,* February 2, 1992.

21. Anderson, *Revolution,* pp. 267–68.

22. *Newsweek,* November 15, 1982, p. 90.

23. The episode is described in detail by Anderson, *Revolution,* pp. 269–71.

Chapter Twenty-Four

1. "By 1973, fixed prices on more than three thousand goods had brought on food shortages and a booming black market in everything from chickens to cement. Import tariffs averaging 105 percent on 5,125 different items had sealed off most foreign trade. Hundreds of private companies had been taken over by the state, some by violence, others through the exercise of an obscure forty-year old law, still others by legal purchase—and most were operating at substantial losses. The government was financing a 55 percent fiscal deficit by printing money, thereby generating inflation that exceeded a 1,000 percent annual rate during Allende's final months in office." Claudia Rosett, "Looking Back on Chile, 1973–84," *National Review,* June 1, 1984, p. 25.

2. Larry A. Sjaastad, "What Went Wrong in Chile," *National Review,* September 16, 1983, p. 1128 (italics in the original).

3. Victor Lasky, *Turning Defeat into Victory: The Soviet Offensive against Chile* (New York: American-Chilean Council, 1975).

4. Rosett, "Looking Back on Chile," pp. 25–26.

5. All later unattributed quotes are from the notes that I dictated at the time—as it happens not in Chile but a few days later at the Fijian Hotel in the Fiji Islands, where we took a brief break on our way to Australia.

6. I also wrote him several times in later years to ask for clemency and release of prisoners whose cases were brought to my attention.

7. I later gave essentially the same lecture under the title "The Fragility of Freedom" at Brigham Young University in December 1975, and published a revised transcript as "The Line We Dare Not Cross" in *Encounter,* November 1976, pp. 8–14. An excerpt was also published as "The Path We Dare Not Take" in *Reader's Digest,* March 1977, pp. 110–15.

8. Orlando Letelier, "Economic 'Freedom's' Awful Toll," *The Nation,* August 28, 1976, p. 137.

9. Rosett, "Looking Back on Chile," p. 25.

10. *San Jose Mercury News,* February 11, 1978, p. 3b.

11. First quote from Robert and Frances Tracy, "Chile Revisited," dated June 22, 1978. Second quote from Maryann Mahaffey, "Chile Suffers in Friedman Economy," *Detroit Free Press,* July 3, 1978, p. 9A.

12. The first, Claudia Rosett, *New York Times,* July 3, 1983; the second, Steven K. Beckner, *Washington Times,* August 18, 1983; the third, Larry A. Sjaastad, *National Review,* September 16, 1983.

13. *Vanguardia,* March 1977, translated by Gloria Valentine.

14. I am indebted to Rafael Rodriguez for these data.

Chapter Twenty-Five

1. *Oriental Economist,* December 1976, p. 30.

2. The *Nihon Keizai Shimbun* has, I believe, the largest circulation of any paper in Japan, and, like the *Wall Street Journal,* has a number of regional editions. In 1964 it established an associated Japan Economic Research Center, of which Milton became an honorary member, and on which he could call for any data about Japan that he might wish to get. In addition, he had occasionally been interviewed by U.S. reporters over the years and had written a few brief pieces for them. They publish a weekly English digest of their daily paper that Milton finds the most useful source of current information on Japan.

3. Our subsequent trips were in 1969, 1970, 1972, 1978, 1980, 1985, and 1988. In addition, I visited Japan without Rose in 1983.

4. The project on which I was advising Chiaki resulted in a major volume on Japanese monetary history, including long time series on money stock, prices, income, etc.: Kokichi Asakura and Chiaki Nishiyama, *A Monetary Analysis and History of the Japanese Economy, 1868–1970* (Tokyo: Sobunsha, 1974).

5. Two other overseas special advisers were Franco Modigliani of MIT and James Tobin of Yale. Tobin also gave keynote addresses at these two conferences.

The title of my first keynote address was "Monetarism in Rhetoric and in Practice"; of the second, "Monetary Policy in a Fiat World." Both were published in *Bank of Japan Monetary Studies,* a journal started by the new institute, and the second formed the basis for chapter 10 of my book *Money Mischief.*

6. On February 7, 1990, the Reuters news agency reported, "The Tokyo Stock market is headed for a 'terrible crash,' U.S. economist Milton Friedman predicted in an interview with an Italian newspaper [*Italia Oggi*]." Within days, the Japanese market did have a "terrible crash," and I attained temporary notoriety for a successful prediction. The coincidence in timing was pure chance. My comment was based on long-run considerations: "At current exchange rates," I told the newspaper reporter who interviewed me, "the total capitalization of the Tokyo Stock Exchange represents between 40 and 50 percent of the total value of all shares in circulation in the world. No one can tell me that that corresponds with reality." I went on to say that the anomaly could be corrected only by a "deep fall of its exchange rate or a heavy drop in prices on the Tokyo exchange."

7. *Bank Markazi Iran Bulletin* 9 (March–April 1971): 700–712.

8. *Money Mischief,* pp. 40–41.

Chapter Twenty-Six

1. The man in charge of public relations for Proposal C commented afterwards that this was the public-relations coup that he was going to tell his grandchildren about. I was being flown around the state in a private plane by Bill Rickenbacker, one of the fellow founders of the National Tax Limitation Committee. At every stop we were beseiged by local reporters and citizens curious to see what a newly minted Nobel laureate looked like.

Chapter Twenty-Seven

1. Those lectures were published as Milton Friedman, *Money and Economic Development* (New York: Praeger, 1973).

2. Milton Friedman, "Israel's Other War," *Newsweek,* August 22, 1977, p. 57.

3. Milton and Rose Friedman, *The Tyranny of the Status Quo* (San Diego, New York, and London: Harcourt Brace Jovanovich, 1984), p. 3.

4. See my discussion of this episode in *Money Mischief,* pp. 239–42. The reform owed much to the pressure and advice from the United States coordinated by George Shultz, as secretary of state, and Allen Wallis, as undersecretary of state for economic affairs.

5. In a 1991 lecture at the Heritage Foundation, Daniel Doron argued that the view, which he admits to holding himself as late as 1988, "that socialism played an essential role in the resettlement of what was then desolate Ottoman Palestine" is a "myth" that was propagated by "Eastern European Zionist leaders." He argues that far from promoting the development of Israel, the insistence on socialist policies inhibited "the growth of middle-class entrepreneurship." See Daniel Doron, "Israel's Economic Challenge: How the U.S. Can Help," *Heritage Lecture 350,* delivered September 20, 1991 (Washington, D.C.: Heritage Foundation, 1991).

Chapter Twenty-Eight

1. Allen, chancellor of the University of Rochester, was also serving as chairman of the Corporation for Public Broadcasting, the government's appointed agency to oversee the Public Broadcasting System, and to distribute appropriated funds.

2. Peter Bernstein "The Man Who Brought You Milton Friedman," *Fortune,* February 25, 1980, pp. 108–12.

3. Leo Rosten, a fellow student of ours at Chicago and a close friend ever since, has already come into our story in Chapter 4. Ben Rogge was a professor at Wabash College, who codirected the Volker summer schools at which I gave the lectures that were the basis for *Capitalism and Freedom.* He was a skilled speaker and had been the presenter in a number of television documentaries.

4. Laurence Jarvik, *PBS* (Rocklin, Cal.: Forum, 1997), pp. 278–79. The final chapter of the book (chap. 13) is devoted to *Free to Choose.*

5. Of the money raised, approximately $2.5 million went for the cost of producing the shows. The rest of the money raised went for promotion. The price level is now roughly two-and-a-half times its level in 1977, so $3 million in 1977 would be the equivalent of $7.5 million today.

6. He was also at the time secretary of the Mont Pelerin Society. An adviser of Margaret Thatcher, she conferred a peerage on him after she was named prime minister, so he is now Lord Harris of High Cross.

7. Another partner in Video Arts was John Cleese of *Monty Python* fame. The firm had been particularly successful in producing training films and did a good deal of work in the United States, enough so that it had an office in Los Angeles.

In later years Jay authored or coauthored and produced two enormously popular TV series on BBC, *Yes, Minister* and *Yes, Prime Minister,* that satirized government bureaucracy. Many of the episodes were directly related to themes from *Free to Choose.* Both series have been repeatedly shown on PBS stations in the United States.

8. I had wanted Jay to be the producer, but he protested that he was too old for so active and exhausting a role. In the event, we had the best of both worlds: Jay's intellectual assistance in planning the programs and their content, and Latham's extraordinary abilities in carrying out the actual filming and constructing of the final programs.

9. Quoted from a letter to us from Bob dated October 17, 1977.

10. The videotapes were titled *Milton Friedman Speaks* (New York: Harcourt Brace Jovanovich, 1980). A complete transcript, including the question-and-answer session, accompanied the videotapes.

11. Eben Wilson, personal letter, December 5, 1996.

12. Letter from Mike Latham dated February 27, 1979.

13. The Temple of Moss is the popular term for the Zaiho-ji Buddhist Temple grounds. The temple's landscape garden is one of the oldest gardens in Kyoto.

14. My loose translation: "It so happens that the issues referred to in these programs have already been largely treated in the productions of ANTENNE 2."

15. My loose translation: "It turns out that those responsible for the programs of ANTENNE 2, notably the Bureau of Information, have chosen, in order to interest the public in economic and social problems, to discuss these questions directly in newspapers and journals, rather than to air a series the length and technical character of which would discourage the viewers in advance."

16. Rose was a member of the board of directors of the foundation.

17. Steve Calabrese, Libertarian; Richard Vigilante, Conservative; Harry Crocker III, Conservative; Gary Jenkins, Liberal; Lee S. Liberman, Libertarian; David Brooks, Social Democrat; Carola Mone, Libertarian.

Chapter Twenty-Nine

1. The discussants for the various programs are for "Power of the Market": David Brooks and James Galbraith; "Tyranny of Control": Michael Walker and Steven Cohen; "Freedom and Prosperity": Gary Becker and Sam Bowles; "The Failure of Socialism": Henry Leven and Gordon Tullock; "Created Equal": Michael Kinsley and Tom Sowell.

2. The introducers of the various programs are for "Power of the Market": Arnold Schwarzenegger; "Tyranny of Control": George Shultz; "Freedom & Prosperity": Ronald Reagan; "The Failure of Socialism": David Friedman; "Created Equal": Steve Allen.

3. Videotapes of both the original and the later program can be obtained from Free to Choose Enterprise, 9008 Main Place, McKean PA 16426-0662.

Chapter Thirty

1. I refer of course to the Russian satellites—Poland, Czech Republic, Hungary, East Germany—and the Baltic states—Latvia, Lithuania, and Estonia.

2. Lewis M. Branscomb, letter dated October 15, 1980. Mr. Branscomb was the chairman of the Committee on Scholarly Communication, which was a joint project of the Council of Learned Societies, National Academy of Sciences, and the Social Science Research Council.

3. The letter from Qian Jun-rui was dated November 17, 1979, from Lo Chengxi, November 19, 1979.

4. Quoted from Milton Friedman, "Report to Committee on Scholarly Communication with the People's Republic of China on Trip to China, September–October, 1980" (submitted May 1981).

5. A few comments on some aftereffects of our visit: On returning from China, I mailed various pieces of literature to eighteen people whom I had met in China and who had expressed an interest in one or more items. The items that I mailed included autographed copies of *Free to Choose,* and a variety of my publications on money.

In addition, four students at three different institutions whom I had not met wrote to me as a result of my visit. Three were either in the process of translating or proposed to translate various works of mine. The extensive correspondence that resulted consisted partly of my answering questions by the translators about the items they were translating. In addition, I wrote a special preface for the Chinese edition of *Price Theory.* All told, I believe that three other books of mine were published in Chinese in China between our first and second visits: the lectures that I gave in 1980, *Free to Choose,* and *Milton Friedman's Monetary Framework.* Others have been published in Chinese in Taiwan. The original English version of the 1980 lectures were published in Milton Friedman, *Friedman in China* (Hong Kong: Chinese University Press for the Hong Kong Centre of Economic Research, 1990).

I believe that *Free to Choose* was either withdrawn or allowed to go out of print. At any rate, when we saw the editor of the *World Economic Herald* in 1988, he expressed the intention of publishing a new translation of the book. Tiananmen Square ended that project along with the *Herald,* whose courageous editor was imprisoned.

6. Steven N. S. Cheung, "Silhouettes," chap. 6 of *Friedman in China,* p. 98.

7. Winston Churchill and Henry Kissinger are examples of the first category: great men, but when they touched on an economic matter, they almost invariably got it wrong. Solzhenitsyn is an example of the second category: in his book, the *Cancer Ward,* he describes accurately how free-market medicine would operate without ever having experienced it—a great feat of the imagination. Another example is my former University of Chicago colleague, Leo Szilard, the great physicist and chemist who first discovered the principle of the chain reaction, and, indeed, patented it. He was repeatedly reinventing economic theorems, and getting them right.

8. *Chinese University Bulletin* (Hong Kong), supplement no. 19, twenty-fifth Anniversary Lecture Series (April, 1990), pp. 58–67.

9. Personal letter, January 20, 1989.

10. Personal letter, March 15, 1989.

Chapter Thirty-One

1. Quoted from "The Sea Ranch Owner's Manual," prepared by the Communications Committee of the Sea Ranch Association.

2. Among other precautions, rather than driving a car, he rode a motorcycle to his office or other destination to be less identifiable, varied his routes at random, and hired someone to case his destination for possible suspicious circumstances. In view of the number of political assassinations in Guatemala during the period in question, these measures were evidence of reasonable caution, not paranoia.

3. Muso writes in "My Remembrance and Comments on the Founding of the University Francisco Marroquín and Its Antecedents," "If the Mont Pelerin Society hadn't existed, it is probable that we would have discarded the idea of founding a university. . . . The contact that we had with these people in the academic world made us more aware that the intellectual crisis of our time, principally in the universities, was worldwide." (Typewritten draft of translation of Spanish original, p. 7.)

Muso was president of the Mont Pelerin Society, 1978–80.

4. One conference was held at Sea Ranch.

5. In James Gwartney, Robert Lawson, and Walter Block, *Economic Freedom of the World, 1975–1995* (Vancouver, B.C., Canada: Fraser Institute, 1996), pp. vii–viii. Since this was written, another volume has appeared: James Gwartney and Robert Lawson, *Economic Freedom of the World: 1997 Annual Report* (Vancouver, B.C.: Fraser Institute, 1997).

6. The latest Heritage volume is Kim R. Holmes, Bryan T. Johnson, and Melanie Kirkpatrick, *1997 Index of Economic Freedom* (New York and Washington: Heritage Foundation and Wall Street Journal, 1997).

7. David Friedman, *The Journal of Legal Studies,* March 1979, pp. 399–415.

8. The other recipients of the medal on this occasion were Malcolm Baldrige (posthumously), Pearl Bailey Bellson, Irving Brown, Warren E. Burger, Jean Faircloth MacArthur, J. Willard Marriott (posthumously), and David Packard.

9. Herewith the topics common to the two meetings: "Free" Enterprise or Competitive Order; Modern Historiography and Political Education: The Future of Germany; The Problems and Chances of European Federation; Liberalism and Christianity; Contra-Cyclical Measures; Full Employment and Monetary Reform; Wage Policy and Trade Unions; Taxation, Poverty and Income Distribution; Agricultural Policy; The Present Political Crisis.

Epilogue

1. Alexis de Tocqueville, *Democracy in America,* Anchor Books ed. (Garden City, N.Y.: Doubleday & Company, Inc., 1969), p. 692.

→ Bibliography ←

Anderson, Martin. *Revolution: The Reagan Legacy.* Stanford, Calif.: Hoover Institution Press, 1990.

———. "The Making of the All-Volunteer Armed Force." In *Richard Nixon: Cold War Patriot and Statesman,* edited by Leon Friedman and William Levantrosser, pp. 171–83. Westport, Conn.: Greenwood Press, 1991.

Anderson, T. W., and Milton Friedman. "A Limitation of the Optimum Property of the Sequential Probability Ratio Test." In *Contributions to Probability and Statistics,* edited by I. Oklin and others, pp. 57–69. Stanford: Stanford University Press, 1960.

Ando, Albert, and Franco Modigliani. "The Relative Stability of Monetary Velocity and the Investment Multiplier." *American Economic Review* 55 (September 1965): 693–728.

Asakura, Kokichi, and Chiaki Nishiyama. *A Monetary Analysis and History of the Japanese Economy, 1868–1970.* Tokyo: Sobunsha, 1974.

"Bali." In *Encyclopaedia Britannica,* 1970 ed.

Baltimore, David, and S. E. Luria. "The Laureate." Letter to the Editor, *New York Times,* October 24, 1976.

Bangs, Robert. Review of *Roofs or Ceilings? The Current Housing Problem* by Milton Friedman and George J. Stigler. *American Economic Review* 37 (June 1947): 482–83.

Bartley, Robert L. *The Seven Fat Years.* New York: Free Press, 1992.

Beckner, Steven K. "Friedmanism Is Exonerated in Chilean Debacle." *Washington Times,* August 18, 1983.

Berger, James O. "Sequential Analysis." In *The New Palgrave: A Dictionary of Economics,* edited by John Eatwell, Murray Milgate, and Peter Newman, 4:312–13. New York: Stockton Press, and London: Macmillan Press, 1987.

Berliner, Michael S., ed. *Letters of Ayn Rand.* New York: Dutton, 1995.

Bernstein, Peter. "The Man Who Brought You Milton Friedman." *Fortune,* February 25, 1980, pp. 108–12.

Bordo, Michael D., ed. *Money, History and International Finance: Essays in Honor of Anna J. Schwartz.* Chicago: University of Chicago Press, 1989.

Brady, Dorothy S., and Rose D. Friedman. "Savings and the Income Distribution." In *Studies in Income and Wealth,* no. 10, pp. 247–65. New York: National Bureau of Economic Research, 1947.

Cagan, Phillip. *Determinants and Effect of Changes in the Money Stock, 1875–1960.* New York: National Bureau of Economic Research, 1965.

Chambers, Whittaker. *Witness.* New York: Random House, 1952.

Cheung, Steven N. S. "Silhouettes." In *Friedman in China,* by Milton Friedman, pp. 97–104. Hong Kong: The Chinese University Press for the Hong Kong Centre for Economic Research, 1990.

Citizens' Committee on Human Rights and Foreign Policy. "Advising Chile." Letter to the Editor, *Newsweek,* June 14, 1976.

Clark, John Maurice. *Studies in the Economics of Overhead Costs.* Chicago: University of Chicago Press, 1923.

———. *Preface to Social Economics: Essays in Economic Theory and Social Problems.* Edited by Moses Abramovitz and Eli Ginzberg. New York: Farrar & Rinehart, 1936.

Cohen, Susan. "Economist Sees Good, Bad in Chile Regime." *San Jose Mercury News,* February 11, 1978.

Cohn, Peter. "Radicals Plan Friedman Protest; Harberger Also Accused of Role." *Chicago Maroon,* October 3, 1975.

"Commons, John R." In *Encyclopaedia Britannica,* 1970 ed.

Conference on Research in National Income and Wealth. *Studies in Income and Wealth.* Edited by Milton Friedman. Vols. 1–3. New York: National Bureau of Economic Research, 1937–39.

"Congratulations." Editorial, *Wall Street Journal,* October 15, 1976.

Crocker, George. "New Torch Burns." *San Francisco Chronicle,* March 7, 1965.

Cross, Rod, ed. *The Natural Rate of Unemployment: Reflections on 25 Years of the Hypothesis.* Cambridge and New York: Cambridge University Press, 1995.

Davenport, John A. "Reflections on Mont Pelerin." *The Mont Pelerin Society Newsletter,* special supplement, July 1981.

Davis, Steven J., and John Haltwanger. "Gross Job Creation, Gross Job Destruction, and Employment Reallocation." *Quarterly Journal of Economics* 107 (August 1992): 819–63.

Delaware Income Statistics Compiled from Income Tax Returns for 1936, 1937, and 1938. Vol. 1. Newark: Bureau of Economic and Business Research, University of Delaware, 1941.

De Prano, Michael, and Thomas Mayer. "Testing the Relative Importance of Autonomous Expenditures and Money," *American Economic Review* 55 (September 1965): 729–52.

"A Dialogue with General Secretary Zhao Ziyang." Translated by Ronald W. C. Teng and Na Liu from the Chinese version edited by Steven N. S. Cheung. *Hong Kong Economic Times,* January 26, 1989.

Doron, Daniel. *Israel's Economic Challenge: How the U.S. Can Help.* Heritage Lecture 350, delivered September 20, 1991. Washington, D.C.: Heritage Foundation, 1991.

Douglas, Paul H. "Are There Laws of Production?" *American Economic Review* 38 (March 1948): 1–41.

Douglas, Paul H., and Aaron Director. *The Problem of Unemployment.* New York: Macmillan Company, 1931.

"A Draconian Cure for Chile's Economic Ills?" *Business Week,* January 12, 1976.

Eccles, Marriner. *Beckoning Frontiers: Public and Personal Recollections.* Edited by Sidney Hyman. New York: Knopf, 1951.

Economic Report of the President, January 20, 1964.

Eisner, Robert. "The Permanent Income Hypothesis: Comment." *American Economic Review* 48 (December 1958): 972–90.

Expo '70 Official Guide. Osaka, Japan.

Farzin, Y. H. "The Time Path of Scarcity Rent in the Theory of Exhaustible Resources." *Economic Journal* 102 (July 1992): 813–30.

Fifty Years of Economic Measurement: The Jubilee of the Conference on Research in Income and Wealth. Edited by Ernst R. Berndt and Jack E. Triplett. Studies in Income and Wealth, no. 54. Chicago: University of Chicago Press, 1990.

"Fireworks in U.W. Econ Department as Instructor May Get $3500 Prof's Job." *Capital Times* (Madison, Wisconsin), May 14, 1941.

Fodor's 90 Eastern Europe. New York and London, 1990.

Friedman, David. *The Machinery of Freedom: Guide to a Radical Capitalism.* New York: Harper & Row, 1973; 2d ed., LaSalle, Ill.: Open Court, 1989.

———. "Private Creation and Enforcement of Law." *The Journal of Legal Studies,* March 1979, pp. 399–415.

Friedman, Milton. "Professor Pigou's Method for Measuring Elasticities of Demand from Budgetary Data." *Quarterly Journal of Economics* 50 (November 1935): 151–63.

———. Review of *Seasonal Variations in Industry and Trade* by Simon Kuznets. *Journal of Political Economy* 43 (December 1935): 830–32.

———. "Marginal Utility of Money and Elasticities of Demand." *Quarterly Journal of Economics* 50 (May 1936): 432–33.

———. "The Use of Ranks to Avoid the Assumption of Normality Implicit in the Analysis of Variance." *Journal of the American Statistical Association* 32 (December 1937): 675–701.

———. "A Comparison of Alternative Tests of Significance for the Problem of **m** Rankings." *Annals of Mathematical Statistics* 11 (March 1940): 86–92.

———. "Discussion of 'The Inflationary Gap' by Walter Salant." *American Economic Review* 32 (June 1942): 308–20.

———. "The Spendings Tax as a Wartime Fiscal Measure." *American Economic Review* 33 (March 1943): 50–62.

———. "Lange on Price Flexibility and Employment." *American Economic Review* 36 (September 1946): 613–31.

———. "The Marshallian Demand Curve." *Journal of Political Economy* 57 (December 1949): 463–95.

———. "The Case for Flexible Exchange Rates." In Milton Friedman, *Essays in Positive Economics* (1953; see below), pp. 157–203.

———. "Choice, Chance, and the Personal Distribution of Income." *Journal of Political Economy* 61 (August 1953): 277–90.

———. *Essays in Positive Economics.* Chicago: University of Chicago Press, 1953.

———. "The Methodology of Positive Economics." In Milton Friedman, *Essays in Positive Economics* (1953; see above), pp. 3–43.

———. "Why the American Economy is Depression Proof." *Nationalekonomiska föreningens förhandlingar* (Stockholm), no. 3 (1954), pp. 58–77. Reprinted in Milton Friedman, *Dollars and Deficits* (1968; see below), pp. 72–96.

———. "The Role of Government in Education." In *Economics and the Public Interest*, edited by Robert A. Solo, pp. 123–44. New Brunswick, N.J.: Rutgers University Press, 1955.

———. "The Indian Alternative." *Encounter* 8, no. 1 (January 1957): 71–73.

———. *Theory of the Consumption Function.* Princeton: Princeton University Press for the National Bureau of Economic Research, 1957.

———. "The Report of the Commission on Money and Credit: An Essay in *Petitio Principii*." *American Economic Review* 52 (May 1962): 291–301.

———. *Inflation: Causes and Consequences.* Bombay: Asia Publishing House for the Council for Economic Education, 1963. Reprinted in Milton Friedman, *Dollars and Deficits* (1968; see below), pp. 21–71.

———. "Can a Controlled Economy Work?" In *The Conservative Papers*, pp. 162–74. Introduction by Melvin R. Laird. Garden City, N.Y.: Doubleday & Co., Anchor Books, 1964.

———. "The Goldwater View of Economics." *New York Times Magazine*, October 11, 1964.

———. "Friedman & Keynes." Letter to the Editor, *Time*, February 4, 1966.

———. Communication on "A Free Market in Education." *The Public Interest*, no. 3 (Spring 1966), p. 107.

———. "Why Not a Voluntary Army?" In *The Draft: A Handbook of Facts and Alternatives*, edited by Sol Tax, pp. 200–207. Chicago: University of Chicago Press, 1967.

———. "The Negro in America." *Newsweek*, December 11, 1967.

———. "The Role of Monetary Policy." *American Economic Review* 58 (March 1968): 1–17.

———. "The Higher Schooling in America." *The Public Interest*, no. 11 (Spring 1968), pp. 108–12.

———. "Decentralizing Schools." *Newsweek*, November 18, 1968.

———. *Dollars and Deficits*. Englewood Cliffs, N.J.: Prentice-Hall, 1968.

———. "Invisible Occupation." *Newsweek*, May 5, 1969.

———. *The Optimum Quantity of Money and Other Essays*. Chicago: Aldine, 1969.

———. "Welfare: Back to the Drawing Board." *Newsweek*, May 18, 1970.

———. "Social Responsibility of Business." *New York Times Magazine*, September 13, 1970.

———. "Paul Samuelson." *Newsweek*, November 9, 1970.

———. "Monetary Policy for a Developing Society." *Bank Markazi Iran Bulletin* 9 (March–April 1971): 700–12.

———. "Why the Freeze Is a Mistake." *Newsweek*, August 30, 1971.

———. *An Economist's Protest*. Glen Ridge, N.J.: Thomas Horton & Daughters, 1972; 2d ed., 1975.

———. "The Need for Futures Markets in Currencies." In *The Futures Market in Foreign Currencies*, pp. 6–12. Chicago: International Monetary Market of the Chicago Mercantile Exchange, 1972.

———. "Homogenized Schools." *Newsweek*, February 28, 1972.

———. "A Family Matter." *Newsweek*, April 10, 1972.

———. "Prohibition and Drugs." *Newsweek*, May 1, 1972.

———. "Busing: The Real Issue." *Newsweek*, August 14, 1972.

———. "Frustrating Drug Advancement." *Newsweek*, January 8, 1973.

———. "Interview: Milton Friedman." *Playboy*, February 1973.

———. "Barking Cats." *Newsweek*, February 19, 1973.

———. "Milton Friedman–Sir Dennis Robertson Correspondence." *Journal of Political Economy* 81 (July–August 1973): 1033–39.

———. *Money and Economic Development*. New York: Praeger, 1973.

———. "The Voucher Idea." *New York Times Magazine*, September 23, 1973.

———. "Economic Miracles." *Newsweek*, January 21, 1974.

———. "Schools at Chicago." (Remarks at the 54th annual Board of Trustees Dinner for Faculty, University of Chicago, January 9, 1974.) *The University of Chicago Record*, 1974, pp. 3–7.

———. "Comments on the Critics." In *Milton Friedman's Monetary Framework*, edited by Robert J. Gordon, pp. 132–77. Chicago: University of Chicago Press, 1974.

———. "FEO and the Gas Lines." *Newsweek*, March 4, 1974.

———. "Comment: 'Are Externalities Relevant?'" In *Nonpublic School Aid: The Law, Economics, and Politics of American Education*, by E. G. West, pp. 92–93. Lexington, Mass.: D. C. Heath & Co., Lexington Books, 1976.

————. "Homer Jones: A Personal Reminiscence." *Journal of Monetary Economics* 2 (1976): 433–36.

————. *Price Theory*. Rev. and enlarged ed. Chicago: Aldine, 1976.

————. Reply to Citizens' Committee on Human Rights and Foreign Policy, "Advising Chile." Letter to the Editor, *Newsweek,* June 14, 1976.

————. "The Line We Dare Not Cross." *Encounter,* November 1976, pp. 8–14. (An excerpt was also published as "The Path We Dare Not Take" in *Reader's Digest,* March 1977, pp. 110–15.)

————. "After the Election." *Newsweek,* November 15, 1976.

————. *The Nobel Prize in Economics, 1976.* (Remarks about receiving the Nobel Prize, Income Distribution Conference sponsored by the Hoover Institution, January 29, 1977.) Stanford, Calif.: Hoover Institution Press, 1977.

————. "How to Ration Water." *Newsweek,* March 21, 1977.

————. "Nobel Lecture: Inflation and Unemployment." (Lecture delivered in Stockholm, December 13, 1976.) *Journal of Political Economy* 85 (June 1977): 451–72.

————. "Israel's Other War." *Newsweek,* August 22, 1977.

————. "A Progress Report." *Newsweek,* April 10, 1978.

————. "The Message from California." *Newsweek,* June 19, 1978.

————. "The Limitations of Tax Limitation." *Policy Review,* no. 5 (Summer 1978), pp. 7–14.

————. "Standards of Morality." *Newsweek,* December 18, 1978.

————. "Implementing Humphrey-Hawkins." *Newsweek,* March 5, 1979.

————. "Jerry Brown's Kiss of Death." *Newsweek,* March 26, 1979.

————. "A Warning on Rent Controls." *San Francisco Chronicle,* April 23, 1979.

————. Testimony of May 17, 1979. In *Hearings on Proposals for a Constitutional Amendment to Require a Balanced Federal Budget,* before the Subcommittee on Monopolies and Commercial Law of the Committee on the Judiciary, U.S. House of Representatives, 96th Cong., 1st and 2d sess., pp. 121–59. Serial no. 67. Washington: Government Printing Office, 1980.

————. Introduction to *New Individualist Review.* A Periodical reprint. Indianapolis: Liberty Press, 1981.

————. "An Open Letter on Grants." *Newsweek,* May 18, 1981.

————. "Free Markets and the Generals." *Newsweek,* January 25, 1982.

————. "Laws That Do Harm." *Newsweek,* October 25, 1982.

————. "Washington: Less Red Ink." *The Atlantic,* February 1983, pp. 18, 20–24, 26.

————. "What Price Oil?" *Newsweek,* March 21, 1983.

————. "Monetarism in Rhetoric and in Practice." *Bank of Japan Monetary and Economic Studies* 1 (October 1983): 1–14.

————. "Busting the School Monopoly." *Newsweek,* December 5, 1983.

————. "Why Deficits are Bad." *Newsweek,* January 2, 1984.

————. *The Meaning of Freedom.* (The twelfth Sol Feinstone Lecture delivered at the United States Military Academy, West Point, September 26, 1984.) West Point, N.Y.: United States Military Academy, 1985.

————. "Monetary Policy in a Fiat World." *Bank of Japan Monetary and Economic Studies* 3 (September 1985): 11–18.

————. "My Evolution as an Economist." In *Lives of the Laureates: Seven Nobel Economists,* edited by William Breit and Roger W. Spencer, pp. 77–92. Cambridge: MIT Press, 1986.

————. "Right at Last, an Expert's Dream" (My Turn column). *Newsweek,* March 10, 1986.

————. "Arthur Burns." In *In Memoriam: Arthur Burns, 1904–1987,* pp. 7–11. Washington, D.C.: Board of Governors of the Federal Reserve System, 1987.

———. Introduction to *The Merits of Flexible Exchange Rates: An Anthology*, edited by Leo Melamed. Fairfax, Va. George Mason University Press, 1988.

———. "A Proposal for Resolving the U.S. Balance of Payments: Confidential Memorandum to President-elect Nixon." In *The Merits of Flexible Exchange Rates: An Anthology*, edited by Leo Melamed, pp. 429–38. Fairfax, Va.: George Mason University Press, 1988.

———. "Any Reaction to Friedman's Travels?" Letter to the Editor, *Stanford Daily*, October 27, 1988.

———. "Collaboration in Economics" (an appreciation of Anna J. Schwartz). In *Money, History, and International Finance: Essays in Honor of Anna J. Schwartz*, edited by Michael D. Bordo, pp. 247–50. Chicago: University of Chicago Press, 1989.

———. "Using the Market for Social Development." *Cato Journal* 8 (Winter 1989): 567–79.

———. "Free Markets and Free Men." *The Chinese University Bulletin* (Hong Kong), supplement no. 19, 25th Anniversary Lecture Series (April 1990), pp. 58–67.

———. *Friedman in China*. Foreword by Richard Y. C. Wong. Hong Kong: The Chinese University Press for the Hong Kong Centre for Economic Research, 1990.

———. "How to Sell Government Securities." *Wall Street Journal*, August 28, 1991.

———. "Vouchers No Threat to Church-State Split." Letter to the Editor, *Wall Street Journal*, December 31, 1991.

———. "Oodoov Economics." *New York Times*, February 2, 1992.

———. "Parental Choice: The Effective Way to Improve Schooling." (Excerpts of an address before the Commonwealth Club of California on August 7, 1992.) *The Commonwealth*, August 31, 1992, pp. 514–16, 521–23

———. "Déjà Vu in Currency Markets." *Wall Street Journal*, September 22, 1992.

———. "Do Old Fallacies Ever Die?" *Journal of Economic Literature* 30 (December 1992): 2129–32.

———. "A Memorandum to the Government of India 1955." In *Foundations of India's Political Economy*, edited by Subroto Roy and William E. James, pp. 163–76. New Delhi, Newbury Park, and London: Sage Publications, 1992.

———. *Money Mischief: Episodes in Monetary History*. New York, San Diego, and London: Harcourt Brace Jovanovich, 1992.

———. "Parental Choice: An 'Evil' Proposal?" *Liberty & Law 2*, no. 1 (Winter 1993): 1, 3, and 8.

———. "The Folly of Buying Health Care at the Company Store." *Wall Street Journal*, February 3, 1993.

———. "The Second Industrial Revolution." *Far Eastern Economic Review*, October 28, 1993.

———. "The Case for Choice." In *Voices on Choice: The Education Reform Debate*, edited by K. L. Billingsley, pp. 91–101. San Francisco: Pacific Research Institute for Public Policy, 1994.

———. "Public Schools: Make Them Private." *Washington Post*, February 19, 1995.

———. "Voucher Wars Revisited." *National Review West*, September 11, 1995.

Friedman, Milton, ed. *Studies in the Quantity Theory of Money*. Chicago: University of Chicago Press, 1956.

Friedman, Milton, and Wilbur J. Cohen. *Social Security: Universal or Selective?* Rational Debate Seminar. Washington, D.C.: American Enterprise Institute, 1972.

Friedman, Milton, with the assistance of Rose D. Friedman. *Capitalism and Freedom*. Chicago: University of Chicago Press, 1962, 1982.

Friedman, Milton, and Rose D. Friedman. *Free to Choose*. New York: Harcourt Brace Jovanovich, 1980.

————. *Tyranny of the Status Quo.* San Diego, New York, and London: Harcourt Brace Jova-novich, 1984.

Friedman, Milton, and Walter Heller. *Monetary vs. Fiscal Policy.* New York: W. W. Norton & Co., 1969.

Friedman, Milton, Harold Hotelling, Walter Bartky, W. Edwards Deming, and Paul Hoel. "The Teaching of Statistics." A Report of the Mathematical Statistics Committee on the Teaching of Statistics. *Annals of Mathematical Statistics* 19 (March 1948): 95–115.

Friedman, Milton, and Simon Kuznets. *Income from Independent Professional Practice.* New York: National Bureau of Economic Research, 1945.

Friedman, Milton, and David Meiselman. "The Relative Stability of Monetary Velocity and the Investment Multiplier in the United States, 1897–1958." In *Stabilization Policies,* a series of research studies prepared for the Commission on Money and Credit, pp. 165–268. Englewood Cliffs, N.J.: Prentice-Hall, 1963.

————. "Reply to Ando and Modigliani and to DePrano and Mayer." *American Economic Review* 55 (September 1965): 753–85.

Friedman, Milton, and Robert V. Roosa. *The Balance of Payments: Free versus Fixed Exchange Rates.* Washington, D.C.: American Enterprise Institute for Public Policy Research, 1967.

Friedman, Milton, and L. J. Savage. "The Utility Analysis of Choices Involving Risk." *Journal of Political Economy* 56 (August 1948): 270–304.

————. "The Expected Utility Hypothesis and the Measurability of Utility." *Journal of Political Economy* 60 (December 1952): 463–74.

Friedman, Milton, and Anna J. Schwartz. "Money and Business Cycles." *Review of Economics and Statistics* 45, part 2, supplement (February 1963): 32–64.

————. *A Monetary History of the United States, 1867–1960.* Princeton: Princeton University Press for the National Bureau of Economic Research, 1963.

————. *Monetary Statistics of the United States.* New York: Columbia University Press for the National Bureau of Economic Research, 1970.

————. *Monetary Trends in the United States and the United Kingdom.* Chicago: University of Chicago Press for the National Bureau of Economic Research, 1982.

————. "Alternative Approaches to Analyzing Economic Data." *American Economic Review* 81 (March 1991): 39–49.

————. "A Tale of Fed Transcripts." *Wall Street Journal,* December 20, 1993.

Friedman, Milton, and George J. Stigler. *Roofs or Ceilings? The Current Housing Problem.* Popular Essays on Current Problems, vol. 1, no. 2. Irvington-on-Hudson, N.Y.: Foundation for Economic Education, September 1946.

Friedman, Rose D. *Poverty: Definition and Perspective.* Washington, D.C.: American Enterprise Institute for Public Policy Research, February 1965.

————. "Milton Friedman: Husband and Colleague." *Oriental Economist,* May 1976–February 1977; April 1977; August 1977.

Galbraith, John Kenneth. *A Life in Our Times.* Boston: Houghton Mifflin Co., 1981.

Goldwater, Barry M. *With No Apologies.* New York: William Morrow, 1979.

Goldwater, Barry M., with Jack Casserly. *Goldwater.* New York: Doubleday, 1988.

Gwartney, James, Robert Lawson, and Walter Block. *Economic Freedom of the World, 1975–1995.* Vancouver, B.C.: Fraser Institute, 1995.

Hammond, Bray. *Banks and Politics in America: From the Revolution to the Civil War.* Princeton: Princeton University Press, 1957.

Hammond, J. Daniel. *Theory and Measurement: Causality Issues in Milton Friedman's Monetary Economics.* Cambridge and New York: Cambridge University Press, 1996.

Hanna, Frank A., Joseph A. Pechman, and Sidney M. Lerner. *Analysis of Wisconsin Income.* New York: National Bureau of Economic Research, 1948.

Harberger, Arnold C. "Setting the Record Straight on Chile." Letter to the Editor, *Wall Street Journal,* December 10, 1976.

Hardin, Charles M. *Freedom in Agricultural Education.* Chicago: University of Chicago Press, 1955.

Hartwell, R. M. *A History of the Mont Pelerin Society.* Indianapolis: Liberty Fund, 1995.

Hayek, F. A. *The Road to Serfdom.* Chicago: University of Chicago Press, 1944; Golden Anniversary ed., with new Introduction by Milton Friedman, 1994.

———. *Hayek on Hayek.* Edited by Stephen Kresge and Leif Wenar. Chicago: University of Chicago Press, 1994.

Hendry, David F., and Neil R. Ericsson. "An Econometric Analysis of U.K. Money Demand in *Monetary Trends in the United States and the United Kingdom* by Milton Friedman and Anna J. Schwartz." *American Economic Review* 81 (March 1991): 8–38.

Hester, Donald D. "Keynes and the Quantity Theory: A Comment on the Friedman-Meiselman CMC Paper." *Review of Economics and Statistics* 46 (November 1964): 364–68.

Hirsch, Abraham, and Neil de Marchi. *Milton Friedman: Economics in Theory and Practice.* Ann Arbor: University of Michigan Press, 1990.

Holmes, Kim R., Bryan T. Johnson, and Melanie Kirkpatrick. *1997 Index of Economic Freedom.* New York and Washington: Heritage Foundation and Wall Street Journal, 1997.

Hotelling, Harold. "The Economics of Exhaustible Resources." *Journal of Political Economy* 39 (September 1931): 256–71.

Houthakker, H. S. "The Permanent Income Hypothesis." *American Economic Review* 48 (June 1958): 396–404.

"Inflationary Effect Certain: U.S. Economist's View of India's Deficit Financing." *The Statesman* (Calcutta), March 17, 1956.

Jarvik, Laurence. *PBS: Behind the Screen.* Rocklin, Calif.: Forum, 1997.

Johnson, Alvin. "Obituary, John Bates Clark." *Economic Journal* 48 (September 1938): 572–76.

Kandell, Jonathan. "Chilean Junta Resisting Critics." *New York Times,* September 21, 1975.

Keran, Michael. "Monetary Policy and the Business Cycle in Postwar Japan." In *Varieties of Monetary Experience,* edited by David Meiselman, pp.163–248. Chicago: University of Chicago Press, 1970.

Keynes, J. M. *The General Theory of Employment, Interest and Money.* New York and London: Harcourt Brace and Co., 1936.

Keynes, J. M. *How to Pay for the War: A Radical Plan for the Chancellor of the Exchequer.* London: Macmillan & Co., February 1940.

Klein, L. R. *Economic Fluctuations in the United States, 1921–41.* New York: Wiley, 1950.

Kneeland, Hildegarde, and others. *Consumer Incomes in the United States.* Prepared for the National Resources Committee. Washington, D.C.: Government Printing Office, 1938.

———. *Consumer Expenditures in the United States.* Prepared for the National Resources Committee. Washington, D.C.: Government Printing Office, 1939.

Knight, Frank H. "The Ricardian Theory of Production and Distribution—Part II." *Canadian Journal of Economics and Political Science* 1 (May 1935): 171–96.

———. "The Case for Communism: Why I Am a Communist, by an Ex-Liberal." In *Research in the History of Economic Thought and Methodology,* Archival Supplement 2, edited by Warren J. Samuels. Greenwich, Conn.: JAI Press, 1991.

Kuznets, Simon. *Seasonal Variations in Industry and Trade.* New York: National Bureau of Economic Research, 1933.

Kuznets, Simon, and others. *National Income, 1929–32.* Prepared for the U.S. Department of Commerce. S. Doc. 124. U.S. Congress, Senate, 73rd Cong., 2d sess., 1938.

Lampman, Robert J. "Essay II, The Milton Friedman Affair at Wisconsin, 1940–1941." In *Economists at Wisconsin, 1892–1992,* edited by Robert J. Lampman, pp. 118–21. Madison: Department of Economics, University of Wisconsin–Madison, 1993.

Lasky, Victor. *Turning Defeat into Victory: The Soviet Offensive against Chile.* New York: American-Chilean Council, 1975.

Letelier, Orlando. "Economic 'Freedom's' Awful Toll." *The Nation,* August 28, 1976.

Lewis, Anthony. "For Which We Stand: II." *New York Times,* October 2, 1975.

Leys, Simon. *Chinese Shadows.* New York: Viking Press, 1977.

Lucas, Robert E., Jr. "Tobin and Monetarism: A Review Article." *Journal of Economic Literature* 19 (June 1981): 558–67.

———. "Review of Milton Friedman and Anna J. Schwartz's *A Monetary History of the United States, 1867–1960.*" *Journal of Monetary Economics* 34 (August 1994): 5–16.

Mahaffey, Maryann. "Chile Suffers in Friedman Economy." *Detroit Free Press,* July 3, 1978.

Marshall, Alfred. "The Present Position of Economics" (1885). Reprinted in *Memorials of Alfred Marshall,* edited by A. C. Pigou, pp. 152–74. London: Macmillan & Co., 1925.

Martz, Larry. "A Nobel for Friedman." *Newsweek,* October 25, 1976.

Mayer, Thomas. "Friedman's Methodology of Positive Economics: A Soft Reading." *Economic Inquiry* 31 (April 1993): 213–23.

Meigs, A. James. *Free Reserves and the Money Supply.* Chicago: University of Chicago Press, 1962.

Meiselman, David, ed. *Varieties of Monetary Experience.* Chicago: University of Chicago Press, 1970.

Melamed, Leo. *Escape to the Futures.* New York: John Wiley & Sons, 1996.

Millis, H. A. *How Collective Bargaining Works: A Survey of Experience in Leading American Industries.* New York: The Twentieth Century Fund, 1942.

"Milton Friedman, the Chilean Junta and the Matter of Their Association." An exchange of letters among Nobel Laureates: Friedman with Baltimore and Luria, and with Wald and Pauling, *New York Times,* May 22, 1977, sec. 4.

Mintz, Morton. "Should the FDA Be Dismantled?" *Washington Post,* February 4, 1973.

———. "The FDA: Battling and Embattled." *Washington Post,* February 5, 1973.

———. "FDA Counterattacking New Wave of Critics." *Washington Post,* February 6, 1973.

Miron, Jeffrey A. "Empirical Methodology in Macroeconomics: Explaining the Success of Friedman and Schwartz's *A Monetary History of the United States, 1867–1960.*" *Journal of Monetary Economics* 34 (August 1994): 17–25.

Mitchell, Wesley C. *Business Cycles.* Berkeley: University of California Press, 1913.

———. *Business Cycles,* vol. 1: *The Problem and Its Setting.* New York: National Bureau of Economic Research, 1927.

———. *Lecture Notes on Types of Economic Theory.* New York: Augustus M. Kelley, 1949.

———. *What Happens During Business Cycles: A Progress Report.* New York: National Bureau of Economic Research, 1951.

Mitchell, Wesley C., and Arthur F. Burns. *Measuring Business Cycles.* New York: National Bureau of Economic Research, 1945.

Moggridge, D. E. *Maynard Keynes: An Economist's Biography.* London and New York: Routledge, 1992.

Morrison, George. *Liquidity Preferences of Commercial Banks.* Chicago: University of Chicago Press, 1966.

Myrdal, Gunnar. *An American Dilemma: The Negro Problem and Modern Democracy.* New York: Harper & Brothers, 1944.

Nef, John U. "James Laurence Laughlin (1850–1933)." *Journal of Political Economy* 42 (February 1934): 1–5.

Nixon, Richard M. *The Memoirs of Richard Nixon.* New York: Grosset and Dunlap, 1978.

"Nobels and Smears." Editorial, *Wall Street Journal,* December 10, 1976.

Perlman, Mark. "Jews and Contributions to Economics: A Bicentennial Review." *Judaism* 25 (1976): 301–11.

Phelps, Edmund S. "Phillips Curves, Expectations of Inflation and Optimal Unemployment over Time." *Economica,* n.s., 34 (August 1967): 254–81.

Popper, Karl. *The Logic of Scientific Discovery.* London: Hutchinson, 1959.

———. *Conjectures and Refutations.* New York: Basic Books, 1962.

Rattner, Steven. "Economist in the Public Cause." *New York Times,* October 15, 1976.

Report of the President's Commission on an All-Volunteer Armed Force. New York: Macmillan, Collier Books, 1970.

Rosett, Claudia. "An Aborted Economic Test." *New York Times,* July 3, 1983.

———. "Looking Back on Chile, 1973–84." *National Review,* June 1, 1984.

Rosten, Leo. *The Joys of Yiddish.* New York: McGraw-Hill, 1969.

Ruiz, Gumersindo. "Experiencias a tener en cuenta: Una estabilización sin resultados." *Vanguardia,* March 1977.

Rukeyser, Louis. "Friedman Won His Nobel Prize on a Battleground of Academia." *Baltimore Evening Sun,* October 22, 1976.

Rukeyser, Muriel. *Willard Gibbs.* 1942. Paperback ed. New York: E. F. Dutton Co., 1964.

Salant, Walter. "The Inflationary Gap: Meaning and Significance for Policy Making." *American Economic Review* 32 (June 1942): 314–20.

Savage, L. J. *Foundations of Statistics.* New York: Wiley, 1954.

Schultz, Henry. *The Theory and Measurement of Demand.* Chicago: University of Chicago Press, 1938.

Selden, Richard, ed. *Capitalism and Freedom: Problems and Prospects,* Proceedings of a Conference in Honor of Milton Friedman. Charlottesville: University Press of Virginia, 1975.

Shils, Edward. "Robert Maynard Hutchins." In *Remembering the University of Chicago,* edited by Edward Shils, pp. 185–96. Chicago: University of Chicago Press, 1991.

Shoup, Carl, Milton Friedman, and Ruth P. Mack. *Taxing to Prevent Inflation.* New York: Columbia University Press, 1943.

Silk, Leonard. *The Economists.* New York: Basic Books, 1976.

Sjaastad, Larry A. "What Went Wrong in Chile." *National Review,* September 16, 1983.

Slutsky, Eugen. "The Summation of Random Causes as the Source of Cyclic Processes." *Econometrica* 5 (April 1937): 105–46. (A revised English version of the article originally published in Russian in 1927.)

Smith, Adam. *The Theory of Moral Sentiments.* 1759. Reprint. New Rochelle, N.Y.: Arlington House, 1969.

Smith, Bruce D. "Mischief and Monetary History: Friedman and Schwartz Thirty Years Later." *Journal of Monetary Economics* 34 (August 1994): 27–45.

Solzhenitsyn, Aleksandr I. *Cancer Ward.* New York: Dial Press, 1968.

Souter, Ralph. *A Prolegomena to Relativity Economics.* New York: Columbia University Press, 1933.

Statistical Research Group. *Sequential Analysis of Statistical Data: Applications.* Edited by Harold A. Freeman, M. A. Girschik, and W. Allen Wallis. New York: Columbia University Press, 1945.

———. *Selected Techniques of Statistical Analysis for Scientific and Industrial Research and Pro-*

duction and Management Engineering. Edited by Churchill Eisenhart, Millard Hastay, and W. Allen Wallis. New York and London: McGraw-Hill Book Co., 1947.

———. *Sampling Inspection: Principles, Procedures, and Tables for Single, Double, and Sequential Sampling in Acceptance Inspection and Quality Control Based on Percent Defective.* Edited by Harold A. Freeman, Milton Friedman, Frederick Mosteller and W. Allen Wallis. New York and London: McGraw-Hill Book Co., 1948.

Statkowski, Jozef. *Poland—Old and New.* Warsaw: M. Arct, 1938.

Stigler, George J. *Memoirs of an Unregulated Economist.* New York: Basic Books, 1988.

Tax, Sol. *Penny Capitalism.* Chicago: University of Chicago Press, 1963.

"The Timeliness of Milton Friedman." Editorial, *Financial Times* (London), October 15, 1976.

Tobin, James. "The Monetary Interpretation of History: A Review Article." *American Economic Review* 55 (June 1965): 464–85.

———. "The Natural Rate as New Classical Macroeconomics." In *The Natural Rate of Unemployment: Reflections on 25 Years of the Hypothesis,* edited by Rod Cross, pp. 32–42. Cambridge and New York: Cambridge University Press, 1995.

Tocqueville, Alexis de. *Democracy in America.* Garden City, N.Y.: Doubleday & Company, Anchor Books, 1969.

"U.S. Business in 1965: The Economy, 'We Are All Keynesians Now.'" *Time,* December 31, 1965.

Vilnay, Zev. *The Guide to Israel.* 5th ed. Jerusalem, 1962.

Viner, Jacob. "Cost Curves and Supply Curves." *Zeitschrift für Nationalökonomie* 3 (1931): 23–46. Reprinted in American Economic Association, *Readings in Price Theory,* pp. 198–232. Chicago: Richard D. Irwin, 1952.

Viorst, Milton. "Friedmanism, n. Doctrine of Most Audacious U.S. Economist; esp. Theory 'Only Money Matters.'" *New York Times Magazine,* January 25, 1970.

Wald, Abraham. *Sequential Analysis.* New York: John Wiley Sons, 1947.

Wald, George, and Linus Pauling. "The Laureate." Letter to the Editor, *New York Times,* October 24, 1976.

Wallis, W. Allen. "The Statistical Research Group, 1942–1945." *Journal of the American Statistical Association* 70, no. 370 (June 1980): 320–30.

Walters, Alan. "Friedman, Milton." In *The New Palgrave: A Dictionary of Economics,* edited by John Eatwell, Murray Milgate, and Peter Newman, 2:426. New York: Stockton Press, and London: Macmillan Press, 1987.

⇥ Index ⇤